WORDS OVER WAR

WORDS OVER WAR
Mediation and Arbitration to Prevent Deadly Conflict

Edited by
Melanie C. Greenberg
John H. Barton
Margaret E. McGuinness

CARNEGIE COMMISSION ON PREVENTING DEADLY CONFLICT

CARNEGIE CORPORATION OF NEW YORK

ROWMAN & LITTLEFIELD PUBLISHERS, INC.
Lanham • Boulder • New York • Oxford

ROWMAN & LITTLEFIELD PUBLISHERS, INC.

Published in the United States of America
by Rowman & Littlefield Publishers, Inc.
4720 Boston Way, Lanham, Maryland 20706
http://www.rowmanlittlefield.com

12 Hid's Copse Road
Cumnor Hill, Oxford OX2 9JJ, England

British Library Cataloguing in Publication Information Available

Library of Congress Cataloging-in-Publication Data

Words over war : mediation and arbitration to prevent deadly conflict / edited by
Melanie C. Greenberg, John H. Barton, and Margaret E. McGuinness.
    p. cm.— (Carnegie Commission on Preventing Deadly Conflict)
    Includes bibliographical references.
    ISBN 0-8476-9892-0 (alk. paper)—ISBN 0-8476-9893-9 (pbk. : alk. paper)
    1. Pacific settlement of international disputes. 2. Intervention (International law) 3.
Mediation, International. I. Greenberg, Melanie C. II. Barton, John H. III. McGuinness,
Margaret E. IV. Carnegie Commission on Preventing Deadly Conflict series.

KZ6010 .W67 2000
341.5'2—dc21   99-051392

Printed in the United States of America

♾ ™ The paper used in this publication meets the minimum requirements of American
National Standard for Information Sciences—Permanence of Paper for Printed Library
Materials, ANSI/NISO Z39.48-1992.

/2723114

To Anna Rose and Jed, who I hope will inherit a more peaceful world.
Melanie Greenberg

In the hope that our work will be useful to future peacemakers.
John Barton

To my parents, Bill and Madeleine McGuinness.
Margaret McGuinness

ABOUT THE
Carnegie Commission on Preventing Deadly Conflict Series

Carnegie Corporation of New York established the Carnegie Commission on Preventing Deadly Conflict in May 1994 to address the threats to world peace of intergroup violence and to advance new ideas for the prevention and resolution of deadly conflict. The Commission is examining the principal causes of deadly ethnic, nationalist, and religious conflicts within and between states and the circumstances that foster or deter their outbreak. Taking a long-term, worldwide view of violent conflicts that are likely to emerge, it seeks to determine the functional requirements of an effective system for preventing mass violence and to identify the ways in which such a system could be implemented. The Commission is also looking at the strengths and weaknesses of various international entities in conflict prevention and considering ways in which international organizations might contribute toward developing an effective international system of nonviolent problem solving. The series grew out of the research that the Commission has sponsored to answer the three fundamental questions that have guided its work: What are the problems posed by deadly conflict, and why is outside help often necessary to deal with these problems? What approaches, tasks, and strategies appear most promising for preventing deadly conflict? What are the responsibilities and capacities of states, international organizations, and private and nongovernmental organizations for undertaking preventive action? The Commission issued its final report in December 1997.

The books are published as a service to scholars, students, practitioners, and the interested public. While they have undergone peer review and have been approved for publication, the views that they express are those of the author or authors, and Commission publication does not imply that those views are shared by the Commission as a whole or by individual Commissioners.

The Carnegie Commission Series

Published in the series:
Bridging the Gap: A Future Security Architecture for the Middle East, by Shai Feldman and Abdullah Toukan
The Price of Peace: Incentives and International Conflict Prevention, edited by David Cortright
Sustainable Peace: The Role of the UN and Regional Organizations in Preventing Conflict, by Connie Peck
Turkey's Kurdish Question, by Henri J. Barkey and Graham E. Fuller
The Costs of Conflict: Prevention and Cure in the Global Arena, edited by Michael E. Brown and Richard N. Rosecrance
Light Weapons and Civil Conflict: Controlling the Tools of Violence, edited by Jeffrey Boutwell and Michael T. Klare
Opportunities Missed, Opportunities Seized: Preventive Diplomacy in the Post–Cold War World, edited by Bruce W. Jentleson
The Ambivalence of the Sacred: Religion, Violence, and Reconciliation, by R. Scott Appleby
Words over War: Mediation and Arbitration to Prevent Deadly Conflict, edited by Melanie C. Greenberg, John H. Barton, and Margaret E. McGuinness

Forthcoming:
Preventive Negotiation: Avoiding Conflict Escalation, edited by I. William Zartman

For orders and information, please address the publisher:
Rowman & Littlefield Publishers, Inc.,
4720 Boston Way, Lanham, MD 20706
1-800-462-6420
Visit our website at http://www.rowmanlittlefield.com

Selected Reports Available from the Commission

David Hamburg, *Preventing Contemporary Intergroup Violence,* founding essay of the Commission, April 1994.
David A. Hamburg, *Education for Conflict Resolution,* April 1995.
Comprehensive Disclosure of Fissionable Materials: A Suggested Initiative, June 1995.
Larry Diamond, *Promoting Democracy in the 1990s: Actors and Instruments, Issues and Imperatives,* December 1995.
Andrew J. Goodpaster, *When Diplomacy Is Not Enough: Managing Multinational Military Interventions,* July 1996.
John Stremlau, *Sharpening International Sanctions: Toward a Stronger Role for the United Nations,* November 1996.
Alexander L. George and Jane E. Holl, *The Warning–Response Problem and Missed Opportunities in Preventive Diplomacy,* May 1997.
John Stremlau with Helen Zille, *A House No Longer Divided: Progress and Prospects for Democratic Peace in South Africa,* July 1997.
Nik Gowing, *Media Coverage: Help or Hindrance in Conflict Prevention,* September 1997.
Cyrus R. Vance and David A. Hamburg, *Pathfinders for Peace: A Report to the UN Secretary-General on the Role of Special Representatives and Personal Envoys,* September 1997.
Preventing Deadly Conflict: Executive Summary of the Final Report, December 1997.
Gail W. Lapidus with Svetlana Tsalik, eds., *Preventing Deadly Conflict: Strategies and Institutions,* Proceedings of a Conference in Moscow, Russian Federation, April 1998.

Scott Feil, *Preventing Genocide: How the Early Use of Force Might Have Succeeded in Rwanda*, April 1998.

Douglas Lute, *Improving National Capacity to Respond to Complex Emergencies: The U.S. Experience*, April 1998.

John Stremlau, *People in Peril: Human Rights, Humanitarian Action, and Preventing Deadly Conflict*, June 1998.

Tom Gjelten, *Professionalism in War Reporting: A Correspondent's View*, June 1998.

John Stremlau and Francisco R. Sagasti, *Preventing Deadly Conflict: Does the World Bank Have a Role?*, June 1998.

Edward J. Laurance, *Light Weapons and Intrastate Conflict: Early Warning Factors and Preventive Action*, July 1998.

Donald Kennedy, *Environmental Quality and Regional Conflict*, November 1998.

George A. Joulwan and Christopher C. Shoemaker, *Civilian-Military Cooperation in the Prevention of Deadly Conflict: Implementing Agreements in Bosnia and Beyond*, December 1998.

Essays on Leadership (by Boutros Boutros-Ghali, George Bush, Jimmy Carter, Mikhail Gorbachev, and Desmond Tutu), December 1998.

M. James Wilkinson, *Moving Beyond Conflict Prevention to Reconciliation: Tackling Greek-Turkish Hostility*, June 1999.

Graham T. Allison and Hisashi Owada, *The Responsibilities of Democracies in Preventing Deadly Conflict: Reflections and Recommendations*, July 1999.

Preventive Diplomacy, Preventive Defense, and Conflict Resolution: A Report of Two Conferences at Stanford University and the Ditchley Foundation, October 1999.

Arturo Valenzuela, *The Collective Defense of Democracy: Lessons from the Paraguayan Crisis*, December 1999.

David A. Hamburg, *Perspectives on Prevention: Preventing Contemporary Intergroup Violence, Education for Conflict Resolution*, December 1999.

To order *Power Sharing and International Mediation in Ethnic Conflicts* by Timothy Sisk, co-published by the Commission and the United States Institute of Peace, please contact USIP Press, P.O. Box 605, Herndon, VA 22070, USA; phone: (800) 868-8064 or (703) 661-1590.

Full text or summaries of these reports are available on the Commission's website: http://www.ccpdc.org

To order a report or to be added to the Commission's mailing list, contact:
Carnegie Commission on Preventing Deadly Conflict
1779 Massachusetts Avenue, NW, Suite 715
Washington, DC 20036-2103
Phone: (202) 332-7900 Fax: (202) 332-1919

Contents

Foreword

This volume of case studies would have been impossible when I was secretary of state in the Carter administration in the late 1970s. Not even the most prescient diplomat at that time could have looked beyond the Cold War and predicted the collapse of the Soviet Union; the destruction of the Berlin Wall; the fall of apartheid in South Africa; and the wave of democracy sweeping through Eastern Europe, Africa, and Latin America. Moreover, we could not have foreseen the rise of a vibrant international community, with one remaining superpower; a United Nations working without the constraints of the superpower rivalry; and a vast array of international and regional organizations, both official and unofficial.

The challenge that faces us is to coordinate and marshal our resources to prevent deadly conflict; to use joint initiatives and alliances to moderate and help resolve conflict; and to remain engaged in the reconciliation, rebuilding, and peacemaking processes. This challenge presupposes a level of intervention that would have been unfathomable in previous eras. The UN Charter prevents external intervention in the internal affairs of a member nation, and this norm of sovereignty was virtually unbreachable during the Cold War. Since then, however, a new norm has developed favoring the rights of individuals to peace and security.

This volume discusses at length the changing international arena and the role of the international community in mediating deadly conflict. The studies represent a fascinating cross section of conflict in the post–Cold War era. Many of the conflicts considerably predate the past decade, but were resolvable only with the end of the bipolar system.

Three of the chapters in this book, Croatia, Bosnia, and South Africa, are especially close to me not only in that they illustrate the nadir and zenith of violence and conflict resolution over the past ten years, but because I experienced them personally as a mediator.

Under the auspices of the United Nations, in a process paralleling Lord Carrington's European Union mediation, I was able in December 1991 to mediate an accord between Franjo Tudjman, leader of the Croats (and president of independent Croatia), Slobodan Milosevic, and local Serb leaders in Croatia. The plan placed 10,000 peacekeeping forces on the ground and set up UN Protected Areas in and around Serb-held territory, on the condition that the Yugoslav National Army would retreat and Serb irregulars would surrender their weapons. The plan also allowed for the return of refugees to their homes.

From September 1992 to May 1993, Lord David Owen and I, as cochairmen of the International Conference on the Former Yugoslavia, mediated the horrific conflict raging in Bosnia–Herzegovina. Shortly after the declaration of Bosnia's independence, Croatian forces under the indirect control of Franjo Tudjman and Serbian forces led by Radovan Karadzic (acting with the full—if undeclared—support of Slobodan Milosevic) grabbed huge areas of territory contiguous to their home states. They drove Bosnian Muslims from their homes, razed villages and mosques, and destroyed architectural treasures like the Mostar Bridge.

Lord Owen and I faced wrenching issues in the philosophy and process of how the conflict should be resolved, and in the implementation of the potential solution. We had to decide, in choosing the principles behind the Vance–Owen Peace Plan, whether we should try to retain the ideal of multiethnic coexistence or essentially partition the country to reflect the ethnic cleansing and military gains on the ground. Negotiating the plan among the Bosnian Muslims, the Bosnian Croats, and the Bosnian Serbs illuminated the fissures within the Muslim and Serbian negotiating teams (a dynamic alluded to by other mediators in this volume) and the difficulties of reaching a settlement when there is severe conflict within one or more delegations.

Lord Owen and I chose to stand by a solution that preserved the heterogeneity of prewar Bosnia. According to the plan, Bosnia would be divided into ten provinces: three with a Serb majority, two with a Croat majority, three with a Muslim majority, one with a mixed Croat–Muslim majority, and Sarajevo, which would be mixed with a power-sharing arrangement between the ethnic groups. This map agreement, backed up by constitutional principles and significant ground forces, would reverse much of the ethnic cleansing that had taken place and would force significant rollback of Serb advances.

I am often asked whether Lord Owen and I should have negotiated with men who would later be indicted by the War Crimes Tribunal in The Hague. My response to this is that, much as I might have been repelled by the acts of many of the leaders with whom I negotiated, they were the only men empowered to make peace, and peace in the end was the most important goal.

In many ways, the South African peace process was the mirror image of Bosnia and other conflicts in this volume. Whereas other leaders played on the fears of minorities to whip up nationalist fervor, in South Africa the white minority finally relinquished power to the black majority. Leaders, rather than seeking ethnic strife, sought out areas of agreement with the other side and worked together on a process of power sharing and reconciliation. While there was certainly significant bloodletting during the years of the negotiations, the solidity of the leadership, the vibrant civil society that had been developing, and the sense that there was no going back to the apartheid regime allowed the negotiations to move forward. The Goldstone Commission allowed for the truth of the apartheid years to emerge in a way that encouraged catharsis and honesty without vengeance.

The vast differences in the experiences between Bosnia and South Africa highlight the importance of this book of case studies on mediation. Only by studying different forms of mediation, and at the same time by comparing controlled variables, can we begin to understand how to make mediation more effective and how to use it in our arsenal of tools for preventing deadly conflict. Mediation cannot occur in a vacuum. Rather, it is most often effective when other tools—sanctions, financial assistance, the promise of ongoing international involvement in reconciliation and rebuilding activities, military force in the form of peacekeeping or peace enforcement—can be called into play by the mediator. Once a vibrant civil society is established, its characteristics—a free press and rule of law, freedom to elect just leaders, freedom from fear and poverty, and willingness to accept help from the international community—lay the groundwork for mediation. I sincerely hope that this volume will inspire future mediators in their search for peace and reconciliation.

Cyrus R. Vance, Cochair
Carnegie Commission
on Preventing Deadly Conflict

Preface

This book originated at a conference in New York in the fall of 1996, sponsored by the Carnegie Commission on Preventing Deadly Conflict and based on a background paper prepared by Robert Badinter, a member of the French Senate and former minister of justice. The subject of the conference was techniques for international conflict resolution. Lively discussion arose about the feasibility of current dispute resolution mechanisms (mediation, arbitration, etc.) and the possibility for new, creative methods of conflict resolution drawing on both the traditional diplomatic mechanisms and the emerging and very successful commercial mechanisms. John Barton, a professor from Stanford Law School, had views that differed enough from some of those expressed by the group that he offered to prepare a conceptual paper outlining them. A number of weeks later, Jane Holl of the Carnegie Commission on Preventing Deadly Conflict proposed that we follow up the conference with a study of a number of specific cases of actual dispute resolution. The result was this edited volume, financed by the Carnegie Commission, that closely compares twelve conflicts of the post–Cold War period and the role of international intervention in resolving the disputes. Our goal was to examine the role of international organizations in dispute resolution, to analyze the tools and forms of leverage mediators used in successful (and unsuccessful) mediations, and to suggest which structures are most effective for international mediation. We also set out to examine how particular characteristics within the conflicts and the disputing parties themselves affect the outcome of mediation, and to suggest, based on our findings, potential new avenues for conflict resolution. The theoretical framework and information about how we chose the cases is laid out in the introduction to this volume.

The case authors include political science graduate students and graduate-level law students, who brought great sophistication and energy to the project. They wrote first drafts of their case studies, drawing on the framework developed by Professor Barton, Melanie Greenberg, and Margaret McGuinness with thoughtful help from Professor Alexander George of Stanford University and Stephen Stedman, senior research scholar at the Stanford Center for International Security and Cooperation. The group of case authors, together with the editors, worked as a coordinated unit during this drafting process. We held meetings to discuss emerging themes of the book and seminars focusing on particular areas of mediation. Interviews with mediators and key participants were another important element of the case-writing process. The Carnegie Commission on Preventing Deadly Conflict was able to provide high-level access to mediators and government officials. Authors traveled to Oslo, El Salvador, London, South America, Central Asia, New York, and Washington to interview mediators and primary participants and held interviews by phone when travel was not feasible. These personal discussions greatly enhanced our understanding of mediation dynamics.

In September 1997, the panel of international lawyers who had originally met in New York the previous year reconvened to discuss the case studies and findings. The meeting was tremendously useful in clarifying our terms, sharpening our hypotheses, and finding common elements between the case studies. Case authors attended this meeting and augmented their cases in light of those discussions.

The completed volume represents not only the creative work of the case authors, but also the significant intellectual energy of a number of others. The editors wish to thank, foremost, the Carnegie Commission on Preventing Deadly Conflict, specifically, Jane Holl, Esther Brimmer, and Thomas Leney, for their exceedingly generous financial and intellectual support of the project and the great lengths to which they went to help our case authors make contact with busy, high-profile diplomats and government leaders for their case studies. David Hamburg and Cyrus Vance took a deep personal interest in the project and helped shape our findings with their insight and wisdom. Professor Alexander George, a member of the Commission, spent a great deal of time with us at the beginning of the project, helping to organize our framework and giving generously of his expertise in the case study method. Robert Lande demonstrated remarkable skill and patience with us as the Commission's editor.

Our deep thanks go to the case authors, without whose work and persistence this project would have been impossible. We offer our gratitude to Daniel Froats and Frances Cook, case authors who left the project early because of outside professional reasons, for their help in understanding national minority issues and Bosnia.

We thank the international lawyers who spent time with the manuscript and with the case authors, hammering out the difficult questions at our September 1997 meeting: Philip Allott, Robert Badinter, Abram Chayes, Antonia Chayes, Hans Corell, Lori Damrosch, Theodor Meron, Oscar Schachter, and Paul Szasz.

We owe great thanks to Stanford Law School, for its support of the project, and especially to Susan French, who efficiently managed the travel, financial, and logistical arrangements of the project. Her talents and wonderful spirit kept the authors and editors unified and were key to bringing the manuscript together at the end. A special thanks is also owed the librarians and staff of the Stanford Law Library for their valuable assistance.

The Stanford Center for International Security and Cooperation (formerly the Stanford Center for International Security and Arms Control, CISAC) supported the book from the beginning and gave us significant assistance as it developed. Thanks, especially, to Stephen Stedman for the time and energy he gave the authors in developing the theoretical framework for the book; to David Holloway for his wisdom and insight into international conflict resolution; to Michael May and Scott Sagan for agreeing to make the book part of CISAC's research agenda; to Lynn Eden for her probing questions; and to Barbara Platt and Helen Neves for their support in administering the project.

Thanks to Byron Bland, Lee Ross, Lorelei Kelly, Maude Pervere, Jonathan Greenberg, and Elizabeth Borgwardt of Stanford University for their deep commitment to conflict resolution, and for the many informal discussions that helped shape our ideas about conflict resolution and prevention. A special thanks to former Secretary of State Warren Christopher, who took time to read an earlier manuscript of this book, and whose own work on the role of negotiators provided inspiration.

Special thanks to our research assistants, Mike Grenier and Pat Sherman, for their tireless work on the final version of the manuscript.

Melanie Greenberg thanks her husband, Lawrence Greenberg, for his thoughtful comments on issues of conflict resolution and his support throughout the process. John Barton thanks the entire research team, and especially Melanie Greenberg and Margaret McGuinness, for their effort, cheerfulness, ideas, and competence. Margaret McGuinness thanks her colleagues at Stanford Law School, whose friendship and intellectual camaraderie were a great source of energy throughout the project.

Finally, we wish to thank the dozens of diplomats, politicians, military officials, lawyers, and academics from around the world who gave generously of their time and wisdom to share with us the lessons of their own mediation experiences. Drawing from their experiences, we hope this book will contribute to a better understanding of the role of mediation.

Abbreviations and Acronyms

ANC	African National Congress [South Africa]
ANPOBAM	The Association of Aral Sea Basin NGOs
ARENA	Nationalist Republican Alliance Party [El Salvador]
ARF	Association of Southeast Asian Nations Regional Forum
ASEAN	Association of Southeast Asian Nations
AWB	*Afrikaner Weerstands Beweging*
AZAPO	Azanian People's Organisation
BBTG	Broad Based Transitional Government [Rwanda]
BVO	Basin-wide Agency for Water Allocation [Soviet Union/Aral Sea Basin]
CCB	Civil Cooperation Bureau [South Africa]
CDN	Conseil National de Développement [Rwanda]
CDR	Coalition pour la Défense de la République
CEPL	Communauté Economique de Pays des Grand Lacs
CGDK	Coalition Government of Democratic Kampuchea
CIS	Commonwealth of Independent States
CISAC	Stanford Center for International Security and Arms Control [now known as the Stanford Center for International Security and Cooperation]
CODESA	Conference for a Democratic South Africa
COSATU	Congress of South African Trade Unions
COPAZ	Government Peace Commission [Guatemala]
CPP	Cambodian People's Party
CSCAP	Council for Security Cooperation in the Asia-Pacific Region
CSCE	Conference on Security and Cooperation in Europe
DK	Democratic Kampuchea
DPRK	Democratic People's Republic of Korea [North Korea]
DUP	Democratic Unionist Party [Ireland]

EBRD	European Bank for Reconstruction and Development
EC	European Community
ECMM	European Community Monitoring Mission to Yugoslavia
EEZ	Exclusive Economic Zone
EPC	European Political Cooperation
EU	European Union
EU-TACIS	European Union's Technical Assistance for the Commonwealth of Independent States
FAFO	Institute for Applied Social Science
FAR	Forces Armées Rwandaises
FMLN	Farabundo Martí National Liberation Front
FRY	Federal Republic of Yugoslavia
FUNCINPEC	United National Front for an Independent, Neutral, Peaceful, and Cooperative Cambodia [known by its French acronym]
G-7	Group of Seven Industrialized Nations
GoR	Government of Rwanda Negotiating Coalition
HDZ	Croatian Democratic Union
IAEA	International Atomic Energy Agency
IBA	Independent Broadcast Authority [South Africa]
ICAS	Interstate Council for Addressing the Aral Sea Crisis
ICFY	International Conference on the Former Yugoslavia
ICJ	International Court of Justice
ICKKU	Interstate Council for Kazakhstan, Kyrgyzstan, and Uzbekistan
ICSDSTEC	Interstate Commission for Socio-Economic Development and Scientific, Technical and Ecological Cooperation [now known as the Sustainable Development Committee]
ICTY	International Criminal Tribunal for the Former Yugoslavia
ICWC	Interstate Commission for Water Coordination [Aral Sea; formerly the IWMCC]
IDASA	Institute for Democracy in South Africa
IEC	Independent Electoral Commission [South Africa]
IFAS	International Fund for the Aral Sea
IFOR	Implementation Force
IFP	Inkatha Freedom Party
IGO	Intergovernmental Organization
IMC	Independent Media Commission [South Africa]
IMF	International Monetary Fund
INLA	Irish National Liberation Army
IRA	Irish Republican Army
ISAR	Institute for Soviet-American Relations

IWMCC	Interstate Water Management Coordinating Commission [Aral Sea]
JAP	Joint Action Plan
JIM	Jakarta Informal Meeting
JNA	Yugoslav People's Army
JPMC	Joint Political Military Committee [Rwanda]
KEDO	Korean Peninsula Development Organization
KPNLF	Khmer People's National Liberation Front
LWR	Light-water Reactor
MDR	Mouvement Démocratique Républicain
MRND	Mouvement Révolutionnaire National pour le Développement
MWe	Megawatt Electric
NATO	North Atlantic Treaty Organization
NGO	Nongovernmental Organization
NMOG	Neutral Military Observer Group
NP	National Party [South Africa]
NPT	Nuclear Non-proliferation Treaty
NSC	United States National Security Council
OAS	Organization of American States
OAU	Organization of African Unity
ONUCA	United Nations Observer Group in Central America
ONUSAL	United Nations Observer Mission in El Salvador
OSCE	Organization for Security and Cooperation in Europe
P-5	Permanent Five Members of the United Nations Security Council
PA	Palestinian Authority
PAC	Pan-Africanist Congress [South Africa]
PKR	People's Republic of Kampuchea
PLO	Palestine Liberation Organization
PNL	Picton, Nueva, and Lennox Islands
PSD	Parti Social Démocrate [Rwanda]
RENAMO	Mozambican National Resistance
ROK	Republic of Korea [South Korea]
RPF	Rwandan Patriotic Front
RSF	Republican Sinn Fein
RTLMC	Radio-Télévision Libre des Mille Collines [Rwanda]
SACP	South African Communist Party
SADC	Southern African Development Community [pre-1994 known as SADCC]
SADCC	Southern African Development Coordination Conference
SDLP	Social Democratic and Labour Party [Ireland]
SDS	Serbian Democratic Party
SFOR	Stabilization Force

SFRJ	Socialist Federal Republic of Yugoslavia
SNC	Supreme National Council [Cambodia]
SOC	State of Cambodia
TEC	Transitional Executive Council
TO	Slovene Territorial Defense Units
UDA	Ulster Defense Association
UDF	United Democratic Front [South Africa]
UDP	Ulster Democratic Party
UNAMIC	United Nations Advance Mission in Cambodia
UNAMIR	United Nations Assistance Mission for Rwanda
UNDP	United Nations Development Program
UNEP	United Nations Environmental Program
UNHCR	United Nations High Commissioner for Refugees
UNICEF	United Nations Children's Fund
UNITA	National Union for the Total Independence of Angola
UNOMIG	United Nations Observer Mission in Georgia
UNOMSA	United Nations Observer Mission to South Africa
UNPA	United Nations Protected Area
UNPROFOR	United Nations Protection Force
UNSC	United Nations Security Council
UNSCR	United Nations Security Council Resolution
UNTAC	United Nations Transitional Authority in Cambodia
USAID	United States Agency for International Development
UUP	Ulster Unionist Party
WARMAP	Water Resources Management and Agricultural Production in the Central Asian Republics
WEU	Western European Union

Maps

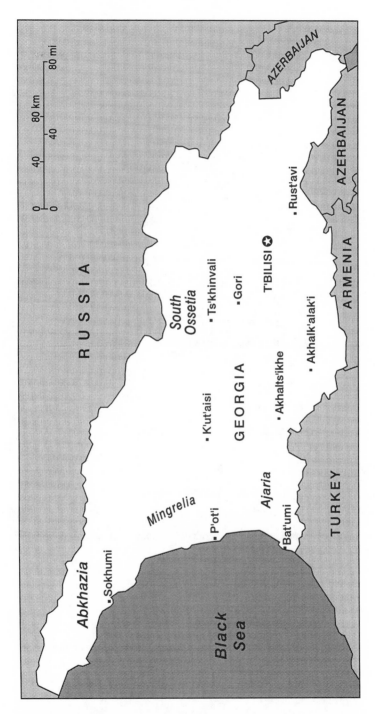

Chapter 1: Abkhazia. Courtesy of the Perry-Castañeda Library Map Collection, University of Texas at Austin (1997).

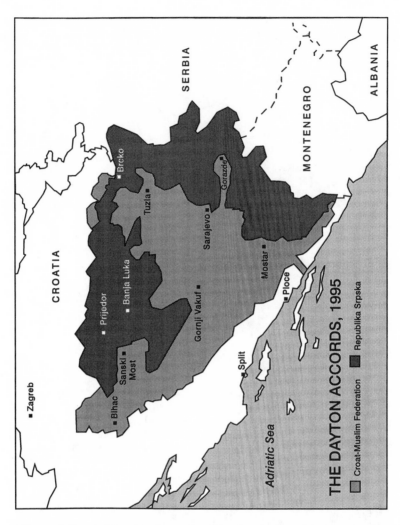

Chapter 2: Bosnia (showing the results of the Dayton Accords). Courtesy of the U.S. Department of Defense.

Chapter 3: Croatia, (showing UNPROFOR deployment areas). Reprinted with permission of the Brookings Institution Press, from *Balkan Tragedy: Chaos and Dissolution after the Cold War,* by Susan L. Woodward (1995).

Chapter 4: Territories Occupied by Israel Since June 1967. Courtesy of the U.N. Department of Public Information (3243 rev. 2, June 1991).

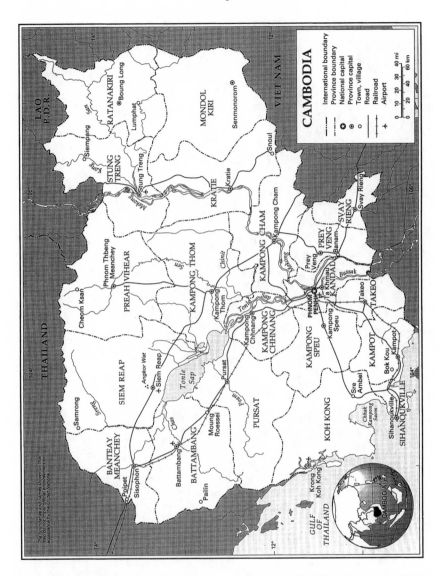

Chapter 5: Cambodia. Courtesy of the UN Department of Public Information (3860 rev., August 1995).

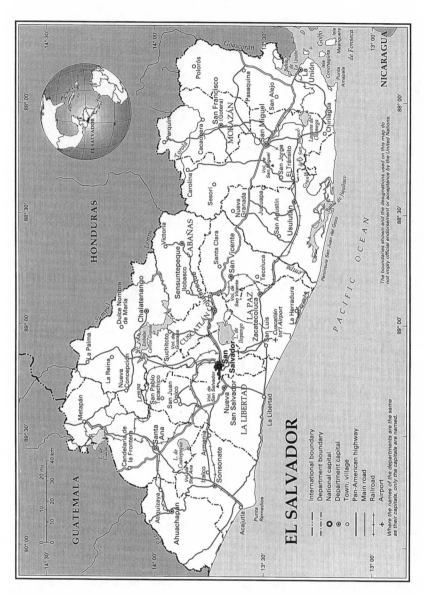

Chapter 6: El Salvador. Courtesy of the UN Department of Public Information (3903, August 1995).

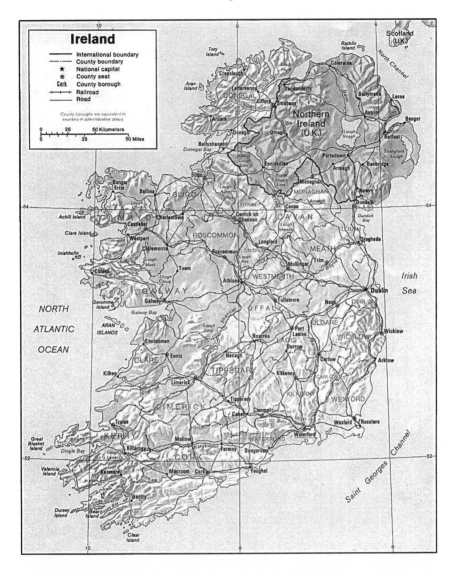

Chapter 7: Northern Ireland. Courtesy of the Perry-Castañeda Library Map Collection, University of Texas at Austin (1982).

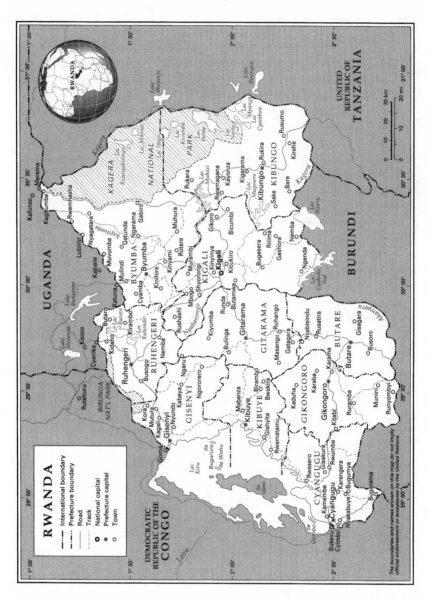

Chapter 8: Rwanda. Courtesy of the UN Department of Public Information (3717 rev. 1, December 1997).

Chapter 9: South Africa. Courtesy of the Perry-Castañeda Library Map Collection, University of Texas at Austin (1995).

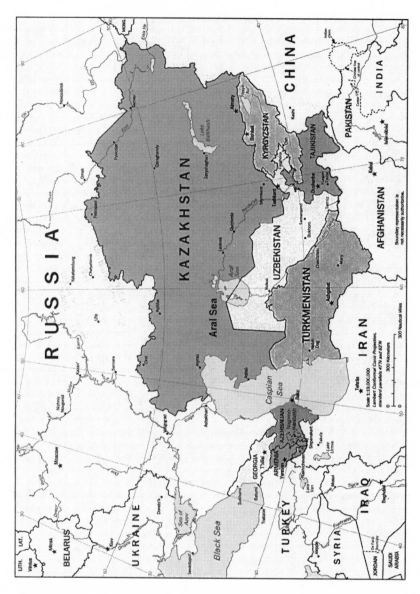

Chapter 10: The Aral Sea Basin. Courtesy of the Perry-Castañeda Library Map Collection, University of Texas at Austin.

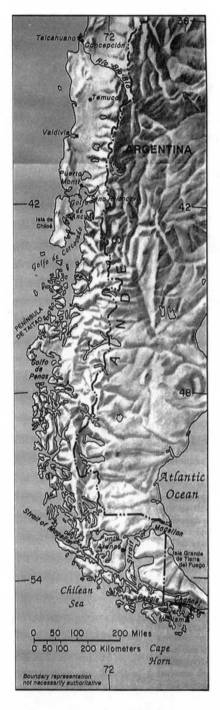

Chapter 11: The Beagle Channel. Courtesy of the Library of Congress Federal Research Division, from *Chile: A Country Study,* ed. Rex A. Hudson (Washington, D.C.: GPO for the Library of Congress, 1994).

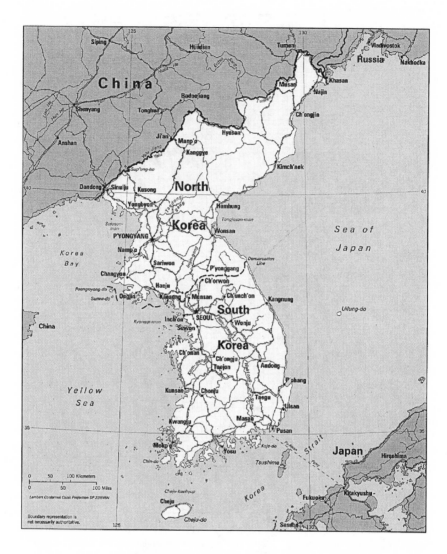

Chapter 12: The Korean Peninsula. Courtesy of the Perry-Castañeda Library Map Collection, University of Texas at Austin (1993).

Introduction: Background and Analytical Perspectives

Melanie C. Greenberg, John H. Barton, and Margaret E. McGuinness

W E EMBARKED ON this project to reach a better understanding of how third-party intervention might lead to successful conflict resolution in the post–Cold War era. We wrote the book with the conviction that the international community can play a helpful role in creatively and aggressively addressing deadly conflict, through mediation, arbitration, and the development of international institutions to promote reconciliation. We realize, of course, that mediation often comes too late to adequately address or prevent the humanitarian dimensions of deadly conflicts or to ensure that conflict does not erupt again. Nevertheless, we feel strongly that mediation can be a highly effective tool for creating resolution of war and/or disputes underlying wars when used at specific and appropriate phases of deadly or potentially deadly conflict.

There are other intelligent, comprehensive, and insightful books and articles addressing the conflicts and disputes we have examined. (The case authors drew extensively from many of these excellent academic histories, which are listed in the bibliography.) This volume is unusual in that it focuses primarily on the negotiated resolutions to the conflicts, rather than the history of the conflicts themselves. Furthermore, we designed a systematic framework for examining each intervention, in order to draw consistent conclusions across a wide variety of cases. The framework for our comparison and an explanation of our choice of cases follow below.

As the title of this book suggests, we see a role for both arbitration and mediation in international conflict resolution. We expected to find a wide range of legal institutions, including judicial and arbitration bodies, operating in the cases we examined. To our surprise, as discussed in the final, synthesis chapter, we found that international courts and arbitration bodies play an important role in resolving many narrower international disputes, but they do not figure prominently in deadly conflict threatening the very nature of states. While bodies such as the Conciliation Commission of the Organization for Security and Cooperation in Europe, the International Court of Justice, and the European Court for Human Rights have made important rulings on territorial and human rights issues, they have not been granted the mandate to rule on the complex issues of sovereignty and minority rights that play a key role in so many of our cases. There are already signs, however, of international legal bodies having a more significant impact on the resolution of large-scale conflict, as in the Hague War Crimes Tribunals for Bosnia and Rwanda and the nascent International Criminal Court. In the future, other bodies might be able to rule on a broader range of issues than currently possible and play a more influential role in resolving political conflict.

Choice of Cases

The chapters in this volume focus on cases where mediation by a nonparty to the conflict constituted the primary form of intervention. We chose our cases because they are among the most complex and interesting conflicts of the post–Cold War period and are representative of the range of difficult issues currently facing the international community in this new era. (The Beagle Channel case represents the one outlier, having been resolved during the Cold War period.) The cases are divided into three rough categories: separation of nations, integration of nations, and intermediation in noncivil conflicts.

The cases involving separation of nations—Abkhazia, Bosnia, Croatia, and the West Bank—have several elements in common. The definition of sovereignty proves to be a polarizing concept that makes peaceful, ambiguous coexistence impossible. Minority rights become an integral concern, as ethnic groups find themselves stranded outside their homeland after secession. In all four of these cases, mediation efforts began while the hostilities on the ground still raged, constantly shifting the parties' incentives to compromise.

In the cases involving integration of nations—Cambodia, El Salvador, Northern Ireland, Rwanda, and South Africa—the primary challenges were to end hostilities and to build new, national institutions in the wake of vicious, bloody, and divisive civil wars. Ensuring political power sharing, the vetting and integration of military forces, building new representative bodies and civil institutions, protecting minority rights, establishing judicial processes for exposing the truth of prior atrocities, and enabling reconciliation became key substantive elements of the mediations in these cases. Among these, the process of transition in South Africa was extraordinary because these issues were negotiated directly by the parties themselves without the aid of an outside mediator.

The cases involving mediation in noncivil conflicts are novel either for their subject matter or the form of intervention. We included the Aral Sea Basin water dispute not only as a demonstration of how conflicts over natural resources may threaten to become a major source of violence and turbulence in the post–Cold War era, but also because it illustrates the creative approach the World Bank took as a mediator. The Beagle Channel case, a territorial dispute between Chile and Argentina in the late 1970s and early 1980s, is significant because the Vatican mediated the conflict and directly averted a descent into armed conflict. The North Korean nuclear crisis illustrates not only the potential of second-track diplomacy, but also the power that a potential nuclear threat can have to galvanize international attention and create incentives for concessions.

Emphasis on Legal Perspective

We approached this study primarily from a legal perspective. As lawyers and legal academics, we were concerned with issues of process, legal principle, rules and development of law, and the role of law in mediated agreements. While bringing this lawyer's bias, we were not limited by this perspective and also examined concepts familiar to specialists in international relations and international security: the development of international institutions, the use and behavior of incentives and sanctions in mediation, the concept of "ripeness" for conflict resolution, and security dilemmas in civil wars. Where possible, we asked questions about whether mediators embraced or avoided concepts of international law; whether law provided avenues for creative solution, or stifled potential solutions; and whether new law was established in particular conflicts.

Theoretical Framework

It was critical in our analysis to ask a set of consistent questions across the various cases. While we did not expect to find a checklist of necessary and sufficient conditions for carrying out a successful mediation, we hoped to draw out general characteristics of mediators and mediating processes that might lend themselves to successful outcomes. We set out to develop a theoretical framework that would pose questions about the nature of the dispute, the organization of the mediation, the implementation process, and the role of various international actors in each mediation. Several scholars and articles were particularly helpful to us in devising the framework. Stephen Stedman gave a very helpful seminar to our case authors, focusing on issues of mediator leverage, flexibility, problem solving, and learning from past failure. Two pieces of scholarly writing by Stedman also proved invaluable, focusing on peace processes in civil wars.[1] Professor Alexander George helped us think through the case study method and provided wise guidance on mediation issues.[2] As discussed in further detail below, William Zartman's work on "ripeness" for conflict resolution was pivotal in our thinking about the mediation process,[3] and Thomas Princen's thoughtful analysis of intermediaries in international conflict was also influential to our studies.[4] The basic framework from which we worked follows below.

Nature of the Underlying Conflict

Our first task was to describe the nature of the underlying conflict. In some cases, this was relatively straightforward. In the Beagle Channel case, for example, the dispute was strictly territorial, with the conflict arising out of different interpretations of boundary lines and ownership rights. The Aral Sea Basin case was more complex in its multiple layers of dispute. The desiccation of the Aral Sea was the most immediate aspect of the crisis, but underlying that crisis were issues of sovereignty, state succession, and the collapse of empire as five newly independent states attempted to build new regimes for resource allocation (and in the process learn how to work together on larger issues). In the former Yugoslavia, the cases of Croatia and Bosnia had elements of both interstate and civil war, with the parties constantly reassessing their negotiation strategies in light of external support, territorial gains on the ground, and the costs and benefits of federation versus independence. The cases of Northern Ireland and the West Bank represented protracted political disputes that each required disaggregation of the most controversial issues to create consensus on the process of mediation.

The Role of Legal Principles in the Dispute

We were very interested in the extent to which *principles and legal issues* were central to the disputes. We knew that sovereignty as a legal principle would permeate the cases, with sovereignty a major issue in Abkhazia, Bosnia, Northern Ireland, the West Bank, and the Aral Sea Basin. We were curious to investigate whether other international legal principles, such as recognition of human rights, either contributed to the underlying dispute or figured prominently as an element in the mediation itself. We also wanted to examine what role standing bodies, laws, and legal institutions had played in adjudicating, advising, or lending guidance in the form of prior precedent on any of these legal principles.

The role of international law and legal principles in the substance of mediated agreements was a key question. What we found did not surprise us: in nearly all of the cases, principles of democracy, procedural transparency, rule of law, and the establishment of particular conflict resolution mechanisms made up the backbone of most agreements between the parties. In several cases—Bosnia, El Salvador, Rwanda, and South Africa—war crimes tribunals or truth commissions played major roles as institutions applying the principles of international humanitarian law in the post-conflict reconciliation process.

Organization of the Key Intervention and Major Actors

Questions involving the choice of the mediator/arbitrator, the selection of parties to the conflict and their representatives, and the role of the international community in intervening in the dispute were central to our analysis of how the interventions were organized.

Choice of Parties

The cases pay substantial attention to the choice of parties and the mechanisms for encouraging them to participate in some form of negotiation. Case authors examine the reasons that particular parties were chosen, the extent to which the parties represent the various interests underlying the conflict, the motivations the parties had for entering negotiations, the political limitations they faced, and the possibility or threat that other actors might have been chosen (and the implications of that choice). "Spoiler" parties and extremists play an important role in many of the conflicts we examined, and case authors analyze how mediators dealt with the spoiler problem.

Choice of Mediators

The choice of mediators proved to be a fascinating question throughout the book. Case authors studied the role of international and regional organizations in providing mediators, analyzed how earlier failures led the parties to choose the ultimately successful mediator, and examined the conditions under which the mediator agreed to enter the mediation. We were also concerned with different typologies of mediation and how mediators chose among various mediation styles. These typologies and styles form a spectrum of mediation, from "good offices," or "facilitator," to "problem solving" to "manipulating" the parties. We analyzed the credibility of the mediators along this spectrum and the possibilities for moving along the spectrum in the course of a given mediation.

Role of the United States, Regional Organizations, International Organizations, and Nongovernmental Organizations

As the last remaining superpower, the United States played at least a marginal role in most—and a major role in several—of the peace processes we examined. We sought to analyze what role (if any) the United States played in setting up the mediation or otherwise influencing the parties to the conflict or events that affected the conflict. We also wanted to assess how the parties perceived U.S. influence. Specifically, we looked at what the United States had done to assist, obstruct, or otherwise influence the outcome of the mediation.

International organizations (especially the United Nations), regional organizations (the Organization of American States, the Organization for Security and Cooperation in Europe, the European Union), and nongovernmental organizations (the Carter Center, the Norwegian Institute for Applied Social Science) played critical roles in almost all of the cases studied. We examine how the influence of these groups can be as highly effective, and also as potentially harmful, as that of any governmental entity.

Form and Specific Mechanisms of Intervention

Of course, we spent a great deal of time studying the specific forms and mechanisms of the mediations themselves. By interviewing mediators and parties, we gained a sense of what was successful and what failed. In the disputes we studied, we found that contemporary conflicts are moving further and further from the traditional pattern of secret resolution by and between career diplomats and politicians. Among the important questions in assessing the form of the process were whether the negotiations were face to face or indirect, the role of formal meetings as opposed to side discussions, whether the key officials dealt directly with each other or indirectly through representatives, whether the discussions were secret or public (and whether their existence was secret or public), and whether the negotiations were carried out uninterrupted over a short time period or during a long series of discussions with breaks in the talks.

Further questions included: Under whose auspices was the mediation conducted, i.e., unofficial, unilateral, regional, or United Nations? What procedures were used, e.g., shuttle diplomacy, proximity negotiations, secret negotiations, talks? What arrangements were made for communications between the negotiators and their various constituencies? Was public information or fact-finding an important part of the intervention, and, if so, how did fact-finding occur? What type of advocacy or expertise (legal, military, etc.) was important? Were public confidence-building gestures, e.g., Sadat's trip to Jerusalem, important?

In examining the day-to-day functions of the mediator, we sought to clarify the precise roles of the intervenors. We looked at their role in injecting new ideas into the process and their ability to develop, propose, and, if necessary, impose settlements through the application of external pressures and incentives. We examined their ability to transmit information; sponsor meetings; convey legal opinions and interpretation; and suggest, facilitate, or make public confidence-building gestures. We also wanted to learn about roadblocks the mediators encountered, such as lack of access to funding for the negotiation process, lack of important intelligence information, language problems, a shortage of staff, or a lack of detailed knowledge about the conflict.

In considering the formidable range of issues inherent in most deadly conflicts, we wondered whether it was possible for the mediator to separate out certain elements of the dispute in order to focus on a smaller number of questions. If so, did they start off with "easier" questions as confidence-building measures to the process and build gradually to the harder questions? Did the parties establish an agenda of issues prior to the negotiations, and did the mediator have the authority to broaden the scope of the discussions if necessary?

What Factors Were Relevant to Shaping the Result?

We would have expected the relative power of the parties, their access to resources, and the depth of their commitment to the outcome to be key factors in shaping the results of the negotiations. We wanted to delve deeper, however, and examine how other dynamics, such as principle and leverage on the part of the mediator, might have affected mediated outcomes.

Principle and Justice Questions

In some circumstances, principle and justice questions are obviously important. We were concerned about how mediators invoke questions of principle and justice and whether they ever choose to gloss over these issues in the interest of gaining peace. When mediators do invoke principle, when does principle matter? How are principles invoked: through legal or similar arguments by various parties? Through United Nations resolutions? Through adherence to or formation of treaties? Through appeals to public opinion over the heads of the negotiating parties? We also asked whether and how often principle and justice questions are left for the implementation process.

Leverage of the Mediator

All mediators act with a subtle balance of persuasion, coercion, and leverage; the cases in this volume analyze how persuasion, coercion, and leverage operate together in each conflict resolution process. The role of outside rewards and sanctions is critical in examining the mediator's leverage. Incentives such as foreign aid and actions of the International Monetary Fund (IMF)/World Bank, and threats such as sanctions, embargoes, criminal prosecution of leaders, and military force, can strengthen the mediator's hand in reaching agreement. Often, of course, these are merely implicitly threatened or promised; they are frequently not within the full control of the intervenors, and the linkage is not often explicitly made in public statements.

In analyzing leverage, we sought to illuminate how the mediator affected the subjective, objective, and normative environments in the mediation process. A mediator could affect the objective environment by providing peacekeepers, side payments, rewards, and military or political retaliation against spoilers. A mediator could demonstrate normative leverage by conferring legitimacy on a particular party that had not previously been included in the peace process—or illegitimacy on a party that had once been included. The mediator might influence the subjective environment by altering the parties' perceptions of an issue or each other, by problem solving or actively working to build trust.

A successful mediator needs to be able to look at past attempts that have failed and should be in tune with changes in events and among parties. The cases analyze how well or badly mediators learned from earlier failures, others' as well as their own. Similarly, we looked at how mediators reacted to potential failure of a current process: Would the mediator threaten to break off talks (and would this provide leverage), or would it be more appropriate to muddle through?

Public information is an important tool of leverage: public expression of new facts or of neutral judgments can significantly affect the further freedom of action of the parties. The cases examine the role of the press and media vis-à-vis both the parties and the mediator, and how parties and mediators use or abuse the media during the mediation process.

Finally, moral suasion by the mediator cannot be overlooked, as is evident in the Beagle Channel case. We realized that leverage based on morality is not always clear-cut, so we sought out instances in which principle, morality, and pressure to "do the right thing" played an important role in the mediation process.

Success and Implementation of the Mediated Agreement

It is difficult to define success in the context of mediation. Does success mean simply an end to hostilities? And does ending hostilities mean a permanent end, or simply a cease-fire? Is a solution that ends the fighting but rewards war crimes and ethnic cleansing a successful one? These normative questions are difficult, but we sought in each case to analyze several criteria for success.

Of course, success cannot ultimately be determined until the implementation period of the agreement is well underway. The implementation period for a mediated agreement is very fragile. Often, the time after a negotiated peace can be even more violent than the period leading up to the mediation. Stephen Stedman lists four reasons that this period is so fragile: signing a peace agreement does not necessarily mean that the parties prefer peace to war, parties might opt to risk the benefits of peace for another try at war and total victory, cheating is common in implementation, and rogue elements might continue to fight even if their leadership has signed a peace agreement.[5] More broadly, in an era in which public opinion may reward a well-publicized partial agreement, it is certainly possible that there can be formal agreements that do not adequately resolve the underlying conflicts. An important part of each case in this volume, therefore, deals with implementation issues.

We were especially interested in the question of spoilers, particularly how extremists were integrated or excluded from the mediation process and whether such exclusion adversely affected the implementation phase. We also wanted to examine whether the parties charged with implementing the mediated agreements had been involved with the negotiation process itself or had otherwise coordinated implementation plans with the signatories to the agreement. Another fascinating question about implementation focuses on the role of ambiguity in negotiated agreement: When is ambiguous language a helpful tool for "selling" an agreement, and when does it become a barrier to successful implementation of an agreement?

Specific Lessons Learned

Finally, even though the cases in this volume vary tremendously in their contexts and scope, we asked for each case to end with a conclusion exploring what larger lessons might emerge that could be useful for future mediators. In examining failures, we were particularly interested in the lacunae or failings of the international dispute management system.

Overarching Themes

In addition to the framework set out above, we were concerned with three larger, overarching themes. The first involves the question of ripeness, the second speculates on the "value added" by the mediator, and the third focuses on special issues concerning intrastate conflict.

Ripeness

A critical element of all our cases was the concept of "ripeness," or when a conflict is most amenable to mediation. William Zartman developed the concept of ripeness, which he describes as a point at which the parties have reached a "mutually hurting stalemate." Inherent in the stalemate is a realization that neither party can win the conflict unilaterally, yet each side maintains the ability to hurt the other. At such a point of ripeness, the parties might be amenable to negotiation, in order to realize at least a portion of their desired gains and to eliminate the threat from an opponent who is still able to wound, if not kill. A key challenge for the mediator is to present a mediated agreement as a way out of the stalemate and to make the parties view the outcome as an acceptable (or even preferable) alternative to a unilateral "win."

Pinpointing a moment when a mutually hurting stalemate has occurred is extremely difficult. Cambodia provides one example of absolute war-weariness on all sides of the conflict. But even there, only when the war-weariness matched external events was a cease-fire made possible. In El Salvador, for example, it was clear that both parties had reached a stalemate (and acknowledged it as such when they sought mediation). Yet, military hostilities continued to take place during the peace talks, operating as an alternate means to achieve gains. In Bosnia, the parties themselves seemed to feel no particular stalemate: they used many of the mediation efforts as tools in the war and as opportunities to delay and buy time before resuming hostilities on the ground. In Bosnia, it was ultimately the international mediators who felt the need to intervene—and then only when the international community felt pushed to the breaking point by the atrocities and humanitarian disasters occurring in the former Yugoslavia.

One unfortunate problem with the term "ripeness" is the implication that the moment for ripeness only occurs once, after a particular process leading up to that moment (as a fruit slowly matures to the point of ripeness, at which point it can be picked). In fact, ripeness can occur—or, in some cases, can be "created"—at many times along the spectrum of a conflict. Mutually hurting stalemates arise at different phases in a conflict and can be broken as one side gains military strength, wins an election, gains additional financial resources, or perceives some advantage over its adversary. It might be more helpful to think about ripe moments as "windows of opportunity" that occur at various moments throughout the conflict. When open, these windows of opportunity can be exploited by a mediator, who can help transform the moment into a situation promoting compromise by all parties.

Another question arises as to how an outside mediator might force ripeness. This can happen in very blatant ways, as when a mediator draws upon force to level the playing field (e.g., the North Atlantic Treaty Organization's retaliatory bombing of the Bosnian Serbs prior to the Dayton talks) or on its ability to influence international economic assistance. It might also operate in very subtle ways, as the mediator frames a solution in a way that makes the current situation feel less optimal than a mediated outcome (for example, when the Vatican used its influence on the parties to the Beagle Channel dispute to convince them that both would suffer greatly from a territorial war). Finally, however, we recognized that an analysis of ripeness often leads to a tautological conclusion: Ripeness occurs at that moment which we recognize in hindsight as the time the parties came together to find a negotiated solution; it fails to occur when the parties continue fighting. To avoid this tautology, we found it useful to compare when and how windows of opportunity were exploited in one instance, but how and under what circumstances a similar window of opportunity was not seized in another.

Value Added by the Mediator

We were also concerned about whether, in the final analysis, mediators "added value" to the negotiation between the parties and to the resolution of the conflict. "But for" and counterfactual analyses are always difficult, but we wanted to examine whether the parties themselves, without a mediator, might have eventually reached agreements, whether a different form of mediation at a different time might have been more successful, or whether the mediator did everything possible to bring the parties to the point where each could maximize its gains and minimize its losses.

Special Qualities of Intrastate Wars

Many of the cases involve intrastate, or partially intrastate, conflicts: Abkhazia, Bosnia, Croatia, El Salvador, Cambodia, Rwanda, and South Africa. Intrastate conflicts demonstrate particular dynamics that make negotiation or mediation especially difficult. Parties often consider intrastate disputes to be a one-time, zero-sum game for control over the country.[6] Pathological leadership can prevent a leader from ever being brought to compromise, even if short-term compromise might lead to more stable power.[7] A demonized view of the "enemy" can keep parties from compromise and make transparent communication about the future, free from stereotype, difficult.[8] Given these formidable barriers to conflict resolution, we wanted to analyze how mediators dealt with irrational leaders, helped humanize the enemy at the negotiation table, and changed the parameters of the conflict from a zero-sum game to some element of power sharing and nation building.

We also wondered to what extent mediation legitimized opposition or nongovernmental groups. Does the fact that the mediator even talks to groups not recognized by the government lend legitimacy to these groups? Is this positive or negative? In intrastate conflicts, which often have a populist or social basis, it can be argued that there is a greater requirement for knowledge, awareness, and public education (which go against the goals of secrecy and quiet trade-offs inherent in many mediations). With intrastate disputes becoming the norm rather than the exception, more data and theoretical work are needed to understand the dynamics of these deadly conflicts. These cases shed some light on the difficulties of and possibilities for mediation in such conflicts.

Capturing a Moving Target

One of the joys and difficulties of working on this book was the constant shift in events on the ground. When the Northern Ireland chapter was originally drafted, the parties were at a low point in the process, and a negotiated resolution seemed unlikely. A year later, two of the participants received the Nobel Peace Prize for the historic Good Friday Agreement. Similarly, the ongoing Oslo process has experienced backsliding; threats of collapse; and in October 1998, hopes for realizing a lasting final resolution of West Bank territorial issues. As of this writing, in Bosnia, SFOR (NATO Stabilization Force) troops remain in position two years after the scheduled withdrawal of the peacekeeping force, and hard-line nationalists have won the most recent elections. Yet despite the continuously changing terrain of these cases, we believe that the central lessons we have drawn from the mediations are lasting and durable and can offer general themes for the future. The chapters in this book represent a sample of the conflicts that proved susceptible to mediation or resolution in the immediate post–Cold War period; they are not the last. We hope that they will illuminate the potential for intelligent, creative, determined, and skilled mediators in situations of deadly conflict and will inspire new forms of intervention for preventing and resolving the deadly conflicts of the future.

Part One

Separation of Nations

W E CHOSE THE Abkhazia/Georgia conflict, the secession of Bosnia and Croatia from the former Yugoslavia, and the Oslo negotiations over the status of the West Bank and Israeli-occupied territories to illustrate problems of secession, state succession, and separation of nations. These cases vary in their historical and political contexts and in the mediation processes that led to an eventual cessation of active hostilities. However, several common themes weave throughout each case and highlight the specific challenges of reaching resolution in conflicts involving secession.

Ironically, perhaps, a primary principle of international law often presents the main barrier to a negotiated settlement in these cases: sovereignty. When placed in opposition to another basic principle of international law, self-determination, the demand of sovereignty is a zero-sum game. In each of these cases, the party seeking to secede sought full rights of nationhood. Sovereignty posed a serious problem for the original state in cases where significant minorities remained in the seceding body, or where the seceding body controlled important land or resources. Solutions short of sovereignty, such as autonomy in key areas of political life, trade, and education, combined with an overreaching confederation, might have made an agreement possible. In each case, the extreme nature of the conflict tended to rule out compromises on sovereignty, and international law did not provide a good road map for the gray areas short of sovereignty. The current world order, still reflective of the seventeenth-century Westphalian statist system, tends to reward full sovereignty; membership in the United Nations and other key diplomatic trappings of modern statehood are not bestowed on substate entities. While mediated agreements in these cases effectively brought active hostilities to an end, the resulting agreements left all parties unhappy, to one degree or another, with the legal result.

Another serious issue facing seceding states is that of minority rights. The rights of national minorities left stranded from the "motherland" created serious stumbling blocks in the mediations. Furthermore, some of the bloodiest fighting of the conflicts occurred within radicalized pockets of minority areas (Bosnian Serbs in Bosnia, Serbs in the Krajina region of Croatia, Jewish settlers in the West Bank). A related problem is refugees, especially where ethnic cleansing has occurred. The refugees not only place a strain on the original state, to which the refugees often stream back (even if their families had been living in the now autonomous region for centuries), but also on neighboring states, creating regional tensions that must then be addressed along with the dispute between the original parties.

Regional organizations played an important role in the Abkhazia, Bosnia, and Croatia conflicts, but with mixed results. On the one hand, the regional organizations were well placed to understand the conflict and were highly motivated— by geography and economic interests—to resolve it. On the other hand, states and entities within the regional organizations often had competing agendas, making unified action and decision making difficult.

These cases suggest a need for an independent judicial body that might one day be able to rule on or provide guidance about issues such as eligibility for secession, taking into account the adequacy of minority rights guarantees and state capacities to manage refugee flows.

1

Multilateral Mediation in Intrastate Conflicts: Russia, the United Nations, and the War in Abkhazia

Arthur Khachikian

Overview

THE ABHKAZIA CASE illustrates a dispute over the independence or autonomy of a portion of a newly independent state. Specifically, the Georgia/Abkhazia conflict is a secessionist ethnic conflict taking place between a parent state (Georgia) and an intrastate minority (Abkhazia), in the wake of the collapse of the Soviet Union. The case is interesting not only because of its historical context, but also because of the "dual mediator" model in which a clearly interested party (Russia) and two neutral international bodies (the United Nations and the Organization for Security and Cooperation in Europe, OSCE) cooperate to mediate a complex dispute. In this particular dual mediator situation, Russia was able to use coercion and political leverage to influence the parties, while the United Nations and the OSCE lent legitimacy and the power of international norms to the process. The case also highlights the difficulties of mediating in the shadow of international law, where the Scylla and Charybdis of "territorial integrity" and "self-determination" stand in the way of compromise over the issue of sovereignty. Finally, the case is an important illustration of "subcontract" peacekeeping.

Timeline

1990 **August:** The Abkhaz Declaration of Sovereignty.

1991 **March:** Georgia boycotts the referendum on preserving the Soviet Union while Abkhazia takes part and votes to remain a part of the Soviet Union.

1992 **February:** The Abkhaz Declaration of Independence. **August:** Georgian troops cross into Abkhazia. The beginning of war. **September:** The Moscow cease-fire; the first UN mission arrives.

1993 **July:** The Gudauta cease-fire. August: UN Observer Mission (UNOMIG) deployed. **September:** The Abkhaz offensive. Abkhazia restored in its prewar borders.

1994 **April:** Moscow talks. The Declaration on Measures for a Political Settlement and the Quadripartite Agreement on the Return of Refugees and Displaced Persons signed. **May:** The Agreement on Cease-Fire and Separation of Forces signed. **July:** The UN Security Council expands the mandate of UNOMIG. **November:** Abkhazia adopts a constitution declaring itself a sovereign state and elects its president.

1995 **February–April:** The sides locked in a stalemate over the political status of Abkhazia. Negotiations in Geneva and Moscow fail. The beginning of the political stalemate.

1996 **January:** The Commonwealth of Independent States (CIS) Heads of States Council imposes economic sanctions on Abkhazia.

Background

Subject of the Dispute

The case of Abkhazia belongs to the category of secessionist ethnic conflict taking place between a parent-state and an intrastate minority ethnic group. The primary issues of the Abkhazia conflict concern the status of the Abkhaz, a Muslim minority group, and their claims to a territorial homeland within the predominantly Christian Republic of Georgia. During the Soviet era, both sides had a place in the Soviet Union's hierarchy of nationalities: Georgia carried the status of a union republic, with the nominal right of secession and state sovereignty, while Abkhazia was classified as an autonomous republic within Georgia.

When the conflict began in the final days of the Soviet Union, the Abkhaz asserted a claim to full independence. The Abkhaz have since relinquished the claim to full independence, but they agree to remain within Georgia only as a part of a confederative arrangement whereby they would have the status of an equal member. Georgia is willing to go no further than a federative arrangement in which Abkhazia would be a part of the sovereign Georgian state, with the broadest possible scope of autonomy. The parties, caught between these two positions, have reached a stalemate, and the negotiation process is at an impasse.

Brief History of the Conflict

As is the case with many other ethnic conflicts, the dispute between Abkhazia and Georgia involves conflicting historical claims of the two sides. Both Georgians and Abkhazians view themselves as the indigenous population of the contested territory and the opponent—as migrants. After the end of the Russian Empire, in the early years of Soviet history, Abkhazia enjoyed a short period of formal sovereignty as a union republic within the Soviet Union (1921–31). It was subsequently incorporated into Georgia as an autonomous republic. In the years that followed, the demographic composition of Abkhazia changed significantly as a result of the Georgianization policy of Lavrentii Beria and the Tbilisi leaders. From the 1930s through the 1950s the Abkhazian component of the population declined steadily, and according to the most recent data, from the 1989 census which reflected the situation before the outbreak of hostilities, the Abkhazians constituted only 17.8 percent of the population, i.e., 93,000 people.

In the final years of the Soviet Union the friction between Tbilisi (the Georgian capital) and Sukhumi (the Abkhaz capital) intensified. The Abkhaz often turned to Moscow to secure privileges in the areas of language, education, and political representation in their autonomous republic, while Moscow supported the rebellious republic in order to control the independent-minded Georgian government in Tbilisi. The nationalist policies of the first post-Communist leader of Georgia, Zviad Gamsakhurdia, aggravated the tension. These policies were a more energetic continuation of the previous attempts of Tbilisi toward Georgianization in linguistic, cultural, and educational areas. The Georgians living in Abkhazia, on the other hand, resented the overrepresentation of the Abkhaz in the local government, which no longer corresponded to the actual demographic balance: the Abkhaz had become a minority while holding the majority of seats in the legislative and executive bodies.

The "War of Laws"

In August 1990 the Abkhazian Supreme Soviet declared sovereignty, which was promptly annulled by the Georgian Supreme Soviet. While Georgia boycotted the referendum of March 1991 on the preservation of the Soviet Union, Abkhazia participated in it and overwhelmingly demonstrated its allegiance. In February 1992 the Georgian Parliament voted to return to the pre-Soviet Constitution of 1921, that of the independent Georgian Republic; Abkhazia followed by declaring its return to the Constitution of 1925, according to which it is a union republic within the Soviet Union. In early 1992 the Supreme Soviet of Abkhazia declared independence from Georgia.

Escalation to Violence and the Main Stages of the Armed Conflict

In August 1992 the Georgian armed forces under the leadership of Defense Minister Tyngiz Kitovani crossed into Abkhazia and seized Sukhumi. The war continued with changing success. The Abkhaz enjoyed the support of certain

Russian military units (from whom they received large amounts of ammunition) and their ethnic kin from the Northern Caucasus, who fought as volunteers on the Abkhaz side. The first cease-fire was negotiated in September 1992 in Moscow by the representatives of Georgia, Abkhazia, and Russia, but it was soon violated. The second cease-fire agreement was signed by these sides in Gudauta (Abkhazia) in July 1993. It was violated again in September 1993, with the sudden Abkhazian offensive that expelled the Georgian forces from the territory of Abkhazia. The most recent agreement on cessation of hostilities was signed in Moscow on April 4, 1994, and was largely observed by both sides. However, efforts to find a comprehensive political settlement have not been successful to this day.

Claims of the Sides and Their Legitimization: The Existing International Legal Framework

The Georgian side invokes the norm of territorial integrity and inviolability of borders of the sovereign Republic of Georgia, which were recognized by the international community after the collapse of the Soviet Union in December 1991. This claim was repeatedly supported by the UN Security Council, as well as by the OSCE and other international actors. The Abkhaz side claims that since Abkhazia was an autonomous republic within Georgia under the old Soviet constitution, by seceding from the Soviet Union and denouncing its constitution on its territory, Georgia thus invalidated Abkhazia's status as a part of Georgia. The relationship between the two units needs to be renegotiated as that between two equal legal entities. (A similar argument was used in the dispute over the status of the Aaland Islands after Finland's independence from Russia after World War I.)

As this example demonstrates, intrastate conflicts are not an area in which international law is easily applicable or particularly useful. Its contradictory principles, such as self-determination vs. territorial integrity, nonintervention and sovereignty vs. human rights, legitimate the conflicting claims of the sides. Other provisions of international law create additional obstacles for recognizing and negotiating with intrastate groups. (A more detailed discussion of these issues will follow later in the chapter.)

Key Interventions and Major Actors

Brief History of International Interventions

Phase 1: Deescalation

At the time when the first cease-fire agreement was signed by Georgia, Abkhazia, and Russia in Moscow on September 3, 1992, the sides issued an appeal to the United Nations and the OSCE to assist in its implementation. According to the agreement, the territorial integrity of Georgia was to be respected, the refugees were to return to their homes, the legitimate authorities of Abkhazia were to resume their functions, and the Georgian forces on Abkhazian territory were to be reduced. A tripartite committee composed of Georgian, Abkhazian, and Russian representatives was to be created to monitor the agreement. However, the cease-fire collapsed on October 1, 1992.

The first UN Mission was sent to the region in September 1992. The second followed in late October 1992, to explore the possible forms of UN involvement, in consultation with the OSCE. Two of the UN civilian personnel remained on the spot. After he was appointed as special envoy of the secretary-general to Georgia in May 1993, Edouard Brunner took part in bringing the sides to the negotiation table and finding a political solution to the conflict. The sides supported an active UN role in the peace process. The United Nations pursued a three-track peace process: consolidation of the cease-fire, continuation of negotiations, and involvement of third-party countries, particularly Russia, in the first two tasks. It was proposed to convene a peace conference under the auspices of the United Nations and to deploy UN observers in the area. However, another cease-fire concluded in May 1993 broke down in two weeks.[1]

In July 1993 the secretary-general proposed to deploy UN military observers in the area. When a new cease-fire agreement was concluded on July 27, through the mediation of Russia, the way was cleared for implementing this proposal. The UN Observer Mission was deployed in August 1993 and established its headquarters in the Abkhazian administrative center of Sukhumi.[2]

On September 16, 1993, the cease-fire broke down again. The Abkhaz launched a surprise offensive, with the support of Russian military detachments; retook the capital city of Sukhumi; and restored the *status quo ante bellum* in Abkhazia. The Security Council condemned the violation of the cease-fire by the Abkhaz forces as well as numerous violations of international humanitarian norms by both sides.

In October 1993 both sides held discussions with the special envoy in Geneva. In November similar discussions were held with the Russian deputy foreign minister. In the same month the peace process gained new momentum with the first round of discussions with both sides in Geneva. The talks took place under the auspices of the United Nations, with the Russian Federation playing the role of a facilitator and the OSCE invited as a participant.[3]

A Memorandum of Understanding was signed by the parties in the presence of representatives of the United Nations, OSCE, and Russia on December 1, 1993. The sides pledged not to use force against each other and to exchange prisoners of war, facilitate the repatriation of refugees, etc. No progress on the main political issues was reported. The second round of negotiations in January 1994 in Geneva produced a joint communiqué with some positive results on essentially the same issues, as well as an agreement on the deployment of peacekeeping forces, but still no breakthrough on the political issues.

Phase 2: Search for Settlement

During the third round of talks in February 1994 in Geneva, the sides faced the necessity of addressing the main political issue of the conflict—the status of

Abkhazia. The special envoy presented them with a draft political declaration that included a provision recognizing the territorial integrity of Georgia. The Abkhaz declined to sign any document containing such a statement, leading to the failure of negotiations. Yet another round of talks in New York in March 1994 had a similar fate, and again, the issues of territorial integrity and the status of Abkhazia were the main reasons for failure. The Security Council passed a resolution calling for both sides to resume the peace process, while at the same time reaffirming the sovereignty and territorial integrity of Georgia.

These issues remained unresolved during the Moscow talks in April of 1994. However, the sides succeeded in signing two important documents—the Declaration on Measures for a Political Settlement of the Georgian-Abkhaz Conflict and the Quadripartite Agreement on Voluntary Return of Refugees and Displaced Persons. The issue of the return of refugees was thus disentangled from the question of the status of Abkhazia, although the implementation of this agreement became very problematic and was eventually linked back to the larger political issues. The return of refugees was not just a humanitarian, but also a very important political problem, since the return of about 200,000 Georgian refugees to Abkhazia would have tilted the demographic and, correspondingly, the political balance in the republic. (Before the exodus of Georgian and other refugees from Abkhazia, the Abkhaz comprised a minority on the territory of their republic). Hence the reluctance of the Abkhaz authorities to allow the refugees' return prior to the resolution of larger political issues.

According to the Declaration on Measures for a Political Settlement of the Georgian-Abkhaz Conflict, Abkhazia would have its own constitution, legislation, and appropriate state symbols, such as anthem, emblem, and flag. Article 7 of the declaration postulates that "The parties held discussions on distribution of powers on the understanding that any agreement on this issue is part of a comprehensive settlement and will only be reached once a final solution to the conflict has been found." However, the same article lists issues on which agreement had been reached: foreign policy and forging economic ties, border guard agreements, customs, energy, transport, communication, ecology, human rights, and the rights of national minorities.

Furthermore, on May 14 the sides signed the Agreement on a Cease-Fire and Separation of Forces. This agreement provided for cooperation between the CIS peacekeeping forces and the UN Observer Mission in Abkhazia. Both the CIS peacekeeping forces and the UN observers had essentially the same task: to monitor the implementation of the May 14 agreement.

In July 1994, a few months after the sides signed the "Declaration on Measures for a Political Settlement of the Georgian-Abkhaz Conflict" and the Quadripartite Agreement, the Security Council authorized a further increase in the UNOMIG forces and expanded its mandate to include observing the operation of the CIS peacekeeping forces. The decision to expand the UN Observer Mission in Abkhazia was made at the same time as the UN authorization of the U.S. action in Haiti. This event gave birth to a new term—"subcontract peacekeeping"—which was coined by a number of analysts to describe a practice in which an international organization authorizes individual states to carry out peace-keeping and other activities. Some reports alleged that there was an informal understanding between Russia and the United States according to which the two nations traded each other's approval for the operations in Abkhazia and Haiti respectively. The AP news agency reported on August 2, 1994:

> Russia supported the UN endorsement of a Haiti invasion only after Washington gave its blessing to Russia's military intervention in the Republic of Georgia, State Department officials say. The officials, asking not to be identified, said the Russians never made the link explicit but suggested in many consultations that there should be equity in the way the UN Security Council acts. By its resolution 937 the Security Council increased the strength of its observer mission and expanded its mandate to include observation of the CIS peacekeeping forces.[4]

This practice of "subcontract" peacekeeping and mediation did not go unquestioned. The representative of Pakistan, on behalf of a number of countries, expressed his concern with involving regional actors in such activities, "especially when such countries have direct political interests in the area of the conflict." Other countries stressed the necessity of pressing on with multilateral mechanisms of conflict mediation and settlement, while recognizing the usefulness of the United Nations-CIS/Russia model.

Two more rounds of talks followed with the participation of the UN special envoy, in July 1994 in Sochi and in August–September 1994 in Geneva. Further progress was reached regarding the issue of the return of refugees, although this issue was later "reintegrated" into the larger political agenda by the Abkhaz side, for the reasons mentioned earlier.

The differences over the core political issues remained unresolved. At the next round of talks in November 1994 in Geneva, another attempt was made to outline elements of the future status of Abkhazia. The sides agreed to consider the draft, but the Georgians rejected it in December 1994 in view of the changing situation. In November 1994 the Abkhazian Parliament adopted a constitution. Article 1 declared Abkhazia to be a "sovereign democratic state." A statement issued by Abkhazia called for the continuation of talks with Georgia with the objective of creating a "union-state of two equal subjects." The next move of the Abkhaz side was the inauguration of Vladislav Ardzinba as the president of the republic in December 1994. Georgia vigorously protested to the Security Council, and Georgia's president issued yet another statement reaffirming the territorial integrity and sovereignty of Georgia. The political negotiations had reached a stubborn impasse.

The talks resumed in Geneva in February 1995. For the first time, the sides agreed on some elements of the political settlement. It included the establishment of a "federal legislative organ" and a "supreme organ of executive power." However, the sides remained divided on the issue of the territorial integrity of Georgia and the federal character of the future state, while agreeing on its borders within those of the Georgian Republic of 1991.

Russia prepared another draft of the political settlement in April 1995. This draft provided for a federative arrangement between the sides whereby Abkhazia would be granted certain powers. The Georgian representatives stated that a federation was as far as Georgia was prepared to go. The Abkhaz interpreted this as an offer of autonomy, not equal membership in a union-state, and rejected the agreement.

In summary, since the beginning of negotiations in 1992 the sides only slightly altered their positions with regard to the political settlement. Abkhazia no longer sought full independence and agreed to stay within a single state with Georgia, although on an equal footing, while Georgia was now ready to provide a great deal of autonomy to Abkhazia short of granting it equal status; in other words, the two sides are still divided over whether they should have a federative or a confederative relationship with one another (see the previous section on the existing international legal framework). This stalemate continues at the time of this writing, despite all diplomatic efforts on the part of Russia and the United Nations.

Phase 3: Bringing Pressure to Bear

Throughout the conflict the UN Security Council and Russia emphasized the territorial integrity and sovereignty of Georgia as a basis for any settlement. This position implied that both of these actors were not impartial with regard to the sides from a normative point of view. Soon the moral pressure changed into more practical measures. In January 1996 the Council of Heads of States of CIS blamed the Abkhaz side for the failure of talks and preventing the return of refugees. A decision was taken imposing economic sanctions and other measures against Abkhazia, namely closing the Abkhaz-Russian border and imposing a blockade of its Black Sea coast. Russia subsequently implemented these decisions, although the enforcement of the blockade had a mixed record and fell short of satisfying the Georgian side.

At present, the political process is in a stalemate. Economic conditions in Abkhazia have been rapidly deteriorating, especially after its access to the outside world through the Russian border and the Black Sea was restricted. The Georgian economy, on the other hand, is now growing at a fast rate; the country also receives large amounts of foreign aid. The new Georgian Constitution left open the provisions for a federal structure of the Georgian state, to allow for greater flexibility of the Georgian side during negotiations.

Timing of Mediation and Ripeness of the Conflict

A critical issue for the success or failure of mediation in conflicts is the issue of timing. It is widely accepted that mediation can only be successful when the conflict in question is "ripe" for it, i.e., at a window of opportunity when the conflicting sides are ready to end the hostilities and accept the intervention of a mediator. William Zartman describes this condition as a mutually hurting stalemate that emerges either after a recent or before an impending catastrophe, when unilateral solutions are blocked, the "underdog" starts rising, and the victor's power is declining.[5]

Just when the conflict is ripe for settlement is not entirely clear; the theorists of conflict mediation are divided on this issue.[6] Some argue in favor of early intervention, before violence flares up and makes reconciliation difficult. Others support late intervention, when the military solutions are exhausted and the sides have no alternative to peace—in the words of Stephen Stedman, when the fear of continuing war is high, and the fear of settlement is low.[7]

Thomas Princen argues that when there is an asymmetry of power between the sides intervention at a later stage may be effective—once the stronger side gives up its hope for unilateral victory.[8] This argument may be pertinent for intrastate conflicts for two reasons. First, intrastate groups are often weaker than the parent states, are usually not as well organized and armed as the latter (in the absence of powerful external supporters), and have no access to international assistance. Given this disparity, the parent-state may have reasons to believe that it can successfully suppress the rebellion at an early stage to preempt further complications. Secondly, the norm of nonintervention and nonrecognition of the rebels prevents external involvement, mediation, or negotiation with the intrastate group. Furthermore, in the eyes of the parent-state, negotiating with the rebels means admitting defeat and granting them an equal status, with the prospect of future independence. In the classic era, the change of status from rebellion to belligerency entitled the belligerent to receive external support and diplomatic recognition. This was usually viewed as the first step toward independence. Therefore, the parent-state may have good reasons to resist any external involvement and attempt to suppress the rebellion in the first place. The Georgian attack on Abkhazia in 1992, led by Tyngiz Kitovani, was an attempt to "pacify" the recalcitrant republic before the conflict became internationalized.

However, the issue of "ripeness" is problematic in the Abkhaz case for one very important reason—both the Abkhaz and the Georgians (although not to an equal extent) at different stages of the conflict have received significant external support from elements within the Russian military. The factor of external support changed the calculations of the warring sides to a very important degree, in fact becoming one of the decisive factors in these calculations. As long as either side could count on this support, it could foster the hope of prevailing in the war. Therefore, the point of military exhaustion was unreachable without the cooperation of the forces that stood behind the military assistance to the sides.

At the latter stage of the conflict in Abkhazia, after the last major eruption of violence in September 1993 during the Abkhaz offensive, the conflict entered into a condition of stalemate; using the typology of Zartman, it became a "grinding crisis." According to his observation, one of the sides in these types of crises is a "leftover national liberation movement or runaway client seeking independent legitimacy and recognition."[9] As the conflict in Abkhazia demonstrates, this condition of stalemate may continue for quite a long time without leading to a settlement.

In summary, if one were to generalize from the Abkhaz experience, it would appear that in conflicts involving interests of major powers and the presence of external sources of support for the conflicting sides, the "ripeness" of the conflict for resolution is closely linked not only to the positions of the sides themselves but also to the positions of these powers and external supporters.

Form and Specific Mechanisms of Intervention

The Multiple Mediator Model

The conflict in Abkhazia provides an intriguing example of international mediation in violent conflict. The mediation was carried out by a number of mediators simultaneously, with a corresponding division of responsibilities among them. Importantly, these roles and functions, as well as the tools and sources of leverage, were different, although the efforts of the mediators were mutually coordinated, complemented each other, and aimed at the same result.

The two main actors in this mechanism were the United Nations and Russia. The formal formula for their cooperation was United Nations + regional organization (CIS), with Russia playing the main role in the latter. Another international organization, the OSCE, had a participant role as an observer. The formula of negotiations was as follows: they were taking place under the auspices of the United Nations, with Russia playing the role of facilitator, and with the participation of OSCE representatives. In practice, the interaction of the two main actors, the United Nations and Russia, was taking place as a parallel and coordinated process. When the United Nations convened negotiations in Geneva, Russia offered its assistance and performed as a facilitator. When Russia convened negotiations in Moscow, the United Nations was informed and the special envoy of the secretary-general took part.

This parallel process included the deployments of the Russian peacekeeping forces and the UN observers in the field. The two had the same mandate—to monitor the implementation of the May 14, 1994, agreement. The representatives of Russia and the United Nations exchanged letters describing the forms and methods of mutual cooperation. The provisions for their cooperation were outlined in the Agreement on Separation of Forces of May 1994.[10] The division of labor and the different roles and capabilities of the United Nations and Russia were brought to light in the aftermath of Geneva talks in February 1994 under the auspices of the former. After the sides failed to reach an agreement and the talks collapsed, Russia successfully used its leverage to induce the sides to sign approximately the same document in April 1994 in Moscow.

Another interesting actor in the international mediation efforts in Abkhazia was a group of states called "The Friends of Georgia" that included the United States, the United Kingdom, France, Germany, and Russia. The role of this group consisted of sponsoring a number of important decisions of the UN Security Council and the secretary-general, as well as supporting the activities of the United Nations with a concerted effort.

Different Roles of Mediators

The mediation in the Abkhaz conflict was carried out by a number of international actors who worked in a coordinated manner forming a joint mediation mechanism. These actors created a certain division of labor among themselves, using different, although mutually coordinated, tools and methods of influencing the conflicting sides (See figure 1.1 for the multiple mediation mechanism). Moreover, among the mediators themselves there existed a relationship of mutual dependence and influence.

The main tool of the United Nations and OSCE was that of legitimization and recognition. The UN decision to endorse the activities of Russia in the Abkhaz conflict implied a conferral of legitimacy to Russia's leading role in the resolution of this conflict, while the deployment of international observers symbolized this legitimacy and provided a tool for monitoring the activities of the Russian forces. The UN Security Council, by passing numerous resolutions reaffirming Georgia's territorial integrity and refusing to recognize Abkhazia's independence, legitimized the Georgian position and put considerable pressure, moral and political, on the Abkhaz side.

Russia, on the other hand, had considerable leverage in the practical realm of the conflict. In the absence of other volunteers, Russia provided its troops for the peacekeeping mission. Both sides in the conflict are heavily dependent on Russia for their military, economic, energy, and other needs. Vital routes linking the region to the outside world run through Russian territory. Both sides in the conflict are armed with Soviet/Russian-made weapons, and they have to turn to Russia to replenish their arsenals. This wide range of tools in the hands of Russia allows it to put considerable pressure on the sides; using that it can facilitate the process of settlement. For example, when the United Nations failed to induce the sides to agree

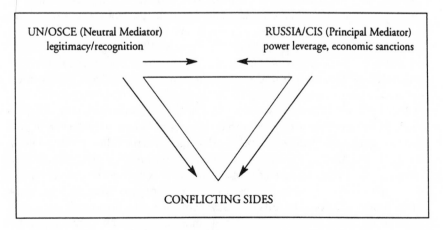

Figure 1.1
The Multiple Mediator Mechanism

on a draft political document in February 1994, Russia stepped in to use its leverage. As a result, an identical agreement was signed in Moscow in April 1994.[11]

After the CIS Heads of States meeting in January 1997, a decision was taken
to impose economic sanctions against Abkhazia. Russia carried out the implementation of this decision. Russian ships enforced the blockade of the Abkhaz
Black Sea coast, while Russian troops closed the border between Abkhazia and
Russia. Although it remains unclear how consistently the blockade was enforced, its consequences were very grave for the Abkhaz economy, which has declined rapidly, while the economy of Georgia is currently on its way to recovery,
boosted by significant amounts of foreign assistance.

In summary, a wide number of tools were used to influence the sides in the
Abkhaz-Georgian conflict. These ranged from moral and political pressure to
legitimization to economic rewards and sanctions to military assistance to the
sides. At present, the Georgian side demands more decisive measures against
the Abkhaz, including a more effective blockade and a more active role of the
Russian peacekeeping troops in the return of Georgian refugees to Abkhazia.
The Russian side, however, argues that these measures would mean a transition
from peacekeeping to peace enforcement for which it has no international
mandate.[12]

The model of "dual mediation" is not without precedent in international practice. Stedman describes this as a "good cop-bad cop" model, referring to the informal division of labor between Alvaro de Soto, the special representative of the
UN secretary-general, and the patrons of the warring sides in El Salvador.[13]
While the former performed the function of a neutral mediator, the latter were
called upon to exert pressure on recalcitrant sides when neutral mediation
failed. The trade-off here, as Stedman notes, is that the presence of multiple mediators with different interests may lead to disunity among them.[14] In this case,
however, there was remarkably little disunity.

A number of theorists of conflict mediation provide different typologies of
roles that mediators can play. Kressel cites the reflexive, nondirective, and di-
rective roles. Touval and Zartman distinguish between communication facilitation, formulation, and manipulation.[15] Princen differentiates between neutral and principal mediators.[16] This case strikes a balance between many of
these roles, with some gaining prominence and others receding at various
points in the conflict.

Mediators can have different resources or tools of leverage at their disposition. Raven mentions such resources as reward, coercion, referent, legitimacy, expertise, and information.[17] Rothschild cites the following sources of
leverage—purchase (rewards), insurance (guarantees), and legitimacy
(recognition of claims and status of the sides).[18] Particular roles may corre-
spond to particular resources—institutions and organizations, such as international organizations, have legitimacy, expertise, and communication and
procedural strategies—the resources of states may go as far as manipulative
strategies.[19] Different types of conflicts may require different types of mediators.[20] Kleiboer notes that in conflicts involving recent violence, mediation

may be best conceived in terms of "power brokerage," i.e., the relationship of power between the mediator and the conflicting sides becomes paramount.[21] This is certainly the case in Russia's relationship with both Georgia and Abkhazia.

The Factor of Interest and Impartiality

Can a mediator have selfish interests of his or her own in the given conflict? According to some theorists, this may not necessarily be a contradiction in terms. Princen, for example, distinguishes between a principal mediator, who has interests in the contested issues and resources to bear, and a neutral mediator, who has neither of the above. The principal mediator changes the structure of the bargain into a three-way interaction, offering carrots and sticks to the sides. The neutral mediator targets the mode of interaction among the disputants, helping them to reconfigure the bargain, by using the strategy of information pooling, among other tools.[22] Zartman goes as far as to say that "military aid to one side does not prevent the donor from also being an effective conciliator, especially if the aid is used to bring concessions from the aided party."[23] Touval and Zartman distinguish between "defensive" and "expansionist" motives of this type of mediator.[24] Partiality and interest in these cases are a source of leverage over the conflicting sides and, given the good will of the mediator, can be used to achieve settlement. The Abkhazia case is particularly interesting in this regard, because the principal mediator (Russia) was able to provide carrots and sticks, while at the same time allowing the United Nations and OSCE (the neutral mediator) to attempt to change the mode of interaction between the disputants in more subtle ways.

Key Factors in Shaping the Result

Russia's Increasing Assertiveness in the Region

The beginning of Russian involvement in this conflict was marked by Abkhazia's appeal to Russia as a "guarantor of stability in the region," which Abkhazia made after the Georgian offensive in September 1992. This appeal was initially made on the pages of the Russian newspaper *Pravda* and then repeated in the Abkhaz Declaration of September 18, 1992.[25] Russia's interests in this conflict were numerous. First, Russia sought to prevent the spillover effect of secessionism, which, given its own problems in Northern Caucasus and elsewhere in the Russian Federation, it could not afford. Next, the conflict afforded the opportunity for a gradual "rediscovery" of its strategic interests in the Transcaucasus and on the Black Sea coast. Finally, the attacks on the Russian military deployments in Georgia, which aroused agitation among the Russian military and political circles, made it difficult for the Yeltsin administration to stay out. These intertwining interests found their official expression in the statement Russian Foreign Minister Kozyrev made on September 8, 1992, in which he declared that the Transcaucasus is a realm of traditional Russian interests. This statement was repeated by Russian Defense Minister Pavel Grachev, who stressed the strategic importance of the Black Sea coast for Russia.

In February 1993 Russian President Yeltsin delivered a speech in which he asked that the international community grant "special powers" to Russia "as a guarantor of peace and stability in the region." On March 3, 1993, Russia presented the United Nations with a document regarding its role in peacekeeping on the territory of the former USSR. In the summer of 1993 a similar document was presented to the OSCE.[26] In another document, Russia proposed that the CIS be regarded as a regional organization, which should be used in peacekeeping operations. The granting of a UN mandate to the CIS/Russian forces in Abkhazia in July 1994 and the dispatch of UN and OSCE observers were the first instances of such a recognition of Russia's activities in this conflict.

These pleas were later replaced by a confident assertion of Russia's role. In a joint statement by the Russian Foreign Ministry and the Ministry of Defense on March 29, 1994, it was declared that Russia did not need further legitimization and was not asking the permission of the United Nations or OSCE for its operations in the Near Abroad. Foreign Minister Kozyrev stated in June 1994 that Russian peacekeeping is "already legitimate to 150 percent."[27]

At the same time, Russian diplomatic initiatives in the region started to bear fruit. On September 15, 1993, Russian Defense Minister Grachev linked signing the treaty on Russian military presence in Georgia with the settlement in Abkhazia.[28] In October 1993 Georgia joined the CIS, in return for which it received Russian military assistance in guarding its railways and halting the advances of the rebel forces in Western Georgia and Abkhazia. In the following years Georgia signed an agreement authorizing the deployment of Russian military bases on Georgian territory, a Treaty on Good Neighborly Relations with its northern neighbor, and a number of other documents cementing Georgia's ties to Moscow. Georgian leaders openly declared that Georgia's reincorporation into the CIS, the agreement to host Russian troops on Georgian territory, and other diplomatic steps were made based on the political and military necessity of that time; in other words, Georgia was forced to agree to Russian military bases and to CIS membership by the defeat in Abkhazia. Some observers went further, suggesting that the entire Abkhaz campaign was sponsored by Russia as part of a strategy aimed at bringing Georgia back into its sphere of influence. At the same time, Georgian leaders explicitly stated that Georgia's continuing cooperation with Russia was contingent on Russian help in returning Abkhazia to Georgian control.

The Russia-Georgia rapprochement immediately aroused fears among the Abkhaz that Moscow was going to tilt to the Georgian side. These fears were aggravated by Russia's implementation, however spotty, of the economic sanctions imposed by the CIS against Abkhazia and the closure of Abkhazia's borders on the land and sea. The Georgian side, on the other hand, was not satisfied with Russia's efforts and urged more decisive Russian pressure on Abkhazia.

This dissatisfaction found its expression during Shevardnadze's visit to Washington in the summer of 1997, during which he declared that Russia has "exhausted her potential" as political mediator and military peacekeeper in the Caucasus, including in the Abkhazia conflict, calling for an end to Russia's "monopoly" on managing regional conflicts. Nevertheless, Russia's special role manifested itself yet again in August of 1997 with the visit of the Russian Foreign Minister Primakov to the region, during which, in a surprise move, he brought together the Abkhaz and Georgian leaders to hold direct talks in Tbilisi. However, this effort, as many previous ones, failed to produce a political settlement: the two sides merely signed a joint statement pledging to renounce force, demonstrate patience and mutual esteem, and settle differences peacefully through negotiations both directly and under Russian mediation with UN, OSCE, and CIS participation. At the same time, Russian President Boris Yeltsin made a statement on August 25, 1997, in which he reasserted Russia's exclusive role in the settlement of this conflict, which it was not ready to surrender to the United States, and declared that "the U.S. will never send its soldiers" to the buffer zone between the sides.[29]

The Role of the United States

At the early stages of the conflict the United States did not have a direct interest or immediate involvement. The American participation in the mediation process was part of a larger international effort and was channeled through international organizations such as the United Nations and OSCE as well as the group of states called "Friends of Georgia," which included, apart from the United States, Russia, Germany, France, and the United Kingdom.

There were several indications that this conflict and the area in general were marginal to U.S. interests. The 1994 mandate for the UN observer mission in Abkhazia implied recognition of Russia's leading role in this area. The United States declined Shevardnadze's request to send its troops as a part of the peacekeeping force in Abkhazia, which he made during his visit to the United States in the spring of 1994. It is symbolic that during the press conference after Shevardnadze's meeting with President Clinton the American reporters focused their questions on the incident in Waco, Texas.

However, the situation started to change when the region acquired strategic importance for the West with the development of the Caspian oil fields. After long deliberations, the international oil consortium composed of leading oil companies of the world chose Georgia and Russia as the two routes for transporting the early oil from Azerbaijan to the Mediterranean Sea. Hence, the growing importance of Georgia and the necessity of restoring stability in the region, including the settlement of the Abkhaz conflict, came to the attention of the United States and other Western powers.

The change in U.S. policy toward Georgia became noticeable during Shevardnadze's visit to Washington in July 1997. During this visit, President Clinton assured Georgia of continuing U.S. economic aid and endorsed the plan of transporting the "main" Azerbaijani oil through Georgian territory. The United States emphasized its support of Georgia's territorial integrity and Georgia's proposals for a UN-sponsored international conference to settle the Abkhazia conflict, with the participation of the OSCE, Russia, and the "Friends of Georgia" group of countries, led by the United States and Germany.

The Role of International Law

Earlier in the chapter it was argued that certain provisions of international law could hinder rather than facilitate the settlement of intrastate conflicts. The introductory section illustrated how a number of contradictory principles, such as self-determination, territorial integrity, nonintervention, sovereignty, and human rights, legitimate the conflicting claims of the sides. The section on the timing of mediation (ripeness) discussed how the principles of nonintervention and nonrecognition impede negotiations and mediation at the early stage of these kinds of conflicts. In the words of Zartman, there exists a perception that "meeting is recognizing and recognizing is approving." He continues to say that

> Usually, recognition is a goal of higher priority to the [national liberation] movement than victory in the crisis, in part because recognition is the precondition to any success. Recognition and legitimization permit negotiation, once they have been attained, conflict resolution can come into play to regularize the new status quo.[30]

The third way in which international law can impede conflict resolution in such instances is by imposing rigid categories in terms of which the sides must define the settlement, making their gains relatively indivisible and irreversible. The main building block of the international legal system is the sovereign nation-state (however ambiguous and controversial this category might be). Only the sovereign and independent nation-states are subjects of international law. As for other entities and categories, their place in the international legal system is marginal; the only form in which international law relates to them is by moderating and constraining the behavior of the main actors, the nation-states (with, for example, minority and human rights provisions). While a number of forms of accommodation within the category of a nation-state exist (e.g., autonomy, federation, etc.), international law does not provide any guidelines or regulations regarding these. Such forms of accommodation are therefore chosen on an ad hoc basis, in an environment of a "legal vacuum." See figure 1.2.

The bottom part of the figure designates the possible settlement ranges for intrastate ethnic conflicts. They are ranked in the order of increasing concessions for the intrastate group and decreasing sovereignty of the parent-state: from cultural autonomy to territorial autonomy to federation to confederation, etc. The upper part of the figure shows how the positions of the sides regarding these settlement ranges changed over time and whether or not an agreement has been reached between them. As becomes evident from the figure, the area in which resolution of such conflicts is to be found lies outside of the traditional understanding of sovereignty, in the "fuzzy" or "soft" sovereignty area. For example, autonomy and federation can be understood as constrained forms of sovereignty, confederation as "joint" sovereignty. While the figure may not reflect with

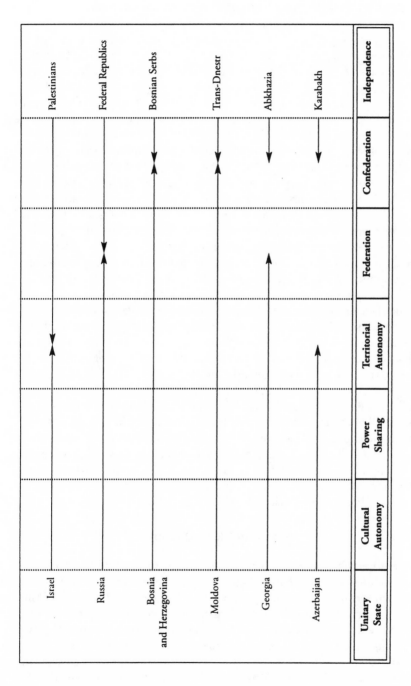

Figure 1.2

sufficient accuracy the precise terms of specific agreements and the stances of the sides, it nevertheless provides a good illustration of this trend.

Despite these forms of accommodation, sovereignty remains a very difficult object to divide, especially if the sides, having engaged in a violent conflict, have good reasons to be concerned about their security. The world does not contain many states with ethnically divided and decentralized armies. Power sharing (consociationalism) may often be successful, but it is not very effective if there is a large power disparity among the sides.[31] Besides, institutional arrangements containing power-sharing provisions, such as constitutions, do not guarantee anything in and of themselves.[32]

As a result, even when there is a possibility of reaching an agreement on a number of specific issues, the sides may not be able to define it in terms of the categories that are imposed on them by international law. The Abkhaz-Georgian agreement of April 1994 illustrates this quite clearly. As a result of the Moscow talks in April of 1994, the sides signed the Declaration on Measures for a Political Settlement of the Georgian/Abkhaz Conflict. Abkhazia, according to Article 6 of this agreement, could have its own constitution, legislation and appropriate state symbols, such as anthem, emblem, and flag. The sides also agreed on such issues as foreign policy and economic ties, border guard agreements, customs, energy, transport, communication, ecology, human rights, and the rights of national minorities. However, they failed to agree on the main political issue—the status of Abkhazia.

In February 1995 in Geneva the sides made further steps toward reaching a settlement by agreeing to establish a "federal legislative organ" and a "supreme organ of executive power" in the future common state. For yet another time, the issue of territorial integrity of Georgia and the federal vs. confederal character of the future state led to the failure of talks. Time and time again, the "big concepts" got in the way of issue-specific deals on which progress was made.

Essentially, the difference between war and peace in Abkhazia is the difference between the concepts of "federation" and "confederation," or between a single and joint sovereignty. Unfortunately, international law does not provide anything in-between; the first term implies a single state with indivisible sovereignty, the second—an association of individual sovereign units. As a result, the political stalemate in Abkhazia continues to the present day.

Success of the Mediation

There are a number of criteria for determining the success or failure of mediation. Some analysts argue that mediation is successful when the conflicting sides cease hostilities and accept the mediator. Others suggest that the success of mediation is in reaching a political settlement of the conflict in question.[33] Depending on the choice of these criteria, the international mediation in Abkhazia can be considered either a success or a failure.

To the extent to which the conflict was deescalated and the sides engaged in a process of negotiations facilitated by external mediators, this mediation has been a success. To the extent to which the sides failed to reach a political settlement on the key disputed issues (namely, the relationship between Abkhazia and Georgia), as well as the unresolved fate of approximately 200,000 Georgian refugees who fled from Abkhazia, this mediation has been a failure so far.

This dilemma raises another important question: Should deescalation and cessation of hostilities precede a political settlement or should the political settlement come first? In its activities in the former Soviet Union republics, Russia has clearly ascribed to the first point of view: Russian peacekeeping forces have been deployed in areas of active military conflict before any significant steps toward political settlement were made. In international practice, the opposite is the case: Peacekeeping forces are deployed only after an agreement on cessation of hostilities is signed and some progress is made in reaching a political settlement.

This difference can be explained by the fact that apart from the Russian peacekeeping deployments, there are numerous other ways in which the Russian presence is felt in these areas. These deployments are also backed up with many other sources of leverage over the sides. Secondly, given the proximity of this area to Russian borders and interests, Russia can hardly afford the luxury of waiting until these conflicts burn themselves out before attempting to step in and stop the war. The critics of this approach argue that such interventions artificially freeze the conflict at a certain stage, leading to a political stalemate, which is the case in Abkhazia today. While this is certainly true, it remains unclear whether a natural way to solve conflicts is to allow for a unilateral victory of one side over the other (if there is a disparity of forces) or a complete exhaustion of both sides (which, as was mentioned earlier, may never happen if the sides have powerful external supporters).

Conclusion

The experience of the Abkhaz-Georgian conflict allows one to make the following generalizations and recommendations.

1. International mediators need to make a step from "big concepts" to "small deals." Mediation in intrastate ethnic conflicts should not seek to invoke international legal categories and principles for initiating mediation efforts, carrying out negotiations, and finding a political settlement. At each stage of this process international norms are capable of impeding rather than facilitating the process of successful mediation. The mediators should instead seek to help the sides conclude "small," issue-specific agreements; transcend rigid legal categories; disaggregate the contested issues; and find innovative forms to cement these agreements, even if that entails compromising such fundamental concepts as sovereignty. The "myth of Westphalia," to use Stephen Krasner's expression, should be dispelled. The future of intrastate conflict settlements lies precisely in the area outside of the traditional understanding of sovereignty, if sovereignty ever existed in its "pure" form. Deviations from the norm of sovereignty were made in the past (in fact, as Krasner shows, in its very

"cradle"—the Treaty of Westphalia[34]) and they continue to be present in the international system of our times.

2. If the conflict in question is taking place in an area of vital interests of one or more major powers, then "exhaustion-induced" techniques (i.e., waiting for the sides to wear each other out before stepping in) will not succeed. These outside powers are unlikely to wait until the conflict burns itself out before they become involved. External involvement and assistance to the sides will then periodically boost the forces of belligerents and perpetuate the conflict in question. In these situations, international mediators will be well advised to include these external actors in their mediation efforts and to use the leverage of the actors to bring the sides to the table of negotiations and conclude an agreement. At the same time, the international mediators should use their own leverage over these powerful external actors to monitor and control their activities. This mechanism of multiple mediators, each having different sources of leverage, forms, and methods of interaction with the sides, has shown some promise in the case of Abkhazia and may be used in other conflicts under similar circumstances.

2

From Lisbon to Dayton: International Mediation and the Bosnia Crisis

Melanie C. Greenberg and Margaret E. McGuinness

Overview

IN JANUARY 1992, while visiting Sarajevo, United Nations Secretary-General Boutros Boutros-Ghali referred dismissively to the conflict in Bosnia as "a rich man's war," unworthy of the international attention it was garnering.[1] Whatever the secretary-general might have felt about Bosnia in the grim hierarchy of post–Cold War conflict, this war has become a paradigm of modern civil war and the failure of international intervention. The war in Bosnia illustrates not only the virulence of nationalism in the hands of unprincipled leaders, but also the challenges of coordinating an effective, principled international response to such conflicts. Bosnia, more than any other conflict, shattered the optimism of the international community and exposed fatal weaknesses in the very institutions that were to have sustained peace and democracy in the new world order.

In answer to the idea that democracy would ultimately bring about a peaceful world, Bosnia demonstrated that the formality of elections and expression of democratic principles were alone not enough to sustain peace and multiethnic ideals. Indeed, Slobodan Milosevic used the Yugoslavian democratic process to drive the engine of his own nationalist agenda, and even the Bosnian Serbs draped themselves in the formal trappings of referenda, assemblies, and elections. Bosnia made embarrassingly clear that, contrary to the exclamation of Jacques Poos, then-president of the European Community (EC), the "age of Europe" had not yet dawned. Despite a series of sustained and concerted mediation attempts, Europe was unable to provide an external military or political solution to the Bosnia crisis. UN peacekeeping forces, whose principles of consent and consensus represented the optimism of post–Cold War international military thinking, were exposed as a poor fig leaf for the Western powers' lack of military and political will to bring about a peace that could be kept. Only when the United States, backed up by the military muscle of NATO, finally took hold of the intervention did the crisis begin to lift in Bosnia.

This chapter examines the causes and nature of the war, then the failed mediation attempts by the European Community and the United Nations, and finally the Dayton Conference and the methods employed by the mediators to bring an end to the immediate conflict. The history of intervention in Bosnia is one of missed opportunities, failure of the international institutions charged with the maintenance of international peace and security, and lack of political will on the parts of the parties and the mediators to enforce agreements. In the end, the case demonstrates how war-weariness of the parties, combined with the political and military clout of the United States and NATO, finally resulted in an end to the fighting.

Timeline

1914　Archduke Ferdinand, heir to the Austro-Hungarian throne, is assassinated in Sarajevo by a Bosnian working on behalf of Serb nationalists.

1918　The Kingdom of the Serbs, Croats, and Slovenes is established.

1929　The Kingdom is renamed Yugoslavia.

1941　Germany and Italy invade Yugoslavia. The Ustashe fascists take power in Croatia; a puppet fascist regime is installed in Serbia.

1945　Socialist Federal Republic of Yugoslavia is established. Bosnia-Herzegovina is one of the six constituent republics.

1980　Yugoslavian President Josip Broz Tito dies.

1989　**September:** Slovenian assembly declares independence and autonomy from Yugoslavia.

1990　**April:** Franjo Tudjman and Croatian nationalists win elections in Croatia on platform of succession from Yugoslavia. December: Slovenes vote for independence.

1991　**January:** Slobodan Milosevic announces intent to annex all Serb lands in a greater Serbia, in the event Yugoslavia ceases to exist. **June 21:** U.S. Secretary of State James Baker visits Belgrade. **Dec. 23:** Germany, Belgium, and Denmark recognize Croatia and Slovenia.

1992　**Jan. 15:** The European Community (EC) extends formal recognition to Croatia and Slovenia. **Feb. 29–Mar. 1:** Bosnia holds a referendum on independence; 99.4 percent vote for independence (but Bosnian Serbs boycott the referendum). **Mar. 2:** Bosnian Serbs erect roadblocks throughout Bosnia. **Mar. 3:** Bosnian government declares independence. **Mar. 18:** Cutileiro Plan signed (dividing Bosnia into three ethnic cantons); rejected by Bosnian President Alija Izetbegovic on Mar. 25. **Mar. 27:** Bosnian Serbs declare autonomous Republika Srpska in Bosnia. **Apr. 6–7:** The United States and the EC recognize the independence of Bosnia-Herzegovina; United States formally recognizes Croatia and Slovenia; United States ends financial sanctions against Bosnia, Croatia, Macedonia, and Slovenia. **Sept. 3:** UN and EC peace negotiations begin, with Cyrus Vance as UN representative and David Owen as EC representative. **Sept. 14:** UN Security Council expands UNPROFOR (United Nations Protection Force) mandate to conduct humanitarian aid throughout Bosnia (UNSCR 776). **Oct. 9:** UN Security Council establishes no-fly zone over Bosnia (UNSCR 781).

1993   **Jan. 2:** Vance–Owen Peace Plan unveiled (dividing Bosnia into ten provinces). Rejected by Bosnian Serbs. **March:** Muslim–Croat alliance breaks down and fighting starts between the two groups. **April:** U.S. Secretary of State Warren Christopher visits Europe to garner support for "Lift and Strike" policy. **Apr. 2:** Cyrus Vance resigns and is replaced by Thorvald Stoltenberg. **Apr. 16:** United Nations declares Srebrenica as a "safe area" (UNSCR 819); this status extended to Sarajevo, Tuzla, Zepa, Gorazde, and Bihac on May 6 (UNSCR 824). **May:** United States and Europe announce "Joint Action Plan" (never implemented). **May 25:** UN Security Council establishes War Crimes Tribunal (UNSCR 827). **July 30:** Owen-Stoltenberg Plan signed; collapses several days later when Bosnian Serbs break cease-fire.

1994   Muslim–Croat war in Bosnia. **Feb. 5:** Sarajevo marketplace massacre. **Feb. 9:** Cease-fire agreement reached on heavy artillery around Sarajevo. **Feb. 23:** Bosnian Muslims and Bosnian Croats sign cease-fire. **Mar. 1:** First NATO air attack in Bosnia. **Mar. 18:** Framework Agreements signed, establishing the Muslim–Croat Bosnian federation and confederation between Bosnia and Croatia and ending conflict between Bosnian Croats and Bosnian Muslims. **April:** Serbs attack Gorazde. **Apr. 25:** Contact Group established (foreign ministers of France, United States, Germany, Russia, and the United Kingdom plus EU and UN representatives). **May 10:** Washington Accords signed: creates Bosnian-Croat Federation. **July 6:** Contact Group peace plan announced, giving 51 percent of territory to Muslim–Croat Federation and 49 percent to Bosnian Serbs. **July 11:** Bosnian Serbs seize control of UN "safe area" Srebrenica. **July 25:** Fall and capture of UN "safe area" Zepa by Bosnian Serbs. **August:** Milosevic slaps embargo on the Bosnian Serb government in Pale. **Nov. 7:** International War Crimes Tribunal issues first indictments. **Nov. 21:** NATO launches "pinprick" air attacks on Serb air bases at Ubdina in retaliation for Serb attacks in western Bosnia in violation of the "no-fly" zone. **Nov. 25:** Ratko Mladic's forces take 150 UN peacekeepers hostage in retaliation for NATO bombing. Contact Group Plan remains on table. **Dec. 23:** Former United States President Carter negotiates a cease-fire for the winter months.

1995   **Feb. 20:** Milosevic rejects Contact Group Plan. **Mar. 7:** Bosnia and Croatia form military alliance against the Serb forces in their countries. April: EU negotiator Carl Bildt takes lead in international diplomatic efforts. **May 1:** Croatian army action against Croatian Serbs in Western Slavonia. **May 25:** NATO bombs Serb positions in retaliation for Serb attacks on Sarajevo and other UN safe areas. **May 26:** Mladic retaliates by taking 350 UN personnel hostage, as "human shields" against further NATO attacks. **June 18:** UN hostages released. EU begins to debate withdrawal of UNPROFOR troops; United States discovers it would be obligated to assist in withdrawal. **July 11:** The fall of Srebrenica; an estimated 8,000 Muslims executed by Bosnian Serb forces. **Aug. 5:** Croatian "Operation Storm" retakes the Krajina after one day of fighting. **Aug. 19:** Three American envoys killed in accident on Mt. Igman during shuttle diplomacy. **Aug. 28:** Serbs mortar the Sarajevo marketplace, leaving thirty-five dead. **Aug. 30:** NATO launches operation "Deliberate Force," massive air attacks on the Bosnian Serb positions near Sarajevo. **Sept. 8:** Foreign ministers of Croatia, Bosnia, and Serbia come to-gether for peace talks. Milosevic officially agrees to act as negotiator on be-half of Bosnian Serbs. **Sept. 12:** Bosnian-Croat Federation launches mas-sive offensive against Bosnian Serbs. Regains significant Serb-held territory. **Sept. 26:** Parties agree on framework for Bosnian Constitution: the cre-ation of a unitary Bosnia with two autonomous entities—the Muslim–Croat Federation and a Serb republic. **Oct. 12:** Bosnia, Croatia, and Bosnian Serbs agree to cease-fire. **Oct. 30:** U.S. House of Representa-tives passes HR 247 expressing House's intent that any peace agreement not require deployment of U. S. ground troops in Bosnia. **Nov. 1:** Dayton Peace Conference begins. **Nov. 21:** Presidents Tudjman, Milosevic, and Izetbe-govic initial the General Framework Agreement. **Dec. 4:** First NATO troops arrive in Bosnia. **Dec. 14:** Official signing ceremony of Dayton Peace Ac-cords in Paris. **Dec. 20:** In accordance with the Dayton Accords, United Na-tions turns over all peacekeeping to the Implementation Force (IFOR).

1996   **Jan. 19:** IFOR completes separation of combatants and weapons. **Feb. 18:** UN and Federal Republic of Yugoslavia(FRY) sanctions on Bosnian Serbs lifted. **Mar. 19:** All of Sarajevo comes under Bosnian government control. **June 19:** UN ends arms embargo on former Yugoslavia. **Sept. 14:** First fed-eral elections in Bosnia. **Oct. 1:** UN ends economic sanctions on the FRY. **Nov. 30:** First conviction at War Crimes Tribunal. **December:** The Stabi-lization Force (SFOR) succeeds IFOR.

Background

Bosnia represents a difficult case for true believers in mediation. The classic mediation model, in which a disinterested neutral helps the parties reach con-sensus on their own terms, was ineffective in resolving the Bosnia conflict, as evidenced by the failure of the Vance–Owen peace process and a long string of other agreements and cease-fires that were either rejected outright or signed and subsequently broken. The process that led to the Dayton Accords and ulti-mately ended the violence imposed a virtual partition of the country, albeit within a unified internationally recognized state, which could only be enforced through the presence of a multinational military force backed by NATO and the United States. This process was, at least formally, called mediation (some preferred the term "mediation with muscle"). The diplomatic, logistical, and technical aspects of the mediation adhered strictly to the models of shuttle and later proximity talks facilitated by an active third-party mediator, the United States. But here, unlike the Oslo Channel, for example, the mediating party was not a neutral, but a deeply interested and indispensable party to the implementation of the peace itself. The general map of Bosnia and the political implementation agreements reached at Dayton were in large measure determined through the iterative negotiations preceding the conference. Nevertheless, the United States played an indispensable role in bringing the parties together and convincing them not that this peace was the best peace, but that none of them could expect a better outcome.

We include this chapter in the volume on mediation not only because Bosnia is a hallmark of post–Cold War conflict, but also because it illustrates the incompatibility and inherent tension between mediation and military intervention. We will attempt to trace not only why traditional mediation attempts failed, but why more active intervention—introduced within a context of mediation—was successful in ending the fighting.

The violence in Bosnia did not come as a surprise to the international community. Even before the official secession of Bosnia from Yugoslavia, preparation for violence was widespread enough, and an escalation of future violence ominous enough, for the European Community to intervene in the dispute. In 1991, the UN Security Council imposed an arms embargo against Yugoslavia (effective as to all the constituent states that subsequently seceded from Yugoslavia), which remained in place throughout the Bosnian war. The embargo had the unintended effect of strongly favoring the Serbs, who started the war with a huge advantage in arms, and benefited early on from JNA (Yugoslav People's Army) support. The arms embargo followed trade sanctions that had been set in place earlier, as well as cuts in foreign aid from the United States in May 1991 (a decision the United States reversed soon after).

A series of mediation attempts preceded the Dayton Accords, but each of them was plagued by the same flaws that allowed a continuing escalation of violence in the conflict. First, the concept of "ripeness" was turned on its head in the Bosnia mediations. Rather than waiting for a window of opportunity in which the parties might be willing to negotiate, the mediators often worked reactively, pressing forward just after a particularly grisly episode in the war (such as the Serb boycott of the independence referendum, the 1992 mortar attack, or the surrender of Srebrenica and Zepa in 1994) that had captured public attention. Mediation in these instances was spurred not by the demand of the parties, but by public pressure to "do something" about the Bosnian crisis.

Second, the map-drawing aspects of most of the mediation plans threatened the process from the beginning. Apart from the Vance–Owen Plan, none of the mediation efforts attempted to create a multiethnic state in Bosnia, and none of the plans sought to alter the boundaries of Bosnia to allow for more realistic states. Rather, the plans rewarded Serb and Croat aggression by granting them territory that they had taken by force and "ethnically cleansed" in clear, repeated, and horrific violations of international legal norms. Ironically, this ethnic cleansing made the map-drawing exercises easier by creating chunks of "pure" territory that could be awarded to the victor.

Third, there was no true military muscle or unified political actor to back up mediated agreements. The UNPROFOR troops were strictly a humanitarian force, with orders to be neutral even in the face of blatant Serb aggression. As the conflict escalated, their role became more and more peripheral, until, in a grim metaphor for their own institutional failure, UNPROFOR troops were themselves held hostage. The "dual key" activation system, under which the United Nations would have to approve of any NATO military action in Bosnia (a near impossibility under the leadership of UN Secretary-General Boutros Boutros-Ghali), was another symbol of the West's reluctance to use force initially. Once the United States made the decision to support NATO air strikes, the dual key system was successfully dismantled.

Finally, none of the early mediation efforts could have been successful without the support of the United States, which during the early years of the Clinton administration had displayed reluctance to commit ground troops to any international humanitarian efforts or to assist in enforcement of any mediated agreements. Even though the United States had no intention to act militarily, it nonetheless intervened in the European mediation efforts by communicating with the Bosnian government and encouraging it, at times, to hold off for a better agreement. Not until 1994, when the United States supported the creation of the Muslim–Croat Federation, took the lead in the Contact Group mediation efforts, and supported NATO air strikes to assist the Federation's efforts on the battlefield, did the conflict in Bosnia start to make real progress toward peace. No matter how robust and energetic the European mediation efforts might have seemed, American policy played a determinative shadow role that could make or break the mediation efforts. With each description of the European mediation process, we will highlight the American response and its effect on peacemaking in Bosnia.

In addition to specific policy and historical issues, Bosnia raises questions about the role of humanitarian assistance and the misapplication of ethical assumptions about humanitarian aid within the context of conflict resolution. One implicit tenet in the conflict resolution and reconciliation literature holds that any conflict resolution process, even a flawed one, is preferable to no process at all. In Bosnia, where some of the processes themselves arguably contributed to worsening the crisis, that tenet cannot be considered absolute. However noble and well-intentioned the goals of the UN/EU mediation process and interim cease-fire agreements may have been, many observers have argued that the long periods of negotiation and mediation between 1992 and 1995 allowed the Bosnian Serbs and Croats enough time to carry out their war goals without a countervailing military threat from the international community.

The international community's adoption of a humanitarian assistance program in Bosnia also complicated the crisis. There is no question that humanitarian aid—from both governmental and nongovernmental sources—provided essential assistance to the civilians under siege during the war. But the inability of UNPROFOR to provide a secure environment for the delivery of aid stymied humanitarian relief. International organizations and UNPROFOR itself frequently were made unwitting accomplices to Serb atrocities and forced ethnic cleansing. The inadequacy of this type of intervention emboldened Serb aggressors and forced the Bosnian government to look to sources beyond the United Nations for military assistance. Viewed cynically, the humanitarian assistance program was a fig leaf that the Western powers used as a substitute for more forceful military intervention.

The Bosnian crisis, accompanied as it was by the worst atrocities committed in Europe since the end of World War II, also raises the difficult question of whether justice was sacrificed in the pursuit of peace. Whether the Dayton Accords can be called a "just" peace continues to be a central theme in analysis of the postconflict state, and will likely continue to be debated for at least a generation. The Dayton Accords may have ended the immediate violence, but they did so at the expense of a strong Bosnian state, which today resembles a partitioned entity, rather than a multiethnic democracy. Furthermore, the agreement consolidated under Bosnian Serb and Bosnian Croat control huge tracts of territory that these parties had ethnically cleansed during the war. The establishment of the International Criminal Tribunal for Former Yugoslavia and its ongoing efforts to indict, arrest, and prosecute war criminals may help ensure that some measure of substantive justice is meted out. But true reconciliation has yet to take hold. Resolution of the current crisis in the Balkans—the war in Kosovo and its accompanying humanitarian catastrophe—will be essential to any lasting and just peace for Bosnia.

Key Interventions and Major Actors

Theories of the Conflict

The Balkans have for centuries been a flash point for conflict, the result of their geographical locus as crossroads between East and West; Europe and the Middle East; Roman Catholicism, Christian Orthodoxy, and Islam; and, historically, the Austro-Hungarian and Ottoman Empires. The spark igniting World War I occurred in Sarajevo, when a Serbian nationalist assassinated Archduke Franz Ferdinand of Austria and his wife, Countess Sophie Chotek.[2] After World War I, southern Slavs came together as the Kingdom of the Serbs, Croats, and Slovenes, later to be known as Yugoslavia. Vicious partisan fighting between Serbs and Croats during World War II left deep scars upon these groups, even when Yugoslavia was reconstituted under the communist dictator Josip Broz Tito. Tito ruled for over forty years under the motto of "brotherhood and unity," expertly dividing power among different ethnic groups throughout the six republics of

Yugoslavia[3] and prohibiting the expression of nationalist sentiment that might undermine the ideal of Yugoslavia.

Nationalism, in a particularly virulent form, was the poison that killed the federation of Yugoslavia. When Tito died, and the Cold War drew to a close, the multiethnic fabric of Yugoslavia began to unravel. Nationalist leaders in Croatia, Slovenia, and Serbia flexed their muscles, causing the delicate balance in Yugoslavia's exceedingly complex federal presidential system to totter. Theories abound as to why these nationalists were able to lead their constituents into such deadly violence, and why a country in which Serbs, Croats, Bosnian Muslims, and others had lived in peaceful coexistence for two generations (and had been intermarrying for centuries) so quickly disintegrated.

Early in the war, many outside observers fell into the trap of explaining the conflict as the manifestation of "ancient hatreds," dating back for centuries between the peoples of the region.[4] But this theory is largely dismissed by historians and political scientists, who argue instead that nationalist leaders expropriate images of ancient conflict as propaganda to arouse fear in their constituents for very modern purposes, such as territorial power grabs. "Ancient hatreds" are simply a pretext for modern war aims, and by themselves neither inevitably lead to war nor permanently block efforts for peace. As Richard Holbrooke argues,

Yugoslavia's tragedy was not foreordained. It was the product of bad, even criminal, political leaders who encouraged ethnic confrontation for personal, political and financial gain. Rather than tackle the concrete problems of governance in the post-Tito era, they led their people into war.[5]

Another misleading theory of the conflict claimed that the war in Bosnia was a religious war, between Catholic Croats, Orthodox Serbs, and Muslim Bosnians. While it is true that different religions were involved, and that the religious leaders of each group at times helped fuel the nationalist fires, this war was not about the expression of religion. A survey conducted in 1985 in Bosnia found that only 17 percent of the population characterized themselves as religious believers.[6] Bosnian Muslims, for example, are among the most secularized Muslims in the world, and even the leaders of the other ethnic groups attended services or used symbols of their faith only when it suited their nationalist aims.

Other explanations more accurately portray the complexities of the conflict's origins, applying economic analysis of Yugoslavia to account for the rise of nationalist leaders who preyed on fears of minority populations.[7]

The most compelling theory of the conflict, however, emphasizes the central role played by the personal and nationalist ambition of Serbian President Slobodan Milosevic and Croatian President Franjo Tudjman. Well before either of the countries broke off from Yugoslavia, each leader had plans for expanding the territory of his republic to include large swaths of Bosnia, and in Serbia's case, significant portions of Croatia. It has been argued that while Tudjman is a true nationalist, enveloping himself in the trappings of Croatian glory, Milosevic simply played the nationalist card as a way of procuring territory for a Greater Serbia, of which he would be supreme leader.

Ultimately, the conflict in Bosnia became the struggle for the very survival of Bosnia as a separate entity. Serbian forces threatened to annex huge swaths of land into Serbia proper, and President Tudjman intended to engulf most of Western Bosnia into Croatia. While the original goal of the Bosnian government was to keep in place a multiethnic state, as the military situation became more dire, the government simply sought a survivable state. Had Croatia and Serbia recognized their territorial goals, Bosnia would have become a sliver of a country, stripped of its historically multiethnic culture, surrounded by enemies, and of only questionable economic or political viability. Though the rhetoric of multiethnicity was never completely lost in the mediations surrounding Bosnia, the underlying central goal of the mediation attempts was to expand Bosnian territory lost in the war to ensure a viable state.

Slobodan Milosevic set loose the Yugoslavian tempest in April 1987, in his dramatic speech in Kosovo. While Serbs are a minority in Kosovo, they hold a disproportionate share of powerful jobs in the region and consider the area of utmost symbolic and historical significance to Serbian culture. It was there in 1389, at the battle of Kosovo Polje, that the Serbian King Lazar decided to enter the heavenly kingdom rather than fight, allowing the Turks to defeat the Serbs. In his speech, Milosevic invoked history and promised to be the protector of the Kosovo Serbs. Two years later, after further consolidating his power in Serbia and gathering a loyal crowd of demonstrators to follow him, Milosevic delivered an even more powerful speech to the Kosovo Serbs that included ominous foreshadowing of the nationalist battles to come.[8]

The speech allowed Milosevic to demonstrate how quickly he could mobilize a million Serbs from around Yugoslavia; its subtext of Serb nationalist ambitions was clear to the rest of the country.[9] Between 1987 and 1991, Milosevic outmaneuvered his mentor Ivan Stambolic to become president of Serbia and manipulated the constitutional leadership of Yugoslavia to create more power for Serbia (which built a strong alliance with Montenegro). In 1990, Milosevic, through his agents, provoked a rebellion among Serbs living in the Knin region of Croatia, helping to spark the bloody Serb–Croat conflict, which only ended in 1991, after international intervention in the form of mediation and the stationing of UN peacekeepers. (See the chapter on Croatia in this volume.)

In 1991, convinced that Yugoslavia was collapsing and eager to expand their own republics, Franjo Tudjman and Slobodan Milosevic held a secret meeting in Karadjordjevo, at which they determined to divide up large chunks of Bosnia.[10] The agreement did not last long, however, before Serbia ratcheted up the fighting in Croatia and gained control of over 30 percent of Croatia. When Croatian police attacked Serb police and civilians in Knin and other enclaves in Eastern Slavonia (territory contiguous to, and coveted by, Serbia), Milosevic successfully called in the JNA, confirming that the powerful military had become his pawn. The fighting between Serb paramilitary groups and Croatian defense forces was bloody and brutal. A central goal of the fighting was to clear out Croatian civilians from Serb-held territory, a practice that became known as "ethnic cleansing." The siege of Vukovar in September 1991 epitomized the horror of the fighting: Serb irregulars razed the entire Croatian town, executed thousands of Croatian men, and buried bodies in mass graves.

As the Serb–Croat conflict raged, declarations of independence by Slovenia, Croatia, and, later, Bosnia and Macedonia, drew the European Community and the United Nations further into the Yugoslavian drama. Slovenia's declaration of independence was followed by a quick and relatively bloodless battle with the JNA. Slovenia had no significant Serb minority, and Milosevic was reasonably content to let it slip away from Yugoslavia without a bruising fight. With the secession and subsequent international recognition of Croatia and Bosnia, however, the intensity of the conflict in Bosnia flared dramatically.

Legal Principles Surrounding Secession Contribute to the Escalation of Violence

Croatia's declaration of independence set off a flurry of international diplomatic and legal activity. Germany was the first country to recognize Croatia, an action that many found precipitous and dangerously premature.[11] The independence issue in Bosnia proved as explosive as in Croatia. The Badinter Commission formed to arbitrate the legality of the Croatian secession had ruled that as a matter of international law Bosnia satisfied the primary criteria for sovereignty, but only if all three major political parties (Serb, Bosnian Muslim, and Croat) agreed to independence in a referendum. On February 29–March 1, 1992, Bosnia held the referendum, but the Bosnian Serbs refused to participate. In the referendum, 99.4 percent of the voters supported independence.[12] On March 2, Bosnian Serbs erected roadblocks throughout Bosnia. On March 3, President Izetbegovic announced the independence of Bosnia; fighting broke out immediately between Serbs and members of the de-facto Croat–Muslim alliance. On March 27, Radovan Karadzic declared the independence of "Republika Srpska"—a political entity comprising the ethnically Serb areas of Bosnia—with its headquarters in Pale, less than fifty kilometers east of Sarajevo. On April 7, the United States and the EU officially recognized independent Bosnia-Herzegovina and quickly lifted the economic sanctions against Bosnia, Croatia, Slovenia, and Macedonia, keeping the sanctions against Serbia-Montenegro that had been in place since 1991.

International recognition of Bosnia, which the United States strongly supported (in part to take momentum away from the Germans, who had taken the lead in recognizing Croatia), has been described by some analysts as the first misstep of the international community. By backing full sovereignty for Bosnia, they argue, the United States and Europe gave all three parties the incentive to posture and prepare for war so that the strongest party would be in the best political position at the time of recognition.[13] Recognition also gave the Bosnian government the expectation that the international community would come to Bosnia's defense as a sovereign state, with full rights under the UN charter. Such recognition, they hoped, would completely delegitimize the Bosnian Serbs.

Pre-Dayton Mediation Attempts

As early as 1991, politicians and commentators in Europe realized that a holistic approach to the unraveling of Yugoslavia was needed, and that the crisis would not end with Croatia and Slovenia. One commentator wrote, "The European Community should anyway aim to convene as quickly as possible a constitutional conference at which Yugoslavia's future can be battled over by politicians, not soldiers. Nothing should be ruled off the agenda of such a conference—not even the recreation of a new, looser Yugoslavia... [I]f the borders within Yugoslavia are to be rearranged, it is vital that this can happen through bargaining rather than through more bloodshed."[14] The European Community, in conjunction with the United Nations, set in motion a series of mediation attempts to resolve the crisis in Bosnia. All the agreements reached under these plans followed the classical mediation model, yet they were likely doomed to fail because of the West's reluctance to provide the ground troops that would have been necessary to implement the plans. The Bosnian Serbs, realizing that the West was unlikely to intervene, became adept at playing along with the process, while at the same time holding on to the 70 percent of the country they had grabbed by 1992 and pushing relentlessly for more. A firm believer in mediation and conflict resolution processes would probably say that any good-faith mediation efforts would have been better than none and that if a consensual process were possible for restoring peace in Bosnia, it should have been sought at all costs. A more cynical view is that mediation processes and limited humanitarian interventions early in the war simply masked the West's unwillingness to commit its own troops, a lack of will that permitted the Bosnian Serbs more time to commit their program of ethnic cleansing. Whether there were realistic alternatives to the European peace efforts, or whether the war was simply not ripe for political resolution, the fact is that none of these early mediation efforts succeeded.

The Carrington–Cutileiro Mediation, March 1992

Early in 1992, as the Bosnians were on the verge of declaring independence, the European Community stepped in to mediate. José Cutileiro, who had been chairing the EC committee overseeing issues of Croatian and Slovenian sovereignty, extended the committee's mandate to Bosnia, in conjunction with another EC mediator, Lord Carrington. While this might have been a time to work on creative constitutional ways of keeping Bosnia together as a multiethnic state, the negotiators accepted the political realities on the ground and the parties' contention that "the internal conflict was ethnically based and that the power-sharing arrangement of the coalition should translate into a triune state in which three ethnic parties divided territorial control among them."[15] The failure of the negotiators to push for constitutional protections for minorities and creative governing arrangements to mitigate the heat of ethnic conflict was a critical early failure. The Lisbon Agreement, or Cutileiro Plan, was signed on March 18,

1992, but within a week Bosnian President Izetbegovic and Bosnian Croat leader Mate Boban reneged on the terms, both hoping to secure a more profitable agreement at a later time.[16]

Out of the range of television cameras, Serb irregulars continued to terrorize Muslim villages along the Drina River in Eastern Bosnia, an important Serb territorial goal because of the region's direct proximity with Serbia. In a breathtaking sweep of the country, Serb forces managed to gain hold of nearly 70 percent of Bosnian territory in only three months, a percentage that did not change significantly until the Muslim–Croat offensive in the summer of 1995. In response to a May 1992 UN Security Council resolution, the JNA withdrew from Bosnia back into the rump Yugoslavia. Rather than stabilizing the military situation in Bosnia, the withdrawal provided the Bosnian Serbs with a windfall in armaments and expertise: the JNA left behind most of its Bosnian-born Serb commanders, and a large cache of artillery and materiel.[17] The Serbs deployed ghastly measures to "cleanse" Bosnians and Croatians from Serb-held land. Families were forced from their homes and robbed of all money and valuables, their houses then burned or bombed to make return impossible. Men, women, and children were separated and sent to detention centers. There, women and young girls were repeatedly raped. Men were either killed outright and dumped in mass graves or held and subjected to torture, sometimes to be killed later.[18]

In the summer of 1992, television broadcasts of the concentration camp Omarska in the Prijedor region of Bosnia prompted moral outrage in the world at large. Echoes of the Nazi death camps were clear: men with skeletal arms and empty eyes, living in squalor and humiliation, facing imminent death. Around the same time, international aid workers in Bosnia began to feel used as collaborators to Serb aggression, a theme that would repeat itself throughout the Bosnian war. In July 1992, Bosnian Serb leaders assured UNPROFOR and UN High Commissioner for Refugees (UNHCR) workers in Croatia that the Muslims streaming toward the Croatian border were leaving voluntarily.[19] Aid agencies helped the Muslims to safety, only to learn that these people had actually been forced from their homes under horrendous circumstances.[20]

As the violence raged in Bosnia over the summer of 1992, international intervention was lukewarm. In May 1992 the United Nations imposed strict financial sanctions against Serbia and Montenegro (Resolution 757) in an effort to force Milosevic to rein in Karadzic and Mladic. NATO and the Western European Union (WEU) staged military exercises in the Adriatic, but they had no enforcement power to board ships loaded with contraband. This signaled to Croatia that it could break the arms embargo without consequences and signaled to the Bosnian Serbs that NATO would not take action against them.[21]

Aside from encouraging Bosnia's independence in 1992, the United States' reaction to the conflict was muted. In June 1992, it made more explicit its preference for a solution acceptable to the Bosnian Muslims and multiethnic groups over the Serbs and Croats,[22] yet continued to hold back militarily and diplomatically. President George Bush was recovering from huge outlays of military and political capital in the Gulf War and was consumed with the break-up of the former Soviet Union and the burgeoning Madrid process on peace in the Middle East. His administration was not eager to expend military and political resources on Bosnia. He sent Secretary of State James Baker to Yugoslavia in June 1991 to inform Slovenia and Croatia that the United States would not recognize them if they chose to secede. He weakened this statement, however, by making it clear that the United States would not use force to intervene in the case of a Serbian attack on Slovenia or Croatia. While Baker was clearly concerned about the potential for carnage in the former Yugoslavia, he felt strongly that the United States didn't "have a dog in this fight."[23]

The Vance-Owen Peace Plan, September 1992–June 1993

Horrified by the violence in Bosnia, and hopeful that the EC's change to British leadership in the spring of 1992 might galvanize the peace process in the former Yugoslavia, on September 3, 1992, the European Community, in conjunction with the United Nations, established the International Conference on the Former Yugoslavia (ICFY). The chairmen of the conference, former British member of Parliament and Foreign Secretary Lord David Owen (representing the EC) and former U.S. Secretary of State Cyrus Vance (representing the United Nations), were charged with establishing a lasting cease-fire and reversing the effects of ethnic cleansing. The United Nations passed resolutions extending the UNPROFOR mandate to Bosnia and allowing it to deliver humanitarian aid to Sarajevo and other areas of Bosnia under siege.[24] The Vance–Owen peace process was an exercise in classical mediation. The mediators caucused with the parties about their aims and concerns, tried to find areas of overlapping interests, and attempted to gain consensus on a common document. The mediators had no leverage or power other than the parties' goodwill (a resource in short supply in the former Yugoslavia at the time). The humanitarian mission set up by the United Nations, for all the help it gave civilians, did not give the mediators the military leverage they might have needed and forestalled more powerful military action by NATO.

During the fall of 1992, Owen and Vance met with the parties, including Milan Panic (a Yugoslavian-born pharmaceutical company magnate from California, hand-picked by Milosevic to be prime minister of Serbia) and Dobrica Cosic (a highly influential Serbian intellectual, appointed by Milosevic to be president of the rump Yugoslavia). Vance and Owen specifically included Milosevic in their discussions, not believing that he would remain long in the shadows of Panic and Cosic.[25] One issue of great concern to Lord Owen was the lack of leverage the negotiators held over the parties, especially the recalcitrant Bosnian Serbs. In an effort to stop Serbian air attacks on civilian targets (Serbian forces, with full access to JNA matériel left in Bosnia, far out-gunned Croatian Serbs and Bosnian Muslims, who were also subject to the UN arms embargo), Owen pushed for the UN Security Council to establish a "no-fly zone" over Bosnia, and for NATO to enforce it. Despite the enactment of the zone by UNSC Resolution 781, British and French officials, concerned about the welfare of their troops on the ground, actively resisted aggressive enforcement of the no-fly zone. The military "stick" that Owen had counted on for leverage turned out to be a mere willow branch until enforcement became more aggressive in 1993.[26]

Meanwhile, in the fall of 1992, Owen and Vance worked on the principles that would ultimately become the Vance–Owen Peace Plan. Revealed formally in Geneva in January 1993, the plan promised to reverse the trend of ethnic cleansing and partition by creating a country in which interdependence between ethnic groups was the only choice. Under the plan the country would be divided into ten "cantons," three with a Serb majority, two with a Croat majority, three with a Muslim majority, and one with a mixed Croat–Muslim majority. Sarajevo, the tenth canton, would be governed through power sharing among the three ethnic groups. The Republic of Bosnia would retain a weak central government, with each province keeping a significant degree of power.[27]

The Vance–Owen Plan, as negotiated, had significant strengths and weaknesses. On the positive side, Bosnia would remain intact as a country and as a multiethnic state (even if divided into seemingly untenable segments), and no international frontiers would need to be changed. More importantly, no country would have been "annexed or obliterated from the map, no state created within a state."[28] On the negative side, the plan would reward the Serbs with more land than they had had before the war, meaning ethnic cleansing would have been rewarded; the plan would have to be enforced by military troops to oversee land swaps and to maintain the peace; and the central Bosnian government would likely be too weak to rule over the divided entity.[29]

By March 1993, with the help of intense international pressure on the Bosnian government, Owen and Vance had convinced the Bosnian Croats and Bosnian government to agree to the plan. Each side, however, accepted the Vance–Owen Plan, with deep reservations: none of the parties really believed that it stood a chance, but signing the plan would win each of them valuable political points from the West. The Bosnian Croats, led by Mate Boban, accepted the plan almost immediately, because it gave them a wide swath of land with a Croatian majority, directly contiguous to Croatia's border. If the plan succeeded, the western part of Bosnia could become de facto a part of Croatia. If the plan failed, the Croatian military could move to annex the region into Croatia anyway.[30]

The Bosnian Muslims initially balked at the plan because it did not provide for a strong central government and did not return all of the land occupied by Serb forces. For the Bosnian Muslims, signing the Vance–Owen Plan was a gamble and an admission that they had no other options.[31] Even though the Bosnian Muslims realized that the Bosnian state would be weak under the plan, they also had faith that the plan would never be enacted because of Serb intransigence (and continued Serb intransigence might lead to at least a lifting of the arms embargo).

The Bosnian Serbs were angered by the plan, which reduced their territory from 70 percent to approximately 43 percent of Bosnia. Furthermore, none of the areas with a Serb majority under the Vance–Owen Plan was directly contiguous with Serbia, and the precious Posavina Corridor (a land bridge between Serbian-held territory in Bosnia and Serbia proper) fell outside their allocated regions.[32] To increase pressure on the recalcitrant Bosnian Serbs, who saw victory on the battlefield as preferable to the cantonment idea, Vance and Owen threatened Milosevic's Serbia: If the Bosnian Serbs did not sign the plan by April 26, Serbia would be punished with even longer and tighter sanctions;[33] at the same time, NATO began more aggressive enforcement of the "no-fly zone."[34]

In response, Milosevic played a cagey game, on one hand seeming to make concessions and agreeing to the plan, while on the other giving assurances to the Bosnian Serbs that the plan would never be implemented. Milosevic calculated that, by signing the plan, he could convince the West to withdraw economic sanctions. He also operated under the certainty that, even if the Bosnian Serbs failed to implement the agreement, the West would not step up its military force. In negotiating with Owen, Milosevic asked for three concessions, concerning the Posavina Corridor, the voting procedures for the interim presidency, and the nationality of personnel policing Serb-held land being turned over to the Muslims.[35] While he was convinced that he could avoid sanctions and gain goodwill by signing the agreement, he was also certain that the Serbs could sign the plan, and then obstruct its implementation, much as they had done in Croatia the year before.

Lord Owen makes an astonishing admission in his memoirs regarding these negotiations with Milosevic. Owen writes that, in fact, he realized that the plan would never even reach that stage."[36] Owen was able to make these tacit concessions to Milosevic because, even though they were not what the Bosnians thought they had signed, "[i]t was in the nature of the Vance–Owen Plan ... that it leant itself to radically different—even contradictory—interpretations."[37] While some degree of creative ambiguity can often be helpful in peace agreements, the mediator's admission of the *Rashomon* quality of this peace plan illustrates the shaky nature of the consensus and understanding behind the plan and the dubious viability of the plan if not enforced militarily.

Milosevic made a show of persuading Karadzic to accept the Vance–Owen Plan. Karadzic at first refused to sign, insisting that the plan had to be approved by the Bosnian Serb Assembly. Predictably, the plan was voted down by the Assembly. At a high-pressure meeting in Greece, Karadzic was "brow-beaten" by Milosevic to sign. Karadzic did sign, but with the proviso, once again, that the Bosnian Serb assembly ratify the plan.

At this point, Vance announced that he was stepping down from the ICFY process, to be replaced by Thorvald Stoltenberg. Owen proclaimed that it was "a bright, sunny day" for the Balkans.[38] But the sunshine quickly turned to thunderstorms when the Bosnian Serb Assembly once again failed to ratify the plan. Almost immediately following the Bosnian Serb rejection, the United States began a public campaign for an alternative process to the Vance–Owen Plan. The Vance–Owen Plan was officially dead, and with it the last hopes for a multiethnic state in Bosnia.

Role of the United States in the Vance–Owen Process

The United States played a critical role in the failure of the Vance–Owen Peace Plan. The negotiation phase of the Vance–Owen Plan took place in the early months of President Clinton's new administration. Whereas Clinton had taken a tough stance on Bosnia during the presidential campaign, his Bosnia policy became more ambiguous after he assumed office. On one hand, Clinton argued that the Vance–Owen Plan was unworkable, yet on the other hand he appointed an envoy—Reginald Bartholomew—to the negotiations and pledged to join with the United Nations and others in enforcing the plan.[39] Secretary of State Warren Christopher soon retreated from this pledge of military support, arguing that "[i]mplemention did not necessarily mean deployment of U.S. ground forces."[40] In Senate testimony two months later, Christopher argued for a strict test of whether the United States should intervene with force. The criteria were a strong echo of the "Powell Principles": a clearly stated goal; a strong likelihood of success; an exit strategy; and broad, substantial public support.[41] It was clear to David Owen that, in the eyes of the United States, these criteria were not met and that U.S. military support would not be forthcoming. Rather than openly supporting the Vance–Owen Plan, Secretary of State Christopher instead traveled to Europe to garner support for an alternate strategy proposed by the United States: "Lift and Strike." This policy aimed to level the playing field by first lifting the arms embargo only for the Bosnian government. The second element of the policy was to launch NATO air strikes against Serb targets. In what was one of the gravest miscalculations of Clinton policy in the former Yugoslavia, "Lift and Strike" was summarily and consistently rejected by the Europeans. Europe was opposed to the plan in part because it so openly subverted the Vance–Owen process, but also because of the fear that it would endanger European peacekeeping forces already on the ground. (The rejection also carried more than an implicit suggestion by the Europeans that the United States, which had committed no troops to the UN peacekeeping effort, was hardly in a position to dictate military strategy.)[42]

Around the time of the "Lift and Strike" policy debacle, President Clinton fell back on the "ancient hatreds" rhetoric, admitting that the Yugoslavia crisis was intractable. The United States publicly backed off both the Vance–Owen Plan and "Lift and Strike," settling into several months of inaction on Bosnia. Christopher testified to Congress that the conflict was "a problem from hell"[43] and started to talk about "containing" the war, rather than resolving the underlying conflict.[44] He went so far as to try to equalize the extent of atrocities between the three groups: " 'There were atrocities on all sides . . . It's easy to analogize [Bosnia] to the Holocaust. . . . But I never heard of any genocide by the Jews against the German people.' "[45] The United States and the United Nations made the choice of describing the conflict as a three-sided civil war, rather than a war of aggression by the Serbs. Rather than calling on the allies and organizing a military force, as the United States had done over Kuwait (where, arguably, more tangible U.S. interests were at stake, as well), the Western allies simply sent out an inadequate humanitarian force to forestall stronger military action. This strategy had tragic results, as illustrated by the fall of Srebrenica.

Srebrenica and the Failure of UNPROFOR

Events on the ground in Bosnia further compounded the political failure of the Vance–Owen agreement. The most tragic event in the spring of 1993 was the capture of Srebrenica, a Muslim enclave in Eastern Bosnia, by Serb forces. The surrender of Srebrenica set in motion a string of events that would eventually "humiliate the UN Protection Force, destroy the Vance–Owen Peace Plan, fatally undermine the credibility of the UN Security Council, and threaten to split the NATO alliance."[46] Srebrenica, a town in the Drina mountains close to the Serbian border, had become home to thousands of Muslim refugees who had been "cleansed" from neighboring towns and villages. Refugees were forced to sleep in the open air, and Serb forces blocked aid convoys from entering the city. Muslim forces in the town sent out raids on Serbian villages, enraging Serb forces and inviting revenge attacks. In March 1993, Serb forces shelled Srebrenica despite an agreement worked out by UNPROFOR Commander Philippe Morillon, who, upon visiting Srebrenica, was held hostage by Muslim citizens until he promised to bring security to the embattled town. At the beginning of April, the Serbs issued a surrender order through the UNHCR, requiring that the Bosnian government surrender within forty-eight hours. Furthermore, they required that the UN forces help in the surrender by evacuating and disarming over 60,000 people under the critical (and gloating) eye of Bosnian Serb military commander Ratko Mladic.[47]

The 1993 surrender of Srebrenica illustrates the untenable position of the UN peacekeeping forces. Not only were they forced to take part in the surrender of the town, but they also bore witness to a horrible scene of Serb violence even after the area was declared "safe." Under the noses of the few Canadian forces left in Srebrenica, the Serbs lobbed a mortar shell into a group of teenagers playing soccer at the high school. The carnage was indescribable.[48] Yet while this was clearly a Serb attack, UN officials told the press that the Serbs were firing in response to a Muslim attack (they later retracted the statement since there was no evidence of Muslim aggression).[49] This manipulation of the truth reflected the lengths to which the United Nations would go not to name Serbian forces as aggressors. To do so would be to shatter the myth of "neutrality" under which the peacekeepers operated, a neutrality under which all parties were equally guilty. This manipulation of the press was also evident in the UN description of the fall of Srebrenica, which never used the word "surrender."[50]

Srebrenica exposed UNPROFOR for what it was: a poorly planned humanitarian-effort force that was an ineffective substitute for the kind of military force needed to stop the atrocities. Rather than lift the arms embargo so that the Bosnians could fight on a level field, or send in troops to combat Serb aggression, the United Nations sent in peacekeepers with no mandate to make or enforce peace. UNPROFOR's only mandate was to secure the delivery of food, medicine, clothing, and other humanitarian aid.[51] This use of peacekeeping forces for these purposes was unprecedented in the absence of a cease-fire and represented the first time that the UN Security Council sent "a neutral military force, a peacekeeping force, into a country where there was not peace to keep."[52] (The example was soon followed in Somalia in December 1992, with disastrous consequences.) The Muslims quickly realized that the UN blue helmets lacked both the capacity and mission authority to protect them from territorial incursions by Serbs and Croats. UN peacekeepers often found themselves unwitting aiders and abettors to the Serb ethnic cleansing campaign, while officially clinging to a policy of neutrality vis-à-vis the warring factions. The work of UNPROFOR was constrained by several internal contradictions to the UN mission plan. First, while the Bosnian Muslims and government expected UNPROFOR troops to protect the sovereignty of Bosnia as a UN member state, UNPROFOR's sole mandate was to provide humanitarian aid under the presumption that all three parties to the conflict were equivalent—equally deserving of humanitarian assistance, and equally culpable in whatever war crimes and atrocities were being committed. Because the Serbs were more heavily armed and had been more aggressive in conquering Muslim territory, the Bosnian Muslims argued that such a declaration of neutrality on the part of the United Nations was tantamount to siding with the Serbs.[53] The Muslim position had merit, given that all humanitarian missions operate under the principle of consent: the UN force commanders needed consent from whoever held the territory to permit aid convoys to pass through to needy civilians. The Bosnian Serbs used the consent requirement to humiliate UN forces and, on numerous occasions, used the required procedures of consent as de facto indications of recognition of Republika Srpska's political authority. Although the Security Council added weapons and funding to UNPROFOR as the war continued, the central humanitarian nature of the mission was not altered. Without the political will—of the parties or the international community—to hammer out a peace agreement, there was no peace to enforce and thus no prospect for adjusting the mission of UNPROFOR from peacekeeping to peace enforcement.

The insufficiency of a purely humanitarian mandate became painfully obvious following the reactive designation of Srebrenica as a "safe area," by UN Security Council Resolution 819 on April 16, 1993, one day after the surrender of Srebrenica. (The Security Council later extended the "safe area" designation to Sarajevo, Tuzla, Zepa, Gorazde, and Bihac, all towns with majority Muslim populations.) Even though the term "safe area" was politically, militarily, and legally ambiguous, for the first time, "the international community had committed itself—morally, if not in any effective practical sense—to the protection of one side in the war against the other."[54] But this commitment exposed dramatically the limitations of the peacekeeping forces: they remained *peacekeeping* forces, not peace enforcement forces, and were never given the mandate or the military equipment to enforce the "safe areas" in any meaningful way. Furthermore, the safe area concept dashed the illusion of UN neutrality and pitted the United Nations against the Serbs.

Yet the United Nations was not willing or able to use force to deter or punish the Serbs. While the resolution on safe areas allowed the United Nations to call for close air cover to counter violations of the safe area, it required two steps of approval, the so-called dual key policy (another bureaucratic obfuscation that kept the West from providing the firepower needed to contain the crisis). First, the UN Security Council would have to approve a request from the secretary-general for military action. Second, the NATO Council would have to approve the use of NATO forces for air support. This created great tension between the United States (who supported air power, largely because it had no troops on the ground and was not willing to send them) and Europe (who wanted to protect their troops from fire and manipulation), and between the UN and NATO.[55] Boutros Boutros-Ghali initially requested 34,000 troops to police the safe areas, yet member nations only committed 7,000.[56]

The concept behind the safe areas, while never entirely clear, seemed to call for withdrawal of Bosnian Serb military units to create demilitarized areas. These areas, however, were neither demilitarized nor safe. Muslims used these areas as rest and recuperation centers, and as bases for raids into Serb territory. The Serbs, perceiving these areas as military bases for Muslims, had no compunction about attacking them, risking their own exposure to NATO attack.[57]

As if the surrender of Srebrenica and the collapse of the Vance–Owen Peace Plan in the spring of 1993 were not enough fuel to add to the conflagration already raging in Bosnia, the fragile Croat–Muslim alliance disintegrated at about the same time. Encouraged by the "legitimacy" granted to them by the Vance–Owen Plan, the Bosnian Croats began "cleansing" the territory contiguous to Croatia of Bosnian Muslims, committing atrocities against the Muslims similar to those that were carried out by the Serbs. Reacting to the news of Srebrenica with fear of a flood of Muslim refugees, Croat forces captured several Muslim enclaves and murdered dozens of civilians. Forced evictions, murders, and rapes followed, and the Bosnian government realized that it was being squeezed out of existence by the Croats to the west and north and the Serbs to the east and north.[58] Finally, after years of appealing to Western governments for help, the Bosnian Muslims (aided by weaponry and other support from Islamic countries subverting the arms embargo) took matters into their own hands and fought back.[59] They recaptured a triangle of territory in Central Bosnia and secured communication lines among spread-out Muslim enclaves. The fighting was brutal, and the violence of the Croat–Muslim conflict led many proponents of "no action" in the West to declare, inaccurately, that "all sides are equally guilty."[60]

Healing Transatlantic Rifts with the Joint Action Plan

In May 1993, the matrix of international actors and organizations working (or not working) on the Bosnian issue suddenly shifted. The United States, along with Britain, France, Russia, and (later) Spain, introduced the Joint Action Plan (JAP), a program of containment that severely undermined the earlier UN–EC peace efforts. The JAP was an attempt by France and Britain to heal the transatlantic rifts over the issues of the former Yugoslavia[61] and provided a means for Russia to take a more active role in the peacemaking process. Bringing Spain aboard at a later date added credibility to the claim that this was a legitimate "European" initiative that could rival the EC's official talks under the ICFY. The irony of the plan was that, despite its name, the Joint Action Plan contemplated no specific "action" on the part of the sponsoring powers.[62] The JAP's underlying premise was "containment"—sealing off the Bosnian borders against Serb and Croat incursions, placing a contingent of troops in Macedonia to avoid spread of the conflict, and expanding the safe areas to include six Muslim towns. While the substance of the plan was on its face fairly innocuous, the consequence of yet another plan was to completely kill off what remained of Vance–Owen and any hopes for a multiethnic Bosnia. While the JAP maintained the shell of the Vance–Owen "process," it gutted the Vance–Owen Plan by approving the Serbs' territorial gains, setting the stage for a future ethnic partition of Bosnia, and implying once again that no force would be used to impose a plan for peace in Bosnia.[63] David Owen was particularly critical of that part of the JAP that called for a UN Security Council resolution to expand the Muslim safe areas.[64] NATO commanders had similar concerns; NATO Secretary-General Manfred Worner asked, "'What does safe mean? Who defends whom? What are the rules of engagement? Where is the connection to the next step—that of withdrawing Serbian forces? What weapons may be used?'"[65] Owen was also bitter that the United States—in order to renege on an earlier obligation to commit troops to Bosnia—had poisoned what he viewed as a just and workable agreement (his own), gone behind his back to establish a competing plan that killed any hope of a unified Bosnia, abandoned its support of the Bosnian Muslims and the ideal of a multiethnic state, and capitulated to the Bosnian Serbs by allowing them to keep territory they had gained in the war. The most positive and lasting element of the JAP, however, was the establishment of the War Crimes Tribunal at The Hague with a mandate to investigate and prosecute all violations of international humanitarian law in the area of the former Yugoslavia.

The Last Gasp for European Peacemaking: The Owen–Stoltenberg Plan, Summer 1993

Whatever humiliation David Owen might have felt at the ignominious defeat of the Vance–Owen Plan, he agreed to continue the EC mediation efforts with Cyrus Vance's UN replacement, Thorvald Stoltenberg. Rather than try to create a plan that would appeal to all sides, or that would attempt to impose a just solution, Owen and Stoltenberg agreed to accept proposals from the parties themselves. This mediation strategy exposes the true failure of classical mediation.

Mediation often depends on proposals suggested by the parties involved. The mediator, in face-to-face talks or shuttle diplomacy, finds common ground among the proposals and works out a consensus that is fair and pleasing to both sides. However, mediators are wary of accepting such plans when there are clear power imbalances between the parties. In these cases, mediators must use great personal leverage to equalize the incentives and gains of each party.

In this case, Owen and Stoltenberg did not have such leverage, and the plan put forth by the Bosnian Serbs and Croats was unfair by any measure. In accepting the plan, Owen frankly stated that he "did not expect to be able to claim that what they achieved was an 'honorable settlement.'"[66] Furthermore, Owen severely compromised the Bosnian Muslim delegation by accepting into the negotiations Fikret Abdic, a successful Muslim businessman—and warlord—from Bihac, in the western region of Bosnia. Owen and Stoltenberg declared that they would rather deal with Abdic than with President Alija Izetbegovic,[67] a position that undermined the negotiating power of President Izetbegovic (who still retained the loyalty of the Bosnian Muslim military), and his negotiating team.

The plans put forward by the Bosnian Serbs and Bosnian Croats (with the full backing of their respective patron governments in Belgrade and Zagreb) allowed only 30 percent of Bosnia for the Muslim population, with no access to the sea or crucial transportation routes. The only principled role for the mediators at this point was to press for arrangements that might be minimally acceptable for the Bosnian Muslims (even as the Serbs were tightening their stranglehold on Sarajevo by mounting weapons on the top of Mount Igman). Eventually, all three parties agreed to a version of the plan they had discussed while sailing the HMS *Invincible*, but, in what was a recurring pattern, Izetbegovic renounced the plan and reneged on his earlier agreement to its provisions.

Despite the failure of the *Invincible* agreement, during the fall of 1993, Owen and Stoltenberg attempted to continue the peace process and to strengthen the leverage of the ICFY. They reached out to the foreign ministers of the major European powers and convinced them to participate in the negotiation process with the parties to the war in Yugoslavia. The exercise was partially fruitful, in that, while still operating primarily within the framework of the Owen–Stoltenberg Plan, it increased the Muslim share of Bosnia to 33.5 percent, with the means of defending its own borders. The plan was nevertheless doomed to fail because the European leaders wanted American support for and involvement in the plan, specifically NATO enforcement of boundaries it established. The Clinton administration, however, despite a growing chorus of voices within the government and on Capitol Hill calling for lifting the arms embargo, stonewalled and refused to engage. Owen felt that the United States' unwillingness to engage not only prolonged the war in Bosnia, but also gave the Muslims the freedom to back out of any deal—as they had done at one point or another with the four past proposals—without the spirit of compromise.[68]

Key Factors in Shaping the Result

The military situation in Bosnia continued to worsen. By mid-1995, the United States and the Western Europeans were faced with the spectacle of a humiliating withdrawal of the UN humanitarian mission—a withdrawal for which NATO had already committed to provide military support. Confronted with such a public and humiliating failure of all prior international efforts to mediate a solution to the war, the United States and its allies finally were compelled to make a more effective political and military commitment to resolving the conflict. Several events helped ensure that a comprehensive diplomatic and military effort, when it finally came in September 1995, would succeed. The creation in 1994 of the Muslim–Croat Federation, and the subsequent boost it gave to the Bosnian government forces, was the first crucial step toward eventual peace. The subsequent formation of the Contact Group, in which the United States played a key role, established a more effective mechanism through which the Western powers and Russia could work together. The Contact Group Plan, calling for a 51 percent–49 percent division of the territory of Bosnia between the Bosnian Serb entity and the Muslim–Croat Federation was rejected by the parties but eventually became the blueprint for the Dayton Peace Plan. To get the parties to Dayton, all sides had to reach a point where they could be persuaded that there were no more gains to be made on the battlefield.

The United States was spurred on to deeper involvement by the worsening humanitarian situation and horrific war crimes committed by the Bosnian Serbs against the Bosnian forces and civilians. Domestic opinion had turned to support a unilateral lifting of the arms embargo and military support of Bosnian government troops. Further, the Republican-led Congress that took office in January 1995 supported unilateral action and seemed unconcerned about the international legal ramifications or potential damage to the United States' multilateral commitments from such a decision. The Clinton administration thus had incentive to take a leading role in the mediation and to act more forcefully in its diplomatic efforts to urge the parties toward a final settlement. This section addresses the factors that led to the final diplomatic and military interventions, and which convinced the parties to meet in Dayton.

The Washington Framework Agreement and the Muslim–Croat Federation

In the wake of the latest failure of the Joint Action Plan and the Owen–Stoltenberg map proposal, the United States appointed a new special envoy and focused on Bosnia with renewed vigor. As noted earlier, throughout 1993 and early 1994, war between the Bosnian Muslims and Bosnian Croats (supported by Zagreb and strengthened by the presence of over 30,000 Croatian soldiers) raged in western and central Bosnia, accompanied by reports of Croat atrocities against local Muslim populations and possible war crimes.[69] In addition to these massive human rights violations, the intense fighting between the Bosnian Muslims and Croats weakened both parties' ability to hold back Serb aggressions and increased the isolation of Muslim strongholds from supply lines. Led by Special Envoy Charles Redman and Ambassador to Croatia Peter Galbraith, the United States worked behind the scenes and apart from the ICFY to broker a cease-fire between the Muslims and Croats and to lay the groundwork for the creation of the Bosnian Federation.

To bring about the cease-fire, which would prove a crucial turning point in the war, Redman and Galbraith exerted considerable pressure on Tudjman to withdraw Croatian forces on the ground in Bosnia. The United States made clear that in return for this important step, it would recognize and support the international boundaries of Croatia, including areas that were then Serb-occupied.[70] Two events hastened Croatia's move toward reconciliation with the Bosnian Muslims. On February 5, 1994, a Serb artillery shell hit a Sarajevo marketplace, killing ten civilians. This grisly attack provoked international indignation and led to a NATO ultimatum forcing the withdrawal of Serb heavy artillery from around Sarajevo. At about the same time, the United Nations issued an ultimatum to Croatia, calling on it to pull its forces out of Bosnia within two weeks. The (temporary) success of the NATO ultimatum to the Serbs lent the international peace efforts an air of confidence that gave the Croats a sense that the time was right to seek peace with at least one of its enemies. Furthermore, these developments forced Tudjman and his top leadership to face the stark reality that because of Croatia's behavior, it was threatened with international sanctions and isolation, not the integration and trade with the international community that he envisioned for his newly independent country.

Given the continuing strength of the Bosnian Serb forces, the Bosnian government forces had an incentive to end the battle with the Croats; they could not carry on credibly against two battlefield enemies. At this time, the Bosnian government looked increasingly upon the United States as partisan to its position in the war: Bosnian sovereignty above all else. The stepped-up American diplomatic activities and increasing public outcry in the United States that "something be done" to stop the atrocities being committed against the Muslims led the Bosnian government of President Alija Izetbegovic to trust and rely on the good offices of the United States in ways that continued up through Dayton, but which at times would create a false sense of unity of purpose that caused tension and frustration between American mediators and Bosnian officials. Nevertheless, this sense of trust made it easier for the United States to suggest solutions to the Bosnian government.

Redman's planned federation of the Muslim and Croat elements in Bosnia—based on a cantonment plan proposed earlier by Croat politician Ivo Komsic—and subsequent confederation with Croatia were accepted in principle by the Croatian government. The details were left to be worked out in Washington, where Redman and Galbraith led short, intense proximity talks with the Bosnian and Croat delegations. The agreement, at least on paper, appeared to be an essential first step to a comprehensive resolution. The Federation created one Bosnian entity to represent the interests of both the Muslims and Croats in negotiations with the Serbian parties on behalf of all the other peoples of Bosnia.[71] As long as Washington remained engaged and supportive of the Federation, the paper alliance led to some important changes on the ground: several joint military operations against the Serbs; the shipment of arms to Muslim forces through Croatian territory; and most important, a cessation of battlefield hostilities between the Muslims and Croats.

The Contact Group Plan: The 51 Percent–49 Percent Solution

After convincing the Bosnian Serbs to comply with the NATO ultimatum in February, Russia appeared, finally, to be exercising its influence on the side of peace. Redman and Russian Deputy Foreign Minister Vitaly Churkin hoped to seize the momentum of the Washington Agreement and the ultimatum to the Bosnian Serbs to bring about a comprehensive cease-fire. Their hopes were dashed with the Serb bombing of the UN safe area of Gorazde in eastern Bosnia in early April 1994. The United Nations responded to the attack on Gorazde by approving NATO air strikes. The resulting series of attacks on Serb positions in Gorazde was almost negligible; the press pronounced them mere "pinpricks." The attacks were effective enough, however, to enrage Serb military commander Ratko Mladic, who took 150 UN personnel hostage during a reprisal attack against the Bosnian-held enclave of Tuzla. The ineffectiveness of the air strikes—and the clear signal that there was no consensus among the NATO countries to do anything more—deflated the peace process, leading the Bosnian government to dig in for a longer war.[72]

In the next weeks, the Bosnian Serbs would act with such impunity as to shake the international community, which had seemed unable to reach consensus on future use of air power. Significantly, Mladic and Karadzic treated their sponsors in Belgrade and Moscow with the same contempt as NATO and the United Nations, an error that would ultimately cut them out of the final peace process.

With the ICFY peace process and subsequent mediation attempts dead letters, the United States and Russia sought to push the mediation in a new direction. The so-called Contact Group was created, with representatives from the United States, Russia, Germany, France, and the United Kingdom (the latter two the only members of the group with peacekeeping troops on the ground in Bosnia) along with representatives from the United Nations and EU. The Contact Group was an important shift from the EU effort because it included the two powers viewed as indispensable to a lasting agreement: the United States and Russia. David Owen's insight into the importance of U.S. involvement would apply not only to the Contact Group but also Dayton itself: "You had to find a way where the Americans were involved in the nitty-gritty of negotiations and in dirtying their hands in a settlement which they had then had to go out and support."[73] The Contact Group appeared to reflect the right composition of countries to overcome attempts by either side in the war to exploit divisions within the international community, as had been done during the failure of "Lift and Strike." But even coordination within a group as small as five countries proved too unwieldy to make it effective in addressing the problems in Bosnia.[74]

Under the strong leadership of Redman and Churkin, the Group did manage to create a new peace plan which would allow Bosnia-Herzegovina to retain its international borders but would allocate internal control of the territory between the Federation (51 percent of the territory) and the Bosnian Serbs (49 percent of the territory). (At the time of the proposal, the Serbs controlled about 70 percent of the territory of Bosnia.)[75] The maps were drawn up by the Contact Group and not unveiled to the parties until June. Karadzic rejected the map out of hand. But Milosevic, by now fed up with what he saw as Karadzic straying too far from Milosevic's plans for greater Serbia, told the Russians that he would agree with the plan. Bosnian Prime Minister Haris Silajdzic was unhappy with the maps, noting that in awarding certain towns to the Serbs, the Contact Group "rewarded genocide and ethnic cleansing . . . the solution especially in eastern Bosnia has serious deficiencies and some genocide areas like Prijedor are going to be controlled by those who committed those crimes."[76]

Threatened by U. S. statements that it would unilaterally lift the arms embargo, the Group of Seven Industrialized Nations (G-7) hastily endorsed the plan—which was described to the parties and those outside the Contact Group as "take it or leave it"—and dispatched European foreign ministers to the Balkan capitals to negotiate with the parties, including Karadzic. Under serious pressure from Milosevic, Karadzic took the plan to the Republika Srpska Assembly, which, as it had with the Vance–Owen Plan, refused to vote an unqualified yes. As Peter Galbraith described it, "they found it impossible to decide which 20 percent to give up."[77] Milosevic quickly turned on the Bosnian Serb leadership in Pale, slapping an embargo on them and, at least publicly, distancing himself from Karadzic.

The decision of the Bosnian Serbs to reject the plan excluded them from all further peace negotiations. But the Contact Group had no counterproposals or efforts to add to the plan. For the next months, the plan would remain on the table but with no action on the ground. Milosevic announced the creation of an enforced border between the FRY and Bosnia-Herzegovina, but evidence indicated that the border was "porous." Observers speculated that Milosevic in fact never intended to enforce the weapons embargo and support continued to leak through.[78]

Worsening Violence and an Effective NATO Response:
The United States Plans the Endgame

Between late 1994 and the final fall of Srebrenica in July 1995, the situation on the ground in Bosnia remained grim. The Serbs deftly manipulated both the UN and NATO decision-making processes by pushing forward and then withdrawing in the face of threats or pinprick air strikes, only to resume fighting in short order. In December, former President Jimmy Carter negotiated a cease-fire agreement with Karadzic and Mladic, but it lasted only through the winter months. Emboldened by the inability of the United Nations and NATO to reach consensus on the use of force, and counting on continuing U.S. reticence to commit ground troops in the region, the Serbs seized 350 UN peacekeepers as "human shields" in retaliation for NATO air strikes against Serb weapons caches. The event reportedly shook President Clinton, who directed that his national security team examine a new approach, what one National Security Council (NSC) official called "the Endgame Strategy" to bring about a comprehensive settlement, end the atrocities, and terminate the ongoing humiliations of the UN and NATO.[79]

A number of factors influenced the Clinton administration to abandon its reluctant stance in Bosnia and to take the lead in seeking a lasting solution to the conflict. In June 1995, newly elected French President Jacques Chirac increased pressure on the United States by threatening the withdrawal of UNPROFOR troops, whose impotence to stop the fighting had been exposed in the humiliating hostage-taking episode. In Chirac's view, either international intervention had to be stronger, which would require greater participation by the United States, or the international community should withdraw.[80] Much to the apparent surprise of President Clinton, U.S. officials realized that in the event of UNPROFOR withdrawal, NATO—and thus U.S. ground troops—would be obligated to assist in the pull-out: NATO Op-Plan 40–104 called for the United States to provide 20,000 of the 60,000 troops that would be required for an "evacuation force."[81] Almost unintentionally, through a series of decisions in Washington and at NATO headquarters in Brussels, the Clinton administration had painted itself into a corner. A troop commitment became inevitable, either as an accompaniment to withdrawal of a failed international peacekeeping force, or as an accompaniment to implementation of a peace plan. The fall of the UN-designated safe area of Srebrenica would leave the United States with no politically or strategically acceptable alternative to the latter approach.

On July 6, 1995, Bosnian Serbs began shelling Srebrenica, which fell to Serbian troops just five days later—a year to the day after the first Serb assault on the town.[82] Dutch UN peacekeeping troops were held hostage and looked on helplessly as the invading Serb forces separated the men and women who had found refuge at the UN compound, leading the men and boys to mass execution sites. Human rights organizations estimate that over 7,000 Muslims—out of a total population of 30,000—were murdered following the fall of Srebrenica. More than any other single incident in the war, the fall of Srebrenica seemed to provoke a near-unanimous condemnation of the Serbs and a call for a decisive international response.

In late 1994, the United States had opened up a new and direct channel of negotiation with Slobodan Milosevic.[83] The channel had been reopened with the approval of the Europeans, who had been playing the lead role in the ongoing international mediation efforts since May 1994 following the failure of the Contact Group Plan. (Former Swedish Prime Minister Carl Bildt served as chief European negotiator.) Richard Holbrooke, who assumed the post of assistant secretary of state for European and Canadian Affairs in late 1994, appointed his deputy, Robert Frasure, as the conduit to Milosevic. The strategy was to keep drumming into Milosevic's head the devastating effects of the economic embargo against the FRY and to try to convince him to exert some control over the leadership in Pale.

As the new White House strategy and the Milosevic channel converged, the events in Srebrenica pushed the administration toward one inexorable conclusion: to achieve peace, the United States would have to make a serious political and, for the first time in the war, military commitment. Two weeks after the slaughter at Srebrenica, the allies and the United Nations changed the "dual key" policy, to allow UN military representatives on the ground, not UN bureaucrats in New York, to call for NATO air support.

Events gained momentum when Croatia launched "Operation Storm" and in an army offensive lasting less than a week, retook the Krajina and drove over 100,000 Serbs from the area. The United States did not protest the action—despite reports that the Croatian government forces were doing to the Krajina Serbs exactly what the Bosnian Serbs had done in Bosnia, namely ethnic cleansing. (Croatian activities in the Krajina were later investigated by the War Crimes Tribunal.) Spurred on by Croatian success in the Krajina, the Bosnian government troops also began an offensive and began to retake territory from the Bosnian Serbs.

As the gains on the ground provided momentum for Clinton's new diplomatic initiative, the U.S. Congress was also lighting a fire under the administration. On August 11, both the House and Senate voted to unilaterally lift the arms embargo in the event UNPROFOR withdrew from Bosnia. Such a withdrawal seemed imminent following the hostage taking and the failure of the United Nations at Srebrenica, and although Clinton vetoed the bill, pressure from Capitol Hill added another layer of urgency to the new effort.

Substantively, the administration's "Endgame Strategy" differed little from the Contact Group Plan, still on the table. It envisioned a 51 percent–49 percent division of the territory between the Federation and the Bosnian Serbs. Procedurally, however, it shifted United States attention away from the concerns of the Bosnian Muslims to a more hard-line approach to Sarajevo. In what became known as the "lift and leave" approach, the United States made clear to Bosnian President Izetbegovic that he would have to come to the final negotiating stage willing to compromise. If the Bosnian government blocked any agreement acceptable to all sides, the United States would lift the arms embargo, but not do anything more—no training, no military support. The United States garnered approval for this new approach from the Europeans, who welcomed the belated arrival of the Americans to a military-political solution and realized that the United States would move forward with the initiative with or without them. Most significantly, the United States was prepared to make Bosnia the highest foreign policy priority. On August 14, the president named Richard Holbrooke as chief U.S. negotiator to the effort and made clear that Holbrooke received the full backing of Secretary Christopher and the president himself.

Mount Igman Tragedy

On August 19, just days after Holbrooke and his team set out on an intense round of shuttle diplomacy between the Balkan capitals, three U.S. officials on the negotiating team were killed when their armored personnel carrier slid off the dangerous Mount Igman road leading to Sarajevo. The effect of this loss of life on the U.S. diplomatic effort in Bosnia cannot be underestimated.[84] First, the deaths of State Department Deputy Assistant Secretary Robert Frasure, NSC adviser Colonel Nelson Drew, and Advisor to the Secretary of Defense

Joseph Kruzel, marked the first American lives lost in the conflict and spawned even more attention in the U.S. media to American diplomatic efforts in the region. Second, the loss had an enormous personal impact on the surviving members of the negotiating team and on U.S. officials in Washington. Indeed, the deaths lent almost a crusade-like zeal to the American team and appeared to give President Clinton a renewed sense of resolve to find peace, so that their lives would not have been given in vain.[85] Holbrooke recommenced his shuttle diplomacy efforts just days after the last memorial service for his fallen colleagues.

Almost as if to spite Holbrooke's ongoing shuttle efforts, Bosnian Serbs launched shells into the crowded marketplace in Sarajevo for the second time in as many years, this time killing thirty-seven civilians. The immediate response was a U.S.-coordinated effort to launch NATO airstrikes to take out the heavy weapons and communications sites that once again laid siege to the city and people of Sarajevo. The aim of the shuttle shifted after the bombings, when it became clear to Holbrooke that NATO intervention had considerably accelerated the speed of the process. In order to lay the groundwork for a later, more comprehensive settlement, the Holbrooke team focused the shuttle efforts on obtaining small, limited interim agreements between the parties that would bring them closer together.[86]

The shuttle team—with new replacements for those who had died on Mount Igman—proved more effective than the prior Contact Group arrangement that had required extensive consultations between the national representatives and between the representatives and their own foreign and defense ministries. Drawn entirely from the U.S. government—but representing each national security organ that would be essential to the enforcement of the peace, Department of State, National Security Council, Joint Chiefs of Staff, and the Office of the Secretary of Defense—the group possessed the expertise to handle the broad range of military and political issues at stake and a rare single-mindedness of purpose.[87] Given the intensity of the negotiations during the early weeks of September 1995, the small size of the shuttle team, the careful balance of military and diplomatic personnel, and Holbrooke's sense of historic opportunity enabled them to endure the physical challenges while keeping focused on the ultimate goal.

In this way, the Bosnia peace process was reduced from the early multinational aspirations of the ICFY to a small cadre of American diplomats and military officials. The Bosnian Serbs tried once again to involve former President Jimmy Carter in the process. But Holbrooke took steps to close off that channel from the U.S. side, and by September, he and his team succeeded in making themselves the sole conduit of negotiations between the three heads of state. At the same time, however, diplomatic efforts maintained at least an air of U.S.-European cooperation; the Contact Group remained in place as a mechanism for consultation; and the United States was acutely aware that whatever progress was achieved through the shuttle would require the blessings of the European Union and Russia.

Bombs Creating "Ripeness" for Conflict Resolution

Holbrooke, a master of the media who recognized that perceptions of progress can have as much effect on a negotiating process as actual substantive steps, moved quickly to capitalize on the NATO air strikes. In rapid succession, he organized a meeting for the foreign ministers of Bosnia, the Federal Republic of Yugoslavia, and Croatia to discuss a general framework for later negotiations. (The same methodology was employed effectively in Oslo and in Northern Ireland.) He performed superhuman shuttle trips—visiting more than four cities in a single day. His team created a sense of inevitable momentum (including a side-trip to Athens to resolve the problem of Greek recognition of independent Macedonia), even when they knew that the parties were far apart.[88]

At the same time, Holbrooke worked feverishly to insure that the United States would remain firm in its support for NATO bombing in the absence of a real cease-fire from the Bosnian Serbs. While he publicly denied that his diplomatic activities and the timing of bombings had any connection,[89] he worked to ensure that the bombings were continued up through the foreign ministers' meeting. The tactic worked. At the meeting of the foreign ministers, the parties agreed to the crucial basic principles that would form the basis of the general framework agreement signed at Dayton, including the recognition of Bosnia's external border and the adoption of the 51 percent-49 percent territorial allocation of the Contact Group Plan.

Form and Specific Mechanisms of Intervention

As the shuttle talks progressed and the Holbrooke team emerged as the sole mediator (albeit with the "approval" and backing of the Contact Group), the question arose as to where the final peace conference should be held. The Europeans, of course, felt that such a conference should be held in Europe, and Carl Bildt investigated holding it in Sweden. Holbrooke, however, felt strongly that a venue in the United States would best maximize the opportunity for achieving agreement. In a pivotal message to President Clinton, Holbrooke argued:

> [W]e had already invested so much national prestige in the [Bosnia] effort that our priority had to be to maximize success, rather than reduce the cost of failure. A meeting site in the United States would give us physical and psychological control of the process; any other site would reduce our leverage dramatically. . . . The American peace initiative, which had already brought a lifting of the siege of Sarajevo and other benefits, had been a powerful signal that . . . "America is back." The choice of venue would be *the* key indicator of how serious and committed we were.[90]

On October 4, President Clinton approved holding the conference in the United States, one day before the formal cease-fire agreement was signed by all the parties. The cease-fire was to take effect on October 10, which gave the Croatians and Bosnians five days to consolidate gains on the ground and acquire new territory. The conference was scheduled for November 1, 1995, thus ensuring that the momentum of the process would be maintained. By November 21, the parties reached agreement on a map and constitutional framework under which the three factions would share power within a unified Bosnian state.

Choice of Parties and Mediators

In the Bosnian crisis, more than almost any other post–Cold War conflict, the international community did not reach a clear consensus as to who the "parties" to the conflict actually were. The complex origins of the dispute and shifting alliances led many to question whether Slobodan Milosevic possessed de facto control over the Bosnian Serbs, or if the proper negotiating partners should be Republika Srpska President Karadzic and Serb military leader Mladic. By mid-1995 a consensus was forming, at least on the U.S. side, that despite his protestations to the contrary, and despite the formal embargo and the apparent splits between Belgrade and Pale, Milosevic held the key to stopping Bosnian Serb aggression and ending the war. The United States thus took a firm position that it would no longer negotiate with Mladic and Karadzic, the two men who had agreed to the Carter-brokered cease-fire during the previous winter and who had continued to negotiate temporary pauses with the UNPROFOR commanders in Sarajevo.

By this time, Karadzic and Mladic had been indicted by the War Crimes Tribunal in The Hague, and were being referred to in press accounts as "indicted war criminals." The dissonance between the purported will of the international community and the rule of international law on the one hand, and the political reality that two indicted war criminal were still calling the shots on behalf of the Bosnian Serbs on the other, had a powerful effect on the Bosnian narrative. The failures of the ICFY process, of the Europeans, and of the United Nations were underscored—indeed, mocked—by the lawless Bosnian Serb leaders who still had the power to cut deals with UNPROFOR commanders and former U.S. presidents.

The United States therefore had at least three reasons to cut Pale out of the direct mediation. First, strategically, the United States held leverage over Milosevic, who was becoming increasingly anxious to end the international embargo against the rump-Yugoslavia and begin rebuilding its domestic economy. Second, morally, and for the sake of preserving international legal norms, it could not be "neutral" as to the question of war crimes and suspected war criminals (this was also a practical consideration, since if Mladic and Karadzic traveled internationally, they would be subject to arrest under the tribunal indictment). Third, Karadzic and Mladic had not acted as rational actors in any of the previous mediation efforts; once they became international outlaws, any remaining incentive for them to act rationally or responsibly would have been removed. By choosing to negotiate officially only with Milosevic, the United States eliminated the potential spoilers to the process and felt that they had achieved maximum leverage over the Serbs in case of backsliding.[91] To lend some "legitimacy" to the selection of negotiators, the official Serb delegation was in name a joint

FRY–Republika Srpska delegating including Pale-based representatives. But Milosevic spoke for the combined delegation.

Croatian President Franjo Tudjman unquestionably represented the interests of Croatia in the Bosnia crisis. First and foremost, he wanted final resolution of Eastern Slavonia and final demarcation of the Croatian international border. His agreement would clearly be needed on any maps delineating Bosnia's international borders. In addition to Tudjman, the Croatian leaders from the Federation were also invited to the talks to negotiate on their own behalf on a host of second-track issues, and, perhaps most importantly, on the allocation of territory within Bosnia between the Muslim–Croat Federation and the Serb entity.[92]

The Bosnian government was represented by President Alija Izetbegovic, Prime Minister Haris Silajdzic, and Foreign Minister Mohammed Sacirbey. The Washington Accord creating the Muslim–Croat Federation required that the Federation act as one voice in all future peace negotiations. Yet the division of responsibility was unclear and required some discussion at Dayton to determine which levels of the Federation could legitimately speak and on what issues. Izetbegovic's Bosnian government team also benefited from some international expertise, in the person of Richard Perle, a former assistant secretary of defense in the Reagan administration, and several other non-Bosnian lawyers and experts.[93]

The decision to allow Holbrooke to act as lead mediator and U.S. negotiator, and not a more senior official such as Secretary of State Christopher, was unusual. Earlier mediation models, like Camp David, would have suggested parity between the seniority of the mediator and the representatives of the parties (head-of-state negotiators in Camp David were brought together by a head-of-state mediator). Yet Holbrooke's personal reputation for toughness, tenacity, and "bulldozing bluntness," combined with the fact that he had already spent hundreds of hours dealing with the key figures and understood their strengths, weaknesses, and personal foibles, suggested that he would be effective. Quite intentionally, the United States wanted Holbrooke to be himself: to push, prod, cajole, and, some would say, coerce the parties into agreement. His was not the role of a neutral or disinterested mediator who was there simply to facilitate the talks. The United States wanted an agreement, one that was acceptable to all the parties, but one that also could be enforced through a peacekeeping implementation force on terms acceptable to the United States and NATO. To do so, the United States would need to assert the "psychological control" that Holbrooke had earlier suggested to Clinton. Further, Holbrooke and Christopher felt that Christopher's lack of a formal role would ratchet down expectations. A failure by Holbrooke would not loom as large as a failure by the secretary of state or the president. In addition, by assigning Holbrooke the lead, the United States precluded the Europeans and other nonparty participants and observers to the talks from insisting on higher-level representation.[94]

Representatives of the other Contact Group countries were also present, along with representatives of the organizations that would help implement the agreement, the EU and OSCE. Almost conspicuously absent were representatives of the United Nations. After the conference got underway, Assistant Secretaries of State John Kornblum and Robert Gallucci handled direct discussions with the Europeans and the Contact Group on a host of second-track issues, including elections, a constitutional framework, and the creation of an international police force to implement the agreement.[95] The American team included Robert Owens and other lawyers with expertise in international law.

Form of Intervention: Proximity Talks with Muscle

In choosing the site for the peace talks, and the form of the mediation, the U.S. team attended to every detail, including the sleeping, eating, and recreational facilities that would be available to the principal participants during the meetings. Wright-Patterson Air Force Base in Dayton, Ohio, was chosen first for its location. It was isolated, thus ensuring secrecy and security during the talks; it was not near any major media centers, thus reducing the temptation that one or another party would attempt public grandstanding during the talks. Most importantly, Dayton was close enough to Washington to allow Secretary of State Christopher or other American officials to fly in on short notice when personal intervention with one or another of the parties was needed, which Christopher did on several key occasions, including the final forty-eight-hour marathon that led to the final map agreement.

Wright-Patterson also offered the perfect physical configuration. The American hosts transformed visiting officers' quarters into temporary guest houses for each of the delegations. The key delegations—Bosnia, Croatia, and Serbia/Republika Srpska—were clustered together with the American delegation, all within short walking distance of one another. The buildings were so close that from the ground floor rooms, delegations could look out and see who was in their suite at any given time.[96] The European delegation was housed just off this main cluster.[97] This arrangement proved key throughout the negotiations, when, for example, during talks with one of the parties, the Americans could suggest a direct conferral with another party—right across the quadrangle. Consciously following the Camp David model, the American team created the perfect setting for proximity talks, which would allow members of the mediating team to shuttle back and forth between the principals, without requiring the principals to meet face-to-face.[98]

By staging the peace talks at a military installation, the Americans were also perhaps sending a not-so-subtle message about the role military might would play in the resolution of (or failure to resolve) the conflict. Also, Dayton sat in the middle of a "middle American" state, one settled heavily by eastern and central Europeans. That the U.S. delegation could point to the people of Ohio as an example of multiethnic harmony contributed to Dayton's appeal.[99] Most importantly, however, by holding the talks on its own territory, the United States demonstrated unequivocally that there would be no peace without its sanction. The location clearly contributed to the unique dynamic of a peace process that was defined, sponsored, and mediated by a nonparty to the conflict. The isolated site, combined with Holbrooke's oftentimes combative and overbearing personality, created an atmosphere that convinced the parties that Dayton was the last best chance for peace.

Getting to an Agreement

With the venue chosen, the delegates agreed upon, and a general agenda of the conference established, the parties met at Wright-Patterson Air Force Base from November 1 to 21. Holbrooke describes the process from his perspective in detail in his memoir:

> It is a high-wire act without a safety net. Much work must precede the plunge into such an all-or-nothing environment. The site must be just right. The goals must be clearly defined. A single host nation must be in firm control, but it is high risk for the host, whose prestige is on the line. The consequences of failure are great. But when the conditions are right, a Dayton can produce dramatic results.[100]

As Holbrooke has noted, the results—an agreement on a map and a framework for implementation—were not foreordained. The day-to-day cajoling, agreeing, backsliding, and frequent bullying that went on gave a unique dynamic to the process. But because the details of the physical environment had been attended to, the American hosts were able to serve not just as facilitators to the talks between the parties, but as active negotiators.

As one example of that control, Holbrooke and Secretary Christopher capitalized on Christopher's absence from the talks to create a "false" sense of urgency and internal deadlines on issues. On November 14, after two weeks of little progress on the main issue of the Bosnia map, Christopher was scheduled to visit the conference site to "check in" with the parties. In a message to Christopher, Holbrooke urged him to use his visit to lay down a "closure or closedown" ultimatum to the parties. "[Your trip] now becomes a last warning to get serious ... with the clear message that when you return we must have either closure or closedown ... You can jump-start this conference by a combination of pressure, rhetoric, and direct involvement on some issues where you can break a logjam."[101] During his visit, Christopher had strong words for the Bosnian delegation: "[President Clinton] will no longer assist your government if you turn out to be the obstacle to an agreement in Dayton."[102] Christopher noted to all the delegates that he expected progress before his next visit, in two days.

The next day, another example of the American negotiators' ability to push the negotiations forward came when Holbrooke seized on an opportunity in the Officers' Club, where many delegates came to eat their meals. With Holbrooke seated with Milosevic at one end of the dining hall, and his assistant seated with Haris Silajdzic at the other end of the hall, Holbrooke began what he calls "the napkin shuttle." Holbrooke walked across the room and told Silajdzic that "Milosevic is willing to talk about Gorazde." He then returned to Milosevic and said "Silajdzic is ready to discuss Gorazde." With this simple dissembling,

Holbrooke got the two sides to begin sketching out ideas on the back of a napkin that was carried back and forth between the tables. After an hour, Silajdzic agreed to join Milosevic at his table. While they did not reach agreement on any issues that evening, Holbrooke notes it was an important breakthrough—the first time the two sides sat down together to discuss territory.[103]

The U.S. team had a "captive audience" and also used that to its advantage. The Department of Defense representatives set up advanced computer-imaging technology to help the parties visualize terrain and allocations of land corridors, while at the same time sending a message about the reliability of U.S. intelligence sources and reminding all present of the military power it possessed.[104] After "playing" with the mapping computer program for two hours one evening, Milosevic agreed to considerable concessions on the land corridor leading to Gorazde.[105]

These scenes were repeated throughout the final days of the conference. As Holbrooke notes, "Negotiations have a certain pathology, a kind of life cycle almost like a living organism."[106] At one point, when Holbrooke feared the team might lose the momentum necessary to bring the talks to fruition, he attempted to impose a "false deadline" and got caught in a gambit that he himself terms, in retrospect, "pathetic." On November 19, Holbrooke and Christopher set out to push for agreement before the end of the day. To create the impression that it was "closure or close-down" time, the members of the U.S. delegations packed their bags and had them picked up to be taken to the airstrip. Holbrooke's staff then set out to collect the bills of the various other parties. No one bought the ruse; the parties refused to pay their bills, and the Americans' luggage was returned to their rooms.

If nothing else, however, even that failed incident, coming just two days before the actual agreement, demonstrates the creativity (some would say underhandedness) of an aggressive and goal-oriented negotiator. When the agreement did emerge, it was a result of marathon efforts by Holbrooke and Secretary Christopher, who lent the authority and full weight of the United States to the closing rounds in which the final territorial issues were resolved.

The Role of International Law and Nongovernmental Organizations

Out of necessity, Holbrooke's shuttle team had focused on immediate first-track issues: obtaining a cease-fire agreement and persuading the heads of state to negotiate a framework agreement on the map and constitution.[107] Even as the team was dealing with larger political issues, it realized that the main impediments to negotiation were territorial. The territorial questions were compounded by the growing sense—particularly on the part of the Bosnian Federation—that continued fighting would result in more regained territory and a better result. The negotiating effort did not completely ignore the second-track elements of political and civic reconciliation and discussion of legal forms, but simply chose to allow other parallel efforts to address these in the background. Nevertheless, the second-track issues would emerge to dominate media coverage and thus influence the actions of the shuttle team. The issue of war crimes, minority rights, refugee resettlement, and reconciliation in a country that had known nothing but war and hatred for over three years posed difficult substantive and legal issues that had to be addressed to achieve peace.

In tackling these issues and the general need for rebuilding institutions of a civil society, nongovernmental organizations played an important role. Beginning early in the war, the Soros Foundation and other NGOs provided essential humanitarian assistance in the form of life-sustaining aid as well as support for civil institutions (a free press, legal infrastructure, open political dialogue, religious organizations). Assistance to these institutions and participation by larger international organizations dedicated to establishing rule of law, providing resettlement assistance, and rebuilding key elements of the Bosnian infrastructure became even more important during the Dayton implementation phase.

War Crimes, Genocide, and the War Crimes Tribunal

As noted earlier, the events of the summer of 1992 shocked the world's conscience and made clear that for the first time since World War II, war crimes and crimes against humanity were being committed on European soil. To many international lawyers and human rights observers, the Serb "ethnic cleansing" of Muslim areas that they conquered during the war, as well as Croat activities during the 1993–94 Muslim–Croat war represented clear cases of genocide.[108] The United States and many European governments, however, did not publicly refer to the term "genocide."[109] This was not accidental. In addition to wanting to avoid the damaging political image of standing idly by while peoples were being exterminated in the heart of Europe, the Western powers were aware that acknowledgment of genocide would trigger duties and obligations under the Genocide Convention.[110]

Nevertheless, as human rights organizations and television crews broadcast to the world the details of the atrocities—including mass killings, torture, and mass rape—the international community took measures to address the war crimes. Separate from the process that was being pursued by the increasingly ineffective ICFY, the UN Security Council was seized by the issue, and in accordance with the JAP discussed earlier, finally voted to create the International Criminal Tribunal for the Former Yugoslavia through the adoption of Resolution 827 in 1993. Invoking Chapter VII authority, which lends it the power to take any necessary steps in the face of a "threat to international peace and security," the Security Council created the first international tribunal for prosecution of a range of war crimes and crimes against humanity.[111] Although the tribunal was plagued with lack of funds and technical cooperation from key Western powers, through the tenacity of its chief prosecutor, Richard Goldstone (who took leave from his position on the newly created Constitutional Court of South Africa), and personnel support from the U.S. government, the Tribunal began to investigate and document the crimes committed in the former Yugoslavia.[112]

In September 1994, the Tribunal issued its first indictment and in February

1995, indicted the two top Serb leaders, Radovan Karadzic and Ratko Mladic, for war crimes and crimes against humanity. The indictment had the long-term effect of isolating them from the diplomatic process. Although the indictments proceeded on a track independent of the various mediation efforts, as Goldstone himself acknowledges, the indictments of Karadzic and Mladic had the ultimate effect of ensuring that the Bosnians would finally come to table. As long as those two were recognized by international actors as speaking on behalf of the Bosnian Serbs (as they had been by a string of UNPROFOR commanders who negotiated cease-fires with them), the Bosnian government was unlikely to sit down to negotiate. Izetbegovic and his supporters simply could not stomach making a deal with them. The indictments had the unforeseen consequence of removing these potential "spoilers" from the process.

For the rest of 1995, the work of the Tribunal had an effect on the procedure, and, perhaps most importantly, on the legal substance of all subsequent peace negotiations. Goldstone's work clearly created external pressure to deal with war crimes and other human rights issues in concert with a military solution. In September 1995, while Holbrooke's team shuttled between the warring parties, the Tribunal amended the indictments of Karadzic and Mladic to include command responsibility for the massacre at Srebrenica, a move which some on the negotiating team criticized as reflecting poor timing. Goldstone admits that the prospect of Dayton "certainly spurred us on to investigate Srebrenica with an eye to a second indictment. Had there been no Dayton . . . the second indictment would have come out a month or two later."[113] Nevertheless, he properly concludes that whether the indictment had come out before, during, or after Dayton, the prosecutor would have been criticized by one side or another for poor timing. What mattered was the investigation and indictment. The sheer magnitude of the horror of Srebrenica demanded that it become a top priority for the Tribunal, regardless of what direction the peace process was taking.

The work of the Tribunal would not be short term. Cooperation by the parties to the conflict with the Tribunal's investigations and prosecutions was essential to any lasting peace agreement. By 1995, it had become clear from the examples of the Truth Commissions in El Salvador and South Africa that a successful transition from civil war to peace and the building of civil society required some form of accounting for the atrocities committed on all sides during the time of conflict. The Tribunal, which was originally viewed with skepticism as a fig leaf for the Western powers' unwillingness to commit to a military solution to the war, emerged as a key element of the Dayton Accords. That it became a key component of peace implementation surprised even Goldstone, who up until the initialing of the final agreement feared "that the Tribunal was going to be sold down the river at Dayton," a view he notes that was shared generally in the American and European media.[114] "I got informal assurances from some of the parties at Dayton [including representatives from the United States] that that wouldn't be so," Goldstone adds, "but there were sufficient doubts." Indeed, the announcement by State Department Spokesman Nicholas Burns that cooperation with the Tribunal would "not be a showstopper" sent Goldstone mixed messages. He took his case to the press and in a late-night interview with the *New York Times*, on the eve of Dayton, made clear his position that there could be no peace without cooperation.[115] From Goldstone's perspective, taking the issue to the media made it almost impossible for the parties and mediators to sweep the Tribunal under the rug.

"Ripeness": Could the War Have Been Stopped Earlier?

The question of whether a conflict is "ripe" for resolution, as traditionally applied by dispute resolution scholars, is enormously complicated in Bosnia. While the William Zartman definition of ripeness occurring at a time of "mutually hurting stalemate" has come to be widely accepted in the scholarship on international mediation, Bosnia appears to defy that ontology. One can point out specific battlefield moments that could be characterized as "mutually hurting" (for example the intense Muslim–Croat fighting in 1993–94), but trying to tie the timing of Dayton to a mutual stalemate on the ground is difficult. This is the case, in part, because the major parties still believed up until the Dayton Accords that they had incentive to continue fighting. While war-weary, the Bosnian government continued to feel aggrieved—by the atrocities committed in the name of Serb nationalism; the destruction and ongoing siege of their once beautiful, multiethnic capital; and the devastation caused by those opposed to a unified Bosnian state. The Bosnian Serbs, emboldened by their battlefield victories and acting with impunity in the face of an apparently impotent international peace process, never reached a point where a cease-fire, much less peace, became a goal.

Most importantly, however, Bosnia represents a case that inverts Zartman's ripeness scenario: In Bosnia, it was the outside intervenors—the mediators themselves—who determined when the situation was ripe for resolution.[116] Early mediators primarily responded to pressure caused by media images of atrocities in Bosnia: they considered the conflict "ripe" for resolution not because the parties themselves had grown weary, but because the situation had gone too far for the rest of the world to stomach.

The ultimately successful intervenor was the United States. It was able to influence the situation on the ground sufficiently to create a window of opportunity for conflict resolution. With the power of NATO to back it up, the United States was able to effect change on the battlefield—through the NATO air campaign, the training of the Croatian Army, and explicit and implicit encouragement of the Bosnian-Croat offensive in the late summer of 1995. But the United States also used its leverage to discourage the Federation from taking back any land that exceeded the 51 percent–49 percent division of territory already contemplated in the Contact Group Plan, thus significantly predetermining the substantive outcome.[117] So, while the parties may not have fought *themselves* to a "mutually hurting stalemate," they did realize that outside powers prohibited either side from reaching a better situation on the battlefield.

The hand of the United States was further strengthened when the sanctions the international community had placed on the Yugoslav rump state in 1991 began to take a serious toll on the Belgrade economy. This gave Slobodan Milosevic the incentive once again to take control over the superficially autonomous Pale leadership, which in turn lent him the unique ability to negotiate (and enforce) an end to the war on behalf of the Bosnian Serbs. In the end, the international community, which for so many years had failed to act decisively or effectively to end a conflict which so clearly threatened regional economic stability and international legal norms, was able to force the "ripeness" of the situation.

This raises an important question about timing: If the international community, led by the United States, was able to create a window of opportunity for conflict resolution in August and September of 1995, could it have done so at an earlier moment? The answer must surely be that the international community could have created the same incentives for each of the parties three years earlier than Dayton. As the last United States Ambassador to Yugoslavia Warren Zimmermann has pointed out:

> When war broke out in Bosnia . . . the United States was not so impotent. The Bosnian war confronted two successive American administrations with the first test of their leadership in Europe since the end of the cold war—a test that, until much too late, they failed to pass. The aggression in Bosnia by Milosevic, Karadzic and the Yugoslav army went far beyond the bounds of any Serbian grievances, real or imagined, against the Muslim president, Alija Izetbegovic. Had NATO met that aggression with air strikes in the summer of 1992, I believe that a negotiated result would soon have followed.[118]

The United States "Lift and Strike" proposal of April 1993 might have achieved the same kind of forced ripeness to a solution—and also would have saved lives. But because the Europeans rejected the formula, and the United States, led by a new administration, was unprepared to press the point by committing large numbers of its own troops to any peacekeeping effort, the opportunity passed.

Others have described this "missed opportunities" analysis as facile. They argue that to demonstrate a "missed" opportunity, one must show that the action to be taken was indeed possible in the first place. The missed opportunity most frequently cited is the failure to deploy NATO air strikes in 1993. Given the domestic political environment in which President Clinton was operating in mid-1993, and the myriad other foreign policy crises demanding his attention and complicating the relationships within the NATO alliance (e.g., Somalia, the Middle East Peace Process), it is too easy to say in hindsight that something could have been done. Nevertheless, the Dayton process teaches that once the United States has decided that an issue lies at the heart of its national interest, and it throws adequate resources and senior-level attention at the problem, its power and credibility can be effective in bringing about a solution. For the United States and its Europeans allies, therefore, the central lesson of Dayton is the continuing indispensability of the United States to security in Europe.

On a more general level, Dayton offers some lessons about the use of persuasion and leverage. Here, the parties with the most leverage were those who had the power to affect the military outcome of the war and to affect the economic progress of the area over the long term. In the end, this meant that the United States possessed the most leverage. Europe could not act effectively without the United States, which had withheld its support from the earlier peace efforts. Once the United States had made the political decision to apply its leverage, it was able to do so in a way that gave it an enormous power of persuasion over the parties. Perhaps more so than any other postwar conflict, Bosnia was susceptible to an externally imposed solution.

NATO as Peacemaker and Peace Enforcer

NATO's involvement in Bosnia, through the air strikes that helped shift military and political expectations on the ground and through the Implementation Force that was a necessary precondition to a permanent framework for peace, demonstrated that at least in the circumstances of this case, a regional security organization can play an effective role, even where one or more of the parties does not perceive it to be neutral. Indeed, the actions NATO took prior to the cease-fire were not neutral in the sense that UNPROFOR had defined neutrality. Quite the contrary, NATO acted in deliberate retaliation to Serb aggression and to level the playing field—which proved an essential element to the success of the Bosnian offensive in August-September 1995.

As the only security institution that binds the United States to Europe, NATO made it inevitable that the United States would be involved in Bosnia. The ignominy and irony of the vision of American NATO troops intervening to support the withdrawal of European peacekeeping troops was a key factor in U.S. decision making. Further, NATO was an institution in search of a mission. As U.S. Senator Richard Lugar said at the time, NATO had to "Go out of area or go out of business." In other words, with the collapse of the Soviet Union and the Warsaw Pact, NATO was beginning to seem obsolete.

Although UNPROFOR was partially successful in maintaining the flow of humanitarian supplies during the harshest days of the war, given its dismal failure in maintaining order and its lack of credibility with any of the warring factions, the UN could not have carried out an effective peacebuilding/peacekeeping mission in postwar Bosnia. And in light of the danger of renewed fighting and deep divisions between the parties that would linger long after the hot war had ended, a well-equipped force was required to create a secure environment in which civilian rebuilding could begin. A multinational observer force outside of UN control would therefore also be inadequate.

The composition of the Implementation Force (IFOR) offered the alliance the perfect opportunity to test the capabilities of the U.S.-sponsored Partnership for Peace program (in which states in central and eastern Europe can acquire affiliate status in the alliance as a way station to full membership), as well as to extend the hand of cooperation to Russia when Russia was feeling threatened by NATO expansion plans. An out-of-area peacekeeping/peacebuilding mission combining troops from the United States and Western, Central, and Eastern Europe would send a strong signal about the viability of the Clinton administration's

NATO policy. France's decision in September 1995 to reintegrate with the NATO command structure, twenty years after De Gaulle evicted NATO from France, added further momentum to the idea that NATO could carry off the mission.

Was Dayton a "Just" Peace?

While the Dayton Accords put an end to the immediate fighting (and an earlier intervention might have saved tens of thousands of lives, prevented subsequent war crimes, and saved millions of dollars in destruction and damage), it is not clear that imposing mediation reaches a just result for the parties. Upon agreeing to the final map at Dayton, Bosnian President Izetbegovic said, "It is not a just peace. But my people need peace."[119] With those words he summed up the views of many Bosnians, and some non-Bosnian advisers to the Bosnian delegation who believed that Dayton was unjustly forced upon the Bosnians.[120] Indeed, some observers now argue that Holbrooke pushed the Bosnians too hard, pressing for a cease-fire at a time when the Federation forces could have made further gains on the battlefield and providing them with further leverage against Milosevic. Again, however, hindsight offers few clues about what actually could have happened had a different tack been taken. Questions of justice, as in other postconflict situations, may not be resolved for another generation.

Justice can mean different things for different parties to the conflict, outside intervenors and the victims of perpetrators of atrocities. Prosecutions of international crimes committed during the war is one type of corrective justice that can be achieved. Prosecutions also play an important role in establishing a record of atrocities committed and helping victims achieve a sense of closure. They make sense as a means to enforce the international rule of law and the need for accountability where domestic legal institutions are incapable of supporting a legal process. But the prosecutorial approach is at best an imperfect tool, capable of redressing only a small number of crimes and punishing a small number of perpetrators. The fact that Karadzic and Mladic are still at large, at the time of this writing, more than four years after their indictments serves as a reminder of the weaknesses of the prosecutorial model. Institutional protection for minorities and the establishment of civil institutions are important elements of the internal process of reconciliation and rebuilding. Full exploration of the past is also an element of moving on toward a just future. Arguably, however, leaving the Republika Srpska as an intact political entity may have worked to undermine a sense of justice and actually created an impediment to bringing about full compliance with the arrest warrants of the tribunal.

Conclusion

At this writing, three and a half years after the signing of the Dayton Accords, the multinational Stabilization Force is still on the ground in Bosnia. Hundreds of international NGOs and government-sponsored organizations have set up shop in Sarajevo and around Bosnia to assist in the physical, psychological, and civic rebuilding of a country devastated by over three years of war. The success of Dayton is thus difficult to measure, as the agreement itself dictated the terms for the elections, governmental structure, and constitutionally enforceable legal norms. There are signs of success in the normalization of daily life and the rebuilding of the economy. There are also political failures, such as the firing of the Serbian president by EU High Representative Westendorp in early 1999. The struggle between the Serb majority and the Albanian ethnic minority in Kosovo and the intervention of NATO in March 1999 to attempt to halt the atrocities certainly point, at a minimum, to the incompleteness of Dayton as a political solution to the overarching problems of political control in the Balkans. The horrors of Kosovo may also provide lessons for future mediations about the cost of failing to address larger looming regional political crises.

Those who crafted the Dayton Accords and the initial implementation of the Dayton cease-fire view the mediation as a success in bringing about an end to the hostilities, which was their primary objective and one that none of the four prior mediation efforts achieved. Former United States Defense Secretary William Perry notes, for example, that Dayton was successful in achieving several immediate objectives that the U.S. government set out. First, the parties were separated and order was restored. Second, the fighting and atrocities were stopped, with a minimum loss of life on all sides. Third, a broad-based multinational force was put in place to create a secure environment in which civilian operations could be carried out. But these were all short-term measures. Whether Dayton ultimately succeeds in bringing a lasting peace to Bosnia— one that will survive the withdrawal of the international security force—requires a closer look at implementation methods and postconflict efforts toward reconciliation.[121]

3

Croatian Independence from Yugoslavia, 1991–1992

Alan Hanson

Overview

THE WAR IN Croatia in 1991–92 presented the European Community (EC) and UN mediators with an exceedingly complex dispute that would ultimately spread even more violently into Bosnia-Herzegovina. The war occurred in the sundown of Yugoslavia, as its constituent republics battled the federal center (which had essentially been co-opted by the Serbs, under Slobodan Milosevic and his vision of a Greater Serbia). The fighting in Croatia pitted Croatian nationalist forces against Serbian minority paramilitaries backed by the powerful federal army, the Yugoslav People's Army (JNA). The fighting was vicious, giving birth to the term "ethnic cleansing." Lord Carrington, appointed by the European Community to mediate the dispute, put in place a carefully planned, multistep process that would build confidence between the parties and would buy time to find a peaceful solution to the nationalist pressures in Yugoslavia. His efforts, though, were stymied by the EC's lack of military force to back up negotiated agreements.

The United Nations also intervened in the conflict, working closely with the EC process. Cyrus Vance, operating as the UN mediator, was able to implement a successful cease-fire agreement and an agreement calling for the Croats to take down blockades around JNA installations. A UN peacekeeping force entered Croatia, allowing JNA troops to withdraw from Croatia and protecting zones in which borders between Croatia and Serbian-held territories were disputed.

While this peacekeeping force effectively carried out the cease-fire agreement, it also gave Serbia the opportunity to redeploy troops in Bosnia–Herzegovina, the next battleground for Serb supremacy.

Further mediation efforts over the political future of Croatia were stymied by Germany's early decision to recognize Croatia's independence, in spite of the Badinter Commission's recommendations that Croatia was not yet ready for independence. This decision severely split the EC at a time when they needed to present a unified face in the Maastricht process. It also led to the downward spiral of violence in Bosnia, which faced even higher stakes in the independence process.

This chapter chronicles the background of the conflict, analyzes the mediation efforts by the EC and the United Nations, and describes the strategic behavior of the Croats and Serbs. It also explains why the spheres of international law and military aggression clashed so tragically in the Croatian conflict.

Timeline

1990   **July 2:** Declaration on Sovereignty of the State of Slovenia adopted by Slovenian Assembly. **Sept. 28:** Constitution of Republic of Serbia promulgated. **Oct. 1:** Serbian Autonomous Region of Krajina (renamed Serbian Krajina Republic) proclaimed by the Serbian people in Croatia. **Dec. 22:** Constitution of the Republic of Croatia promulgated.

1991   **Apr. 11:** Meeting of presidents of Yugoslav republics concerning constitutional reorganization of Yugoslavia. **June 25:** Republics of Slovenia and Croatia declare independence from Yugoslavia; Yugoslav Federal Parliament refuses to recognize secessions; Federal Executive Council issues decree empowering defense minister and interior minister to deploy frontier units of JNA to safeguard state frontiers. **June 27:** JNA units deployed in Slovenia. **July–August:** Outbreak of fighting in Croatia between Serb paramilitaries and Croatian National Guard. **July 4:** Slovene Territorial Defense (TO) units surround JNA bases in Slovenia; armed skirmishes between JNA and Slovene TO; Serbian Democratic Party (SDS) formally recognizes the independence of Slovenia. **July 7:** Brioni Accord; European Community Monitor Mission (ECMM) established; withdrawal of JNA in Slovenia to barracks. **July 18:** Total withdrawal of JNA from Slovenia ordered by Yugoslav presidency. **Aug. 26:** Town of Kijevo, Croatia, destroyed by Serb paramilitaries and Knin Corps of the JNA led by Colonel Ratko Mladic of Serbia. **Sept. 1:** Cease-fire agreement signed by presidents of the six Yugoslav republics in Belgrade. **Sept. 7:** EC Peace Conference on Yugoslavia opens. **Sept. 14–30:** Croatian National Guard blockades JNA barracks and installations across Croatia; siege of Vukovar by Serb paramilitaries begins. **Sept. 25:** United Nations appoints Cyrus Vance as the personal envoy of the UN secretary-general on a mission of peace to Yugoslavia (UNSCR 713). **October–November:** JNA leads assault on Vukovar, attacks Dubrovnik, Osijek, and other Croatian towns; Vance begins negotiations for a UN Peacekeeping Operation. **Oct. 4:** EC Peace Conference divided into two working groups—"two tracks"—regarding (i) constitutional reorganization of Yugoslavia and (ii) attaining a cease-fire in Croatia. **Oct. 14:** Bosnian representatives ratify proclamation of sovereignty in Bosnian parliament. **Oct. 18:** Arrangements for a general settlement proposed by Lord Carrington at the EC Peace Conference; Carrington brokers cease-fire agreement among Serbia, Croatia, and the Socialist Federal Republic of Yugoslavia (SFRJ). **Nov. 1:** Treaty provisions for new relations between Yugoslav republics proposed by Carrington at the EC Peace Conference. **Nov. 8:** EC adopts Declaration of Suspension of the Trade and Cooperation Agreement with Yugoslavia. **Nov. 23:** UN brokers cease-fire agreement, the Geneva Accord, among SFRJ, Croatia, and Serbia. **Nov. 27:** UN Security Council Resolution 721, considering deployment of UN Peacekeeping Operation on recommendation of secretary-general, special envoy of secretary-general and permanent representative of Yugoslavia to the United Nations. **Nov. 29:** Opinion No. 1 of the Arbitration Commission of the Peace Conference on Yugoslavia, concerning Yugoslavian dissolution and succession. **November–December:** Concept for a UN Peacekeeping Operation in Yugoslavia formalized by Cyrus Vance and Marrack Goulding. **Dec. 8:** Agreement signed, providing for deblocking of JNA barracks and facilities in Croatia. **Dec. 10:** Letter from UN secretary-general to the Dutch foreign minister warns of the danger of premature recognition of Croatian independence. **Dec. 15:** UN Security Council approves the creation of UN Peacekeeping Operation in Yugoslavia with mediator to enable Yugoslav republics to settle disputes through the EC Peace Conference (UNSCR 724). **Dec. 15–16:** European Political Cooperation (EPC) Ministerial held in Brussels to discuss question of recognition of Yugoslav republics. **Dec. 16:** EC Declaration Concerning the Conditions for the Recognition of New States invites Yugoslav republics to apply for recognition by December 23, 1991. **Dec. 23:** Germany unilaterally recognizes Croatian and Slovene sovereignty.

1992   **Jan. 2:** Geneva Implementing Accord signed. **Jan. 9:** Serbian Republic of Bosnia-Herzegovina (renamed Republika Srpska) proclaimed by ethnic Serbs in Bosnia-Herzegovina. **Jan. 11:** Opinion Nos. 5 and 7 On The Recognition of Croatia and Slovenia issued by the EC and its member states; Croatia fails to satisfy recognition criteria. **Jan. 14:** United Nations dispatches military liaison officers to Yugoslavia. **Jan. 15:** EC recognizes Croatian and Slovene sovereignty. **Feb. 3:** SFRJ endorses UN Peacekeeping Operation. **Feb. 6:** Croatia endorses UN Peacekeeping Operation. **Feb. 11:** Assembly of Serbian Krajina Republic endorses UN Peacekeeping Operation. **Feb. 21:** UN Security Council creates UN Protection Force (UNPROFOR) (UNSCR 743). **Feb. 23:** Statement on Principles for New Constitutional Arrangement for Bosnia and Herzegovina (the Lisbon Agreement) proposed. **Mar. 8:** Deployment of UNPROFOR begins in Croatia. **Apr. 6:** EC recognizes sovereignty and independence of Bosnia-

Herzegovina. **Apr. 7:** United States recognizes sovereignty and independence of Bosnia-Herzegovina, Croatia, and Slovenia. **Apr. 8:** Civil war
breaks out in Bosnia-Herzegovina; Serb paramilitaries and JNA units
jointly attack predominantly Muslim town of Zvornik. **August:** EC Peace
Conference on Yugoslavia ends.

Background

The Peace Conference on Yugoslavia, sponsored by the European Community
(EC) and cochaired by Lord Carrington of the United Kingdom and EC Minister Hans van den Broek, was the best failed opportunity for a comprehensive
general settlement of the crisis in Yugoslavia. Opening on September 7, 1991,
amid civil war in the Republic of Croatia precipitated by its declaration of independence from Yugoslavia, the Conference aimed to reorganize the constitutional structure of the Yugoslav federation into a loosely allied group of independent republics. The Conference closed, officially, in August of 1992 after the
Yugoslav civil war had proliferated from Croatia into the Republic of Bosnia-
Herzegovina. For all intents and purposes, however, the end of the EC Peace
Conference came about abruptly on December 23, 1991, nine months earlier, the
day that a reunified Germany broke ranks with EC foreign policy on Yugoslav
unity and unilaterally recognized Croatia's sovereignty prior to the EC's recognition schedule. This so-called "premature" recognition by Germany arguably
had several effects: it (i) formally established Yugoslav federal dissolution, (ii)
eliminated Croatia's interest in participating in ongoing negotiations about Yugoslavia's constitutional future, (iii) shifted the focus of the crisis from Croatia
to Bosnia-Herzegovina, and (iv) precluded any further efforts for a general settlement to the Yugoslav crisis by the EC or any other multilateral institution.[1]
Furthermore, German recognition may have established a precedent for the
early recognition of belligerent nations claiming self-determination under international law. Of course, there were additional factors involved in ending the
Peace Conference. Primary among them, the EC was unable to halt the fighting
in Croatia through the diplomatic means provided by the Conference.

Starting in October of 1991, shortly after the EC Peace Conference opened,
the United Nations began its own diplomatic intervention in Yugoslavia, aimed
specifically at achieving a sustainable cease-fire in Croatia. Former U.S. Secretary of State Cyrus Vance, serving as special envoy of UN Secretary-General
Javier Perez de Cuellar, led several peacekeeping missions to Yugoslavia. These
missions eventually resulted in the establishment of protected zones in the areas
of most heavily concentrated fighting within Croatia and to the deployment of
a multinational protection force to enforce the terms of the peace therein, all
overseen by the United Nations. Specific in aim, narrower in scope, and different in motive than the EC Peace Conference, the UN peacekeeping missions
achieved something that the Conference could not: a cessation of hostilities in
Croatia. The EC's inability to stop the fighting seriously undermined its ability
to reach a political solution to the Yugoslav crisis.

Inasmuch as they both sought a cease-fire in Yugoslavia, the EC Peace Conference and the UN Peacekeeping Operation shared a common aim. Germany, too, shared this aim. In fact, the quest for an end to the fighting provided the rationale for Germany's early recognition of Croatian sovereignty: A sovereign nation enjoys the benefits and protections of international law, so it is better equipped to deter armed aggression. But through recognition Germany was interested in quelling hostilities solely in Croatia, regardless of the potential effects of early recognition upon the EC Peace Conference and the other Yugoslav republics. By contrast, the EC and the United Nations both took a broader view of the conflict, aspiring to completely end or prevent all hostilities stemming from the crisis.

Viewed together, the interventions of the EC, the United Nations, and Germany provide important lessons for international peacekeeping from a perspective of collective security policy and action. Their combined efforts have been described as mediation a la carte,[2] a menu of distinct diplomatic policies and procedures among which the Yugoslav parties could pick and choose depending on their immediate interests at any given time. Aside from circumstantial overlap (which was significant) between the EC and UN mediations and Germany's participation in the European Political Cooperation (EPC) council of EC Foreign Ministers, the separate diplomatic interventions of the EC, the United Nations, and Germany in the Yugoslav crisis were neither systematically integrated nor based upon a set of shared institutional rules. Consequently, the overall international diplomatic intervention in Yugoslavia during this period produced ambiguous results.

Key Interventions and Major Actors

The EC was the first international player to intervene in Yugoslavia, beginning in the summer of 1991. Several factors led to the Europeans taking a leadership role in mediating the crisis. The United States, the sole superpower remaining after the breakup of the Soviet Union, was preoccupied with the Persian Gulf War throughout much of 1990–91 and had no vital American interests to protect in the Balkans. Both President George Bush and Secretary of State James Baker believed that the destabilization of Yugoslavia was a European security issue because of its proximity to Western Europe. Deputy Secretary of State Lawrence Eagleburger and Bush's advisor on national security, Brent Scowcroft, doubted America's ability to influence the course of events in Yugoslavia without an unpopular and potentially protracted military engagement.

At the same time, the Western European powers asserted a claim to intervene in the Yugoslav crisis through the auspices of the EC. The EC member states had recently ratified treaty provisions on European Cooperation in the Sphere of Foreign Policy through the Single European Act on September 9, 1985, which provided the legal vehicle establishing the EPC (European Political Cooperation), the primary policy-making institution of the EC during the Yugoslav crisis. Several of the representatives signing the Act on behalf of their respective countries, such as Hans Dietrich Genscher for Germany and Hans van den Broek for the Netherlands, became key players in future EPC policy discussions on Yugoslavia. Additionally, EC member states had ties with particular Yugoslav nationalities, stemming from the period of the first and second world wars, the United Kingdom and France with the Serbs and Germany with the Croats. For instance, the United Kingdom and France helped create the unified Yugoslavian State in 1918, in part to ensure protection of Serbs living outside Serbia. Germany maintained a longstanding "guest worker" (*gastarbeiter*) relationship with ethnic Croats, and a large Croat population resided permanently in Germany. Finally, nearly half of Yugoslavia's current trade was conducted with EC member states. Thus, intervening in Yugoslavian internal affairs promised an effective method of drawing Yugoslavia deeper into the Western European economic and political fold, broadening the scope of EC diplomatic influence, and limiting the need for outside intervention in the European sphere after creation of common foreign policy institutions among EC member states.

The immediate cause of the armed conflicts in Slovenia and subsequently in Croatia arose from their June 25, 1991, declarations of independence from the SFRJ, which threatened the territorial integrity of the Yugoslav state. The Yugoslav civil war originally began as a "limited policing action" of the federal Yugoslavian army, the JNA, within the Republic of Slovenia to Croatia's north, and escalated within Croatia after the withdrawal of the JNA from Slovene territory.

The ultimate cause of the civil war in Yugoslavia, however, can be traced to a conflict that arose between two competing concepts of nationalism after the death of Yugoslav President Josep Broz Tito in April 1980. Tito's death destabilized the political balance of power from the mid to late 1980s. The first concept of nationalism emphasized the national unity of Yugoslavia. Favored by Yugoslav Communists, particularly among the leadership of the JNA and other institutions of the federal government, this concept supported centralized political and economic power. The second concept of nationalism was grounded in ethnic identity and supported independence for certain Yugoslav republics in which a particular ethnic group predominated, namely, for the Slovenes in Slovenia and the Croats in Croatia. This form of ethnic nationalism combined longstanding historically and culturally based claims to independence with a desire to break free from the political and economic yoke of Yugoslavia's centralized socialist system. A variant of this concept of nationalism also surfaced around 1986 in Serbia, stressing the Serbs' separate historical origins (in Kosovo) and claiming long-term political and economic exploitation of the Serb people by the Slovenes and Croats. Serb nationalism expressed the desire to consolidate the power of Yugoslavia into Serb hands.

From the late 1980s until 1991, Slobodan Milosevic, chief of the Serbian Communist Party and president of Serbia from 1987, supported Yugoslav unity. During this period, Serbia and the Communist leaders of the federal government maintained a nominal alliance that forestalled international consensus concerning Serb aggression, since it was carried out in the name of Yugoslav sovereignty. From 1989 to 1991, Milosevic also drew upon Serb ultranationalism to foment dissent against the anti-Yugoslav nationalism of non-Serbs—Croats, Slovenes, Albanians—idealizing the Serbs as the true protectors of Yugoslavia. After the Slovene and Croatian secessions in 1991, Milosevic openly embraced Serb nationalism to justify territorial expansion of Yugoslavia into Serb-populated areas of non-Serb republics, with the intention of creating a Yugoslav successor state in which all Serbs could live united. The manipulative blending of these two historically opposed concepts of Yugoslav nationalism based in ideological unity and ethnic identity characterized Milosevic's politics during the initial years of the Yugoslav crisis. What may at first have seemed to the international community a defense of Yugoslav (multinational) unity by Milosevic was soon revealed to be a dangerous Serbian expansionist program.

The tension between these competing nationalist concepts became politically manifest in 1988–89 when Milosevic staged political coups in the two Serbian Autonomous Provinces of Vojvodina and Kosovo, replacing the existing Communist Party leadership of both provinces with political allies loyal to Serbia. This stratagem held significant implications for control of the Yugoslav federal government and of the JNA. The ruling institution of federal power in Yugoslavia, the Yugoslav head of state, was the Federal Presidency, an eight-member ruling council composed of one voting representative from each of the six constituent republics and the two autonomous provinces. After the Vojvodina and Kosovo coups, with these two votes firmly in its grip, and factoring in the vote of the Republic of Montenegro, Serbia's traditional ally, Serbia controlled half the votes of the Federal Presidency after 1989. No significant federal action could be taken without its explicit approval. This power enabled Serbia to force amendments to its constitution through the Federal Presidency, stripping Kosovo and Vojvodina of their constitutional autonomy and absorbing them into the Serbian Republic proper.

As a counter to Serbian hegemony, Slovenia proposed a package of amendments to its constitution that included a right to secede and increased control over the disposition of its resources within the federal system. Although these amendments were rejected by the vote of the Federal Presidency led by Serbia, Slovenia was intent upon adopting them, unilaterally if necessary, and relations between Serbia and Slovenia deteriorated. As with many of Milosevic's political power grabs, although Serbia's constitutional amendments were clearly hegemonic, they did not outwardly challenge the basic socialist unity of Yugoslavia; on the contrary, they increased the centralization of power. By contrast, Slovenia's amendments openly challenged the territorial integrity of the Yugoslav state in such a way as to provoke the response of the federal government and through it the federal army, the JNA.

At the same time that Slovenia flexed its nationalist muscle, nationalist conflict intensified within Croatia, spurred by Croat nationalists who asserted political control over the republic and pushed for separation from Yugoslavia. In 1989, the leading nationalist party in Croatia, the Croatian Democratic Union (HDZ), led by former JNA general Franjo Tudjman, won 57 percent of the seats in the first national parliamentary elections authorized by the Croatian Communist Party and saw Tudjman vaulted to the presidency of the republic. Tudjman's main political platform consisted of a pledge to deliver Croatian independence. The Croatian Serbs were caught unprepared and unorganized for the national elections and were grossly underrepresented in the parliament as a result.[3] The only Serb members elected to the parliament came from the radical Krajina area of Croatia, where Serbs had created the SDS in response to Croat nationalism prior to the elections. But the SDS was not able to mobilize ethnic Serbs from throughout Croatia in time to protect Serb national minority rights. The new Croatian constitution promulgated by an overwhelming majority of the new parliament renounced the hitherto protected status of ethnic Serbs as a separate constituent nation embedded in the old constitution and defined Croatia as the sovereign state of the Croatian nation.[4] In response, the SDS in Krajina began building its own national governmental entity in order to preserve the rights that had been stripped away and to enhance the sovereignty of Croatian Serbs.

When the Republics of Slovenia and Croatia embraced nationalist platforms, Milosevic and Serbian leaders shifted away from their Communist centralist alliance and adopted a pan-Serb vision of controlling as much of the Yugoslav federation as possible if and when it dissolved. Milosevic took the view that Slovene and Croat nationalism would lead inevitably to the dissolution of Yugoslavia and that the only subsequently valid organizational constituents of Yugoslavia would be the national peoples. Consequently, only the nations, not the republics, in Milosevic's view, had the right to secede from the federation, and the borders separating the republics therefore held merely administrative significance. Despite this shift, Serbia and the JNA's aims still overlapped to a large degree. With Yugoslav unity on the verge of destruction, the Slovenes and the Croats considered the JNA to be an occupying army of a foreign government encroaching on their sovereignty. Throughout the Serb-dominated regions of Yugoslavia, however, including those in Croatia, the Serbs considered the JNA the legitimate military force of the Yugoslav state. Such an alliance corresponded with Milosevic's intention to create a Yugoslav rump state succeeding to the legal status of the former Yugoslav federation if Croatia and Slovenia were to secede.

During the spring of 1991, the Krajina Serbs began asserting their own independence through actions hostile to the Croatian government. Radical SDS members seized government police stations and erected barricades at the entrances of Serb-populated towns. Krajina unilaterally declared itself an independent Serb territory within Croatia. Unrest also developed in a region of Croatia on the border of Serbian Vojvodina known as Eastern Slavonia, where SDS activists and local Serbs began erecting barricades. Armed Serb village patrols formed in both Krajina and Eastern Slavonia, and the SDS demanded Eastern Slavonia's annexation to Serbia, along with Krajina's independence. The pan-Serb concept had become a formidable ideological force. In turn, ultranationalist members of the Croatian HDZ provoked armed conflicts in Serb-populated villages. The Serb–Croat conflicts evolved into a pattern of localized fighting, village by village, within the regions where the ethnic mix between Croats and Serbs was thickest: Krajina, Western Slavonia, and Eastern Slavonia. But the federal government would not allow the Croatian Republic government to handle the unrest internally. When the Croatian government dispatched troops of the Croatian National Guard into Krajina to quell the fighting, the JNA intervened and mobilized inside Croatia on the pretext that individual republics were not permitted to maintain standing armies of their own. The JNA intervention represented to the leaders of both Slovenia and Croatia the willingness of the JNA to interfere in the internal affairs of the republics and perhaps, they reasoned, redraw the internal boundaries of the Yugoslav state to carve out the disputed regions.

Thereafter Slovenia began preparations for a formal secession from the Yugoslav federation. The final steps toward disintegration of the federation were imminent. The leaders of the Yugoslav republics and members of the federal government held summit talks across the country in an attempt to stop the dissolution, but failed to make progress. One of the main difficulties of the talks concerned the interpretation of the right to self-determination: who should get it, how exercised, territorial dimensions, etc. Although the Helsinki Final Act of 1975 maintains the right of nations to self-determination, it also upholds the principle of the inviolability of state borders, a seeming contradiction when applied to Yugoslavia's multinational federative system. Self-determination in the context of imminent federal dissolution was interpreted in three ways, according to each of the parties' respective interests. The Communists argued for the inviolability of federal borders; the Slovenes and Croats argued for self-determination as applied to the constituent republics, preserving current republican borders intact upon sovereignty; and Milosevic, on behalf of Serbia, espoused the right to self-determination of the constituent nations, raising serious doubts about the territorial status quo, since the Serb nation was spread throughout several Yugoslav republics.

From the beginning of the Yugoslav crisis, the international community, including the EC, supported maintaining Yugoslavian unity as opposed to fragmenting the state into independent and unassociated republican constituents. As a first response, the United States and the EC provided trade incentives and economic aid to the Yugoslav federal government to encourage Yugoslavia's transformation from a coercively centralized socialist regime into a capitalist liberal democracy that would be more tolerant of national ethnic differences. Federal Prime Minister Ante Markovic, who held office from 1989 to 1991, tried to introduce free-market reforms into the federal system, but most of these encountered resistance from the leaders of Slovenia, Croatia, and Serbia, all of whom sought greater control over their individual republic's resources within the federal scheme. The EC's official foreign policy concerning Yugoslavia at this time endorsed maintaining Yugoslav unity and denounced ethnic nationalism of all stripes. Evincing this view, French Prime Minister Edith Cresson proclaimed, "Yugoslavia cannot be part of Europe unless she remains united."[5] Prior to the summer of 1991, the EC and all of its member states, including the United Kingdom, France, and Germany, agreed that separatism could not solve the crisis and that Yugoslav unity should be supported.

On June 25, 1991, both Slovenia and Croatia declared independence. On the same day, the federal parliament convened and voted not to recognize the secessions. Additionally, Prime Minister Ante Markovic issued a decree empowering the defense minister to deploy JNA units to safeguard state frontiers and territorial integrity. The JNA was promptly deployed.

After the JNA deployment into Slovenia, the Slovene Territorial Defense (TO) units rallied to surround and block JNA barracks and cut off water and electricity lines. Several armed skirmishes between the Slovene TO and the JNA occurred between June 27 and July 6, 1991. On June 27, 1991, the EPC Council of EC Ministers met and agreed not to recognize the Slovene and Croat secessions and called for the restoration of the constitutional order and territorial integrity of Yugoslavia. The EC dispatched a troika of foreign ministers, Jacques Poos of Luxembourg, Gianni de Michelis of Italy, and Hans van den Broek of the Netherlands, to help mediate the Slovene conflict at the federal and republican levels. The troika met informally with the leaders of Slovenia, Croatia, and the federal government and brokered a cease-fire agreement that, in exchange for the withdrawal of JNA troops to their barracks, imposed a three-month suspension on Slovene and Croat independence. During this moratorium period, preparations were to be made for convening negotiations for a comprehensive settlement to the constitutional crisis afflicting Yugoslav unity, which would include all concerned parties and be led by the EC.

The cease-fire/withdrawal was formalized by the Brioni Accord of July 7, 1991, which established several necessary conditions for general settlement negotiations under the auspices of the EC. These conditions included the following: (i) reversion of border security to the status quo without JNA policing; (ii) control of border-crossings into Slovenia by the Slovenian police, in conformity with federal regulations; (iii) lifting of blockades of JNA facilities and return of JNA troops to barracks; (iv) removal of blockades of roads; (v) deactivation of Slovene TOs; and (vi) return of all JNA facilities and equipment.[6] The Brioni Accord also provided for the close monitoring of the cease-fire, deblocking, and implementing withdrawal through deployment of a monitoring mission in Slovenia and, if necessary, Croatia. The monitoring body, the ECMM, was composed of both civilian and military monitors, all of whom were unarmed. Its mandate was to help stabilize the cease-fire and monitor the implementation of the Brioni Accord commitments.

Although the EC clearly endorsed a foreign policy supporting Yugoslav unity, the Brioni Accord, in effect, spelled the end of the Yugoslav federation, because it placed only a moratorium on the implementation of Slovene and Croatian independence, not a prohibition on their right of unilateral secession. Over the objections of Prime Minister Ante Markovic, EC Minister van den Broek was said to have railroaded the agreement through to confirmation with the aid of Serbia and Slovenia, without ever addressing the contested issue of self-determination. When the Federal Presidency voted to withdraw JNA troops from Slovenia, Slovenia effectively acquired de facto independence. Croatia's road to independence would not be so easy, however. Serbia and the SDS officially sanctioned

Slovene secession, because it could be used to uphold secession along national lines, there being no other national peoples dwelling in significant numbers in Slovenia than Slovenes. But they violently opposed Croat independence. The Serb population predominated in several regions in Croatia and these Croatian Serbs looked upon Serbia as their nation-state, and Serbia upon them as national constituents of Serbia.

After the Brioni Accord took effect, and without the withdrawal of the JNA from Slovenia, the conflict in Croatia between Serb paramilitaries and the Croatian National Guard heated up considerably. Serb paramilitary forces increased their hold over disputed Croatian territory through their access to arms and equipment from the JNA and Serbia. JNA lieutenant and Serb national, Ratko Mladic (who later commanded Serb forces in the Bosnian war), was posted to head the JNA corps in Knin, the capital of Krajina. Thereafter the JNA began openly fighting alongside Serb irregulars, providing weapons and infantry support to the paramilitary fighters. Together in this way, Serb paramilitaries and JNA forces leveled the village of Kijevo and followed a pattern of joint aggression throughout the war in Croatia.

The origin of the civil war in Yugoslavia stemmed from several overlapping sources of conflict: ethnic enmity, national chauvinism, and federal/Serb hegemony. In addressing those courses of conflict, the EC Peace Conference included on its mediation agenda such issues as constitutional structure, ethnic autonomy, national self-determination, and federal state succession.

Form and Specific Mechanisms of Intervention

The EC Peace Conference on Yugoslavia

Following the Brioni Accord of July 7, 1991, and preparations for EC-sponsored general settlement negotiations, the EC authorized the Peace Conference on Yugoslavia and appointed Lord Carrington the chair.[7] The EC Peace Conference constituted the EC's primary mediation vehicle during the first year of the Yugoslav crisis.

Under the terms of the August 27 declaration, the EC Peace Conference was established in conjunction with an arbitration procedure through which participants in the Conference could submit their differences for judicial consideration. The Conference's arbitration commission (the so-called Badinter Commission) was composed of five members chosen from the Constitutional Courts of EC member countries, two of whom were appointed by the Yugoslav Federal Presidency and three by the EC, and was chaired by Judge Robert Badinter of France. Officially convening the Peace Conference depended upon two related prerequisites. The first prerequisite was the signing of a cease-fire agreement among the six republics and the federal government by September 1, 1991, providing for the (i) unconditional cessation of fighting in Croatia, (ii) immediate disengagement and withdrawal of all parties to the conflict, (iii) disarming of paramilitary and irregular forces, (iv) demobilization of the Croatian National

Guard, (v) withdrawal of the JNA to barracks, and (vi) joint implementation of a cease-fire agreement by the Croatian National Guard, the JNA, and paramilitary forces. The second prerequisite was the expansion of the mandate of the ECMM to include monitoring the implementation of this cease-fire.[8] Serbia initially objected to the ECMM extension, but quietly relented when the EC foreign ministers made the opening of the Conference contingent upon the extended ECMM role. The EC believed that continued instability in Yugoslavia would prevent productive negotiations from taking place.

The EC Peace Conference was held initially at the Peace Palace in The Hague. It brought together the following parties: representatives of the Yugoslav Federal Presidency, then headed by Stipe Mesic from Croatia, and Federal Defense Minister Veljko Kadijevic; the presidents of the six Yugoslav republics, Milan Kucan of Slovenia, Franjo Tudjman of Croatia, Slobodan Milosevic of Serbia, Alija Izetbegovic of Bosnia-Herzegovina, Momir Bulatovic of Montenegro, and Kiro Gligorov of Macedonia; and representatives of certain EC member states. The Conference did not include non-state representatives, such as the leaders of the breakaway Krajina region of Croatia. EC Foreign Affairs Minister Hans van den Broek cochaired the Conference with Carrington.

The decision to appoint Carrington as chair was one of the least contentious the EC would make regarding the Yugoslav crisis. Carrington was a veteran diplomat, a former British foreign secretary, whose reputation stemmed from the settlement he had negotiated in 1979 to the conflict over independence of Rhodesia (renamed Zimbabwe following independence) between the government of Prime Minister Ian Douglas Smith and the insurgent Zimbabwe African National Union led by Robert Mugabe. Carrington was known in the diplomatic community for his honesty, integrity, and firmness of purpose. In the Rhodesian settlement, Carrington followed a phased negotiation strategy, in which constitutional issues were addressed first, followed by issues relating to the transition of rule and cease-fire.[9] He believed that this stepped approach allowed momentum to build in the negotiations and reduced the maneuvering space of the participants. Over ten years later in the Conference on Yugoslavia, Carrington employed much the same negotiation formula.

In Carrington's hands, the purpose of the EC Peace Conference was arranging (or rearranging) the constitutional future of the Yugoslav federation. Carrington's Conference agenda had two phases: The first gave priority to constitutional issues of association between the six republics, and the second deferred the more contentious issues, such as national self-determination and border changes, until after the constitutional points were satisfactorily resolved. In this way, Carrington sought to preserve viable federal infrastructure and institutions, create a renewed sense of unity among the republics, and advance a set of constitutional norms that would condition each republic's autonomy. Addressing and resolving these issues, Carrington hoped, would preclude the need for the second phase of negotiations. Issues relating to the cease-fire were not originally conceived as part of the Conference plan, because the prerequisite cease-fire agreement had been executed on September 1 in Belgrade and the expanded

ECMM set in place to oversee its implementation. Finally, under no circumstances were Slovenia and Croatia to gain EC recognition of their sovereignty until reaching an overall settlement through the framework of the Conference.

After several plenary sessions of the Conference during September 1991 that familiarized the participants with the main constitutional issues and a range of possible solutions, Carrington issued three foundational principles for guiding the Conference's future course. If all agreed, the constitutional restructuring of Yugoslavia would fundamentally entail:

(a) A loose association or alliance of sovereign or independent republics;
(b) Adequate arrangements for the protection of minorities, including human rights guarantees and possible special status for certain areas;
(c) No unilateral changes in borders.[10]

In the context of Carrington's two-phase negotiation agenda, the three foundational principles reflected a broad accommodation of the participants' interests that conformed with standards of international law but did not alienate any of the participants from the Conference's ultimate goal of a general settlement. The EC's interests, for example, as represented by Carrington, remained with Yugoslav unity, that is, some form of alliance among the republics. In Carrington's view, the republics were the legal constituents of the Yugoslav federation that would survive in case of its dissolution. His conception permitted each republic the degree of sovereignty it desired, while preserving as much as possible of the existing federal infrastructure, such as economic relations and common markets, legal standards and treaties, transportation and utilities facilities, common currency, foreign affairs and joint security.

Among the republics, Slovenia pushed for sovereignty and rejected all but very limited common institutional arrangements. Croatia showed a willingness to share institutions on an intergovernmental basis wherein its own independence was assured. Macedonia favored the idea of independence, as evidenced by its Declaration of Sovereignty and Independence of September 17, 1991, and accepted regional economic ties with other republics. Montenegro remained a strong ally of Serbia and was prepared to join with it in a Yugoslav rump state. Bosnia-Herzegovina maintained a neutral stance concerning its own independence and provisionally stood by a pre-Conference plan authored by Izetbegovic and Gligorov proposing an asymmetrical federation composed of Serbia and Montenegro, with Bosnia-Herzegovina and Macedonia as constituent but autonomous republics. Of all the republics, Serbia's interests were the most unyielding and extreme. In case of dissolution, Milosevic intended for Serbia to succeed to the legal entitlements of the former Yugoslavia and insisted that all ethnic Serbs throughout the federation live in one Yugoslav state.

To Carrington, such pan-Serb interests were completely out of the question and endangered the Conference's very existence. He countered them with the phased negotiation strategy and appeasement through strong constitutional rights. Carrington hoped that ensuring Serbia of minority protections and au-

tonomy for Serbs living within other republics (the second of the two fundamental principles) would satisfy its interests in Serb safety and unity, without
needing to broach the issue of Serb self-determination. He hoped thereby to de-
fer indefinitely the issue of Serb self-determination, and its corresponding issue
of republican border changes, to the vanishing point of the Conference. Thus the
three foundational principles represented, in part, a Serbian containment strategy utilizing protracted, phased negotiations as a tool.

On October 4, 1991, after several plenary sessions of the Peace Conference, all
of the Conference participants informally agreed to accept the three principles
as parameters of continued talks. Additionally, Carrington, Milosevic, Tudjman,
and Kadijevic agreed to divide the Conference into two working groups focusing on political (constitutional) issues, on the one hand, and military (cease-
fire) issues, on the other, the so-called "twin-track" approach. Under the twin-
track organization, Lord Carrington would continue to lead the political
discussions and Minister van den Broek was put in charge of the military negotiations. Cease-fire considerations signed their own track in the negotiation
process because the September 1 cease-fire agreement had failed from its inception, and this failure had undermined the Conference negotiations from the
outset. Contrary to EC intent, the Conference had been convened while hostilities among the Croatian National Guard, Serb paramilitaries, and the JNA continued to erupt. In fact, since September 7, the fighting in Croatia had escalated
dramatically.

Lord Carrington and Minister van den Broek dealt with the cease-fire failure
in two ways: forging new cease-fire agreements and focusing talks on the particular issues impeding a cease-fire. Carrington personally negotiated a second
cease-fire agreement at Igalo on September 17, 1991, among the Republics of
Croatia and Serbia and the Yugoslav minister of defense in the form of a political
statement in which each party pledged to exert every influence to end the fighting immediately.[11] Minister van den Broek and Carrington jointly chaired an October 4, 1991, meeting on cease-fire issues at The Hague, attended by Tudjman,
Milosevic, and Kadijevic. The meeting focused on two specific points of the
cease-fire implementation as being particularly important to correcting the
cease-fire failure: (i) on the part of Croatian authorities, immediately lifting the
blockade of JNA garrisons and other facilities and (ii) on the part of the JNA,
withdrawing and relocating its units in Croatia with the assistance of EC monitors.[12] Minister van den Broek alone chaired another cease-fire meeting on October 10, 1991, among the same participants. The topic at this meeting concerned
the extent to which the JNA would fully withdraw from Croatia after implementation of Croatian deblocking. To this question, Kadijevic reserved his response
pending a ruling by the four-member rump Yugoslav Federal Presidency.[13] The
rump Federal Presidency, shortly thereafter, predicated full withdrawal of the
federal army upon a general political settlement among the parties and so could
not guarantee that deblocked JNA troops and equipment would not be re-de-
ployed within Croatia. Minister van den Broek also chaired an October 18 cease-
fire meeting attended by Tudjman, Milosevic, and Kadijevic to discuss further

the issues of deblocking and evacuation of JNA barracks. As a result of this meeting, all the participants signed an agreement obligating each party to give immediate instructions to their respective forces for (i) an immediate and unconditional cease-fire, (ii) immediate deblocking of all JNA barracks and installations in Croatia, and (iii) evacuation of JNA barracks and installations according to a time schedule to be determined by a special tripartite cease-fire working group in Zagreb.[14] The EC therefore appeared to make progress on problematic cease-fire issues.

On the political track, however, the progress of the Peace Conference underwent a serious breach at the plenary session held on October 18, 1991, when Carrington formally presented a comprehensive plan for the constitutional reorganization of the Yugoslav federation entitled "Arrangements for General Settlement" (the Carrington Plan). Article I, the core of the Carrington Plan, consisted of a restatement of the three fundamental principles; the remainder of the plan enumerated specific terms of cooperation between the republics in the areas of human rights and rights of ethnic and national groups (Article II); in other areas of cooperation, such as economic relations and foreign affairs (Article III); and in institutional arrangements for effecting the plan (Article IV).[15] When Carrington took a formal poll of the participants' acceptance of the plan, Serbia, despite approvals registered by the other five republics, including Montenegro, rejected it, specifically citing disagreement with Article I, the very principles to which Milosevic had previously agreed on October 4.

Milosevic was thought to have changed his mind about Serbia's commitment to the principle of human rights protections and special status for ethnic groups.[16] Although he was nominally satisfied with the protections as they applied to enhanced autonomy for Serbs in Croatia, he was apparently not prepared to protect the rights of ethnic groups residing in Serbian territory—namely, the Kosovo Albanians, though they constituted the overwhelming majority of the population there. According to Milosevic himself, however, Serbia was dissatisfied with the Conference's refusal to elucidate the following issues: the Yugoslav entity entitled to the right of self-determination (i.e., the republics or the peoples), the conditions of lawful secession from the federation, the status of internal (administrative) and external (state) frontiers under the Helsinki Final Act and the Paris Charter, and the terms conditioning succession to the Yugoslav state, all of which Carrington had strategically deferred until the second phase of negotiations.[17]

On October 30, 1991, Serbia and Montenegro jointly proposed an amendment to Article I of the Carrington Plan providing for Serbian succession to the Yugoslav state comprising the territory of all nonseceding republics. Carrington immediately rejected the proposed amendment as a declaration of Serbian territorial ambition that he could no longer keep at bay. The combined effect of this justifiable rejection and Carrington's suppression of issues having anything to do with Serb self-determination or Yugoslav succession removed any Serbian interest in continuing discussions for a general settlement. The Conference never moved beyond this sticking point. All along, knowing of Serbia's extremist stance, Carrington ignored Serbia's interests by refusing to put the issues on the table for serious consideration. But he really had no other choice under standards of international law.[18] Carrington's delay tactics made the best of a bad situation with Serbian aggression. Carrington believed that given enough opportunity for face-to-face discussions with Milosevic under Conference auspices, emphasizing Serb autonomy without Serbia, he could bring Milosevic around to a more reasonable negotiating position, while avoiding the complete breach that an up-front, frank assessment of his expansionist interests would surely have caused sooner. In fact, Carrington never had any intention of seriously broaching the question of Serb self-determination and its necessary concomitant, Croatian (and Bosnian) partition. Addressing such interests was diplomatically almost inconceivable at the time because of the lack of supporting precedent under international legal norms of federative dissolution, and Carrington did not want to appear to capitulate in any way to Serbian aggression. Nonetheless, Carrington also had to contain Serbia as best as he could through diplomatic engagement, because Serbia possessed by far the greatest military force in the federation, mightier than all the other republics combined. Such manipulative diplomacy was the EC's only tool for disengaging Serb forces.

The second major impediment to progress toward a general settlement was the persistence of war in Croatia. What Serbia would never achieve through negotiations with Carrington, the Serbs were certain to capture on the ground, and they pursued their military goals unwaveringly. For instance, October 4, the day on which all the Conference participants agreed to the fundamental principles of peace, coincided with the fiercest attack of the Croatian war to date by Serbian forces. A combined Serb–JNA force bombarded Vukovar in Eastern Slavonia from the ground and the air and attacked the city hospital. Since the beginning of September, the city had endured regular bombardments and constant sniper attacks (a siege tactic later famously repeated in Sarajevo) until less than a third of the population remained. The cease-fire agreements were utterly ineffectual at stopping such attacks. In addition to the September 1 and September 17 cease-fires, Carrington personally negotiated up to six more cease-fire agreements by the middle of October 1991. The EC in general, primarily through Minister van den Broek, had negotiated a total of ten cease-fires since the end of July 1991.[19] By November 1991, Serb–JNA forces controlled nearly a third of Croat territory through steady military application.

The failure of the cease-fire agreements was a major source of criticism of Carrington and the Carrington Plan in the international press, particularly by EC member state Germany, and led to an increasing level of tension among EC members regarding their collective foreign policy position on Yugoslavia. The United Kingdom and France continued to appeal for Yugoslav unity and stood behind the EC Peace Conference efforts; Germany strongly backed Croatian sovereignty and therefore pushed for a policy of recognition at the earliest possible date. German Foreign Minister Hans Dietrich Genscher argued for an early recognition policy on the theory that Milosevic was using the Conference as a stalling tactic to gain time for advancing his military ambitions in Croatia.

Immediate recognition of Croatian sovereignty, Genscher argued, would repel the Serb–JNA advance by recharacterizing the JNA as an occupying army and Serb paramilitaries as belligerents under international law. Independence would afford Croatia both the right to crush the Serb insurgency within its borders, unhindered by JNA interference, and the protections of other sovereign nations and institutions against Serbian-Yugoslav encroachment of its sovereign boundaries. The German early recognition policy, strongly backed by Germany's pro-Croatia lobby, threatened to destroy the Peace Conference and any hope of a general political solution to the Yugoslav civil war. Both Carrington and van den Broek understood that early recognition spelled disaster for the Conference and especially for the Republic of Bosnia-Herzegovina, because as soon as Croatia gained recognition, two events would inexorably occur: Croatia would lose incentive to abide by the terms of the Carrington Plan, and the center of the Yugoslav conflict would shift to Bosnia-Herzegovina. German recognition of Croatia and its effect on the mediation efforts are discussed in more detail later in this chapter.

A fatal weakness of the EC's negotiation efforts was its lack of a credible military force to counter Serbia's expansionist aggression. In lieu of a standing army to repulse Serb–JNA aggression, the EC had at its disposal only the ECMM to monitor implementation of the various cease-fire agreements. The ECMM was not a peacekeeping army. Monitors were unarmed and were not necessarily trained as soldiers. The ECMM mandate, set forth in two Memoranda of Understanding on July 13, 1991, and September 1, 1991, relating to the Brioni Accord and the cease-fire agreement of September 1, respectively, included provisions for overseeing the deblocking of JNA facilities, immediate withdrawal of all parties from areas of hostility, disarming of paramilitary forces, demobilization of the Croatian National Guard, and withdrawal of JNA troops to barracks. Each of the individual parties was responsible only for implementing the provisions of the cease-fire that related to it, and the ECMM was responsible for monitoring, evaluating, and reporting on, but not enforcing, the implementation. The ECMM did, however, undertake to forge local cease-fire and other humanitarian agreements between the parties in conflict.[20]

The failure of the cease-fire agreements can also be explained in part by the failure of the ECMM to oversee their implementation. This problem was recognized by the EC as early as September 19, 1991, in an EC declaration on Yugoslavia conceding that the ECMM was no longer able to perform its duties because of the continued violence in Croatia.[21] Outfitted only with communications and surveillance equipment, the EC monitors operated solely in areas where the cease-fire had verifiably taken effect. They could not possibly have assisted the implementation of troop withdrawal, disarmament or demobilization, as none of these actions was forthcoming from the relevant parties and monitors could not be expected to intervene in the hostilities. The EC monitors were in a better position to aid deblocking of JNA facilities. Apparently, however, they did not fully understand the importance of lifting the Croat blockades for achieving a sustainable cease-fire in Croatia. The ongoing hostilities limited the ECMM's intelligence-gathering capacities.[22] The primary reason that the ECMM did not help implement the deblocking aspects of the cease-fire agreements was its bias in favor of the Croatians against the JNA and Serbs.[23] The ECMM knew that the Croats would face a substantial danger of JNA troop and equipment redeployment within Croatia if they deblocked the JNA installations, and so the ECMM refrained from doing so. Whatever the weaknesses of the ECMM might have been, the fact remained that Carrington and the EC needed a sizeable army, not simply an unarmed force, to implement and enforce the terms of the cease-fire agreements and to stabilize the situation on the ground. Before the hostilities in Croatia had escalated to civil war, there had been talk among politicians in Germany of committing a peacekeeping force in Yugoslavia composed of troops from the Western European Union (WEU).[24] Since the EC was now incapable or unwilling to commit a multinational peacekeeping force in the midst of the Croatian war, the responsibility to intervene devolved upon the United Nations, which had had over forty years of peacekeeping operation experience using multinational peacekeeping troops.

UN Mediation

In April 1992, the United Nations began deploying nearly 10,000 troops of a UN Protection Force into four UN Protected Areas within the Republic of Croatia. The Republic of Croatia had appealed for UN troops since the start of the war in July 1991. Beginning in September 1991, coincident with the opening of the EC Peace Conference, the United Kingdom, France, and other EC member states lobbied the UN Security Council for a peacekeeping operation to halt the interrepublic hostilities. EC ministers understood that a reliable cease-fire was essential to the Peace Conference's success. Against JNA and Serb armed forces, a peacekeeping army would be necessary if diplomatic means proved ineffective for halting the conflict. Chapter 7 of the UN Charter places a great responsibility upon the UN Security Council for enforcing international peace, and this provided authority for deployment of a UN peacekeeping force in Yugoslavia. The Helsinki Final Act of 1975, the founding charter of the main collective security institution in Europe, the Organization for Security and Cooperation in Europe (OSCE), conferred no comparable responsibility on the EC or its member states, nor did the EC have a standing military force to utilize for peacekeeping purposes.

UN Peacekeeping Missions/Geneva Accord

Responding to international demands, the Security Council took initial action to intervene in the Yugoslav crisis in Resolution 713 on September 25, 1991, pursuant to which UN Secretary-General Javier Perez de Cuellar dispatched former U.S. Secretary of State Cyrus R. Vance as his personal envoy on a mission of peace to Yugoslavia.

Between October and December of 1991, Vance conducted four separate missions under the Resolution 713 mandate. On each mission, he was accompanied by former U.S. Ambassador to the German Democratic Republic Herbert S. Okun, his special advisor, as well as J.P. Kavanaugh, senior officer in the cabinet of the secretary-general, and H. Heitmann, political affairs officer for research and collection of information. Sir Marrack Goulding, UN undersecretary-general for special political affairs, joined the third and fourth missions. Collectively, the UN peacekeeping missions had one primary aim, to secure and maintain peace in Yugoslavia. In this regard, the missions overlapped with the political and cease-fire tracks of the EC Peace Conference and Monitoring Mission. The UN missions benefited from the progress made by Carrington and van den Broek in negotiations, shared intelligence gathered by the ECMM, and offered support to the EC mediation effort where it was consistent with UN policy. Yet the UN missions, as an independent collective security intervention of the UN, also maintained a critical distance from the EC experience of mediating the Yugoslav crisis to date, allowing the United Nations to act as a corrective to the errors in policy, strategy, and implementation undermining EC efforts to achieve peace. Most importantly, the UN held at its disposal the critical means of incentive for achieving peace: the promise of a UN peacekeeping force deployed in Croatia, which all of the relevant parties believed benefited their individual interests. Throughout the four missions and especially during the third and fourth, Vance conducted head-to-head discussions with a broad group of Yugoslavia-wide politicians (federal, republican, and local) to create a peacekeeping plan that would achieve a sustainable cease-fire in Croatia.

Vance undertook his first mission to Yugoslavia between October 11 and 18, 1991. In this period, Vance visited all six republics of Yugoslavia and met with the presidents of each and with representatives of the federal government. Vance and Okun worked in close association with both the EC Peace Conference and the ECMM to understand the significant factors controlling the Croatian conflict. They attended the two plenary political sessions of the EC Peace Conference held during that week and met and conferred with Lord Carrington individually, the Council of Ministers of the EC, and with German Foreign Minister Hans Dietrich Genscher, who was also serving as the chairman of the Conference on Security and Cooperation in Europe (CSCE) at the time. Vance attended the October 18 cease-fire track meeting chaired by Minister van den Broek that resulted in the commitments of Croatia, Serbia, and the JNA to immediate deblock JNA installations and schedule withdrawal of JNA units. Finally, Vance and Okun were briefed by the head of the ECMM, Ambassador Dirk Jan van Houten, and other EC monitors concerning the current findings and status of ECMM operations and problems related to attaining a stable cease-fire.[25]

By the end of Vance's second mission to Yugoslavia, November 3–9, 1991, Vance and his advisors devised a strategy for reaching a sustainable cease-fire that consisted of three parts: first, a final, definitive cease-fire agreement signed under UN auspices by all parties to the conflict; second, overseeing the implementation of deblocking of JNA installations and withdrawal of JNA units from Croatia; and third, deployment of an armed UN peacekeeping force in contested territories of Croatia for the purpose of enforcing the terms of the cease-fire agreement. All aspects were essentially interdependent in the sense that the ultimate aim, deployment of UN troops, completely hinged upon first attaining a stable cease-fire, and attaining a stable cease-fire required deblocking of JNA installations and withdrawal of JNA troops. JNA officials briefed Vance and Okun on the relation between deblocking and cease-fire. Finally, Vance would not authorize deployment of UN troops until the necessary preparations were in place.

The third mission took place between November 17 and 24, 1991, at the end of which the planned cease-fire agreement, the Geneva Accord of November 23, 1991, was signed by Tudjman, Milosevic, Kadijevic, and Vance. The terms of the Geneva Accord were substantially the same as the terms of the cease-fire-track agreement signed on October 18 among the same Yugoslav parties at the cease-fire meeting led by van den Broek.[26] Vance considered the Geneva Accord a definitive cease-fire agreement, because he made it explicitly clear to all the parties that their full compliance with its terms constituted an unconditional prerequisite to deployment of UN peacekeeping forces.

Unlike all of the EC-negotiated cease-fires, the Geneva Accord eventually stuck. Certainly, the chief reason was the contingency of UN troop deployment. Additionally, the Geneva Accord succeeded, according to Ambassador Okun, because of the attention that Vance and Okun paid to the implementation and progress of deblocking and evacuation of JNA barracks and installations. In fact, the implementation of the cease-fire was directly dependent, in the view of JNA leadership, upon the implementation of deblocking of JNA installations. For instance, during the week of November 25, just after the signing of the Geneva Accord, shelling in Croatia resumed and the deblocking/withdrawal process slowed down, more or less simultaneously. Senior defense officials in Belgrade informed Vance that in their view these two developments were linked. Vance therefore urged full resumption and the earliest conclusion of deblocking and withdrawal, while stressing the need for full and immediate implementation of the Geneva Accord.[27]

The fourth UN mission to Yugoslavia, December 1–9, 1991, accomplished several important elements of a sustainable cease-fire. Picking up from meetings they had initiated during the third mission, Vance and Goulding held head-to-head discussions, intending to define the conditions for a peacekeeping operation acceptable to the parties that would be affected by a UN troop deployment: Milosevic, Tudjman, Kadijevic, Ante Markovic, Izetbegovic; Milan Bobic and Goran Hadzic, the Serb leaders from Krajina and Eastern Slavonia, respectively; Stjepan Kljuic, leader of the Democratic Croat Party of Bosnia-Herzegovina; and Radovan Karadzic, leader of the SDS of Bosnia-Herzegovina. The result of these meetings was Vance and Goulding's "Concept for a United Nations Peacekeeping Operation in Yugoslavia"[28] issued on December 11, 1991, after the end of the fourth mission. Additionally, during the fourth mission, Ambassadors Okun and van Houten negotiated a deblocking agreement, which laid down guidelines for expediting the deblocking process and resolved all outstanding issues for blockade-lifting of JNA facilities and relocation of JNA and personnel and equipment outside Croatia, all to be completed by the first of the new year.[29]

Deblocking and Withdrawal

Vance had asked Ambassador Okun during the third mission to oversee the deblocking process, which was essential to implementing the Geneva Accord. Following the end of the third mission, Okun stayed in Yugoslavia to assess the status of deblocking. The Croats persistently blockaded JNA barracks and installations because the Croats were outmanned and vastly outequipped and because they wanted to bring international attention to their claim of independence. On November 26, 1991, Okun began traveling to JNA facilities throughout Croatia in order to address the difficulties that slowed the pace of deblocking implementation up to this point. Okun and Ambassador van Houten of the ECMM visited facilities in Split on November 29–30 to supervise the deblocking operation there, as well as other facilities along the Dalmatian coast of Croatia. On December 3, 1991, during the period of the fourth mission, a serious difficulty arose when Croatian National Guard members blockaded the ZMAJ military aircraft repair and maintenance facility outside Zagreb. Both JNA leadership and Croatian authorities informed Vance that the disposition of the ZMAJ plant and equipment represented a potential point of breakdown in the whole deblocking and evacuation process.[30] Prior to adopting an agreement setting the terms of JNA withdrawal from Croatia, blockading presented the only effective strategic option to prevent further JNA mobilization inside Croatia, but without deblocking the JNA refused to agree to a cease-fire and to the JNA's withdrawal from the republic.

The ZMAJ problem precipitated the need for a deblocking agreement, which Ambassadors Okun and van Houten jointly wrote and negotiated. The agreement was signed for Croatia by Vice-President Dr. Mate Granic and for the JNA by General Andrija Raseta, commander of the Fifth Army District, on December 8, 1991. The agreement resolved several significant issues, such as (i) devising a formula for sharing outstanding equipment at various JNA installations, including ZMAJ; (ii) removal of land mines surrounding several JNA installations; and (iii) evacuation of all JNA garrisons in Croatia according to a set timetable.[31] According to Okun, the impediments to deblocking implementation had not derived from a lack of interest on behalf of the parties, but from a tendency of the parties to haggle over details of implementation and from the ECMM's failure to aid implementation because of its bias in favor of Croatian sovereignty. EC monitors apparently viewed the JNA as an occupying army supporting Serb insurgency. Before the UN intervention, deblocking would have worked solely to the JNA's advantage. But even after Vance had taken control of the cease-fire process, these problems were exacerbated by the inefficient procedures followed by EC monitors posted at JNA facilities, who continued working without any sense of urgency. The deblocking agreement substituted definite rules for such ad hoc procedures.

By the time of the Okun–van Houten agreement, both Croatia and the Yugoslav federal government had clear interests for implementing the deblocking agreement: The Croats wanted the JNA out of Croatia, and the JNA wanted its troops and their families (by this time overwhelmingly Serb) released so they could return home. The conflict at the federal level between the JNA and Croatia had reached a stalemate, because the JNA could do nothing further to prevent Croatian secession.

Ambassadors Okun and van Houten were able to use the premise of a comprehensive peacekeeping agreement as leverage to convince the Yugoslav and Serbian leadership to withdraw deblocked troops and equipment from Croatia. The comprehensive peacekeeping agreement would include a reliable cease-fire, withdrawal of the JNA and Croatian troops, and the deployment of peacekeepers. The UN force was attractive to the Serbs because it would free up JNA troops for redeployment elsewhere and would put a neutral force in contested areas. Because the Croats knew that the Serbs were holding out for peacekeeping forces they felt more confident that Serb forces would not redeploy at a later date. Especially since Vance emphasized that there would be no deployment of UN peacekeeping forces in Croatia until a cease-fire under the Geneva Accord had lasted for six weeks, unblocking JNA facilities did not create the same potential for redeployment as deblocking would have prior to UN intervention. The troops were thus pressured to withdraw by the interdependence of withdrawal, cease-fire, and UN troop deployment. Indeed, deblocking and evacuation of JNA barracks and installations were as essential to implementation of the Geneva Accord as the implementation of the Geneva Accord was essential to the UN Peacekeeping Operation.

UN Peacekeeping Operation

Vance and Goulding's Concept for a UN Peacekeeping Operation, issued on December 11, 1991, started with the premise, stated in part one of the text, that it was an interim arrangement for creating necessary conditions of peace and security to enable negotiation of an overall settlement under EC auspices (i.e., the EC Peace Conference on Yugoslavia) to proceed, without prejudicing the outcome of that negotiation.[32] The concept plan had the full cooperation of Lord Carrington and contained several key elements that the EC Peace Conference and Monitor Mission had helped to establish.

The UN Peacekeeping Operation consisted of two main parts: (i) the designation of four areas inside Croatia as United Nations Protected Areas (UNPAs), where the fighting among the Croatian National Guard, the JNA, and Serb and Croat irregulars was most heavily concentrated; and (ii) the complete demilitarization of the UNPAs through troop withdrawal and disbandment and deployment of a United Nations Protection Force (UNPROFOR) in the UNPAs in order to maintain the cease-fire and suppress fighting on a local level between national ethnic groups after troop withdrawal.[33] The UN Peacekeeping Operation did not draw upon a cease-fire agreement to which any representatives of any Serb or Croat irregular force was party (no such agreements existed) but only upon the Geneva Accord. The four UNPAs were located in Eastern Slavonia (sector East), Western Slavonia (sector West), and Krajina (sectors North and South), and UNPROFOR's duties included disarming all irregular forces in the protected zones and assisting the humanitarian agencies of the United Nations in the return of persons displaced from their homes by the fighting. The withdrawal of the JNA, once problematic, presented no further technical difficulties following Okun and van Houten's deblocking agreement.

Vance and Goulding conducted head-to-head meetings with all of the parties affected by the Peacekeeping Operation, but primarily with Tudjman, Milosevic, Kadijevic, and Federal Prime Minister Ante Markovic, each on several different occasions, in order to discuss the Peacekeeping Operation's elements and terms. In addition, Ambassador Okun personally met with President Tudjman in December of 1991 to further persuade him to accept the plan after he had voiced misgivings. The SFRJ and Croatia were interested in withdrawal, because by the fall of 1991, the war had become, with respect to their constitutional conflict, a stalemate, neither side able to win its objectives on the ground. The JNA was not able to restrain Croatia from seeking independence, and Croatia was not able to repel the JNA from Croatian territory. Tudjman's particular interests in the Peacekeeping Operation included ending the war, securing the withdrawal of the JNA from Croatia, and working on a general political settlement under peaceful conditions. Yet he was concerned that the UNPAs would consolidate territory inside Croatia for eventual annexation by Serbia. Okun argued in response to Tudjman's doubts that the UN plan would give Croatia time to build up its army or that the EC Peace Conference would reach a peaceful settlement, and that in either case Croatia would soon be internationally recognized within its present borders.

On behalf of Serbia and the Serbs, Milosevic supported the UN Peacekeeping Operation, because he wanted to consolidate the territorial gains that Serb forces had made in the war against Croatia. The deployment of UNPROFOR troops, he thought, would replace an actively resisted JNA-Serb military occupation with a neutral, passive occupying force of the United Nations that would accomplish two of his aims. It would preserve Serb territorial gains for future inclusion into the Yugoslav successor state and release JNA-Serb forces from the Croatian conflict for redeployment in Bosnia-Herzegovina to fight for Serb territory in that republic.

At this stage of the discussions, the cooperation between Lord Carrington and Secretary Vance proved essential, because the parties were participating simultaneously in the EC Peace Conference and the UN Peacekeeping Operation discussions. Because there was not a millimeter of difference between Lord Carrington's views and the views of Vance concerning the cease-fire, Croatia, the SFRJ, and Serbia were prevented from playing one intermediary off against the other in pursuit of better terms to the military compromise since each party had his own, but very different, reasons for supporting UN troop deployment.

The Peacekeeping Operation discussions often returned to the territorial dimensions of withdrawal and deployment procedures. Disagreement by the parties over these issues led Vance and Goulding to devise the UNPA/UNPROFOR peacekeeping innovation. The usual way of withdrawing armed forces in UN peacekeeping operations is known as "green line" withdrawal, requiring each party in the conflict to retreat several kilometers to either side of an inviolable border, the "green line." This technique had been employed by the United Nations in Cyprus, for example, for separating Greek and Turkish nationals. Croatia wanted the green line drawn along its republican boundaries, thus completely ridding JNA forces from Croatian territory upon withdrawal. Yugoslavia and Serbia wanted the line to track the front lines of the armed conflict at the withdrawal date, thus provisionally expanding Yugoslav territory significantly into Croatian land. The right of republican self-determination and territorial integrity (confirmed by the Badinter Commission's opinions of January 11, 1992) supported Croatia's claims. The SFRJ–Serbian cause was enhanced by a claim for national autonomy of Serbs inside Croatia, but was undermined by the principle regarding no unilateral change in borders contained in the Helsinki Final Act. The UN view of the conflict affirmed both sides' right to take up arms under standards of international law, recognizing that a belligerent party in a civil war possesses a legitimate right to wage war and a sovereign state possesses a legitimate right to use force in order to protect its territorial integrity from belligerents; however, the sole purpose of the Peacekeeping Operation was attaining peace in the region, not mediating questions of territorial allocation. The UNPA/UNPROFOR solution therefore designated these disputed territories protected zones overseen by the United Nations, from which the troops of both parties were required to evacuate upon withdrawal, and into which UN troops would be deployed. Vance and Goulding never for a moment doubted that the territory designated as UNPAs was legally anything other than Croatian.

The UNPA/UNPROFOR solution derived from two points of overlap with the EC negotiations for a general political settlement led by Carrington. First, Vance drew upon the commitments that Tudjman and Milosevic had made to the three foundational principles of October 4, specifically the principle regarding no unilateral changes in borders, which was directly applicable to the withdrawal issue. Second, Vance drew from the human rights provisions of the Carrington Plan, with respect to comprehensive arrangements for the protection of human rights and special status for certain groups and areas, which Tudjman had fully accepted and Milosevic had accepted in relation to Serbs living in Croatia. These points of overlap formed the cornerstone of the UNPA/UNPROFOR concept.

In the UNPA/UNPROFOR context, the first point prohibiting unilateral border changes clarified that the UNPAs did not affect territorial distribution between Croatia and Yugoslavia. The second point assuring human rights and group protections addressed the problem of ethnic cleansing that had become widespread in the contested regions, which the UNPAs and UNPROFOR would help remedy. All of the parties in the conflict denied any responsibility for ethnic cleansing, so the United Nations had to deal with substantial numbers of refugees and internally displaced persons on its own. For example, after Croatia regained military ground in Western Slavonia, 20,000 Serbs were expelled during the month of November. Most of the Serbs fled to Banja Luka in Bosnia-Herzegovina, where the retreating JNA had moved. Tudjman explained this refugee flight to Okun as Serb civilians voluntarily accompanying the Yugoslav army. The UNPAs allowed for repatriation of the expelled populations and insulated local communities against further civilian expulsions. The UNPA/UN-PROFOR concept also derived from the fact that in mixed Croat-Serb areas where fighting had been concentrated, there were no clear "green lines" that could be drawn to separate local ethnic groups and halt their localized fighting. In light of this fact, Vance characterized the UNPA/UNPROFOR plan as "ink spot" deployment. The UNPA/UNPROFOR concept represented a human rights-maximizing alternative to the usual "green line" military withdrawal used in traditional UN peacekeeping operations, the first in UN history.

With the UN Peacekeeping Operation plan in place after Vance and Goulding's concept paper of December 11, its implementation depended only upon the cessation of JNA–Croatian National Guard hostilities for a period of six weeks. Since a sustainable cease-fire was dependent on deblocking and withdrawal of JNA forces, the six-week cease-fire test period could not begin until after deblocking and withdrawal were completed. Accomplishing this would take the remainder of the month of December and the beginning of January, according to the withdrawal timetable agreed upon by the Zagreb tripartite cease-fire working group and under the terms of the Okun–van Houten deblocking agreement, which, according to Okun, required that equipment and installation division between the JNA and Croatian government be completed by January 1, 1992. Deblocking and withdrawal proceeded according to this schedule.

After the January 1, 1993, completion date, the Accord Implementing the Cease-fire Agreement of 23 November [34] was promptly signed under UN auspices by Colonel-General Raseta of the JNA, who had also signed the deblocking agreement on behalf of the JNA, was signed by Croatian Defense Minister Gojko Susak, and was witnessed by Vance on January 2, 1992. The Implementing Accord fixed the start date of the six-week cease-fire test period, after which the UNPROFOR troops would be deployed, provided the cease-fire held and Vance authorized deployment. Because of these measures, a sustainable cease-fire was within grasp, pending the formalities of deblocking and withdrawal implementation, and there were no outstanding issues or conflicts that could derail its progress; indeed, nothing did. On February 21, 1992, seven weeks after the Implementing Accord, the UN Security Council issued Resolution 743 on Vance's recommendation, authorizing deployment of UNPROFOR troops in the Croatian UNPAs.

Under this timeframe, the EC Peace Conference, with the support of UN intervention, was shed of its largest impediment, the inability to attain a sustainable state of cease-fire, and, for the first time since its inception on September 7, the participants anticipated political track negotiations unhampered by persistent war. Strangely, EC member state Germany chose precisely this period to break ranks with EC foreign policy on Yugoslavia and unilaterally recognize Croatian sovereignty.

German Recognition

Between December 1991 and January 1992, EC member state Germany placed immense pressure on the EPC council of Foreign Ministers to recognize Croatian sovereignty, succeeding finally on January 15, 1992, when the EC extended formal recognition to Croatia. This was the culmination of an effort by the German political elite to secure Croatian independence despite the backing of the majority of EC ministers for a general political settlement under the Carrington Plan.

As early as July 2, 1991, a week after the Slovene and Croatian declarations of independence, Germany publicly criticized EC policy on Yugoslav unity and, in opposition to this policy, promoted Croatian sovereignty. Against French President François Mitterand and British Prime Minister John Major's support for the principle of Yugoslav territorial integrity, German Prime Minister Helmut Kohl touted Croatian independence, relying for legal support on the right of self-determination in the Helsinki Final Act, which Germany had previously invoked to authorize its East–West reunification.[35] The split in EC policy regarding Yugoslavia from this time forward was clear. At the time of the EC's first intervention in Yugoslavia when the ministerial troika negotiated the Brioni Accord of July 7, 1991, Germany nominally complied with the majority EC position supporting unity, yet simultaneously pursued its own early recognition policy against Yugoslav officials and in the international press. In early July 1991, Germany threatened to cut off economic aid to Yugoslavia if the Federal Presidency did not withdraw JNA troops immediately from Slovene and Croat territory. By August 1991, after the JNA withdrawal from Slovenia but not from Croatia, Germany enlarged these threats to include recognition of the sovereignty of Croatia. At all times, Germany's threats were intended to pressure Yugoslavia into a cessation of hostilities against Croatia, the same goal advanced by the EC Peace Conference; however, Germany's actions were not made in support of the Conference or in solidarity with the EC but toward its own political objectives. Later, when Germany set the process of unilateral recognition in motion, its actions were carried out despite their effects upon the Conference and upon the EC's position as chief intermediary in the Yugoslav crisis.

Carrington said on a number of occasions that Germany's unilateral recognition of Croatia destroyed the EC Peace Conference and any remaining chance for a general political settlement to the Yugoslav crisis. The German recognition, according to Carrington, removed the only incentive for Croatia to remain involved in the discussions for constitutional reorganization of the SFRJ. Furthermore, as a result of Croatia's independence, the recognition of republican sovereignty precipitated the escalation of the conflict from a constitutional crisis concerning republican secession from the SFRJ (with an undercurrent of Serb territorial aggression) to a full-scale civil war over the partition of the state of Bosnia-Herzegovina among its national ethnic groups: Serb, Croat, and Bosniak.

From the outset of its intervention in Yugoslavia, the EC as a whole followed a policy of withholding recognition of republican sovereignty outside of an orderly process of dissolution, for fear of the precedent that early recognition might set. Before the opening of the EC Peace Conference in September 1991, Germany agreed to a compromise with France, the United Kingdom, and the rest of the EC member states to hold off on recognition pending the Conference's outcome. This compromise was confirmed at an Extraordinary Ministerial Meeting of the EPC council of Foreign Ministers in Rome on November 8, 1991, where it was decided that recognition of individual Yugoslav republics could only be made within the framework of an overall political settlement that included guarantees for the protection of the human rights of national and ethnic groups.[36] The EC ministers at the Rome meeting also imposed trade sanctions against Yugoslavia, immediately suspending its trade and cooperation agreements and stripping Yugoslavia of its preferred trading status with the EC. The Rome meeting represented the EC policy of using, in lieu of its nonexistent military force, all available sanctions to obtain a cease-fire, while allowing the EC Peace Conference to proceed according to Carrington's protracted negotiations agenda. France and the United Kingdom believed that an early recognition schedule would simply accelerate the war in Croatia onto several fronts at the same time by causing the fighting to spread to all areas of Yugoslavia with significant Serb populations.

By contrast, Germany acted to obtain a cease-fire as quickly as possible through early recognition. Germany believed that early recognition would force the JNA to withdraw immediately from Croatia, and Serb irregulars to immediately suspend their localized attacks, because of the international protections against armed incursion and foreign occupation accorded sovereign nations. Despite the UN progress on cease-fire issues leading up to the deblocking agreement of December 8 and the Peacekeeping Operation Concept of December 11, Germany intensified its early recognition campaign for several reasons: The recognition deadline imposed pursuant to the Brioni Accord negotiations had terminated; Germany felt dissatisfaction with the progress of cease-fire on the ground; and political pressure for recognition continued to mount inside Germany.

Germany promoted the recognition timetable devised by the EC ministerial troika prior to the opening of the EC Peace Conference. The original moratorium on Croatian (and Slovene) independence negotiated by van den Broek, Poos, and de Michelas at the end of June 1991, in connection with the Brioni Accord of July 7, 1991, was for a period of three months. Germany argued that when this moratorium period expired during the first week of October 1991, Minister van den Broek brokered, on behalf of the EC Peace Conference, an agreement with Tudjman, Milosevic, and Kadijevic at a cease-fire track meeting on October 4 to further suspend recognition of Croatia (and Slovenia) for another two months from that date, but no later. Thus, as Germany understood it, recognition had been slated for the first week of December 1991. Furthermore, outbreaks of fighting attributable to the JNA continued throughout the Conference term and persisted even after the signing of the Geneva Accord. For example, there were additional JNA artillery attacks on Osijek, the capital of Eastern Slavonia, and naval shelling targeting Dubrovnik on December 6, 1991. Germany believed that recognition of Croatian sovereignty presented the only option for putting a stop to this ongoing aggression. Additionally, Germany took Serbia's rejection of the Carrington Plan for an indication of bad-faith negotiations, a "double strategy" of blocking negotiations for a political settlement while waging a war of territorial conquest against Croatia.[37] Germany also interpreted the Badinter Commission's first opinion, issued on November 29, 1991, concerning the questions of Yugoslavian succession and republican secession, to mean that the SFRJ was in the process of dissolution from a federal state into constituent components. But perhaps the most compelling factor of the mix was the mounting domestic pressure from political elites in Germany calling for Croatian recognition. After Croatia and Slovenia declared independence, the Christian Democratic Union, the Christian Socialist Union, the Social Democratic Party, and the Federal Democratic Party, all the major political parties in Germany, adopted a policy supporting recognition and pressed the German government to act. The reunification of Germany convinced the political elites that self-determination represented an antidote to Cold War ills. In addition, newspapers such as the *Frankfurter Allgemeine Zeitung* portrayed Croatia as committed to European values, i.e., democracy, and caricatured the Serbs as non-European communists. Based upon these factors, the German leadership (Kohl and Genscher, in particular) decided that recognition was timely, appropriate, and necessary.

During this period of UN cease-fire progress and increasing EC–German policy strife, the United Nations clearly understood the negative repercussions of early recognition and informed Germany of its position. Just after the deblocking agreement was signed, Secretary-General Perez de Cuellar dispatched a letter to Minister van den Broek on December 10, 1991, stating in explicit terms that premature, selective recognition of Croatian independence would lead to disastrous consequences for the EC Conference and for the Republic of Bosnia-Herzegovina.[38] Furthermore, Carrington knew that premature unilateral recognition of Croatia by Germany would effectively force the EC to pose the question of recognition to every remaining Yugoslav republic, and President Izetbegovic of Bosnia-Herzegovina could not refuse to declare independence in the current political climate of nationalist separatism and Serb aggression. Given that Bosnia-Herzegovina was composed of three nationalities, and ethnically dominated by Serbs, independence from Yugoslavia and Serbian hegemony was the only Bosnian option short of partition. Such a declaration of independence by Bosnia-Herzegovina would certainly trigger a civil war of great proportions among Serbs and Croats, each allied with their own national republic, and Muslims (Bosniaks) over territorial control of the Bosnian state. The reason that Lord Carrington had deferred questions of republican sovereignty to the second phase of the Peace Conference was precisely to suppress this sort of interethnic conflict from coming to the fore and completely destroying the frayed fabric of peace.

In the first week of December, Genscher announced to the EC that Germany had gained the backing of Italy, Austria, and, perhaps, Poland for its early recognition plan. After December 11, 1991, Genscher informed the EC ministers that

Germany planned to break ranks with EC foreign policy and recognize Croatian sovereignty unilaterally. In light of the impending German defection, the EPC Council of Foreign Ministers convened in an Extraordinary Ministerial Meeting on December 15–16 to settle the recognition issue between the German coalition and other EC member states. The risk of German defection presented a serious challenge to the spirit of the Treaty of European Union that was being finalized concurrently at Maastricht during the months of December and January. The Maastricht Treaty set forth terms of Common Foreign and Security Policy, among other fields of cooperation, among EC member states. In order to preserve the appearance of Maastricht unity before the final signing of the treaty on February 6, 1992, the EC foreign ministers finally capitulated to Minister Genscher's threat.

On December 16, 1991, the foreign ministers issued a set of recognition guidelines entitled "Conditions for Recognition of New States," and the EC formally invited all Yugoslav republics that desired independence to declare their intentions and apply to the EC for formal recognition by December 23, 1991. As a primary precondition of sovereignty, the Conditions for Recognition required that new states: (i) respect provisions of the UN Charter, the Helsinki Final Act, and the Charter of Paris; (ii) guarantee national and ethnic group rights and autonomy in accordance with the CSCE framework; and (iii) respect the principle of inviolability of borders and demonstrate adequate control over territorial frontiers.[39] The suitability of each republic's application for recognition under these guidelines would be evaluated by the Badinter Commission by January 11, 1992. In spite of the rules of democracy and human rights the guidelines advanced, Germany pushed ahead with Croatian recognition anyway, even before the results of the Badinter Commission evaluation. On December 23, 1991, Germany unilaterally recognized the sovereignty of Croatia and Slovenia, preempting the Badinter Commission's opinion as to their qualifications. When it issued its opinion on January 11, 1992, the Badinter Commission found that in all significant respects, Croatia failed, without reservation, to qualify for EC recognition under the EC guidelines. Concurrent with the issuance of the Badinter Commission opinion regarding Croatia, Genscher proclaimed that it did not legally have binding effect for EC member states, because it was a device of arbitration not of international law. And on January 15, 1992, the EC , as a whole following Germany's lead, recognized Croatian sovereignty despite the findings of its own arbitral tribunal.

Conclusion

The German early recognition policy was not instrumental to attaining a cease-fire in Croatia, although the cessation of hostilities coincided more or less perfectly with the recognition of Croatian sovereignty by Germany and the EC. Cease-fire was attained because JNA troops withdrew from Croatia and Croatian Serbs laid down their arms, pursuant to the terms of the UN Peacekeeping Operation. But the withdrawal of JNA troops must also be seen as part of a process of withdrawal and redeployment through which Serbian President Slobodan Milosevic was able to close down and contain one front, in Croatia, and open up another, in Bosnia-Herzegovina, within his systematic program of interrepublican armed aggression and conquest. Coincident with the Croatian recognition and cease-fire, Milosevic pressed forward with a military campaign in Bosnia-Herzegovina throughout most of 1992 and beyond, undeterred by the international recognition of Bosnian sovereignty in early April of that year. Recognition did not protect Bosnia against JNA and Serb-led attack (or Croat-led), nor would it likely have earlier protected Croatia unless there had been other strategic reasons convincing Milosevic of the benefit of withdrawal. Toward Milosevic's ultimate goal of consolidating Serb-populated territory for a new Yugoslav successor state,[40] the larger Serb territory in Bosnia presented a major incentive to withdraw forces from Croatia under the then prevailing circumstances: (i) success of JNA's Croatia campaign, (ii) recognition of Croatian sovereignty, and (iii) implementation of the UN Peacekeeping Operation. After Bosnia, though, there was nothing left to gain.

Thus, while Germany's recognition of Croatia was no more than an accessory to the UN-backed cease-fire and withdrawal, it equally cannot be held responsible for the proliferation of the Yugoslav civil war into Bosnia-Herzegovina. The JNA's pattern was clear: intervene in republics that had declared sovereignty or that had responded militarily to Serb insurgency. Whether or not Germany and the EC had pressured the Bosnian leadership to declare sovereignty in December of 1991 by virtue of Croatian recognition, the issue of Bosnian sovereignty may have reached critical mass within the near term anyway, the only questions being how soon, under what circumstances, and with what repercussions. The Bosnian Parliament, for example, had already passed a resolution on Bosnian sovereignty on October 14, 1991, in the absence of Serb representatives, who had walked out in protest. Ethnic tensions on a local level had increased in Bosnia-Herzegovina during the term of the EC Peace Conference, and the radical-separatist SDS was gaining a greater ideological hold over the Serb population.

What influence the Peace Conference could have exerted upon these developments in Bosnia had Germany and the EC not recognized Croatian sovereignty depends upon several factors. The German "premature" recognition accelerated a process of dissolution that inevitably would have occurred, at least in part, and that was scheduled to proceed after agreement on terms of a general settlement under EC auspices. In general, the difference is one of degree of control over the dissolution process. Early recognition removes the opportunity that a mediator might otherwise have had to control the effects that recognition, in a particular political context, produces, which in the case of Yugoslavia were disastrous and inexorable. Carrington's deferred recognition plan tried to exert control over a high-stakes dissolution process distorted by interethnic enmity and conditioned by a history of violence involving local, republic, and federal actors. Clearly Germany's early recognition strategy eliminated in one move this entire mediation approach, and henceforward necessitated a much tougher engagement of Milosevic and Serb aggression than the EC was capable of pursuing but which may have been more appropriate all along. The EC's decision to generally extend recognition to those republics that desired sovereignty signaled the advent of a force-dependent phase of intervention requiring input from stronger mediation players than the EC.

However, if the focus remains on the EC's general settlement strategy as it was played out, the significant question is how much more effective the EC could have been in containing Yugoslav-Serb territorial aggression, in convincing Milosevic to accept a diplomatic settlement to the issues driving the Yugoslav dissolution, and, therefore, in averting Germany's call for early recognition. In this regard, the EC could have increased the effectiveness of its mediation effort in several ways: by threatening the use of military force; eliminating policy ambiguities among its member states and representatives; and addressing the interests, legitimate or illegitimate, of all the concerned parties, particularly Serbia's.

The UN Peacekeeping Operation clearly demonstrated the effectiveness of armed deployment in forcing JNA troops out of Croatia. Whether an earlier military intervention—that is, before JNA–Serb forces had achieved their tactical aims in Croatia—would have succeeded is debatable.[41] An examination of the long-term disposition of the disputed Croatian territory shows that the territory remained Croatian after the term of the Peacekeeping Operation, largely because the Croatian army substantially increased its strength in the interim. The Croatian Serbs could not match the strength of the Croatian army without JNA military support and Belgrade's political backing. It is unlikely that military intervention by the EC or the United Nations would have prevented the Bosnian war had the EC been capable of making a credible military threat against the JNA and Milosevic, since the Republic of Bosnia-Herzegovina, where the issues that drove dissolution forward were magnified, represented the true core of the Yugoslav conflict. It is more likely that an earlier threat of military intervention could have bought enough time for Carrington to force further political concessions from Milosevic and impede the pace of conflict escalation, which would have given Western powers the opportunity to reevaluate their mediation strategy.

The EC mediation effort was also undermined by the ambiguity and vagueness of its mediation goals. The ambiguous policy positions adopted by the EC and its member states, supporting Yugoslav unity at certain times and self-determination at others, damaged the EC's integrity as mediator in the eyes of the Yugoslav parties. Furthermore, these policies were articulated as broad goals rather than specific actions that the EC required of the Peace Conference participants. For example, in February 1991 (and on many other occasions) EC foreign ministers called for maintenance of unity and territorial integrity for Yugoslavia, but on March 13, 1991, the European Parliament adopted a resolution reflecting the political positions of certain EC member states, saying that the Yugoslav republics should be free to determine their own future (i.e., self-determination).[42] This ambiguity and vagueness created uncertainties that "led each of the contending Yugoslav parties to believe that its actions would not be punished, but rather, that after a brief interval of time, they would be accepted and perhaps supported"[43] by the European governments. Such belief was not mistaken on the part of the contending Yugoslav parties, since it was grounded in opportunities for manipulating mediation outcomes in their favor produced by the broadly, ambiguously defined goals of the mediator.

The most prominent example of such an outcome was the laying of an early recognition foundation by EC mediators that allowed the Yugoslav parties to gain control over the self-determination issue, each in a way supportive of its own aims. The seed of early recognition was planted in the EC's official mediation effort during negotiations for the Brioni Accord of July 7, 1991. There the EC troika's official policy position expressed support for Yugoslav unity, but its contradictory actions as mediator helped a Slovene-Serb coalition attain de facto independence for Slovenia, without negotiating the specifics of Slovene self-determination or establishing the rules of self-determination as applied to the other republics or the terms controlling Yugoslav succession. This lack of specificity fueled both Slovene and Croatian secession, and the cause of pan-Serb self-determination. The resulting three-month moratorium placed upon the Slovene and Croat secessions imposed a separate, accelerated recognition schedule upon EC mediators. EC Minister van den Broek reinforced this schedule under the auspices of the EC Peace Conference three months later in an agreement among Tudjman, Milosevic, and Kadijevic that extended the three-month moratorium through December 1991. This time frame contradicted Carrington's settlement and contingent recognition schedule. Selective recognition played into Serbia's hands, because it cleared Serbia's path to Yugoslav succession. Germany's early recognition plan for Croatia was thus, in concrete terms, an outgrowth of a policy ambiguity existing within the policy-making institutions of the EC that had already insinuated itself into the EC mediation effort and been exploited by Yugoslav actors.

The primary reason for the EC's policy ambiguity was its relative institutional youth at the time of the Yugoslav crisis. In contrast to the UN strict rule-based procedures and broad mediation experience, the relatively young and inexperienced EC had not worked out internal rules of policy making and diplomatic procedures. The EC's diplomatic foundation remained strongly tied to an outmoded system of regional influence that put European powers into competition with each other over the sphere of influence that each commanded. As in the nineteenth century and earlier, such influence hewed along lines of long-standing imperialist alliances between individual European member states and particular Balkan nations. When Yugoslavia began to dissolve, the EC was not sufficiently institutionally developed in collective foreign affairs to have fully revised such regressive diplomatic concepts.

The final way that the EC's mediation efforts could have been improved goes to the heart of the reasoning behind Carrington's two-phase negotiation strategy. A phased negotiation strategy deferring hard or contentious issues to a later phase of negotiations may be appropriate when the contending parties have reached a stalemate or are fairly evenly matched in terms of their military strength and/or political legitimacy. They are therefore more likely to agree to first-phase concessions that reduce their leverage, or maneuvering room, with respect to second-phase, hard issues. However, when one or more of the contending parties is possessed of dominant military strength and cloaked in the trappings of state sovereignty, as Milosevic was with respect to Yugoslavia, a phased negotiation strategy may backfire. Dominant military strength cannot be easily reduced by negotiations. Such a powerful actor may refuse to be controlled by restrictions stemming from early-phase agreements, as Serbia did when Milosevic retracted his acceptance of the second of Carrington's three fundamental principles, if its later-phase interests are not timely, separately, or comprehensively addressed. A mediator must get at the interests driving the dominant military force, if he cannot counter that force, because an actor with overwhelming military strength will almost always pursue its goals on the ground if its interests are not being sufficiently addressed on the table.

Why Carrington refused to countenance Serb self-determination and Yugoslav succession, given the military strength that Milosevic possessed, is not hard to understand in relation to then prevailing standards of international law, but may have been a less than optimal negotiation strategy in the Yugoslav context. The mediation goal need not have been outcome determinative, such as partition or any other result that would have violated international legal standards, but purely strategic. By discussing Serbia's unconscionable interests, Carrington could have sized up Milosevic's ultimate aims more effectively and discerned where he might have been willing to compromise. And—although this is unlikely in light of Belgrade's subsequent military campaign in Bosnia—he may have convinced Milosevic to quit pursuing his aims militarily and instead exclusively use the venue provided by the EC Peace Conference. The failure of the EC-brokered cease-fires signaled the need to fully discuss the underlying issues propelling the conflict forward. However, Carrington's branding of Serbia's interests as non-negotiable may have caused Milosevic to pursue Serb self-determination and Yugoslav succession by violent means all the more insistently. By suppressing Serb interests at the EC Peace Conference on Yugoslavia, Carrington's two-phase negotiation strategy may have heightened the urgency of Milosevic's pan-Serb military campaign.

Germany's early recognition seemed the only way to respond forcefully to Milosevic and other Yugoslav leaders in lieu of using military means, which the EC and its member states would not commit to using. But this is precisely what an early recognition policy implies: the use of military force, if necessary, to protect the sovereign state against invasion—the military force of one or more nation states. During the Bosnian war, other states such as the United States eventually stepped in to fulfill the military responsibility that the German early recognition policy had instigated. Henceforward the international community will think very carefully about use of early recognition as a diplomatic tool.

4

The Oslo Channel: Benefits of a Neutral Facilitator to Secret Negotiations

William J. Bien

Overview

THIS CHAPTER EXAMINES the remarkable breakthrough in the Middle East peace process achieved through direct, back-channel negotiations between Israel and the Palestinians, and the indispensable role played by the Norwegians who acted as architects, sponsors, and hosts of those direct talks. This case suggests that neutrality, above all else, is an essential trait of a mediator who seeks not to cajole or influence the outcome of a mediation, but to get the two sides talking. Significantly, in contrast to the concurrent Washington talks and the continuous active shuttle diplomacy carried out by the United States, the Oslo channel took place in absolute secrecy. Away from the daily media deadlines and the pressures of their respective constituencies, the two sides were able to build mutual trust over time. This trust enabled the mediation to develop from exploratory talks between unofficial emissaries of the parties, to full-fledged official negotiations in which the negotiators on each side were vested with the full authority of the highest Israeli and Palestine Liberation Organization (PLO) officials. The case is also significant in that neither a large power nor an international organization was involved as a sponsor or mediator. On the contrary, the Oslo Channel represents the success of a grassroots nongovernmental organization (NGO), which, working closely with a sponsor government, was able to overcome the political (and legal) stumbling blocks to commencing direct talks. Because of the unique and long-standing nature of the dispute, and the existence of the concurrent multilateral and bilateral negotiations in Washington, the facilitator did not need to carry carrots or sticks. The outcome of the talks was a framework for an ongoing process, the implementation of which would require the involvement and sponsorship of the larger international community.

Timeline

1948 State of Israel established.

1964 PLO established.

1967 Six-Day War. Israel occupies the West Bank, East Jerusalem, Gaza, and Sinai. United Nations adopts Resolution 242 calling for "establishment of just and lasting peace in the Middle East."

1968 Egypt begins "war of attrition" against Israeli forces in the Sinai.

1973 Egypt and Syria attack Israel on Yom Kippur. Israel prevails after sixteen days of fighting.

1977 Egyptian President Anwar Sadat visits Jerusalem.

1978 U.S. President Jimmy Carter mediates the Camp David Accords. Egypt and Israel settle the Sinai dispute and establish diplomatic relations.

1982 Israel invades Lebanon.

1987 Palestinian Intifada uprising erupts in the West Bank and Gaza.

1990 Iraq invades Kuwait. Under UN auspices, United States organizes military coalition against Iraq. Arab members of Gulf War coalition pressure United States to resume Palestinian-Israeli talks.

1991 **Mar. 6:** U.S. President George Bush announces that a comprehensive Middle East peace must rest on UN resolutions 242 and 338 and the concept of territory for peace. **March–October:** Secretary of State James Baker meets with Palestinian leaders in the occupied territories, including Hanan Ashrawi and Faisal Husseini. Syria, Jordan, and Israel agree to participate in Madrid Conference on Middle East Peace sponsored by the United States and the Soviet Union. **May:** Bush administration ties U.S. loan guarantees to Israel to a moratorium on Jewish settlements in the West Bank. **June–August:** Bush asks Congress to delay consideration of loan guarantees for Israeli settlements; Baker oversees selection of Palestinian–Jordanian delegation to Madrid Conference. **September:** Invitations sent to conference participants; Faisal Husseini on behalf of Palestinian–Jordan delegation reserves the right to raise any issue seen as important, including the right of PLO to be involved in later negotiations. **October:** Norwegian Foreign Ministry sponsors the Institute for Applied Social Science (FAFO) to research the economic conditions in the Gaza Strip. Terje Rod Larsen, director of FAFO, establishes diplomatic and informal connections with Israeli and Palestinian leaders that he will later rely on while facilitating negotiations between the two sides. **Oct. 30:** Madrid Conference begins, establishing dual tracks of multilateral negotiations and bilateral negotiations among Israel and its Arab neighbors. PLO indirectly supervises Palestinian members of the Palestinian–Jordanian delegation.

1992   **Spring:** Labor Party wins the Israeli parliamentary elections after promising diplomatic resolution of tensions with the Arab community. **May:** Norwegian Foreign Ministry arranges secret, exploratory discussion between Israeli Deputy Foreign Minister Yossi Beilin and Faisal Husseini, leader of the Palestinian delegation to the Madrid Conference. **December:** Labor Party introduces bill in the Knesset to repeal ban on meetings between Israel and the PLO. Exploratory meetings between later participants in the Oslo Channel secretly occur in London during a Madrid Conference Seminar. Israel's representative is a private citizen who is a friend of Yossi Beilin. Israel and the PLO ask the Norwegian Foreign Ministry to arrange back-channel negotiations.

1993   **January:** Norwegian Foreign Ministry authorizes FAFO to sponsor the negotiations. **Jan. 20:** First negotiations held under the cover of an academic conference. Israeli representatives are private citizens. **February–March:** Negotiations continue between Palestinian representatives and private Israeli citizens who secretly report to Yossi Beilin. Negotiators exchange draft versions of the Declaration of Principles. **March:** PLO negotiators state that they will not continue negotiating with private Israeli citizens. Rod Larsen unsuccessfully asks Beilin to upgrade the Israeli delegation by including government officials. Negotiations continue due to public messages voiced by Israeli and PLO leaders about the secret negotiations. **April:** Negotiations break down temporarily because of the absence of Israeli government officials. After confirming that the PLO chief negotiator was well placed in the PLO, Beilin and Foreign Minister Shimon Peres add Uri Savir, director general of the Israeli Foreign Ministry to the talks. **May:** Negotiations produce a revised draft of the Declaration of Principles. **June:** Negotiations temporarily break down. **July:** Negotiations resume but break down again. Norwegian facilitators intervene with PLO and Israeli leaders on behalf of the talks. Negotiations resume and continue intermittently throughout the month. **August:** Successful conclusion of negotiations about the Declaration of Principles. Foreign Ministers Peres and Holst meet with Secretary of State Christopher to request U.S. support for the negotiated accord. The three agree that the United States would show its support by holding the signing ceremony at the White House in September 1993. **August–September:** Intense negotiations over Israeli–Palestinian mutual recognition are mediated by Foreign Minister Holst, and finally succeed. **Sept. 13:** Signing ceremony at the White House.

Background

Pre–Gulf War History

In 1882, the first group of Jews returned to the area of Palestine in fulfillment of the new ideas of Zionism. This population movement has continued ever since and was greatly intensified as a result of the Holocaust. It has naturally led to tensions with Arab residents of the area. The shape of today's disputes over the West Bank can be traced back to the patterns of settlement in Palestine under the British Mandate between World Wars I and II and to the management of conflict between Israel and its neighbors since that nation's independence in 1948.[1]

At the end of World War I, the United Kingdom and France divided the areas of the Middle East, formerly under control of the Ottoman Empire, into spheres of influence. The area of Palestine became a British Mandate and, in the Balfour Declaration of November 2, 1917, the British government promised the Zionist community a Jewish homeland in Palestine. Jewish immigration continued, albeit slowly during this period, and tensions began to arise between the Jewish and Arab communities, with violent conflicts resulting in significant loss of life erupting in 1929 and 1936.

Through the end of World War II, the United Kingdom regularly adjusted its Palestine policy in favor of either the Jewish or Arab side, typically in response to and often provoking further conflicts. In response to the 1936 conflicts, the United Kingdom proposed partition, which at that time was summarily rejected by the Arabs. In 1939, the United Kingdom revoked its support and acceptance of the idea of an independent Jewish state and issued a new proposal for a commonly managed state to be organized over a ten-year period. The Jewish community saw this as a betrayal of the Balfour Declaration. At the end of World War II, in spite of strong U.S. support for the Jewish community and the establishment of a Jewish homeland, a cause which was bolstered by the horrific disclosures of the Holocaust, the British continued to view strategic relations with Arab Palestinians and surrounding Arab states as more important than those with the Jewish community. The result of British pro-Arab policies were frequent attacks on British forces by Jewish terrorists seeking independence. The British government concluded that it could not afford the military effort to impose partition on the Arabs, and in February 1947, they turned the issue over to the newly created United Nations. Although the UN effort was boycotted by the Arabs, a UN study recommended partition, and the General Assembly (under its authority over mandates) approved a detailed partition plan, General Assembly Resolution 181, in November 1947. The resolution, supported by the Jewish community, authorized the partition of the Mandate into an Arab state, a Jewish state, and an internationally supervised territory linking the two states on May 15, 1949. The British left.

Jewish and Arab communities jockeyed for influence and control over the territories that the resolution defined; terrorist actions by irregular units of each side escalated. After establishing control over the territory allocated to the Jewish community under Resolution 181, Jewish forces declared the independent state of Israel on May 14, 1948. Less than twenty-four hours later, regular armies of Egypt, Jordan, Syria, Lebanon, and Iraq invaded the new country. Although the Arab forces posted initial gains and the fighting was intense—costing more than 6,000 Israeli lives—the Israeli military prevailed and conquered not only the territory allocated to it in Resolution 181, but also significantly more, defining the effective territory of the nation until the 1967 war. An armistice—but not a settlement—was negotiated under UN auspices in the spring of 1949. Under the armistice, the Gaza Strip was held by Egypt, the West Bank by Jordan. These were among the areas populated by those Palestinians who had sold or lost their land, a group that increased over time as a result of Israeli policies favoring Jewish land ownership and discouraging Arab land ownership.

Three more wars took place. The first was in large part a response to internal Egyptian developments—in 1956, Israel joined with France and the United Kingdom to attack Egypt, which had nationalized the Suez Canal. Although their military actions were successful, the United States pressured them to back down, and a UN-supervised truce, including a UN interposition force, was imposed between Israel and Egypt in the Sinai.

The 1967 war contributed most directly to Israeli–Palestinian conflict over the West Bank. The period was one of great tension between Israel and its neighbors, erupting from time to time in border incidents and aerial dogfights between Israel and Syria. Egypt, encouraged and supported by the Soviet Union, made serious threats against Israel; obtained the support of Jordan; and, to pave the way for its forces, successfully sought the departure of the UN peacekeeping force from the Sinai. In the face of this threat, Israel preemptively—and very successfully—attacked Egypt, Syria, and Jordan, initiating what became known as the Six-Day War. By the end of the brief but intense conflict, Israel had pushed Arab forces out of the West Bank, East Jerusalem, Gaza, and the Sinai. It thus occupied many of the regions to which Palestinian Arab refugees had fled during the 1948 conflict. The future status of these occupied territories has dominated Israeli–Arab diplomacy ever since.

Later in 1967, as part of its ongoing effort to mediate the dispute, the UN Security Council adopted Resolution 242. The resolution called for the "establishment of a just and lasting peace in the Middle East," that would include the "[w]ithdrawal of Israeli armed forces from territories occupied in the . . . conflict," and respect for the "sovereignty, territorial integrity and political independence of every State in the area." It also called for a "just settlement of the refugee problem" and requested that the secretary-general promote the necessary agreements. A measure of the careful wording of the resolution is that the language dealing with Israeli withdrawal from occupied territories *in the conflict* was adopted after the Council rejected language calling for withdrawal from all occupied territories.

In spite of the UN effort and hopes that this resolution would provide a formula for peace through creation of an Arab community under some form of self-government in the West Bank in return for Arab recognition of Israel's right to exist in peace, peace efforts stalled, and the parties moved toward further conflict. Three years before the 1967 war, a number of Palestinian refugee groups had formed the PLO, led by Yassir Arafat, which made the destruction of Israel a cornerstone of its charter. Following the 1967 conflict, the PLO began to develop resistance efforts in the West Bank and organized a number of terrorist attacks. In 1968, the PLO began to operate out of Lebanon. At the same time, Egypt launched a "war of attrition" against Israel's defense forces in the Sinai, a conflict that ultimately involved airstrikes by both sides. Israeli forces also began to engage in regular conflict with PLO forces in Lebanon. Egypt and Syria then took matters into their own hands and attacked Israel on October 6, 1973. This surprise attack—coming on the Jewish holy day of Yom Kippur—presented a significant military challenge to Israel, which experienced a fallback before achieving a victory after sixteen days.

Shuttle Diplomacy and the Origins of the Peace Process

Through his "shuttle diplomacy" mediation efforts, U.S. Secretary of State Henry Kissinger played a key role in securing disengagement agreements between Israel and Egypt following the Yom Kippur War. His intense shuttling between the Israeli, Egyptian, and Syrian capitals reaped important early agreements that would establish the United States as the central mediator to the larger Israeli–Arab conflict and lay the groundwork for eventual discussion of the status of the occupied territories. In 1974 Kissinger also explored potential rapprochement between Jordan and Israel on the issue of the West Bank, but the time was not yet ripe for placing the status of the occupied territories on the table.

The Israeli political situation changed radically in 1977, when Menachem Begin's conservative Likud party defeated the Labor party that had led the nation since independence. The Begin government, much in contrast with public expectations, moved to settle the conflict with Egypt. Despite its defeat, Egypt had acquitted itself well enough in the 1973 war that its leaders were in a position of relative strength at home, and psychologically able to make concessions necessary to peace; they were also motivated by economic pressures. Further, Egypt had, in 1972, expelled Soviet military advisers who had been present since the 1950s. Egyptian President Anwar Sadat, in what became the key symbolic gesture of Egyptian–Israeli rapprochement, visited Jerusalem in 1977 and addressed the Knesset. His trip laid a dramatic foundation for a resolution of the dispute. President Jimmy Carter backed the peace effort with the full weight of the United States and served as the essential mediator to the 1978 Camp David Accords. These accords, reached through proximity talks hosted by President Carter at Camp David, established diplomatic relations between Israel and Egypt and provided a framework for the resolution of a host of issues between the two states and a first step toward reconciliation with other Arab states. As the first Arab state to recognize Israel, Egypt would play an important role in all diplomatic efforts to resolve Israeli–Arab disputes. The Begin government was also successful in reducing border tensions with Jordan.

At the same time, however, the Begin government took a maximalist position vis-à-vis the West Bank and immediately began a substantial campaign of Jewish settlement in that area. The creation of large-scale Jewish settlements in the West Bank would make it more difficult for future Israeli governments to appear credible in any discussions of reversion to Palestinian control. Not surprisingly, the disputes between Israel and the PLO grew in intensity, involving both conflicts in the

West Bank and attacks by PLO forces in Lebanon against Israel itself. Israel responded by invading Lebanon in 1982. The ensuing brutal conflict resulted in many civilian casualties and accusations of atrocities committed by Israeli allies in Lebanon. Although Israel achieved its immediate military goal, it paid a heavy cost in loss of public support, both among its own population and abroad.

Having been forced from its base in Lebanon, the PLO moved its headquarters to Tunis, despite the city's distance from the occupied territories. Although support for the PLO was strong within the West Bank, the PLO's distance—both geographically and politically—from the action became apparent when the powerful Intifada uprising erupted under local underground leadership in the West Bank and Gaza Strip in December 1987. The PLO later gave political and financial support to the Intifada movement, but the breadth of support for the Intifada challenged the PLO's monopolistic leadership of and grip on the Palestinian resistance to Israel's occupation of the West Bank and Gaza. New political groups with ideologies more extreme than the PLO's leading Fatah faction gained popularity in the occupied territories during this period, including the ultra-radical Hamas organization, which was supported by Syria and Iran. Chairman Arafat, however, used the Intifada to advance a new agenda for the PLO by sending representatives to the occupied territories to coordinate PLO actions with local resistance groups, such as the militant Muslim Brotherhood, and to shape the goal of the Intifada toward the establishment of an independent Palestinian state in the occupied territories that would peacefully coexist with Israel. More militant Palestinians, however, disagreed with this moderate solution and separatist groups like Hamas called for an Islamic Palestine with borders that would conflict with Israel's borders.

Israel's government, now a national coalition led by Prime Minister Yitzhak Shamir, treated the Intifada as a coordinated program of terrorism and regarded Arafat's proposal for peacefully coexisting states as a threat to Israel's territorial integrity. Israel responded with an "iron fist" policy that attempted to crush the popular uprising. The iron fist policy, however, carried a price. The Israeli army's repressive techniques—mass arrests, beatings, and tear gas attacks—intensified Palestinian support for the Intifada. International and domestic criticism of Israel's handling of the Intifada increased.

Throughout this period the United States pressured Israel to negotiate a resolution of the occupied territories with the Palestinian people. Prime Minister Shamir delayed such negotiations by proposing in 1989 that Israel would hold elections of Palestinian negotiators from the occupied territories; he slowly worked out the details of this proposal throughout 1989 and 1990. At the same time, his government continued to quell the Intifada and also to promote settlements in the occupied territories. The Likud party committee imposed conditions on Shamir's election plan, including a reaffirmation that Israel would not relinquish any land and that it would continue building Jewish settlements in the West Bank and Gaza. Palestinian representatives rejected the plan because of these conditions. Other efforts were made—Egypt's President Mubarak put forward a ten-point plan in 1989, and the United States pushed for a more procedural approach. Both proved unacceptable to the more conservative Israeli political groups.

The Gulf War and the Madrid Conference

Iraq's August 1990 invasion of Kuwait and the threat its force posed to overall security in the region, and, more immediately to U.S. ally and major oil producer Saudi Arabia, diverted America's attention from the Israeli–Palestinian conflict. In the ensuing Gulf War, the United States, through the formation of a UN-backed military coalition to counter Iraqi aggression, developed even closer ties to its Arab allies. At the same time, Iraq's open aggression toward Israel—including Iraqi scud missile attacks on targets within Israel—made clear that a conclusion of the war would require a more comprehensive settlement of the broader Arab–Israeli conflict. Saudi Arabia and Egypt led the Arab states in pressing the United States to pursue Palestinian–Israeli talks after the war was over. When a cease-fire with Iraq was reached, the administration of President George Bush, in close coordination with Egypt and other members of the Gulf War coalition, vigorously pursued a negotiated resolution to the conflict in the occupied territories. The total military defeat of Iraq had displayed the unsurpassed superiority of the U.S. military; the breakup of the Soviet Union left the United States in a unique position to wield its power to bring the parties to the seemingly intractable dispute together.

The Intifada in the West Bank continued throughout the war. Prime Minister Shamir continued his pro-settlement policy and resisted efforts toward any negotiated resolution of the Palestinian conflict. Chairman Arafat of the PLO, however, seriously weakened his credibility—both vis-à-vis Israeli moderates and the world community—by supporting Iraqi leader Saddam Hussein in the war against the U.S.-led coalition. Hamas, backed by Iran (which had fought a long and bloody war with Iraq throughout the 1980s), was given additional reason to distrust Arafat. This political miscalculation also cost him traditional supporters of the Palestinian cause in the oil-rich Gulf states. As a result, by the end of the war in early 1991 many of the Arab nations that had once provided significant financial support to the PLO had stopped or substantially reduced these subsidies. Faced with these problems, the PLO had to quickly reassert its leadership of the Palestinian cause before the new extremist groups displaced the PLO's leadership in the occupied territories. Thus, the PLO had much to gain by entering negotiations as representatives of the Palestinians.

The historical window of opportunity having been pushed open, President Bush reinvigorated U.S. policy toward the Israel–Palestinian conflict and took the lead in pushing for a comprehensive solution to the territorial issues. Before a joint session of Congress in March 1991, he emphasized that a comprehensive Middle East peace must "be grounded in . . . the principle of territory for peace." This statement directly challenged Shamir's approach to the future of the occupied territories. Later in the year, it became clear that the president might oppose new loan guarantees for Israel unless he obtained an Israeli response to his request for a freeze on new Jewish settlements in the West Bank. Although a show-down on this issue was ultimately avoided, the loan guarantees were an important leverage point for the United States: Israel needed capital to build housing for the new flow of refugees from the collapsing Soviet Union. Faced with this pressure, Shamir agreed to participate in an international conference aimed at addressing the Arab–Israeli conflict in a comprehensive structure that would also address a host of other regional issues. Shamir continued to resist, however, any suggestion that Israel would trade any of the land it had occupied since the 1967 war for peace with its neighbors—the so-called "land for peace" requirement. He also refused to negotiate directly with any members of the PLO.

Secretary of State James Baker and his team, organizing the proposed Madrid Conference, therefore drew together a group of notable Palestinians who resided in the occupied territories and had only indirect relations with the PLO, including Hanan Ashrawi and Faisal Husseini, to serve as representatives of the Palestinian people. Because of his weakened political position, Arafat accepted the arrangement and the related requirement that the Palestinians participate only as members of a Jordanian-Palestinian team. This latter demand reflected Israel's fear that direct negotiations between Israeli officials and Palestinian representatives (even those not part of the PLO leadership) would be tantamount to Israeli recognition of Palestinian independence.

The Madrid Conference, held in October and November 1991, led to the Washington-based bilateral and multilateral negotiations between Israel and its Arab neighbors that continued throughout 1992 and 1993. The Washington talks made little substantive progress and served more as a public relations forum for the negotiators than as a forum for resolution of the conflict.[2] During the first eight rounds the United States sought to serve as a neutral facilitator and did not intervene on substantive issues until the ninth and tenth rounds in 1993. Faced with a breakdown in the talks at that point, the United States proposed a measure that addressed the parties' main concerns as a way to bridge the gap that separated them and to continue the negotiations.

This intervention demonstrated the difficulties facing a mediator intervening with the negotiating parties. In private conversations with Norwegian officials during the Oslo Channel discussions, Yassir Arafat exclaimed that over 75 percent of the text from the U.S. bridging proposal was taken from earlier Israeli proposals. In Arafat's mind this demonstrated significant U.S. bias in favor of Israel and against the Palestinians; he did not view the United States as being capable of filling the role of a neutral facilitator.[3]

Despite these difficulties, the Madrid Conference and the subsequent Washington talks were the essential backdrop for the Oslo Channel. First, these diplomatic talks weakened the normative barriers to bilateral talks between Israel and Arab nations that had developed over the past half century of conflict and demonstrated that Israeli and Palestinian representatives could negotiate with each other. They also provided a multilateral framework for organizing substantive areas of negotiation, such as water rights. Second, and more importantly, the Madrid Conference revitalized Israel's peace movement, which shifted the balance of power between the Likud and Labor parties. In the 1992 Israeli elections, societal fatigue with both the Intifada and its accompanying violence and the seemingly unending and unfruitful Washington talks resulted in the election of a Labor government, led by Yitzhak Rabin, on a platform that promised an Israeli deal trading the creation of an autonomous Palestinian region for the end of the Intifada within nine months after the election. Labor would make the "land for peace" deal that Likud had earlier rejected. Finally, the Washington talks provided the needed public distraction and "cover" to allow a secret channel to proceed undiscovered and unpressured by public scrutiny.

Form and Specific Mechanisms of Intervention

The 1993 Oslo Peace Accords earned late Israeli Prime Minister Yitzhak Rabin, former Foreign Minister Shimon Peres, and PLO Chairman Yassir Arafat the Nobel Peace Prize. The story of how the breakthrough to the Declaration of Principles—the essence of the accords—was achieved astonished the world community. Away from the bright lights and intense scrutiny of the public peace process that was being carried out in Washington, a small group of Norwegian, Israeli, and Palestinian academics began informal discussions that would culminate in the historic Rabin-Arafat handshake on the south lawn of the White House on September 13, 1993. The agreement paved the way for the creation of the Palestinian Authority and the establishment of Palestinian autonomy in Gaza and small portions of the occupied West Bank. The agreement would also prove fragile, and subsequent backsliding on both sides has frequently appeared to threaten an enduring settlement of the dispute.

Despite that fragility, the process begun in Oslo permanently shifted attitudes on both sides about what could be achieved. Perhaps most important, it overcame the seemingly insurmountable block of direct negotiations between the PLO and Israel—a key step toward eventual peaceful coexistence. The success of that psychological and behavioral transformation can be credited to the extraordinary efforts of the mediators of the Oslo Channel.

The Oslo Channel occurred in two distinct phases: the pre-negotiations and the actual negotiations. The pre-negotiations, which occurred between February 1992 and April 1993, consisted of the Norwegian intermediaries arranging face-to-face talks between representatives of the PLO and the Israeli Labor government and facilitating the initial unofficial meetings between these representatives. According to Terje Rod Larsen, the chief facilitator of the talks, the objectives of this phase were to establish trust among the disputants' negotiators, move the disputants' negotiators into an environment where they were insulated from the current pressures of their dispute so they could develop a commonality of personal values, and motivate the disputants' negotiators and their superiors to believe that a solution was possible. To achieve these goals the facilitators arranged meetings in a neutral, relaxed environment and deliberately personalized the relations between the negotiators.

The second phase, the period of actual negotiations, proved to be a critical time for the facilitators because the parties hardened their positions and closely scrutinized the other side's proposals. These actions exacerbated the tensions between the negotiators, and disputes occurred frequently; during this period the facilitators helped the parties resolve their disputes and achieve the solution they had envisioned in the pre-negotiation phase. The Norwegians' experience suggests that a facilitator's methods for accomplishing these goals are varied. As a preliminary matter the facilitator should maintain an atmosphere of calm. At times this was done by injecting some humor into the proceedings and at other times by spending equal amounts of time privately discussing each party's grievances with them. If the substantive efforts fail and the talks begin to collapse, the facilitator will have to use as leverage the respect and trust that the parties have developed for him during the pre-negotiation phase to persuade them to resume the negotiations. If the facilitator intervenes to keep the talks going while the parties are still present at the negotiating site, he can ask the negotiation leaders to review their differences one last time before leaving the talks. If this approach fails and the talks truly break down then the facilitator would have to travel to each party's headquarters to ask them to resume the talks. The groundwork laid by the Norwegians during the pre-negotiations was thus crucial to the success of the later substantive talks.

Pre-Negotiations

True to this form of laying the groundwork early, Norway's pre-negotiation of its secret channel began during the beginning stages of the Madrid Conference. Because it had already developed strong working ties with the Israeli government, the Norwegian Foreign Ministry focused on strengthening its non-governmental ties with the PLO. As will be explained below, relationships with NGOs were an essential feature of the Oslo Channel and are a common aspect of most Norwegian diplomatic efforts.[4]

In order to establish these ties, the Foreign Ministry partly subsidized an economic study conducted by a Norwegian think tank about raising the standard of living in Gaza. The think tank was FAFO, directed by Terje Rod Larsen. In addition, FAFO and the Foreign Ministry shared contacts they had made in the region. This cooperation began to pay dividends when Norwegian Deputy Foreign Minister Jan Egeland recommended that Larsen meet with Abu Ala, the director of the PLO's economic enterprises, who had authored a study about the economic development of the occupied territories. This meeting proved to be key; Abu Ala later became the leader of the PLO delegation to the Oslo Channel.[5]

The Norwegian Foreign Ministry explored the use of confidence-building measures while FAFO continued the Gaza study and developed further contacts in the region.[6] The Foreign Ministry also suggested to Israeli government officials and local Palestinian leaders that Norway could provide a discreet forum for meetings between the Israeli government and Palestinian leaders. The Likud government had not taken up any of the Norwegian offers. In May 1992, however, FAFO organized a meeting between Yossi Beilin, a Labor Party MP close to Shimon Peres who advocated direct negotiations with Palestinians, and Faisal Husseini, the leader of the Palestinian element of the Jordanian–Palestinian delegation to the Madrid talks. This meeting was important because it confirmed for Beilin that Israel would have to negotiate directly with the PLO rather than simply negotiating with notable Palestinian citizens if Israel was to resolve the conflict in the occupied territories peacefully. In their conversation, Beilin asked Husseini if the Palestinians in the occupied territories would support the Labor Party in the elections held later that month. Husseini answered that if Labor or the Israeli government wanted support from the Palestinians then Labor or Israel would have to ask PLO representatives for their support.[7] This answer was probably still fresh in Beilin's mind when he chose to initiate secret discussions in Norway between Israel and the PLO.

After the Labor Party won the spring 1992 elections, Shimon Peres became foreign minister and Beilin was named deputy foreign minister. Privately, both men entertained the idea of direct negotiations with the PLO. Although Prime Minister Rabin had promised that Israel would negotiate peace in the occupied territories in return for autonomous rule within nine months of the election,[8] they cautiously prepared for this possibility by first organizing support in the Israeli Knesset for repeal of the ban on meetings between Israeli government officials and the PLO. It wasn't until December 1992 that the possibility of a Norway Channel crystallized. That month the Knesset introduced the bill to revoke the ban on Israeli–PLO meetings and a close friend of Yossi Beilin, Professor Yair Hirschfield, privately met with Abu Ala in London. The Knesset repealed the ban in January.

Hirschfield and Abu Ala were both in London attending an economic development seminar associated with the Madrid Conference. Hanan Ashrawi suggested to Hirschfield (attending the conference as a private advisor to Beilin), that Hirschfield privately meet Abu Ala, who was present to guide (unofficially) the Palestinian delegation's participation in the seminar and in a discussion of Ala's paper on development in Gaza. Aware that it was still illegal for Israeli officials to meet with PLO officials, Hirschfield decided not to inform Beilin of the proposed meeting, and asked Larsen to organize the secret meeting with Ala. Impressed by Ala's ideas, Hirschfield later described the meeting to Beilin who suggested that Hirschfield and Ala continue their discussion in Oslo at a later time.

Uncertain whether Hirschfield represented an official probe by Beilin or was just a well-meaning private adventurer, Ala asked Abu Mazen, a high-ranking PLO leader who oversaw the organization's foreign affairs, for permission to continue this dialogue in Oslo. Willing to explore new options to the moribund Washington talks, Mazen authorized the meeting. In late December 1992, Ala asked Larsen to organize a clandestine meeting. A crisis on the ground, however, threatened to kill this back channel before it began. In January, Israel deported a large number of Hamas militia members into the Lebanese desert, a move that was quickly criticized internationally. Amidst escalating tensions on the ground, Egeland and Larsen persuaded Beilin to send Hirschfield to meet Ala secretly to begin discussions about the conflict.

Beilin gave the go-ahead for the talks that same month, and the Norwegian Foreign Ministry authorized FAFO to invite representatives of Israel and the PLO to Sarpsborg, Norway.[9] Larsen prepared FAFO for the first meeting of the back channel, which convened on January 20, 1993, under the guise of an academic conference about the living conditions in the Gaza Strip. The seminar was a brilliant cover for the actual negotiations that were to occur because it enabled all parties to deny the existence of the negotiations and to describe the meetings as academic exchanges.

The initial talks, however, were far from perfect. The asymmetrical delegations that each side had sent had made them inherently awkward. The Israeli team consisted of two academics, Ron Pundak and Yair Hirschfield, who were close associates of Yossi Beilin. Beilin had chosen them to serve as his proxies because of the official ban on meetings between Israeli government officials and PLO representatives. The PLO team consisted of high-ranking PLO officials and direct representatives of Chairman Arafat: Abu Ala; Hassan Asfour, Abu Ala's aide; and Maher El Kurd, an assistant to Arafat. The informal demeanor of the Israeli academics did not match the PLO's formalism. The academics' lack of official standing and inability to represent official positions exacerbated these stylistic differences and provided little assurance to the PLO that it was finally meeting proxies of decision makers in the Israeli government.

Geir O. Pederson, a Norwegian diplomat whom the Foreign Ministry seconded to the back-channel talks, explained that although both parties knew that Israel could not initially send official government representatives,[10] the PLO representatives did not want to expend effort and political capital talking to well-meaning intellectuals. Similar "unofficial" talks—between private Israelis and Palestinians and between Israeli officials and Palestinians who were not PLO members—had occurred regularly since World War II, with little substantive progress to be shown for the efforts.[11]

Despite these misgivings and the history of prior failed talks, Abu Mazen chose to send the PLO representatives to Sarpsborg in hopes that the Norwegians could eventually establish direct negotiations between the PLO and the Israeli government. Although the PLO representatives accepted that they would have to talk initially with just the two Israeli academics, they wanted reassurances that these men truly represented decision makers within the Israeli government. The Norwegian facilitators' credibility on this point was important. The Norwegian team reassured the PLO representatives that Hirschfield and Pundak were Beilin's representatives, and that Beilin, in turn, had a direct line to Peres. In addition, the Norwegians provided assurances to the PLO representatives that Prime Minister Rabin supported the Peres–Beilin decision to open the Oslo Channel. This was a particularly important point: Rabin was known for years as a hard-liner when it came to the PLO; the PLO was understandably skeptical that Rabin would endorse the talks.

Pederson notes, however, that the Norwegian team cannot be credited as fully responsible for reassuring the PLO. Instead, he believes the combined effect of Norwegian reassurances, PLO intelligence reports about Hirschfield and

Pundak, and confidence-boosting measures by the Israelis themselves improved Palestinian confidence in the Oslo Channel. Additionally, the PLO representatives may have reasonably concluded that Beilin had deputized Hirschfield and Pundak in response to Husseini's suggestion in his first meeting with Hirschfield that Israel should talk directly with the PLO about the key issues in dispute.

Disaggregation of Particular Elements

Acting upon Abu Ala's suggestion, the parties agreed at the start of the talks not to review the historical causes of the dispute but to consider instead how to build peaceful relations between the parties. To the Israelis' surprise, Abu Ala suggested that the peace process should start with an Israeli withdrawal from the economically depressed and crime-ridden Gaza Strip, a favorite proposal of Shimon Peres that the PLO had frequently rejected because they feared that Israel would hand over only Gaza and not the more prosperous West Bank. Most importantly, both sides agreed to negotiate a declaration of principles on the issues that divided them and on the future interaction between the PLO and Israel.

The negotiations continued in February and March. After receiving approval for further negotiations both teams returned to Norway in February and drafted a rough version of the Declaration of Principles. This draft set the terms for an autonomous Palestinian authority and a framework for a final resolution of the dispute. The draft also introduced the concepts of a gradual return of occupied land to Palestinian control and Palestinian governance of civil affairs within the occupied territories.[12] The negotiations, however, stalled in March because of the negative effects of violent unrest in the occupied territories and the PLO's concern that Israeli government officials were still absent from the talks.

Feeling that they had exhausted the potential of meeting informally with private citizens, the Palestinians threatened not to return for later rounds unless the Israeli delegation included government officials. Later that month, Larsen traveled to Tel Aviv to ask Beilin to add government representatives to the Israeli team. Beilin was unable to comply. Despite this failure, public comments obliquely supportive of the proposals made in the Oslo Channel by both Rabin and Arafat encouraged both teams to return to Norway.

This optimism proved short-lived. In April, at the fourth meeting of the negotiators, the asymmetry of the negotiating teams continued to create a problem for Abu Ala. Larsen stepped in at this critical juncture to facilitate a resolution of this procedural issue that was threatening the future of the talks. Beilin agreed to honor Abu Ala's request if Ala could prove that he had a large degree of influence over the PLO's internal and foreign affairs. Larsen then arranged for a test of Ala's control of Palestinian negotiators involved in a multilateral round of the Madrid Conference discussing refugee affairs. The test was simple in theory but difficult to implement. Beilin secretly forwarded a text to Larsen for delivery to Ala. Ala was asked to ensure that the Palestinian delegation sponsor this text in the refugee negotiations. Given the tight time frames of the exchange, Larsen barely succeeded, but the Palestinian team at the refugee talks unknowingly approved a passage drafted by the Israeli Foreign Ministry.[13] Satisfied by this demonstration of control, Beilin asked Foreign Minister Peres to upgrade the Israeli delegation. On May 15, Peres and Prime Minister Rabin agreed to send Uri Savir, the newly appointed director general of the Foreign Ministry, to the next Oslo negotiation.

Key Interventions and Major Actors

Actual Negotiations: Israeli Security Placed on the Table

With the addition of Uri Savir to the talks, the back channel changed from exploratory discussions to official "government to government" negotiations, and thus entered the second phase: actual negotiations. At his first meeting with the Palestinian negotiators in May 1993, Savir took a hard line and explained to Abu Ala that, above all else, security was Israel's main concern and that Israel would insist on retaining control of security powers related to the occupied territories. Moreover, he stated that any agreement between the parties should exclude a resolution of Palestinian claims to Jerusalem. After consulting with Abu Mazen by phone, Abu Ala accepted both requests, which impressed Savir. Given the polemic discussion of these issues in the public Washington negotiations, Savir had not expected the PLO representatives to accede so quickly or willingly to these demands as preconditions to negotiations about Palestinian autonomy.

After the session ended Savir asked Peres to add an experienced international attorney to the Israeli team so that the parties could negotiate a legally sound agreement. Working cooperatively, Peres and Rabin appointed Yoel Singer, a former military associate of Rabin who had participated extensively in earlier Middle Eastern negotiations. Singer reviewed the draft Declaration of Principles produced in the second session of the back channel and declared it an unworkable document. Nevertheless, Savir's description of the PLO representatives' views about Israeli–PLO cooperation impressed Singer as the basis for a sound agreement; he agreed to attend the next negotiation.

At the June meeting Singer startled the Palestinian side because he relentlessly questioned Abu Ala about the practical details concerning the framework concepts the parties had discussed earlier. For two days Singer queried Ala about the practical details of implementing an autonomous Palestinian government and the willingness of the PLO to concede Israeli control over Israeli settlements in the West Bank. After the negotiations Abu Ala and Abu Mazen concluded that this extensive questioning and his prior military association with Rabin meant that Singer was Rabin's representative at the talks and that Rabin was now extremely interested in the channel.

After the meeting, Singer drafted a new Declaration of Principles based on Ala's responses and on the issues raised in the public Washington talks.[14] This new declaration, presented to the Palestinians on July 3, 1993, shocked the

Palestinian team. From their perspective this new draft contradicted the earlier draft and rejected all the Palestinian input into the first draft. The Palestinians felt a sharp betrayal of the trust they had begun to develop with the Israeli team. Despite some efforts to overcome the ensuing arguments over the drafts, the talks began to break down again.[15]

Both teams returned home to confer with their superiors about what to do next. Although discouraged, the teams returned to Norway on July 10, 1993, on their superiors' orders. The PLO team, however, chose to respond to Singer's surprise with one of their own. They introduced a twenty-five-point proposal for an autonomous Palestine and its relations with Israel and refused to discuss Singer's proposal unless the Israeli team first considered this new counterproposal. The key differences between the two proposals—the designation of the PLO as the governing authority of the new autonomous government and a demand that the PLO control a passageway between Gaza and Jericho—proved too large a roadblock to a resumption of talks. Both teams returned home empty-handed.

Following this breakdown, the Norwegian facilitators intervened on both governmental and nongovernmental levels. Foreign Minister Johan Holst, Deputy Minister Egeland, Pederson, Mona Juul (also an officer in the Foreign Ministry), and Larsen traveled to Tel Aviv and Tunis to confer with Rabin and Peres and with PLO Chairman Arafat about the feasibility of further meetings. In these meetings, the Norwegians encouraged both sides to continue the secret talks and resolve their differences. They also received letters of commitment to the process from Rabin and Arafat and conveyed them between these leaders. In addition, Larsen and Juul answered endless telephone queries by leaders of the negotiating teams about the other side's positions on the differences that had become apparent at the last meeting. After Larsen hosted a similar confidence-building meeting between Ala and Hirschfield in Paris, the teams agreed to return to the negotiating table.

The negotiators' work became even more difficult in late July and August. In the talks beginning July 24, 1993, the Palestinians refused to rescind their July 10 draft or to accept Singer's July 3 draft as the basis for an official agreement. The parties had little choice but to painstakingly review each text and compare the points raised in each draft item by item. After another day of unsuccessful talks, both parties threatened to withdraw permanently, blaming their mediator, Larsen, for the misunderstandings that divided them. At the brink of total collapse, Larsen drew on the personal rapport he had developed with Savir and Ala, the principal negotiators, to arrange an emergency meeting between them. During this meeting Savir offered a solution to the impasse: Israel would formally recognize the PLO in a separate agreement if the teams worked to reconcile the two draft Declaration of Principles.

To accomplish this latter task, Larsen suggested that the teams divide the remaining substantive issues into two sets: issues about Israeli security and issues about the transfer of Gaza and Jericho to PLO control. He also suggested that each team assume responsibility for revising one set so their superiors would find it acceptable. Savir agreed to assume responsibility for Israeli security issues; Abu Ala agreed to be responsible for Gaza and Jericho autonomy issues.[16] During the next two weeks both teams tirelessly reviewed and revised these proposals. When the teams reconvened on August 13, 1993, however, their work proved fruitless.

Although both sides now agreed to attach an agenda for final talks to the framework document (which began to be known as the Declaration of Principles), the parties could not resolve their differences over the timetable of Israel's withdrawal from Gaza and Jericho or resolve the issues embodied in UN Resolutions 242 and 338, which stipulated that all parties should return land occupied during war and respect each other's security needs. Another sticking point was how the election of leaders of the Palestinian Authority should be conducted in Jerusalem. This issue was especially difficult because Israel was concerned about the security of Israelis who remained in these areas after the withdrawal.[17] Abu Ala felt that he could resolve these remaining differences with a phone call to PLO headquarters in Tunis, but the PLO leadership rejected his proposals, and talks once again collapsed.

Active Mediation by the Norwegians during the Final Round

Two weeks later Shimon Peres reactivated the channel during an official state visit to Scandinavia. On August 17 he called Norwegian Foreign Minister Johan Holst and asked to meet secretly in Stockholm, Sweden, that night for a "make or break" meeting.[18] The Norwegian entourage quickly assembled to travel—in secret—to their neighbor's capital to meet Peres. The audacity of this move was worthwhile because it stimulated the final negotiating session of the Oslo Channel. Peres and Singer greeted Holst on his arrival and explained that they wanted to complete the negotiations that night so Peres could sign a treaty when he made an official visit to Oslo on August 19, 1993. Peres asked Holst to facilitate a telephone negotiation between himself and Singer and Arafat and the rest of the PLO's senior leadership to discuss the remaining divisive issues. Throughout the night and until the next morning Holst acted as the spokesperson for both sides by communicating both sides' proposals and suggesting various options that they could select. One by one, the sides resolved their differences on the security of the settlers, details of the transfer of governmental power in Gaza and Jericho, and the location of the Palestinian government (referred to as the Palestinian Authority, PA) headquarters. The terms of the Declaration of Principles were then finalized.

The Role of the United States

Almost immediately after the delegations had initialized the draft Declaration of Principles on August 19, Israeli Foreign Minister Peres and Norwegian Foreign Minister Holst flew to the United States to brief Secretary of State Warren Christopher about their success. They also asked him to pronounce the Declaration as a product of the Washington talks. Their request reflected the important role the United States had played and would continue to play as a close ally and financial supporter of Israel and as the one remaining power that could apply pressure to both sides to stick to the agreement. In addition, the request signaled that the negotiations between the PLO and Israelis would soon have to change from secret negotiations facilitated by a small country, whose main diplomatic asset was a low profile and the accompanying ability to keep the talks secret, to public negotiations mediated by a major power such as the United States, which could use its diplomatic, economic, and military resources to motivate the signatories to implement their agreement.

Although impressed by the Declaration of Principles, Secretary Christopher and his senior envoy for Israeli–Arab issues, Dennis Ross, recommended that the United States not take credit for the Declaration of Principles. In their view, such a move would be quickly seen by the media as an attempt to take the credit for work done by Norway. Christopher therefore suggested that the United States could lend support to the Declaration of Principles by hosting the signing at a public White House ceremony. The United States also agreed to participate in subsequent talks between Israel and the PLO. Additionally, Christopher and Ross suggested to Holst and Peres that Israel should include language in the mutual recognition agreement (which Israel and the PLO had not yet negotiated) requiring the PLO to accept responsibility for preventing "any violent attacks by its constituent agencies" before Israel would officially recognize the PLO.[19]

The meeting between Holst, Peres, and Christopher, however, was not the first time that the parties had briefed the United States about the Oslo Channel. Norway had frequently briefed U.S. diplomats during the pre-negotiation phase. In November 1992, Jan Egeland informed Dan Kurtzer, a State Department specialist on Middle Eastern affairs, that Norway had established ties between Israeli and Palestinian leaders.[20] Following the initial meeting in Sarpsborg, Egeland invited the U.S. State Department in January 1993 to send observers to the talks,[21] and in a February 1993 meeting then Foreign Minister Thorvald Stoltenberg described the progress of the secret negotiations to Secretary Christopher. At a later meeting, Foreign Minister Holst shared a draft copy of the Declaration of Principles with Secretary Christopher. The relatively quiet position that the United States took on the secret Oslo talks suggests that although American foreign policy makers might have seen the Oslo Channel as a promising forum, it was not a forum in which the United States could have participated (because of a policy of no direct negotiations or contact with the PLO), or indeed would have been an effective participant.

The Role of Other Third Parties

The United States was not the only third-party government tangentially involved in the Oslo Channel. Throughout the negotiations both the PLO and Israel relied on Egypt to confirm the political influence of negotiators who participated in the Oslo Channel and exchanged messages through Egyptian intermediaries. For instance, Israeli Foreign Minister Peres asked Egyptian President Mubarak to establish secret connections between Israel and the PLO during the later months of 1992. In April 1993, the PLO leadership asked Egyptian Foreign Minster Amre Musa to confirm that Israel truly perceived the Oslo negotiations as a serious endeavor. Additionally, the PLO later relied on Egyptian Foreign Ministry attorneys during the final rounds of the negotiations. The role of Egypt in Oslo underscores how crucial the resolution of the Israeli–Egyptian dispute through the Camp David Accords was to the ongoing process of finding a comprehensive solution to the Israel–Palestinian conflict.

The United Nations did not actively participate in the Oslo negotiations because the parties desired to maintain the secrecy and speed of the back channel. In retrospect this decision makes sense because it is unlikely that a large public body like the United Nations, which relies on the consensus of its members to make policy decisions, could support secrecy or speed in decision making. Nevertheless, the United Nations and the World Bank did become essential players in the implementation stage of the Oslo Accords, leading the coordination of international efforts for economic support of the development of the PA and fostering economic cooperation between the PA and Israel.

Mediator Takes on an Active Role

Foreign Minister Holst's involvement in the negotiations wavered between facilitation and mediation during the final negotiations in August concerning the mutual recognition agreement. Pressured by increasing press scrutiny after the August 19 signing of the Declaration of Principles and the approaching deadline of the mid-September signing ceremony at the White House, Holst directly participated in the negotiations between the Israelis and the PLO. Unlike Larsen's neutral facilitation, Holst recommended to the Palestinians that they accept Israel's version of the mutual recognition letter—the document separate from the Declaration of Principles dealing with recognition of Palestinian autonomy—because it was the best deal that they could get.[22] Although this move was necessary because of the time pressures involved, it was a risky tactic because it tarnished the Norwegians' neutrality, which could have developed into a rift between the PLO and the Norwegian team if the negotiations had continued later than expected. Because everyone knew that this was the final stage of the negotiations, they accepted Holst's intervention as necessary to overcome final disagreements. On September 4, the negotiating teams reconciled the remaining differences and finalized the mutual recognition letter.

Success of the Mediation

The Oslo Channel's limited success would not have been possible without the preceding changes in the political climate in the Middle East and the special efforts of the Norwegian facilitators. The Gulf War, the collapse of the Soviet Union and the Eastern Bloc, and political changes in the Middle East created a need in both the PLO and in Israel to address their dispute through diplomatic channels. Capitalizing on this new situation, the Norwegian facilitators created a special, neutral environment in which the Israelis and PLO could negotiate. The Norwegians' creation of a neutral setting and nurturing of common bonds among the negotiators during the pre-negotiation phase, and their later advocacy of the peace process during the actual negotiations, were necessary for the negotiations' success. The next section more closely examines how these factors ensured the effectiveness of the Oslo Channel and how the facilitators influenced the talks and resolved disputes between the parties.

Interviews with the Norwegians who facilitated the Oslo Channel suggest that the secret talks added two key elements to the political resolution of the Israeli–Palestinian dispute. First, the channel's secrecy enabled representatives of both Israel and the PLO to negotiate directly—which had never occurred before. Second, Deputy Foreign Minister Egeland believes that Oslo's secret meetings between the PLO and the Israelis overcame the problem that had hamstrung the Madrid–Washington talks: the lack of direct representation of the PLO. In his opinion, establishing direct negotiations substantially improved the chances of achieving a lasting resolution because, unlike prior attempts in which private Israeli and Palestinian citizens had discussed their dispute, the negotiators in Oslo could actually effect fundamental changes in both Israeli and Palestinian policy.[23]

Ripeness

Structural ripeness of the dispute was a necessary precondition of the Oslo Channel and distinguishes it from the public Israel–Palestinian talks held as part of the Madrid Conference. As William Zartman points out in his article "Explaining Oslo," ripeness was not present at the Madrid Conference at its inception in 1991 because a mutually hurting stalemate, a necessary element of ripeness, did not exist then.[24] A mutually hurting stalemate harms both parties enough to motivate them to resolve their differences as quickly as possible through negotiations.

Shamir's Likud government and the PLO were not equally hurt in 1991 and thus were unequally motivated to negotiate their differences. The PLO was highly motivated because unless it could quickly produce results at the negotiating table its weakened relations within the Arab world and the growing strength of the Hamas movement threatened to topple its leadership of the Palestinian cause. The events of 1990, however, had not maligned Shamir's government as much as the PLO—while the Intifada continued, his administration and the Israeli military still controlled the occupied territories. Shamir's major concern was to assuage the U.S. calls for negotiations between Israel and its Arab neighbors. Thus, as he had done in 1988 and 1989 through his half-hearted proposal of Israel negotiating with representatives elected by Palestinians in the occupied territories, Shamir acceded with the U.S. request to the point where he could deflect criticism of the settlement program in the West Bank. As a result, the Israeli team participated in the negotiations with the Palestinian–Jordanian team with the intent of "merely registering a presence" and not with the goal of resolving the substantive differences between the two delegations.[25] Ironically, Israel's participation in the Madrid Conference brought about a mutually hurting stalemate. As the Madrid Conference talks bogged down in Washington, popular Israeli opinion soured about the lack of success. Combined with the latent dissatisfaction about the ongoing Intifada, the discontent became a seed for change. In the 1992 national elections the Labor Party capitalized on those dynamics by making a quick diplomatic resolution of the Arab–Israeli conflict a central plank of its platform. After winning this election in the spring of 1992 the Labor Party had to consider serious diplomatic negotiations as a way to fulfill its campaign promise.

The stagnant nature of the Washington talks, however, meant that the Labor government had to consider alternatives to the Washington forum. Hence, its interest in the Oslo Channel. Concurrently, the leadership of the PLO was looking for a forum other than Washington where it could directly negotiate with the Israeli government. The impetus for this search arose from Arafat's need to negotiate directly and rapidly with Israel in order to secure his power over the Palestinian resistance movement and stature within the Arab community. The concurrent need of both sides to diplomatically resolve their dispute created a moment of ripeness for the Oslo Channel, which the Norwegian, Israeli, and Palestinian participants skillfully seized.

Added Value of the Neutral Facilitator

Ripeness by itself, however, does not guarantee a successful mediated resolution of a conflict.[26] The record of the Oslo Channel suggests that successful negotiations sometimes require an intermediary whom both parties trust as a neutral facilitator. Deputy Foreign Minister Egeland believes that to differing degrees, both the Israelis and Palestinians chose Norway to sponsor their back channel because its benign reputation made it a trustworthy broker. Both parties viewed Norway as a neutral host because it had maintained a positive relationship with Israel since its inception without ignoring Palestinian claims.[27]

Norwegian–PLO relations were positive because of the efforts of Norway's preeminent statesman, the late Foreign Minister Thorvald Stoltenberg. Stoltenberg visited PLO Chairman Arafat in Tunis for the 1981 New Year holiday, and during this visit Arafat asked Stoltenberg to assist the PLO in contacting the Israeli government discreetly. Stoltenberg's later 1983 attempt to arrange such a back channel failed, however, when extremist Palestinian assassins murdered the PLO representative before the meeting began. Subsequent to that attempt, Stoltenberg and the Norwegian Foreign Ministry maintained positive ties with the PLO, including donations of humanitarian aid.[28]

In addition to its reputation for neutrality in the Israeli–Palestinian dispute, Norway brought well-defined rules on how it would avoid taking sides and convince the negotiators that it would remain neutral throughout the negotiations. The foundation of these rules is a categorization the Norwegian diplomatic community uses to define different types of diplomatic intermediaries: passive technical hosts, active facilitators, and interested mediators.[29] A passive technical host merely provides a neutral setting and then disengages himself from the proceedings; an example of this is Switzerland's sponsorship of technical negotiations in Geneva. An active facilitator also provides a neutral setting, but in addition ensures that the parties develop personal and respectful relations with each other. Also, an active facilitator will serve as a personal conduit of information, referred to as a "go-between" by the Norwegian diplomats, between the parties during breaks in the negotiations. In contrast, an interested mediator is actively involved in the negotiations and is strategically interested in the negotiators' substantive positions. Such a mediation runs the risks of the parties perceiving him as biased.

Of these three types, the Norwegian facilitators consciously chose to remain active facilitators as much as possible because they believed that only the Israelis and the Palestinians could solve their problems and that both had relied too long on outside parties to force them to solve their disagreements.[30] According to a Norwegian facilitator, their constantly expressed commitment to neutrality convinced the parties that they were negotiating only the parties' interests instead of negotiating the parties' interests and the interests of the third-party negotiator.[31] The Norwegians took a highly active role in providing a neutral, transparent process. To reinforce this commitment, the Norwegians took great pains to stay neutral and not to show any favoritism, and to provide scrupulously fair procedures and support services. For example, they provided equivalent cars, drivers, rooms, meals, and other amenities. In addition, they accepted both parties' complaints about the perceived unfairness of the established procedures, allowing the parties to vent their frustrations at a third party rather than at each other.[32] These steps turned out to be very important, because Abu Ala, the leader of the PLO delegation, was extremely sensitive about procedural fairness.

Throughout the talks the parties instinctively tried to turn the Norwegian hosts into allies for their causes by asking them for opinions and interpretations of the other side's points or to suggest solutions for disputes. Except for Holst's action in the final round of the negotiations, however, the Norwegian team declined to take positions on any issue or involve themselves in any substantive way. This approach became very important during the actual negotiations when the tensions between the teams intensified. The Norwegians did not just passively observe the actual negotiations phase, however. Their involvement in the negotiations increased as they assumed more active go-between roles and employed leverage to induce the parties to continue negotiating. In between negotiation sessions, the Norwegian facilitators actively conveyed messages between Tel Aviv and Tunis. The Norwegians constantly confirmed with the sending party their understanding of these messages, in order to avoid showing bias or to be seen as biased by conveying incorrect messages that favored one side.

Their transferal of these messages depended somewhat on the messages' content and the actual context of the negotiations. If the Norwegians thought the elements of the messages did not have any value except to damage the other party, they would then try to screen these elements out of the messages they conveyed. They were aware, however, that they could not do this in every case. The Norwegians believed that each side's unaltered messages canceled each other out because each party used them equally.[33] During protracted disputes, the Norwegians also used the act of conveying messages to create positive momentum and to encourage the sides to meet again.

After the Israelis upgraded their delegation, and the negotiations intensified, Larsen and the other facilitators used moral persuasion as leverage to continue the talks. Larsen was the best suited to do this because of the close relationships he had built with the negotiating teams during the pre-negotiations. For instance, at a critical juncture in the July 24 meeting he persuaded Abu Ala and Uri Savir to return to the negotiating table, if only as a gesture to Larsen and the rest of the Norwegian facilitators. It is important to note, however, that Larsen only used positive messages to persuade the parties. He did not try to legitimize one side over the other by criticizing a team or by threatening that FAFO would not continue to sponsor the negotiations if the parties walked away, because he felt that these negative persuasive methods had limited long-term value.[34]

During the actual negotiations between May and August, both parties used coercive negotiating tactics intensively. In an interview for this study, Larsen recalled that some of these tactics included frequent threats to end the negotiations and abruptly depart if the negotiators could not resolve a heated conflict, Israeli threats to switch their negotiating efforts from the PLO to the Syrians, and the PLO's threats to resume the Intifada but to supply the Intifada resistance with guns rather than stones.[35] When these coercive threats frequently stalled the negotiations, Larsen and Juul intervened with both team leaders and persuaded them to resume the talks. These interventions included actual visits where they called upon the negotiation team leaders five or six times to plead for resumption of the talks.[36]

Larsen also allowed the parties to blame him for the breakdowns, letting them vent their anger and frustration at him and not at the other side. Larsen stressed that this type of action is critical for a facilitator's success. Above all else, he noted that a facilitator must not "lash back" at the negotiators, because he would then become a party to the conflict, jeopardizing his neutral position in any later talks.[37]

The Importance of Secrecy

Both Israel and the PLO knew that Norway had previously organized back-channel negotiations for international actors with publicly intractable differences. Through their contacts with the Norwegian Foreign Ministry and Norwegian NGOs like FAFO, both Israel and the PLO knew that Norway was willing to capitalize on its isolated location to host negotiations that could easily evade media scrutiny. In addition, all the parties knew that FAFO's involvement in the process lent plausible deniability to their discussions. According to Egeland, everyone involved in the Oslo Channel knew that if the negotiations failed, the Norwegian Foreign Ministry would publicly attribute the meetings between the PLO and the Israeli representatives to their participation in an academic seminar that FAFO had sponsored.[38] The plausibility of such a denial decreased significantly when the Israelis sent government officials to the negotiations because this action reversed years of political opposition to such talks.

Unlike the concurrent Madrid–Washington talks, the Oslo Channel was completely secret. The media and other political actors didn't expect Norway to serve as a back channel and didn't inquire about the string of seminars that FAFO held for the Israeli and Palestinian participants. According to one Norwegian facilitator of the Oslo Channel, it remained a secret until the final stage, and this secrecy allowed the parties to develop a common understanding, ignore current conflict between them, and avoid playing to the media. This secrecy, which is the hallmark of a back-channel process, also lowered the level of commitment each party had to make in the pre-negotiation phase. This lower level of commitment enabled the parties to freely explore untraditional solutions and to brainstorm together more effectively than their counterparts in Washington, who were negotiating publicly.[39]

In contrast, the constant media coverage of the Washington talks seemed to motivate the negotiators there to express their bargaining positions publicly. The media scrutiny also led participants to turn press releases about the negotiations into commentaries on political developments that occurred in Israel and the occupied territories during the negotiations. The press devoted their coverage to the most contentious points; this attention exacerbated differences between the parties. These running commentaries hardened bargaining positions and harmed the parties' perceptions of each other. In addition, the news coverage of the Madrid Conference exacerbated the constituencies' perception of the differences separating the negotiators.

The critical shortcoming of the Washington talks was the PLO's absence. The Shamir government's requirement that only Palestinians who were not members of the PLO and who resided in the occupied territories participate in negotiations with the Israeli government, and that they participate in the Washington talks as members of the Jordanian delegation, manifested Israel's long-standing policy of excluding the PLO and tacitly implied that Palestinians were citizens of either Israel or Jordan—not independent. Despite these intentions, the Palestinian delegation's need to consult with the Tunis-based PLO leadership on every matter of importance demonstrated to the Israeli side who the true decision makers were for the Palestinian people, and by implication, that Israel could not resolve the instability in the occupied territories without negotiating with the PLO.

This is not to say that back-channel negotiations by themselves can resolve long-standing complex disputes. On the contrary, the facilitators recognized that private, back-channel negotiations like the Oslo Channel should complement public negotiations or confidence-building measures like the Madrid Conference or the Oslo Accords' important symbolic public signing ceremony at the White House, because such public events positively influence the public's attitude of the negotiated resolution.

Participants in the Oslo Channel recognized the benefits of these conditioning effects. They thus had intended to use the Oslo Channel for candidly discussing solutions to impasses in the Madrid–Washington talks. In fact, when they began the Oslo Channel, both Israel and the PLO intended to feed proposals developed there to the public negotiations held in Washington. As the Oslo talks progressed, however, the parties recognized that the negotiations were much more productive than the Madrid–Washington talks and chose to turn the Oslo Channel from a supportive forum to the main event. Moreover, fears of leaks at the Washington talks motivated both parties to transform the secret Oslo talks into the main forum and to isolate it from the public talks. Both teams, but especially the Israeli side, feared that their Washington-based colleagues would leak sensitive details discussed in the Oslo Channel to the press before the negotiators could complete their deal. Once leaked, they feared these details would inflame the passions of opponents to the peace process on both the Israeli and Palestinian sides and cause the press to ask the Washington-based negotiators for comments on the details. Given the atmosphere in Washington, it was probable that these comments would lead to confrontations between the delegations rather than the constructive resolution of their differences.

Close Cooperation between States and Nongovernmental Organizations

The secrecy that surrounded the Oslo Channel was not a simple matter that the Foreign Ministry created by itself. Acting alone, the Norwegian government could not have achieved this secrecy because its sponsorship of successive meetings of PLO and Israeli representatives would have eventually attracted media attention. Instead, the Norwegian Foreign Ministry needed to cooperate with an NGO with routine operations that could shroud the talks in plausible deniability. FAFO satisfied this criteria because its academic research and seminars provided a plausible cover for the meetings between the PLO and Israeli representatives.

FAFO's role as the host of most of the negotiation rounds was critical to the Oslo Channel's success because it allowed both parties to deny that the talks were diplomatic negotiations and instead to characterize them as academic discussions, avoiding legal or political problems. FAFO also provided a truly neutral environment for the negotiations. As an NGO, it didn't have a reputation for bias or strategic interests in the region. Instead, along with Norway in general, it had a reputation for nonstrategic, humanitarian assistance to the region.

Until the Oslo Channel's final stages, when Foreign Minister Holst actively negotiated the mutual recognition letter between Yassir Arafat and Shimon Peres, the Norwegian Foreign Ministry and FAFO acted as equal partners. According to Mona Juul, this cooperation was necessary for the success of the process. FAFO provided the necessary neutral environment and plausible deniability

while the Norwegian foreign ministry lent the official support and status necessary to induce both parties to overcome their final differences.

Given the level of secrecy that the Norwegians created through this public–
private cooperation it is important to consider whether other countries could
achieve similar results using the same model. In other words, could other countries duplicate secrecy similar to the level that protected the Oslo Channel
through cooperation between their foreign service and NGOs? Since factors
unique to Norway had solidified this dynamic well before the Oslo Channel it
would appear difficult for a large power with less intimate relations with its nongovernmental sector to duplicate the Norwegians' success. In its dealings with
many areas of the world the Norwegian Foreign Ministry and Norwegian NGOs
symbiotically share financial resources, foreign contacts, and substantive expertise because Norway's diplomatic resources are limited. This mutual reliance may
be difficult to achieve in countries where governments and NGOs have a history
of independent action because of greater resources or legal restrictions on governmental contacts.

Conclusion

The aftermath of the Oslo Channel suggests that back-channel diplomacy conducted by a neutral facilitator with inadequate strategic resources may not motivate the parties themselves to implement the deal later. Unlike a strategically
interested mediator equipped with deployable military and economic resources, there is little that a neutral facilitator can later do to motivate the parties to fulfill the promises they had made in the agreement. In the context of the
Middle East, the Oslo Accords are a perfect contrast to the Camp David Accords,
where President Carter used both military and economic assistance as induce-
ments to the parties to later overcome their differences and implement the
agreement.

These shortcomings, however, should not deter future negotiators from using
back-channel diplomacy. Secret back-channel diplomacy enables the parties
privately to discuss the issues away from media pressure, and forces them to use
a small number of negotiators, thus enhancing the personal understanding that
disputants can gain of each other. Future intermediaries should keep the Oslo
Channel parameters in mind if they construct a back channel.

1. The disputants sent very small negotiating teams, three or four representatives each, to enhance the personal intimacy and secrecy of the exchanges between the negotiators;
2. The facilitators shielded the negotiators from the press, maintained an environment that forced them to interact together around the clock, and
   treated the parties equally on all procedural matters;
3. Especially during the initial phase, the facilitators attempted to manage the
   interactions between the disputants to ensure that they developed personal relationships and a common culture. To achieve this the facilitators

initiated conversations about characteristics that the negotiators shared in common, such as humor and families.

The objective of these steps was to develop a cohesive bond of shared values, communication phrases, and respect among the negotiators during the initial phase. Terje Larsen, the principal facilitator of the Oslo Channel, described the process as being one where he fashioned an almost tribal mentality among the negotiators, meaning that they treated each other as close colleagues and occasionally as friends who possessed conflicting goals, rather than as enemies. An interesting aspect of this humanization of the negotiating relationships was that the negotiators soon developed a private collection of jokes and phrases that they would use either to break the tension or communicate ideas in a shorthand manner during the later negotiation rounds.

All of the primary facilitators interviewed, including Larsen, Juul, and Egeland, also believe that the public Washington talks were a necessary prerequisite and backdrop to the secret Oslo Channel. Their collective remarks indicate that the Madrid–Washington talks were a major step toward the official direct negotiations between the parties that the Oslo Channel achieved. The Madrid-Washington talks were the first time that the Israeli government had publicly and officially talked with Palestinian decision makers rather than just vetting small groups of influential Palestinians in the occupied territories about the peace process.[40]

The Norwegian intermediaries expressed that, in hindsight, they view secret, back-channel diplomacy as a complement to, rather than a replacement of, public diplomacy. A serious weakness of back-channel negotiations is that secret negotiations do not "condition" the societies for the agreement and the compromises on each side that are necessary for dispute resolution. Only the political elite represented by the negotiators are given an opportunity to understand the need to compromise. Back-channel negotiations might more appropriately serve to complement public negotiations, which in turn can serve to educate the public on both sides of the dispute about the key issues and the likely points that must be reconciled. The internal tension to this point is clear: by conducting public negotiations, one risks the secrecy that is necessary for an effective back channel.

It is possible to measure the effectiveness of back-channel negotiations by determining whether they succeed in establishing direct negotiations between the parties and in setting the stage for later public resolution of the disputants' differences. The Oslo Accords achieved both these goals. The larger resolution of the dispute, beyond the framework of Oslo, has been left to successive agreements and negotiations between the parties, which as of this writing, are ongoing. The escalation of tensions between Israel and the Palestinian Authority since the Likud government took power in 1996 and the uneven implementation and partial backsliding—on both sides—on promises set forth in the Oslo Accords and the later agreements make it difficult to call the Oslo Channel a complete success as a mediation to the overall conflict. More specifically, the differences in Israeli opinion and policy about the Oslo Accords raise some questions about the influence of back-channel negotiations on societal attitudes about the dispute. The Oslo Channel in itself did not guarantee peace; instead, it created a foundation that the Israelis and Palestinians can choose to build upon or to tear down. The other benefit of the Oslo Channel was that it empowered the participants to negotiate their dispute without relying on intervention by a strategically interested third party like the United States or the Arab Council.[41]

The violence that erupted in the occupied territories, which has marred the implementation of the Oslo Accords, suggests that a single moment of ripeness may not provide a strong foundation for a complete solution of complex disputes like the Palestinian-Israeli problem. Nevertheless, as Oslo demonstrates, one moment of ripeness can serve as the essential first link in a chain of subsequent ripe moments that may lead to successful negotiations of the underlying conflict.

Part Two

Integration of Nations

THE CHAPTERS ON Cambodia, El Salvador, Northern Ireland, Rwanda, and South Africa illustrate the problems involved with resolving civil wars and protracted internal disputes and, in the unique case of South Africa, internal divisions and violence resulting from the apartheid system. The most difficult obstacle to overcome in these cases is often the zero-sum, winner-take-all mentality that is common to each party to a civil war. The mediation process requires shepherding the parties to a stage where they are willing to create a system of power sharing and full representation, using the mediation to build trust between the parties, laying the foundation for joint institutions, and beginning to establish reconciliation mechanisms. The journey from war to reconciliation can be challenging for both mediators and parties. Spoilers play an especially dangerous role in the resolution of civil conflict and can effectively derail a mediation process through propaganda or with well-placed violent attacks against military or civilian targets.

The period of implementation following cease-fire and framework agreements can be extremely fragile, with the potential (as in Rwanda) for rapid devolution into conflict, sometimes even bloodier than the original civil war. El Salvador and Rwanda illustrate polar examples of success and disaster in the implementation process that can be traced to the strengths and weaknesses of the underlying mediation efforts. Sometimes, violence in the implementation period can serve to bring the main parties together in opposition to a "spoiler," strengthening the resolve of moderates to continue the peace process, as occurred in Northern Ireland following the August 1998 bombing in Omagh.

It is striking in these cases that even in the post–Cold War period, regional organizations played a very minor role in the mediation processes. In Cambodia, the Association of Southeast Asian Nations (ASEAN) was consulted, but it did not actively assist the mediation. In El Salvador, the Organization of American States (OAS) did not command sufficient trust from the parties. In Rwanda, the Organization of African Unity (OAU), then under the leadership of Mobutu Sese Seko, had not been successful in facilitating earlier talks and was only marginally involved in the Arusha Accords. The OAU was also not involved in South Africa's extraordinary internal negotiations over the transfer of power. The United Nations played a supporting role at key moments in South Africa but was not actively involved in the substance of the negotiations. In Northern Ireland, the European Union did not become involved in the conflict, deferring to the sovereignty of Britain as a member state and its consequential right to resolve disputes within its jurisdiction.

In these cases reconciliation must occur not only at the governmental level, through the creation of new institutions for power sharing, but also at all levels of civilian society. While the mediation processes take the first critical steps toward peace, great attention must be paid in the postconflict phase to develop civilian institutions that promote ongoing reconciliation. In the cases of South Africa and El Salvador, truth and reconciliation commissions served as fora for uncovering the truth of the conflict, acknowledging victims and perpetrators of injustice, and promoting national healing through forgiveness. In Rwanda, international and domestic criminal tribunals were established to punish at least a proportion of the perpetrators of the genocide. In Northern Ireland religious groups and other grassroots organizations continue their efforts to bridge gaps between Catholics and Protestants. No institution can by itself ensure peace, however, and the failure of Rwanda and the backsliding in Cambodia and Northern Ireland demonstrate how the fragility of the postconflict stage can be shattered when the interests of all parties, including spoilers, have not been adequately addressed during the mediation stage.

5

The 1991 Cambodia Settlement Agreements

Tali Levy

Overview

IN ITS INTERVENTION to resolve the civil war in Cambodia, the United Nations entered in the form of the permanent members of the Security Council (P-5): China, France, Russia, the United Kingdom, and the United States. The mechanism was one of active mediation by representatives of the P-5, who negotiated a settlement framework among themselves, which was then accepted by the Cambodian parties. As in the case of El Salvador, Cambodia represented a ripe opportunity, in the context of the collapse of the Soviet Union and the end of the Cold War, for the former adversaries and historical sponsors (with the exception of the United Kingdom, which was historically disinterested) of the competing Cambodian factions to reach agreement on previously intractable issues. The war-weariness of the parties to the conflict left them more than ready to reach a peace.

UN resources, through the United Nations Transitional Authority in Cambodia (UNTAC) and the United Nations High Commissioner for Refugees (UN-HCR), proved invaluable for repatriation of refugees and administering elections. Issues of war crimes and amnesty were more difficult to resolve and went unaddressed by the United Nations. While this "housekeeping at the end of the Cold War" may have provided the great powers with an effective mechanism for resolving their interests and entanglements in the Cambodian conflict, the ultimate result for Cambodia has been less than successful. The study shows that the

P-5, when working together, can marshal considerable resources to build post-conflict economic and political structures. Nevertheless, without the active participation and consensus of the key players in the intrastate dispute, and without adequately dealing with potential spoilers, a solution imposed from the outside may prove unworkable once the outside sponsors withdraw from the process.

Timeline

1953 Cambodian independence.

1955 Sihanouk abdication; Royalist government.

1963 U.S. border incursions in Cambodia; Sihanouk cuts ties with the United States.

1970 **Mar. 18:** Lon Nol coup d'état; Sihanouk removed as head of state.

1975 **Apr. 17:** Khmer Rouge (KR) seize Phnom Penh, begin program of emptying cities; Establishment of Democratic Kampuchea (DK).

1976 Sihanouk to Beijing; Pol Pot consolidates power.

1978 **Dec. 25:** Vietnamese invasion of Cambodia.

1979 **January:** Vietnamese seize Phnom Penh, install Heng Samrin government; People's Republic of Kampuchea. **Nov. 14:** UN General Assembly passes first of a series of annual resolutions on Cambodia, calling for self-determination and the withdrawal of foreign forces. General Assembly requests the secretary-general to use his good offices in seeking a solution to the conflict.

1980 **July 13–17:** UN General Assembly's International Conference on Kampuchea attended by seventy-nine states, including DK, but boycotted by Vietnam and Soviet bloc states because of the conference's emphasis on condemning the Vietnamese invasion without mention of the Khmer Rouge genocide or human rights concerns.

1982 **June 22:** Coalition government-in-exile forms and occupies Cambodia's seat at the United Nations, maintaining the Democratic Kampuchea name. Sihanouk formally leads the coalition, which along with his party—the United National Front for an Independent, Neutral, Peaceful, and Cooperative Cambodia (FUNCINPEC)—includes the DK and the Khmer People's National Liberation Front (KPNLF).

1987 **December:** Sihanouk and Hun Sen meet in France.

1988 **January:** Indonesian foreign minister convenes continued "cocktail talks" between Sihanouk and Hun Sen. **July 25–28:** Jakarta Informal Meeting (JIM I) convened, bringing together the four factions, the Association of Southeast Asian Nations (ASEAN), and Cambodia's neighbors.

1989 **Feb. 19–21:** JIM II. **July 30:** Paris Conference on Cambodia is convened by France and Indonesia as copresidents, but fails to each a resolution on the Cambodian conflict.

1990 **January:** Representatives of the P-5 begin meetings on Cambodia in January, culminating in the August 1990 announcement of a framework to an agreement. **Sept. 9–10:** The four Cambodian factions meet in Jakarta and announce their acceptance of the framework and the formation of a Supreme National Council (SNC), the embodiment of Cambodian sovereignty. **Sept. 20:** UN Security Council adopts Resolution 668, endorsing the framework agreement. **Nov. 26:** Meeting in Paris, the P-5 and copresidents (France and Indonesia) agree to the draft text for the agreement, which is presented to the SNC in December in Paris.

1991   **Apr. 22:** Temporary cease-fire announced, taking effect on May 1. **July 16–18:** Beijing meeting in which Sihanouk is elected SNC president. P-5 plus Indonesia meet in Beijing with Sihanouk. **Aug. 26–30:** Pattaya meeting of SNC, with representatives from the United Nations, France, and Indonesia, with progress on military matters. P-5 plus Indonesia meeting in Pattaya. Joint meeting of copresidents, P-5, and SNC. **September:** November 1990 text revised; United Nations Advance Mission in Cambodia (UNAMIC) plans announced. **Oct. 16:** UN Security Council establishes UNAMIC, deciding to send it immediately upon the signing of the agreement (UNSCR 717). **Oct. 23:** Paris Conference reconvenes; Agreements on a Comprehensive Political Settlement of the Cambodia Conflict signed by representatives of nineteen states. **Nov. 9:** UNAMIC arrives in Cambodia.

1992   **Jan. 9:** UN Secretary-General Boutros Boutros-Ghali appoints Yasushi Akashi his special representative for Cambodia. **Feb. 28:** UNTAC is established by the Security Council. **Mar. 15:** The first members of UNTAC, under the leadership of Akashi, arrive in Cambodia. **Mar. 30:** The UNHCR commences the repatriation of 360,000 refugees along the Thai–Cambodian border. **June–July:** DK representatives first signal their intent not to comply with UNTAC and its demobilization efforts. **Oct. 5:** Voter registration period commences, amid continuing noncompliance of the DK.

1993   **Apr. 13:** The DK announces its withdrawal from the election process and abandonment of its Phnom Penh office. **May 23–28:** Elections held with 90 percent participation. **June:** Following the threatened secession in the east, prompted by the Cambodian People's Party's (CPP) failure to achieve a majority in the elections, Sihanouk announces the formation of an Interim Joint Administration between CPP and FUNCINPEC leaders Hun Sen and Norodom Ranariddh. **June 10:** Election results are released: FUNCINPEC wins 45 percent and the CPP wins 38 percent. **June 14:** The Constituent Assembly, reflective of the election results, is sworn in and begins constitutional deliberations. **Sept. 24:** Cambodian Constitution adopted. Sihanouk elected king of the Kingdom of Cambodia and announces the formation of a coalition government in which Prince Norodom Ranariddh is the first prime minister, and Hun Sen is the second prime minister. The Constituent Assembly becomes a legislature. **Dec. 31:** UNTAC completes its withdrawal.

Background

On October 23, 1991, the participants in the Paris Conference on Cambodia signed the Agreement on a Comprehensive Political Settlement of the Cambodia Conflict.[1] While the signatories to the Agreement included four Cambodian factions, eighteen other states signed the Agreement, and the P-5 members were integral to the ultimate settlement. To a great degree, the Cambodia case represents neither mediation nor arbitration. Rather, the Agreement resulted from an outright negotiation between the P-5 members, each with different interests in settling the Cambodia conflict, in the context of extricating themselves from waning and increasingly anachronistic Cold War allegiances. The result of that negotiation was then presented to, and largely accepted by, the Cambodian factions.

The extent to which the Agreement was in fact accepted by the Cambodians is, however, questionable, as evidenced by the various factions' actions during the implementation of the settlement, beginning with the Khmer Rouge non-participation in the settlement and culminating in the July 1997 coup d'état. Although the settlement agreements had been heralded as a major success, exemplifying the new role the United Nations could take on in the post–Cold War world, critics of the settlement and its outcome foreshadowed the instability of the coalition government that emerged following the elections.

General Historical Context

The preamble of the Agreement specifically recognizes Cambodia's "tragic recent history."[2] To understand the conflict and its settlement, it is essential to outline that recent history and, stepping further back, the historical context that created the conditions for that tragedy. The following brief account pays particularly close attention to foreign involvement in Cambodia. Indeed, because this chapter focuses on the changing interests and alliances of states external to the internal conflict, it is important to highlight those states' involvement over time in Cambodia.

Cambodia is situated between Thailand to the west, Laos to the north, and Vietnam to the east, and its history is replete with border wars with its neighbors. In the early nineteenth century, Cambodia alternately fell under both Thai and Vietnamese control, cementing deep-seated national sentiments of bitterness toward the Vietnamese and subordination to the Thai.[3] Cambodia enjoyed a brief period of independence before its 1863 establishment as a French protectorate. France thus has had the most long-standing Western involvement in Cambodia and, indeed, throughout Southeast Asia.

The French suppressed a Cambodian national rebellion in 1886 and then bolstered their domination by crowning successive cooperative kings throughout the tenure of the protectorate. By the 1940s, French colonialism in Indochina was coming to an end. A royal death allowed the 1941 installation of a new king, and the French chose nineteen-year-old Norodom Sihanouk, with the expectation that this young monarch would be malleable and amenable to their interests and policies. But Sihanouk did not toe the line, and indeed turned on the French, extolling Khmer nationalism. By 1945 he declared Cambodian independence, which was ultimately granted in 1953. Sihanouk abdicated the throne and entered politics in 1955, forming a national front government.

During his rule, Sihanouk aligned himself internationally with China and domestically with left-leaning Cambodians. In 1963, he cut off U.S. military and economic aid; nationalized foreign trade; and by 1965, when the United States was fully engaged in the Vietnam War, completely severed diplomatic relations. Sihanouk proclaimed Cambodian neutrality, but secretly formed an alliance with Hanoi. The North Vietnamese thereafter stationed troops in and shipped military supplies through Cambodian territory, leading to a U.S. response with the infamous secret B-52 bombings ordered by the Nixon administration.

Sihanouk ruled until 1970, when he was deposed in a coup d'état orchestrated by his prime minister, Lon Nol. Following the coup, Sihanouk embraced the Cambodian Communists, whom he had earlier christened "les khmer rouges." The United States supported Lon Nol, who presided over a notoriously corrupt government until the April 1975 Khmer Rouge seizure of Phnom Penh. The Khmer Rouge emptied the cities and initiated a radical and brutal agrarian revolution, accountable for the deaths of over a million Cambodians from overwork, starvation, disease, and mass executions. Although this ruthless regime's rule would later be referred to in diplomatic code as "the universally condemned policies and practices of the past," the international community at the time did not act to intervene in what is now recognized as genocide.

China and North Korea backed the Khmer Rouge, and its leader Pol Pot, throughout its reign of terror. The Khmer Rouge government, known as Democratic Kampuchea (DK), began mounting border attacks on Vietnam, leading ultimately to the late-1978 Vietnamese invasion and subsequent occupation of Cambodia, beginning in 1979 and lasting a decade. Following the Vietnamese invasion, hundreds of thousands of Cambodians fled to the border with Thailand, where 350,000 individuals who were not resettled elsewhere remained in refugee camps until their 1992 repatriation.

The Vietnamese-installed government consisted of former Khmer Rouge military commanders who had defected during the DK rule. Hun Sen, one such Khmer Rouge lieutenant colonel, came to power in the mid-1980s as prime minister of the People's Republic of Kampuchea (PRK), renamed the State of Cambodia (SOC) in 1989. The Vietnamese-backed administration had to face the fierce opposition of three unlikely allies, unified only in their hostility toward the PRK.[4] The Khmer Rouge had allied with two non-Communist resistance factions: the royalists led by Sihanouk and his son Prince Norodom Ranariddh, organized politically in 1982 as the United National Front for an Independent, Neutral, Peaceful, and Cooperative Cambodia (known by its French acronym, FUNCINPEC), and the Khmer People's National Liberation Front (KPNLF), led by the West-leaning former prime minister Son Sann and with links to the former Lon Nol government.

The PRK had to fight two sizable and exhausting battles against the opposition. First, a guerrilla war raged throughout the period. The Khmer Rouge continued to be armed and supported by the Chinese, who were strongly opposed to any Vietnamese efforts to establish Indochinese dominance, and Thailand, who feared Vietnamese expansionism and wanted to maintain a separate

Cambodia as a buffer between themselves and a potentially hostile Vietnam. Meanwhile, the royalists and the KPNLF, known as the non-Communist resistance (NCR), were funded by the West, with backing by the United States, France, and the United Kingdom, as well as the member states of ASEAN.[5] Vietnam's support for the PRK was predicated on tremendous financial backing of Hanoi by the Soviet Union. Thus, Cambodia in the 1980s represented a typical Cold War proxy battlefield.

Second, on the diplomatic front, the international community, led by the United States—nursing deep wounds inflicted during the Vietnam War—refused to recognize the PRK, pointing to Vietnam's illegal invasion and occupation of a sovereign state. With only the backing of the Warsaw Pact countries, the PRK could not unseat the Khmer Rouge from Cambodia's UN General Assembly seat. Vietnam and the Soviet bloc states boycotted the 1981 UN General Assembly's International Conference on Kampuchea, which condemned the Vietnamese invasion of Cambodia without reference to the Khmer Rouge genocide or human rights concerns. The Khmer Rouge retained the seat until 1982, when the Cambodian government-in-exile, the Coalition Government of Democratic Kampuchea (CGDK) (composed of the Khmer Rouge, FUNCINPEC, and KPNLF), formed and took over the seat. The CGDK held the seat, under the name "Democratic Kampuchea" until the 1991 signing of the Paris Peace Agreement. Throughout the 1980s, the international community therefore found itself in the awkward and uncomfortable position of favoring the notorious and genocidal Khmer Rouge over the illegal Vietnamese occupiers.

Negotiation and Mediation History

The ultimate success in achieving the 1991 Agreement must be seen as the culmination of a long diplomatic process. Earlier efforts, both regional and international, had failed. But at each step, the issues became more clearly focused, narrowing the agenda and setting the stage for the final settlement.

Efforts at mediation of the Cambodia conflict began in the early 1980s, with Rafeeuddin Ahmed, the secretary-general's special representative for humanitarian affairs in Southeast Asia, visiting the region several times, and the General Assembly passing annual resolutions calling for peaceful settlement of the Cambodia conflict and withdrawal of foreign (read: Vietnamese) forces. The Soviet bloc countries voted against each of these resolutions. These early efforts proved entirely fruitless until 1987, when Hun Sen and Prince Sihanouk met in France.

Prior to the so-called "cocktail talks" between Sen and Sihanouk, the French had initiated discussions with Sihanouk in an effort to convince him that the French were serious and committed to mediating a settlement of the conflict. Sihanouk was initially reticent, arguing that China had been consistently reliable and hospitable to him. He was ultimately convinced that the French were serious and that Paris should be the location of settlement discussions. Moreover, Hun Sen and Vietnam refused any plan for Hun Sen to meet Sihanouk at his residence-in-exile in Beijing. The French offered Paris as a "neutral" meeting ground, given the equally large Cambodian and Vietnamese expatriate communities resident there.

Once the "where" had been agreed to, complicated issues arose over the "how": Should the meeting occur in a neutral place, or should Hun Sen call upon Sihanouk and pay tribute to him? Sihanouk insisted that Hun Sen request a visit, and Hun Sen acceded to the formality.[6] Thus, the process commenced with face-to-face meetings between Hun Sen and Sihanouk in Fère-en-Tardenois, a suburb of Paris, in December 1987 and January 1988. Though the meetings boasted no substantive achievements, the forum provided an opportunity for Sihanouk and Hun Sen to express their positions, paving the way for a regional effort at a settlement.

In the region, the Cambodians, along with representatives from the ASEAN states, Vietnam, and Laos, had their first opportunity to gather when Indonesian Foreign Minister Ali Alatas sponsored the Jakarta Informational Meetings (JIM I & II). Though the meetings, held in July 1988 and February 1989, did not come close to reaching an agreement, they set the terms of the negotiations and identified a need for international involvement in achieving a settlement. Indeed, the agenda at the JIM meetings foreshadowed the ultimate agreement, including discussions of a substantial UN role, though Vietnam and the PRK adamantly opposed such a solution.[7] Moreover, each meeting provided a forum for the parties to state their positions and concluded with Consensus Statements expressing the need to remain engaged and keep working toward an agreement.[8] The JIM meetings were essential steps in demonstrating to the parties that a negotiated solution was possible.

The parties agreed on the goal of achieving an "independent, sovereign, peaceful, neutral, and nonaligned Kampuchea on the basis of self-determination and national reconciliation."[9] The dispute centered on how to achieve that goal through an acceptable power-sharing arrangement. The CGDK, China, ASEAN, and the United States favored a quadripartite government that would replace a dissolved PRK and CGDK prior to the administration of elections. Vietnam and Hun Sen insisted on a quadripartite council, leaving the PRK bureaucracy in place up to and through the elections.[10] Advocates of the quadripartite government viewed this approach as an untenable legitimization of the Hun Sen government, fearing that any election administered with the PRK bureaucracy in place would give Hun Sen unfair advantages of incumbency. To the PRK and Hanoi, dissolution prior to elections would be unacceptably threatening as it might create a vacuum that would allow the Khmer Rouge to return to power.[11] Both plans envisioned a cease-fire, but a cease-fire would necessarily be predicated on resolving the deadlock over power sharing.

In 1985, Vietnam had pledged to withdraw all its troops from Cambodia by the year 2000. But by April 1989, feeling the press of sharply decreasing Soviet assistance, Vietnam announced it would completely withdraw its forces by September 1989. French Foreign Minister Roland Dumas responded by announcing that France would join Indonesia in cochairing an international conference on Cambodia.[12] The Paris Conference on Cambodia convened for a month in July and August of 1989, but despite high hopes, ended without reaching a settlement. The Conference's failure can be attributed to substantive and procedural issues, in addition to the unstable international situation—fissures in the Soviet Bloc and events in Afghanistan and China.

The main substantive sticking point remained the issue of power sharing among the four Cambodian factions, including whether the Khmer Rouge would be part of an interim government. Failure to reach an agreement on this point ultimately doomed the Conference. Other intractable issues included the scope of a UN role and the mechanism for achieving a cease-fire. Furthermore, Hanoi and the PRK insisted on attaching the label "genocide" to the 1970–75 Pol Pot rule, while China and the NCR complained bitterly about the extent of Vietnamese settlers in Cambodia.[13]

The first Paris Conference also faced procedural problems, faltering under the strain of so many involved parties and interests. In addition to the four Cambodian factions, the P-5 and twenty other countries were present. The rationale for involving the international community—so that the ultimate agreement would be witnessed and guaranteed—backfired in that too many countries complicated the work of the conference.[14] Seating the Cambodian parties at the Paris Conference emerged as a formidable problem, with disputes centered over who would represent Cambodia. Claude Martin, director of the French Foreign Ministry's Asia-Pacific Division, solved the problem by positioning the four delegations side by side, in order of age, behind a long blue sign that read "Cambodge" (French for Cambodia).[15]

Finally, the Paris Conference suffered from the unpredictable external influence of international events in Afghanistan and China. In Afghanistan, the Soviet-installed regime continued to hold out against the U.S.-supported Mujahideen freedom fighters. According to Singaporian diplomat Tommy Koh, Hanoi may have seen this as an analog and assurance that the PRK too would survive against the opposition.[16] Additionally, the Tiananmen Square massacre, which occurred immediately preceding the conference, altered the dynamic between Vietnam and China at the conference.[17] Following Tiananmen, the international community had given China the diplomatic cold shoulder. China was therefore pleased to be invited to an international meeting. Prior to Tiananmen, China had little incentive to engage the Vietnamese in negotiations.

The Vietnamese announcement of a September 1989 troop pull-out further altered the landscape of the negotiations, both for the SOC and the international community, which had long held the Vietnamese occupation as the major impediment to a settlement. According to one French official, the Chinese had assumed that in one to two years they would be in a better position to negotiate with Vietnam. However, post-Tiananmen, the Chinese could no longer afford to stall Cambodia negotiations, since this was the one arena where the international community was not shunning them. Hanoi, acting on this weakened Chinese position, miscalculated by assuming that China would accept any proposal and, in turn, force the Khmer Rouge to accept any peace terms. Thus, Hanoi and the PRK pushed too hard and refused to compromise, leading in large part to the failure of the conference.[18] As noted by Richard Solomon, then assistant secretary of state for East Asia and Pacific affairs and the top U.S. negotiator, the 1989 effort ultimately failed because China and Vietnam were constantly at each others' throats. Vietnam insisted on not stabilizing the position of Hun Sen. However, to the Khmer Rouge and China, allowing Hun Sen SOC authority only meant continued Vietnamese colonialism, an outcome they could not abide.

Prior to the Paris Conference, Congressman Stephen Solarz, chair of the U.S. House Committee on Asia and the Pacific, attempted in vain to convince the administration of President George Bush to adopt a new approach to the power-sharing impasse. While on a trip to Southeast Asia in the spring of 1988, Solarz visited Site B, a royalist refugee camp on the Thai/Cambodian border, and met with Prince Norodom Ranariddh, Sihanouk's son. Discussing the power-sharing problem with Ranariddh over lunch, Solarz thought of an arrangement that could "square the circle": a trusteeship under the UN Charter. A trusteeship would allow the existing PRK government to remain in place without the NCR accepting its legitimacy, while simultaneously allaying NCR fears of a rigged election. Moreover, the PRK could retain its bureaucracy while rejecting the quadripartite government proposal.[19] Though the U.S. administration did not embrace his idea, Solarz succeeded in pitching it to Australian Foreign Minister Gareth Evans. The two met in New York in October 1989, following the failed Paris Conference. Evans lamented the domestic difficulty he faced in supporting the quadripartite government solution—he had suffered severe criticism for supporting a plan that would include the Khmer Rouge. For Evans, Solarz's idea had substantive appeal and political attraction, and Solarz needed a figure with greater standing than himself to champion it.[20]

Evans went public with the idea in a speech in November 1989 and then dispatched Michael Costello, deputy secretary of the Australian Department of Foreign Affairs and Trade, to sell the proposal at thirty meetings in thirteen countries over the course of twenty-one days in December 1989 and January 1990.[21] Initially, the response to Solarz's proposal was tepid;[22] a trusteeship would be legally impossible under the UN Charter, which prevents the application of the trusteeship system to UN member states.[23] However, the so-called "Red Book" proposal that Evans had subsequently developed dropped the "trusteeship" phrase, substituting the idea of an enhanced UN role that would place Cambodia's civil administration under the supervision and control of the United Nations up to and throughout a UN-administered election. "Clearly," lauds Professor Michael Haas, "the Evans proposal had elements of genius: If the UN handled interim governance, the issue of power sharing would no longer exist."[24]

The P-5 members met in January 1990 to discuss the Australian proposal, thereafter taking over the primary negotiating role. The momentum had been building—from the initial core French efforts to convince Sihanouk to become involved, to the inclusion of Hun Sen, and then to an expansion to the other Cambodian factions. The hope had been that there could be an internal settlement, which could be ratified and guaranteed by neighboring countries and the international community. But the process had stalled in 1989. It was only after the P-5 engaged and seized the issue that the Cambodians were forced to reach an agreement. This chapter will focus on the P-5 negotiations, which ultimately reached an agreement centered on an enhanced—and unprecedented—UN role in establishing institutions capable of carrying out civilian reconciliation and nation building.

Key Interventions and Major Actors

Choice of Parties

From the outset, the SOC, the Khmer Rouge, FUNCINPEC, and KPNLF were involved and included in the negotiations. Each of the nongovernment factions' participation was indicated by their hope of gaining power through elections, and in the case of Hun Sen, legitimating his power in the face of a retreating Vietnam. Critics of the talks point to the inclusion of the Khmer Rouge.[25] According to diplomats involved, however, the Khmer Rouge had to be included because of the insistence of the Chinese. The Khmer Rouge, along with China, were in the strong position of playing the role of "spoiler" and blocking the settlement. But for domestic political reasons, the United States could not allow the appearance that the Khmer Rouge was being built up politically. Diplomats finessed the problem through "smoke and mirrors": the SNC ultimately included the Khmer Rouge as individuals, rather than as an organization.[26]

Everyone agreed that because of his status as a symbol of national authority, Prince Sihanouk would be the key to a workable agreement. Because he manifested legitimacy, no one wanted to play politics without the cover of his support. All the parties viewed him as the only person who could reconcile all the sides, indeed, as perhaps the only individual who could be a new Cambodia's legitimate head of state. Sihanouk had at one time been allied with or supported by each of the key parties in the negotiation, including France, China, and the United States.[27] Even Hun Sen recognized that because Hanoi installed him, he lacked legitimacy and thus would be unable to rule Cambodia alone. Without Sihanouk's participation, the Khmer Rouge fighting would continue indefinitely. The international community also recognized the importance of Sihanouk; the P-5 strongly urged the Cambodian factions to elect Sihanouk as president of the SNC.

Yet Sihanouk was not always easy to work with.[28] One U.S. diplomat described accompanying Secretary of State Baker to an eleven AM meeting with Sihanouk. Prince Sihanouk greeted Baker with a glass of champagne, which the secretary politely declined. Sihanouk thereupon set the glass down on the floor for his dog to lap up. Some diplomats—sometimes frustrated by Sihanouk's inability to focus on what would happen in Cambodia postsettlement (other than his luxuriating at the palace with morning champagne)—privately dubbed Sihanouk the "White Rabbit." Other diplomats, however, saw Sihanouk as the only Cambodian politician who had any vision for his country.

Role and Interests of the Key International Actors

Each of the P-5 states had complicated interests and roles to play in the negotiations. Aside from the United Kingdom, which remained relatively disinterested (but filled an important role because of its perceived neutrality), the remaining P-5 states each had ties to one of the factions. France, like the United States, supported the NCR (FUNCINPEC and KPNLF). China played patron to the Khmer Rouge, though it also had strong ties to Sihanouk. And the Soviet Union's interests lay with its client-once-removed (via Vietnam), the SOC. Simultaneously, however, each of the P-5, particularly China and the Soviet Union, wanted to extricate itself from its client and its prior interests, which in the winds of change in 1989–90 were fast becoming anachronistic vestiges of the Cold War. Regardless of their unconcealed desire to disengage from the conflict, both the Russians and the Chinese were motivated to secure the "best possible compromise for their client party as they were going out the door," according to John Bolton, who participated in the negotiations as the U.S. assistant secretary of state for International Organization Affairs.

Although the P-5 states were officially and technically mediators of the conflict between the four Cambodian factions, they were also akin to parties in a multistate negotiation. Other than the United Kingdom, each P-5 state had a strong interest in the outcome, and at one level they were negotiating the terms of their disengagement from the conflict. On the other hand, although each of the parties' motivations differed, each had a common purpose: to settle the Cambodian conflict. Richard Solomon likened the network of interests and shifting alliances to layers of an onion, with external diplomatic processes peeling away to expose internal political maneuvering at the core between China and Vietnam.

China

China's interests were perhaps the most complex of the P-5 states. Indeed, it is significant that three of the four assistant secretary-level P-5 representatives to the settlement agreement were rewarded by their governments for their efforts with immediate subsequent posts as ambassadors to China.[29] China's major interest was in preventing Vietnam from establishing Ho Chi Minh's dream of an "Indochina Federation" in Southeast Asia. Ultimately, China wanted to cut the Khmer Rouge loose, weary of continuing to support and be associated with the universally condemned pariah group.

Dating back to the Vietnamese occupation of Cambodia, China's interests in the conflict were motivated by Beijing's three overlapping objectives in Indochina: the reduction of a Soviet presence in the region and along China's southern periphery, a Vietnamese withdrawal from Cambodia, and the dissolution of the Vietnamese-backed government in Phnom Penh.[30] China made "normalization" and the holding of a Sino–Soviet summit contingent upon a Soviet cutoff of Vietnam's bankrolled presence in Cambodia. The Soviet Union acceded, leading to the 1989 announcement that Vietnam would withdraw its forces, and in May 1989, Mikhail Gorbachev went to Beijing for an historic meeting with Deng Xiaoping. Thereafter, China lost leverage against Vietnam, both because the Soviet Union had already accomplished the goal of Sino-Soviet rapprochement and because without the economic carrot, the Soviets no longer controlled the financial reins in Vietnam.[31] Accordingly, China's backing of the Khmer Rouge became its source of power and leverage in Indochina.[32] Nevertheless, by 1989, China had achieved two of its three goals.

Finally, immediately following the Tiananmen Square massacre, the international community shunned China—diplomatically, politically, and economically. Whereas Solomon viewed Tiananmen as playing merely a minor role in Chinese motivations to engage in the talks, John Bolton saw Tiananmen as crucial to Chinese actions. China found itself isolated, and the P-5 Cambodia process offered a way to engage the United States and others. In the Security Council, China would not have to face hurled insults of "Butchers of Beijing." Moreover, Bolton characterized China as being motivated less by the dynamic with Vietnam than by the ultimate desire to get out of their bad investment in the Khmer Rouge, which they viewed as no longer worth supporting.

Regardless of the consultation with and involvement of other states, Solomon stresses that the Vietnam–China issue was at the core. The settlement process had many godfathers, including the Australians and even the Japanese, but the real power issue was between China and Vietnam in the context of fading Russian influence.

The Soviet Union

The Soviet Union's interests have to be understood in the context of the fall of the Berlin Wall, and the rapid disintegration of the financially crippled and declining empire. Solomon recalled a conversation in the final stages of the negotiations when his Soviet counterpart, Igor Rogachev, complained to him of the Soviet decline. Additionally, the Sino–Soviet rift was warmer following Gorbachev's visit to China in May 1989. The Soviet Union was thus increasingly disengaging from Vietnam, and the decision to stop funding had led to the advanced schedule for withdrawal of Vietnamese troops from Cambodia. The Vietnamese were isolated because of the Soviet decline, yet the Soviet representative, Rogachev, represented Vietnam's (and thus Hun Sen's) interests in the P-5 talks. Vietnam was, in turn, motivated by the aspiration that cooperation in the Cambodia process would pave the way for full diplomatic relations with the United States and China, along with full economic and political participation in the international community.[33]

The United States

Numerous factors contributed to the increased interest of the United States in reaching an agreement in the Cambodia conflict. The United States had taken a "passive but supportive" role during the 1989 effort. Following the failure of the

1989 Paris Peace Conference, Secretary of State James Baker decided that perhaps the time had come for the P-5 to become involved. Moreover, following Tiananmen, the United States had no direct diplomatic talks with the Chinese; the Cambodia discussions were viewed as one forum within which to engage China.[34]

The instability in the region affected Thailand, and, more importantly, ASEAN. The United States, along with its ally Thailand, wanted to stop Vietnam's quasi-colonial involvement in Cambodia. As the Vietnam War and its aftermath came to a close, the United States had increasingly desired normalized relations with Vietnam. Lord Gilmore, the high-ranking British representative, expressed his constant sensitivity to the extreme difficulty the United States had in dealing directly with Vietnam, given the history, background, and depth of feelings involved.

Finally, a domestic element shaped the timing of U.S. involvement. Following the Tiananmen Square massacre in June 1989, Democrats in Congress had taken the offensive to demonstrate the Bush administration's insensitivity to human rights issues. Congressman Chester Atkins and Senator Alan Cranston, among others, were vocal critics with sizable Cambodian constituencies. For the Democrats, the continuing conflict in Cambodia became a human rights rallying-cry, and they pointed to U.S. complicity in its support of an arrangement that included the genocidal Khmer Rouge. Moreover, because of the vacuum left by the Vietnamese troop withdrawal, there was a fear that the Khmer Rouge would rise again and the killing fields would reemerge. Richard Solomon recalled testifying before Congress during the period and "getting beat up" by questions about why the United States had not stood against genocide in Cambodia. Indeed, Congressman Jim Leach insisted that Pol Pot should be tried as a war criminal by an international tribunal, and 203 Congress members signed a petition pressuring Baker to cut the Khmer Rouge out of the deal.[35] A typical U.S. media criticism lamented the government's Cambodia policy: "While the Bush Administration refuses to consider dealing with the Phnom Penh government, it looks to the sponsors of the Tiananmen Square massacre and to the genocidal Khmer Rouge for commitments to an orderly democratic process in Cambodia."[36]

The Congressional Democrats preferred the Hun Sen government, but the administration viewed support of Sen as completely untenable. Solomon recounted a triumphant moment in Congress when Congressman Stephen Solarz humiliated Congressman Atkins by emphasizing that Atkins had no alternative credible settlement mechanism. Although Solarz and Atkins were both Democrats, Solarz grilled Atkins, exposing Hun Sen as a Vietnamese surrogate whose authority the Chinese would block at all costs.[37] According to Solarz, U.S. support for Hun Sen would have indefinitely prolonged the stalemate; the opposition would clearly never have accepted the result. Instead, Solarz argued at the time that the Khmer Rouge could be eliminated as a political force by in fact being included in the political settlement. Under a plan that would allow for free and fair elections, the Cambodian people could determine their destiny, and the Khmer Rouge would likely lose. History would bear out that desired outcome.[38]

Solomon credits Secretary of State James Baker with seeing the necessity of taking the political lead on the issue of human rights and of making it clear that the Bush administration was not soft on genocide. Thus, U.S. involvement in the Cambodia settlement talks gave the Bush administration an opportunity to get off the defensive. As long as the United States could work with the P-5 to keep the negotiations alive, the administration would be seen as involved in a process to undermine the Khmer Rouge, or at least not be regarded as collaborating with the Khmer Rouge.

France and the United Kingdom

France, with its long history of colonial involvement in Indochina, was arguably eager to get back into the region. According to rumors, the French made the symbolic gesture of digging up an old throne from a warehouse so that Sihanouk could sit with appropriate regalia, hearkening back to the days when the French actually seated Sihanouk as king. The French viewed themselves as proprietors of the process, and the other P-5 states acceded to their desires to conclude the conference in Paris, making it look as French as they could, according to Solomon. John Bolton perceived a strong French sentiment to validate their continued membership as permanent members of the Security Council through the use of the P-5 mechanism.

It was this motivation that led to France's enthusiasm to create and devise a role for the P-5 to find an answer to the Cambodia question. The P-5 talks were not derived from UN policy. Instead, the French pushed the idea and, according to Bolton, played on the Bush administration's fears of negative domestic publicity for allowing the specter of the Khmer Rouge to reemerge from the jungle. Gilmore gave the French, and Claude Martin in particular, far more credit as the conference instigator and "leader of the dance." He praised Martin's "remarkable performance" in using the British to play a mediation role because he recognized that the British had the least politically at stake.

The United Kingdom was officially disinterested in Cambodia. Gilmore, however, expressed the British desire to play a role in an international settlement, particularly one that properly used the P-5 mechanism to persuade the conflicting parties. The United Kingdom had a substantial interest in its dealing with the Chinese on the issue of Hong Kong. Hong Kong, at the time still under British control, was inundated with Vietnamese refugees, confronting the United Kingdom with difficult repatriation issues. Thus, the British generally hoped for greater stability in Southeast Asia. Because of the Tiananmen Square massacre, the United Kingdom's relationship with China was strained, and the settlement process offered a chance to engage the Chinese.

One of the most important aspects of the P-5 process was the possibility it offered the parties for a neutral, disinterested, balanced process for settlement. The United Kingdom, as the most disinterested P-5 state, took the role of the neutral party. To that end, Gilmore took upon himself the task of briefing the Japanese and the Australians throughout the process. Each time the P-5 met, Gilmore held separate follow-up meetings with high-level representatives from Australia and Japan. Because the P-5 needed the support of other interested major countries, he had to make sure that everyone remained in the picture to avoid a sense of grievance that the P-5 had taken over the process. Occasionally, Gilmore spoke to representatives of the ASEAN countries as well.

Australia, Indonesia, and Japan

Australia and Indonesia played indispensable roles in the mediation efforts leading up to the engagement of the P-5 mechanism (Indonesia through its role in JIM I & II and the cosponsorship of the first Paris Conference and Australia through its advocacy of the enhanced UN role). Though they were briefed throughout and contributed ideas, they were not actively involved in the P-5 process. But to the extent that the Framework Document reflected earlier narrowing of the issues, both countries played pivotal roles. Moreover, following the adoption of the Framework Document, Indonesia played a key part, along with France, in pitching the agreement to the Cambodia factions and securing the terms of the final agreement.

Japan, with increasing market interest in Southeast Asia, had an economic interest in Cambodian stability. More important, according to John Bolton, the P-5 had an interest in engaging Tokyo in the hopes that Japan would contribute financially to the proposed UN mission to Cambodia. Bolton recounted the repetitive and resounding Japanese response—"No taxation without representation"—in their continuing campaign to gain a permanent seat on the Security Council. Because of Japanese inexperience in international negotiations, they contributed nothing of substance to the mediation itself. But the desire for future Japanese commitment to Cambodia was reflected in the appointment of Yasushi Akashi as the head of UNTAC and the deployment of Japanese peacekeepers as part of the UNTAC mission.[39]

Form and Specific Mechanisms of Intervention

For a full decade, attempts at achieving a settlement had proved fruitless: UN efforts, regional diplomacy (JIM I & II were successful in bringing the parties to the table), and the 1989 French-Indonesian cosponsorship of an international conference had each failed to settle the conflict. Although these earlier efforts proved necessary in setting the terms of the debate, ultimately, the P-5 representatives, over the course of six meetings held in New York and Paris between January and August 1990, hammered out the Framework Document. The P-5 presented the Cambodian factions with the completed Framework Document, which the factions signed, and urged them to form a Supreme National Council (SNC) to embody Cambodian sovereignty during the transitional period, which they formed. The P-5 handed the task of negotiating the specific agreements back to France and Indonesia, cochairs of the first Paris Conference.

The P-5 took the initiative, with prodding from the French. According to Gilmore, Claude Martin and he came up with the idea of using the Security

Council, but getting out from under the New York machinery. Thus, instead of using their respective permanent missions to the United Nations, the P-5 states dispatched high-level diplomats from their capitals, and the P-5 talks alternated between Paris and New York. This entirely unusual approach meant that the representatives came directly from their foreign affairs ministries, giving them a freedom of maneuverability that would not have been possible in the more formal atmosphere of New York. Because the representatives were at the vice ministerial level, they spoke with authority that derived directly from their respective capitals. Clearly, the P-5 capitals would not have dispatched such high-level diplomats to lengthy international negotiations without the general will to work for a real solution and find a final settlement to the problem. Moreover, Gilmore repeatedly emphasized the importance of the personal nature of the talks, where the representatives all came to know and respect each other. It was crucially important to the achievement of a settlement that all the representatives got along. The shuttling between New York and Paris made the diplomats like a "traveling circus," and they shared in running "If it's Thursday, this must be New York" jokes.

France, the United States, and the United Kingdom conducted the majority of the work in the settlement talks, reflecting the routine operation of the P-5. Indeed, the British, French, and Americans always met first, before joining the others. They viewed their job as fencing in the Cambodians, while pulling in the Russians and Chinese. Bolton recalled someone drawing circles on a napkin schematically representing the P-5 dynamic: at the center a large circle with the United Kingdom, France, and the United States; two lines radiate out like antennae to smaller circles on the left and right, labeled "China" and "Russia."

During the P-5 negotiations, the Cambodian factions were only peripherally involved. The P-5 carried out their meetings in private, with each of the states briefing their client Cambodian factions, and Gilmore briefing the Japanese and Australians. The United States briefed the various NCR factions, whose interests were more or less aligned. Yet while Solomon deemed it necessary to consult with the NCR, the United States felt it would work out elements of the agreement that would protect the NCR interests. France kept Sihanouk apprised of the negotiations, but apparently Sihanouk lamented his noninvolvement in the P-5 talks, complaining that he didn't even know what the P-5 representatives were discussing.[40]

The goal was to keep the other interested parties, particularly the Cambodians, involved, but distanced from the negotiations. Gilmore attributed the failure of the Paris talks in 1989 to the fact that all the Cambodians were present. "From Sihanouk downwards, in mass ranks" the Cambodian presence made negotiation quite impossible. The resonant image of Paris in 1989 was the four Cambodian factions sitting side by side at a table behind the "Cambodge" nameplate. According to Lord Gilmore: "It was exactly the wrong atmosphere to get anything done because everyone was playing to his gallery. It was a recipe for no progress at all." As discussed above, the first Paris Conference indeed suffered from the presence of numerous parties, including the four Cambodian factions. But the dissent over power sharing was the substantive impediment to an agreement. In 1990, the P-5 avoided the substantive logjam by limiting the number of parties and focusing on the relevant issues: "To proceed to an end game, the issues and the actors needed to be reduced in number."[41]

Rafeeuddin Ahmed, as the UN diplomat involved, did not succeed in his early offers to the parties to use the secretary-general's good offices. Nor could Ahmed and other UN civil servants offer solutions that involved an enlarged UN role. According to Steven Ratner:

> The concept of UNTAC thus originated from outside the Organization, from several diplomatic players seeking a way out of the ongoing impasse. Indeed, this had to be so: Ahmed and his team could not have proposed such a far-reaching plan, for the permanent members of the Security Council would have likely regarded it as irresponsible for international civil servants to make such an overture. Just as had occurred with the Namibia settlement plan, the powerful and interested states had to design and back the idea first, with UN officials providing intellectual legwork, but not leadership, along the way.[42]

Indeed, according to Lord Gilmore, throughout the P-5 talks, Rafeeuddin Ahmed was informed of the progress of the talks as a courtesy, but was not at all involved in the negotiations. Ahmed, however, was "available in the wings"[43] to provide intellectual and logistical support. The United Nations played a significant part during the P-5 negotiations by dispatching fact-finding missions to study communications and infrastructure, existing administrative structures, and other important on-the-ground conditions.[44] Moreover, UN administrators in New York produced the working papers that facilitated and informed the work of the P-5.[45]

Though Gareth Evans's initiative broke the power-sharing logjam and instigated the P-5 process, Australia was largely shut out of that process. Australia provided working paper resources to the P-5, based on a fact-finding mission to Cambodia, and pledged $1 million to finance additional UN fact-finding missions to Cambodia.[46] Yet, "Evans was frustrated by the snail's pace of the peace process as well as a snub from France's Dumas that Canberra's work did not pass Gallic muster."[47]

Following the adoption of the Framework Document, the P-5 delegated to France and Indonesia, the cochairs of the first Paris Conference, the task of negotiating the Framework into an agreement.[48] Although the Cambodian factions extracted some changes—most notably the SOC's insistence on 70 percent rather than full demobilization[49]—the final agreement faithfully tracked the Framework Document.

Key Factors in Shaping the Result

"Fencing in" the Parties

Lord Gilmore describes keeping the pressure constant on the Cambodian factions, "fencing them in," and not allowing them "off the hook." But he acknowledged that the main incentive to the Cambodian parties was their acceptance of the fact that civil war could not rage forever and that outside benefactors would not support them indefinitely. Moreover, as discussed above, each of the parties had a stake in participating in the settlement talks because they each lacked a necessary element for total dominance in Cambodia: Hun Sen and the Khmer Rouge both lacked international legitimacy; the NCR lacked control on the ground. Thus, the fencing was predicated on the Cambodian realization that they *had* to come to an agreement—they were ready to have their arms twisted. Once the negotiations reached the level of P-5 involvement, the Cambodian factions knew they would not be allowed out, and were ready for a settlement.

Perhaps the greatest pressure came from the realization on the part of each of the Cambodian factions that international attention could not remain indefinitely focused on attaining a solution. The P-5 settlement talks were in some sense the ultimate appeal. On the ground, war had failed, and the parties were war-weary. Regional solutions had failed. The 1989 conference, too, had failed. The P-5 countries were now involved, offering the Cambodians their final shot at an internationally brokered settlement.

Indeed, each of the parties had internal incentives to cooperate. The NCR factions had every incentive to participate, as "the UN built them a game," according to Solomon. The NCR knew they would no longer get military support from the United States or ASEAN. Similarly, Hun Sen knew that the Vietnamese could not continue to maintain support for the SOC without commensurate aid from the Soviet Union. And, because of his party's decade-long rule, in which the party became entrenched down to the village level, Hun Sen felt confident he could win any elections. The Khmer Rouge knew they would lose Chinese support and therefore stayed in the game, notwithstanding their ultimate withdrawal prior to the elections. Thus, as each faction felt increasing apprehension that their respective patron states were disengaging and would no longer provide support, they feared that their enemy's benefactor might not. In that context, resolution of the conflict would be a less risky alternative.

"The Window of Opportunity"

In the Cambodia case, timing was crucial to the parties' participation in the settlement. But it would be an oversimplification to merely look to "ripeness" or war-weariness of the Cambodian parties. The extent of violence and war-weariness could hardly be exceeded in Cambodia. A civil war had been raging for over two decades, and 350,000 refugees were camped along the Thai border. Moreover, as discussed above, each of the Cambodian factions was facing the cut-off of foreign-supplied armaments and funding. Additionally, each party understood that it had some leverage, but lacked a complete set of advantages necessary for total dominance. The Khmer Rouge held the UN seat, but controlled only limited areas on the ground in Cambodia and faced tremendous international isolation and condemnation. The NCR had international backing, but neither political nor military power on the ground. And, finally, although Hun Sen held political power, he lacked either international recognition or control over Khmer Rouge-dominated regions of the country. For Hun Sen, the lack of international legitimacy, and the consequent inability for himself and Cambodia to be considered legitimate international players, drove his need for the process. Thus, internally, the conflict was certainly ripe for settlement.

But perhaps more significant in the Cambodia context was the dynamic at play at the international level. "The time was just right," reflected Gilmore, "it had come at a moment when people wanted to get this thing off their backs." The patron states' interests and desire to end the Cambodia conflict aligned, and, according to Lord Gilmore, Claude Martin recognized and seized the moment that the window had opened. The Soviet empire had unraveled, ending support for Vietnam. Simultaneously, Vietnam recognized the importance of compromise with Cambodia in pursuit of the greater prize of restoring diplomatic relations with the United States and China.

As the P-5 engine began revving, Washington proposed the "Baker Initiative"— a pledge for the United States, China, the Soviet Union, and Vietnam to immediately cut off assistance to their respective Cambodian client factions. China rejected the proposal. However, by the final August 27–28, 1990, meeting, when the Framework was unveiled, China took the pledge and followed it up with a secret meeting in Chengdu, China, with the Vietnamese. This turning point meeting occurred in the wake of (and beyond the confines of) the P-5 settlement talks. Both Vietnam and China (as backers of the best-armed factions) were integral to the settlement. But Vietnam had been reticent to agree to the P-5 approach, which threatened the future of the SOC. In the Chengdu meeting, September 3–4, 1990, Hanoi swallowed its pride and accepted a deal in which both countries agreed to pressure their respective clients to sign on to the Framework approach.[50]

Additionally, according to Richard Solomon, China extracted another key concession from the Vietnamese at Chengdu. The Chinese felt strongly negative toward Vietnamese Foreign Minister Nguyen Co Thach, and at Chengdu they demanded that he be purged. The Vietnamese conceded and dismissed Thach, and, according to Solomon, the final settlement proceeded *because* Thach was out of the picture. This demand was China's "pound of flesh."[51]

Role of International Law

The key international legal challenge was crafting an international intervention in the face of the international community's reticence to invoke Chapter VII enforcement action, and the limitation of trusteeship arrangements to non-UN member states under the UN Charter.[52] According to Professor Steven Ratner, who at the time was a lawyer at the State Department, Chapter VII enforcement "never received serious consideration owing to the [Security] Council's unwillingness to impose a large UN presence on Cambodia without any agreement by the factions, especially in view of the Council's reluctance to invoke chapter VII before the Persian Gulf war."[53] The solution involved the creation of a Supreme National Council (SNC), the embodiment of Cambodia's sovereignty, which could then invite a UN action in its territory, in the form of UNTAC.

The idea for the SNC had been floating around for a while, but was reinvigorated by Australia following the first Paris Conference's failure to bridge the power-sharing impasse. The P-5 included the SNC in the Framework Document and urged the Cambodian factions to accept the framework wholesale and form an SNC. The P-5 specifically called for Sihanouk to be chosen as president of the SNC, but left the composition of the SNC up to the Cambodian factions.[54] In September 1990, when the Cambodian factions accepted the P-5 Framework Document, they formed the SNC.[55] In July 1991, at the behest of the P-5, the factions finally elected Prince Sihanouk as president of the SNC.[56]

The SNC composition reflected a careful balance of interests. Twelve individual Cambodians formed the SNC: six from the SOC, and two each from the DK, FUNCINPEC, and KPNLF. Thus, instead of a quadripartite-type distribution of votes, the SNC was evenly split between the SOC and the CGDK. On the other hand, SNC decisions had to be made by consensus voting, thus allowing for a Khmer Rouge veto.[57]

Although the SNC posed difficult international law questions, it was hardly a relevant force. Solomon called it "symbolic," and John Bolton dismissed it as "giving new meaning to 'fig leaf' " and recounted the standing joke that the "purpose of the SNC was to raise the Cambodian national flag in the morning, and take it down at night." Regardless, the composition of the SNC became one of the most contentious issues between the Cambodian factions. Hun Sen considered Sihanouk to be the head of the royalist party, but Sihanouk wanted Ranariddh to be the head, so that Sihanouk himself would not have to occupy one of the SNC positions allocated to the royalists. Sihanouk won that battle and was instead elected president of the SNC. However, ultimately, Sihanouk won the battle and lost the war. Sihanouk wanted to avoid being "kicked up" to being king. He wanted to be the head of state. An anonymous French official suspected that Hun Sen and Ranariddh had a secret power-sharing agreement from the beginning, in which Sihanouk would become king, and they would share the real political power.[58]

Conclusion

Because of the still unfolding developments in Cambodia, this chapter does not focus on the implementation of the agreement. UNTAC was a $2.5 billion operation and succeeded in administering elections with an extraordinary 90 percent turnout, though the preelection phase was marked by political violence, with assassinations and fierce attacks on Vietnamese residents of Cambodia. Before the elections, the Khmer Rouge withdrew from the agreement, and as the election results showed that FUNCINPEC would emerge victorious, Hun Sen threatened to reject the results. To avoid a backslide into civil war, Ranariddh conceded to a coalition government in which the ministries were split between Hun Sen's Cambodian People's Party (CPP) and FUNCINPEC; Ranariddh was named first prime minister and Hun Sen second prime minister.

In the end, the Khmer Rouge pulled out of the settlement and refused to participate in the elections or allow UNTAC to enter areas under its control (though it did allow for the repatriation of refugees). The Khmer Rouge asserted that UNTAC had failed to take full control over the five areas (defense, finance, foreign affairs, information, and public security) delegated to it by the SNC under the agreement. As a result, according to the Khmer Rouge, the Hun Sen/SOC government had retained political power. Most significantly, the failure of the Khmer Rouge to comply meant that UNTAC could not carry out the cantonment and disarmament of the Khmer Rouge troops.

Historian David Chandler summarizes the result of the negotiations:

> The Paris Accords of 1991 allowed [the] larger powers a chance to dissolve alliances with Cambodian factions and to retreat from the responsibilities of patronage while appearing to save face. The "free and fair" elections of 1993 celebrated these arrangements, and delivered the country into the hands of a range of former clients, recently set free and enjoined by their increasingly indifferent patrons to be friends.[59]

Unfortunately, the Cambodian factions never were, nor would be, "friends."

Perhaps the most positive outcome of the UNTAC presence relates to the spread of the concept of human rights and political freedoms. For the first time, a free press emerged, along with a strong indigenous human rights NGO community, which organized to address issues such as prison reform, freedom of association, economic development, and women's empowerment. Under UNTAC, Cambodia acceded to international instruments related to human rights, including the International Covenant on Civil and Political Rights, as well as the Convention against Torture and other Cruel, Inhuman, or Degrading Treatment or Punishment. And following the elections, and the establishment of the Kingdom of Cambodia, a constitution was adopted, which on its face encompassed all vital international human rights standards.

Diplomats interviewed were extremely wary of drawing broad lessons from the Cambodia case study. Each stated adamantly that every situation is *sui generis*. In the Cambodia case, the uniqueness took the form of "housekeeping at the end of the Cold War," in John Bolton's words. Invoking Richard III, David Gilmore emphasized the importance of the "time and tides which wait for no man" and the importance of catching the "witching moment."

Although it may not be possible to generalize from the Cambodian example, specific lessons can be gleaned. One lesson is that the United Nations can provide a neutral outlet for settlement if the parties want to use its mechanisms. The United Nations can prepare to step in and provide the backstopping necessary to help set the terms of its involvement. But it may not possess the leverage to initiate the engagement. The Cambodian case also clearly demonstrates that progress and momentum can build over time; whereas initial efforts may fail to achieve a final agreement, they can serve to bring the parties together, air and focus issues, and set future agendas. "Failures" can thus be viewed as steps in an overall process. The Cambodian case also offers a powerful example of stepping outside the context of the main stumbling blocks to resolution to seek creative legal and political solutions. Power sharing between the four factions confounded and frustrated all the parties involved. The Solarz/Evans solution of creating an SNC mechanism obviated and circumvented the issue.

The UN efforts in Cambodia were largely heralded as a success by the international community. The results to date, however, particularly the July 1997 coup and the elections one year later, have clearly subdued that initial euphoria and the characterization of the implementation phase as a success for the United Nations. At worst, the UN mechanisms can be viewed as having been manipulated by the P-5 members to jettison increasingly irrelevant and undesirable Cold War obligations, imposing an externally forged agreement on the Cambodian factions without then following through to assure that the parties would abide by the agreement. Ironically, the very factor that may have made the settlement agreements possible, that the Cambodian factions were only peripherally involved in the negotiations, may have ultimately led to the failure of the agreements to achieve a lasting peace in Cambodia.

6

El Salvador

Barbara Messing

Overview

EL SALVADOR IS a textbook case for effective mediation by the United Nations. By 1990, the conflict in El Salvador had reached a stalemate. After the end of the Cold War, the conflict in El Salvador no longer represented (if it ever did) an important battlefield between the forces of democracy and communism. The parties to the conflict, a conservative government with a strong but uncontrollable military and a highly organized and effective guerilla movement (Farabundo Martí National Liberation Front—the FMLN), realized that neither side could win the war decisively. Two incidents in 1989 galvanized international pressure for peace and forced the parties to seek mediation. In November 1989, the FMLN staged a battle in the wealthiest areas of San Salvador. The battle was effective in the short term, but it angered the local population, which made it clear that civilians had no desire to take up arms or continue the civil war. In December 1989 the murder of six Jesuit priests by the military brought international condemnation and the realization within and outside El Salvador that the military would never be professionalized. Recognizing the need for peace, the parties sought out the United Nations to mediate the dispute, after eliminating other possibilities such as the Organization of American States (OAS).

Alvaro de Soto, named as special representative to the conflict by Secretary-General Perez de Cuellar, worked with the parties over nearly two years to orchestrate a comprehensive agreement. Following de Soto's well-crafted framework, with the support of an influential Group of Friends and constant behind the scenes communication with the United States, the parties agreed to end the hostilities, reform the armed forces, and create new civilian institutions. The agreement was so broad-reaching that it was referred to as a "negotiated revolution." This chapter examines the background to the El Salvador dispute, the elements that made the conflict particularly ripe for resolution, the techniques de Soto used to skillfully mediate the dispute, and the implementation process of the historic agreement. Drawing on interviews with many of the major participants, it provides personal insights into the reasons for the success of the mediation (and roadblocks that occurred along the way).

Timeline

1979   Military coup.

1980   Outbreak of Civil War.

1981   José Napoleón Duarte joins the junta and assumes leadership at the end of the year.

1982   FMLN launches its "final offensive" for a popular rebellion.

1983   United States begins giving military support and training to the Salvadoran military.

1984   Duarte defeats the rightist candidate Roberto D'Aubuisson in a run-off for the presidency.

1986   **November:** Secretary-general of the United Nations and the secretary-general of the OAS jointly offer assistance for peace efforts in Central America.

1987   **August:** Presidents of Costa Rica, El Salvador, Guatemala, Honduras, and Nicaragua sign Esquipulas II Agreement in support of peace in the region.

1989   **March:** Alfredo Cristiani elected to presidency. **July:** UN Security Council expresses support for Esquipulas II and the use of the secretary-general's good offices to help stabilize the region. **September:** Government of El Salvador and the FMLN agree to initiate a dialogue. **November:** FMLN offensive. **December:** Central American presidents sign a declaration inviting the United Nations to mediate in the region. Two FMLN leaders meet with UN official Alvaro de Soto in Montreal, Canada, to ask the United Nations for help in bringing an end to the conflict.

1990   **January:** In New York, the president of El Salvador formally requests UN help in bringing an end to the conflict. **April:** Geneva Agreement is signed, laying out a framework for negotiations with four objectives: ending the armed conflict, promoting democratization, guaranteeing respect for human rights, and reconciling Salvadoran society. **May:** Government and FMLN agree on an agenda and timetable for negotiations in Caracas. **July:** Parties sign the San José Agreement on Human Rights.

1991   **April:** In Mexico City, the government and FMLN agree to constitutional reforms regarding the armed forces and the judicial and electoral systems. The parties also agree to the establishment of a Commission on the Truth. **May:** United Nations Observer Mission in El Salvador (ONUSAL) is established with a twelve-month mandate to monitor compliance with the agreements. **September:** At the secretary-general's invitation, President Cristiani joins the negotiations at UN Headquarters in New York. Government and FMLN agree to a tightened future agenda and to substantive issues on the armed forces, the police force, land transfer programs, and the establishment of the National Commission for the Consolidation of Peace (COPAZ.) **December:** Secretary-general invites Cristiani to New York to finish remaining issues on the agenda. Government and FMLN sign the Act of New York, which completes all substantive issues of the peace process.

1992 **Jan. 13:** All outstanding issues are resolved and the two parties sign New York Act II. **Jan. 16:** Formal signing of peace agreement in Mexico City. **Feb. 1:** Official cease-fire begins.

Background

From spring 1980 through January 1992, El Salvador was immersed in a bloody civil conflict that claimed over 75,000 lives. In October 1979, reformist officers of the Salvadoran military led a coup deposing the old regime of General Carlos Humberto Romero. Following the coup, a succession of juntas composed of both civilian and military members ruled the country, demanding redistribution of economic and political power. The conservative armed forces and members of the oligarchy responded with a campaign of terror and assassination against activists of the reform movement. Utilizing both clandestine and public methods of intimidation and violence, including the use of death squads, the military's actions wreaked havoc on the Salvadoran population.[1]

Antigovernment violence erupted, with attacks on military targets, takeovers of radio stations, and bombings of newspaper headquarters. The civilian members of the junta resigned in January 1980, and José Napoleón Duarte, a leading Christian Democrat, became a member shortly thereafter. By the end of 1980, with U.S. sponsorship and military agreement, Duarte assumed the presidency of the junta. Conservatives controlled the urban areas, and the survivors of the reform movement fled the country and joined the guerrillas in the mountains. By the spring of 1980, the country had descended into civil war. Five Marxist groups that sought armed opposition to the government in the name of social justice created a united guerrilla front known as the Farabundo Martí National Liberation Front (FMLN).[2]

The impact of the civil war in El Salvador reached far beyond its borders. The Reagan administration focused on El Salvador as a key case in its crusade against communism in the Western Hemisphere. The United States increased its military and economic assistance to the Salvadoran military, despite the massive human rights abuses and killings perpetrated by the armed forces. Reagan argued that the social unrest was the result of subversive tactics orchestrated by Soviet Union puppets.

The United States and the Salvadoran army became allies to preserve their perceived security interests: the armed forces (and their right-wing allies) supported elections, civilian governments, and limited reforms that were necessary for congressional support of the administration's policy in exchange for institutional preservation, military assistance, and their own aggrandizement.[3]

The ten years of war that followed were devastating to El Salvador. Over 75,000 people were killed, and more than one million Salvadorans became refugees or internally displaced persons. Death squad killings, disappearances, arbitrary detention, and other acts of brutality directed primarily against civilians were attributed to the government or to government supporters. The FMLN was also responsible for murder and violence, although on a much lesser scale, assassinating mayors and judges and committing acts of sabotage against community targets.

In March of 1989, the ultra-right Nationalist Republican Alliance Party's (ARENA) candidate, Alfredo Cristiani, defeated Duarte. During the history of the conflict, ARENA had viciously opposed political change with a paramilitary wing whose death squads worked with army units to murder thousands of perceived opponents, including Archbishop Oscar Arnulfo Romero. Cristiani's overwhelming victory demonstrated two key elements: the erosion of Duarte's political base and the failure of the United States' policy of providing an alternative to the oligarchy and the FMLN.[4] A Georgetown University graduate and member of the Salvadoran elite, Cristiani had risen through the ranks as Roberto D'Aubuisson's[5] protégé and represented the pro-business interests of ARENA. One of the small group of moderates within the party, Cristiani pledged during his campaign that he would seek an end to the armed conflict and stated that he felt a strong personal commitment to reaching a peace settlement during his term.[6] Importantly, Cristiani had the support of D'Aubuisson, which gave him the ability to pursue a negotiated settlement despite the resistance to negotiations by the powerful conservative members of ARENA.

Two internal incidents in the fall of 1989 were key in the shift from war to peace talks and reverberated internationally as well: the November 1989 offensive launched by the FMLN and the murder of six Jesuit priests by members of the Salvadoran military. The November offensive was more than a military maneuver for the FMLN. The FMLN leadership believed that the offensive would serve as the spark necessary to ignite a popular rebellion against the government and military. To the surprise of the military, the FMLN gained control over many parts of San Salvador. Wealthy San Salvadorans were shocked and surprised to have a civil war being fought within their neighborhoods of fifteen-foot walls. Even the fenced-in compound of the luxury Sheraton Hotel was penetrated by the FMLN forces. The secretary-general of the OAS, a visitor to El Salvador at the invitation of the Salvadoran government, was a guest at the Sheraton when the FMLN invaded. After being told (incorrectly) that the FMLN had come to the Sheraton to take him hostage, he was evacuated in an armed military vehicle in a dramatic rescue by the Salvadoran government.

Despite the military successes of the November offensive, the FMLN's dream of a popular rebellion never materialized. The FMLN realized that the civil war could not be sustained without the popular insurrection it had sought. Rather than inspiring the populace to take arms, the offensive had an effect not predicted by the FMLN leadership. After nearly a decade of civil war, Salvadorans were tired of the bloodshed and resented the FMLN for jeopardizing the safety of the city. Militarily, the FMLN had conducted their largest offensive, and the aftermath left them with both weakened forces and limited weaponry. Thus, as a result of the successful, yet failed, offensive, and the dramatic change in the international climate following the end of the Cold War, by February of 1990 all five constituent organizations of the FMLN came to the conclusion that the immediate priority was negotiations.

The FMLN's November offensive had real implications for the Salvadoran government and military as well. The government and the armed forces were forced to recognize that the FMLN still had significant military capabilities and concluded that the Salvadoran military could not win the war. Although the armed forces believed the FMLN were formidable combatants, they believed with certainty that the FMLN would never be able to win a war either. However, the prospect of another decade of low-intensity, and at times high-intensity, conflict in the small country forced the government and military to consider entering negotiations. In December of 1989, six Jesuit priests, their cook, and her teenage daughter were killed in their residence by members of the military. This shocking and brutal action attracted worldwide attention and signified to sectors both within and outside El Salvador that the military would never be able to be professionalized.[7]

The November 1989 FMLN offensive and the killings of the Jesuits fundamentally altered the strategy and tactics of the FMLN, the Salvadoran government and armed forces, the Bush administration, and the U.S. Congress. All parties concluded that negotiations aimed at achieving a cease-fire and political settlement were the best available policy option. President Cristiani reflected recently, "the two major incidents of the November offensive and the assassinations of the Jesuit priests, ugly as they were, created a sensation that there was no other way out."[8]

Key Interventions and Major Actors

Choice of Parties

The United Nations

The United Nations intervened at the request of both the FMLN and the government of El Salvador. In November 1989, a few days prior to the Costa Rica summit, FMLN leaders Salvador Samayoa and Ana Guadalupe Martinez flew to Montreal to meet with Alvaro de Soto of the United Nations. They met in Montreal rather than at UN Headquarters in New York, because the United States refused to issue visas for the two FMLN leaders. Alvaro de Soto was the executive assistant to Secretary-General Perez de Cuellar and the personal representative of the secretary-general to the Central American peace process at the United

Nations. De Soto became the secretary-general's personal representative, because of the latter's interest in following the events taking place in the region. At this initial meeting, Martinez, Samayoa, and de Soto discussed the possibility of having the United Nations mediate a peace process in El Salvador. De Soto described for Samayoa and Martinez what an initiative or diplomatic effort by the secretary-general would look like, and the three also discussed the relations between the secretary-general and the Security Council. Apparently, the FMLN was extremely concerned that the Security Council could have an influence on the secretary-general that wouldn't favor a negotiation.[9] De Soto, having witnessed earlier failed negotiation attempts, explained to Samayoa and Martinez that the United Nations would serve as a mediator only if the FMLN agreed to allow the United Nations to have full control over the process and to commit themselves to completing the peace process. From the start, the goal of the UN intervention was not simply to promote dialogue, but to reach a peace agreement. By all accounts, the meeting went well between the parties.[10]

President Cristiani also sought the assistance of the United Nations. Cristiani flew to New York and made a formal request to Perez de Cuellar at the end of January 1990. The sequence of events that laid the foundations for this request varies, depending on who recounts the background. Prior to Cristiani's meeting with Perez de Cuellar in New York, de Soto met with Cristiani at the inauguration of the president of Honduras in the second half of January of 1990. De Soto had gone to Tegucigalpa to discuss with Cristiani the mechanics of UN involvement and also to tell him that the United Nations had been approached by the FMLN. At the inauguration, Cristiani informed de Soto that he was going to formally request the secretary-general's help, and he carried a letter that he intended to deliver in person to the secretary-general later that month.

Prior to this, Oscar Arias had been persuading Cristiani to ask the secretary-general for assistance, and Arias, along with the five Central American presidents, issued a joint statement formally inviting the United Nations to mediate peace in the region. Cristiani had a meeting with the Central American presidents at the San José summit in December of 1989 and, according to Arias, Cristiani was actually "forced" into accepting UN intervention by Arias and other Central American presidents.[11] Cristiani said he came to this decision of his own volition, and David Escobar Galindo, a close personal friend of Cristiani and a member of the government negotiation team, concurs, recalling that Cristiani sought a peace agreement from his first days as president-elect.[12] Says Cristiani, "At the beginning they probably thought I was bluffing—'this guy can't be serious, he comes with the death squad, offers a peace process' . . . [e]veryone thought that, probably, at least outside the country and in the FMLN, except Ellacuria."[13] FMLN leader Salvador Samayoa has another explanation for Cristiani's seeking out the United Nations. He believes that Cristiani only went to the United Nations because of pressure from the U.S. government.[14] Bernard Aronson, assistant secretary of state for inter-American affairs, states that while the United States did urge Cristiani to negotiate, he also had his own set of pressures that brought him to the United Nations.[15]

David Escobar Galindo recalls that Cristiani set up the January meeting with Secretary-General Perez de Cuellar in New York to receive his assurance that the meeting would not simply promote dialogue, but rather would finish the process. Cristiani clarified his position, explaining "[w]hat we had to get was something within the process that would generate pressure on the FMLN to not do 'weird stuff' and so the idea came up of calling the Secretary-General and asking for an intermediation process."[16] Cristiani believed that the United Nations would act as a safeguard to ensure that negotiations would continue. On April 4, 1990, UN Secretary-General Perez de Cuellar announced publicly that the United Nations would oversee a political settlement.

The FMLN Negotiation Team

The FMLN negotiation team was made up of representatives of the five organizations of the FMLN, including Salvador Samayoa, Ana Guadulupe Martinez, Shafik Handal, Salvador Sanchez Ceren, and Joaquin Villalobos. Although the FMLN acted publicly as one organization, the five factions had ideological differences and struggled internally over strategy and tactics for winning the war throughout the conflict. In addition, some of the members were more interested in negotiating a settlement than other members, who believed that a military victory was still possible. While the head of the negotiation team was Shafik Handal, the government team viewed Villalobos and Sanchez Ceren as having more control over the outcome of the process. Cristiani recalled that the agreements depended on their approval. "Even if Shafik wouldn't agree, if Villalobos and Sanchez Ceren decided it was time, Shafik had to continue even though he was part of the PC and had more international support than the others ... our perception was that if things were going to end, it's because Villalobos and Sanchez Ceren say it's going to end."[17]

The Government Negotiation Team

Cristiani handpicked the members of the government negotiation team, selecting high-ranking members of the armed forces, an intellectual and personal friend, and members of the Ministry. Cristiani believed that members of the team complemented each other: Santamaria and Torres were both lawyers who were familiar with the constitution and "were keen on that sort of thing ... they were the people who would watch out for illegalities."[18] About his choice of Escobar Galindo, Cristiani says that he "was more a university person, philosophical, a strong optimist, a person who lifts your spirits."[19] General Vargas had an essential role on the team: "his role was to make the armed forces feel as if they weren't being double crossed at the table."[20] Although Cristiani was not a regular member of the team, he was actively involved with the decision making, and de Soto and members of his own team spoke with him often during negotiations as his approval was key to the agreement process. Cristiani formally joined the team, in a sense, when he came to New York in both September and December of 1991 at the request of the secretary-general. His presence was intended to bring the process seriousness and momentum and allow peace to be reached.

Windows of Opportunity to Resolve the Conflict

The UN intervention was not the first effort at dialogue between the FMLN and the Salvadoran government. There had been previous attempts at negotiations during the conflict. Two meetings between the FMLN and President Duarte in 1984 and 1985 were hoped to be the beginnings of negotiation, although these meetings were futile for two reasons. First, Duarte lacked the political power to effect any substantial agreement, as he did not have real control over the military. In addition, both sides still believed that a military victory was still possible. In 1987, following the Esquipulas II agreement, two more rounds of talks were held, but these also failed to establish an ongoing process. Later, Cristiani initiated dialogues with the FMLN when he became president in 1989, but these talks broke down when the military attacked the headquarters of a labor federation in San Salvador.

However, the negotiations that began in 1990 took place in a very different climate. For the Bush administration, the U.S. military advisers, and the Salvadoran army and government, the November offensive destroyed any illusion that the FMLN was fading away as a military threat. Although there was considerable sentiment that the offensive was very costly militarily for the FMLN, there was also growing conviction that continuing to pursue a military strategy to defeat the FMLN would not produce significant results for many years.[21] The armed forces reflected on the experiences of some of their Latin American neighbors and determined that El Salvador should not fall into the same trap of unending internal strife as Colombia and Peru.[22] General Vargas noted that even if the military did eventually win, this victory would be hollow when contrasted with the destruction of lives and property. Also significantly, the defeat of the Sandinistas in Nicaragua had a number of implications for the climate in El Salvador. For the FMLN, the defeat signified the loss for one its main supporters, the Sandinista government. In the Bush administration, the defeat accelerated policy changes toward Central America. For the Salvadoran people, it was an example of the ability to find peace after years of conflict.

Indeed, the climate in El Salvador was ideal for a negotiated settlement. De Soto pointed out that El Salvador fit the model of a "mutually hurting stalemate," as conceived by William Zartman. Zartman posits that chances for negotiated political settlement increase when the conflict hurts the two sides more in war than it would if they reached peace. At the end of 1989 El Salvador had reached this point. In essence, the November 1989 offensive demonstrated two things that were key to approaching a resolution to the conflict through negotiations. First, the offensive demonstrated that the FMLN could not win the war, and they were not able to generate a popular uprising. When they tried to hand out weapons, the people said no. It also demonstrated that the government could not win by military methods. The conflict could not be resolved. This combination of factors kept the momentum in the peace process. "The negotiations were about the government trying to get the FMLN to stop the war, and the FMLN trying to exact out of the government the necessary reforms—reforms that would allow the FMLN to say 'okay, we have gotten something out of this,' and that was the quid pro quo."[23]

Role of the United States

Even prior to the November offensive, the Bush administration had indicated to Salvadoran officials that the decline of the Cold War and the changes taking place in Eastern Europe, together with U.S. budget problems, made it unlikely that Congress would continue to provide aid at the level of the 1980s. This diminishing assistance affected the military and government greatly. On top of this, outrage in the United States over the killing of the Jesuits produced strong pressure in Congress to cut off future military assistance to El Salvador. In addition, the invasion of Panama in December of 1989 and the defeat of the Sandinistas in February of 1990 eliminated even the appearance of a regional threat, and the administration could no longer justify its policy in El Salvador.[24] Secretary of State James A. Baker's testimony before Congress in February of 1990 formally marked the Bush administration's change in policy: he called for a negotiated settlement to the conflict.[25]

The U.S. Congress's role was significant as well. By controlling the foreign and military aid on which the armed forces depended, they were able to influence the military's conduct during the negotiation. The armed forces were compelled to be flexible, because the pressure Congress exerted was substantial. During the previous decade, the United States had given an estimated $4 billion in military and economic aid to El Salvador, a country with only five million people.[26] Alvaro de Soto remarked, "I think it had a definite role in spurring along the negotiations, because the key area where concessions had to be made by the government was in the area of the armed forces."[27]

Form and Method of the Intervention

Both the FMLN and the El Salvadoran government believed that the United Nations was the only institution able to mediate a peaceful settlement. Although the United Nations had not had a significant role in the region prior to this instance, Costa Rican President Oscar Arias laid the foundation for such involvement. Costa Rica had historically been a neutral and uninvolved country, and Arias molded his presidency around the search for peace and stability in the region. In 1987, Arias introduced the Esquipulas II Accord, in which the five presidents of Central America agreed to involve the United Nations in the verification of any accords made by the government in the search for peace and democracy in the region.

Both the FMLN and the government agreed that the two other potential mediators, the Roman Catholic Church and the OAS lacked key elements to negotiating a long-term settlement. The Church, for example, had attempted to promote dialogue between the two parties at various points in the conflict. However, the FMLN and the government agreed that the Church lacked the international scope and authority that both sides thought would be essential to reaching a resolution, and the efforts were rejected by both the government and the FMLN. In addition, the conflict was rooted in political causes and had many international links that could not be effectively addressed by the Church. In addition, although the Church functioned well as a facilitator of communication, the country was extremely polarized, and both sides sought a third party outside the country.[28] Also significantly, vis-à-vis the ripeness component, neither side was prepared to come to the table at that time, with both sides still believing a military victory was possible.

Both the FMLN and the Salvadoran government eliminated the OAS as a possible mediator. Former Assistant Secretary of State for Inter-American Affairs Bernard Aronson notes that historically, "the OAS never has had a peacekeeping function, thus it would have been harder for them to put forth the machinery."[29] Moreover, the conflict in El Salvador had a dimension beyond Latin America.[30] The FMLN, for their part, believed that the OAS was too closely tied to Washington. Cuba and the Soviet Union were not member states of the OAS, which Samayoa said made it "impossible" to have used it. Cristiani agreed, stating that they needed to get the United States and the Soviet Union to agree to stop support for the war simultaneously. "The OAS could not get the US and USSR to the table. The United Nations can . . . [t]hey see each other every day."[31] Both sides agreed that the OAS did not have the international authority they believed was necessary for the agreements.

In addition, a previous attempt to involve the OAS "went down in flames."[32] The FMLN's November 1989 offensive began while the General Assembly of the OAS was meeting in Washington. During the assembly, Nicaragua proposed that the secretary-general of the OAS undertake a mission to El Salvador to see if the OAS would undertake negotiations. Before the draft resolution could be proposed by Nicaragua, the foreign minister of El Salvador preempted it and invited the secretary-general of the OAS to El Salvador. When the secretary-general arrived in El Salvador, the press asked him if he was there to see if a peace could be brokered. The foreign minister of El Salvador interrupted him, saying that the secretary-general had come merely to observe and report. De Soto believed that the government was not interested in negotiations at this time, because it was early enough in the offensive that they believed they would succeed militarily. Shortly after the secretary-general's arrival and check-in at the Sheraton Hotel, an FMLN patrol came down the volcano adjacent to the hotel and entered the building. As mentioned earlier, the secretary-general thought that the FMLN had come in to capture him, and the Salvadoran armed forces said that this was indeed the case. Thus, the army proceeded to carry out a dramatic operation to rescue him. Meanwhile, the FMLN stated that they had not the slightest intention of capturing him and had been communicating with the United States through the entire situation because a group of U.S. servicemen was staying at the hotel. Says de Soto, "[t]hrough all these circumstances, the attempt to play a diplomatic role failed miserably."[33]

Thus, the United Nations became involved in the Salvadoran conflict under the auspices of their good offices. The involvement was unorthodox on two levels: First, the United Nations did not normally involve itself in internal conflicts; and second, the United Nations had not had a history of involvement in Latin America generally.[34] The negotiation had four goals: to put an end to the conflict, to broaden democracy in El Salvador, to guarantee respect for human rights, and to bring about the reconciliation of Salvadoran society.[35]

Key Factors in Shaping the Result

Role of the United Nations

The United Nations played an essential role in the resolution of the conflict. First, many key members of both the FMLN and the Salvadoran government had faith in the organization's ability to broker a peace agreement. As noted by members of the FMLN, and the Salvadoran government and military, the United Nations was the only organization in which all interested parties were signatories. In addition, the United Nations had already established its credibility in the region through its role as an observer of previous dialogues between the parties. The UN Observer Group in Central America (ONUCA) had accustomed people to accepting UN involvement in the region, and the organization had made contacts over the years on a confidential and informal basis with the FMLN.[36]

In addition, both the FMLN and the government recognized the limited number of organizations that could help negotiate a peace agreement. General Vargas of the Salvadoran negotiation team remarked, "Personally, I didn't have trust in the United Nations—but I also didn't have distrust. . . . We had an ideological and political conflict, and we needed a person that could come in between the parties—an intermediary."[37] His opinion, echoed by members of both the FMLN and the government team, was that the United Nations was selected more out of necessity than conviction. De Soto stated that with Contadora and the OAS eliminated, "it was only natural that they would come to the United Nations, if only by a process of elimination."[38]

Also significantly, the parties independently and unilaterally approached the United Nations for assistance and agreed to the mediation parameters laid out by the United Nations to ensure that the process moved toward peace. Moreover, the United Nations, on its part, made the Salvadoran peace process a priority. de Soto had a personal interest in the region and had been serving as the special assistant to the secretary-general on Latin America for two years prior to the beginning of the process.

Ripeness of the Conflict

As discussed earlier, the conflict in El Salvador had reached a pivotal stage when the two parties sought UN assistance. Internally, both sides had independently come to the realization that neither could win. Also significantly,

President Cristiani came from the right-wing ARENA party and had the confidence of the military and the support of D'Aubuisson. Oscar Arias pointed out that "the military only accepted UN intervention when a right-wing President like Cristiani came into power."[39] In contrast, when Duarte was president, the military had no confidence in his power. Oscar Arias recalled a conversation in a meeting in Tesoro Beach, El Salvador, with Duarte and the former defense minister Carlos Vides Casanova. Recalls Arias, "We were having lunch, and I said to Duarte, 'I believe we will need to change the Constitution in order to have elections, and I said to Casanova, 'what do you think of this idea?' and he said, 'if you do that, and President Duarte does that, I'll be forced to have a coup d'état.' "[40]

Also significantly, Cristiani came into office seeking peace, believing that the time had come to find a political solution.[41] Being a member of ARENA with the support of D'Aubuisson, and from a landed family of El Salvador, Cristiani had the political ties and credentials that Duarte lacked. D'Aubuisson's support of Cristiani was significant both personally and politically to Cristiani. Revered by the extreme right, D'Aubuisson served as a link between Cristiani and the conservative members of ARENA. D'Aubuisson openly supported the peace process and played a key role in maintaining support of the process from within the party until his death from cancer in February of 1992. Still, throughout the peace process, Cristiani was sensitive to the nervousness among certain members of Salvadoran society, and he would arrange breakfast meetings to calm the fears of various sectors of the elite.

Regionally, the Central American presidents were putting pressure on the government of El Salvador to reach a negotiated settlement, and the conflict in Nicaragua had ended. Internationally, the Cold War had ended, the Bush administration's financial support and interest in continuing the conflict dissipated, and the Soviet Union's and Cuba's interest decreased correspondingly. In addition, as discussed earlier, Congressional aid had decreased as a result of the military's assassination of the Jesuits.

Role of U.S. Policy

The United States sent public signals to the FMLN that they would support a negotiated settlement and urged Cristiani to enter a peace process.[42] Even prior to the elections in 1989, the FMLN floated a proposal to have a cease-fire, and Secretary of State Baker stated publicly that the proposal was worthy of consideration.[43] Although the United States never came to the negotiation table and formally proposed suggestions, they did participate behind the scenes through discussions with the parties and met regularly with de Soto. Prior to the November offensive, Father Ellacuria came to Washington to meet with State Department officials and discuss a possible peace agreement.[44] A week after the offensive, Hector Silva came to the State Department to discuss issues around a peace agreement, particularly the purging of human rights violators from the army.[45] While the relationship between the Salvadoran government and the U.S.

Department of State was more public, the FMLN also received information from the Department of State through nonpapers and correspondence, including security guarantees and the State Department's positions.[46] In addition, Aronson published an article in the *Washington Post* expressing the State Department's position on the talks and testified in support of the negotiation process in front of Congress. The FMLN and officials from the State Department also had direct contacts. Relatively early in the process, an official from the State Department went to the Mexico City talks to interact with the FMLN. Both the FMLN and the government praised Aronson's role in the process.

The U.S. Congress played an important role in the Salvadoran military's acceptance of the peace agreements. Congress put pressure on the Salvadoran military to support the process by reducing military assistance. Aronson recalled that military aid was suspended for six months without announcing it during the peace process to put pressure on the military, and there was always an implicit sanction of cutting off all military support.[47] U.S. Representative Joseph Moakley was extremely active in leading the House in this area and introduced legislation with strong House support that would have effectively eliminated military funding entirely. According to one expert, the Bush administration, though supportive of the process, "appeared to balance every step to help protect Cristiani's right flank, appease U.S. officials who wanted to take a harder line against the FMLN, and avoid a perceived potential loss of influence within the Salvadoran army."[48]

The Bush administration offered its support to the UN mediation, but they did not always agree with de Soto's management of the process. Overall, the U.S. government shared de Soto's strategy and would try to use its influence to help the process. However, there was a perception at the State Department that he was too lenient with deadlines that were important to moving the process forward.[49] In addition, de Soto appeared to put more pressure on the government than on the FMLN.[50] There was tension at times between de Soto and the U.S. government, and at one point anonymous State Department sources criticized his diplomacy skills in the *New York Times*.[51]

Pressure from the Ongoing Conflict

The end of the Cold War in the late 1980s slowed the flow of weapons, training, funding, and political support, but the door to negotiations opened only after the government of El Salvador and the FMLN wearied of the fighting amid the realization that no military solution was in sight. Although both sides were exhausted from the nine years of war, the fighting continued throughout the negotiations. Both sides identified the ongoing conflict as a crucial factor in reaching a peace agreement. De Soto recalls that "what kept the pressure was that the FMLN never stopped the war." In November 1991, the worst fighting since the beginning of the process took place. The FMLN believed that the government would only make concessions under military pressure.

Some of the negotiation team members said it was difficult at times, with the

war continuing throughout the process. But they also believed the war was instrumental in keeping the momentum toward an agreement. When asked if it
would have been possible to reach a peace agreement had a cease-fire occurred
earlier in the peace process, Escobar Galindo, Ruben Zamora, de Soto, Cristiani,
Samayoa, and Vargas all agreed that it would have not been possible. Escobar
Galindo remembers that it was difficult to negotiate with the war going on
around them, but when the teams came to the table they would leave those battles outside the room.

Group of Friends

In a number of unmediated conflicts, UN member states would independently organize a "Group of Friends" composed of ambassadors or other envoys
sent directly from the member state governments. The Groups of Friends would
primarily act behind the scenes as advisors or providers of services to the
process and particular partners over the course of the negotiation. Such a group
was organized for El Salvador, and both the FMLN and the Salvadoran government found the presence of the Group of Friends a useful part of the negotiations. The Group of Friends included Mexico, Venezuela, Costa Rica, and Spain.
De Soto consulted with the ambassadors of the Group of Friends countries, as
did members of the FMLN and government negotiation teams. In addition, the
Group of Friends provided valuable financial support to the process. Many of
the peace talks were held in Mexico, and the Mexican government provided the
financial resources to conduct the process. The governments of Costa Rica and
Venezuela also financed talks. Cristiani believed that, at times, the financial support allowed the Group of Friends to influence the parties' actions. Toward the
end of the process, for example, the FMLN stalled the negotiations by bringing
up new issues not on the agenda. At this time, members of the FMLN were staying in Mexico. According to Cristiani, the government of Mexico urged the
FMLN team to continue with the agenda, indicating that Mexico's hospitality
and financial support would not be indefinite. When asked about this alleged
pressure, Samayoa of the FMLN disagreed with this assessment, saying that
Mexico put no pressure on the FMLN.

Further, the Group of Friends actively assisted in bringing the two parties together. The Group of Friends had the trust of both sides, as its participation was
related to the desire that El Salvador reach a negotiated settlement. It was viewed
as an amalgam of neutral parties that could bring an outside perspective to the
process. Before traveling to New York at the secretary-general's request in the final days of the negotiation in 1990, President Cristiani called the members of the
Group of Friends and asked if they believed that an agreement could be reached.
When he received a commitment from the Group of Friends that they would put
pressure on the FMLN to reach an agreement, he agreed to come—"not that
they took sides—I could never get them to take our side, and that's what made
them so valuable." Cristiani says that the Friends were able to give finishing
touches that the United Nations was unable to give and the Friends also gave

helpful advice: "Don't kill another soul, because you want to get a little bit further."

Mechanisms of Mediation

De Soto had the trust of Perez de Cuellar and was given the authority to conduct the negotiations with his judgment. Because the Salvadoran government and the FMLN were not speaking to each other, de Soto's first task was to establish a framework to bring the parties together. Throughout February and March 1990, he shuttled back and forth between the FMLN in Mexico and the government in San Salvador. During this period the FMLN leadership, which included Shafik Handal, Ana Guadalupe Martinez, Salvador Sanchez Ceren, and Salvador Samayoa, took turns meeting with de Soto. De Soto believes that during this period they were sizing him up. By the end of March they had come up with an agreement, but the United Nations decided that high-level representatives from the parties should sign the agreement formally in Geneva.

De Soto had studied past attempts at negotiations in the El Salvador conflict, identified the flaws, and organized a structure to overcome these problems. He had participated as a witness with an OAS representative at talks held in October 1989 in Costa Rica, which he described as a "deeply flawed diplomatic exercise." Ordered by the Church (a combination of the Salvadoran Episcopal Hierarchy and representation from the Holy See) and run by two delegates from the Salvadoran Episcopal hierarchy, the talks took place in a rest home for nuns. The negotiation was to be conducted through direct talks, with the government seated at one side of a long rectangular table, the FMLN facing them on the other side of the table, and the observers seated at the ends.

De Soto recalls: "[E]veryone was in a very bad mood and they were haranguing each other, and one of the first things someone said is 'what these people are saying is absolutely horrendous, and I want to tape this,' and suddenly everyone was putting their electronics on the table, and I knew at that moment that nothing else was going to come out of this ... [t]hat is one of the basic rules—no taping." In addition, de Soto quickly learned the necessity of limiting relations with the press. At the Costa Rica meeting, the delegates would leave every half-hour to brief the press on the situation and, not surprisingly, little was accomplished.

In the beginning weeks, the United Nations established with the parties the manner in which the negotiations would be conducted. The government wanted the negotiations to be direct, while the FMLN thought direct negotiations would be ineffective without the president or the head of the armed forces at the table. The FMLN believed that the most effective negotiation would be done indirectly, through the secretary-general's representative. Thus, the parties came to an agreement on a "two track approach." In this approach, the mediator would shuttle between the parties to understand and communicate their positions, and eventually the two sides would come together and create the agreements. According to de Soto, it was also established that the secretary-general's representative would play an active role, which would allow him to actually present ideas toward proposals. (The Salvadoran government team disagrees, saying de Soto's role limited him to hearing what each side said and then communicating it to the other side without his own intervention.) De Soto said, "What happened was much of what they agreed on was proposed by us, because mistrust was such that if either presented a proposal, the other side would reject it."[52]

In the beginning stages of establishing the framework, de Soto utilized a negotiation technique that he learned at the UN Law of the Sea Conference: the single negotiation text technique. De Soto would meet with each of the parties separately, ask questions, and on the basis of the meetings, draft a proposal that he believed would be a compromise. After presenting the proposal to both sides, de Soto would elicit comments and then revise it. After seven weeks, de Soto was able to bring agreement on all but a few issues, and those remaining issues were resolved in unpublicized direct talks in Mexico on March 27. The parties gathered in the early afternoon and by 2:00 A.M. had reached an agreement. Although the agreement was reached in Mexico, the parties met for the formal signing of the agreement in Geneva, Switzerland, in April. This first momentous agreement became known as the "Geneva Agreement."

The Geneva Agreement included many elements to ensure that the peace process moved forward. From his experience at the Costa Rican talks, de Soto concluded that it would be impossible to reach agreements when the parties were constantly seeking out the press. Thus, one of the components of the Geneva Agreement was that de Soto and the secretary-general were the only people authorized to speak with the press about the peace process.[53]

The Geneva Agreement also allowed the secretary-general or his representative to contact whomever he thought necessary during the peace process. This allowed de Soto to travel to El Salvador and meet with union members, church leaders, opposition leaders, nongovernmental organizations, and other interested parties. The Geneva Agreement also stipulated that the secretary-general or his representative could consult any government during the process, and this proved useful as well. At the start of the process, the secretary-general consulted with the governments of Cuba, the United States, and the Soviet Union to ensure that they would not undermine the process and received a reasonable commitment from each of them.

In April 1990 in Geneva, both parties officially signed an agreement that permitted UN-mediated negotiations. A month later in Caracas, the parties established an agenda for the talks and agreed to approach the negotiation in three stages: negotiations on key issues to permit an agreement on a cease-fire; renewed negotiations on the first issues to reach more definitive agreement; and ultimately, final accords that would represent culmination of the previous negotiations.[54] The issues identified for the negotiations included changes in the armed forces, human rights guarantees, strengthening of the judicial system, reforms of the electoral system, constitutional reforms, a pact over economic and social problems, and UN verification.

The negotiation process was extremely difficult at times, with most of the difficulties arising from the armed forces issues and the constitutional reforms. The eventual passage of the constitutional amendments for specific reforms was a significant victory for the peace process. Despite a huge backlash from the extreme right, pressure from the European Community, the Group of Friends, the five Central American presidents, the U.S. Congress, the Bush administration, and last minute phone calls by the U.S. ambassador secured the passage of the amendments.[55]

The negotiation of the armed forces issue began in Mexico in June 1990 with the discussion of demilitarization and military impunity. The parties could not come to an agreement on this topic, but the first substantive agreement on human rights emerged from the process, an agreement that de Soto states he "pulled out of his hat."[56] In August more talks on the issue continued, with no success. The deadlock led the secretary-general to announce that all future negotiations would be conducted in secret.

Going into the negotiations, one of the FMLN's key goals was the elimination of the armed forces, but it modified this stand during the negotiations to integrating the FMLN combatants into the existing military. Coming to any agreement on FMLN participation in the armed forces proved elusive. The army was resistant to having their former adversaries in their barracks, while the FMLN suggested that members of their forces join the officer corps. The army also did not want a purge of human rights abusers, nor did they want to discuss military impunity. Talks were foundering, and the difficulties were only exacerbated by the absence of the principal decision makers. In August 1991, in a significant demonstration of the increasing support for the process, Secretary of State Baker joined with the Soviet Union's minister of foreign affairs to issue a joint statement calling on the secretary-general to take an active role in reviving the stalled talks on the armed forces issue. The secretary-general invited the General Command of the FMLN and President Cristiani to come to New York to discuss the issue of the reintegration of the FMLN into society. The outcome was a success. Perez de Cuellar correctly surmised that the pressure created by a trip to New York would allow the parties to reach an agreement on the armed forces issue. The parties also agreed to create an agenda for the negotiation of outstanding issues.

Relationship with De Soto

The FMLN and the government agree that de Soto took his role as a negotiator very seriously and put a significant amount of time into the process. He shuttled back and forth dozens of times to set up the framework at the commencement of the process. In addition, he mobilized resources for their discussions. His team-member Pedro Nikken also was praised for his ability to produce compilations of negotiations efficiently on his laptop computer.

In interviews with some of the key players in the peace process, there was some belief that de Soto brought his own agenda to the negotiating table. Escobar Galindo believed that de Soto wanted to extend his power beyond the negotiation of a peace agreement; in sum, he sought to transform the country and develop institutions. Vargas believed that de Soto used the peace process as an opportunity to make the institutions more liberal than the reality of the country demanded. Cristiani argues that de Soto's personal agenda kept de Soto from being trusted by either side, stating that he thinks "the real issue for a mediator should be how to gain trust from both sides, not how to gain distrust from both sides." Samayoa and Zamora did not view de Soto's proposals as creating the problems that Cristiani described, although Samayoa did recall that "at times, the trust of de Soto was high and at times very low."[57]

Ruben Zamora notes that de Soto was generally perceived as antimilitary, a trait that the FMLN liked and the military disliked.[58] Both Vargas and Cristiani also were offended by de Soto's characterization of the armed forces. Vargas stated, "He painted us [the armed forces] as primitive, and the military as savages. He had misdiagnosed the problem."[59] Cristiani concurred, complaining that de Soto "believes that all military are dictators, doesn't believe that there are democrats within the rank and file of the armed forces, and believes that the military are ogres who go out shooting people, this Hollywood impression, with dark glasses and shiny medals all over the place."[60] According to Vargas, this perception of de Soto's antimilitary bias heightened tension within the armed forces.

Relationship between the Parties

Both sides remarked upon the camaraderie and respect that existed between them. When asked if it was difficult to maintain good relations as war was taking place outside the negotiations, each person agreed that the battles outside had to be separate from the negotiation process. Samayoa viewed the relationship as mutually respectful and concluded that this respect was very important to the peace process. Escobar Galindo recalls that relations were thoughtful, cordial, and nonaggressive from the first meetings. In fact, General Vargas liked the opposition's negotiation team members so much that his team members teased him that he was going to divorce his wife and marry one of the FMLN leaders.

In contrast, de Soto perceived the relationships between the negotiating parties differently.

> It was difficult into the end. The stress was much greater than in Guatemala, but the adversaries were more formidable, because the Salvadoran guerrillas had actually penetrated the cities, holding the army at check. A lot of them had known each other and were on a first name basis, but the antipathy was so obvious that little came out of direct contacts.[61]

Relationship between the Parties and Their Constituents

Although the negotiations were not public, El Salvador was a polarized state, and both the FMLN and the Salvadoran government met with their constituencies throughout the process. The FMLN and government teams consulted and received feedback on relevant issues, recognizing that popular support was essential for the long-term success of the agreements. For the government, this included meetings with the business sector, the military sector, and the political parties, among others. As discussed earlier, Cristiani would have breakfast meetings with members of the oligarchy to keep them abreast of the negotiations. To manage the fears of his peers in the armed forces, Vargas convened seminars with his co-officers to discuss the agreements, and the participants wrote their opinions on aspects of the discussions anonymously and gave them to Vargas to review. The FMLN also held meetings with their constituents throughout the process, including the unions, political parties, and the working sectors of El Salvador.

End of Perez de Cuellar's Term

One factor that contributed to the timing of the peace process was the conclusion of Perez de Cuellar's tenure as secretary-general. In conversations, the parties and de Soto stated that they felt pressure to reach a settlement before the end of Perez de Cuellar's term. Although there was momentum in the process and a peace agreement was in striking distance in the final months of his term, there were a significant number of areas where little, if any, progress had been made. Perez de Cuellar's departure became a true deadline, because everyone assumed that if he left the office without a settlement the process would lose momentum. During the September talks, Cristiani visited with Boutros Boutros-Ghali, the incoming secretary-general. According to de Soto, Boutros-Ghali told Cristiani that he would be wise to strike a deal, because he could not guarantee that he would make the Salvadoran peace process a priority, and it would be months before he would be ready to take on the project. Cristiani, on the other hand, recalls that the meeting with Boutros-Ghali had a more positive spin. His recollection is that Boutros-Ghali said that he was committed to continuing the peace process with full speed.

The talks that took place at the end of December 1991 were conducted under the intense time pressure of Perez de Cuellar's departure. The secretary-general called Cristiani to ask if he could come to New York, stating that he believed that the process could be concluded before he left. Cristiani confirmed with the Friends that they would put pressure on the FMLN to reach an agreement and came to New York. The talks, under intense international pressure, included Cristiani, Perez de Cuellar, and a high-level U.S. delegation. Although at the time the atmosphere was intense, Cristiani recalled that the meetings in December were fun and even theatrical, because of the Perez de Cuellar deadline. Cristiani also believes that Perez de Cuellar had a personal motivation to strike an agreement. Because Perez de Cuellar wanted to have a political career in Peru, Cristiani believed that a peace agreement would be a gold star on his record at the United Nations. The negotiations were filled with gamesmanship. Perez de Cuellar was supposed to leave for vacation with his wife on the evening of December 31, 1991. According to Cristiani, Perez de Cuellar would say that he promised his wife he would leave for the Bahamas at six, so he was leaving. Cristiani would then call a press conference saying that if Perez de Cuellar leaves, "I'm taking the next plane down to Salvador and to hell with this process!" The secretary-general's departure pressured both sides to come to a resolution on the issues quickly, and the parties reached an agreement at midnight of the new year. The agreement, known as the Act of New York, completed the negotiations on all substantive issues of the peace process. The Act of New York also stipulated that a meeting would take place at the beginning of January 1992 to set a timetable for the implementation of the agreements and the reintegration of the FMLN into civilian life.

On January 16, 1992, in an emotional celebration in Mexico City, the parties held the ceremonial signing of the peace agreement. Secretary of State James Baker joined President Cristiani in congratulating the FMLN leaders on the historic agreement. The presidents of both Mexico and Spain and the secretary-general also came to the ceremony to offer their support and congratulations.

Success of the Mediation

Following the signing, the United Nations continued to be closely involved with the peace process in El Salvador. The reforms proposed in the El Salvador peace accords were aimed at dismantling the underlying causes that led to the conflict, and thus the peace process has been described as a "negotiated revolution."[62] United Nations peacekeepers monitored the cease-fire, separation of forces, and formal end of hostilities. The United Nations also sent down experts in human rights, civilian policing, and economic development to institute reforms in the major civilian institutions. In addition, the United Nations placed observers at the elections, ensuring that they met democratic standards and were conducted fairly and justly.

The implementation of the agreements did meet some obstacles. Because the final stages of the negotiation process were conducted with great speed, many of the agreements were vague and had to be interpreted and reinterpreted. The secretary-general sent Marrack Goulding to El Salvador to handle the negotiations over the implementation of the agreements and to tie up loose ends. Implementation fell behind schedule in several crucial areas, including the demobilization of troops, purification of the armed forces, and transfers of land to facilitate the reintegration into civilian life of both sides' combatants. Confidence in the peace process was jolted by the discovery of illegal arms caches being maintained by the FMLN and by a spate of summary executions carried out by armed illegal groups, killings which called to mind the "death squad" assassinations of the civil war years. However, despite these setbacks, the implementation process moved forward.

Conclusion

Overall, the UN intervention is viewed as a success: it resulted in a "negotiated revolution."[63] Unlike other peace accords, the peace agreement in El Salvador sought not only to end the military conflict, but also to reform the structural problems of Salvadoran society. Following the negotiations that took place in early 1992, FMLN members put down their arms, and have since become a political force in El Salvador. In the March 1997 elections, only the second vote since the war, the FMLN more than quadrupled the number of city halls under its control and almost doubled its representation in the Salvadoran Congress.[64] Thus, although the original agenda of the FMLN, the elimination of the armed forces, was sacrificed, the FMLN gained enormous political strength. Cristiani, interviewed shortly after the elections, wondered if the negotiations were not too successful, because his party has lost so much politically. Economically, the country has rebounded as well, and the war is behind it. In perhaps a telling anecdote to the extent of goodwill between the former enemies, General Vargas and FMLN leader Salvador Samayoa now cohost a radio talk show together, one of the most popular programs in El Salvador.

When asked to give recommendations for future negotiations, all the parties emphasized the unique circumstances of the El Salvador peace negotiations that would make comparisons to future negotiations difficult. Most significantly, the negotiations succeeded because the conflict was ripe for peace. Moreover, external pressures or sanctions did not force the parties to the table; rather, internal and self-imposed pressures gave them the will to reach agreements. Despite the uniqueness of the conflict, the parties did offer more general recommendations for future negotiations.

De Soto believes that a good framework is essential for a successful negotiation and that the mediator should spend all the time necessary to perform this task well. In addition, de Soto noted he had never seen a successful negotiation that pandered to the press, and thus secret negotiations provide more avenues for reaching agreements. General Vargas offered a more general recommendation for the negotiations, stating that the agreements should address the underlying issues and parties' interests, as well as reflecting the general will of the country. To do this, a mediator who knows the roots of the conflicts is important, and the parties themselves should be able to identify these issues on behalf of their own constituencies. Escobar Galindo agrees with Vargas, stating that a successful negotiation will have a mediator who has a good understanding of the conflict and the parties' demands. Cristiani, remembering his frustration with de Soto, offers the recommendation that the mediator should be impartial and convey to each side the opposition's demands. He argues that a mediator simply confuses the issues by implanting his own opinions into the discussions.

Bernard Aronson, like de Soto, emphasized the need for mediators to maintain neutrality in the negotiation process and avoid the appearance of political biases.[65] Aronson also highlighted the importance of a large and visible investment by international actors in the peace process. An internationalized process allows the parties to have friends and allies to push them in a positive way toward decision making. In addition, having a process with international involvement allows the parties to make concessions that their constituents would not ordinarily allow them to make. As an example, the eventual success of the negotiations on constitutional reforms could not have happened without the pressure from numerous international actors. Finally, the international community's involvement helps secure economic aid to implement the agreements after the process.

As a final recommendation, both the Salvadoran government and the FMLN leadership concurred that peace can only be reached if both sides are under substantial pressure to find a solution. In the Salvadoran conflict, this required keeping the conflict ongoing throughout the negotiation process.

7

The Role of International Mediation in the Northern Ireland Peace Process

Kevin King

Overview

PROTESTANT LEADER DAVID TRIMBLE and Catholic leader John Hume shared the 1998 Nobel Peace Prize for their brave negotiation efforts in the decades-old Northern Ireland conflict. Success in the negotiation was by no means fore-ordained, however: the negotiation effort required new initiatives between Britain and Ireland; creative solutions for separating the issue of decommissioning from the substantive agenda of the talks; great patience and courage on the part of the participants; and active intervention by an international body, led by former U.S. Senator George Mitchell. The talks were governed by what came to be known as the "Mitchell Principles," which tied political participation in the talks with the renunciation of violence. After nearly two years of intense negotiation, Senator Mitchell set a final deadline for agreement for Good Friday, April 9, 1998. This deadline galvanized the parties, and with direct encouragement and support from President Bill Clinton and Prime Minister Tony Blair, the parties reached an historic agreement in April 1998.

This chapter traces the complex history of the conflict, analyzes earlier peace efforts, and examines why the talks led by George Mitchell ultimately succeeded. While the agreement alone is not enough to heal the rift between the Catholic and Protestant communities, it created important multilateral institutions that will allow both communities a strong voice in determining their future and in managing any future tensions. The agreement was tested on August 15, 1998, when a Republican bomb in the market square of the town of Omagh killed twenty-eight and injured over two hundred civilians. Rather than setting in place a spiral of violence directly after the traditionally tense marching season, the horror of the bombing made both sides step back from the brink and embrace the principles that they had so strongly endorsed in the May 1998 referendum following the signing of the agreement.

Timeline

1801   Ireland is formally declared a part of the United Kingdom.

1912   The British government puts forward a new Home Rule Bill that would have provided for home rule through a single parliament for a unified Ireland. Home Rule Bill passes in 1914. World War I forces the postponement of further consideration of home rule.

1916   Irish leaders, disappointed with the failure of the Home Rule Bill and seeking more complete independence, organize an Easter uprising in Dublin. The uprising fails to receive wide support, and British forces put it down. Following the uprising, guerrilla fighting continues between the newly named Irish Republican Army (IRA) and the Royal Ulster Constabulary.

1920   The Government of Ireland Act provides for the partition of Ireland into a six-county north and a twenty-six-county south, each with its own government and parliament.

1921   The Anglo-Irish Treaty creates the Irish Free State as a self-governing unit within the United Kingdom. The Anglo-Irish Treaty is followed by civil war in the south between pro- and antitreaty forces. Pro-treaty forces prevail in 1923.

1949   The Irish Free State becomes a republic and leaves the British Commonwealth. The British Parliament adopts the Ireland Act, which confirms the status of Northern Ireland as part of the United Kingdom of Great Britain.

1968   The civil rights campaign begins in Northern Ireland.

1969   British troops deployed in Derry and Belfast.

1972   The Northern Ireland Parliament is suspended and direct rule is introduced. Henceforth, Northern Ireland is ruled from Westminster.

1981   The Anglo-Irish Intergovernmental Council is established at the Thatcher-Haughey Summit.

1985   The Anglo-Irish Agreement establishes the Anglo-Irish Ministerial Conference and Joint Secretariat.

1986   Sinn Fein drops abstentionism from its constitution. If elected, Sinn Fein candidates will take their seats in the Dail, the Republic of Ireland's Parliament.

1988   The first round of secret talks are held between John Hume, leader of the Social Democrat and Labour Party, and Gerry Adams, leader of Sinn Fein.

1990   Northern Ireland Secretary Peter Brooke initiates the three-strand formula for talks between Northern Ireland's primary political parties and British and Irish governments. Strand 1 of the talks break down after ten weeks.

1992   The three-strand talks resume. An official Unionist delegation meets an
            Irish delegation in Dublin under Strand 2. Negotiations end inconclusively.
1993   Renewed Hume–Adams talks deliver peace proposals to Irish government.
            The British and Irish governments issue the Downing Street Declaration.
1994   **August:** The IRA announces a unilateral cease-fire. October: The Com-
            bined Loyalist Military Command declares a cease-fire on behalf of Protes-
            tant paramilitaries.
1995   **February:** The Irish and British Governments publish *A New Framework
            for Agreement,* more commonly referred to as the Joint Framework Docu-
            ment. **November:** The Irish and U.K. governments issue a communiqué
            announcing the creation of an International Body to provide an indepen-
            dent assessment of the decommissioning issue.
1996   **January:** The International Body issues its report on the decommissioning
            issue recommending disarmament in stages during substantive negotia-
            tions. Shortly after the report's release, the British government proposes an
            election in Northern Ireland to establish a constituent assembly from which
            teams of negotiators would be chosen to represent the Republican and
            Unionist parties in multiparty negotiations. **Feb. 9:** The IRA terminates its
            seventeen-month cease-fire by exploding a bomb in the Docklands area of
            London. **May 30:** Elections are held in Northern Ireland to select represen-
            tatives to all-party negotiations, which are scheduled to begin on June 10.
            Although Sinn Fein has its best electoral showing ever, it is banned from the
            opening of negotiations because of the IRA's continuing military cam-
            paign. **June 10:** Delegates from Northern Ireland's political parties gather
            in Belfast for the Opening Plenary Session of negotiations. Shortly after ne-
            gotiations begin they deadlock over the issue of decommissioning.
1997   **March:** After eight months of stalemate over the issue of decommissioning,
            the Opening Plenary Session is suspended pending the approaching British
            general election and local elections in Northern Ireland. **May 1:** British vot-
            ers elect the Labour government of Tony Blair to replace the paralyzed Con-
            servative government of John Major. **June:** The British government offers
            Sinn Fein admission to the peace process if the IRA declares a "genuine"
            cease-fire and observes it for six weeks. **July 19:** After a joint appeal from
            Gerry Adams and John Hume, the IRA accepts the offer and renews its
            cease-fire. **July 24:** Both the Democratic Unionist Party and the U.K.
            Unionists walk out of the negotiations. **August:** The British and Irish gov-
            ernments sign an agreement establishing the Independent International
            Commission on Decommissioning. **Sept. 15:** Sinn Fein negotiators pledge
            their adherence to the Mitchell Principles and take their seats at the multi-
            party talks. **Dec. 22–Jan. 20:** Loyalist extremists detonate three car bombs
            in Northern Ireland. In possible retaliation for the first of these attacks, the
            Irish National Liberation Army, a Republican paramilitary group not
            bound by the IRA cease-fire, murders the leader of the Loyalist Volunteer
            Force in the Maze prison in Belfast.
1998   **Jan. 26:** The British and Irish governments expel the Ulster Democratic

Party (UDP) from the negotiations for four weeks, after the Ulster Freedom Fighters—a Unionist paramilitary group with whom the UDP is affiliated—is tied to a string of sectarian killings. **February:** Sinn Fein is expelled for two weeks from the negotiations in response to IRA killings of a Loyalist paramilitary and a "punishment" killing of a Catholic drug dealer. Recognizing that the rising tide of violence threatens to unravel the peace process, George Mitchell announces that the deadline for completion of the negotiations has been moved up from May to April 9. **Apr. 10:** After weeks of intensive negotiations, the parties to multiparty talks declare that they have reached an agreement. **May 22:** The people of Ireland, north and south, overwhelmingly approve the Northern Ireland peace agreement in separate referendums. **Aug. 15:** Republican extremists opposed to the peace process detonate a bomb in the market town of Omagh, in Northern Ireland. The blast kills twenty-eight and injures over 200. Instead of halting the peace process, however, the attack appears to strengthen momentum toward peace and reconciliation in both the Protestant and Catholic communities.

Background

On May 22, 1998, voters across Ireland went to the polls and overwhelmingly approved an ambitious peace plan intended to free the island from one of this century's most enduring violent conflicts. The peace plan, which reflects a joint understanding of the principles and processes that will determine Northern Ireland's political future, is the culmination of almost two years of sustained negotiations made possible only through international intervention and mediation.

The international mediation, which was originally requested by the Irish and British governments to facilitate negotiations and end the stalemate over the timetable for decommissioning weapons, ultimately took on a role and significance much greater than its original mission. Following publication of recommendations on decommissioning, international mediators assumed prominent roles in the multiparty talks, adding objectivity and legitimacy to the peace process—preconditions necessary for Northern Ireland's warring paramilitaries to make a successful transition from violence to political dialogue. Freed from the constant threat of violence, political parties on both sides of Northern Ireland's communal divide were able to forge a compromise agreement.

This chapter examines the Northern Ireland peace process, focusing on the flexible role of international mediation in forging the historic "Good Friday" Peace Agreement. It begins by framing the conflict with a brief overview of Ireland's troubled history, Northern Ireland's society, and the parties to the conflict. It then proceeds to trace the origins of the peace process from the early 1980s through the Downing Street Declaration of 1993. Against this introductory framework, the chapter launches into a more in-depth analysis of the conflict's "ripeness" for negotiations themselves and the evolving role of mediation within the context of the Northern Ireland peace process.

Since Northern Ireland emerged as a political entity in 1921, its history has been marked by varying degrees of low intensity violence, consisting primarily of paramilitary and terrorist attacks on both civilian and military targets. Over the past twenty-nine years alone, the violence has resulted in over 3,400 deaths and 20,000 injuries.[1] The economic impact of the conflict has also been severe, costing the United Kingdom an estimated £3 billion per year and the Republic of Ireland roughly a quarter of its annual budget.[2]

Although the focus of this chapter is the period from 1921 to the present, the roots of the conflict are inseparable from the larger tragedy of Anglo-Irish relations and extend back over eight centuries to the initial Anglo-Norman conquest of Ireland. Over this long history, the conflict has acquired multiple dimensions. What originated as primarily a religious and ethnic struggle has evolved into essentially an intercommunal fight for self-determination. Instead of losing relevance, however, religious and ethnic divisions continue to divide Northern Ireland and contribute to intercommunal tensions.

Historical Context

The religious and communal structure of Northern Ireland dates back to 1602, when the English defeated Hugh O'Neill's uprising. This was one of many conflicts between Irish and English communities on an island governed incompletely by England and, since the uprising was supported by Spain, was also part of the broader conflict between Catholic and Protestant in Europe. When O'Neill and his supporters fled, the English declared their lands forfeited to the Crown and began a systematic pattern of English and Scottish settlement in this "plantation" of Ulster. Although there were plans to completely eliminate the Irish from this region, those plans were executed only imperfectly, leaving a mix of religions and ethnic communities in the area. The settler community's close ties with, and loyalty to, London translated into economic and political power, which in turn fostered resentment in Ireland's native Catholic population.

Tensions deepened when James II, a Catholic, fled to Ireland after the "Glorious Revolution" of 1688 in England, and, with Ulster help, was defeated by William of Orange at the Battle of the Boyne in 1690. English policy treated the native Irish throughout the island as traitors and formally discriminated against them, for example, denying them the vote as well as inheritance rights. By the middle of the eighteenth century, Catholics owned less than 5 percent of the land.[3] Conflicts naturally continued. They intensified at the end of the eighteenth century when the ideas of the French Revolution spread to Ireland, reflected in another bloody revolution, supported by the French. Although the English successfully put down this rebellion, they sensed the need for reform and developed a plan for both Catholic emancipation and integrated governance of both England and Ireland through one Parliament in Westminster. Ireland was formally declared a part of the United Kingdom in 1801, but Catholic emancipation would not be achieved until 1829.

The great famine of the late 1840s was a turning point in the history of Ireland. This famine killed nearly one million people (out of a population of eight million) and led another million to emigrate, primarily to the United States.[4] The famine reflected the enormous poverty of Catholic Ireland and at the same time the relative economic prosperity of Ulster. Ultimately, the famine led to broad-scale popular action in the Catholic areas, exemplified by the Land League, which selected specific (typically English) oppressive landlords and ostracized them through mass meetings and the refusal to provide services. This period also witnessed the rise of nationalist societies, such as the Irish Republican Brotherhood (the forerunner of the IRA), that were dedicated to overthrowing the Union by force.

British governments sought to deal with these issues, as through the 1881 Land Act, strengthening the position of tenant farmers against their landlords. But radicalization continued. Home Rule legislation was considered in Westminster during the late 1880s and evoked the opposition of Ulster Protestants. On the Catholic side, Irish nationalism grew among both intellectuals and the working people, with the spread of organizations such as the Gaelic Movement. In response to internal political pressures, the British government put forward a new Home Rule Bill in 1912 that would have provided for home rule through a single parliament for a unified Ireland, with that parliament ultimately subject to Westminster (as were others in the Commonwealth). The bill was initially blocked by the House of Lords and went through several readings. This gave Ulster oppositionists time to threaten an uprising of their own, organize volunteer forces, and obtain support from some of the military as well as from the police who stood by while arms were illegally consigned to the volunteers. The Home Rule Bill did pass in 1914, following discussion of arrangements for Ulster to opt out, but these arrangements were not resolved, and formal implementation of home rule was to be postponed until the end of World War I. The discussions, however, contributed to the ultimate postwar division and establishment of two separate parliaments, one for the Catholic south in Dublin and one for Ulster in Belfast.

Irish leaders, disappointed in the Home Rule Bill, seeking more complete independence, and taking advantage of Britain's attention to the war, organized an Easter uprising in Dublin in 1916. The uprising failed to receive wide support, and British forces put it down after a week's fighting but then inflamed popular resentment against them by executing the leaders. A number of the Irish politicians elected to Westminister refused to take their seats and instead met on their own in 1919 to proclaim their sole authority over Ireland. Guerrilla conflict continued between the newly named Irish Republican Army (IRA) on the one hand and the Royal Irish Constabulary, the famous "Black and Tans," on the other. Finally, the guerrilla effort succeeded; the British and Dublin negotiated a settlement in 1921, creating the Irish Free State. In 1949, this state became a republic and left the Commonwealth. Northern Ireland remained part of the United Kingdom but was given its own parliament in Belfast with certain limited powers, including policing, education, and social services.

The partition of Ireland was never intended to provide a permanent solution to the Anglo-Irish conflict. Consequently, although it had the effect of shifting the geographical locus of the conflict, it did nothing to address the intercommunal tensions and resentments at its core. The subordination of Catholics prior to partition was perpetuated, and even intensified, after Northern Ireland became a distinct political entity. Northern Ireland's Protestant majority used the newly acquired instruments of government to entrench itself and hold down the Catholic minority. Although Britain retained considerable financial power over Northern Ireland, it chose to make little use of this instrument to force reform. Gerrymandering, discrimination, and segregation were prevalent and persisted for over forty-five years.

Rampant inequalities ultimately led to Northern Ireland's destabilization and political disintegration. Beginning in the early 1960s, the Catholic community began to organize and demand an end to Protestant abuse of political and economic power. By 1968, a nonviolent civil rights movement modeled after its U.S. counterpart had emerged from Northern Ireland's Catholic community.[5] Attempts by the Catholic community to bring about peaceful change, however, resulted in violent clashes with Northern Ireland authorities and segments of the Protestant community. These clashes in turn led to the resurgence of the IRA. In 1969, in the face of a rapidly deteriorating security situation, British military forces were called in to maintain law and order.

The British intervention of 1969 marked the end of Northern Ireland's relative independence and set the present context for the conflict. As the number of British troops in Northern Ireland grew from initially a few hundred to 30,000 at one point in 1972, so did British involvement in the daily affairs of Northern Ireland.[6] Although the British implemented reform policies, the presence of the army created new problems. The security state dictated by IRA and other paramilitary violence was not conducive to the exercise of human rights and civil liberties. In the summer of 1971, British and Northern Ireland authorities, in an effort to break the IRA, instituted a policy of internment under which Catholics suspected of involvement with the IRA were arrested and held without trial. By the spring of 1972, 900 individuals were being held, many of them innocent.[7] Many of these detainees were questioned by authorities and subjected to harsh and demeaning interrogation techniques.[8] Amidst escalating violence and British involvement, it became increasingly difficult for the British to prop up the local government. In March 1972, the United Kingdom imposed direct rule and disbanded the Northern Ireland Parliament. Although direct rule was originally intended to be a temporary measure, both communities possessed the power to thwart any attempt at reform. Northern Ireland thus entered a state of political deadlock. With the exception of a three-month period in 1974, Northern Ireland was governed directly from Westminster until the summer of 1998.

Northern Ireland's Communal Divide

The modern legacy of Northern Ireland's tragic history is a society severed into two distinct communities—one Irish-Catholic and Nationalist, the other settler (i.e., Scottish, Welsh, or English)-Protestant and Unionist. The divide that exists between the communities consists of a complex layering of differences that transcends religion and encompasses ethnicity, culture, historical experience, and social class. Together, these differences force the communities apart, reducing opportunities for cross-community contact and relationships.

Northern Ireland's communal divide is wide. The Catholic and Protestant communities tend to live in separate areas, attend different schools, and often work in different settings.[9] Demographics illustrate a clear tendency for people in Northern Ireland to live in areas populated primarily by members of their own community. This phenomenon appears to be driven by a search for security. As Kevin Boyle and Tom Hadden observe, "[i]t takes only one brick through a window or one scribbled graffiti to make a family move out of a mixed into a safer area."[10] This self-imposed segregation extends to formalized education. Virtually all of Northern Ireland's primary and secondary schools are segregated. Ireland's first integrated school was not established until 1981. Currently, there are only thirty-three integrated schools in Northern Ireland (twenty-two primary and eleven post-primary) with a total enrollment of about 7,000 students, or roughly 3 percent of the relevant population.[11]

Despite efforts by the British Government to combat employment discrimination, wealth and class disparities continue to plague Northern Ireland, though to a much lesser extent today than two decades ago. The Catholic community in Northern Ireland has always had a higher rate of unemployment than the Protestant community.[12] In 1991, Northern Ireland experienced an overall unemployment rate for male workers of 20 percent. Broken down by community, the male unemployment rate among Protestants was only 13.9 percent, compared to male unemployment among Catholics of 28 percent.

The disproportionate unemployment rate for the Catholic community helps to explain its downward-focused wealth profile compared to that of the Protestant community.[13] The average income for Protestant households tends to be larger than the income of Catholic households. In 1992, for example, the average income for Protestant households in Northern Ireland was £290 a week compared to £264 for Catholic households—roughly a 10 percent disparity. These statistics belie an even greater disparity, since the average Catholic household of 3.2 persons is larger than the average Protestant household of 2.5 persons.[14]

The divide that exists between Northern Ireland's two communities has traditionally presented a formidable obstacle to peace and reconciliation. Not only does it help perpetuate cross-community animosities and intolerance, it can also, during times of intercommunal tension, generate a siege mentality and radicalization. The root of this mentality is insecurity—for Catholics arising from their minority status and their history of persecution and subordination, for Protestants arising from concerns about their future ability to preserve their cultural identity and remain independent from the Republic of Ireland. This dynamic is particularly evident during Northern Ireland's "marching season," when Unionist hard-liners insist on parading through Catholic neighborhoods in tribute to the Protestant victory over the Catholics in July 1690.

Members within both the Protestant and Catholic communities have tried over many years to build bridges between the groups. Hundreds of grassroots meetings, often sponsored by churches, religious groups, and nongovernmental organizations (NGOs), have sought common ground in the conflict. While these activities are beyond the scope of this chapter, the grassroots movement has played a crucial role in priming the communities for peace and creating an atmosphere in which an ultimate agreement might flourish.

The Parties to the Northern Ireland Conflict

The conflict in Northern Ireland is an intercommunal struggle over the political future of the province. The principal antagonists are the province's Protestant and Catholic communities, each represented by political movements that embody their political aspirations. These movements, referred to generally as Unionism and Nationalism, are not monolithic, but encompass numerous factions and subgroups. The roles of the British and Irish governments are historical in origin and place them in the center of the peace process.

Unionists

Northern Ireland's Unionists are united in their primary objectives: a Northern Ireland independent from the Republic, under Protestant control, and part of the United Kingdom. The two primary Unionist political parties in Northern Ireland are the Ulster Unionist Party (UUP) and the Democratic Unionist Party (DUP). Although they differ on domestic social and political issues, both parties are united in their rejection of unification with the Republic of Ireland and in their support for Northern Ireland's continued status as a province within the United Kingdom. Of the two parties, the DUP is the more antinationalist.

The common position among Northern Ireland's Unionists with respect to the United Kingdom, however, belies complex motives. As Joseph Ruane and Jennifer Todd note, the reasons for valuing ties with the United Kingdom vary.

> Some do so because they feel a deep sense of loyalty and affinity with the British world or fellow British subjects, others because of a commitment to what Arthur Aughey has called the "idea of the Union." Others value particular British institutions or traditions . . . or the British economic subventions. For still others the union serves a purely defensive function—it is a defense of Protestant interests against Roman Catholicism and a united Ireland. For many, there is a strong conditional quality to their support; if the benefits ceased, loyalty would no longer be assured.[15]

These various motivations merge in a complex relationship between London and Northern Ireland—characterized by both loyalty and distrust.

A number of Unionist paramilitary groups exist, the largest of which is the Ulster Defense Association (UDA). Traditionally, Unionist paramilitary violence has been reactionary, shadowing Republican violence. The 1990s, however, have witnessed a surge in Unionist killings, with Unionist paramilitaries for the first time killing more victims than their Republican counterparts.[16]

Nationalists

The primary objective of Northern Ireland's Nationalists (or Republicans) is the unification of Ireland. The nationalist movement is overwhelmingly comprised of Catholics. Although 80 percent of Northern Ireland's Catholics support the goal of Irish unification, the community—and the Nationalist movement—is split over how and when unification should be achieved. The differences over unification are reflected in the two primary Nationalist political parties: the Social Democratic and Labour Party (SDLP) and Sinn Fein, the political wing of the IRA. The SDLP is the largest Catholic political party in Northern Ireland, holding approximately two-thirds of the Catholic vote. It favors a united Ireland achieved through constitutional means that secure Protestant participation. For the SDLP, the goal of a united Ireland is a long-term aspiration—the major obstacle being the intransigence of Northern Ireland's Protestant community. The SDLP's principal rival for Catholic votes in Northern Ireland is Sinn Fein, which favors the immediate unification of Ireland and the removal of British forces from the island. As its ties with the IRA suggest, Sinn Fein has traditionally viewed the use of political violence, in the form of bombings and assassinations, as a strategic necessity.

The IRA is by far the largest of the Republican paramilitary groups. It is a well-financed and well-equipped force of about 400 principal members. For almost three decades, the IRA has waged an armed campaign against Northern Ireland's security forces and the civilian Protestant community. During that time, the IRA is believed to be responsible for the deaths of approximately 1,800 people. After declaring its cease-fire in 1994, the IRA continued to police the Catholic community and carried out a number of "punishment beatings" and killings of suspected drug dealers. This policing function reflects the traditional IRA rejection of the Northern Ireland police, the Royal Ulster Constabulary, which is overwhelmingly Protestant in religious affiliation.

The United Kingdom

The official British position is that Northern Ireland is a part of the United Kingdom. The British government traditionally has viewed the conflict as an internal matter and resisted efforts to "internationalize" the conflict. In 1985, in a major change of policy, the British government recognized the Republic of Ireland's "special interest" in the affairs of Northern Ireland.

Since 1969, the British military has maintained a large presence in Northern Ireland. British troop strength in the province currently stands at approximately 17,000. This presence has frequently been targeted by nationalist paramilitaries.

Despite the large military presence, the British government has repeatedly insisted that it possesses no selfish economic or strategic designs in Northern Ireland and that it will uphold the democratic wish of the majority of citizens in Northern Ireland on the issue of whether they prefer to support the Union or a sovereign United Ireland.

The Republic of Ireland

The Republic of Ireland, which is approximately 95 percent Catholic, never relinquished its claim to the entire island following partition in 1921, as reflected in the Republic's Constitution, Articles 2 and 3 of which assert jurisdiction over all of Ireland's original thirty-two counties. Since its acceptance of the Anglo-Irish Agreement in 1985, however, the Republic's claim to all of Ireland has given way to the recognition that unification will require the approval of a majority in Northern Ireland.

As part of the Anglo-Irish Agreement a standing Intergovernmental Conference, served by a permanent Joint Secretariat composed of Irish and British civil servants, was established to permit the Republic of Ireland to put forward proposals on British policy toward the province. The Republic has tended to use its influence over the formulation of British policy in Northern Ireland to strengthen the position of the SDLP, whose emphasis on slow constitutional change and recognition of the need for intercommunal tolerance is more in line with the objectives of the peace process, as reflected in the 1985 Anglo-Irish Agreement, the Downing Street Declaration, and the 1995 Frameworks Documents.

Key Interventions and Major Actors

Origins of the Northern Ireland Peace Process

The multiparty negotiations that culminated in the Good Friday Agreement are simply the final phase of a larger process, the origins of which can be traced back to the early 1980s, and improved Anglo-Irish relations. Beginning with the first Anglo-Irish summit between British Prime Minister Margaret Thatcher and Irish Taoiseach (Prime Minister) Charles Haughey in 1980, bilateral relations that had for decades been characterized by discord were transformed and came to be defined by a relatively high degree of cooperation and mutual support. Over the next fifteen years, British and Irish officials worked together to produce a series of joint agreements, declarations, and initiatives that set the structure of negotiations and identified fundamental principles upon which a political resolution to the conflict could be based. Although these developments preceded multiparty negotiations, each moved the peace process forward and contributed to its successful conclusion. The key developments during this period included the Anglo-Irish Agreement, the failed Brooke-Mayhew Initiative, and the Downing Street Declaration.

The Anglo-Irish Agreement of 1985

The first tangible manifestation of the new relationship between Dublin and London was the 1985 Anglo-Irish Agreement ("the Agreement"). The Agreement was intended to strengthen constitutional nationalism against the IRA—an idea that found support not only among British officials, but also within the Republic. The Agreement accomplished this objective by institutionalizing the emerging partnership between Dublin and London and recognizing the legitimate interest of the Republic of Ireland in the affairs of Northern Ireland. The momentous nature of the Agreement arose from its creation of a standing Intergovernmental Conference, served by a permanent Joint Secretariat composed of Irish and British civil servants. Within the Conference, the Republic of Ireland is permitted to put forward proposals on British policy toward the province, for the first time giving Irish Nationalists a voice in the formulation of British policy in Northern Ireland. Almost as important as the Conference itself were the relationships that emerged from the negotiations. Key figures in London and Dublin developed relationships of trust, which reinforced and provided resiliency to the peace process.

The Brooke-Mayhew Initiative

In January 1990, newly appointed British Secretary for Northern Ireland Peter Brooke initiated an effort to bring the major political parties of Northern Ireland to the negotiating table. The Brooke initiative differed from earlier efforts to create a dialogue between the parties to the conflict because of the central role played by the Republic of Ireland. The Intergovernmental Conference and the Joint Secretariat established under the 1985 Anglo-Irish Agreement not only guaranteed formal Irish government support for the effort, but also brought them into the process as a cosponsor of the effort. After more than a year of relentless effort, Brooke announced a three-strand framework for the talks, designed to take account of the different facets of the Northern Ireland conflict: Strand 1 was intended to address the relationships between the parties in Northern Ireland; Strand 2 was intended to take account of the relationship between Northern Ireland and the Republic of Ireland; and, finally, Strand 3 was designed to address the relationship between the Republic of Ireland and the United Kingdom. Despite efforts taken to initiate the talks, they faltered from the outset. The Strand 1 talks conducted under Brooke's supervision bogged down over procedural matters and were not successfully concluded. Strands 2 and 3 were initiated by Brooke's successor, Patrick Mayhew, and concluded similarly to Strand 1.

Nevertheless, the initiative marked a significant contribution to the peace process. Although bringing political parties from Northern Ireland's two communities together and initiating dialogue was a considerable achievement in itself, the three-strand formula devised by Brooke remained the basic framework for negotiations throughout the remainder of the peace process. In addition, the failed initiative provided a valuable lesson regarding the limits of Britain's role in the process. Although Brooke's determination and personal attributes are credited with making the talks possible, his position as British secretary for Northern Ireland hopelessly complicated his role in the negotiations. Brooke is said to have seen himself as a facilitator, using reasoning, persuasion, the control of information, and the suggestion of alternatives to bring about a negotiated settlement.[17] However, as a representative of a party to the negotiations, he could not be impartial. As one observer noted, during the process "[h]e used the resources of his position as Secretary to employ leverage and coercion, he attempted manipulation of the parties, he was a fully involved member of the negotiating triad."[18]

The Downing Street Declaration and the 1994 Cease-fires

Despite the failure of the Brooke–Mayhew Initiative, the peace process progressed. On December 15, 1993, Irish Taoiseach Albert Reynolds and British Prime Minister John Major issued a Joint Declaration, commonly referred to as the Downing Street Declaration, setting out both governments' understanding of the origins of the conflict, its character, their common interest in resolving the conflict, and principles upon which a peace process could be founded. The professed goal of the Irish and British governments was the creation, through a process of political dialogue, of "institutions and structures which, while respecting the diversity of the people of Ireland, would enable them to work together in all areas of common interests."[19]

At the heart of the Declaration were the principles of self-determination and democracy (i.e., respect for the consent of the majority). Britain asserted in the Declaration that it possessed no selfish economic or strategic designs in Northern Ireland and affirmed that it "[would] uphold the democratic wish of a greater number of people of Northern Ireland on the issue of whether they prefer to support the Union or a sovereign United Ireland."[20] The Irish government, for its part, noted that "it would be wrong to attempt to impose a united Ireland, in the absence of the freely given consent of a majority of the people in Northern Ireland" and accepted that "the democratic right of self-determination by the people of Ireland as a whole must be achieved and exercised with and subject to the agreement and consent of the majority of the people of Northern Ireland, and must, consistent with justice and equity, respect the democratic dignity and the civil rights of both communities."[21]

The Declaration, while mandating that the pursuit of political objectives must be settled by exclusively peaceful and democratic means, held out an open invitation to paramilitaries positioned outside of the "legitimate dialogue." Paragraph 10 of the Declaration stated that "[d]emocratically mandated parties which establish a commitment to exclusively peaceful methods and which have shown that they abide by the democratic process, are free to participate fully in democratic politics and to join in dialogue in due course between the Governments and the political parties on the way ahead."[22] The Declaration thus presented paramilitaries with a choice: renounce violence and participate in the peace process or risk political marginalization.

The IRA spent the months immediately following the Declaration seeking clarification of its meaning. However, on August 31, 1994, the IRA called for a unilateral cessation of its military operations. Republican splinter groups, including the Irish National Liberation Army (INLA) and Republican Sinn Fein (RSF), refused to commit to the cease-fire. Nevertheless, the IRA announcement was followed on October 13 by a cease-fire declared by the Combined Loyalist Military Command on behalf of Protestant paramilitaries.

A Window of Opportunity for Conflict Resolution

According to I. William Zartman, the success of mediation is tied to the perception and creation of a "ripe" moment. He identifies three dimensions that determine the suitability of a moment for conflict resolution: the intensity of the conflict, the alternatives available to the parties, and the power relations among the parties.[23]

The IRA cease-fire of August 1994 was a turning point in the Northern Ireland peace process. It reflected a willingness on behalf of Republican paramilitaries to engage in serious political dialogue—an essential ingredient that had been missing from the peace process since its slow beginning in the early 1980s. Without Republican participation, the negotiations offered little or no hope of yielding a political settlement that would end, or at least curtail, Republican paramilitary violence. However, with Sinn Fein and the IRA on board, the stage was set for achieving meaningful progress. British Prime Minister John Major echoed this sentiment, when he stated following the IRA cease-fire that the then existing situation in Northern Ireland offered the "best opportunity for peace in twenty-five years." The Republican decision to participate in negotiations toward a political settlement was driven by the prevailing military stalemate in Northern Ireland and was actively encouraged and reinforced by the Clinton administration.

The Military Stalemate and the Emergence of a Republican Political Strategy

By the mid-1990s, it was clear to all those involved in the Northern Ireland conflict that a point of military stalemate had been reached. Neither Nationalists nor Unionists possessed the military or political resources necessary to guarantee fulfillment of their political aspirations. But whereas other political parties were engaged in the political process, Sinn Fein and the IRA remained politically marginalized because of their continued reliance on violence. Without the participation of Sinn Fein and the approval of the IRA, there was little hope in forging a meaningful peace agreement.

For the IRA, the stalemate meant the implicit failure of its military campaign: twenty-five years of violence had failed to achieve the unification of Ireland or force the withdrawal of British troops. Moreover, the ongoing cycle of violence was undermining support for Republican paramilitaries within the Catholic community. The Catholic community—despite its Nationalist tendencies—

remained strongly in favor of peaceful change in Northern Ireland and disapproved of the violent methods employed by the IRA and other Republican paramilitaries. The stalemate thus left the IRA and its political wing, Sinn Fein, no choice but to turn to a new strategy and a new forum for pursuing their goals. In the words of Richard McAuly, press secretary for Gerry Adams,

> Republicans had long accepted that this was a war that nobody could win. And in that context, what do you do? The obvious answer is you try to find some way of bringing the different enemies together, preferably around a table, and work out some way of negotiating a settlement.[24]

The politicization of the Republican movement began only after the hunger strikes of 1980 and 1981, which attracted unprecedented attention and sympathy for the Republican cause. From a standing start, within three years Sinn Fein was capturing over 13 percent of the vote in Northern Ireland (representing 40 percent of Northern Ireland's Catholic vote). The evolution of a political component in Republican strategy accelerated in the second half of the 1980s with the unprecedented decision to allow Sinn Fein representatives to take their seats in the Republic of Ireland's parliament and Gerry Adams's secret negotiations with John Hume, head of the SDLP, regarding the future of Northern Ireland. With the IRA ceasefire, however, the transformation of Republican strategy was nearly complete. For the first time, political participation took precedence over the military campaign.

The Clinton Administration as Facilitator

The transformation of Republican strategy was facilitated by the Clinton administration, which recognized and embraced the changes taking place within the Republican movement. In January 1994, seven months before the IRA declared its cease-fire, the Clinton administration ordered that Gerry Adams, president of Sinn Fein, be granted a one-day visa to address a peace conference at the Waldorf Astoria in New York. In justifying his decision, President Clinton noted that "[Gerry Adams's] comments . . . on the questions of violence and the joint declaration . . . justified not a general visa, but a very narrow visa for the purpose of coming to this conference in the hope that it will advance the peace process."[25]

The decision to issue the visa was one of the administration's boldest foreign policy decisions, but also one of its politically safest. The decision was made by the White House against the advice of the State and Justice Departments, and in the face of resistance from the British government. Moreover, it represented a clean break with the traditional "hands off" policy of earlier administrations, which viewed Northern Ireland as an internal British matter. However, the move enjoyed strong support from America's powerful Irish-American lobby. Nancy Soderberg, staff director for the National Security Council, recalls the decision:

> [W]e were getting increasing pressure from Irish America to let him in and I think we were all very skeptical . . . But the more I looked at it, the more I realized it was a win–

win situation for us. If we reached out to Mr. Adams and to Sinn Fein and it helped move them to a peaceful strategy, to help influence the IRA to declare a cease-fire, obviously that's a win.[26]

This initial visa—while influential in its own right—was part of a larger plan to draw Sinn Fein into the political mainstream. The strategy tied administration overtures to Sinn Fein to that organization's commitment to the peace process. Following the IRA's cease-fire declaration, Adams was again allowed into the United States. This second visit was longer than the first and included a warm reception from Senator Edward Kennedy. The culmination of this strategy, however, came in March 1995 when Gerry Adams was allowed to take a two-week tour of the United States that included a personal meeting with the president and fund-raising. The latter ultimately netted $1.3 million for Sinn Fein.

The visas and the subsequent success of Gerry Adams's visits were important factors in securing the IRA cease-fire and eventual participation of Sinn Fein in the peace process. First, the visits—which attracted a great deal of media attention—provided stunning examples to Sinn Fein and the IRA of the political rewards that could be gained by becoming legitimate players in the political process. Second, they gave the IRA and Sinn Fein self-confidence and access to a much wider audience. Finally, the visas convinced them that the United States was committed to seeing the peace process through to a successful conclusion and was willing to seriously consider their views. Taken together, these considerations presented them with their best opportunity to secure their political objectives. Although political participation, with its emphasis on process and compromise, meant that Republican aspirations would not be achieved in the short term, it offered the IRA a better chance for eventual success than the alternative strategy of continued violence and military stalemate.

Form and Specific Mechanisms of Intervention

The IRA's cease-fire in 1994 presented an opportunity for meaningful progress in the peace process. However, it was just that—an opportunity. Moving from cease-fire to comprehensive and all-inclusive political negotiations was a formidable task. The divide between Northern Ireland's communities remained immense.

In February 1995, the Irish and British governments published *A New Framework for Agreement,* more commonly referred to as the Joint Framework Document.[27] The Joint Framework Document represented "a shared understanding reached between [the Irish and British governments] on the parameters of a possible outcome to the Talks" and was intended "to give impetus and direction to the process."[28] Notably, it proposed that negotiations be structured according to the three strand formula arrived at during the Brooke–Mayhew Initiative.[29] In addition, the document applied the principles espoused in the Joint Declaration—namely, self-determination, democracy, and nonviolence.[30]

Although the Joint Framework Document and the previous peace initiatives had moved the process along by establishing a workable framework for negotiations and identifying fundamental principles that would have to be incorporated into any ultimate resolution, the initiatives had not established a solid foundation on which all-inclusive political talks could be based. The major political parties of Northern Ireland had never faced each other in comprehensive negotiations. Moreover, a number of vexing issues needed resolution before the parties would even consider participating in negotiations, the most pressing being how and when to decommission the stockpiles of weapons amassed by Northern Ireland's paramilitaries.

The International Body on Decommissioning

The issue of when and how to disarm Northern Ireland's paramilitaries was one of the most formidable addressed throughout the negotiations. For both Unionists and Republicans, the decommissioning issue took on a symbolic significance out of proportion to its military or political importance. Legitimately concerned about the ease with which paramilitary cease-fires could be terminated, and unwilling to negotiate under the threat of violence, several political parties conditioned their participation in multiparty negotiations on the decommissioning of weapons prior to the start of negotiations. The British government agreed with this assessment and made paramilitary decommissioning a prerequisite for the participation of political parties linked to paramilitary groups. This category encompassed Sinn Fein as well as the Ulster Democratic Party, which is affiliated with the Ulster Freedom Fighters. The IRA, however, had been operating under the understanding that its cease-fire alone would be sufficient to guarantee Sinn Fein's participation. It perceived this new demand as a delaying tactic and a sign of British bad faith. The IRA believed that decommissioning at any time prior to a final political settlement would symbolize defeat. In the words of Gerry Adams, "The British government [was] not simply interested in a gesture. It [was], in reality, demanding the start of a surrender process as a precondition to [multiparty] talks."[31]

To break this impasse, on November 28, 1995, the Irish and British governments issued a communiqué announcing the creation of an International Body to "provide an independent assessment of the decommissioning issue."[32] The communiqué represented a severing of the decommissioning issue from the pre-negotiation process. From this point forward, decommissioning would be handled separately from the preliminary discussions concerning the basis, participation, structure, and agenda of multiparty negotiations. The International Body's mandate concerned solely the narrow issue of decommissioning. Specifically, the International Body was requested to

- identify and advise on a suitable and acceptable method for full and verifiable decommissioning and
- report whether there was a clear commitment on the part of those in possession of such arms to work constructively to achieve full and verifiable decommissioning.[33]

Former U.S. Senator George Mitchell, then serving as a U.S. envoy to Northern Ireland for economic development, was asked to head the International Body. Mitchell was joined on the commission by Harri Holkeri, former prime minister of Finland, and General John de Chastelain, the former head of the Canadian Defense Forum. George Mitchell was an excellent selection to lead the International Body. He was familiar with both the conflict and the prominent figures involved in the process, including British Prime Minister John Major. Moreover, as an American, Mitchell's appointment helped to sustain U.S. support for the peace process.

The International Body was structured as a traditional consultative body without authority to impose its views on the parties. The strategy was to involve a neutral third party to facilitate problem solving through communication and analysis. The communiqué provided the International Body with authority to determine its own procedures, but noted that both the Irish and British governments expected the International Body to meet with the relevant parties and elicit their views on decommissioning.[34] The limited authority and narrow focus of the International Body were most likely necessary to obtain British approval to open the peace process to international involvement. Only months earlier, British Prime Minister John Major rejected a UN offer to hold an international peace conference in Geneva to break the deadlock in the Northern Ireland peace process.[35]

Two series of meetings were held by the International Body: the first in Belfast and Dublin, December 15–18, 1995, and the second in London, January 11–22, 1996. During the course of these meetings, the International Body received oral and written submissions from the various parties to the conflict, including testimony from government officials, political leaders, and church officials. In addition to information received through the formal meetings, the commission received hundreds of letters and telephone calls from members of the general public.[36]

The Report

On January 22, 1996, the International Body issued its independent assessment of the decommissioning issue. Although the International Body found "a clear commitment on the part of those in possession of . . . arms to work constructively to achieve full and verifiable decommissioning," it concluded that this commitment did not extend to decommissioning prior to multiparty negotiations.[37] To address that reality, the International Body advanced a compromise position calling for decommissioning in phases during the negotiations. The International Body argued that decommissioning during negotiations would contribute momentum to the peace process and could serve as a useful confidence-building measure.[38]

Notwithstanding its compromise recommendation, the International Body recognized the need to insulate the negotiations from violence and the threat of violence. To achieve this objective, it recommended that all parties "affirm their total and absolute commitment" to six principles of democracy and nonviolence.[39] These six commitments, which later came to be known as the Mitchell Principles, tied political participation in multiparty negotiations to the renunciation of violence. It was hoped that the use of these Mitchell Principles as conditions for participation in the peace process would ensure that parties approached the negotiations in good faith.

For the Mitchell Principles to be effective as a code of conduct, two conditions had to exist. First, the advantages from participating in the negotiations had to outweigh those presented by violence. If parties believed that they could gain more from continued violence, there would be little incentive to participate in negotiations. Second, the Mitchell Principles had to be backed with a plausible threat of sanctions. In the Northern Ireland context, these preconditions were met. The prevailing military stalemate essentially nullified the military option and consequently enhanced the relative attractiveness of negotiations. Moreover, the threat of expulsion for violation of the Mitchell Principles was real as would subsequently become clear from Sinn Fein's exclusion from the peace process.

To ensure that decommissioning would proceed in an orderly and acceptable manner, the International Body urged the creation of an independent commission, appointed by the governments after consultations with the parties, to supervise the process.[40] The International Body noted that in order to perform its functions adequately, the independent commission would need to be authorized to act independently of the governments and be given appropriate legal immunities. With respect to the method of decommissioning, the International Body recommended that the decommissioning process should (i) be applied in a manner that suggests neither victory nor defeat; (ii) be verifiable; (iii) result in the complete destruction of weapons; and (iv) not expose individuals to prosecution (i.e., the weapons turned over during the decommissioning process should be immune from forensic examination).[41]

In an implied rejection of the International Body's recommendation on the timing of decommissioning, the British government proposed an alternative to multiparty talks that was based on a confidence-building measure identified in the International Body's report.[42] The proposal called for an election in Northern Ireland to establish a constituent assembly from which teams of negotiators would be chosen to represent the Republican and Unionist parties. Under the British proposal, the sole purpose of the elections would be to provide an alternative to the prior decommissioning of weapons. The elected body would not possess legislative or executive powers.

In the short term, the British proposal was a major blow to the peace process, as well as to Anglo-Irish relations. The Irish government, which had warmly welcomed the International Body's recommendation, was caught unprepared by the British action.[43] Irish officials were outraged that they had not been previously consulted on the proposal and criticized the electoral scheme on the basis that it would provide the Unionist majority with a veto over political developments in Northern Ireland. This criticism was shared by Northern Ireland's Nationalist community.[44]

The British government's rationale for not implementing the International Body's recommendations is not entirely clear. The proffered electoral scheme sought to avoid the decommissioning issue—an obstacle that the British had helped to create—by providing an alternative path to multiparty negotiations. To the extent that the proposal decoupled decommissioning and participation in negotiations, the electoral scheme represented a clear victory for Republicans and a concession by the British: it would allow the IRA access to negotiations without having to turn over any weapons. However, in a striking example of the level of distrust and animosity between the parties to the conflict, Republicans cynically perceived the British proposal, not as a victory, but as "yet another obstacle to negotiations" and further proof of British bad faith.

On February 9, 1996, the IRA shattered its seventeen-month cease-fire by exploding a 1000-pound bomb in the Docklands area east of London. The explosion killed two people, injured forty-three and caused $150 million in damage. Within nine days the IRA staged two additional attempted bombings.[45] The termination of the cease-fire did not come as a surprise to many observers. The IRA had declared its cease-fire with the expectation that substantive negotiations would begin within three months. In the weeks preceding the explosion, the IRA and Sinn Fein had repeatedly expressed frustration over the slow pace of the peace process. An IRA statement issued one hour prior to the Docklands blast echoed that frustration: "[t]he cessation [in hostilities] presented an historic challenge for everyone and the IRA commends the leaderships of the nationalist Ireland at home and abroad. They rose to the challenge. The British Prime Minister did not."[46]

Whether decommissioning parallel to negotiations was ultimately feasible is, and will remain, a matter of speculation. Although the International Body had identified parallel decommissioning as a possible confidence-building measure, it is just as likely, given the distrust between the parties, that it would have destabilized the talks. Nevertheless, the measure of the International Body's role in the peace process is not the implementation of its recommendations for resolving the decommissioning issue, but it's significant impact on the larger process. First, the intervention allowed the British government to avoid the dual role, namely that of sponsor of and vital party to the peace process, that handicapped the earlier Brooke-Mayhew initiative.[47] Second, the International Body brought objectivity and legitimacy to the process. Third, adherence to the Mitchell Principles of democracy and nonviolence became the ticket of admission to the peace process and provided the security necessary for the success of the talks.

International Involvement in the Multiparty Negotiations

The period immediately following publication of the International Body's report was one of the low points of the entire fifteen-year peace process. The IRA's termination of its cease-fire shattered hopes across Ireland and the United Kingdom for a quick settlement of the conflict. Accusations of blame for collapse of the negotiations were exchanged between the Irish and British governments.

Within several weeks, however, the situation began to move forward. A compromise blueprint regarding the path to all-party talks was worked out between the Irish and British governments. The blueprint established a two-step procedure. Step one, put forward by the Irish government, called for Northern Ireland's major political parties to participate in Dayton-style proximity talks, in which parties would gather at a single location but not meet face-to-face. Rather, negotiations would be conducted through intermediaries—in this case representatives of the Irish and British governments. It was the hope of the Irish government that proximity talks would create momentum and restore confidence in the overall process. The purpose of the proximity talks would be to hammer out the procedures for step two, the Northern Ireland elections called for by the British. Under the blueprint, the elections would lead directly to all-party talks, which were scheduled to begin on June 10, 1996.

Northern Ireland Forum Elections

The proximity negotiations were held March 4–13, 1996, but were inconclusive. A dispute arose among the parties over the election procedures. The UUP proposed that the elections be based upon the constituencies used in elections for the British Parliament. Under this plan, the Protestants would maximize their representation, thus benefiting the UUP—the largest Protestant political party within Northern Ireland. The UUP proposal was opposed by the SDLP and, oddly enough, the radical DUP. The SDLP and the DUP argued for use of the electoral system used for European Parliament elections, which would increase representation of their respective parties.

Failing to obtain an agreement among Northern Ireland's political parties, the British government promulgated procedures for the election later that month. Voting was set to take place using the constituencies intended for British parliamentary elections. The procedures called for voters in Northern Ireland to elect a 110-member forum, from which delegates to multiparty negotiations would be selected. The top five political parties in each constituency would be allowed to send delegates to the talks based on their proportion of votes cast. Twenty additional delegates, however, would be awarded to the ten parties receiving the highest number of votes province-wide. The date for the election was set as May 30, 1996.

The elections took place as planned. All of Northern Ireland's major political parties took part, including Sinn Fein. Despite bad weather conditions, 65 percent of Northern Ireland's voters turned out. As expected, the UUP and the DUP won the most seats (thirty and twenty-four seats respectively). The SDLP was the leading Nationalist party, receiving 21.4 percent of the vote and qualifying for twenty-one forum seats. In its best electoral showing ever, Sinn Fein qualified for seventeen seats, with 15.5 percent of the vote, but remained barred from the process until the IRA instituted a permanent cease-fire. It is unclear whether the surge in support for Sinn Fein was intended to encourage the IRA to resume its cease-fire or reflected growing Nationalist frustration with the peace process and a radicalization of Nationalist voters. Other Northern Ireland political parties receiving sufficient support to be represented in the forum included the Alliance Party (seven seats), the United Kingdom Unionist Party (three seats), the Northern Ireland Women's Coalition (two seats), the Progressive Unionist Party (two seats), the Ulster Democratic Party (two seats), and a Labour coalition (two seats).

The Opening Plenary Session of Multiparty Negotiations

Delegates from Northern Ireland's political parties gathered in Belfast on June 10, 1996, to open negotiations. The opening of negotiations was marked by the failure to assemble all of Northern Ireland's major political parties, as Sinn Fein was denied entrance to the talks due to the IRA's continuing campaign of violence. Despite the provocation posed by the IRA, the Unionist cease-fire had remained in effect. Consequently, the UDP and the Progressive Unionist Party, both of which had affiliations with Unionist paramilitaries, were allowed to participate in the talks.

The negotiations were structured to begin with an opening Plenary Session, during which the parties would negotiate rules of procedure, create a Business Committee to address unresolved procedural issues, set the agenda for the substantive negotiations, and appoint a subcommittee to address the issue of decommissioning. Substantive negotiations were set to follow the successful completion of the opening Plenary Session and were structured on the three-strand format arrived at by Peter Brooke, former Northern Ireland secretary, during his 1990 peace initiative. Under this formula, Strand 1 negotiations would address the relationships between the various parties of Northern Ireland, Strand 2 negotiations would focus on the relationship between Northern Ireland and the Republic of Ireland, and Strand 3 negotiations would address the relationship between the Republic of Ireland and the United Kingdom. The Subcommittee on Decommissioning would focus solely on the decommissioning issue. Negotiations under all three strands and on decommissioning would parallel one other. Coordination of the entire process fell under the responsibility of the independent chairman of the Plenary Session, who was authorized to convene meetings of the Plenary as necessary. The basis for progress in the negotiations would be the concept of "sufficient consensus," measured by the support of parties that, taken together, constitute a clear majority of the valid poll and between them represent a clear majority in both the Unionist and Nationalist communities in Northern Ireland, respectively. Apart from the opening ceremonies, the negotiations would be closed to the public.

All three members of the International Body were asked by the Irish and British governments to assume positions of responsibility in the negotiations: George Mitchell was asked to assume the chair of the Plenary Session and the Subcommittee on Decommissioning; General John de Chastelain was asked to serve as independent chairman of the Strand 2 negotiations involving the relationships within the island of Ireland, and chair the Business Committee; and

Harri Holkeri was asked to serve as an alternate for any of the independent chairman roles. The Strand 1 negotiations would be chaired by the British government, and the Strand 3 negotiations would be jointly chaired by the Irish and British governments.

Virtually from the moment the talks opened they became mired in intense and acrimonious debate. Led by David Trimble, leader of the UUP, the Unionists bitterly opposed Senator Mitchell's appointment as independent chairman of the Plenary Session, arguing that he was too closely tied to the Irish-American lobby to be impartial. On June 12, after two days of intense negotiations, the UUP split from their fellow Unionists, dropped their objections, and allowed Senator Mitchell to assume the post of independent chairman. With that initial crisis behind them, the parties each formally declared their commitment to the International Body's principles of democracy and nonviolence.[48]

Progress throughout the opening Plenary Session was painstakingly slow. After agreeing on revised procedural rules in late July 1996, the negotiations derailed over the priority to be given to the issue of decommissioning on the agenda. The UUP renewed its demand for decommissioning of paramilitary weapons prior to the beginning of substantive negotiations. The SDLP opposed the UUP plan, arguing that the parties should proceed with parallel decommissioning as called for in the International Body's Report. In March 1997, after eight months of stalemate over the issue of decommissioning, the opening Plenary Session was suspended pending the approaching British general election and local elections in Northern Ireland. The British elections would prove to be a turning point in the negotiation process.

British General Elections

After eight months of stagnation, new life was breathed into the Northern Ireland peace process by the British general election, held on May 1, 1997. British voters voted decisively to replace the paralyzed Conservative government of John Major with the vibrant Labour government of Tony Blair. Although John Major and his government had worked tirelessly in organizing the peace process and initiating dialogue between Northern Ireland's Protestant and Catholic communities, it was becoming increasingly clear that his government lacked the political support necessary for active leadership of the process. From the fall of 1995 through the spring of 1997, John Major watched as his party's majority in Parliament slowly eroded from scandals and defections. By the fall and winter of 1996, his government's political survival had come to rest solely on the votes of Unionist members of Parliament, thus limiting his flexibility to lead the peace process and effectively eliminating his ability to initiate overtures to Sinn Fein and the IRA.

Tony Blair's Labour government, unlike its predecessor, enjoyed broad support, was not beholden to Northern Ireland's Unionists, and was thus free to undertake initiatives to kickstart the negotiations. Shortly after the Plenary Session resumed on June 3, Blair initiated efforts to pull Sinn Fein back into the political process and break the deadlock over decommissioning. In early June, the British government took the controversial step of extending an offer to Sinn Fein and the IRA—Sinn Fein would be allowed to participate in negotiations if the IRA declared a "genuine" cease-fire and observed it for six weeks.[49] Following public disclosure of the offer, Northern Ireland's Unionists demanded that it be withdrawn, vowing to walk out of negotiations if Sinn Fein representatives were allowed to participate. Nevertheless, the Blair government left its offer intact and on July 19, after a joint appeal from Gerry Adams (Sinn Fein) and John Hume (SDLP), the IRA accepted the offer and renewed its cease-fire.[50]

Against this backdrop, progress was also made on decommissioning. In late June 1997, the British and Irish governments presented to the Plenary Session a joint paper expressing their position on decommissioning. The paper was based firmly on the recommendations of the International Body.[51] It called for the total, verifiable disarmament of all paramilitary organizations. In addition, the paper echoed the International Body's call for the creation of an independent commission to oversee the surrender of weapons. Absent from the proposal, however, was a timetable specifying when this process was to occur. It thus left unaddressed the critical issue that had bedeviled negotiators and prevented progress. On July 24, the parties voted on the paper, but failed to achieve sufficient consensus. The proposal was rejected by the UUP, the DUP, and the U.K. Unionists. Angered both over the proposal's lack of a specified timetable for negotiations and the looming prospect of having to negotiate with representatives of Sinn Fein, both the DUP and the U.K. Unionists walked out of the negotiations in protest following the vote. Although the UUP remained in the process, it remained adamant that IRA decommissioning occur as soon as substantive negotiations began.

Despite the lack of consensus among the political parties of Northern Ireland, the British and Irish governments forged ahead and on August 27, 1998, signed an agreement establishing the Independent International Commission on Decommissioning. Two days later, with the preconditions expressed by Blair nearly met, Sinn Fein was formerly invited to participate in the substantive "strand" negotiations, which were scheduled to begin in mid-September. On September 15, 1997, Sinn Fein negotiators pledged their adherence to the Mitchell Principles and took their seats at the negotiations. The first item for discussion was a UUP indictment calling for the expulsion of Sinn Fein from the peace process for violation of the Mitchell Principles.[52] Although it was clear that the governments would not expel Sinn Fein after spending considerable effort and political capital to include them in the process, the indictment was leveled to provide the UUP with political cover. Following rejection of the UUP's challenge and the beginning of negotiations, the UUP could claim that it was forced into negotiations.

As expected, the indictment to expel Sinn Fein was rejected. On September 25, the political parties of Northern Ireland agreed to address the decommissioning issue alongside the strand negotiations and proceed to substantive talks. The UUP, however, remained committed in its refusal to negotiate directly with representatives of Sinn Fein. The UUP's strategy was to engage and negotiate with all of the other parties involved in the process except Sinn Fein. This strategy, which was pursued throughout the remainder of the process, was possible because Sinn Fein's vote was not required to reach "sufficient consensus" under the peace process's procedural rules.

The Final Push

As the three-strand negotiations proceeded throughout 1997 and into 1998, an upsurge in violence cast the peace process back in doubt. Between December 22, 1997, and January 20, 1998, Loyalist extremists detonated three car bombs in Northern Ireland. In possible retaliation for the first of these attacks, the Irish National Liberation Army, a Republican paramilitary group not bound by the IRA cease-fire, murdered the leader of the Loyalist Volunteer Force in the Maze prison in Belfast.

These and other incidents had a direct impact on the faltering negotiations. On January 26, 1998, the British and Irish governments expelled the UDP from the negotiations, after the Ulster Freedom Fighters—a Unionist paramilitary group with whom the UDP is affiliated—was tied to a string of sectarian killings. At the time of the UDP's expulsion, the governments made clear that the party would be allowed to reenter the talks after an unspecified period of time (which turned out to be four weeks) if it remained committed to the Mitchell Principles. In late February 1998, Sinn Fein was expelled for two weeks from the negotiations in response to IRA killings of a Loyalist paramilitary and a "punishment" killing of a Catholic drug dealer. According to Senator Mitchell, enforcement of the Principles—though necessary—came at considerable cost to the peace process in terms of party distraction and lost negotiating time.[53]

Recognizing that the rising violence threatened to unravel the peace process, Mitchell announced that he was moving up the deadline for concluding the peace process from May to April 9, Good Friday. This date, which marks the start of the Easter holiday weekend, is significant to both of Northern Ireland's communities and was strategically chosen by the independent chairman to reinvigorate the talks. In the weeks leading up to the April 9 deadline, negotiations intensified. A draft agreement representing the culmination of all three strands of negotiations was presented to the parties by the independent chairman. As the political parties and governments focused their efforts on the draft document, tensions flared, and rumors circulated that the UUP and the Sinn Fein were on the verge of leaving the process.

Although the midnight deadline of April 9 passed without an agreement, the parties and governments continued negotiating. Tantalizingly close to an agreement, the talks were again almost derailed by the decommissioning issue as senior members of the UUP informed David Trimble that they could not accept an agreement that would allow Sinn Fein into a government "without the IRA having decommissioned a single bullet." This final threat to the process was overcome by assurances from Tony Blair, who provided political cover for David Trimble and the UUP. In particular, Prime Minister Blair assured the UUP that, if the Agreement proved ineffective in dealing with office holders no longer committed to "exclusively peaceful means," the British government would support changes to make it so. Blair also confirmed that he shared the UUP's view that decommissioning measures should commence immediately upon implementation of the Agreement. With these final concerns addressed, the parties presented the Agreement to the people of Ireland for their acceptance in separate referendums, North and South.

On May 22, 1998, the people of Ireland overwhelmingly accepted the Agreement. In the Republic, almost 95 percent of the votes cast were in favor of the Agreement. In the north—where a record 81 percent of voters turned out to register their opinion—71 percent of voters cast their ballots in favor of the Agreement. However, this large margin of victory did little to allay concerns about Northern Ireland's future as nearly half of the province's Unionist voters chose to reject the Agreement.[54] It is feared that such widespread discontent among Unionists may impede implementation of the Agreement.

Overview of the Agreement

The Agreement presented to the people of Ireland is essentially a joint understanding on the principles and processes that will determine Northern Ireland's political future. Under the Agreement, Northern Ireland's political status as part of the United Kingdom remains unchanged. However, the two governments and the political parties of Northern Ireland agree that any future change to the status of Northern Ireland must be based on the democratically expressed wish of the majority of people residing there and carried out through exclusively peaceful means. In accordance with these principles, both the British and Irish governments must relinquish claims to all of Ireland: the British by repealing the Government of Ireland Act of 1920 and the Irish government by modifying Articles 2 and 3 of its constitution.

Under the Agreement, local government is restored to the province. The Agreement calls for the establishment of a 108-member Northern Ireland Assembly to exercise legislative authority on local matters (i.e., those matters previously within the competency of the United Kingdom's six Northern Ireland Government Departments). Executive authority will be held by a "first minister," "deputy first minister," and additional ministers with departmental responsibilities, with all ministerial posts allocated in proportion to party strengths. Legal and institutional safeguards will be implemented "to ensure [that] all sections of the community can participate and work together successfully . . . and that all sections of community are protected,"[55] including the incorporation of the European Convention on Human Rights into Northern Ireland law, the creation of an Equality Commission to ensure equal opportunities and "parity of esteem" between the two communities, and the creation of an independent commission on policing.[56]

Negotiations dealing with the relationship between Northern Ireland and the Republic resulted in the establishment of a North/South Ministerial Council

intended to "develop consultation, cooperation and action within the island of
Ireland—including through implementation on an all-island and cross-border
basis—on matters of mutual interest within the competence of the Administrations, North and South."[57]

At the international level, the Agreement calls for a new British–Irish Agreement to replace the Anglo-Irish Agreement of 1985. This new agreement will
bind both governments to honor the political aspirations of the majority of citizens in Northern Ireland. The new British–Irish Agreement will give rise to two
new institutions: a British–Irish Council and a standing Intergovernmental
Conference. The British–Irish Council will be comprised of representatives of
the Irish and British governments, including the devolved institutions in Northern Ireland, Scotland, and Wales. Its aim will be to "promote the harmonious and
mutually beneficial development of the totality of relationships among the peoples of these islands."[58] The British–Irish Intergovernmental Conference will
subsume both the Anglo-Irish Intergovernmental Council and the Intergovernmental Conference established under the Anglo-Irish Agreement. Its mission
will be to promote bilateral cooperation on matters of mutual interest. In recognition of the Irish government's "special interest" in Northern Ireland, it will
continue to be allowed to put forward views and proposals on nondevolved
Northern Ireland matters (i.e., those matters that are not within the competency
of the Northern Ireland Assembly).

The glaring weakness of the Northern Ireland peace agreement is its treatment of decommissioning. Although the Agreement notes that decommissioning is an indispensable part of the peace process and provides a two-year deadline, it does not establish a firm timetable for disarming paramilitaries, nor does
it establish detailed procedures to be followed.[59] Moreover, political parties affiliated with paramilitary groups are only required to "use any influence they
may have" to achieve decommissioning. Thus, the viability of the Agreement
hinges on the actions of paramilitary groups not directly bound by the text. Indeed, in the months following adoption of the Agreement, IRA representatives
have repeatedly expressed their organization's unwillingness to undertake even
token disarmament.

International Community Support for the Northern Ireland Peace Process

The politics of the Northern Ireland conflict severely limited the opportunities for direct involvement of the international community in the peace process.
Both the British government and Northern Ireland Unionists opposed opening
the peace process to broad international participation, though for somewhat
different reasons. The British position that the conflict is primarily an internal
matter precludes unlimited international involvement on the basis of sovereignty concerns.[60] The chief concerns of Northern Ireland's Unionists, on the
other hand, relate to the desire to maintain control over their political future—
a right they can more effectively enforce in Westminster than before the United
Nations. Despite this resistance to direct involvement, the peace process has en-

joyed indirect encouragement and support from both the United States and the European Union (EU).

The Role of the United States

The Clinton administration deserves considerable credit for its sustained support of the Northern Ireland peace process. The administration, though limited in its ability to directly influence the peace process, voluntarily adopted a facilitating role involving "passive" economic support for Northern Ireland and "active" encouragement and support for parties committed to the peaceful resolution of the conflict.[61] Taken together, U.S. support has been, and continues to be, a positive and valued influence on both the process and the participants.

U.S. economic assistance to Northern Ireland is intended to promote peace by ameliorating the economic conditions that exacerbate the conflict, namely discrimination, wealth disparity, and unemployment. In addition to sponsoring trade missions and conferences to promote U.S. foreign direct investment in Northern Ireland, the United States provides direct funding through the International Fund for Ireland. With an annual budget in the range of $10–15 million, the Fund provides capital for projects that both support economic development and bring members of Northern Ireland's two communities together.[62]

The more prominent component of U.S. facilitation is the administration's active support and encouragement of the peace process. As previously discussed, the United States was deeply involved in facilitating Sinn Fein's decision to enter the political mainstream. The role of the Clinton administration, however, extended beyond the issuance of visas. In the fall of 1995, President Clinton undertook a trip to Northern Ireland specifically to show support for the peace process. His visit marked the first time a U.S. president undertook a trip to the province while in office (and the audience receiving him in Northern Ireland was one of the largest of any of his presidential trips).

The administration's unwavering support for the peace process extended throughout the negotiations and was felt in their final hours. In the early morning hours of April 10, as the parties struggled to hammer out the final details of their historic agreement, President Clinton made personal telephone calls to the various party leaders urging them to go forward with the Agreement. As Senator Mitchell would later observe, these were not cold calls—President Clinton, through his sustained commitment to the process, knew the parties, the issues, and the individuals, all of which added weight to his last minute appeals for peace.[63]

The Role of the European Union

The European Union's influence in Northern Ireland stems from the fact that the conflict exists within its political and economic framework. The issues at the heart of the conflict—territorial sovereignty and self-determination—run counter to the prevailing European trends of economic and political integration. Although it possesses the political resources to influence the conflict, the EU as an institution has been unwilling to undertake sustained and decisive action. Both the Council of Ministers and the European Commission adopted the view that the conflict was an internal affair of the United Kingdom and that direct intervention by the EU could jeopardize Europe's move toward regional integration. Though the EU has not exercised direct influence in the peace process, it has affected events in Northern Ireland indirectly by providing a political forum for the British and Irish governments and economic assistance to the region.

In Europe, the hope has long existed that the EU's movement toward ever-increasing degrees of integration would eventually render the conflicting positions of the two communities largely irrelevant. While European integration did little to dilute the conflicting positions of Northern Ireland's communities, it clearly had an impact on relations between the British and Irish governments. By providing the United Kingdom and the Republic of Ireland with a neutral political forum, the EU played a role in improving relations between the two governments. Within the context of the EU, the government representatives of the United Kingdom and the Republic are treated formally as equals, thus breaking the traditional pattern of Irish subordination. Moreover, the EU provides representatives of both countries with the opportunity to work together and build relations of trust and understanding. The Republic of Ireland's voice in the formulation of British policy in Northern Ireland, as effectuated through the Intergovernmental Conference and Joint Secretariat established under the 1985 Anglo-Irish Agreement, represents a degree of joint sovereignty over Northern Ireland that would have been unthinkable outside the context of European integration.

The EU, like the United States, is also a source of economic assistance for the province. The EU's Peace and Reconciliation Fund for Northern Ireland is budgeted to provide Northern Ireland with $550 million between 1995 and 1999.[64] Like its U.S. counterpart, the EU economic assistance program is intended to ameliorate the economic conditions that exacerbate the conflict.

The EU played a subtler role as well. The Republic of Ireland, for much of the 1990s, prospered financially as a member of the EU. Jobs were created at a strong rate, including a thriving technology sector, and young people who might at one time have left Ireland stayed there to live and work. This prosperity in Ireland was tied at many levels to its participation in the EU and was in stark contrast to the high levels of unemployment and relative poverty of Northern Ireland (when compared to Britain or the Republic of Ireland). The conflict of Northern Ireland became increasingly anachronistic in an era of a strong Europe, and the opportunity costs of the conflict in terms of productivity and prosperity became abundantly clear. A united Northern Ireland, even with ambiguous sovereignty, stands a greater chance of benefiting from European economic growth.

Success of the Mediation

International mediation was essential to successfully forging the Good Friday Agreement. As the failed Brooke–Mayhew initiative illustrated, the troubled history of Northern Ireland and the level of animosity and distrust between the antagonists made it virtually impossible for the British and Irish governments to direct the process themselves. For the peace process to be viewed as objective and fair by all the parties, it required external intervention. Although the need for outside assistance and facilitation was clear, the scope and role of the intervention was not. Looking back over the Northern Ireland peace process, international mediation was extraordinarily flexible and assumed a number of roles during the process. The nature of these roles ultimately hinged on the mediators' relationships with the parties. During the negotiations, the mediation effort attained a progressive level of responsibility and influence. This pattern coincides with increasing trust between the mediators and the parties to the negotiations.

At the outset of negotiations, the intervention took the form of a consultative body, the International Body on Decommissioning. Because the International Body lacked authority to enforce its views and was limited in scope, it posed little risk to individual parties. This lack of authority (as opposed to potential influence) was responsible for the absence of resistance to the international involvement generally, and the International Body's composition in particular. Not until the international mediators assumed positions of influence within the framework of multiparty talks were complaints raised by various parties, but by this time the peace process had developed significantly more momentum.

Senator George Mitchell's appointment as independent chairman of the Plenary Session drew particular criticism and resistance from Unionists suspicious of his alleged ties to the pro-Republican Irish-American lobby. Although he eventually assumed the role of independent chairman, these complaints had the practical effect of severely limiting his ability to undertake initiatives in the short term, reducing his initial role to that of "presiding officer" responsible for setting meetings and imposing time limits.[65] As negotiations proceeded and the parties came to trust him, Senator Mitchell's role in the process became markedly more active and substantive.[66] In this respect, the length of negotiations actually worked to the advantage of Senator Mitchell and the mediation effort. Senator Mitchell remarked that he was able to build trust through a series of small, procedural decisions and was ultimately trusted enough by all parties to make significant procedural and substantive suggestions.[67] The ultimate test of Senator Mitchell's influence came in the final months of the negotiations with his decision to accelerate negotiations. There was a risk that some parties might see the decision to move up the deadline for ending the negotiations as an attempt to manipulate the process and pressure the parties into an agreement. The fact that his decision was not met with criticism and resistance was viewed by Senator Mitchell as a testament to the level of trust that had emerged between him and the political parties.[68]

Conclusion

The successful conclusion of the Good Friday Agreement does not mark the end of the peace process in Northern Ireland. This fact was driven home to Catholics and Protestants alike on August 15, 1998, when Republican extremists opposed to the peace process detonated a bomb in the quiet Northern Ireland market town of Omagh. The blast, which killed twenty-eight and injured over 200, was the single worst attack in almost thirty years of violence in Northern Ireland. But, instead of halting the peace process, the attack strengthened the resolve of those working for peace in both communities. SDLP leader John Hume and UUP leader David Trimble won the Nobel Peace Prize for their brave work in the negotiation process.

Continued bravery and resolve will be needed to overcome the considerable challenges that lie ahead. Implementation of the Agreement, specifically the provisions dealing with decommissioning, will provide an early test of the parties' commitment to peace. Ultimately, if the peace process is to be successful, Unionists and Nationalists will need to develop working relationships based on trust and mutual respect. The strategy underlying the Agreement is to develop these relationships within an institutional framework, as evidenced by the institution-laden nature of the Agreement. These institutions—while easier to create than the relationships they are intended to engender—remain vulnerable to the intransigence and manipulation of political parties, as well as future attacks from extremists opposed to the peace process.

Cutting against these forces that threaten to unravel the achievements of the peace process is the reality of the senseless carnage and destruction that awaits the province should this opportunity be squandered. This reality motivated the parties to negotiate—one hopes it is enough to keep them working for peace.

8

The Arusha Accords and the Failure of International Intervention in Rwanda

Joel Stettenheim

Overview

THE PERIOD FOLLOWING an agreement on ending internal conflict can often be even bloodier and more dangerous than the period before the agreement. The Arusha Peace Accords, which ostensibly ended the ongoing conflict in Rwanda between an exiled Tutsi guerrilla group (the Rwandese Patriotic Front) and the Hutu government of President Juvenal Habyarimana, are a tragic example of a negotiated agreement failing miserably in its implementation. Almost immediately following the signature of the Arusha Accords, Hutu extremists who felt left out of the process and threatened by the results organized a horrific massacre of Tutsi and Hutu moderates. Between 800,000 and one million people died between April and July 1994.

Rather than focusing on the period of the massacre, this chapter examines how the mediation of the Arusha Accords set the stage for what many have described as genocide. The chapter also highlights the unsuccessful mediation attempts leading up to the Arusha Accords; the successful mediation of the Arusha Accords by a highly skilled Tanzanian diplomat, Ami Mpungwe; and the violence following the breakdown of the Accords after the suspicious death of President Habyarimana. The role of regional organizations and other international actors in the pre-Arusha mediations and the Arusha process itself is analyzed. The skill of the mediator in pacing the negotiations, focusing the substance of the negotiations, and using connections with the international community strategically are also examined. The chapter looks at the dangers presented when a bitterly divided party must negotiate with a party of unusual unity and strategic vision, and how the inclusion or exclusion of extremist groups can derail negotiation attempts. The chapter finally highlights the misperceptions arising from a serious lack of intelligence information and the tragedy of peacekeeping forces whose weak mandate and lack of materiel made them impotent to stem the horrendous violence.

Timeline

1860	The Tutsi King Rwabugiri (1860–95) expands his power and creates a centralized state.
1880	The first European explorers arrive in Rwanda.
1899	Germany begins its colonial rule.
1911	An uprising in northern Rwanda is repressed by combined German and Tutsi-led southern forces, creating significant bitterness on the part of the northern Hutu.
1916	Belgium takes over control (under a League of Nations mandate).
1920s–30s	A policy of "ethnogenesis" exaggerates the "ethnic" differences between the Hutu and Tutsi and creates a monopoly Tutsi rule. Ethnic identity cards are introduced.
1959–61	A Hutu "revolution" replaces the Tutsi monarch with an independent Hutu republic controlled by President Kayibanda and southern Hutu political elites.
1973	A coup by Juvenal Habyarimana transfers power to northern Hutu.
1960s–70s	Attacks and repression against the Tutsi result in a refugee population that numbers approximately 600,000.
1990	**Oct. 10:** The Rwandese Patriotic Front (RPF) invades Rwanda.
1990–91	A series of regional mediation efforts are undertaken. The Communauté Economique de Pays des Grand Lacs (CEPL) hosts summits that include the participation of Zaire, Uganda, Burundi, and Tanzania.
1991	**Feb. 19:** The Dar-es-Salaam Declaration produces a refugee agreement that is later used as the basis for the Arusha refugee talks. **Mar. 29:** The N'Sele Cease-fire, although short-lived, formally creates the Neutral Military Observer Group (NMOG). **Sept. 16:** The Gabolite Cease-fire deploys the NMOG. In addition, the control of mediation switches from Zaire to Tanzania. **October:** Low intensity traditional guerrilla warfare by the Force Armées Rwandaises (FAR) sees initial success and is followed by a resurgence of the RPF.
1992	**May 8:** U.S. Assistant Secretary of State for Africa Herman Cohen meets with the RPF and Yoweri Museveni in Kampala, Uganda. **May 10:** Cohen meets with Habyarimana and opposition members, Prime Minister Nsengiyaremye and Foreign Minister Boniface Ngulinzira, in Kigali, Rwanda. **May 24:** PM Nsengiyaremye and FM

Ngulinzira meet in Kampala with the RPF to explore peace talks. **June 6:** The RPF and the Rwandan Government hold preliminary talks in Paris. **June 20:** Government of France's Director for Africa and Maghreb Affairs Dijoud and Assistant Secretary Cohen meet with Ugandan Foreign Minister Ssemmogere and RPF representatives in Paris to strongly encourage talks. **July 12:** The Arusha talks open under the auspices of the Organization of African Unity (OAU). The primary facilitation is delegated to Tanzanian President Ali Hassan Mwinyi and his ambassador, Ami Mpungwe. **Aug. 18:** The Rule of Law Protocol signed. **September:** The power-sharing talks begin. **Oct. 6–31:** The talks on the Framework for a Broad Based Transitional Government (BBTG) continue. An agreement that significantly reduces the scope of presidential powers is reached. The Transitional National Assembly is also created to replace the Conseil National de Développement (CDN). FM Ngulinzira initials the agreement without the authority of Habyarimana. **November–December:** Discussions on the composition of the transitional institutions continue. **Nov. 15:** Habyarimana calls the Arusha Accords "pieces of paper."

1993 **Jan. 5–10:** The distribution of the seats in the BBTG is finalized. The extremist Coalition pour la Défense de la République (CDR) is excluded. **Feb. 8:** The RPF launches an offensive. **June 9:** The Protocol on the Rights of Refugees and Displaced Persons is signed. **June 24:** The Protocol on the Integration of the Armed Forces of the Two Parties is signed. **July 8:** The extremist Radio-Télévision Libre des Milles Collines starts broadcasting. **July 23–24:** A meeting of the MDR expels Faustin Twagiramungu, signaling the beginning of the splintering of the opposition parties. **Aug. 4:** President Habyarimana and RPF chairman Alexis Kanyarengwe sign the Arusha Accords. **Oct. 5:** The UN Security Council approves the United Nations Assistance Mission for Rwanda (UNAMIR), a 2,500-strong peacekeeping force. **Nov. 1:** The UNAMIR forces start arriving. **Nov. 21:** Tutsi military extremists assassinate Burundi Hutu President Ndadaye. The subsequent repression and reprisal killings result in tens of thousands of deaths and over 600,000 refugees. **Dec. 28:** 600 RPF soldiers arrive in Kigali as part of the Arusha Accords.

1994 **Jan. 8:** Deadlocks within the Mouvement Democratique Républicain (MDR) and Parti Libéral (PL) block the convening of the BBTG. **Feb. 10:** Further attempts to convene the government are aborted by the assassination of the Parti Social Démocrate (PSD) leader Felicien Gatabazi and the reprisal killing of Martin Bucyana of the CDR. **Apr. 6:** Habyarimana and Burundi President Ntaryamira are killed when their plane is shot down while approaching the Kigali airport. **Apr. 7:** Interim Prime Minister Agathe Uwilingiyimana is killed along with ten Belgian peacekeepers assigned to protect her. Belgium withdraws its forces. **Apr. 8:** The RPF renews its fighting. **Apr. 21:** UN Security Council resolution reduces UNAMIR from 2,500 to 270 (UNSCR 917). **Apr. 30:** By the end of April at least 100,000 people have been killed, and 1.3 million have become refugees. **July 18:** The RPF declares that the war is over. Almost one million people have lost their lives, and in October the United Nations estimates the war, through death and displacement, has reduced the population of Rwanda from 7.9 million to 5 million.

Background

Three principal interwoven factors allowed a small group of political elites in April 1994 to mobilize tens of thousands of ordinary Rwandan citizens to slaughter between 800,000 and 1,000,000 of their neighbors with gruesome efficiency. This genocide is even more tragic because it occurred after the signing of the Arusha Accords, meant to bring about power sharing between the Hutu and Tutsi. These factors are first, the poverty and high population of the country; second, Rwanda's history of authoritarian rule; and third, the "ethnic" conflict between the Hutu and Tutsi. In reporting the killings, much of the Western media simplistically described the genocide as a spontaneous explosion of long simmering ethnic hatred. A more sophisticated description of the ethnic relations between the Hutu and Tutsi is required, however, not only to understand the true source of the genocide but also the context within which the Arusha Peace Accords were negotiated.

The Hutu and Tutsi ethnic classifications have various historical antecedents, including colonial classifications, clan affiliation, occupational status, "feudal" relations, and ancestral origin. As in numerous long-standing conflicts, there was a range of pre-genocide attitudes toward ethnicity and identity. Most, conscious of the ethnic divide, harbored some suspicions toward the other group; but some viewed the other as anathema and were deeply opposed to a multiethnic Rwanda, and certainly to power sharing. Prior to the genocide, the vast majority of Hutu and Tutsi lived side by side, dispersed throughout the country. With the high poverty rate and history of tensions, the majority of Hutu peasants were susceptible to manipulation by a small band of Hutu elites who were willing to destroy Rwanda in a desperate bid to preserve their power and economic privilege.

Poverty and Population Pressure

Dominated by lush terrain, Rwanda is a land of tremendous physical beauty. The terrain is primarily mountainous with high plateaus. Running along the northwestern region are the Virungu volcanic mountains, familiar to the West through Dian Fossey's gorilla research. The country is blessed with considerable rainfall, and moderate average temperatures; many regions are capable of up to three agricultural growing cycles per year.[1]

The pressures on the land, however, are extreme. A country of only 23,000 square kilometers, Rwanda had a population of 7.15 million people and an annual growth rate of 3.1 percent (1991 census). With the national parks and forests excluded, the average pre-genocide population density was 405 people per square kilometer, the highest in Africa. The northern Rhuengeri region, the most populated, had 820 people per square kilometer of productive land.[2] Most people were poor subsistence farmers. In 1984, 57 percent of the rural households farmed less than one hectare and 25 percent had access to less than half a hectare to support a family of five.[3]

Rwanda's economy was severely injured by the collapse of the international coffee market in the 1980s and by civil war (1990–93). The war's impact was fourfold: 1) the internally displaced people posed a loss to coffee production and an increased demand on government resources, 2) the region controlled by rebels cut off a main export route, 3) the nascent tourist industry was destroyed, and 4) the government's military spending consumed significant resources.[4] In addition, structural adjustment programs demanded by the World Bank and the International Monetary Fund were particularly hard on Rwanda's peasants. The combined effects resulted in the average per capita income falling from U.S. $330 in 1989 to U.S. $200 in 1993, a 40 percent decrease in only four years.[5]

Although there are numerous factors contributing to the genocide, the economic, population, and land pressures were clearly among them. As Rwandan scholar Gerard Prunier commented,

> the decision to kill was of course made by politicians, for political reasons. But at least part of the reason why it was carried out so thoroughly by the ordinary rank-and-file peasant . . . was the feeling that there were too many people on too little land, and that with a reduction in their numbers, there would be more for the survivors.[6]

"Ethnic" Relations and Authoritarian Rule

In orchestrating their genocide, the extremists were able to call upon two interwoven themes from Rwanda's history, its tradition of authoritarian rule and the "ethnic" conflict between the Hutu and Tutsi. For the past two hundred years Rwanda has been governed by a highly organized hierarchical social and political structure that has existed in three distinct forms: a centralized state created by Tutsi kings, a colonial government administered indirectly through the Tutsi, and finally Hutu-controlled dictatorships.

Overlapping and combining with these governing developments was the evolution of the Hutu and Tutsi "ethnic" classification. Always a somewhat fluid identity, the classification has been transformed from a multifaceted social description, often secondary to local clan affiliation, to a more rigid social and political ordering imbued with powerful overtones of intellectual superiority and political and economic dominance. To carry out their plan, the Hutu extremists utilized an administrative structure that provided direct access to and obedience from the peasants. They also manipulated "ethnic" tension through hate-filled rhetoric to create a hysterical climate of fear.

*Precolonial: Creation of Centralized Authority and Development
of "Ethnic" Classifications*

The Hutu, Bantu-speaking agriculturists, appear to have arrived in what is present-day Rwanda around 1000 C.E., slowly displacing the indigenous forest-dwelling Twa. Principally involved in agriculture, many of the Hutu organized themselves into "statelets" by the fifteenth century. These local administrative and political structures were based largely on clan affiliation. As part of a general pastoralist influx from the lakes region from the eleventh to the fifteenth centuries, the Tutsi began arriving in the area.[7] When Tutsi moved into a region there was usually an initial period of peaceful coexistence characterized by trading, Tutsi cattle products for Hutu agricultural goods. Subsequently the Tutsi would often subjugate the local population and establish military and administrative control.[8]

Although by the middle of the eighteenth century the Tutsi dominated the local power structure, they themselves had been assimilated by the Hutu, and the ethnic classifications were flexible. The Tutsi adopted the Hutu language, Kinyarwanda, and incorporated many of their traditions and cults. During this period, the Hutu/Tutsi classification corresponded roughly to occupational status and wealth. Cattle-herders, soldiers, and administrators were generally Tutsi, and the majority of the farmers were Hutu.[9] As symbols of wealth, power, and good breeding, cattle provided a form of social mobility in which a Hutu, and his lineage, could become "Tutsified" if he were able to acquire a sizable enough herd. Conversely a Tutsi who lost all his wealth and needed to cultivate the land would be "Hutuified."[10] Clans, which were multiclass and multiethnic, were arguably a more important form of identification at this time than "ethnicity."[11]

As the Tutsi extended their control, "ethnic" classification began to play a more significant role. From the fifteenth to the nineteenth centuries, the Tutsi rulers of the eastern Nyiginya region expanded their dominance over the neighboring areas. King Rwabugiri, who reigned from 1860 to 1895, was the most influential of the Tutsi kings. During his rule, he greatly increased the centralization of power and created a highly efficient administrative state that extended through much of the country and extracted obedience from even remote areas.[12] He was unable, though, to subjugate the northern and southwestern regions, an important fact for later intra-Hutu and Hutu/Tutsi relations.

Underpinning the royal governing structure on a local level, and important to the development of Hutu/Tutsi relations, was a "feudal" system of patronage, *ubuhake*. Between two men of unequal status, this arrangement involved bonds of loyalty and an exchange of goods and services. Tutsi were generally the patrons with subordinate Tutsi or Hutu as the clients. As a hierarchical system of social organization, *ubuhake* institutionalized socioeconomic differences between the Hutu and Tutsi and created a greater awareness of the "ethnic" classification, particularly among the Hutu. In later ideological battles, *ubuhake* became an important point of contention. For Tutsi ideologues the system was a mutually beneficial partnership, and for Hutu ideologues the system was a form of slavery.[13]

The "ethnic" divisions created during this period were not monolithic, however, and much of the political struggle existed as a fight between the center and the periphery. To dilute remote resistance, the king established an overlapping system of local governance in which up to three chiefs shared power over the basic administrative unit, the hill. The "chief of the pastures" was almost always a Tutsi; the "chief of the land" was usually a Hutu; and the "chief of men," the tax collector, was usually a Tutsi. To complicate the system, the chiefs did not always share control over the same hilltop, and often the king created a patchwork of intertwining rule in a particularly rebellious region.[14]

During this period, the Tutsi elites who held all the highest positions of power almost certainly began to associate their status and privilege with their Tutsi "ethnicity." At the middle-level and lower ranks of the social structure, however, "ethnicity" was simply one factor in determining an individual's social stature. Furthermore, as mentioned above, local affiliations were important in the ongoing struggle against the centralized power of the royal state.

German Colonial Rule (1899–1916) and Belgian Trusteeship (1916–1961): Indirect Rule through Tutsi

The importance of the Hutu/Tutsi "ethnic" classification dramatically increased during the period of European control. With limited resources, the Europeans usurped the royal governing structure of Rwanda and ruled indirectly through the Tutsi. The Europeans actively pursued a policy of "ethnogenesis," a "politically-motivated creation of ethnic identities based on socially constituted categories of the pre-colonial past."[15] The effect of the colonial policies was to exaggerate the economic and political differences between the groups and to provide a theoretical underpinning for the divisions. The organizing principle for colonial rule was the racist Hamitic thesis stating that everything of value in Africa could be traced to Caucasian origin. Early anthropologists identified the Tutsi as Hamites; based on this classification, colonial administrators came to regard and promote the Tutsi as the intellectually superior, naturally aristocratic race.[16]

Acting under this view, the Germans and, especially, the Belgians, transformed the royal governing structure to suit their administrative needs, creating a monopoly Tutsi rule and a rigid ethnic classification system. From approximately 1926 to 1931, the Belgians instituted an administrative reform replacing all Hutu chiefs and deputy chiefs with Tutsi. In 1933, the Belgians introduced compulsory ethnic identity cards that were based on fairly arbitrary criteria.[17] Henceforth, ethnicity was the determining factor for access to education and economic and political privilege. In addition, relations between Hutu and Tutsi were further hardened by the transformation of the previously flexible *ubuhake* system into a mechanism for extracting forced labor. The effect of sixty years of colonial rule was to exaggerate the egos and fortunes of the Tutsi and create a bitter sense of resentment and inferiority among the Hutu.[18]

Independence: Dictatorship and Exploitation of Ethnicity

Four crucial elements of the Hutu/Tutsi relationship emerged during Rwanda's transition to independence and the first and second Hutu republics. These elements are important to understanding the 1990 civil war and the dynamics of the Arusha Accords. First, in the late 1950s, the struggle for power had become defined in ethnic terms. Second, the ascension of the first Hutu republic began a cycle in which power was transferred from one political elite to another in a zero-sum game of winner-takes-all.[19] Third, the large Tutsi refugee population displaced by fighting and repression became the source of the RPF guerrilla army. Fourth, intra-Hutu tensions that developed during the first and second republics (1962–90), mainly between northern/western and southern groups, dominated Rwanda's multiparty democracy and then hobbled the government of Rwanda (GoR) negotiating team during the Arusha Accord negotiations.[20]

The Bahutu Manifesto, signed by nine Hutu intellectuals in 1957, including future president Grégoire Kayibanda, demonstrated that the colonial conception of Rwandan society as defined by the Hutu/Tutsi divide had taken hold.[21] An important statement of principle for the coming Hutu "revolution," the document sought to create a general awareness of ethnic identity among the Hutu masses. It argued that the root of Rwanda's problems was the ethnic conflict between the Hutu and the foreign Hamites, principally the Tutsi. In response, two high Tutsi chiefs wrote letters ridiculing the Hutu and asserting that Tutsi dominance was justified by their military defeat of the Hutu "little" kings.[22]

From 1959 to 1961, a Hutu "revolution" replaced the Tutsi monarch with an independent Hutu republic controlled by Kayibanda and southern Hutu political elites. During the transition, the Belgian authorities and the Catholic Church switched allegiance and supported the Hutu. The change was precipitated in part by a Tutsi attempt to unilaterally gain independence and by generalized guilt over the treatment of the Hutu during colonial rule.

Repression of Tutsi during this period, including a massacre that killed 5,000 to 8,000, led to a massive exodus of refugees into Burundi, Zaire, Tanzania, and Uganda. Violence in Rwanda continued against the Tutsi, particularly in 1963–65 and 1973, and lead to successive waves of exodus. By 1990 the refugee population, including their descendants, numbered almost 600,000.[23] Some of the refugees in Uganda joined in the fight against Idi Amin and Milton Obote. In particular, the future RPF leaders Paul Kagame and Major General Fred Rwigyema were among the twenty-six original fighters who started in the bush with Yoweri Museveni, the president of Uganda.[24]

Juvenal Habyarimana's bloodless coup in 1973 transferred power to northern Hutu. The coup represented not only competition for political control but also a desire for revenge for the subjugation suffered by the northerners early in the century. During the seventeen years of the Habyarimana regime, members of Habyarimana's immediate power circle, the *akazu,* consolidated power at the expense of southern Hutu groups and Hutu from other clans.[25] By the mid-

1980s, members of Habyarimana's Bagogwe clan held 80 percent of the top military posts and dominated the ruling Mouvement Révolutionnare National pour le Développement (MRND), Rwanda's only political party, many of whose leaders were among the main organizers of the genocide.[26] The *akazu,* particularly Habyarimana's wife and brothers-in-law, represented a distinct Hutu subculture whose earlier members had remained independent into the twentieth century until they were defeated by combined German and Tutsi-led southern forces. Fiercely proud of its pre-Tutsi past, this group was deeply suspicious of any reconciliation with the RPF and hostile to moderate Hutu who supported dialogue.[27] Having felt like second-class citizens first to the Tutsi and then to other Hutu, the northerners were loath to relinquish power once having gained control.

During the Habyarimana regime, Rwanda experienced significant economic development. From 1976 to 1990, Rwanda moved from the bottom to the top of a per capita GNP ranking of regional countries. During the 1980s, the World Bank considered Rwanda a relative success. In 1987 its debt was 28 percent of its GNP, one of the lowest rates in Africa.[28] Although Rwanda's human rights record was still problematic, the situation was considered to be improving. Before 1990, no major ethnic violence had occurred during Habyarimana's regime, and, to some extent, he was favored by the internal Tutsi.[29]

Civil War and Multiparty Politics

The early 1990s involved considerable change for Rwanda. First, the RPF began its guerrilla war. Second, as mentioned earlier, the economic crisis placed considerable strain on the government. Third, under internal and external pressure, Habyarimana's regime began instituting multiparty politics.

On October 1, 1990, the RPF invaded northern Rwanda. After initial success, they were pushed back into Uganda by the internationally reinforced Force Armées Rwandaises (FAR). Over the next few years, the fighting settled into a low-level guerrilla war. Significantly motivated by the refugee crisis and their increasingly hostile treatment in Uganda, the RPF had an eight-point political agenda that was directed at reform of the Rwandan government.

Immediately on the heels of the RPF invasion France, Belgium, and Zaire sent troops to aid the Habyarimana regime. By October 4, France had sent 150 members of the 2ème Régiment Etranger Parachutiste to Kigali. Brussels followed with over 400 paratroopers. Mobutu Sese Seko, president of Zaire, sensing an opportunity to gain favor with France and Belgium, sent several hundred of his top Presidential Guard to the aid of his longtime friend Habyarimana. A few days later, after being deceived by a staged attack on the capital by the FAR (armed forces of the Habyarimana and interim governments) itself, France committed an additional 600 troops.[30] Paris continued its support throughout the war and in addition to logistical assistance underwrote and facilitated the purchase of over U.S. $10 million in military supplies.[31]

Because of its desperate economic situation, Rwanda was susceptible to pressure from donor nations, and, first weakly in 1990 and then more forcefully in 1992, Habyarimana's regime instituted political reforms. Initiated by the French military attaché, Lt. Col. Galinie, and then adopted by all donor nations, democratization was seen as a necessary complement to the ongoing negotiations with the RPF. In March of 1991, the MDR was launched and identified itself as the successor to Kayibanda's MDR/PARMEHUTU party. In addition the PSD, which enjoyed principally southern support, and the PL, whose base came primarily from the capital, were formed.[32] Under intense internal and external pressure, Habyarimana formed a new transitional government on April 6, 1992, that included all the major opposition parties. The government was led by Habyarimana, as president, and Dismas Nsengiyaremye, an MDR member, as prime minister.

Form and Specific Mechanisms of Intervention

This section of the chapter presents the Arusha Peace Accords that were negotiated between the RPF and the government of Rwanda (GoR). The Arusha Accords are best analyzed in a tripartite manner: the pre-negotiation phase, the talks themselves, and finally the failed implementation.[33]

Pre-Negotiation: Regional Efforts, Failed Cease-fires, and International Intervention

The efforts leading up to the Arusha talks included ultimately ineffective African initiatives, a series of failed cease-fires, and finally an intervention by the United States and France that brought the parties to the table in Arusha.

The invasion of Rwanda by the RPF in October 1990 immediately prompted significant diplomatic activity. Only days after the invasion, Belgium sent a high-level delegation, consisting of the prime minister, foreign minister, and defense minister, to Kigali in an attempt to resolve the conflict. This group met in Nairobi, Kenya, with President Habyarimana on October 14 and then held talks with the governments of Kenya, Tanzania, and Uganda and with the OAU. The efforts by the Belgian group culminated in a regional summit on October 17 that laid the groundwork for the involvement of neighboring countries and the OAU.[34]

Regional efforts included the sponsoring of cease-fire talks and a series of ad hoc summits. The summits were hosted by the heads of state of the CEPL (members were Rwanda, Burundi, and Zaire) and involved the participation of Uganda, Tanzania, the OAU, and the United Nations. At early meetings Mobutu Sese Seko was chosen as a mediator despite Zaire's military involvement in Rwanda. A monitoring force, the Neutral Military Observer Group (NMOG), was also created. The Dar-es-Salaam Declaration on Rwandese Refugees Problem, signed on February 19, 1991, was the first significant achievement from these summits and later formed the basis for refugee negotiations at Arusha.[35] At this meeting, under pressure from Ugandan President Yoweri Musevini and

Tanzanian President Ali Hassan Mwinyi, Habyarimana also signed the Zanzibar Communiqué that supposedly expressed his commitment to negotiate with all parties in an attempt to resolve the conflict.[36]

The focus of the talks then shifted to cease-fire negotiations that failed because Mobutu was a biased and ineffective mediator[37] and because both sides in turn perceived continued fighting to be to their advantage. The first cease-fire was negotiated and signed on March 29, 1991, in N'Sele, Zaire. The agreement formalized the creation of the NMOG and developed a basis for future talks. Almost immediately after the signing, however, the FAR shelled RPF positions, and fighting continued for several months.[38] A second cease-fire was signed on September 16, 1991, in Gabolite, Zaire. In this agreement, the military leadership of the NMOG shifted from Zaire to Nigeria, and the objectives of a peaceful solution articulated at N'Sele were reconfirmed. After the Gabolite talks, the mediator role passed from Mobutu to Tanzanian President Mwinyi.[39]

The final pre-Arusha stage of the resolution efforts involved the partially coordinated, low-level involvement of France and the United States. In Paris on January 14–15, 1992, Quai d'Orsay's director for Africa and Maghreb convened a meeting with GoR Ambassador Pierre-Claver Kanyarushoke and RPF leader Pasteur Bizimungu where the director encouraged the RPF to stop fighting and the GoR to heed more closely the RPF's demands.[40] During this same time, the Rwandan desk officer at the U.S. State Department, Carol Fuller, was communicating with RPF representatives in Washington. These discussions finally matured into the involvement of Assistant Secretary of State for Africa Herman Cohen, who began a series of interagency meetings that for the next two years oversaw U.S. involvement in Rwanda.[41] Because of the lack of progress in the peace talks throughout 1991, U.S. Ambassador Bruce Flatin in Kigali lobbied for a more active U.S. role. In response, Cohen arranged for a parallel series of meetings with leaders in Kampala and Kigali, where he encouraged negotiations and offered U.S. technical assistance.[42]

From May 8 to 9, 1992, Cohen met with President Musevini and representatives of the RPF in the Ugandan capital. In these discussions Cohen argued that the war was slowly destroying Rwanda's economy and that a military solution was not feasible given that the RPF could not hope to gain more than its small northern enclave.[43] In addition Cohen suggested to Musevini that a negotiated settlement of the refugee problem would serve the dual purposes of easing the internal burden on Uganda and injuring his longtime opponent Habyarimana.[44] Musevini was pleased that the United States did not share France's view that Uganda was the source of the conflict and pledged to use his influence with the RPF. For its part, the RPF expressed an interest in negotiations but asserted that the GoR was refusing to recognize their right to return.

From May 10 to 11, 1992, Cohen met separately with Habyarimana and representatives of the opposition parties. During these meetings, the president again refused to acknowledge the RPF as anything but Ugandans, but expressed a willingness to consider the right of return issue. Cohen's discussions with opposition leaders highlighted two points important to future negotiations: First, he perceived them as true reformers open to change, and second, they were clearly deeply suspicious of the RPF. They feared the rebel force as a throwback to previous aristocratic Tutsi rule and were concerned that the Tutsi would be able to dupe them at the negotiating table. Cohen left Kigali without a promise of negotiations but felt certain that talks were imminent.[45]

The precipitating factor for the start of substantive negotiations was the combined pressure of the United States and France on the RPF to remove its precondition that Habyarimana step down in favor of an interim government. The joint effort occurred when Dijoud asked Cohen to join him on June 20 at the Foreign Ministry Conference Center for a meeting with Ugandan Foreign Minister Paul Ssemmogere. At the meeting Cohen forcefully told Ssemmogere and his military entourage, who he assumed were RPF members, that the United States considered the RPF demands to be unreasonable and expected Uganda to use its considerable leverage with the RPF to create a climate conducive to negotiations. To back-up the demand, Cohen made an implicit threat of the withdrawal of aid. He stated that the refugee situation was sapping limited Western resources, and if the situation were not resolved, then a portion of the assistance currently provided to Uganda would most likely need to be diverted.[46] After the June talks, the RPF and the GoR agreed to meet in Arusha under the auspices of the OAU for comprehensive negotiations. Authority for the talks was delegated to Tanzanian President Mwinyi and the first session commenced on July 12, 1992.

The prestige, moral authority, and leverage introduced by the Western powers were certainly central to achieving an agreement where African efforts had failed. The success is also attributable to the ripeness of the conflict. From 1990 until 1992 both parties in turn felt that there was an advantage to be gained from continued fighting. At first buoyed by its initial victory, the government had hopes that it could defeat the RPF militarily, but by 1992 military victory seemed remote, and the economic crisis was placing considerable strain on the government. As for the RPF, after its initial poor performance, it was interested in improving its negotiating position. RPF leaders, though, realized that they could not win on the battlefield and that negotiations were necessary.

Arusha Talks

The Arusha peace talks were a sophisticated exercise in conflict resolution, but the process was greatly complicated by the internal dynamics of the parties. In theory Arusha was a textbook mediation: All the parties were present at the table, the conflict had reached a window of opportunity for conflict resolution, the root causes were addressed, and a neutral mediator guided the negotiations.[47] In reality, the talks were flawed because the GoR was forced to negotiate not only with the RPF, but also with opposition members of its own party. This meant that while the RPF was disciplined and well organized, the GoR was fragmented. Ultimately the different levels of negotiating competence led to a final settlement that was essentially a victor's deal for the RPF.[48]

To provide an understanding of the negotiating dynamics behind the Arusha Accords, the first part of the next section will analyze the role, objectives, motivations, and strategies of the various parties to the talks. The second part will describe the negotiating process, focusing particularly on the two most contentious issues: the composition of the transitional government and the integration of the armed forces.

Parties to the Negotiations

RPF: Disciplined and United

The RPF was a disciplined and highly effective guerrilla army, and its seriousness and determination expressed themselves in its negotiating approach. A former RPF official described the basis of the party's success at the table as fourfold:[49] 1) they were highly motivated because they felt that they were fighting for a just cause, 2) their strong organization and discipline allowed them to speak unfailingly with one voice, 3) they were in a strong negotiating position because of their military successes, and 4) they were able to more effectively develop support among the observer group.[50]

When the RPF arrived in Arusha, they already had a theoretical structure for their demands and detailed position papers for many of the finer points.[51] The major issues for the RPF were the establishment of the rule of law, a power-sharing arrangement that included a veto over essential government functions, an integration of the national army, and the right of return for refugees. Security concerns were at the core of most of the RPF's positions. Although the final settlement gave the RPF almost all of its demands, observers noted that in some key instances the RPF would probably have settled for less if forced to do so.[52]

Throughout the negotiations, the RPF sought to enlist the government opposition's support in trying to create a post-Habyarimana regime. To this end, they used both enticements and implicit threats. Especially in relation to the rule of law, the RPF argued for the creation of a pluralistic Rwandan society that guaranteed individual rights and was not based on ethnicity.[53] All parties were aware, however, that the RPF was prepared to return to the battlefield if they did not reach an adequate settlement.

GoR: Fragmented

The weakness that the GoR delegation displayed at the negotiating table can be attributed primarily to its fragmented nature but also to a sense of inferiority. The delegation was composed of representatives from the MRND and the opposition parties, MDR, PSD, and PL, which were essentially negotiating the intra-Hutu power dynamics of a future government while at the same time trying to resolve issues with the RPF. The leader of the delegation, Foreign Minister Ngulinzira, an MDR member, commented that it was often more difficult to reach agreement within the GoR than with the RPF. The fragmented nature of the GoR delegation not only led to disorganization and lack of preparedness, but also presented obvious divisions that the RPF was able to exploit.

Throughout the negotiations, Habyarimana vacillated between the moderates who supported some reconciliation and the hard-liners who adamantly opposed it. Several observers feel that he had no intention of abiding by the Accords and that he expected that the French would bail him out of any agreement.[54] In a now famous speech given in November 1992, Habyarimana called the Arusha Accords mere "pieces of paper."[55] Habyarimana later recanted this claim, but his lack of commitment is also used to explain his placing an opposition figure in charge of the GoR delegation. The theory is that he expected the talks to break down and so planned to blame the failure on his political opponents.[56] Ultimately, however, the negotiations reached a settlement, and whatever his earlier stance, many feel that when his plane was shot down, he was intending to proceed with implementation.

The opposition, caught in the middle between Habyarimana and the hard-liners and the RPF, did not have clear and consistent objectives throughout the negotiations. Many were genuine reformers who had common purpose with the RPF on numerous issues, especially the removal of Habyarimana. In addition, they generally did not support the war, as they perceived it as a fight between northern Hutu and the RPF.[57] The opposition was also, however, deeply suspicious of the RPF. They were uncertain about the rebels' true commitment to power sharing, and the RPF's offensive in February 1992 significantly deepened this concern. They were fearful of being taken advantage of by the "Tutsi" RPF, which some viewed as intellectually superior.[58] The opposition was also consumed in its own power struggles that ultimately had a disastrous effect on the implementation of the Accords.

Tanzania: Skilled Mediation

As the primary facilitator,[59] the lead Tanzanian diplomat, Ami M. Mpungwe, demonstrated a sophisticated, theoretical, and practical approach to the negotiations. Mpungwe considered his role to be essentially that of a referee who encouraged the parties, sometimes forcefully, to address seriously their problems by developing a coherent, reasonable agreement for the future of Rwanda. Mpungwe directed the talks in a proscribed sequence and developed and employed various mechanisms and leverage to resolve sticking points. In its efforts, Tanzania was motivated by a variety of interests that were compatible with its role.

The guiding principle for Mpungwe in the talks was the need to establish trust and confidence between the parties. To this end, the talks were disaggregated and moved from the least difficult to the most contentious issues. A cease-fire was established first. This was followed by discussions on the rule of law defining the new political order. As momentum built, the talks next addressed how the new order would be reached: the power-sharing arrangements in the BBTG and the transitional institutions. Finally, when the process had gained significant authority, respect, and momentum, especially in the eyes of the observers, the negotiations tackled the most contentious issue, the integration of the armed forces.

To achieve resolution on problematic issues, Mpungwe employed a variety of measures. First, whenever the talks became contentious, Mpungwe would separate the groups and hold proximity discussions, functioning as an intermediary. To apply leverage, Mpungwe would threaten to withdraw Tanzania as the mediator or to identify one party to the international community as blameworthy. As Tanzania was the only neutral regional party, and a negotiated settlement significantly depended on its involvement, the former threat carried considerable weight. Mpungwe would sometimes condition his use of leverage on the parties reaching a settlement by a specified deadline. In addition, Mpungwe was able to appeal to the international and regional community to apply diplomatic or economic pressure.[60] Finally, once an agreement had been reached, Mpungwe would strengthen commitment by coordinating, prior to its announcement, its immediate recognition by the international community. The statements of support lent the new, sometimes tense, and tentative agreements an aura of international authority.

In undertaking and sustaining the year-long negotiations, Tanzania was motivated by the mutually compatible goals of humanitarian concern, a self-interest in resolving the long-standing refugee problem, and the promotion of regional stability through the development of a sustainable Rwandan government.

OAU: Regional Organization

Having previously refrained from involvement in the "internal" politics of its member countries, the OAU's involvement in the pre-negotiations and the Arusha talks was somewhat remarkable and can be attributed to two principal factors. First, Ugandan President Musevini was chair of the OAU at the time and supported a diplomatic resolution of the conflict.[61] Second, the new secretary-general of the OAU, Salim A. Salim, a Tanzanian, was extremely interested in the organization taking a lead in resolving African conflicts. The United States was supportive of these efforts and provided an initial $U.S. 3–4 million for the NMOG force that was under OAU control.[62]

France: A Dual Policy

In general terms France perceived the English-speaking RPF as a threat to its Francophone hegemony. Although Paris was unfailingly supportive of the Habyarimana regime, it pursued a dual policy of supporting the government militarily while at the same time promoting a negotiated settlement.[63]

The dual policy was principally the result of divisions within the French government, with the Africa Unit at the Elysée Palace on one side and the Ministry of Foreign Affairs on the other. President Mitterand's son, in charge of the

Africa Unit, said immediately following the RPF invasion that France would "send a few boys to help old man Habyarimana."[64] He expected the conflict to be short-lived, but the Africa Unit continued its military assistance even as the conflict continued. Increasingly critical of this approach, the Ministry of Foreign Affairs, as indicated by the Paris talks discussed above, actively supported negotiations as the best solution. They thought the RPF might be able to win militarily but not politically and that the GoR was basically in the opposite situation. The Ministry's objective was a settlement as favorable to Habyarimana as possible. Although France encouraged the negotiations, it was not a disinterested observer. Throughout the talks, Paris championed the GoR position, especially regarding the composition of the government and the integration of the military.

Since the genocide, France has been severely criticized for the material and psychological assistance it provided to the regime. By propping up the government with military and economic aid, France encouraged intransigence on the part of the GoR and provided a shield behind which the extremists were able to develop their desperate plan.[65] The counterargument, however, is that the positions taken by France and the GoR would have ultimately proved to be more sustainable. These issues are discussed more extensively below in the conclusion section.

United States: Technical Resource

From the beginning the United States did not take a primary role in the Arusha process, but acted as a facilitator, providing technical assistance and lending authority to the talks.[66] In 1992 and 1993, U.S. attention was directed elsewhere because of its significant involvement in several other ongoing negotiations in Angola, Mozambique, Ethiopia, Liberia, and Namibia. With its lack of strategic interest in the area, the United States was generally perceived as an effective neutral intermediary. The lower level of U.S. involvement did, however, have its negative consequences, as discussed in the conclusion section below.

As a facilitator, the United States primarily focused its efforts on maintaining an effective process, that is, on aiding the parties in reaching a mutually agreeable settlement. Although in general the United States did not evaluate the content of the agreement, it did occasionally encourage an approach that it thought was more sustainable.[67] After early talks in which the RPF was surprised at its success, Charles Snyder, director of the Office of African Regional Affairs in the U.S. State Department, encouraged the RPF not necessarily to take all the concessions it could win. In particular he suggested that they seek a lower percentage in the military. Early U.S. involvement focused on the development of a workable cease-fire and on helping the parties identify the issues that would need to be addressed in later rounds. In particular, U.S. observers offered advice on the creation and implementation of the cease-fire, the structure of the Neutral Military Observer Group (NMOG), encouraging a feasibly limited mandate, and the operations of the Joint Political Military Committee (JPMC).

As suggested above, the United States generally functioned as an information resource, although it occasionally took a more active role. An example of the former role was the advice that Lt. Col. Marley, political-military advisor, Africa Bureau, State Department, provided on the integration of the officer ranks. The GoR had eight command levels, whereas the RPF had four. In brief meetings with either side, Marley suggested a matrix including considerations of an officer's age, responsibility, and education. Months later when the issue was addressed at the table, both parties presented matrices, and the issue was resolved within thirty minutes. An example of more interventionist involvement came after the RPF offensive in February of 1992, during an extraordinary session of the JPMC that was designed to restart the talks. During negotiations the Rwandan prime minister had agreed to the withdrawal of French forces from Rwanda. Believing that the agreement was not sustainable, the Tanzanians asked Marley to intercede. In separate late night talks, Marley confirmed that the prime minister was not committed to the withdrawal and instead brokered a deal that addressed the RPF's demands and the GoR's security concerns by cutting the French force in half and by limiting its presence to Kigali.[68]

Actual Negotiations

The Arusha talks ran from July 12, 1992, until the signing of the Accords in August 1993. Under the auspices of the OAU, Tanzanian President Ali Hassan Mwinyi and his OAU Ambassador Ami Mpungwe facilitated the talks between the RPF and the GoR. Observers from regional countries, Burundi, Uganda, and Zaire, and the international community, France, Belgium, Germany, the United States, and Senegal, were present at various sessions. A recurring theme during the talks was the tension between the Habyarimana regime and the opposition parties leading the delegation. Repeatedly Habyarimana would veto breakthroughs agreed to by Foreign Minister Ngulinzira that significantly reduced the former's power and the influence in the ruling MRND.[69] The final package of protocols included

- N'Sele amended cease-fire (7/12/1992)
- principle and creation of the rule of law (8/18/92)
- power sharing, the enlargement of the transition government (i.e., inclusion of the RPF), and the creation of a transition parliament (10/30/92 and 1/9/93)
- reintegration of refugees and internally dislocated persons (6/9/93)
- creation of a nationally unified army (i.e., merger of RPF and FAR) (8/3/93)[70]

In addition to establishing a cease-fire, the preliminary session in July 1992 stipulated the agenda for the talks and implemented the JPMC. The JPMC was a forum that ran parallel to the Arusha talks to address military issues, especially cease-fire violations, and although the Committee had no adjudication authority, it proved to be an important safety valve for releasing tensions.[71] Amending previous cease-fires, the new agreement held throughout the negotiations except for a RPF offensive in February of 1992.

The session on the rule of law dealt with the background conditions in Rwanda that the RPF, and the opposition, saw as the roots of the country's instability. In particular, the protocol sought to establish the fundamental rights of the people, including the freedom of expression and the right to life, as articulated by the UN Charter and other internationally recognized fundamental documents. In these negotiating sessions, the RPF argued for the importance of creating a broadly defined pluralistic society. For the RPF pluralism represented not simply multipartyism but a political culture capable of sustaining debate and dialogue. Along these lines, the RPF stressed that the Rwandan people should be indivisible and not identified in terms of ethnicity. The RPF viewed the principles articulated in the rule of law protocol as the theoretical underpinnings on which all subsequent agreements should build and which the parties should seek to reinforce.[72]

Negotiations on the creation of the new government and the transitional institutions proved extremely contentious.[73] They ultimately resulted in an agreement with three key ingredients: one, the extremist CDR party was excluded from participation; two, the power of the government shifted from the presidency to the parliament, with the MRND relegated to a minority position;[74] and three, a majority vote was defined as requiring the concurrence of four parties despite the mention of consensus rule. Elections were stipulated to occur at the end of the transitional period, and a commission was to draft a new constitution that would be approved by a referendum.[75] During the negotiations on November 15, Habyarimana essentially withdrew his support, calling the protocols merely "pieces of paper." Despite Habyarimana's disapproval, Foreign Minister Ngulinzira returned to Arusha in December and continued to negotiate essentially without authority.

On power sharing, the RPF's demand that the CDR be excluded from the government was probably the most significant barrier and stalled talks for several weeks. During this period, Mpungwe separated the parties and along with members of the observer group strenuously lobbied the RPF to allow the CDR to participate in the government. As articulated by one Western diplomat, the logic was that it was better to have the CDR inside the tent than outside, threatening to burn it down.[76] The RPF, however, remained absolutely intransigent.[77] Their reasoning, which ultimately prevailed over Mpungwe, with the agreement of the opposition, was that the extremists were the source of Rwanda's suffering and were bent on destroying any power-sharing arrangement. The best means of controlling them was the quick implementation of the transitional government and the integrated security forces that could check their agitation. As discussed below, this did not occur.[78]

The government's eventual accommodation was based on several factors: The opposition was sympathetic to the RPF viewpoint; the RPF had made it clear that it would readily resume hostilities; and in the eyes of the international community, Habyarimana's commitment to peace would be dubious if he scuttled talks by insisting on the inclusion of a sectarian extremist group. It is unclear, however, if those in Kigali were ever committed to the power-sharing arrangement. Supporters of Habyarimana said they would never be a permanent minority.

During and after the agreement, the Tanzanian facilitators tried to encourage the supporters of Habyarimana by making apparent that the Accords did not represent a conspiracy against him and that he would be guaranteed a fair shot in free elections. To some extent Habyarimana took to heart the facilitators' advice about the possibilities of maintaining power through the new political process. Starting in the spring, he began to manipulate the opposition to change the distribution of power in the new transitional government. The hard-liners, however, reacted violently to their exclusion. During the power-sharing negotiations Col. Bagasora had threatened to bring about "an apocalypse."[79] In late January, over 300 Tutsi were killed in Bagogwe, home to Habyarimana's clan.

The final significant barrier to the conclusion of the Accords were the negotiations on the integration of the armed forces. They were completed in the summer of 1993 and followed the RPF offensive in February. Ostensibly taken in response to the Bagogwe massacre, the offensive doubled the RPF's territory and allowed them to enter the military negotiations having dramatically demonstrated their superiority. The principal difficulty of the negotiations focused on the proportions each side would gain in the new integrated army. The government entered the negotiations proposing approximately a 20 percent share for the RPF as commensurate with their ethnic proportion of the population. The RPF was committed to a fifty–fifty split.

Guiding Mpungwe's mediation was a desire to avoid the situation that had occurred in Angola, in which each faction had retained its own military force. Mpungwe's goal was a reconciliation of the security concerns of the two sides. Given his dedication to the rule of law and a de-emphasis on ethnicity, Mpungwe was not sympathetic to the government's initial offer. He separated the parties and refused to communicate the GoR position to the RPF. The formula developed for settlement involved a horizontal and vertical integration of the security forces.[80] The horizontal balance was achieved by giving the MRND control over the military and the RPF control over the gendarmerie. Vertical checks were instituted by requiring that the two most senior officers at each command level be from opposing sides. For example, if the commander was from the FAR, than the deputy commander would an RPF officer. An additional important lesson from Angola was the decision not to schedule elections until six months after the scheduled integration of the security forces.

After significant effort, the final settlement split the command and control functions fifty–fifty and gave the GoR a sixty–forty advantage in troop composition.[81] When Foreign Minister Ngulinzira agreed to the above formula, Habyarimana flatly rejected it and in fact recalled Ngulinzira. Ngulinzira refused and the negotiations continued for a period during which he had no authority. Ultimately, Habyarimana reshuffled the cabinet. Former Defense Minister and MRND party member James Gasana was placed in charge of the talks, and they recommenced in Rwanda. Angered by Habyarimana's refusal, the RPF demanded an increased representation in the troop levels. During the first week in June, democratic elections had replaced Tutsi leaders with a Hutu president. The removal of the southern Tutsi ally probably contributed to the RPF's insistence on high percentages. After considerable lobbying by Mpungwe and the observers, the RPF returned to its earlier position and a final agreement was achieved.

Signed on August 3, 1993, by Habyarimana and RPF chairman Alexis Kanyarengwe, the Accords called for the inauguration of the transitional government, led by Faustin Twagiramungu, within at least thirty-seven days. Until the arrival of the UN peacekeeping and implementation force, the caretaker government of Agathe Uwilingiyimana was to retain control.[82]

Implementation

Driven by a desperate plan orchestrated by Hutu extremists, numerous factors internal and external to Rwanda led to the disastrous failure of the implementation of the Arusha Accords. Central to the extremists' plans was the development of a rural militia and the manipulation of ethnicity to create a climate of fear. Political infighting by the opposition also contributed to the undermining of the Accords. In addition, an ineffective peacekeeping force, in part the result of a disjuncture between the United Nations and the OAU, failed to propel the peace process or provide the needed security and stability. Finally, pressure by regional countries and the international community was ultimately ineffective.

Although the Accords prescribed a dramatic reduction in the extremists' power, they held control of the military and administrative machinery of the government during the negotiations and the crucial implementation phase. The *akazu* formed the core of the hard-liners and had members in ruling positions in the military, the CDR, and the MRND. Using the regional prefectures and deputy prefectures, they organized and trained local militias, the infamous *interahamwe,* "those who work together," throughout the country. Military documents reveal that the extremists hoped to arm one in ten peasants, often targeting unemployed young men, and developed extermination lists of Tutsi and moderate Hutu.[83] Although these efforts intensified during late 1993 and early 1994, the groundwork for the genocide had begun even while the Arusha talks were in progress.

Paralleling these efforts was a media campaign that effectively exploited events to incite hatred and fear and sow ethnic division among the Hutu masses. Beginning on July 8, 1993, Radio-Télévision Libre des Mille Collines (RTLMC) began broadcasting rhetoric vehemently opposed to the Arusha Accords. A turning point in the implementation occurred with the disastrous events in neighboring Burundi. On October 21, 1993, Tutsi extremist military officers assassinated the newly elected Hutu president, Melchior Ndadye, and began a campaign of repression that resulted in approximately 50,000 Hutu and Tutsi deaths and led to about 300,000 Hutu refugees fleeing into Rwanda.[84] When combined with the installation of a 600-man RPF battalion in Kigali, the extremists were able to paint a dark picture of an imminent Tutsi usurpation of power. With the transitional government not yet in place in Rwanda, the only governmental institution with real power was Habyarimana's presidency. Although the president had clearly been hesitant about the Accords, Mpungwe believes that the assassination of Ndadye allowed the extremists to decisively commit Habyarimana to oppose the Accords.[85] Regardless of Habyarimana's position, numerous observers credit the assassination with allowing the extremists to develop a broad constituency that otherwise might have still supported the transitional government.

During this time, the opposition parties became splintered by personal power struggles that dissolved into ideological and regional divisions. Immediately after the designation of Faustin Twagiramungu (MDR) as interim prime minister by the Arusha Accords, he was expelled from his own party as part of MDR infighting.[86] Habyarimana exploited these divisions among the opposition and used the absence of opposition consent to justify delaying the implementation of the transitional government. On January 8, 1994, the convening of the BBTG was blocked by deadlocks within the MDR and PL. Attempts to proceed on February 10 without the PL were aborted by the assassination of the PSD leader Felicien Gatabazi and the reprisal killing of Martin Bucyana of the CDR.[87] Although the United Nations was able to reestablish order after riots in Kigali, Rwanda was hurtling toward the precipice.

Under pressure from the French, the United Nations had rebuffed efforts by the OAU to take an active role in the implementation and monitoring of the Arusha Accords and had assumed primary responsibility for what would be a completely ineffective peacekeeping force.[88] As the Arusha Accords called for French troops to be withdrawn and replaced with UN blue helmets, it is likely Paris wanted to ensure UN control as an indirect means of maintaining its hegemony. With the OAU's hopes of providing a transitional military presence rejected, there was no monitoring or implementing force on the ground during the crucial, tense six months it took the United Nations Assistance Mission for Rwanda (UNAMIR) to materialize. Once in place UNAMIR lacked much of its essential equipment and was short on even basic supplies such as ammunition.[89] In addition to the resistance shown by the international community, the parties, especially the RPF, pushed for a lower level of involvement for UNAMIR.[90] The mission was further crippled by a toothless mandate that prohibited any involvement should hostilities erupt.[91] After fighting did start, the European battalion of UNAMIR withdrew. The African battalion, however, remained.

Throughout the implementation, the international and regional powers exerted pressure on Habyarimana to abide by the Accords. In Kigali the international diplomatic core was united in relentlessly lobbying the government to fulfill its commitment to the peace process. On April 3, 1994, a group of influential Western ambassadors met with Habyarimana and stressed that the Accords must be implemented. Three days later at a regional summit, the leaders of the neighboring countries and the secretary-general of the OAU harshly reprimanded Habyarimana and reiterated the same point.[92] The problem with this strategy was that Habyarimana may have been a prisoner too and was soon to become a victim of the extremists.

On April 6 the plane carrying Habyarimana and Burundi President Cyprien Ntaryamira, was shot down as it approached the Kigali airport. Even before the missile was fired, the *interahamwe* militias had set up roadblocks around the city and had begun their killing. On April 7, Agathe Uwilingiyama, the appointed prime minister, was murdered in her home along with ten Belgian peacekeepers who were tortured before being killed. As intended, this led to the withdrawal of the European component of UNAMIR.[93] Over the next three months the extremists spread their genocidal mania throughout the countryside. Before the RPF forces were able to take control of the country, nearly one million people had been brutally killed, and approximately two million refugees had poured over Rwanda's borders in the largest and fastest exodus of displaced persons in modern history. [94]

Analysis

Although at the time of the signing of the Arusha Accords many considered it to be the best peace agreement in Africa since Lancaster House, much of the subsequent commentary views the Accords as having contributed to the violence in 1994. Academic critics and participants in the negotiations focus on both the theoretical and practical aspects of the negotiations. The theoretical analyses fault the Accords for not co-opting the extremists or otherwise neutralizing them and question the appropriateness of international pressure.[95] The practical perspectives emphasize the lack of available resources and intelligence.

Some of the academic writing argues that the Arusha Accords broke a fundamental tenet of conflict resolution by failing to give the extremists a stake in the new government.[96] The extremists were driven into a corner first by excluding them from the government and then by removing their control over the military. The hard-liners were left with the stark choice of loss of power or violent opposition.[97] Underlying this view is the unprovable counterfactual argument that the extremists might not have perpetuated their plans had they been included in the government.[98] There is circumstantial evidence for this position. Although the extremists clearly did not support the Arusha process, at least initially they did not regard it as irrelevant. During the BBTG negotiations, they argued ardently for the inclusion of the CDR. At some point during the military discussions, however, they appear to have abandoned interest in the process.[99]

If the extremists were to lose political and military power through implementation of the Accords, then it is argued that some means had to be provided to achieve this. The internal political opposition and the RPF military forces certainly provided some pressure, but the primary implementation mechanism articulated by the Arusha Accords, UNAMIR, was a neutral peacekeeping force not designed or directed to remove the hard-liners. Such an effort, as in Haiti, would have required the disarming of the hard-liners or their removal from the country. Without the removal of hard-liners, the Accords were not a complete and sustainable solution.[100]

The disjuncture between the OAU and the United Nations represents a crucial missed opportunity. Although the OAU lacked training and resources it clearly had the political will to be significantly involved in the implementation and monitoring of the Accords. The OAU repeatedly lobbied for participation, and its troops remained in Rwanda after the fighting began. In the future, cooperative relationships between the United Nations and regional organizations may represent a means of overcoming the perennial lack of political will to undertake remote peacekeeping operations demonstrated by the international community. Such arrangements might be criticized as mercenary, but as with the OAU, these organizations are often interested in addressing their own regional problems and can do so with technical and financial assistance. Ensuring neutrality is a significant concern, but certainly not an insurmountable barrier.

Given the failings in the Arusha Accords and the international community's lack of commitment to implementation, commentators have questioned whether the international community should have aggressively pushed for the acceptance and implementation of the agreement.[101] Peacemaking can be a risky process, and the involvement of the United Nations, the United States, and the Europeans provided a false sense of security for those seeking change.[102] Herman Cohen has suggested that the United States was locked in a routine act of "rote" diplomacy that viewed a cease-fire and negotiations as inherently beneficial.[103] With twenty-twenty hindsight, he suggests that an alternative solution would have been to condemn the RPF invasion from the start and to pursue a more modest plan of encouraging internal political reform before compounding the political and military instability with the introduction of the RPF. This accords with the view of Ian Linden, who described the Arusha Accords as "too much, too far, too fast."[104] It should be again noted that several of the observer groups counseled restraint on the part of the RPF and that the RPF's military strength, combined with the GoR's deteriorating economic situation, placed considerable independent pressure on the GoR. There are strong indications, however, that without significant regional and international pressure, Habyarimana's regime would not have accepted the Accords or proceeded with their implementation.[105]

The practical recommendations from U.S. participants were primarily a response to the low priority that the talks represented for the United States. Both Herman Cohen and Charles Synder commented that the coordination and brainstorming sessions that had been used in other conflicts would have been helpful in Arusha.[106] Using input from all U.S. participants and therefore from all of the parties' perspectives, these sessions developed an overall strategy that provided clear direction for the individual participants in their interactions with the teams. This would have eliminated the fuzzy mandate that instructed U.S. facilitators to simply encourage the groups to reach a mutually agreed settlement. A higher priority would also have meant more continuity, as facilitators would not have been switched from Arusha to other conflicts. In addition, with more resources, the U.S. team would have been able to allocate more personnel to the talks; for example, someone could have been present during the December and January power-sharing talks. While discussing the above points, U.S. participants also noted that the United States purposefully took a less active role so as not to undermine the Tanzanian and OAU mediators.

Crucial to any mediation is good intelligence. Members of the observer community and the academic literature have suggested that those who mediated and implemented the Arusha Accords needed better information.[107] In hindsight the warning signs appear clear, but for many participants at that time the magnitude of the impending crisis was not apparent. Participants and members of the RPF remember dismissing RTLMC precisely because it was so literal and extreme.[108] For some, the January massacres were interpreted as a negotiating tactic. In addition, there was a belief that some killings were the inevitable result of transition. Part of the problem may also have arisen because of the dramatically different atmospheres that existed in Arusha and Kigali. For example, when the Accords were signed, no celebration occurred in the Rwandan capital. Instead the city was dominated by a state of fear, especially acute among the Tutsi population.

The human rights community had been documenting the efforts of the extremists and the disturbing trend they represented. Tragically, what almost no one anticipated before early 1994 were the brutally inhumane lengths to which the extremists were willing to go in their desperate bid to retain power. There are strong arguments that a robust response by the international community could have stopped the killings before they spread throughout the country. What happened instead was that the United Nations, after having insisted on unilateral control, simply withdrew. The civilians, who were being killed by the thousands each day, were abandoned to their fate.[109] Although UN Secretary-General Boutros Boutros-Ghali was perhaps trying to spread the blame, his outrage about the world's inaction was shared by many:

> We are all to be held accountable for this failure, all of us, the great powers, African countries, the NGO's, the international community. It is a genocide.... I have failed.... It is a scandal.[110]

Conclusion

The Arusha Accords stand as a testament to the strength of and the implicit danger represented by third-party intervention. They indicate that even the most carefully crafted resolution is not complete until implemented. They also underscore the deep responsibility of third parties to maintain their full commitment once having accepted the burden of involvement. Especially for small countries, the international community has the power to dramatically alter the course of events. International powers must remain fully cognizant that partial efforts are likely worse than no efforts at all.

9

South Africa: The Negotiated Transition from Apartheid to Nonracial Democracy

Peter Bouckaert

Overview

THE SOUTH AFRICAN case is exceptional in that the parties completely renegotiated their political system with only a minimum of outside intervention and no formal external mediation process. Even though the international community had acted for years against apartheid in South Africa, there was no externally led mediation effort in South Africa during the 1990–94 negotiation period, and the international community remained interested but largely unentangled observers in the negotiation process. The decision of the international community to remain on the sidelines, while offering logistical support and occasional focused intervention (such as Cyrus Vance's mission under the auspices of the United Nations and the UN observer group that followed), was a conscious and appropriate decision, and one that actually aided the parties in reaching their own solution.

In addition to the heroic stature of Mandela and de Klerk, the keys to the success of this remarkable transition were a strong civil society (fostered with help from the international community); a public peace process in which a myriad of public meetings helped generate support for political change; strategic use of help offered by the United Nations and others at key points in the talks; and the establishment of independent, objective structures like the Goldstone Commission to ensure successful implementation of the negotiated agreements. This chapter also highlights how a spoiler group, in this case the Inkatha Freedom

Party, can be cajoled, threatened, and ultimately included in the peace process, avoiding the disastrous outcome brought about by spoilers in the Arusha process in Rwanda.

Timeline

1948   Electoral victory of the National Party (NP).

1985–1990 "Public Peace Process" meetings and secret negotiations between Nelson Mandela and NP officials.

1989   **July 5:** Secret meeting between President P. W. Botha and Nelson Mandela.

1990   **Feb. 2:** President de Klerk addresses the South African Parliament, announcing the release of Nelson Mandela from prison, lifting the ban on the African National Congress (ANC) and other parties, and inviting parties to the negotiating table. **May 2:** Groote Schuur Minute: framework for return of exiles. **Aug. 7:** Pretoria Minute: ANC renounces armed struggle.

1991   **Sept. 14:** National Peace Accord signed by de Klerk, Mandela, and Mangosuthu Buthelezi. **Dec. 1:** CODESA (Conference for a Democratic South Africa) I negotiations, bringing all parties together for talks.

1992   **May:** Resumption of CODESA negotiations. **June 16:** ANC abandons negotiation process. **July:** Security Council Resolution 765 issued, emphasizing responsibility of South African government in stopping violence and urging resumption of the negotiation process; United Nations appoints Cyrus Vance as special representative for South Africa. **July 20–31:** Cyrus Vance visits South Africa. **Aug. 3–4:** Successful general strike organized by ANC. **Aug. 17:** UN Security Council authorizes deployment of UN observers to strengthen structures established under the newly adopted National Peace Accord.

1993   **January and February:** NP and ANC hold secret bilateral meetings and reach agreement on the process and structure of transition to democracy (agreement later rejected by a number of other parties). **May:** Kempton Park talks held, aimed at gaining acceptance from other parties for bilateral agreement.

1994   **Apr. 8:** Summit between Mandela, de Klerk, Buthelezi, and Zulu king Goodwill Zwilithini. **Apr. 27:** Elections held successfully.

Background

In a study of contemporary mediated international and intranational conflicts, South Africa might appear to be an unlikely candidate for inclusion. Although the controversy over apartheid had been one of the preeminent issues on the United Nation's agenda since the founding of that organization, leading to an unprecedented international campaign against apartheid, the international community maintained a relatively hands-off approach during the negotiations period (1990–94). There was no consistent mediation effort in South Africa, and the international community seemed content to remain on the sidelines for much of the time. In essence, the negotiations were convened and conducted by the South Africans themselves.

This chapter will argue that the decision of the international community to remain on the sidelines, while offering logistic support and the occasional focused intervention, was conscious and appropriate. The decision to intervene only when appropriate, and at the invitation of the parties involved, allowed the South Africans to resolve a severe and potentially violent conflict in a constructive, realistic, and viable manner. Thus, a decision not to mediate—where the required capacity exists within the country for direct negotiations—may at times be an option preferable to intervention by mediation.

Because of the limited intervention of the international community and the nonexistence of a central mediator, it will at times be difficult for this chapter to adhere to the structure of the other case studies included in the volume. Many of the issues considered in other case studies, such as persuasion tactics of the mediator, may not be relevant in the South African negotiation context. However, wherever possible, a framework similar to that of the other studies has been attempted in order to facilitate comparison.

The Nature of the Apartheid Conflict: 1948–90

The Domestic Situation

White settlement began in South Africa with the arrival of Jan Van Riebeeck and his small party at present-day Cape Town in 1652. The small colony was supposed to serve only as a supply station for the ships of the Dutch East India Company traveling between Holland and India, but the colony soon grew larger and began moving inland. What was to follow over the next centuries was a complex conflict between the various groups fighting for dominance or survival in the region. The Afrikaners, and the English who soon followed, fought bloody battles against the African tribes of the region. The expansion of the Zulu Nation under King Shaka Zulu led to equally pitched struggles among the various African nations in the country and caused massive population movements.[1] Some smaller nations, such as the nomadic KhoiSan, were virtually wiped out in this conflict.

Whites also fought among each other, especially after the discovery of gold and diamonds in the region. English colonists wanted to claim the South African territory for the British Crown, but faced bitter resistance from the largely rural Afrikaners. During the Anglo-Boer War (1899–1902), the English used concentration camps to isolate Afrikaner women and children from the rebelling Afrikaner guerrillas. Housed in deplorable conditions, between 20,000 and 26,000 inmates of these camps died from malnutrition and disease, in addition to more than 14,000 Africans. Incidents like this—and the Afrikaners' often miraculous survival against incredible odds—helped create a strong desire for survival and a fear of annihilation among the Afrikaners.

Apartheid as an official state policy gained prominence with the electoral victory of the National Party (NP) in 1948, but discrimination long preceded *de jure*
apartheid. Like most colonial societies, South Africa operated under a strict racial-
ist system, and both the Dutch East India Company and the English colonists had
introduced segregationist legislation.[2] In addition, much of the disenfranchise-
ment of the nonwhite population had already been completed by 1948. As African
tribes were defeated on the battlefield, their land was often seized by the victorious
whites.[3] The Land Act of 1913, passed by the English colonial government, had already "reserved" less than 10 percent of the land in South Africa for black settlement, effectively making the indigenous populations aliens in South Africa proper.

Thus, apartheid only consolidated, but did not create, a system of white supremacy in Africa.[4] The next decades brought untold suffering to the nonwhite
populations of South Africa, as the architects of apartheid implemented their
vast social engineering experiment aimed at the complete separation of the
races in South Africa. The influential Report for the Second Carnegie Inquiry
into Poverty and Development in Southern Africa[5] documents in detail the impact of apartheid on the nonwhite population, and only a few illustrative statistics will be offered here. Whites, accounting for only 13 percent of the population, owned an estimated 87 percent of South African land at the end of the
1980s.[6] Only 7 percent of whites in South Africa live below the poverty line,
compared to 67 percent of African households, 38 percent of coloured households, and 18 percent of Asian (Indian) households.[7] The average income of
whites is eight times greater than that of black South Africans. These grave inequalities in wealth distribution along racial lines were created in large part
through programs of job reservation and other discriminatory legislation.

The Regional Impact of Apartheid

The apartheid system had a further detrimental effect on the economies of
the states surrounding South Africa. The socialist-oriented governments of Angola, Mozambique, Tanzania, Zambia, and Zimbabwe were opposed to
apartheid and at times allowed the liberation movements, the ANC and the Pan-
Africanist Congress (PAC), to operate within their borders. In order to counter
this perceived threat, South Africa developed a major destabilization campaign
in the region, which would ultimately lead to military invasions of at least seven
of its neighbors,[8] assassination attempts on foreign leaders, the backing of genocidal dissident groups in Angola (UNITA) and Mozambique (RENAMO),[9] and
the general disruption of regional economies by sabotage of transport systems
and the disruption of oil supplies.[10] By characterizing its interventions as struggles against communism, South Africa was able to solicit support from the U.S.
government for some of its ventures.[11] In response to South Africa's continual
harassment of its neighboring states, the Frontline states formed a regional
body, the Southern African Development Cooperation Conference (SADCC),
which had as its explicit goal to reduce the economic dependence of the Frontline states on South Africa.[12]

The final cost of these interventions is immense. A 1989 UNICEF report estimated that the South African destabilization campaign cost more than 1.3 million lives, at an economic cost of more than U.S. $60 billion.[13] A 1985 memorandum by the SADCC to the Organization of African Unity (OAU) estimated the damage to the SADCC states at more than U.S. $10 billion for the preceding five years.[14] Nelson Mandela estimates the dead at two million and the cost at U.S. $62 billion.[15]

The International Response

The international campaign against apartheid predates the arrival to power of the NP in 1948 and grew from a limited concern over South Africa's treatment of Indian nationals[16] "to become a comprehensive global campaign against apartheid as an ideological basis of legitimate governance."[17] As the decolonization movement gathered speed across the world and the balance of (numerical) power in the UN General Assembly moved toward the newly independent Third World countries, the General Assembly began an increasingly vocal campaign against apartheid, leading to the declaration of apartheid as a "crime against humanity" in 1966.[18]

Compared to the General Assembly's actions, the response of the UN Security Council to apartheid was far more restrained. The Security Council occasionally condemned South Africa and its racist practices after a massacre like the 1960 Sharpeville incident.[19] In 1963, the Security Council described the situation in Southern Africa as "seriously disturbing to international peace" and called for a voluntary arms boycott against South Africa.[20] Frustrated by the unwillingness of the Security Council to take more punitive action, the General Assembly continued to agitate against apartheid and adopted a series of programs designed to "provide legal, educational, and humanitarian assistance to internal and external victims of apartheid."[21] In addition, the General Assembly promoted a global grassroots campaign against apartheid, designed to pressure the abstainers on the Security Council—especially France, the United Kingdom, and the United States—into taking more effective action against South Africa's apartheid regime.[22]

It took a combination of the mounting grassroots campaign, continued General Assembly pressure, and renewed South African belligerence to bring about the mandatory sanctions that had a profound impact on the continuing viability of apartheid. The Soweto riots of 1976, in which schoolchildren protesting the compulsory teaching of Afrikaans were gunned down, detained, and exiled, led the Security Council to impose a mandatory arms embargo on South Africa in 1977.[23] However, the Reagan and Thatcher governments, arguing for "constructive engagement" with, rather than isolation of, South Africa, diminished the chances for more comprehensive sanctions in the early 1980s. Again, it took a mass grassroots campaign under the direction of the Free South Africa Movement, headed by Randall Robinson, to further isolate the South African regime. College protests, divestment campaigns, sit-ins, and protests at the South African embassy ultimately led to the passing of the Comprehensive Anti-Apartheid Act in 1986 over President Reagan's veto. By this time South Africa was a virtual outcast, denied its seat in the United Nations, banished from participation in many international sports, and subject to an almost comprehensive worldwide sanctions campaign.

Form and Specific Mechanisms of Intervention

The Decision to Negotiate and the Process of Negotiations

The South African negotiation process was an intensive four-year process with almost daily developments. The formal negotiation period was preceded by an equally intriguing and important period of secret negotiations and meetings between various citizen groups and the liberation organizations. (This chapter cannot chronicle the entire process, and the reader is referred to other sources for this information.[24]) This section will give an overview of the negotiation process, focusing on the effective negotiation methods used and the role of the international community.

The Public Peace Process, the Secret Negotiations, and Ripeness of the Conflict

The Public Peace Process

Although F.W. de Klerk's groundbreaking address to the South African Parliament in February 1990 provides a convenient starting point for the commencement of formal negotiations, much of the groundwork was laid prior to this time. An important component of the pre-negotiation activity was the myriad of public meetings, which took place between the various groups working toward a settlement in South Africa, the so-called "public peace process." A similar public peace process approach has been used in the context of the U.S.–Soviet Union Cold War conflict, the Arab–Israeli conflict, and the Armenia-Azerbaijan conflict.[25]

One of the first such public meetings took place in 1985 when Piet Muller, editor of the Afrikaans newspaper *Beeld,* and Professor H. W. van der Merwe traveled to Harare to meet with the exiled ANC, ending a long moratorium on such talks.[26] A virtual flood of similar meetings followed. In September 1985, major industrialists—including Gavin Reilly, chairman of the giant Anglo-American Corporation—traveled to Lusaka to meet with the ANC and returned in a positive mood.[27] Many other meetings followed, including an important IDASA-sponsored[28] meeting between Afrikaner intellectuals and the ANC in Dakar, Senegal, in 1987; a similar meeting between 115 South African delegates and the ANC in Lusaka, Zambia, in 1989; and the 1988 Broederstroom meeting between business leaders and the ANC-aligned United Democratic Front (UDF) and Congress of South African Trade Unions (COSATU) inside South Africa.

At the request of ANC President Oliver Tambo, an English mining executive, Michael Young, facilitated a series of twelve meetings in England between prominent Afrikaners (including leading members of the secretive Broederbond, and Willem de Klerk, brother of F.W. de Klerk) and the ANC. Similar opportunities to talk developed at other venues, such as a conference at the Ford Foundation in New York in 1986 attended by Broederbond Chairman Pieter de Lange and several top ANC leaders.[29] These meetings were deeply emotional for both sides and built a bond that would last through four years of difficult negotiations. A great seduction took place[30] as both sides came to realize that they had a strong love of South Africa in common—as one exiled ANC official requested at the closing of the 1987 IDASA conference in Dakar with tears in his eyes, "Kiss the ground for us." The value of these powerful meetings cannot be underestimated. As one observer comments,

> [The meetings] began to melt down the propagandized visions of the enemy that permeated white society during the years of the total onslaught ideology.... These meetings helped inculcate an understanding among political elites on both ends of the spectrum that negotiation could in fact yield a mutually beneficial outcome. In terms of prenegotiation, such track-two diplomacy served to help the parties arrive at a common definition of the problem, explore negotiations as the most attractive alternative available to the players, create a core of moderation in an environment of overwhelming polarization, and begin to lay the groundwork for public acceptance of a negotiated solution.[31]

The Secret Negotiations

The government officially frowned upon any talks with the ANC, branding those who participated as traitors and disloyal. However, it is now clear that the Botha regime was aware of the meetings and closely followed them to "feel out" the ANC without running the political risk of direct engagement.[32] In addition, members of the Botha regime had commenced direct talks with the imprisoned Nelson Mandela in complete secrecy. If the public peace process led to a consensus that negotiations were possible, the secret Mandela-government talks did much to establish the agenda for the negotiations, which were to follow. The meetings came about through a number of miraculous coincidences. In absolute secrecy, Mandela (whose face had not been seen by the public for many years) was being driven around Cape Town and entertaining government officials in his own private cottage in Pollsmoor Prison.[33]

While reassuring the ANC leadership that he was not engaging in substantive negotiations and that the government was not attempting to co-opt him and weaken the ANC, Mandela put his legendary charm to work on members of the Botha government. He rejected a 1985 conditional offer of release, refusing to renounce violence unconditionally and stating that

> I am in prison as the representative of the people and [the people's] organization, the African National Congress, which was banned. What freedom am I being offered while the organization of the people remains banned?... Only free men can negotiate. Prisoners cannot enter into contracts.[34]

Mandela's diary notes at least forty-seven meetings with government officials to discuss future negotiations. In 1989, Mandela wrote a detailed eleven-page memorandum to President Botha summing up his views on possible negotiations, suggesting a two-phase process, first creating the proper climate for negotiations and then proceeding to actual substantive negotiations.[35] Mandela finally met with President Botha on July 5, 1989. A month later, F.W. de Klerk and other members of Botha's cabinet went to visit the ailing president, requesting him to resign because of bad health, and de Klerk acceded to the presidency.

Ripeness

A number of factors accounted for the decision by the NP government to begin the process of formal negotiations in 1990. The end of the Cold War had powerful repercussions in the Southern African region, which had long been a Cold War battlefront. During the Cold War, South Africa was valuable to the West as a bulwark against communism, and one of the main reasons for Reagan's and Thatcher's policy of constructive engagement was the Cold War conflict raging in the region. With the end of the Cold War, South Africa was stripped of its anti-Communist cloak and lost much of its already waning Western support.

With the Communist threat gone, and inspired by the relatively peaceful transitions in Eastern Europe, the major world powers began to pressure both the apartheid government and the ANC to enter into negotiations aimed at a peaceful resolution of the apartheid conflict.[36] The attractiveness of negotiations was certainly enhanced for both parties by the stalemate that existed between the two sides within South Africa. The ANC, through its Charterist[37] allies the United Democratic Front (UDF) and the Congress of South African Trade Unions (COSATU), had succeeded in rebuilding a power base within South Africa and was able to call crippling strikes and other forms of mass action. Its campaign of ungovernability, aimed at making the entire country ungovernable through various forms of mass action, had paralyzed the nation. On the other hand, the NP remained in firm control of the country through its use of military force, and an ANC seizure of power by force remained only a remote possibility. The ANC could not seize power, and the NP could not govern effectively: thus the stalemate.

A negotiated settlement became a more attractive alternative to the NP government as time went on. The consolidation of sanctions in the mid-1980s slowly began to strangle the economy, cutting the growth rate in half and costing the country billions in foregone investment opportunities. The country had been turned into a pariah state, banned from the United Nations, various sport events, and international cultural affairs. The cost of sanctions weighed heavily on South Africans, both on their psyche and their economy. The removal of sanctions and the reintegration of South Africa into the community of nations would prove to be a powerful carrot guiding NP actions. In addition, the NP's power base was slowly eroding. A small number of vocal supporters continued to vote for the reform-oriented Democratic Party, but the real threat to the NP was coming from the far-right which was capturing an increasing share of voters dissatisfied with the NP's attempt to reform apartheid.[38] The increasing pressure from the right wing made piecemeal reform impossible, and caused the NP to search for a more permanent solution to the apartheid quagmire.

Why did the South African parties decide to conduct the negotiations on their own rather than invite an outside mediator? Part of the answer probably lies with the NP's distrust of the international community. The apartheid government had been subjected to an unprecedented campaign by the United Nations and was unlikely to trust an international mediator. The ANC probably had similar apprehensions, especially about U.S. or U.K. mediators who had played too great a role in the Cold War conflict on the subcontinent—often to the detriment of the ANC's Socialist allies. Second, the parties had built a remarkable level of mutual understanding through the public peace process and had already formed a common purpose, however tenuous at the time. They had learned to respect each other's positions and were willing and able to meet for face-to-face talks. Foremost, they saw their problem as a uniquely South African one in need of a South African solution. Direct face-to-face negotiations allowed them to control their own agenda and the pace of the negotiations.

Pre-Negotiations and the Multilateral CODESA Negotiations

Pre-Negotiations

On February 2, 1990, new President de Klerk stunned the nation and the world by announcing the imminent release of Nelson Mandela, and the lifting of the ban of the ANC, the South African Communist Party, and the PAC, and by inviting all parties to the negotiation table. In closing, de Klerk summed up his hopes for the negotiation process:

> History has thrust upon the leadership of this country the tremendous responsibility to turn our country away from its present direction of conflict and confrontation. Only we, the leaders of our people, can do it. . . . The eyes of responsible governments across the world are focused on us. The hopes of millions of South Africans are centered on us. The future of South Africa depends on us. We dare not falter or fail.[39]

The stage for negotiations was now set, but there was still a need to establish ground rules before the commencement of formal negotiations. The ANC responded two weeks after the speech by sending a delegation to meet with de Klerk to discuss talks about talks. The ANC reiterated the demands of its earlier Harare Declaration, which required the release of all political prisoners, the unbanning of all anti-apartheid organizations, the withdrawal of government troops from the townships, and an end to the state of emergency and all political trials prior to the commencement of formal negotiations.

The first substantial agreement, the Groote Schuur Minute of May 2, 1990, provided a framework for the return of exiles by providing temporary immunity and committed the ANC and the government to the route of peaceful negotiations. A few months later, in the Pretoria Minute of August 7, 1990, the ANC suspended its armed struggle and reaffirmed the parties' mutual commitment to negotiations, inviting other political parties to join the process:

> We are convinced that what we have agreed upon today can become a milestone on the road to true peace and prosperity for our country. In this we do not pretend to be the only parties involved in the process of shaping the new South Africa. We know there are other parties committed to peaceful progress. All of us will henceforth walk that road in consultation and cooperation with each other.[40]

The CODESA Process and the Breakdown of the Multilateral Process

Despite the optimism of the ANC and the government, the process of negotiations soon came to take second stage to the rising tide of violence, as the rivalry between the ANC and the Inkatha Freedom Party (IFP) erupted into an all-out war in Kwazulu Natal and the townships surrounding Johannesburg. The ANC accused the apartheid government of complicity in fomenting the violence from the very beginning, and history would later show that elements within the apartheid government had indeed played a central role in the spiral of violence by training Inkatha "hit-squads" and engaging in a dirty tricks campaign aimed at destabilizing and discrediting the ANC. The issue of political violence would remain a central theme throughout the negotiation process and led directly to the most extensive interventions by the international community.

In the meantime, the major parties had come to an agreement to hold an all-party conference to initiate the negotiation process. Major differences about the substance of the talks to take place, and the players who should be involved, continued to hamper the process at this early stage. The ANC wanted a quick handover of power and preferred to leave as much as possible to be decided by a future democratically elected government in which it would likely be the majority power. The governing NP was attempting to add to its clout by including a large number of often overlapping progovernment parties at the negotiation table: it secured representation for the government, the NP (nonvoting), and various homeland leaders, while the IFP argued for the inclusion of an IFP delegation, a Kwazulu Homeland government delegation, and a third delegation for the Zulu monarch.[41]

The first meeting of CODESA (known as CODESA I) in December 1991 ended in uncertainty after Mandela and de Klerk exchanged angry words during the closing ceremony.[42] However, the process was a milestone as it brought all major parties, with the notable exception of the black nationalist AZAPO (Azanian People's Organisation) and the right-wing Conservative Party (CP), together for talks. Five working groups were also established, focusing on the establishment of a free political climate, constitutional principles and the constitution-making process, transitional government, the reincorporation of the homelands, and time frames for the transition movement. Finally, all participants signed a Declaration of Intent in which they pledged themselves to the creation of a "united, nonracial[,] non-sexist state [and] multiracial democracy."

CODESA II and the Breakdown of the Negotiations

By the time the CODESA negotiations resumed in May 1992, there was a perceptible change in the political climate surrounding the negotiations. After losing a crucial by-election to the CP in Potchefstroom, de Klerk took a major political gamble and called for a whites-only referendum on whether or not to proceed with the negotiations. The record turnout of voters returned a 68.7 percent vote in favor of continuing negotiations, a significant boost to the spirits of the NP leadership. According to some observers, the NP negotiators returned to CODESA with a newfound arrogance, thinking that the referendum "had given them both the political and the moral right to demand what they wanted."[43]

The ANC was similarly reconsidering its negotiation stance. Frustrated by the continuing rise in the levels of political violence and the perceived unwillingness of de Klerk to take steps to deal with the issue, the ANC began to threaten to walk out of the negotiations. On June 16, the ANC abandoned the negotiation process in favor of a campaign of mass mobilization. The next day, IFP hostel dwellers attacked the ANC stronghold in Boipatong, killing forty-nine persons, including many women and children. Mandela lashed out at de Klerk, stating that he could "no longer explain to our people why we continue to talk to a government which is murdering our people."[44] The CODESA process had deadlocked anyway over the size of the majority needed to make decisions regarding regional powers, a major issue for the IFP and the NP, which had largely regionally based electoral support.

The UN Intervention

The continuing violence caused Mandela to request the UN Security Council to intervene. On July 15 and 16, 1992, the Security Council held an extraordinary session "on the question of South Africa," inviting representatives of the ANC, PAC, the South African government, and a number of representatives from the homelands (including IFP leader Mangosuthu Buthelezi) to make submissions to the Security Council. The two-day session ended with the adoption of Security Council Resolution 765 (1992), which emphasized the responsibility of the South African government in stopping violence, called upon all parties to cooperate in ending violence, and urged a resumption of the negotiation process. In addition, the resolution requested that the secretary-general appoint a special representative to travel to South Africa and recommend measures to help end the violence and create an atmosphere conducive to negotiations.

Cyrus Vance was soon appointed as special representative for South Africa and visited the country from July 20 to July 31, 1992, meeting with a wide variety of persons. Acting upon the recommendations of Vance and the secretary-general, the Security Council soon authorized, by its Resolution 772 of August 17, 1992, the deployment of UN observers in order to strengthen the structures established under the newly adopted National Peace Accord. The resulting UN Observer Mission to South Africa (UNOMSA) will be discussed later in this chapter.

The Bilateral Negotiations

The Failure of Mass Action

When it pulled out of the negotiation process, the ANC engaged in a program of mass mobilization. A successful general strike on August 3–4, 1992, demonstrated the mass popular support for the ANC and reaffirmed the organization's position as the predominant representative of black interests. Encouraged by the success of the August general strike and the events in East Germany, where a mass mobilization campaign had toppled the Communist government, ANC hard-liners attempted to topple the Ciskei government in a similar fashion on September 7, 1992. However, the Ciskei military opened fire on the ANC marchers, killing at least twenty-eight people. As in 1990, the major parties in South Africa realized that the future of the country could not be determined in the streets, but would require the negotiation table.

The Return to the Negotiation Table

Ironically, the voice of reason came from none other than Joe Slovo, chairman of the South African Communist Party (SACP) and former commander of the ANC's military wing, *Umkhonto we Sizwe.* In an influential article published in the *African Communist,* Slovo argued that the balance of power between the government and the liberation forces made an unconditional surrender on the part of the NP government unlikely.[45] Compromise would be unavoidable, but such compromise could not "permanently block a future advance to nonracial democratic rule in its fullest connotation."

Slovo went on to suggest the possible outlines of a settlement that would be remarkably similar to the ultimate compromise reached between the parties in the Interim Constitution of 1993. He foresaw the creation of a democratically elected constitution-drafting body that would have to abide by certain entrenched constitutional principles. His argument for independent structures to oversee the transition to democracy was similarly adopted.

Slovo listed a number of permissible compromises, most of which were ultimately adopted: a "sunset clause" requiring power sharing for a specified period of time, an informal agreement on regional powers and federalism, an amnesty for past political crimes, and an agreement on job security and retirement compensation for a mostly white civil service. Slovo also suggested a list of impermissible compromises that would permanently prevent the creation of a nonracial, democratic South Africa: a minority veto power during the constitution-writing process, a permanent compulsory power sharing regime; a binding agreement on regional powers and boundaries and any agreement that would prevent the future government from "redressing the racially accumulated imbalances in all spheres of life."

After much heated debate,[46] the National Executive Committee of the ANC adopted the Slovo proposals as its own negotiation guidelines and signaled a willingness to return to the negotiation table.[47] During secret bilateral meetings in January and February 1993, the NP government and the ANC came to an agreement on the process and structure of the transition to democracy, essentially adopting Slovo's strategic perspective. However, the two parties were unsuccessful in selling the democratization pact to the other parties—the agreement was rejected by the IFP, PAC, CP, and AZAPO.

In response to this setback, the government convened the Multiparty Negotiation Process, also known as the Kempton Park talks, in May 1993, in order to gain acceptance for the bilateral agreement from other parties and to work out the final details of the transition. The extreme Right and the IFP walked out of the process and formed the Freedom Alliance, commencing a campaign aimed at delaying the now seemingly inevitable transition. The actions of the Freedom Alliance in fact strengthened and broadened the central coalition in favor of the democratic transition. The assassination of the firebrand ANC leader Chris Hani on April 10, 1993, sparked nationwide unrest but had the unexpected positive result of cementing the election date of April 27, 1994. In the wake of the assassination, it was Mandela who appeared on national television to appeal for calm, signaling the inevitable transfer of authority to come.

The disruptive campaign of the Freedom Alliance proved a miserable, albeit bloody, failure. Perhaps nothing did more to diffuse the "Right-Wing Threat" than the actions of the white Right itself. A takeover of the Kempton Park building by members of the extremist *Afrikaner Weerstands Beweging* (AWB)—well known for their three-sided swastika emblem—devolved into a two-hour reign of general buffoonery. The attempt to rescue the Mangope homeland regime from imminent collapse was similarly embarrassing. Once again, the belligerent AWB arrived, driving through the streets in unorganized throngs randomly shooting at blacks. A combined National Defense and Homeland force soon forced the right-wing militias to retreat, and television crews captured the execution of a carload of right-wingers by an angry black policeman. When put to the test, the once-feared white military threat proved to be little more than an irritating, disorganized menace. In the end, the leader of the "respectable" wing of the white Right, General Constand Viljoen, decided to join the election process and take his chances with democracy.

Bringing the IFP into the process proved more difficult. The notoriously fickle Buthelezi was incensed at being marginalized during the negotiation process, and his IFP warriors had shown their potential for mayhem by playing a central role in the political violence, which had already claimed more than 10,000 lives. Buthelezi would hold out until the very end for an advantageous deal. A high-level summit between Mandela, de Klerk, Buthelezi, and the Zulu king on April

8, 1994, ended in failure, with Buthelezi demanding a delay of the elections. International mediators Henry Kissinger and Lord Carrington, who had played a major role in the Zimbabwean independence talks, arrived in South Africa a week later to attempt a last minute intervention, but left within twenty-four hours because the parties were unable to agree on the terms of reference for the mediators. They left behind a little-known Kenyan negotiator, Washington Okumu, a friend of Buthelezi for over twenty years, who continued to hammer away at the reluctant Buthelezi.

In yet another unexpected development of the transition process, Buthelezi suddenly decided to participate in the elections after all—less than a week before the elections were scheduled to take place and after acquiring a lucrative, secret land deal and a guaranteed, constitutionally entrenched role for the Zulu monarch from the de Klerk government. In the face of immense logistical complications—each ballot required the attachment of an IFP sticker because of the late decision of Buthelezi, and the vast majority of voters had never been able to practice this democratic privilege before—the elections went forward as planned and were relatively peaceful, leading to a successful transition.

The Role of the International Community in the Negotiations: Constructive Support and Encouragement

Building Up the Structures of Civil Society

Although the international community chose to remain largely on the sidelines during the negotiations period, it did play a crucial role at strategic points during the talks. In the first place, the unprecedented worldwide campaign against apartheid played an important role in bringing the parties to the negotiating table. The United Nations and almost every nation in the world condemned apartheid in no uncertain terms, effectively isolating the rogue apartheid state, and imposed crippling sanctions on the country. At the same time, a number of NGOs, businesses, foundations, and governments brought the two sides together to explore the possibility of a peaceful settlement through negotiations. Finally, both the private and public international community made an important contribution toward a peaceful settlement by working to create a vibrant civil society in South Africa. Foreign countries, universities, and foundations provided scholarships for thousands of black South Africans. The Ford Foundation was instrumental in setting up the Legal Resources Centre and the Development Resources Centre, important resources for anti-apartheid activists. Other foundations supported similar enrichment processes. The Aspen Institute invited leading South African jurists such as Richard Goldstone to participate in seminars dealing with human rights, democracy, and similar subjects. Over a period of many years, hundreds of different programs created a vibrant and active civil society and a large pool of worldly, qualified leadership that was able to engage effectively in negotiations.

UNOMSA: The Issue of Violence and the UN Response

During the negotiation period, there were a number of important interventions by the international community, demonstrating the positive role it can play even when not directly mediating a conflict. One of the dominant issues during the entire negotiation period was the issue of political violence, responsible for the deaths of more than 10,000 South Africans and the cause of repeated breakdowns and tensions in the negotiations. The issue of violence was especially volatile in the context of the South African negotiations because the government was repeatedly accused by the ANC of secretly fomenting violence in order to destabilize the ANC. The Goldstone Commission findings and recent revelations at the hearings of the Truth and Reconciliation Commission do, indeed, support at least some of the contentions regarding the involvement of the South African government in violence in South Africa.

As discussed above, Mandela asked for the intervention of the Security Council after the Boipatong massacre of June 17, 1992. The Security Council responded with a two-day hearing, and passed Resolution 765 (1992) strongly urging the government of South Africa to take effective steps to address the violence and requesting the secretary-general to appoint a special representative for a mission to South Africa. Cyrus Vance was thus appointed, and his observations formed the basis of a lengthy report by the secretary-general on the question of violence.[48] In response to the report, the Security Council authorized the deployment of UNOMSA.[49] UNOMSA was deployed in due time, under the leadership of Angela King, the director of the UN's Office of Human Resources Management. Commencing with a staff of fourteen observers, the contingent grew to 100 by October 1993, covering all eleven regions of South Africa.

The UNOMSA mission was not an independent one: its primary objective was to "strengthen the structures of the National Peace Accord to end violence in the country."[50] The National Peace Accord, signed by de Klerk, Mandela, Buthelezi, and twenty-nine political organizations on September 14, 1991, provided the impetus for the establishment of independent watchdog organizations like the Goldstone Commission discussed below. UNOMSA played an important role in ensuring that demonstrations and other types of public protests were adequately planned, by providing channels of communication across the political spectrum and by attending a myriad of meetings as independent observers. Several UNOMSA members with the requisite legal background provided direct logistical support to the Goldstone Commission. The UNOMSA mission was complemented by similar missions on behalf of the Commonwealth, the European Union, and the OAU, and these missions provided an important level of international, independent oversight of the negotiation process.[51] Political violence was not ended because of the presence of a large contingent of independent international observers. But few would disagree with the assessment of the UN secretary-general that "virtually all parties have expressed the view that the presence in South Africa of United Nations Observers has significantly enhanced and reinforced the structures under the National Peace Accord."[52]

The "Failed" Lord Carrington/Henry Kissinger Mediation

The UNOMSA mission demonstrates the type of intervention that the international community chose in South Africa. Instead of sending an international mediator who would take primary control of the mediation, the international community chose to remain largely on the sidelines, encouraging and observing the direct negotiations and intervening at the request of the South African parties where appropriate. Many examples of such limited, focused interventions can be found during the negotiation process. During the early stages of the negotiations, for example, the UN High Commissioner for Refugees, at the request of the government and the ANC, opened an office in South Africa to monitor the return and indemnification of the exiles whose numbers were estimated at between 10,000 and 40,000.[53] When the negotiations bogged down around the issue of federalism and regional powers, the governments of the United States and Germany invited the negotiators to visit their countries in order to see federalism in action.[54] Again, the international community never took charge of the negotiation process but supported the effort in a crucial and effective way.

One of the most direct attempts at mediation occurred barely a month before the elections were scheduled to take place, when seasoned mediators Henry Kissinger and Lord Carrington traveled to South Africa to attempt a mediation aimed at bringing Buthelezi's IFP into the elections. The popular press shouted failure when Kissinger and Carrington left within twenty-four hours because the parties could not agree on the appropriate terms of reference for the negotiations.[55] A closer look at the "failed" mediation reveals a different picture. The dispute regarding the terms of reference centered on the IFP's demand for a delay in the election—a demand which, if met, might have led to widespread unrest in the entire country. If mediation would have taken place, a very strenuous four-year process might have been jeopardized, and the entire democratization pact would have been thrown open for renegotiation. It was simply too late in the process to risk such a potentially destabilizing intervention. By leaving, the mediators sent a powerful message to the disputants: You have accomplished so much and you now need to work this out among yourselves.

But the mediators didn't really leave. They left behind a Kenyan member of their team, Washington Okumu, who was a long-time friend of Buthelezi, Mandela, and de Klerk. Perhaps, as Timothy Sisk suggests, Okumu delivered a message that Carrington and Kissinger could not, the message from a fellow African: "Okumu read [Buthelezi] the African future ... He told him, you are staring into the abyss."[56] Okumu didn't significantly change the sweetheart deal offered to Buthelezi in the previous weeks, but provided "a face-saving exit from the corner in which the IFP had painted itself."[57]

Key Factors in Shaping the Result

Principle and Justice Considerations

What accounted for the almost miraculous success of the South African negotiations, which transformed a pariah security state based on a system of white supremacy into a vibrant and widely celebrated democracy? As I have argued elsewhere,[58] the ideal of nonracial democracy as advocated by the ANC and its allies provided a powerful *inclusive* alternative to the *exclusionist* ideology of apartheid. Unlike many other liberation organizations in Africa and elsewhere that were based on an African (or other nativist) nationalism, the ANC showed a remarkable commitment to the slogan of the 1955 Freedom Charter: South Africa belongs to all who live in it, black or white.[59] Nonracialism provided an alternative to apartheid that guaranteed the continued survival of Afrikaner society, and thus directly addressed the most serious concerns of the Afrikaner community, the fear of annihilation.

The very popularity of the ideal of democratic rule, especially in the post–Cold War era, also significantly shifted the momentum toward the nonracial, democratic majority rule model proposed by the ANC. The idea of minority rule based on a white supremacist ideology was almost universally discredited in the eyes of the world community, as evidenced by the UN International Convention on the Suppression and Punishment of the Crime of Apartheid and the almost universal momentum of the international sanctions campaign against apartheid.

Outside Rewards and Sanctions

The Carrot of Reintegration

By the late 1980s, South Africa had become a pariah state, banished from the United Nations and from participation in international sports and cultural events and significantly hampered from participation in the world economy because of sanctions. Opponents of sanctions argued that they merely reinforced a larger mentality of "us versus the world" among the NP leadership, and sanctions undoubtedly did have this effect, as demonstrated by the finger-wagging, bellicose style of politicians like P.W. Botha. Sanctions also severely constricted the South African economy, and opponents of the sanctions movement were probably correct when they argued that the impoverished black majority would bear the brunt of this economic downturn. But in the final analysis, the sanctions movement did accomplish its primary goal: it played a central role in bringing the South African government to the negotiation table. The importance of the sanctions movement in bringing about change in South Africa is perhaps best demonstrated by de Klerk's almost constant requests for the lifting of sanctions after his February 2, 1990, speech. The world community could certainly dangle a powerful carrot in front of the apartheid government, and the ultimate reintegration of South Africa into the international system was a powerful reward fueling the negotiations.

Official Encouragement and Oversight

Aside from reintegrating South Africa into the world economy and world political system, and celebrating its miraculous transformation, the international community had a powerful influence on the negotiation process by closely following the process and expressing its opinions on developments. Whenever the negotiation process veered off track, the South African parties were bombarded with resolutions of the United Nations, the European Union, and the OAU and statements by various heads of state expressing their views in clear terms. The example of the UN secretary-general's many statements demonstrates a constant involvement with the South African negotiation process, an involvement duplicated by many other organizations and governments. UN Secretary-General Boutros Boutros-Ghali wrote, *inter alia*, to Mandela to argue against mass mobilizations because of the potential for violence,[60] to de Klerk to plead for the continuation of negotiations,[61] to Buthelezi to argue for his participation in negotiations,[62] and to both Mandela and Buthelezi to urge them to take stronger steps in dealing with political violence.[63] He also issued statements condemning the Ciskei massacre,[64] expressing outrage at the right-wing takeover of the Kempton Park building,[65] and congratulating the parties on various accomplishments of the negotiation process.[66] A mere selection of these statements does not do justice to the almost continuous process of consultation between the secretary-general and the South African parties, and this process was multiplied in many ways by the actions of other international organizations and statesmen. Other events, such as the sharing of the Nobel Peace Prize by Mandela and de Klerk, played a similar reinforcing role. Overall, the international community played a crucial "channeling" role by encouraging positive developments and expressing their disapproval of negative and obstructionist developments.

Success of the Agreement and Implementation

The Goldstone Commission as a Model Independent Institution

Even with a substantive compromise in place, there was still a perceived need to develop independent institutions in order to guide the transition process. One useful precedent in the South African context was the Commission of Inquiry into Public Violence, popularly known as the Goldstone Commission after its eminent Chairman Richard Goldstone. The Goldstone Commission was established after the signing of the National Peace Accord in 1991, and its members were chosen by consensus among the three major parties, the ANC, NP, and IFP. During its existence, the Commission soon established a true independence from the government and political influences. Thus, it was able to provide an objective source of information on the issue of political violence.

In dramatic fashion, the Goldstone Commission asserted its independence in November 1992 by raiding the Pretoria offices of a secret military intelligence unit without informing de Klerk prior to the raid. The daring raid turned up evidence of a dirty tricks campaign against the ANC using "a support network of prostitutes, homosexuals, nightclub managers and criminal elements."[67] The secret unit included at least forty-eight members, including such types as the notorious Civil Cooperation Bureau (CCB) operative Ferdi Barnard, who had two murder convictions and an attempted murder conviction on his record. Although de Klerk initially lashed out at the Goldstone Commission for making a "plethora of insinuations, allegations and accusations [which] threatened the credibility of the security forces," his own follow-up commission (the Steyn Commission) apparently substantiated the charges and de Klerk was forced to fire or suspend twenty-three senior Defence Force officers for their complicity in the scheme.[68]

The Goldstone Commission dropped a second bombshell just six weeks before the scheduled 1994 elections, announcing that the Commission had substantive evidence of what had long been suspected: top police officers were and had been involved in training and supplying weapons to the IFP. In an unpublished follow-up report, which was subsequently leaked to the press, Goldstone described a police network of "serious criminal conduct including murder, fraud, blackmail, and a huge operation of dishonest political information."[69] Goldstone did not investigate the actions of the de Klerk government alone. His criticisms of the role of the ANC and the IFP leadership in continuing the cycle of violence were equally biting. But the Goldstone Commission's willingness to stand apart from the government and police its actions is especially important for the present analysis, because it created a set of "rules to the game" that may not have existed in its absence. The creation of such independent, objective structures obviated to some extent the need for a neutral international presence to police the process, although the presence of international observers greatly increased the effectiveness of the Commission, which relied extensively on public opinion for its moral authority.

The Transitional Executive Council, Independent Electoral Commission, Independent Broadcast Authority, and the Election Process

As demonstrated above, one of the greatest threats to the transition process came from the possibility that the government would use its awesome capacity to manipulate the transition process in its favor. The attempted destabilization of the ANC by secret military units has been described above, but similar dangers existed because of the government's substantial control over many media sources. For the election process to be perceived as "free and fair," it was essential that independent bodies similar to the Goldstone Commission be set up to prevent manipulation of the process.

In order to accomplish this goal, the parties agreed to set up a Transitional Executive Council (TEC), with representation from all major parties, with the exception of the IFP, which chose not to participate. The TEC served effectively as a government-in-waiting from December 7, 1993, until the elections in April 1994, although its substantive powers remained unclear. The TEC, with its broad representation, served to level the playing fields considerably, and gave the nongovernment parties an important voice in the governing of South Africa during the run-up to the elections. For example, it was the TEC, in conjunction with the government, that announced the State of Emergency in Kwazulu in March 1994 to address the spiraling violence in the province.

The TEC was assisted in its task of ensuring a free and fair election by the creation of several commissions, most importantly the Independent Electoral Commission (IEC), under the chairmanship of Judge Kriegler; the Independent Media Commission (IMC); and the Independent Broadcast Authority (IBA). The IEC had the daunting task of organizing a free and fair election in a country where the vast majority of voters had never voted before, a country with high levels of illiteracy and no voter rolls that could be used to establish eligibility. Under the circumstances, the IEC was able to pull off a remarkably successful election. The IEC trained approximately 200,000 voting officers and election staffers to be deployed at more than 9,000 polling stations across the country. It also undertook a massive voter education campaign, enlisting the services of numerous NGOs in the process. The IBA and IMC were responsible for guaranteeing the political parties fair access to the South African electorate through the media and ensuring fair coverage in the government-owned press.

Again, the success of these bodies is partially due to the support provided to them by the international community. The United Nations, OAU, EU and the Commonwealth all expanded their observer teams in the run-up to the elections, and it is estimated that up to 6,000 international observers were in place at the time of the election. Despite serious irregularities, all observer organizations declared the elections "free and fair."[70]

Assessing the South African Transition Model

International mediation occurs when a third party attempts to help solve a conflict, which the disputing parties are unable to resolve through direct negotiations. In this sense, it is often a second-best alternative to resolving conflict through direct negotiations. However, mediation and direct negotiation are alternative, complementary tools in the field of international conflict resolution, each one serving a useful purpose under appropriate conditions.

The direct negotiations that brought about change in South Africa resulted in a remarkable reconciliation and a strong sense of national identity and purpose among the vast majority of South Africans. Because it was a solution arrived at by the South Africans themselves, they are proud of their accomplishments when discussing the "solemn pact." By working out the issues among themselves, South Africans were able to overcome the deep polarization of the past. For perhaps the first time in its troubled history, it is indeed possible to talk about a *united* South Africa. This new national unity expresses itself in many ways: the unanimous rejoicing over the World Rugby Cup victory of the Springboks, once a despised symbol of Afrikanerdom, provides a poignant example. National consciousness often revolves around common symbols, and South Africa certainly has a powerful set of national symbols, from its revered President Mandela to its beloved new flag. To any observer of the South African peace process negotiations, the genesis of these symbols can be found in the four years of soul-searching negotiations. The parties to the South African conflict did not just cut a deal: they also developed a powerful new national consciousness.

The direct negotiations also created a pact of remarkable viability, precisely because its details were hammered out by the parties to the conflict, instead of being proposed by a third-party mediator. The negotiators presented real interests and constituencies. Since the negotiators would also be the implementors of any agreement, there was a significant momentum in favor of arriving at a pact that was both acceptable to all parties and realistic in terms of implementation.

The direct negotiation model further carries a relatively low cost to the international community, compared to more involved interventions in, for example, the Palestinian-Israeli conflict, Cambodia, or the former Yugoslavia. The cost of second-track diplomacy and sending international observers is negligible compared to the cost of a high-profile mediation effort (often tied to significant foreign aid promises, as in the case of the Camp David Accords) or military intervention.

Yet the direct negotiation model also carries significant risks. Perhaps most significant is the lack of an independent and neutral rule-enforcing authority. The possibility exists that the government will exploit its dual role as negotiator and governing authority and harness the power of the state to its advantage in the negotiations. Some would argue that the de Klerk government did exactly this during the negotiation period, by its covert support for the IFP, although de Klerk has continually denied any such attempt and has blamed any destabilization campaigns on rogue elements within his government. The creation of independent institutions—the Goldstone Commission, IEC, IMC, and IBA—alleviated this problem to some extent, and the power sharing that occurred through the TEC significantly leveled the playing field during the period before the election.

The unacceptably high cost in human lives, incurred during the negotiation period, should not be ignored, and the ANC, IFP, and the government all carry their share of blame for the high level of political bloodletting. The remarkable accomplishments of the negotiations are marred by the almost daily double-digit body count that accompanied them. One of the subsidiary causes of the violence may have been the near complete distrust of the police in the townships, because of the police's past role in upholding apartheid and its perceived role in aiding the IFP in its war against the ANC. We should recall that one of the primary demands of the ANC in its pre-negotiation Harare Declaration was the withdrawal of troops from the township. The ineffective and deeply distrusted police force was simply unable (or unwilling) to stem the rising tide of violence, and the paramilitary self-defense units of the ANC and Inkatha were little more than private armies. Perhaps, the presence of a UN or OAU peacekeeping force could have garnered the necessary credibility to address the political violence effectively. Considering the size of the country and the widespread diffusion of the political violence, an effective peacekeeping force would have required a costly commitment by the international community.

South Africa faces considerable obstacles in its path to reconstruction, especially in the areas of crime, political reform, and socioeconomic reconstruction.
As I have argued elsewhere,[71] the issue of crime is related to the legitimization
of violence during the apartheid period, serious economic inequalities, and the
ineffectiveness of the police forces. The route to a truly democratic political culture will also present difficulties, partly because of the hegemonic position of the
ANC in the new order and partly because of the political compromises in the
constitution, which seriously stifle interparty dissent. The international community can play only a limited role in the resolution of these issues, aside from
offering logistical support and encouraging further democratic development. In
many ways, these issues are not unique to South Africa and are being faced by
many transitional societies—Russia provides one similar example.

In the area of socioeconomic reconstruction, however, the international community could play a more active role. South Africa faces a daunting task in alle-
viating severe inequalities, which developed under apartheid, and must do so
with limited resources and without endangering its economic growth. International aid and investment have been rather sparse, clearly insufficient to cover
the dire needs of the country. Perhaps the international community would have
been more willing to invest in the South African future if it had been more directly involved in the negotiation process, although other factors such as donor
fatigue are also playing a role. Nonetheless, South Africa's economic recovery
and socioeconomic reforms are crucial to a subcontinent that will clearly benefit from the creation of a vibrant, stable, and democratic economy on its southern tip.

Conclusion

Judged against the predictions of most observers of the pre-negotiation era, the
South African transition has been a remarkable success. The process showed the
power of settlements reached by direct negotiations and provides an interesting
alternative to other recent settlements reached through international mediation.
There are important benefits, which accrue when a nation is allowed to solve its
own problems, in terms of viability of the agreement, likelihood of successful
implementation, and national reconciliation. Although the South African
model, like all negotiation models, is context-specific, several lessons can be
drawn from the experience.

The Value of Investment in Civil Society

The international community invested heavily in building a vibrant civil society and increasing the human capacity of South Africa. International organizations, states, foundations, universities, and NGOs all played a role by funding
scholarships, sponsoring conferences and workshops, and aiding in the establishment of South African NGOs. Together, these thousands of projects created
a vibrant civil society and greatly increased the capacity of South Africans to

carry forth the transition themselves. In an era of donor fatigue, it is important to remember the value of investing in human capacity.

The Public Peace Process

If any single factor could account for the success of the South African negotiations, it would be the remarkable bonds that were formed at the myriad "citizen" meetings during the mid- to late 1980s. Second-track diplomacy, or public peace processes, are a relatively new and understudied component of international conflict resolution. The South African experience illustrates their importance, and they may be one of the most cost-effective conflict resolution tools available. The public peace process is an essential component of any effective conflict resolution system, and the opportunities for public peace process meetings should be multiplied. This requires the creation of centers and the training of professionals specializing in the facilitation of such meetings.

A Model of Direct Negotiation: International Observation, Encouragement, Logistical Support, and Limited Intervention

The South African experience highlights the effectiveness of direct negotiations, but the international community did play an important role in the process. The role of the international community included observing the process, encouraging positive developments, offering logistical support, and interviewing on a limited basis when appropriate. All of these actions complemented the direct negotiation process and played an important role in its ultimate success. They form an attractive and cost-effective alternative to more direct mediation efforts and should be considered as an approach under the appropriate circumstances.

Part Three

Intermediation in Noncivil Conflicts

THE ARAL SEA BASIN crisis, the Beagle Channel dispute, and the nuclear crisis in North Korea do not fall into the category of civil conflict. The Aral Sea Basin illustrates a conflict over natural resources, having the potential to develop into a larger political crisis. The Beagle Channel dispute is our outlier; it was mediated during the Cold War and is the only conflict over a strictly territorial issue in the volume. The North Korean nuclear weapons case is the only one of our chapters to deal explicitly with the threat of weapons of mass destruction.

The cases, despite their very different contexts, are all extraordinary for the creativity displayed in their mediation processes. In the Aral Sea Basin crisis, the World Bank took a highly proactive role in fostering regional cooperation on water issues. An explicit goal of the World Bank's involvement was to help the parties use cooperation over water resources as a preliminary step toward cooperation on larger political issues in the wake of the collapse of the Soviet Union. The Beagle Channel dispute illustrates how the Vatican used its unique moral authority to lead the parties toward a peaceful resolution of a volatile conflict. The North Korean crisis highlights the potential for second-track diplomacy even in highly technical cases involving weapons of mass destruction. It also demonstrates the ability of the mediator to broaden the context of the mediation to resolve a highly dangerous issue.

10

Making Waves: Third Parties and International Mediation in the Aral Sea Basin

Erika Weinthal

Overview

CONFLICT INVOLVING NATURAL resources has become a far more visible and immediate problem in the post–Cold War world, with new challenges for mediators. These disputes are not only complicated in themselves, but can also lead to more generalized political discord (such as how to house and feed "environmental refugees" fleeing ecological disasters). This chapter focuses on the Aral Sea Basin, the scene of an ongoing natural resource disaster in the former Soviet Union. The waters of the Aral Sea Basin, formerly controlled by one sovereign power (the Soviet Union), are now controlled by a number of states with varying claims on the water. Not only are newly sovereign states in conflict about rights to the water and appropriate uses, but domestic actors are making claims about usage as well.

This chapter analyzes the origins of the Aral Sea Basin crisis and examines the history of the dispute over water resources and water quality in the region. The study sheds light on the important (and novel) role of the World Bank, along with other international financial and political institutions, in fostering agreement among the Central Asian states regarding water usage and remedies for the desiccation of the Aral Sea Basin. The World Bank intervened in an innovative and powerful way in the conflict, often acting like a mediator in establishing capacity-building institutions and fostering regional cooperation. The World Bank initially conducted "quiet diplomacy" among the five leaders of the newly sovereign states to help them reach a regional accord, then took a proactive role in building a program to (1) stabilize the environment surrounding the Aral Sea, (2) rehabilitate the disaster zone area, (3) improve management of the international waters of the Aral Sea Basin, and (4) build capacity of regional institutions to plan and implement the above program. In addition, the World Bank (and other international organizations) stimulated and funded civil society-building activities by NGOs (nongovernmental organizations), used leverage to influence the scope and forms of possible solutions, and gave incentives to regional institutions and NGOs to cooperate on water issues. An overarching, if subtle, theme of the intervention was that if the states could cooperate on water usage issues, they could learn to cooperate on other strategic and political issues as well.

Timeline

1989–90 Riots and clashes sporadically erupt in the Fergana Valley, some of which are intimately linked to land and water allocations.

1991 **December:** Soviet Union falls apart, and the Central Asian republics unexpectedly gain independence.

1992 The World Bank launches a series of missions to the region after the five Central Asian states formally request assistance to mitigate the Aral Sea crisis. **Feb. 18:** The five water ministers sign the first agreement on "Cooperation in the Management, Utilization, and Protection of Water Resources of Interstate Sources." Set up of the Interstate Water Management Coordinating Commission.

1993 **Mar. 26:** Several agreements establish the Interstate Council on the Aral Sea Problems, its Executive Committee, and the International Fund for the Aral Sea. **Apr. 26:** The World Bank holds a seminar in conjunction with UNDP (United Nations Development Program)and UNEP (United Nations Environmental Program) in Washington, D.C.

1994 **Jan. 11:** The five heads of state adopt the World Bank regional program to address the Aral Sea crisis. **June 23–24:** Donors conference held in Paris.

1995 **March:** Meeting of the heads of state in Dashhowuz, Turkmenistan. **September:** The heads of state sign the Nukus Declaration.

1996–97 **Winter:** Tension between Kyrgyzstan, Uzbekistan, and Kazakstan over release of water from the Toktogul Reservoir. **Feb. 28:** The heads of state meet in Almaty and decide to streamline the institutions of water management. President Karimov of Uzbekistan is named the new head of the International Fund for the Aral Sea.

Background

Conflict in the Post–Cold War World

The emergence of fifteen Soviet successor states and the reconstitution of East Central Europe has not only reshaped the structure of the international system of nation-states, it has also compelled scholars and policy makers to rethink conventional approaches for understanding international politics. With a world no longer divided between two spheres of influence, the present period of state breakup and reformation forces us to move beyond a narrow emphasis on military issues and high politics to refining our basic assumptions of threats to international security.[1] Dangers no longer derive from the old Cold War rivalry but come from other local and regional conflicts fueled by the changes following the breakup of the Soviet Union. As we approach the twenty-first century, we are returning to concepts of state and nation building, self-determination, and minority rights that characterized the first half of this century, culminating with decolonization in the 1960s.

While many of the post-Communist states are successfully embarking upon unprecedented economic and political transitions, several others have imploded. Moreover, the conflicts that ensued do not resemble previous interstate conflicts of the Cold War era. Rather, most of the conflicts in the former Communist bloc are intrastate, ethnic, and regional in character. Nor do these types of conflicts appear to be the only ones that will define the post–Cold War period.

Environmental issues, such as the question of scarce freshwater resources, represent another arena in which conflicts are likely to emerge.[2] This chapter focuses on the increasingly salient issue of freshwater resource conflicts and their implications for international mediation and arbitration in the post–Cold War era. In particular, it examines the Aral Sea Basin. The breakup of the Soviet Union created a water sharing dilemma for the newly independent Central Asian states over the allocation and use of the rivers of the Aral Sea Basin. Independence transformed a domestic resource system into a problem of international relations.

In contrast to the other chapters, the Aral Sea Basin represents a case in which there was no outright violent conflict despite the great *potential* for conflict brought by the collapse of the Soviet Union. In anticipation of conflict, international actors intervened immediately following independence; hence, their role has constituted one of conflict prevention rather than conflict resolution. Thus, this chapter provides an opportunity to look at new forms of conflict as well as the changing role for the international community in the post–Cold War era. By tracing the process by which third parties worked together with local actors to redesign institutions for the management of the Aral Sea Basin in Central Asia, this chapter attests to an enhanced role for third parties in confronting and mitigating the potential for resource conflicts.

Water Conflict and State Security

Shared freshwater resources present problems for the international system of nation-states because water does not adhere to political boundaries. International rivers by definition are common to several states and usually transcend and/or delineate state boundaries.[3] According to a 1978 UN figure, there are over 200 shared river basins of which thirteen are shared by five or more states, and four are shared by nine or more states.[4] Shared watersheds comprise 47 percent of the total global land area, and more than 60 percent of this is located in parts of the developing world in Africa, Asia, and South America.[5] Cooperative agreements, however, are much more prevalent in the developed industrialized countries than in the developing ones; the volatile Middle East still lacks agreements over the Euphrates-Tigris and the Yarmuk Rivers.[6] John Waterbury points out that in the Middle East there has been just one formal allocative accord signed: the 1959 Agreement between Egypt and Sudan over the Nile, in which only two out of the ten co-riparians are party to the agreement.[7]

While rivers politically divide countries, ecologically they join these same countries together. As a result of the break-up of the Soviet Union, new political borders do not coincide with the physical boundaries of the different natural resource systems that were located within the territorial space of the Soviet Union. For the first time since the decolonization of the 1960s, several river basins are being politically reorganized. In East Central Europe, the breakup of Czechoslovakia exacerbated the controversy between Slovakia and Hungary over the Gabcikovo-Nagymaros dams, a legacy of a 1977 agreement between then-Communist Hungary and Czechoslovakia.[8] Even when Hungary unilaterally suspended construction of its part of the dam project, Slovakia pushed ahead with the completion of its part of the project, diverting water away from the Danube.

This tension between ecological interdependence and the notion of territorially based sovereign nation-states distinguishes environmental resource conflicts from other forms of conflict, and accordingly one of the main challenges in the post–Cold War era will be to determine how to reconcile the dominant principle of territorial sovereignty with the ecological interdependence of a resource system as a basis for cooperation.[9] So far the appropriation of military weapons, technical infrastructure, or even historical monuments has been much easier for the post-Communist successor states than the consolidation of control over shared resource systems, given the new political borders.

The physical composition of an environmental resource system is important for understanding when and how conflicts can take place. In international river systems, the benefits of cooperation are highly asymmetrical and unevenly distributed because of the unique advantage upstream riparian countries have over downstream riparian countries. At times, unilateral action by an upstream country can result in discord such as in January 1990 when Turkey interrupted the flow of the Euphrates for an entire month to fill the huge reservoir behind the Atatürk dam. This decision by Turkey to build a series of dams along the Euphrates, as part of the overall Southeast Anatolia Project to increase its hydroelectric potential and available land for agriculture, has heightened political tension with its downstream neighbors—Syria and Iraq. When the project is finally complete, Syria and Iraq, which greatly depend upon the Euphrates, will find their flow restricted.

In such situations where water is already a scarce resource, it turns into a national security priority, and where political hostilities already exist between co-riparians, water scarcity can further aggravate political tensions.[10] One of the issues that continue to stymie negotiations between Palestinians and Israelis has been how to share the aquifers underlying the West Bank.[11] Water is such a politically sensitive issue in the Middle East that it has also been a target of war. Objections to an Arab plan to divert the headwaters of the Jordan resulted in Israel launching a series of military strikes inside Syria in 1967 against the diversion project.[12]

Besides scarcity issues, environmental externalities that result from the upstream development of a dam project for energy production or when an upstream country dumps large quantities of pollutants into the water system can spark interstate disputes.[13] Unlike scarcity issues, externalities can also flow in the opposite direction from a downstream riparian to an upstream riparian. The downstream construction of a dam for irrigation, hydroelectricity production, or flood control can lead to upstream flooding.

Resource conflicts in the future will be more complex than other forms of conflict because the linkages between resource scarcity and/or quality and conflict are less direct and muted by other social, economic, and political factors.[14] Migrations of so called environmental refugees, resulting from displacement due to environmental resource scarcities or degradation, have begun to generate concern in the world community.[15] If flooding continues in the Ganges Brahmaputra Basin, large segments of the population in Bangladesh may migrate into the adjacent Indian state of Assam, and many warn that when groups intermingle in situations where resources are limited, competition for these resources will exacerbate religious, ethnic, and cultural differences.[16]

The post–Cold War era is already replete with examples of potential conflicts over resources, but unlike the Cold War period, freshwater disputes need not lead to conflict but can invite cooperation. The remainder of this chapter details the potential water conflicts in the Aral Sea Basin and describes the manner in which third parties are intervening with confidence-building measures, thereby attempting to preclude resource conflicts from sharpening political tension between states and within states.

The Aral Sea Basin

Historically, Central Asia has referred to the land between the two rivers—the Oxus and the Jaxartes. These two major rivers of Central Asia—now known as the Amu Darya and the Syr Darya Rivers—originate in the eastern mountains of Central Asia and flow through the Kara Kum (black sand) and Kyzl Kum (red sand) deserts before reaching the Aral Sea. The Aral Sea Basin, a closed drainage system, is the ultimate disposal site for all runoff and discharge from these rivers. The tributaries of the Syr Darya River originate in the Tien Shan mountains of Kyrgyzstan; from there the river runs through Uzbekistan into Tajikistan, back into Uzbekistan, and then finally flows through Kazakhstan until it reaches the Aral Sea. The Amu Darya arises partly in Afghanistan and in the Pamir mountains in Tajikistan and then flows through Uzbekistan into Turkmenistan and reenters Uzbekistan through the Autonomous Republic of Karakalpakstan. Both rivers are fed by snowmelts and glaciers. The Amu Darya, the larger of the two rivers, drains 692, 300 sq km while the Syr Darya drains 493,000 sq km.[17]

Estimated combined flow of the two rivers is 110 km³ of which 73 km³ comes from the Amu Darya and 37 km³ from the Syr Darya.[18]

The Aral Sea Basin in Central Asia, covers about 1.5 million sq km of territory that includes the two southern provinces of Kazakhstan (Qyzlorda and Shymkent), Kyrgyzstan, Tajikistan, Turkmenistan, and Uzbekistan. In addition, smaller portions of the headwaters are located in Afghanistan. About 40 million people live in the basin, with the largest population located in Uzbekistan, 22.8 million. Although Kazakhstan has a total population of 17.1 million, only about 2.5 million live in the basin. There are 4.7 million in Kyrgyzstan, 6.1 million in Tajikistan, and 4.1 million in Turkmenistan.[19] Central Asia is primarily a semi-arid and arid environment where irrigation is essential to sustain agriculture that makes up the bulk of the regional economy. The Aral Sea Basin has three ecological zones: mountain, desert, and the delta region near the sea.[20]

Subject of the Dispute

In 1960 the Aral Sea was the fourth-largest lake in the world, but due to extensive withdrawals for irrigation, the Amu and Syr Daryas no longer reached the sea by the mid-1980s. Diversions for irrigation, undertaken to reclaim marginal lands for the expansion of cotton monoculture, drastically altered the water balance in the sea. By 1989 the sea had shrunk to half its original size; its volume had decreased by two-thirds, and salinity levels in the sea had nearly tripled, wiping out a thriving fishing industry that earlier provided the base of the local economy bordering the sea.[21] The population in the lower reaches of the delta receive severely contaminated water laden with pesticides from agricultural practices upstream and frequently endure dust storms containing the toxic salt residue from the exposed seabed. There are numerous accounts of high rates of respiratory illness, typhoid, paratyphoid, and hepatitis among the population in the near-Aral region.[22]

The water crisis reached epic proportions in the 1980s, coinciding with indications of a severe economic and political crisis within the Soviet regime as a whole. Soviet authorities could no longer disregard earlier warnings from the scientific community regarding the environmental consequences of the indiscriminate use of water for irrigation compounded by inadequate drainage. Waterlogging and salinization of the soil were causing agricultural yields to decline at the same time that the desiccation of the Aral Sea had become visible to the naked eye.

Mikhail Gorbachev initiated combined policies of *perestroika* (restructuring) and *glasnost* (openness) to revitalize the stagnating economy. The latter, in particular, loosened the political reins, enabling grassroots movements to develop environmental platforms with national overtones.[23] Following the example of environmental movements in Russia, where Russian national writers led the battle against the Siberian water diversions, one of the first movements to form in Central Asia was the Committee for Saving the Aral Sea.[24] Central Asian intellectuals, primarily writers, rallied around the Aral Sea as a proxy for long-suppressed questions of cultural survival and regional self-determination. Nationalist movements such as Birlik and Erk also used the desiccation of the sea in their fight against Russian dominance to press for cultural autonomy in issues such as language concerns.[25] Cotton monoculture thus came to represent Soviet exploitation and the lack of control the Central Asians had over their own destiny.

The Central Asian republican leadership supported the claims that these opposition movements levied against Moscow, in turn pressing the center in Moscow for more regional autonomy as a means to strengthen their own authority within the republics. The water crisis accentuated the growing tension between Moscow and the Central Asian leaders over autonomy issues in which questions of scarcity and externalities were linked to broader issues of political and economic control over decision making and control of resources. Most importantly, they wanted Moscow to provide means of redress for the environmental crisis created by Soviet economic policies toward the region.[26]

It should be noted that the Central Asia leadership never demanded independence but rather sought greater autonomy and a response to the Aral Sea crisis within the confines of the Soviet system. Moscow was still seen as providing the all-Soviet solution. As a result of mounting public pressure, the Central Committee of the Communist Party of the Soviet Union and the All-Soviet Council of Ministers issued a decree in the fall of 1988 on measures for the restoration of the destroyed ecological balance in the Aral region and the preservation of the sea.[27] In November 1989 the Supreme Soviet followed with a resolution establishing a research and planning framework for rehabilitation efforts in the Aral Sea region.[28] Subsequently, in 1990 a Government Commission on the Development of Measures for Restoring Ecological Equilibrium in the Aral Region announced a contest for the best ideas for improving the overall situation in the Aral Sea Basin.[29]

The growing tension between center and periphery over the water crisis was not the only area in which disputes were manifesting themselves. Both the titular leadership and Moscow authorities were facing an unprecedented rise in intrarepublic conflicts in which different ethnic groups were competing for control of and access to scarce resources. Parallel to the rise of eco-nationalist movements, there was an upsurge in small-scale ethnic conflict in Central Asia during the last few years prior to the breakup of the Soviet Union. Several of these incidents involved water and land issues. In 1989, Tajiks and Uzbeks quarreled over land and water rights in the Vakhsh Valley; deadly ethnic strife took place between Uzbeks and Meskhetian Turks in the Fergana Valley; and Tajiks and Kyrgyz fought over land and water rights in the Isfara-Batken district along the border of the two republics.[30] Later, in June 1990, violent conflict erupted between Kyrgyz and Uzbeks in Osh, Kyrgyzstan, in which several hundred died. In sum, both environmental and ethnic issues became increasingly salient during the late 1980s.

The Collapse of the Soviet Union: Changing Conditions and Potential Conflict

With the collapse of the Soviet Union in December 1991, the Central Asian republics gained their full independence; however, they were ill prepared for the immediate task of state formation. Domestically, the Central Asian leadership faced numerous challenges linked to the urgency of having to formulate their own political and economic institutions. They also inherited environmental problems and resource-based conflicts that emerged during the last few years of the Soviet Union. Moreover, these became not only domestic problems but were now sources of interstate contention.

With independence, new political borders transcend the physical borders of the principal water system that undergirds the economic and social structure of the region. The creation of five new states has turned the upstream and downstream divisions into politically relevant categories by elevating the status of the titular ethnic groups. As a result, such internal and localized conflicts that transpired between Tajiks and Kyrgyz over irrigation water during the Soviet period now have international ramifications. Moreover, since these micro-level conflicts can reinforce both micro and macro identities, subnational level conflicts can evolve into interstate conflicts. An example is the conflict between Tajiks and Kyrgyz along the new international border in what previously had been the two neighboring districts of Isfara in Tajikistan and Batken in Kyrgyzstan.

In short, disputes previously resolved outside the region by the authorities in Moscow are now left for the Central Asian republics as challenges for which they must devise their own regional solutions. As a consequence, the potential for conflict exists on two levels.[31] First, there are new conflicts between the republics at the interstate level between upstream and downstream riparians, and second, there are internal conflicts between different domestic water users. Furthermore, the previous all-Soviet concepts for improving water management, health, and ecological conditions in the Aral Sea region had to be shelved because of waning Russian interest. In turn, the Central Asian countries at both the international and local levels must reorganize a water system in which demand is very heavy and the benefits of cooperation highly unbalanced and asymmetrical.

Consider the physical structure of the river basin. In the Syr Darya Basin, Kyrgyzstan is now the upstream riparian; Uzbekistan and Tajikistan share the middle course; and Kazakhstan (Shymkent and Qyzlorda provinces) is the downstream riparian. In the Amu Darya Basin Tajikistan is the upstream riparian; Uzbekistan is both a midstream and downstream riparian in which the Autonomous Republic of Karakalpakstan and Khorazm province are downstream to the upstream users. Dashhowuz province in Turkmenistan is also a downstream riparian in the Amu Darya Basin. The situation in the Zarafshon, a smaller drainage basin within the Aral Sea Basin, also has international consequences. The Zarafshon originates in Tajikistan and flows into Uzbekistan, where almost all of its waters are used in Bukhoro and Samarqand provinces before it vanishes in the desert, never reaching the Amu Darya. Three-fourths of Central Asia's population resides in the midstream and downstream territory of the basin; Uzbekistan makes up over half of the basin's population.

The republics that are extremely water poor, Uzbekistan and Turkmenistan, are also the ones most dependent on the water resources from outside their states for irrigated crop production. Currently, 98 percent of Turkmenistan's and 91 percent of Uzbekistan's water supply originates outside their borders.[32] Uzbekistan, it turns out, does not control the sources of the three main rivers, the Syr Darya, the Amu Darya, and the Zarafshon, but uses three-fifths of the regional water supplies for irrigated agriculture.[33] Between 1965 and 1990, cultivated land increased from 2.7 million to over 4.2 million hectares; overall in the Aral Sea Basin, there are approximately seven million hectares of irrigated land.[34]

Although the upstream states are rich in water resources, they lack energy resources; in contrast, the downstream states are poor in water resources, but possess vast oil and gas reserves. The upstream states use much less water but have inherited a significant and potential capacity for generating hydroelectricity. Prior to the collapse of the Soviet Union, Kyrgyzstan and Tajikistan, as upper riparians, did not have much leverage to exercise sovereignty over the upper reaches of the water system since the administrative headquarters of the control works were located in the downstream state of Uzbekistan. Soviet planners created these basin-wide agencies for water allocation (BVOs, the Russian acronym) in the late 1980s to have an executive function—to manage a cascade of reservoirs as well as all the water withdrawal facilities and pumping stations. The BVOs were to control and monitor the flow of the rivers and allocate the flow to the different irrigation canals and direct users in the region. The regional center for the distribution of water from the Amu Darya is located in Urgench, Uzbekistan, and for the Syr Darya in Tashkent, Uzbekistan.[35] However, independence left these agencies with an ambiguous status for the responsibility of interstate water distribution.

The transference of decision-making authority from these basin-wide agencies to domestic actors has already resulted in disputes at the interstate level over the different scenarios for managing the rivers. Kyrgyzstan now controls most of the Naryn River, a tributary of the Syr Darya, on which some of the main hydroelectric stations, dams, and reservoirs are located. The Toktogul Reservoir is the largest and the only one with substantial storage that essentially determines how much water is released to the lower reservoirs along the cascade. The Toktogul Reservoir was intended to meet irrigation demands downstream rather than generate energy. However, due to diminishing energy supplies from Russia and the other Central Asian republics, Kyrgyzstan is experiencing critical energy shortages compounded by severe economic problems. In order to make up for the lack of energy supplies in the winter, Kyrgyzstan has chosen to periodically operate the Toktogul power plant for electricity production during several of the last few winters. When Kyrgyzstan runs Toktogul in the winter, the water released must be diverted to a local depression because of the winter freezing of the lower Syr Darya, and as a consequence the water does not reach the sea. If it is a dry year, Kyrgyzstan can, moreover, reduce the water flow to Uzbekistan in the spring and summer when the demand for irrigation is at its highest peak downstream.

The Toktogul Reservoir is only one example in which the break-up of the Soviet Union has politicized the control and use of hydro-technical assets. The demarcation of new political borders has also elevated the status of various domestic canals such as the Kara Kum canal into issues for international relations. Currently, Uzbekistan and Turkmenistan divide the Amu Darya water at Termez equally between them, but this past allocation could potentially become an international point of contention since Turkmenistan wants to keep extending the canal so that it can add an additional 1.6 million hectares of cultivated land. The lower Amu Darya (another important agricultural region) is shared by Dashhowuz province, Khorazm province, and the Autonomous Republic of Karakalpakstan, and here additional problems have arisen in the past over a canal that Turkmenistan is building away from the Tuyamuyun Reservoir to improve water delivery for the oasis in the lower reaches of the Amu Darya.[36]

Several other potential resource conflicts clearly illustrate how resource issues are intertwined with the broader issues of ethnicity, economic development, and state formation in the post-Soviet context. Territorial borders assume particular significance for the Central Asian states because they were artificially created in the Soviet period. Nonetheless, the Central Asian states are determined to maintain the current borders.

In fact, borders are a sensitive issue for the three countries that share the Fergana Valley: Kyrgyzstan, Tajikistan, and Uzbekistan. Within a territory 300 kilometers in length and 170 kilometers in width, important irrigated areas include Jalal-Abad and Osh (Kyrgyzstan); Andijon, Namangan, and Fergana (Uzbekistan); and Leninabad (now called Khujand in Tajikistan). As previously noted, most of the ethnic conflicts during the Soviet period took place here, often tied to competition for scarce land and water resources. In the Fergana Valley the political borders weave in and out, leaving irredentist populations outside of their titular countries. Moreover, canals that were built to support agriculture in the Fergana Valley now transcend these political borders, leaving provinces such as Andijon without any indigenous water supplies (all its water comes not only from outside the region, but from outside the republic).[37]

The Collapse of the Soviet Union: Rapid Cooperation

Not surprisingly, with the breakup of the Soviet Union, many scholars and policy makers like David Smith assumed that "nowhere in the world is the potential for conflict over the use of natural resources as strong as in Central Asia" for several reasons.[38] First, the Central Asian states inherited the previous system for water management without an authority to guide it. Second, independence introduced new capabilities and new interests among the water users in the basin. Third, faced with an uncertain and rapidly changing political climate, new states should be expected to jealously guard recently acquired natural resources now that each can define its own priorities for water use. By December 12, 1990, the Central Asian republics had already declared sovereignty, asserting their rights to control land, water, and other natural resources within their respective territories.

However, the removal of an external decision-making authority did not preclude, but rather provided, the impetus for the Central Asian leadership to cooperate. As early as November 1991, the ministers of reclamation and water management began to work on developing cooperative management of water resources of the Amu and Syr Daryas.[39] The five ministers of water management signed the first agreement on February 18, 1992, on "Cooperation in the Man-

Table 10.1 Potential Water-Related Conflicts in the Aral Sea Basin

DRAINAGE BASIN	STATES THAT SHARE THE BASIN	POTENTIAL CONFLICTS	NATURE OF THE CONFLICT
SYR DARYA	Kyrgyzstan (upstream), Uzbekistan (midstream), Tajikistan (midstream), Kazakhstan (downstream)	1) Between Kyrgyzstan, Uzbekistan, and Kazakhstan over water releases from Toktogul.	1) Question of energy versus irrigation.
		2) Between upstream agricultural users in the Fergana Valley and Golodnaya Steppe versus downstream users in Kazakhstan near the Aral Sea.	2) Question of both quantity and quality of the water. Agriculture versus potable water.
AMU DARYA	Tajikistan (upstream), Uzbekistan (midstream), Turkmenistan (downstream), and Karakalpakstan in Uzbekistan (downstream)	1) Between two downstream states—Turkmenistan and Uzbekistan in regards to water withdrawals from the Kara Kum canal.	1) Question of quantity.
		2) Other potential conflicts over water sharing in the lower Amu Darya between Uzbekistan and Turkmenistan.	2) Question of quantity.
		3) Between upstream users in Tajikistan (i.e., Vakhsh Valley) and downstream users in Chardzhou and Dashhowuz provinces in Turkmenistan and Khorazm oblast in Uzbekistan and Karakalpakstan.	3) Question of both quantity and quality. Long-term potential conflict between energy versus irrigation.
ZARAFSHON	Tajikistan (upstream), Uzbekistan (downstream)	1) Between upstream users in Pendzhikent, Tajikistan and downstream users in Samarqand, Bukhoro, Uzbekistan.	1) Question of quantity.

Note: The overall Aral Sea Basin comprises several different water basins. Here I have disaggregated several of the basins in order to show the variation in types of conflicts of interests and capabilities.

agement, Utilization, and Protection of Water Resources of Interstate Sources."
The Central Asian states "commit themselves to refrain from any activities
within their respective territories which, entailing a deviation from the agreed
water shares or bringing about water pollution, are likely to affect the interests
of, and cause damage to the co-basin states" (Article 3).[40]

This agreement set up the Interstate Water Management Coordinating Commission (IWMCC—later referred to as the Interstate Commission for Water
Coordination or ICWC), composed of the five water ministers, who would meet
on a quarterly basis to define water management policy in the region and work
out and approve water consumption limits (broken down by growing and non-
growing periods) for each of the republics and for the whole region.[41] The Central Asian states retained the regional centers for distribution (BVOs), as organs
of the IWMCC. According to the agreement, the BVOs are to be largely responsible for implementing decisions regarding water sharing; they still have an executive function with regard to the operation of hydraulic works, structures, and
installations on the rivers. Although with independence these hydrotechnical
assets are the property of the territory upon which they are located, the agreement transfers them to the BVOs for temporary use (Article 9).

Nevertheless, the first stage of international institution building for water management had less to do with mitigating the desiccation of the Aral Sea (environmental protection) than with ensuring that cooperation would be sustained for political reasons in this transitional period. First, transitions entail uncertainty, and
here, especially, shared fears of what the future would hold without the center drove
policy actions.[42] Second, the memory of the Osh riots, along with other small-scale
resource conflicts, continued to loom heavily over early policy decisions. Third,
during the first year after independence rapid cooperation can to a large extent be
explained by inertia—not wanting to disrupt or to depart from past practices.

Unlike other Soviet successor states, the Central Asian states did not seek to
disengage themselves from the Soviet Union, so any change in the previous
structures would only have added more flux and uncertainty. Even after independence the Uzbekistani water minister, Rim Ghiniatullin, maintained that no
matter what kind of political system they would have, a centralized system for
water management would still be necessary.[43] At this early stage, such outlooks
were widespread, since the community of experts was accustomed to working
with one another in an environment relatively free of hostilities; they all knew
and understood one another because they were all trained and brought up
through the same ranks of the Soviet system.

Furthermore, the only other system of water management that had existed in
the pre-Soviet period had been superseded, so the Central Asian leadership
could not revert back to pre-Soviet practices. Scott Barrett, in a study of cooperation and conflict over international river basins, finds that precedent often influences negotiations.[44] During this first phase of renegotiating institutions in
Central Asia, the leadership worked within the confines of the former system,
grafting new institutional structures onto previous ones in order to sustain
cooperation. As a result, the postindependence framework agreements incor-

porated the water sharing rules applied during the Soviet period, which are based on crop requirements and quotas and pay scarce attention to water quality.[45] The Central Asian leadership convened in early 1992 to guarantee largely that the planting season would not be interrupted in the spring.[46]

The Central Asian states initiated the early period of cooperation in the Aral Sea Basin to ensure that the Soviet system was not dissolved before other institutions were introduced or before a vacuum of authority could take hold. However, these unusual circumstances only explain this initial period of cooperation. These agreements were not fixed or exhaustive, which made it unclear whether cooperation would continue or whether conflict would ensue once the states began to develop their own political and economic policies. Moreover, the Central Asian republics needed to amend the agreements to ensure a minimum flow into the Aral Sea and to address the broader question of water quality.[47]

What then explains long-term cooperation and the continuous process of negotiations over institutional design? It is uncertain whether cooperation over the long term would have taken hold if the international community had not been involved since the onset of independence. These newly independent states lacked the institutional and legal basis for international cooperation as well as the methods and knowledge to devise institutional structures for a water basin once controlled by an outside authority. This chapter specifically focuses on the proactive role that the international community has played in the conflict.

Key Interventions and Major Actors

Role of Third Parties

Almost immediately other domestic and international factors pushed the five Central Asian states to approach the international community for assistance in mitigating the desiccation of the Aral Sea. As the poorest of the former Soviet republics, the Central Asia states found themselves cut off from previous financial resources as well as faced with domestic opposition at home. Whereas previously the regional leaderships could rely upon the growing social and eco-nationalist movements as leverage against Moscow to extract resources, now the leadership confronted the same vocal opposition, which was beginning to pose a threat to their weak legitimacy. In this context, the international community became the actor most likely to fill the vacuum left by Moscow's departure.

Toward the end of *glasnost,* interest from members of the international community—intergovernmental organizations (IGOs) and nongovernmental organizations (NGOs)—concerning the Aral Sea crisis was growing. Environmental destruction not only inspired domestic but also international campaigns to save the Aral Sea and preserve the cultures of the Central Asians directly threatened by the desiccation of the sea. For instance, the Aral Sea International Committee based in Sausalito, California, was one of the early active groups following the collapse of the Soviet Union. During glasnost the Socio-Ecological Union, an umbrella environmental organization in Moscow, collaborated with ISAR (formerly the Institute for Soviet-American Relations). In turn, local NGOs in Central Asia were able to establish ties to the West and raise the Aral Sea crisis in international fora. The public protest during the late 1980s resulted in the United Nations Environmental Program (UNEP) signing an agreement with the Soviet Union for a two-year program to develop a rehabilitation plan for the Aral Sea region and near-Aral region. The UNEP prepared a diagnostic study, but with the break-up of the Soviet Union curtailed its program. During this time, the influence of the Moscow-based working groups began to slip while the emerging Aral Sea Basin Program under the World Bank's auspices began to be regarded as the preferred vehicle for finding regional water solutions.[48]

Several geopolitical reasons underlie the entrance of outside actors following the break-up of the Soviet Union. First, with the end of the Cold War, the West sought to enhance the likelihood that democracies and markets would flourish in the successor states of the Soviet Union. Second, Central Asia is considered to be a strategic buffer region, bordering Russia, China, Iran, and Afghanistan. Within Western policy circles, there was a growing fear that Islamic fundamentalism could spread from Iran, and the region was seen as a critical counter to that movement. Third, Kazakhstan inherited some of the Soviet Union's nuclear stockpile. And finally, the region possesses the second-largest oil and gas reserves outside the Middle East, largely untapped during the Soviet regime.

Regarding the water sector, members of the international community feared that as the newly independent states began to undertake national development programs in which water demands could differ from previous allocations, conflicts of interests would arise that did not exist during the Soviet period.[49] The water sector consists of an extensive network of water specialists located in scientific research institutes, planning and construction institutes, water distribution centers, and technical institutes, as well as the hydrotechnicians and farmers who with independence found themselves competing for influence over water use with the energy, industrial, and health sectors. Taking into account the importance of freshwater to economic development for the region, the World Bank concluded that "despite the water agreements signed after independence of the Republics, the potential for future water disputes cannot be ignored."[50]

Moreover, Aral Sea problems represent an area in which consensus could be reached among the actors within the region and outside the region. Here, environmental issues provide a safe means for outside intervention. On the one hand, Western actors could improve their reputation in the region, while on the other hand the newly independent states could solidify their separation from Russia by forging ties to other international bodies.

Form and Specific Mechanisms of Intervention

Induced Cooperation

Although the Central Asian authorities dealt immediately with questions of water allocation, they had yet to confront directly the formidable challenges of the desiccation of the sea. If they continued past practices from the Soviet period, they would also continue to cooperate in destroying the environment. However, domestic and international actors actively sought to counter this inefficient use of water. The international actors could assume the part that Moscow had previously played as a dispenser of financial resources, but instead direct these resources in an environmentally sound manner. Accordingly, actors such as the World Bank took a more "proactive" role in the Aral Sea Basin.

What distinguishes resource conflicts from other conflicts in the post–Cold War period is the manner in which the multilateral financial institutions are trying to prevent as well as resolve them. Assessing the rise of multilateralism in world politics, John Ruggie finds overall that multilateral institutions "appear to be playing a significant role in the management of a broad array of regional and global changes in the world system today."[51] The active role for international actors explains to a large extent why the Central Asian water situation differs from other water conflicts such as those in the developed countries or in other developing countries.

In Western Europe and North America, international river management has to a large degree been successful because interactions take place in a heavily institutionalized setting in which the countries are economically interdependent and relations among them are fairly good.[52] In contrast, developing countries often lack institutional capacity and have insufficient financial and material resources to ameliorate environmental problems. Moreover, most postcolonial states usually view attempts by outside actors to encourage cooperation as an intrusion upon their domestic sovereignty and economic development. Yet, this does not appear to be the case in Central Asia.

International actors are able to take on such a large role because of the sweeping nature of the political and economic transitions underway in the post-Communist states. Unlike other transitions toward democracy and/or markets, the post-Communist transitions are firmly embedded within the international system and rely upon substantial amounts of financial assistance to transform the previous system of state socialism. IGOs play a significant role, especially for countries like Kyrgyzstan that would barely exist without aid. The international community has helped sustain many of these new states in the immediate period following the collapse of the Soviet bloc, through such multilateral channels as the United Nations and regional bodies such as the Organization for Security and Cooperation in Europe (OSCE).[53]

Multilateral Assistance

Following the February 18, 1992, agreement and several subsequent resolutions during April-August 1992, the Central Asian states requested assistance from the World Bank to help mitigate the ecological and health situation near the Aral Sea. The World Bank launched a series of missions to the region in 1992 but did not directly offer financial support at that time. Rather, it suggested it would render assistance once the states had agreed upon a new institutional framework for water management amongst themselves and had developed a list of priorities for water sharing in the region.[54] The Bank invariably stressed the need for regional cooperation.

In turn, the Central Asian states signed in Qyzlorda, Kazakhstan, on March 26, 1993, an agreement on joint activities for addressing the crisis of the Aral Sea and the zone around the sea, improving the environment, and ensuring the social and economic development of the Aral Sea region.[55] This agreement laid out the framework for water management. By early 1994 the Central Asian governments had created two apex institutions to the original IWMCC: the Interstate Council for Addressing the Aral Sea Crisis (ICAS) and the International Fund for the Aral Sea (IFAS). Subsequently, in July 1994, the Interstate Commission for Socio-Economic Development and Scientific, Technical and Ecological Cooperation (ICSDSTEC) was established.

According to the new institutional structure, ICAS and its executive committee (EC) became the leading management organization. The EC, the operational arm of ICAS, is responsible for developing policies and programs for addressing the crisis. ICAS is composed of twenty-five high-level representatives from the five states who meet twice a year to discuss and decide policies, programs, and proposals put forth by the EC. The EC's charter states that it is considered to be equivalent to a sovereign government with full powers to plan and implement programs approved by ICAS. The heads of state also established IFAS to finance the Aral Sea programs based upon contributions from the five states; each basin state should allocate one percent of its Gross Domestic Product to the fund. In sum, the Aral Sea Basin states took these steps to demonstrate to the international community their willingness to cooperate in the management of the basin's waters and to undertake joint projects to mitigate the crisis. As a consequence of these decisions, most of the multilateral financial institutions concentrated their efforts on these new apex organizations.

After a seminar held in Washington, D.C., on April 26, 1993, during which the heads of state presented the new institutional arrangements and reconfirmed their commitment to addressing the Aral Sea crisis, the World Bank and a set of working groups established by the regional organizations felt prepared to forge ahead and list specific projects for financing. During the spring of 1993, the World Bank, in conjunction with the UNEP and the UNDP, worked with the basin states to prepare a program framework for the Aral Sea Basin to be carried out in three phases. The program calls for seven thematic programs and nineteen urgent projects.[56] The five heads of state approved this program on January 11, 1994, in Nukus, Karakalpakstan.

The World Bank, in collaboration with the UNDP and UNEP, subsequently convened a donors conference on June 23–24, 1994, in Paris to raise the initial funding to launch the Aral Sea Basin Program. The program has four objectives: (1) to stabilize the environment of the Aral Sea basin, (2) to rehabilitate the disaster zone around the sea, (3) to improve the management of the international waters of the Aral Sea basin (also referred to as strategic planning and comprehensive management of the water resources of the Amu and Syr Rivers), and (4) to build the capacity of the regional institutions to plan and implement the above programs.[57]

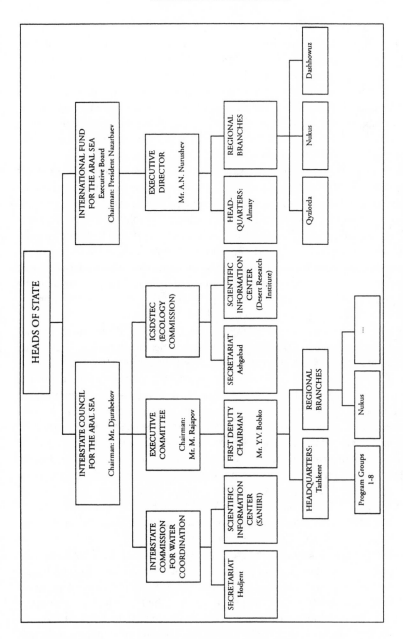

Figure 10.1 Aral Sea Basin Regional Organization (Source: World Bank)

The centerpiece of the program is to coordinate a regional water strategy and to undertake a capacity-building program for these apex organizations and regional distribution centers. The World Bank describes the Aral Sea Program as "designed precisely to promote this regional cooperation."[58] The justification for World Bank and other multilateral assistance is tied to the notion that economic development of the region depends largely upon regional cooperation. Implementation of the first phase of the Aral Sea Basin Program, which is being carried out by researchers from Europe, the United States, and the Central Asian republics, is to cost $470 million.

Multilateral assistance lends itself to larger-scale projects, and this project is clearly multicountry and multisectoral. This program, moreover, illustrates the manner in which the technical and political become interfused with one another. Donors seek to use technical and engineering solutions as confidence-building measures to bring about cooperation. Besides trying to strengthen the apex institutions, all of the World Bank projects were designed to include a capacity-building component. This emphasis on capacity-building arises from a realization that in order to sustain many of these technical projects, such as the drainage project or improving the automatic control systems, rules and procedures are necessary to govern them once the donors pull out.

Working in conjunction with the World Bank, the UNDP has undertaken an "Aral Sea Basin Capacity Development" project.[59] Besides assisting the regional institutions such as ICAS and the Sustainable Development Committee (formerly ICSDSTEC), the UNDP focuses on human resources through training programs at the national level and the promotion of micro-projects to meet urgent human needs, along with increasing community participation through the improvement of health, education, and social sanitation services. For example, UNDP has provided direct assistance for a micro-credit program as well as for the installation of several hundred hand pumps in Karakalpakstan, Uzbekistan. In 1995, the UNDP organized a conference on sustainable development in which all the presidents signed the Nukus Declaration, renewing their overall commitment to the program.[60] Momir Vranes, a UNDP program manager in environment and resources management, described the support of such declarations as an exercise in conflict prevention.[61]

Parallel to the Aral Sea Basin Program, the European Union's Technical Assistance for the Commonwealth of Independent States (EU-TACIS) initiated its Water Resources Management and Agricultural Production in the Central Asian Republics (WARMAP) project in 1994 to support the EC of ICAS and cooperating institutions (at both the regional and national levels) dealing with the Aral Sea crisis. The World Bank, UNDP, and EU-TACIS signed a memorandum of understanding to avoid duplication of projects and to cooperate with one another to reach the overall objectives of the Aral Sea Basin Program. WARMAP concentrated on capacity building, development of water resources management strategies, the creation of a management information system for the EC-ICAS, and improvement of water efficiency in the agricultural sector.[62] Unlike the other aid projects with a technical focus, WARMAP had a specific legal and institutional agenda to create a framework for water sharing based on legal principles in accordance with the Helsinki Rules and the International Law Commission recommendations.[63]

Bilateral Assistance: Role of the United States

Whereas the multilateral assistance programs are large-scale and long-term, the United States focused on bilateral assistance with more specific short-term goals. The Aral Sea was targeted early as an environmental priority because of a visit by then-Senator Al Gore to the region surrounding the Aral Sea in August 1990. As vice president, he made the Aral Sea disaster zone a high priority for United States Agency for International Development (USAID) assistance. Concerning the Aral Sea, U.S. interests were to demonstrate goodwill toward and leadership in Central Asia, develop regional cooperation among the Central Asian states aimed at preventing future conflict over water use, deal with the largest environmental problem in the newly independent states via a multilateral effort that leverages U.S. assistance, and focus U.S. assistance strategy so that Central Asians would associate U.S. assistance with solutions to a priority problem.[64] By targeting public health issues such as water, the United States hoped to establish its credibility in the region.

In order to show the newly independent Central Asian states a U.S. commitment, the U.S. government devised several small-scale, but visible, projects. Following a State Department pledge of $22 million, USAID undertook three concrete projects to improve water quality and public health conditions in the region.[65] In Turkmenistan, USAID installed a demineralized water treatment plant in Dashhowuz province; in Kazakhstan, its focus has been on the installation of replacement pumps in thirty-two wells in the area north of the Aral Sea, along with the installation of chlorination equipment at six pumping stations; in Uzbekistan, USAID is providing water quality improvements for the populations of Urgench in Khorazm province and in Nukus, Karakalpakstan, with the installation of chlorination and chemical equipment at two major water treatment plants. To increase regional cooperation, USAID has also run a series of workshops on water policy and pricing issues. Like the multilateral financial institutions, the United States believes that by encouraging discussion at a technical level on conflict resolution, it can link the issue of water with other talks concerning ethnic conflict and political stability in the region. Overall, the U.S. government has directed its activity to promote the overarching goal of regional cooperation.

Nongovernmental Organizations

In addition to cultivating interstate cooperation through capacity-building programs and technical assistance, outside actors have also stressed the need for more community participation and a role for NGOs in sustaining many of these programs. The UNDP, as a result, focuses on local NGOs as a way to promote sustainable development. Various non-state actors are also attempting to create and reinforce local NGOs as the basis for the emergence of a civil society. For example, ISAR has a Seeds for Democracy Project funded by USAID that dispenses small-scale grants for assisting environmental groups with institutional development, administrative support, and ecological projects. In contrast to the large-scale, multilateral technical and infrastructural projects, outside actors believe that strengthening local environmental NGOs such as the Dashhowuz Ecology Club, Union in Defense of the Amu Darya and Aral Sea in Nukus, Green Salvation in Almaty, Ekolog in Tashkent, For an Ecologically Clean Fergana, and Perzent in Nukus is necessary for both regional cooperation and sustainable economic development to take hold.[66]

Key Factors in Shaping the Result

International actors pursued a variety of approaches, outlined in the preceding section. The World Bank and TACIS are undertaking relatively large-scale multilateral projects that focus on technical assistance and institution building.[67] USAID prefers bilateral, smaller-scale projects that are much more visible. The UNDP, along with non-state actors, is focusing on the creation of local NGOs and community participation in addressing the Aral Sea crisis. Overall, while the international community has had a positive effect on shaping a cooperative rather than conflictual outcome to the Aral Sea problem, some of these approaches have been more successful than others.

Role of Multiple Actors: Intergovernmental Organizations and Nongovernmental Organizations

In the post–Cold War period multilateral approaches are complementing, and in some instances replacing, traditional bilateral forms of diplomacy. In resource disputes, international lending institutions are playing an active and interventionist role as negotiators reaching beyond the tools of financial assistance. Abram and Antonia Chayes observe that in matters of environmental degradation the World Bank weighs other issues such as poverty and income distribution rather than just the economic soundness of the projects it funds.[68] The European Bank for Reconstruction and Development (EBRD), created after the fall of the Berlin Wall to render assistance to East Central Europe and to the former Soviet Union, has overstepped the traditional mandate of an international financial institution. Article one of its charter clearly illustrates a political agenda: "to foster the transition towards open market-oriented economies and to promote private and entrepreneurial initiative in Central and Eastern European countries committed to and applying the principles of multiparty democracy, pluralism, and market economies."[69]

In a study of the formation of environmental institutions, Oran Young observes that "IOs [international organizations] have become a source of leadership in environmental negotiations, a development that makes it appropriate to speak of them as architects of the institutional arrangements emerging from these negotiations."[70] The Aral Sea Basin case bears out the premise that the negotiating arena over environmental resource issues such as water institutions is much broader than other negotiating situations, including multiple actors ranging from multilateral economic institutions to NGOs. In this case, the World Bank deviated from its often cautious and limited approach to international water conflicts and intervened beyond financial and technical assistance, as an active participant in the negotiations. Assessing the Bank's role in the Aral Sea Basin, Syed Kirmani and Guy Le Moigne state that the Bank recognizes the need for diplomatic skills to foster riparian cooperation, or what they refer to as "assisted negotiations."[71]

Moreover, in post-Communist states NGOs assist both IGOs and states in dealing with the problems of the political and economic transitions by operating at the grassroots level that is frequently overlooked in large-scale assistance programs. NGOs are essential for mitigating environmental problems because they help to mobilize domestic actors to push their governments to take action, as well as participate in the monitoring and implementation phase.[72] With the rise of environmental activism throughout the world, the World Bank now consults and includes provisions for NGO involvement in many of its projects.[73] NGOs are playing an important role in post-Communist states by filling the void of a lack of civil society that remains as a vestige of the Communist legacy. Specifically in the Aral Sea Basin, a Dutch organization, NOVIB, has been helping to create an Association of Aral Sea Basin NGOs (ANPOBAM), uniting more than twenty-five Aral Sea Basin NGOs to lobby national and international institutions to reform the principles of water usage in the Aral Sea Basin as well as to increase awareness among the local population on health issues.[74]

Role of Outside Rewards and Sanctions

Most importantly, international actors provide strategic financial incentives to encourage cooperation. Considering the daunting economic and political transitions away from communism, we should not expect the post-Communist states to be better situated than their predecessor to ameliorate questions of resource scarcity and environmental degradation. This is especially true in the Aral Sea Basin case because the Central Asian states are poor and weakly institutionalized. Indeed, international actors are spending large sums of money and time trying to help these new states increase domestic capacity by building the empirical components of statehood. For the post-Communist countries, foreign aid does not have the same negative connotations that it has in postcolonial states, for example in Africa. Foreign aid, especially from the West, at least symbolically enables these new states to join the international community of nation-states and become viable entities apart from Russia.

Many argue that financial and material assistance to developing states must be congruent with the interests of the most powerful actors involved in the issue, usually implying the states and IGOs.[75] However, in transitional states such as the post-Communist states, assistance also becomes a form of side-payment to compensate key domestic interests whose positions are being undermined by the transition.[76] With the breakup of the Soviet system, post-Communist elites no longer have resources from the center at their disposal to channel to local clients as in the Soviet period; financial assistance thus enables new governments to placate domestic interests with compensation from outside actors.

International actors attempt to foster cooperation in numerous ways, such as sponsoring development projects in local communities, undertaking large infrastructural projects, or conducting training programs. In Central Asia financial rewards not only target the top echelons of the political and scientific sectors, but also marginalized groups that are directly affected by the crisis and are politically and physically removed from the leadership. Vast deserts separate the populations in Dashhowuz, Turkmenistan; Aralsk, Kazakhstan; and Nukus, Karakalpakstan, from the capital cities. Programs like USAID's, which are directed at the downstream populations, can relieve the government of the burden of channeling government funds to these areas. In a similar manner, Israelis are helping to introduce water-saving technologies like drip irrigation to increase crop yields while cutting water consumption on pilot farm projects throughout Central Asia.[77] These programs allow multiple international actors, with the permission of the Central Asian governments, to serve as dispensers of compensation in the form of financial and technical assistance.

The international community has tried to leverage its assistance to foster regional cooperation for addressing the Aral Sea crisis as well as to modify Soviet approaches to problem solving. Reforming the Soviet command economy requires rethinking past practices and incorporating economic and social costs into the policy decision-making process. Early in the negotiation process, the Central Asians were still pressing for large infrastructural projects (i.e., interbasin transfers) to replenish the sea, such as reviving the Siberian River Diversion Project or pumping water from the Caspian Sea to the Aral Sea, rather than focusing on more realistic projects that would entail agricultural reform and restructuring water management practices. By restricting what they were willing to finance, the World Bank and other international actors were able to influence the scope and form of possible solutions.

Although the Central Asian states quickly coordinated water policy after the breakup of the Soviet Union, there was recognition within the countries and outside that continuance of past policies would impede economic development and could potentially lead to new disputes over water allocations. Without a firm legal basis to resolve potential disputes caused by diverging interests, outside actors sought to use foreign assistance to offset the new capabilities and interests resulting from the break-up of the Soviet Union and demarcation of the Aral Sea Basin. International actors have used strategic resources to encourage local actors to consider new options for water sharing as well as demonstrating issue linkages between energy and water. For example, USAID has focused on the potential and real disputes over water management schemes for the Toktogul Reservoir.

In the Aral Sea Basin, international actors behave as catalysts in the negotiations, especially in the pre-negotiation phase in which they help bring affected parties together through seminars and workshops to discuss various institutional arrangements for managing water allocations. Although state actors remain the primary actors for negotiating interstate agreements in Central Asia, outside rewards enable international actors to influence the design of new institutions for water management and, more importantly, to take part in the early negotiation phase.

Specific Mechanisms of the Mediation

Multiple actors create different levels of intervention and mediation ranging from heads of state meetings to grassroots campaigns. In Central Asia, we do not find one single actor serving as a mediator in the negotiations over the redesign of water institutions, nor do we find one set of formal negotiations taking place. Rather, the process of redesigning institutional arrangements for water sharing is a conglomerate of events and interventions. Water sharing is complex in the Aral Sea Basin largely because of the highly interdependent and integrated water system, engineered by Soviet planners, that does not conform to the boundaries of independence. Decisions to change the previous system will inevitably infringe upon different economic sectors and political interests across regional, national, and local dimensions.

In general, interstate agreements proceed at the level of heads of state in Central Asia. Considering that water is such an important and sensitive resource for the economic development of the region, outside intervention began at this level as well. Kirmani and Le Moigne describe early World Bank missions to the region as a form of "quiet diplomacy" in which the Bank's director and vice president conducted negotiations with the five heads of state.[78] As part of the Soviet legacy, lower-level bureaucrats will not discuss freely or share information and data until approval is received from the top leadership.

Besides high-level meetings, outside intervention to formulate a regional strategy has primarily centered around the organization of working groups, seminars, and training sessions. The management of an international water basin is complex, requiring interdisciplinary knowledge. However, during the Soviet period, the basin was approached solely in an engineering and technical manner. In contrast, to solve the environmental problems that arose from a system that favored quantity over quality, the negotiations must include actors across disciplines and sectors and must incorporate new forms of knowledge. TACIS points out that just in Project 1 of its WARMAP program, they have contacted twenty-six institutions in the five states, and fifteen of these have provided over 160 local experts. The World Bank working groups also involve a large number of participants, equally representing the basin countries. For international actors to make headway and establish fruitful working relationships with these newly independent states, an approach of inclusion has been essential.

Yet at times, this policy of inclusion also becomes problematic. On the one hand, outside actors must work with the old guard who were responsible for the Aral Sea problem; but on the other, if outside actors overlook the old guard, the program may be subverted. Here, this has resulted in two independent tracks for institution building to foster regional cooperation in water management.[79] As mentioned, the World Bank and other donors such as the EU-TACIS have been working with the five-country ICAS and its related organizations to develop mechanisms for water allocation and management in the Aral Sea Basin. In contrast, USAID has concentrated less on the old water governing infrastructure associated with ICAS and the ICWC, choosing instead to work with another Central Asian regional body, the Interstate Council for Kazakhstan, Kyrgyzstan, and Uzbekistan (ICKKU). Rather than addressing the problem within a framework of the entire basin, USAID has conducted workshops and seminars with ICKKU to develop a more focused regional agreement solely for the management of water releases from the Toktogul Reservoir.

With so much interest and activity on the part of the various IGOs and bilateral aid organizations, duplication and redundancy in many of the programs have been common. Not surprisingly, this multidimensional approach forces local actors to compete amongst themselves for access to international resources; at the same time, it also enables local groups to play outside actors against one another.

Whereas IGOs seek to affect the critical negotiations and decisions that occur at the highest political level, NGOs, in contrast, operate in an untraditional manner when measured against conventional understandings of mediation. In the discussions over new interstate water institutions, many local and international NGOs feel that they have rarely been consulted. Instead, NGOs have chosen to focus their attention on local patterns of water use and health and agricultural practices that directly affect communities living near the Aral Sea.

Role of the United States

The role of the United States in the water sector has not been as significant as that of multilateral financial institutions, primarily because its approach is smaller in scale and more short-term in outlook. As described above, USAID has chosen to tackle two specific problems; first, it has dealt with the issue of water quality, and second, it has focused on a more limited interstate agreement over Toktogul between Kazakhstan, Kyrgyzstan, and Uzbekistan. Overall, USAID's work in Central Asia is largely concentrated on the development and privatization of the energy sector in Kazakhstan and Kyrgyzstan. It is not surprising that Toktogul would become its priority because hydropower has been the main source of electricity for Kyrgyzstan since independence. The seminars held under the auspices of USAID have studied different scenarios for the timing of water releases from the reservoir in order to support the development of agreements demonstrating mutual benefits in exchanging fuel and water resources. USAID views these meetings as means for overcoming the early reluctance on the part of ICAS and the BVOs to negotiate either water allocation or timing issues for the Syr Darya Basin, but at the same time USAID decides who can participate and determines the agenda.

Nevertheless, when it comes to issues of interstate exchange between fuel and water, barter still defines the relationship in Central Asia, and these decisions are made at the heads of state or ministerial level. Although it is clear that there is a need to connect the energy and water sectors, decisions concerning who negotiates must be determined by the respective governments and not by the donor community if international bodies hope to bring about long-term binding agreements.

Role of International Law

Prior to the breakup of the Soviet Union, many principles of water law and legal institutions were immaterial since the question of water use and allocation was solely a domestic issue. Interstate conflict did not exist until independence, so there was no need to have formal agreements. Although a body of international water law exists that could guide water management in the Aral Sea Basin, the Central Asian states have not relied upon the Helsinki Rules and/or the International Law Commission recommendations for devising water management institutions for international drainage basins.[80] International water law, while stressing such principles as equitable utilization, an obligation not to cause harm to other riparian states, and an obligation to exchange relevant information and data, may not be acceptable to new countries in a new international basin because independence gives upstream countries an opportunity for the first time to declare absolute sovereignty.

The international donor and legal community, nevertheless, equates cooperation on the basis of fundamental water law principles with the establishment of an international water basin institution.[81] As such, the impact of international law is indirect. International water law manifests itself through the operational procedures of organizations such as the World Bank, which will not intervene and support projects that contradict the above accepted principles of international water law.[82] In this case, the World Bank did not act on technical principles alone when it informed the Central Asian countries that they needed to draft a basin-wide strategy before funding any concrete projects.

The Central Asian states, in turn, recognized this and quickly devised the new water sharing institutions, which explains why there are so many inconsistencies within the different agreements and their current lack of legal personality. For example, the relationship between ICAS and the ICWC remains unclear given the duplication of functions and responsibilities in their statutes.[83] It should be noted that the first agreement created immediately after independence did not draw upon the above principles of international law at all; instead, this agreement was designed for political reasons to ensure that water allocations, though inefficient, were not disrupted. In Central Asia as in the rest of the former Soviet Union, engineers do the drafting without any legal expertise or economic constraints.

Assessing the impact of international law, Sandra Postel suggests that "in the absence of a formal body of clear and enforceable law, the resolution of international water disputes depends on the negotiation of treaties among neighboring countries."[84] Although organizations like the World Bank can demand water sharing institutions before it renders aid, reopening and/or codifying water allocations and institutional arrangements as treaties in Central Asia remains a political contest and bargaining game. Without a tradition of rule of law, the Central Asian states may confirm the principles of international law in their declarations and statements, but past patterns of prior use and local customs such as a tradition of oral agreements continue to undergird negotiations over water sharing.

Success of the Mediation

For most of the twentieth century, Soviet planners in Moscow promulgated water management policy for all of Central Asia. The challenges of reengineering such a highly mechanized and integrated institutional environment are formidable. While taking into account the magnitude of transforming such a colossal water system, third-party attempts to intervene should be evaluated in regard to the previous centralized Soviet system. Within a period of five years, international actors and local counterparts have taken a number of substantial steps to alter water management practices in Central Asia. Although the pace of change is rapid, many of these mutually agreed upon programs are still at the preparatory phase of implementation, and the initial optimism following the rapid intervention of outside actors has led to both numerous disappointments as well as to some potentially positive surprises.

At the onset, many Central Asians naively expected that the international community could provide overnight solutions. Since Central Asians, especially those living within the disaster zone, consider the desiccation of the Aral Sea to be a global problem and not just a regional one, they have directed their appeals for assistance toward the international community rather than toward their leadership, which in many cases lacks the financial resources and political will to tackle the problem. In addition, many scientists and bureaucrats assumed that the international community could replace Moscow as a dispenser of financial resources to enable them to continue working on schemes to transfer water from outside the region to the Aral Sea.[85] To the dismay of many Central Asians, the international community decided that the Aral Sea could not be saved, only stabilized. Operating within the framework of stabilization, the multilateral financial institutions and other bilateral donors pushed for lessening agricultural dependence upon cotton while introducing more efficient water management techniques such as pricing policies and/or drip irrigation.[86]

Multilateral financial institutions are not willing to finance projects without the proper feasibility studies. The overall objective during the first phase of implementation of most of the Aral Sea assistance programs entailed conducting project reports and feasibility studies as well as trying to strengthen the capacity of the new regional institutions. Since many of these programs did not include rapid response activities, but rather emphasized working groups and seminars, many Central Asians complained that they could not see any concrete results from such a large investment. Parliamentarians in Kyrgyzstan have recently voiced their displeasure with the way the negotiations have progressed.[87] They would like to receive financial compensation from Kazakhstan and Uzbekistan to help maintain the reservoirs on their territory along with obtaining outside investments to complete several other hydroelectric stations that were half built during the Soviet period along the Naryn River.[88]

Regarding the programs for strengthening the institutions for regional cooperation, progress during the preliminary phase was slower than anticipated.[89] Several donor recommendations were never implemented during the early stages. For instance, the Central Asian leadership failed to appoint a permanent chair for the EC, conclude an intergovernmental agreement recognizing the international status of the interstate organizations, and clarify the mandates and jurisdictions of ICAS, the EC, IFAS, the ICSDSTEC, the ICWC, and the BVOs. Moreover, IFAS was unable to meet its mandate to act as a fund for the Central Asian republics to channel money for financing programs addressing the Aral Sea crisis.[90]

Outside mediators, in general, are expected to illuminate how regional cooperation can create win-win situations. However, when some foreign legal experts tried to impose their institutional prescriptions, tension ensued in the subsequent discussions over the form of the current legal institutions for water management.[91] Such attempts to transfer solutions from abroad can increase the resentment and mistrust felt by local scientists, who argue that they already understand the problems and know the answers. However, the World Bank had made it clear that it would not finance large-scale engineering projects; rather, it placed emphasis upon the creation of teams of local experts to identify and prepare specific projects, especially to devise a regional strategy for water management.

Over time learning has taken place on both sides to the extent that various options are now openly discussed between outside actors and local counterparts. Arrigo Di Carlo, leader of the WARMAP program, suggests that time was particularly crucial in establishing trust among the concerned parties.[92] The first few years of creating mechanisms for regional cooperation to address the Aral Sea crisis shows that international actors cannot impose solutions and institutions upon local actors, just as local actors cannot continue past practices at will if they hope to attract financial and technical assistance. The negotiation over new institutional mechanisms for water sharing is an ongoing bargaining process that requires more trust than technical know-how in the early phases.

Several signs of progress are evident, however. Most significantly, the Aral Sea Basin Working Group from Project 1 concluded a version of a Water Resources Management Strategy.[93] By late 1996, the EC had largely completed the preparation phase of Phase 1 of the Aral Sea Basin Program, and the World Bank in conjunction with the EC was beginning an overall review of the program in which it would seek to narrow the scope of the program as well as discuss options for

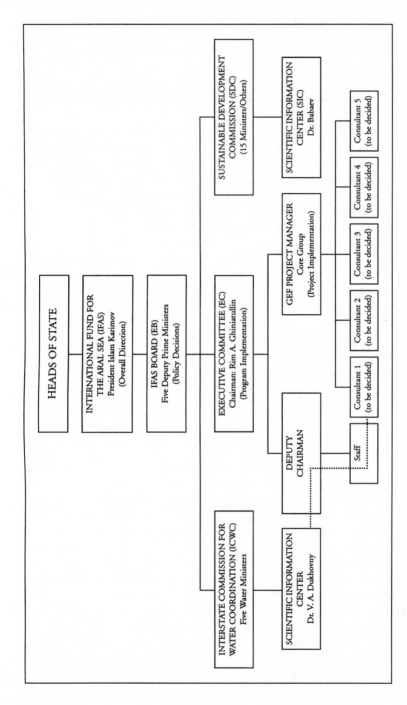

Figure 10.2 Institutional Structure of the International Fund for Saving the Aral Sea, Proposed by the Heads of State in Almaty, February 28, 1997 (Source: World Bank)

clarifying the functions of the interstate institutions. Around the same time, TACIS issued its recommendations for strengthening new institutions.

As much as outside actors are assisting these new states with the sweeping political and economic transitions at hand, many decisions are still made at the level of heads of state. The negotiation process in Central Asia continues to be nontransparent: when the heads of state met in Almaty, Kazakhstan, on February 28, 1997, they surprised many of the donors by deciding to streamline the current institutions for water management. During this meeting, they moved the International Fund for the Aral Sea to Tashkent and turned it into the main apex organization, while also appointing President Karimov of Uzbekistan as its head.

Conclusion

The end of the Cold War has not only changed the nature of conflict in the international system, it has also altered the manner in which international mediation takes place. In the Aral Sea Basin, multiple actors are trying to foster regional cooperation along with attempting to improve the immediate health needs of the population living in the disaster zone. Although many of these third-party actors would not describe themselves as mediators in the traditional sense of diplomacy, the role that they are playing suggests their intervention is broader than simply providing purely technical and financial assistance. In the early stages of World Bank intervention after the breakup of the Soviet Union, the manner in which the Bank rendered conditional assistance illustrates that it played a catalytic role roughly parallel to what a mediator plays in other conventional conflicts. By choosing to support new institutions for water management, the World Bank, along with other donors, sought to prevent the Central Asian states from undertaking individual policies that could result in conflict. Rather, the international community sought to help the Central Asian states sustain regional cooperation over a contentious issue area while adapting to a new political and physical situation.

The breakup of the Soviet Union enabled third parties to intervene. The post-Communist states require tremendous amounts of financial assistance, which has enhanced the role of multilateral financial institutions in these countries. Third-party intervention, in this case, not only affects water management practices but also has implications for the overall process of state formation and economic development in the region. While the multilateral financial institutions, along with other donors and NGOs, ostensibly intervened to solve the water crisis in the Aral Sea Basin, the institutions for cooperation in such new states may be performing other functions rather than just the obvious one of environmental protection. Institutions for regional cooperation may have to do more with the production of security than the protection of the environment. External actors have helped reinforce domestic stability by providing assistance to those whose position could be undermined by the current changes.

Moreover, simply establishing a collection of institutional arrangements provides no assurance that the function of environmental management will be fulfilled. Most of the international community's efforts have concentrated on strengthening the capacity of these new interstate water institutions, but some have pointed out that in order to support these changes, institutional change is also necessary at the national and local levels.[94] In the long term, it will not matter if new interstate allocation and distribution rules are in place if they cannot be enforced at the national and local levels.

It is apparent that this is an ongoing process in which the agreements and institutions are constantly evolving to conform to the sweeping political and economic changes that are taking place simultaneously. The international community has kept the water sharing question on the negotiating table, whereas in many other international water basins, riparian states cannot even get to the table.

11

The Vatican Mediation of the Beagle Channel Dispute: Crisis Intervention and Forum Building

Mark Laudy

Overview

IN 1978, ARGENTINA AND CHILE nearly went to war over a cluster of small islands at the southern tip of South America. The mediation that resolved the
dispute (before blood was shed) was remarkable for several reasons. The mediator was the Vatican, whose supreme moral authority and influence over the
large Catholic populations in each country made it a mediating body that the
parties could not ignore. The Vatican played two distinct roles within the mediation. First, Cardinal Antonio Samoré, the Pope's personal envoy, acted to defuse
the situation by bringing the parties to an agreement that stopped the immediate military crisis. In the next phase, the Vatican crafted a six-year process that
allowed the parties to grapple with increasingly difficult issues. The process was
remarkable because it was flexible enough to accommodate the changing political environments in both countries and because the mediator used a range of
tools to great advantage. This process served to protect a fragile peace between
the countries and ultimately allowed them to create an agreement that has lasted
until this day. The case is also significant in the background role that regional
and legal institutions, like the OAS (Organization of American States) and the
International Court of Justice, played in the process.

Timeline

1881   Argentina and Chile sign the Boundary Treaty of 1881.

1967   Chile unilaterally invokes a 1902 treaty providing for resolution of disputes through arbitration by the British crown.

1971   **July 22:** Argentina and Chile sign an agreement formally submitting to binding arbitration under auspices of British Crown.

1977   **May 2:** Arbitral decision is announced, awarding PNL (Picton, Nueva, and Lennox) island group to Chile and providing for execution of the award within nine months. **May–December:** Direct negotiations regarding implementation of the arbitral award conducted between Chile and Argentina on an ad hoc basis. Negotiations prove unsuccessful.

1978   **Jan. 25:** Argentina repudiates the British arbitral award. **Feb. 20:** Argentine and Chilean presidents execute the Act of Puerto Montt, establishing a formal structure for further direct negotiations. **May–October:** Unsuccessful negotiations held in accordance with the Act of Puerto Montt. Military mobilization accelerated in Chile and Argentina. **November:** Argentina accepts Chilean proposal for mediation. **Dec. 12:** Argentine and Chilean foreign ministers meet in Buenos Aires and are unable to select a mediator. Armed forces at full state of alert. **Dec. 23:** Pope John Paul II informs Chile and Argentina that he is sending a personal envoy to meet with their respective governments. **Dec. 26–Jan. 5:** Cardinal Antonio Samoré arrives in South America and conducts shuttle diplomacy between Buenos Aires and Santiago.

1979   **Jan. 8:** Chilean and Argentine foreign ministers sign the Act of Montevideo, formally requesting mediation by the Vatican and renouncing the use of force. **May 4:** Mediation process officially begins at the Vatican. **May–Summer:** Mediation team gathers background information.

1980   **Fall 1979–May:** Preliminary negotiations on secondary issues, e.g., navigation and fishing rights. **May:** Negotiations begin on territorial sovereignty, maritime boundaries, and straight baselines. **Dec. 12:** Papal proposal for resolution of conflict presented to parties.

1981   **Jan. 8:** Chile accepts papal proposal. **Mar. 17:** Argentina delivers note to Vatican expressing serious objections to papal proposal. **April:** Chilean officials arrested in Argentina. Chile reciprocates. Argentina closes border with Chile. **April–June:** "Mini-mediation" focused on arrests and border closing.

1982   **Jan. 21:** Argentina announces termination of 1972 General Treaty on the Judicial Settlement of Disputes, creating *vacuum juris*. **January–September:** "Mini-mediation" focused on resolving *vacuum juris*. **April–June:** Falkland Islands War.

1983   **Feb. 3:** Cardinal Samoré dies. **July:** Santiago Benadava and Julio Barberi hold discussions and prepare "nonpaper." **Dec. 10:** President Raúl Alfonsín takes office.

1984   **Jan. 23:** Chile and Argentina sign Declaration of Peace and Friendship. **Apr. 14:** Vatican Secretary of State Cardinal Agostino Casaroli meets separately with each delegation, requesting proposals for final settlement. **June 11:** Casaroli delivers final proposal to the parties. Vatican proposal accepted by both Chile and Argentina. **Oct. 18:** Casaroli delivers final text of treaty to the parties. **Nov. 25:** Argentine voters approve treaty in nonbinding national referendum. **Nov. 29:** Chile and Argentine foreign ministers execute Treaty of Peace and Friendship at the Vatican.

Background

The Beagle Channel conflict had its origins in a long-standing disagreement over the contours of the Argentine–Chilean border. The core issue in this dispute was sovereignty over three barren islands to the south of Tierra del Fuego and the scope of the maritime jurisdiction associated with those islands. In the course of attempting to resolve this initial problem, however, the parties confronted several collateral issues of great importance, including navigation rights, sovereignty over other islands in the Fuegian Archipelago, delimitation of the Straits of Magellan, and maritime boundaries south to Cape Horn and beyond.

The exact demarcation of the southern border between Chile and Argentina was a source of contention between the two countries from their earliest days as independent nations in the second decade of the nineteenth century.[1] In 1881, Chile and Argentina attempted to definitively resolve their territorial disputes through a comprehensive agreement known as the Boundary Treaty of 1881.[2] This agreement provided that the border between the two countries would follow the Andes as far south as the fifty-second parallel and would be defined by "the highest summits ... which divide the waters."[3] At the fifty-second parallel, the border was to proceed along a generally eastward course to Point Dungeness, on the northern shore of the Straits of Magellan, just where the Straits empty into the Atlantic Ocean. To the south of the Straits, the 1881 Treaty stipulated that the border would run to the south from Cape Espiritu Santo, on the northern shore of Tierra del Fuego, "until it touches the Beagle Channel."[4] Tierra del Fuego was thus to be divided into an eastern portion belonging to Argentina and a western portion belonging to Chile. Finally, the treaty included a provision for allocation of the islands to the south of Tierra del Fuego: "As to the islands, Argentina will possess Staten Island, the small islands immediately surrounding it, and any other islands that may exist in the Atlantic to the east of Tierra del Fuego and the eastern coast of Patagonia; and Chile will possess all the islands to the south of the Beagle Channel as far as Cape Horn, and any other islands that may exist to the west of Tierra del Fuego."[5]

This language soon led to various difficulties of application. With respect to the Beagle Channel and the islands south to Cape Horn, the key problem was the treaty's failure to specify the eastern terminus of the Channel. Since the Boundary Treaty granted Chile possession of all the islands south of the Beagle Channel, the Channel effectively defined the longitudinal scope of Chilean sovereignty to the south of Tierra del Fuego. It was therefore impossible to definitively separate Chilean and Argentine claims in this region without determining where the Channel ends. The Chilean view was that the Beagle Channel extended well to the east of Navarino Island, and beyond the three smaller islands—Picton, Nueva, and Lennox—which were the focus of the dispute.[6] Under this interpretation, all three islands are south of the Channel, and thus Chilean. Argentina, on the other hand, argued that the Beagle Channel veered sharply to the south along the east side of Navarino Island, making everything to the east of that island Atlantic, and thus, under the terms of the Boundary Treaty, Argentine.[7]

Compounding this dispute was a crucial disagreement concerning the scope of maritime jurisdiction associated with the islands. When Chile and Argentina signed the Boundary Treaty in 1881, international custom restricted territorial waters to a three-mile offshore zone.[8] During the twentieth century, however, changes in the law of the sea greatly expanded that zone; modern maritime custom, as codified in the 1982 UN Law of the Sea Convention, provides for territorial waters extending twelve miles offshore and an exclusive economic zone (EEZ) up to 200 miles offshore.[9] While the 1982 Law of the Sea Convention was not in force during the mediation of this dispute, its principles had already gained virtually universal recognition in the international community.[10] Thus, possession of the islands had the potential to carry with it control of an extensive area of the South Atlantic.

Complicating the situation still further was a Chilean straight baselines decree issued in 1977, establishing a complex system of baselines that would enclose the vast archipelago, extending from the eastern mouth of the Beagle Channel southwest to Cape Horn Island and northwest from the Cape along the Pacific coast of Chile.[11] Argentina had objected to the portion of this system enclosing the islands from the Beagle Channel to Cape Horn, but the Chilean decree remained in effect when the Vatican intervened at the end of 1978. This decree had two important implications for the dispute. First, it extended the platform from which Chile might attempt to project its twelve-mile territorial sea and 200-mile EEZ along an unbroken line from Picton, Nueva, and Lennox Islands (the PNL group) as far south as Cape Horn, thus greatly increasing its potential maritime jurisdiction to the east and southeast. Second, it effectively converted all waters enclosed by the baselines into Chilean internal waters, where navigational rights for Argentina (as well as third-party states) would exist only through explicit agreements with Chile.[12] This made navigational rights a key element of the dispute. Argentina had long regarded the waters surrounding the southern archipelagos as critical to its commercial and military navigation. The Argentine port city of Ushuaia, located on the north shore of the Beagle Channel, was well established as the hub of Argentina's southern fishing fleet, as well as the base from which all Argentine expeditions to Antarctica proceeded. Argentina thus considered its unfettered use of the waters surrounding the Fuegian Archipelago to be a matter of critical importance.[13]

A further point of contention, though one that appears to have been of secondary importance during the mediation, centered on the boundary between the two nations in the eastern portion of the Beagle Channel itself. As noted above, the 1881 Boundary Treaty indicated that the line dividing Tierra del Fuego was to run due south "until it touches Beagle Channel." This language enabled Chile to argue that the border should be drawn along the northern shore of the Beagle, thus making the entire Channel Chilean. This was, in effect, the maximalist Chilean position, advanced sporadically in the years prior to the papal mediation. The alternate Chilean view was that the boundary ran through the middle of the Channel, with the northern half Argentine and the southern half Chilean. An arbitral award issued by the British government in 1977 (discussed below) had fixed the boundary more or less in the center of the Channel, in accordance with this latter interpretation, and this boundary was not disturbed as a result of the mediation. Nevertheless, the issue remained a potential source of conflict with the potential to color other aspects of the negotiations.

As a final matter, the mediation eventually addressed certain long-standing disputes between Chile and Argentina regarding the eastern portion of the Straits of Magellan. Although this issue was initially excluded from the papal mediation, the topic was reintroduced toward the end of the process, when substantial progress had been made toward resolution of territorial disputes in the Beagle Channel area.[14] The issues regarding the Straits closely paralleled those involved in the dispute over the Beagle. Chile and Argentina had never agreed on a boundary marking the eastern mouth of the Straits of Magellan. The Chilean view was that the line marking the eastern end of the Straits runs from Point Dungeness to Cape Espiritu Santo, both of which were explicitly assigned to Chile in the 1881 Boundary Treaty. Under this view, Chile enjoyed sole control of the Straits themselves and was entitled to project an exclusive economic zone 200 miles eastward into the Atlantic. The Argentine position, on the other hand, was that the eastern boundary of the Straits runs along a line originating at Cape Virgins, an Argentine possession on the Atlantic, some ten kilometers east of Point Dungeness. Alternate Argentine arguments placed the southern mouth of the Straits either at Cape Espiritu Santo (in accordance with the Chilean view) or at a point to the southeast controlled by Argentina. These alternate Argentine arguments would award Argentina either complete or shared control of the eastern mouth of the Straits. In either case, Chile would be prevented from projecting an EEZ eastward into the Atlantic.

Interests of the Parties

As the foregoing discussion should make clear, Argentine and Chilean interests in the dispute went well beyond mere possession of the unimpressive PNL island group. The territory at issue was actually quite extensive; it included not only the PNL group, but also an extensive chain of islands ranging south to Cape Horn, along with the potentially extensive maritime areas associated with that territory. If one adds to that the ocean frontage at the eastern mouth of the Straits of Magellan and the vast EEZ that such frontage could potentially generate, the scope of the dispute expands to cover an enormous area of the South Atlantic.

Furthermore, both sides regarded the area in question as having substantial economic and strategic importance. The military authorities of both countries had long regarded the southern zone as crucial to their long-term strategic objectives because of its three interoceanic passages—the Straits of Magellan, the Beagle Channel, and the Drake Passage.[15] Argentina and Chile had always viewed one another as aggressive and potentially hostile neighbors, and each considered control of the southern zone necessary to curtail the perceived expansionist tendencies of the other.[16] This was particularly significant in light of the fact that Argentina and Chile were both controlled by military governments at the time of the Vatican intervention. The economic stakes were also high. For example, the area contained significant, though largely undeveloped, fisheries.[17] Additionally, by the late 1970s Chile and Argentina were convinced that large reserves of fossil fuels were located there. Tierra del Fuego had proven to be a rich source of oil and natural gas, and both governments believed that additional deposits existed in the nearby waters of the eastern Beagle Channel.[18]

The Beagle Channel dispute also had implications for the two countries' respective territorial claims in Antarctica. Chile and Argentina have asserted overlapping claims to sizable areas of Antarctica, and both countries take their claims very seriously. Not only do they view Antarctica as having the potential for future resource exploitation, but they also see it as a linchpin of their broad strategic goals for the southern zone. Furthermore, the two countries have always linked their Antarctic claims to their continental possessions and their claims to the southern passages. Since possession of the disputed territories and maritime zones could drastically realign the two countries' Antarctic frontage, the conflict stood to alter significantly their respective claims to that continent.[19]

The Chilean and Argentine governments shared another common interest in the dispute over the Beagle Channel: the preservation of political capital within their respective governments. By the time of the papal intervention in late 1978, the conflict over the Beagle Channel had become the primary foreign policy imperative of both governments. Nationalist elements in each country made possession of the islands a point of sovereign pride, and the prominence of the issue rendered the dispute highly significant to the internal politics of both Chile and Argentina. In Chile, where President Augusto Pinochet enjoyed absolute authority and was largely unaccountable to other elements within the military, this was a less significant issue. Nonetheless, the conflict tested the confidence and stability of the Pinochet government at a time when it was struggling with other serious pressures. The prolonged economic recession that plagued Chile in the late 1970s and early 1980s, coupled with Pinochet's growing isolation in the international community, made the Beagle Channel dispute a critical testing point for the Chilean dictatorship. Indeed, the dispute was viewed as having such profound implications for the internal politics of Chile that the Pinochet government took the highly unusual step of maintaining a dialogue on the subject with the opposition Christian Democratic Party.[20]

In Argentina, the ramifications of the dispute for internal politics were even greater. The Beagle Channel conflict became a rallying point for extreme nationalist elements within the military junta that controlled the country until

1983. Among many junta members, a conciliatory approach to Chile came to be regarded as a sign of weakness, giving the dispute far-reaching consequences at the highest levels of Argentine politics. This ultimately produced an environment in which relatively moderate decision makers assumed a more confrontational posture due to the fear of removal.[21]

Prior Mediation Attempts

Although Chile and Argentina made a number of unsuccessful attempts to resolve the Beagle Channel problem over the nearly one hundred years that the dispute lingered between them, the most significant antecedents to the papal mediation were the British arbitration of 1971–77 and the period of direct negotiations that began with the issuance of the arbitral award and ended with the Vatican intervention. In one sense, it is somewhat artificial to consider these processes as distinct attempts to resolve the dispute; they are perhaps more accurately characterized as discrete phases of a single ongoing process. Nonetheless, each phase entailed readily distinguishable methods and produced markedly different results.

Between 1915 and 1964, there were no less than five unsuccessful attempts to submit the Beagle Channel controversy to arbitration.[22] Finally, in 1967, Chile unilaterally availed itself of the arbitration mechanism provided for under a 1902 treaty and appealed to the British government to intervene as arbitrator. A period of negotiations between the two disputants ensued, and on July 22, 1971, Chile and Argentina signed an agreement formally submitting the matter to arbitration by the British Crown.[23]

The question submitted for resolution under the 1971 agreement was narrowly focused on the eastern portion of the Beagle Channel, including the islands Picton, Nueva, and Lennox (the PNL group), and their surrounding waters. The court that was to decide the matter was composed of five judges from the International Court of Justice at The Hague. The arbitral court's final award would be submitted to the British Crown, which was authorized to accept or reject the award, but not to modify it. The 1971 agreement provided that if an award was made and approved by the British Crown, it would be binding on both parties. In February 1977, the court submitted its decision to the British government, which approved the award two months later. The arbitral decision, officially announced on May 2, 1977, established a boundary running roughly through the center of the Beagle Channel and extending to the east of the PNL island group. Thus, all three of the disputed islands were awarded to Chile.[24] The arbitral award included a provision requiring the parties to put it into effect within nine months.

Movement toward direct negotiations began almost immediately after the issuance of the arbitral award. On May 5, 1977, Argentina sent Admiral Julio A. Torti to Santiago with a proposal for direct discussions regarding the implications of the arbitral award, particularly maritime boundaries. This overture eventually led to two rounds of discussions, held from July 5 to 8 and October

17 to 20, 1977, with Chile represented by the legal scholar and former Foreign Minister Julio Philippi and Argentina represented by General Osiris Villegas. These talks bogged down as it became clear that Argentina was fundamentally committed to the goal of obtaining islands in the southern archipelago. According to Julio Philippi, "The reason why it was not possible to move forward was the Argentine delegation's groundless attempts to discuss Chilean sovereignty over the islands to the south of the Beagle Channel, both those covered in the British arbitration and those further to the south."[25] Argentina appears to have wasted no time in converting the post-arbitral dialogue—originally intended to focus on implementation of the award and the resolution of collateral issues such as maritime delimitation—into a forum for direct negotiation on the substantive issues underlying the arbitration itself.

Argentina made its next move on December 5, 1977, when Admiral Torti returned to Santiago with a proposal from President Jorge Rafael Videla of Argentina. Although the Argentine proposal apparently conceded the PNL group to Chile, it called for joint ownership of three other islands to the south that the Pinochet government considered unequivocally Chilean: Evout, Barnevelt, and Cape Horn Island. The Torti proposal also provided for a maritime boundary that would extend south for 200 miles along a meridian passing through Cape Horn.[26] Chile regarded this proposal as a thinly disguised attempt to modify the 1881 Boundary Treaty, according to which all islands to the south of the Beagle were Chilean. It therefore rejected the proposal and suggested instead that the foreign ministers of the two countries meet directly to discuss the issue of maritime boundaries. As a result, Argentine Foreign Minister Oscar Montes and his Chilean counterpart, Patricio Carvajal, met on two occasions in December 1977. These discussions proved equally fruitless.[27]

By January of 1978, tensions were building to dangerous levels. On January 10, Chile invited Argentina to submit the matter to the International Court of Justice. But the Argentines, having been defeated in the British arbitration, had little appetite for further juridical proceedings. With armed confrontation beginning to seem like a real possibility, the Argentine and Chilean presidents met in Mendoza on January 19. Although no resolution was achieved, the two leaders agreed to meet again the following month in a final attempt to reach a settlement through direct negotiation, and tensions momentarily eased. The following week, however, as the nine-month period that the arbitral court had provided for execution of its award was drawing to a close, Argentina formally declared the arbitral award void. This development immediately elevated tensions to their most critical level yet. One key Chilean official has asserted that by the time of the Puerto Montt meetings the following month, the possibility of war was every bit as great as it was during December of 1978.[28] Chile denounced Argentina's repudiation of the award and reasserted its suggestion that the dispute be submitted to the International Court of Justice. However, plans for the next presidential meeting moved forward.

On February 20, 1978, Presidents Videla and Pinochet met in Puerto Montt, Chile, where they signed an agreement known as the Act of Puerto Montt. This agreement established a framework for the continuation of direct negotiations regarding the conflict in the southern zone. It did so through the creation of two joint commissions. The first commission was to spend up to forty-five days developing proposals for measures that would improve relations and foster the atmosphere of mutual trust deemed necessary for a resolution of the dispute. The second commission was to address a variety of carefully specified substantive matters, and was to complete its work within six months following approval of the proposals developed by the first commission. The primary task of the second commission was, of course, to establish land boundaries and provisions for maritime jurisdiction in the southern zone. In addition, the commission was to address matters of economic integration, the problem of straight baselines, and issues relating to Antarctica and the Straits of Magellan.[29]

By the beginning of May 1978, the first commission had completed its work. The second commission, headed by legal scholar Francisco Orrego of Chile and General Ricardo Echeverry Boneo of Argentina, then began six months of intense negotiations. Although the parties made some limited progress on questions of economic integration, the core issues proved totally intractable.[30] As the negotiations faltered, military operations accelerated on both sides of the Andes. And in Argentina, military leaders began to seriously consider the idea of occupying the islands.[31] When the second commission's deadline passed at the end of October with no hint of an agreement in sight, both countries began full-scale military mobilizations.

Thus, by the beginning of November 1978, Chile and Argentina no longer had any mechanism for working toward a peaceful settlement, and the situation began to destabilize rapidly. Shortly after the second commission's negotiations came to an end, Chile once again proposed that the dispute be submitted to the International Court of Justice. The unofficial response from Buenos Aires was that Argentina would consider that course of action to be *casus belli*. It was at this point, with direct talks dead and a judicial settlement unacceptable to Argentina, that Chile suggested mediation. Argentina accepted the proposal and the two foreign ministers agreed to meet in Buenos Aires on December 12 for the purpose of selecting a mediator.[32]

As agreed, Chilean Foreign Minister Hernan Cubillos met with his Argentine counterpart, Carlos Pastor, in Buenos Aires on December 12, 1978. Although the two ministers agreed within minutes that the Pope should mediate the dispute, their understanding proved ephemeral. Later that day, as the Chilean delegation was preparing the documents for signature, Pastor called Cubillos to tell him that President Videla, who had approved their choice of mediator, had been stripped of his authority by the junta. Despite hours of frantic diplomatic maneuvering and an uninterrupted meeting of the junta, no agreement could be reached.[33]

The failure of the December 12 meeting convinced many decision makers in both Chile and Argentina that war was both inevitable and imminent. Indeed, it appears that Argentina did finalize its plans for an invasion of the islands during the week following the failure of the Buenos Aires meeting. According to one report, the invasion was firmly set for December 22, but was delayed twenty-four hours due to unfavorable weather. Then on the morning of December 23, Pope John Paul II contacted both governments directly to inform them that he was sending a personal envoy to Buenos Aires and Santiago on a mission of good offices.

Key Interventions and Major Actors

Role of Standing Bodies

Although international organizations and standing bodies of international law were not explicitly invoked during the mediation phase of this dispute, they played a significant role in the events leading up to the papal intervention and remained a part of the backdrop to the mediation itself. In effect, it appears that the parties bargained in the shadow of these institutions, with the implicit threat of recourse to international organizations such as the OAS and the International Court of Justice (ICJ) serving as a Chilean counterpoint to the implicit threat of force that underlay much of Argentina's work at the negotiating table.

Although the OAS did not assume a significant role at any point during the mediation, Chile did invoke this organization as a potential leverage point in the crisis that developed following the failure of direct negotiations in late 1978. In December of that year, when the parties had not yet agreed to accept papal mediation, Chile announced an intention to initiate accusatory proceedings before the OAS, charging Argentina with actions threatening regional peace.[34] Later that month, while the two countries remained deadlocked and war appeared likely, the United States asked the OAS to intervene.[35] The question of OAS intervention became largely moot, however, with the arrival of envoy Samoré on December 26. Although the possibility of recourse to the OAS continued to exist, at least in theory, as an alternative to mediation, none of the negotiators interviewed for this chapter identified that possibility as a factor in shaping the mediation process, or indicated that it was seriously considered at any point.

More significant than the OAS as a potential alternative to the mediation process was the possibility of formalized legal proceedings under the ICJ. Indeed, the ICJ played an indirect role in the Beagle Channel dispute as early as 1971, when the British arbitration began; as noted above, the five judges who sat on the arbitral court were selected from the ICJ, in accordance with the 1971 arbitration agreement. The two countries solidified the role of the ICJ in the following year, when they adopted the General Treaty on the Judicial Settlement of Disputes, an agreement requiring that any conflicts not resolved through direct negotiations be submitted to the ICJ.[36] The 1972 General Treaty had a term of ten years, subject to renewal by the parties. This aspect of the agreement became an important point of negotiations during the mediation phase, when Argentina announced that it would allow the treaty to lapse in 1982. Even before this development, however, the ICJ loomed large as a backdrop to the mediation process. As discussed above, Chile repeatedly invoked the 1972 General Treaty and called for review by the ICJ in the months following issuance of the British arbitral award in May 1977. Argentina consistently rejected that suggestion and ultimately made it clear that if Chile were to unilaterally resort to the ICJ, such action would be regarded as *casus belli*. Key participants from both sides confirmed that this remained the Argentine position throughout most of the dispute.[37]

Choice of Parties

The character of the Beagle Channel dispute made the choice of parties somewhat simpler than in many mediation contexts: Chile and Argentina obviously had to be included, and there were no third-party states with interests sufficient to warrant a place at the negotiating table. To be sure, tensions in the far south were a matter of great concern to neighboring governments; indeed, there was widespread speculation that if war broke out between Chile and Argentina, Peru and Bolivia might seize the opportunity to attack Chile in an attempt to regain territory lost during the War of the Pacific in the nineteenth century.[38] In that event, some strategic analysts thought it possible that Brazil would enter the fray on Chile's side in order to block an Argentine bid for regional hegemony.[39] Such hypotheses were far too tenuous, however, to justify the inclusion of these or other third parties. This was unmistakably a bilateral dispute and was treated as such from the beginning.

The choice of mediator was a more difficult and complex process, because the decision as to *who* should mediate was interwoven with the decision as to *whether* to mediate. The parties considered a number of alternatives following the failure of negotiations under the Act of Puerto Montt in the fall of 1978, including further direct talks and recourse to the ICJ at The Hague. Chile, having prevailed in the British arbitration, sought to capitalize on its legal position through some kind of formalized, juridical method of dispute resolution.[40] Not surprisingly, Argentina preferred a political approach, reflecting its greater military strength and its dissatisfaction with the arbitral award.[41] Viewed from this perspective, mediation represented an intermediate process, one that would incorporate some of the objectivity of a legal proceeding and yet retain the flexibility that Argentina required.

The two countries appeared to reach an agreement in principle to submit the matter to mediation in early December 1978. On December 12, their foreign ministers met in Buenos Aires to choose a mediator. Chile and Argentina had formulated overlapping, but still distinct, sets of criteria for a potential mediator. Chile's primary concern was that the mediator have sufficient power to prevent Argentina from ignoring its proposals or initiating hostilities. According to Hernan Cubillos, Chilean Foreign Minister in 1978, "It had to be a country powerful enough so that the suggestions it would make as a mediator had power behind them . . . And when we talk of power, I'm talking about influence, moral power, political power, economic power." Additionally, says Cubillos, Chile wanted a country "where legal tradition and legality were important and understood more or less the way we understand it. And as we had a very strong legal case and an award in our favor, we felt that we had to have a country that was willing to understand the importance of that settlement and one that respected international law."[42] Based on these criteria, Chile drew up a list of five countries that it would consider acceptable mediators. The Vatican was at the top of the list.

Argentina's priorities were slightly different. Its primary concern was that the mediator be neutral—which for the Argentines meant a willingness to consider the matter on a clean slate, without being constrained by the results of the British arbitral process.[43] Argentina also considered it important that the mediator restrict its deliberations to the specific issues submitted for review by the two parties to the dispute. With these characteristics in mind, Argentina considered such diverse potential mediators as the king of Spain, the United Nations, the queen of England, UN Secretary-General Kurt Waldheim, Henry Kissinger, and the Pope. According to some reports published in the Argentine press, however, the Junta ultimately restricted its potential candidates to friendly governments from outside Latin America, not individuals or neighboring states.[44]

The Vatican was an obvious choice given the parties' priorities. Its leadership of the Catholic Church gave it a moral authority that neither of these overwhelmingly Catholic nations could disregard. At the same time, the Vatican was remote from Latin American politics and more clearly neutral than any alternative state mediator, having no direct or even indirect interests in the dispute whatsoever. But was it the only suitable intermediary? Cubillos seems to believe that any number of countries would have been sufficiently powerful to satisfy Chile's requirements, including Switzerland by virtue of its international stature as a neutral meeting place.[45] Professor Francisco Orrego, a prominent Chilean international legal scholar and a member of the Chilean negotiating team, is of a different view. He feels that no third-party nation would have commanded sufficient authority to adequately constrain Argentina.[46] Dante Caputo, foreign minister of Argentina during the final phase of the mediation, agrees.[47]

One characteristic that appears to have made the Vatican a particularly qualified intermediary is its unique institutional patience. Several of the negotiators interviewed for this paper identified the Vatican's patience as a key factor in producing a peaceful settlement.[48] Samoré himself advised the parties that a successful outcome would require "a bottle of wisdom, a barrel of prudence, and an ocean of patience."[49] As discussed below, the parties remained mired in a stalemate and made little progress toward a settlement throughout much of the mediation period. Indeed, it appears unlikely that anything could have been done to achieve a settlement prior to the reinstatement of democratic government in Argentina at the end of 1983. Under these circumstances, much of the value of the mediation lay in maintaining a forum for peaceful discussions, one that stabilized the formerly volatile environment in the Southern Cone and prevented recourse to the use of force. In effect, the mediation served as a kind of holding mechanism that maintained the status quo until the political developments necessary for a permanent accord had been achieved. The Pope, having a long-term perspective on his mission and being largely unaccountable to any interested constituencies, was almost certainly better suited to such a role than other heads of state. Other governmental mediators, subject to electoral or other political pressures, might be expected to push more aggressively for a quick solution, in the interests of short-term political expediency. In a delicate political environment, such an approach might well have jeopardized the mediation process and returned the parties to the brink of war.

Ripeness of the Conflict

A number of factors converged in late 1978 to make the Beagle Channel conflict more amenable for resolution than it had been at any prior point in the century-long history of the dispute. First, as discussed above, changes in the law of the sea that had occurred over the previous two decades made the territorial issues more pressing than they had ever been before. Second, by the 1970s, the need for regional economic integration had become quite apparent to decision makers on both sides of the Andes.[50] Third, the diplomatic and military face-off that had developed in the wake of Argentina's repudiation of the British arbitral award had brought the situation to an unmistakable crisis point: both sides recognized that unless they established a credible mechanism for achieving a long-term settlement, war was inevitable. Finally, the election of Pope John Paul II in October 1978 gave the parties a willing and uniquely capable vehicle for addressing their differences. The dispute afforded the new Pope the perfect opportunity to demonstrate strong leadership of the Church and to carve out a role for the Vatican in international diplomacy, objectives that were, by most accounts, very important to him.[51] Furthermore, there was a major decennial conference of Latin American Church leaders scheduled for January 1979, which may well have enhanced the Pope's interest in mediating the dispute. The Third General Assembly of the Latin American Episcopate was expected to focus primarily on the role of the Church in the social and political issues facing Latin America.[52]

Despite these incentives and opportunities, however, the dispute was not fully ripe for resolution in late 1978, or even when the delegations arrived in Rome the following May. The reason, quite simply, is that the parties remained absolutely committed to fundamentally irreconcilable positions. Chile, fortified in its convictions by the British arbitral award, was unwilling to make any concessions whatsoever regarding the islands themselves; for the Chileans, it would have been preferable to appeal unilaterally to the ICJ, knowing that such a course would likely mean war, rather than give up any part of the islands. Argentina, for its part, was firmly committed to the goal of attaining islands. Francisco Orrego reports that during one of the early negotiating sessions, a key member of the Argentine delegation flatly declared that unless Argentina received something in the way of islands, there would be war.[53] This version of events is at least partly corroborated by the fact that Argentina had already made plans for an invasion when the Vatican intervened on December 23, 1978.[54] Thus, each party preferred its next best alternative—appeal to the ICJ or direct military action—over a mediated result meeting the other party's minimal requirements. There was, in short, no bargaining range available between their respective reservation values.

What ultimately changed that situation and facilitated the eventual settlement of the dispute was the Falkland Islands War and the subsequent return to democratic government in Buenos Aires. The military government that controlled Argentina from the beginning of the mediation through the fall of 1983 viewed the dispute primarily in geopolitical terms. Given that unsurprising orientation, Argentina was not likely to abandon its pretension to islands—the key Argentine concession in the 1984 Treaty—so long as the junta remained in power. Indeed, key Argentine negotiators have confirmed that an agreement simply could not have been achieved before the Alfonsín government took over in December 1983.[55] It was only after the debacle in the Falklands—which both spurred a return to democratic government and discredited the military's aggressively nationalist agenda in the minds of future voters—that conditions truly ripened for settlement.

Disaggregation of Particular Elements

Notwithstanding the fact that a formal agreement was politically unrealistic prior to 1984, the Vatican did succeed in developing a dialogue between the delegations and in establishing a framework for discussions that enabled the parties to reach agreement very quickly following the reinstatement of democracy in Argentina. One of the keys to this success appears to have been the Vatican's willingness to disaggregate specific elements of the dispute and attack individual points in isolation. For example, in developing the modifications to the British arbitral award that ultimately formed the basis for the 1980 papal proposal (discussed below), the Vatican separated the issue of territorial possession of the islands from the problem of maritime jurisdiction.[56] This was the critical development that ultimately made the settlement acceptable to Argentina, albeit in a form quite different from the one originally proposed by the Pope. The arbitral court, charged with resolving a narrow question of international law, did not have the flexibility to interweave such doctrinally unorthodox, but politically expedient, elements into its result.

Another example of effective disaggregation was the suspension of discussions regarding the Straits of Magellan. This was a particularly important exclusion given the sensitive character of this topic in the wake of the British arbitration. The arbitral award included certain provisions pertaining to the Straits that favored Chile and also tended to support the Chilean view of the Beagle Channel dispute.[57] This was an especially sore point with Argentina, as the Straits had not been included in the 1971 agreement that defined the questions for arbitration. In fact, these apparently superfluous provisions of the arbitral award constituted one of the grounds that Argentina relied upon in declaring the decision null and void.[58] Issues relating to the Straits of Magellan were thus considered potentially inflammatory and were excluded from discussions throughout most of the mediation. In the final months of negotiations, however, when the parties had attained a good working relationship and were moving rapidly toward a comprehensive solution, the subject was reintroduced.[59] The final treaty therefore included provisions resolving the parties' outstanding differences with respect to the Straits.

Similarly, questions regarding Antarctica were carved out of the mediation process.[60] Antarctica was a potentially explosive issue that might well have seriously complicated the negotiations. By keeping this topic off the table, the Vatican was able to address the core issues of territorial sovereignty and maritime jurisdiction without confronting the problem of realigning the parties' respective claims to Antarctica. The 1984 treaty explicitly indicates that nothing in it should be construed to alter the parties' rights with respect to Antarctica.[61]

A final example of the Vatican's disaggregation of particular elements arose in 1982, when Argentina announced its intention to allow the General Treaty on the Judicial Settlement of Disputes to lapse at the end of the year. Expiration of the 1972 treaty could very well have endangered the entire mediation process; Chile might have felt compelled to bring its case to the ICJ before its right to do so under the treaty expired, a course of action which, at best, would have undermined the Vatican's efforts, and at worst might have provoked armed conflict.[62] Recognizing this, the Vatican effectively put the substantive issues aside and for nine months conducted a "mini-mediation," focusing exclusively on the procedural issues surrounding the parties' dispute resolution machinery.[63] These efforts proved successful in September 1982, when Chile and Argentina agreed to renew the General Treaty solely for purposes of the Beagle Channel conflict.

Role of the United States

The United States took the Beagle Channel conflict seriously and attempted to play an active role in resolving the conflict.[64] Nevertheless, U.S. efforts appear to have been important primarily at the margins of the dispute. The Carter administration made it clear at an early stage that the United States would not mediate the dispute but that it would participate in any action by the OAS.[65] Chile and Argentina, for their part, never seriously considered requesting U.S. mediation. Indeed, the United States might not have satisfied Chile's principal requirement that the mediator have sufficient leverage to constrain any Argentine inclination to balk at the results or initiate hostilities. Several negotiators have indicated that despite its vast power and resources, the U.S. government had very little leverage with either country.[66] The Carter administration had been highly critical of each country's human rights record and had suspended arms sales to both. Given that state of affairs, the United States was never viewed as a suitable intermediary. Instead, the United States attempted to use diplomatic channels to discourage the use of force and encourage mediation. For example, it made a substantial, though unsuccessful, effort to pressure Argentina into reducing its military build-up on the Chilean border in November and December of 1978.[67] More significantly, the United States appears to have played a role in convincing the Vatican to assume the role of mediator. In December 1978, Carter's representative at the Vatican, Richard Wagner, held meetings with Vatican Secretary of State Agostino Casaroli in which he encouraged the Vatican to intervene.[68] Even more important, perhaps, were the efforts of George Landau, U.S. Ambassador to Chile. Landau followed the political developments in the Southern Cone closely and relayed his information to the Vatican. Around December 19, 1978, when Landau learned of Argentina's imminent invasion from U.S. intelligence sources, he communicated the need for immediate action to the Vatican. The Pope had already been informed of the planned invasion by its nuncio in Buenos Aires, Pio Laghi, but had apparently decided not to intervene until after Christmas, convinced that Argentina would not attack before then. Landau's information may well have served to accelerate the Vatican's intervention by a few critical days.[69] It thus appears that the United States may have had some impact on the situation despite its relative lack of leverage with the parties, simply on account of its diplomatic and informational resources.

Form and Specific Mechanisms of Intervention

Broadly speaking, the Vatican intervention can be broken down into four distinct periods. The initial phase, beginning with Samoré's arrival in Buenos Aires in late December 1978, was a pure crisis intervention. This was the shortest, but perhaps most critical, period of the entire process. The central feature of this phase was Samoré's shuttle diplomacy, designed to prevent a war and secure an agreement to submit the matter to mediation, objectives that were achieved with the signing of the Act of Montevideo on January 8, 1979. The second phase ran from May 1979, when the two delegations arrived in Rome, through December 1980, when the Pope presented the parties with his proposal for settling the dispute. The third and longest phase, running from the beginning of 1981 until Argentina's return to democracy in December 1983, was characterized by long periods of stalled discussions. The most significant developments during this period were the Argentine repudiation of the 1972 General Treaty; the subsequent effort to fill the juridical vacuum resulting from that repudiation; and the Falkland Islands War, which set the stage for the return to democracy in Argentina. The final phase of the mediation began when Raúl Alfonsín assumed the presidency in Buenos Aires at the end of 1983 and ended with the signing of the 1984 Treaty of Peace and Friendship almost one year later.

Procedures of Mediation

Because the Vatican mediation extended over such a long period of time and involved such strikingly different objectives at different points in the process, it is hardly surprising that the procedures employed evolved substantially over the course of the mediation. In general, it appears that the Vatican's flexibility and adaptability in modifying the format of the proceedings in accordance with the changing tone of relations between the parties may have been one of its most important contributions.

The first phase of the Vatican's intervention was not really a part of the mediation effort at all, but rather a "good offices" mission with the limited objectives discussed above. This phase of the process took the form of shuttle diplomacy; Samoré made four trips across the Andes in December 1978 and January 1979. The Vatican's officially stated position at this point was not to pursue the role of mediator, but merely to gather information and transmit proposals between the two governments. With an eye toward maintaining the strictest possible neutrality, Samoré alternated between the two capitals and was careful to spend roughly equal time with each side. Former Chilean Foreign Minister Hernan Cubillos has indicated that there was virtually no substantive component to Samoré's visits to Chile following his initial meeting with Cubillos but that the papal representative nonetheless spent as much time with Pinochet as with President Videla of Argentina, simply to maintain the appearance of neutrality.[70]

Samoré spent his first week in South America questioning the leaders of the two countries regarding their respective positions and familiarizing himself with the background of the dispute. After this initial information gathering was complete, Samoré began encouraging the two sides to propose procedures for resolving the dispute. Chile favored a papal mediation without any restrictions as to the scope of discussions.[71] Argentina initially insisted that any papal mediation effort be subject to a number of conditions. For example, the Argentines demanded that the arbitral award be considered null and void, and that the mediation be limited to specific topics agreed upon in advance. They also insisted that the mediation be based on an acceptance of the so-called "two ocean principle," defined in terms of a meridian passing through Cape Horn.[72] These conditions remained unacceptable to Chile, leading to a great proliferation of alternative Argentine proposals. During this period, Samoré assumed an active role in transmitting proposals from one side to the other, either directly or through their respective ambassadors. Eventually, Samoré began to draft his own proposals as well.[73] On January 5, 1979, the Argentine junta finally agreed to papal mediation, thus paving the way for the Act of Montevideo.

In the course of working toward a procedural agreement, Samoré had avoided the question of military withdrawal, a point that Vatican sources report to have been one of his key objectives. Samoré considered this issue to be sufficiently sensitive for hard-line elements in the Argentine military that introducing it might have jeopardized the Montevideo agreement. Excluding this question might thus appear to have been another example of the disaggregation strategy that characterized Samoré's management of the dispute throughout the mediation process. In this case, however, the issue could not be put aside for very long; Samoré believed that if the parties maintained the military situation that had developed at the end of 1978, the entire mediation process would be jeopardized, as the slightest provocation could easily turn into outright hostility. He addressed this problem by adding to the Act of Montevideo a provision renouncing the use of force and calling for a military withdrawal. However, Samoré did not reveal this additional language to the parties until they arrived in Montevideo to sign the document on January 8. The Argentines were thus effectively presented with a *fait accompli* and, after much deliberation, accepted the addendum.[74]

After the Pope accepted the parties' request for mediation later that month, the focus of the negotiations shifted from South America to the Holy See. Chile and Argentina sent permanent delegations to Rome at the beginning of May 1979, and the mediation process officially began there on May 4. Samoré continued to serve as the Pope's personal representative during the mediation and continued in that capacity until his death in February 1983.

Samoré and his principal assistant, the Spanish priest Monsignor Faustino Sainz Muñoz, spent the first several months of the mediation process attempting to gain a fully developed view of the parties' positions.[75] Toward this end, Chile and Argentina each submitted papers outlining their views on the conflict, accompanied by whatever documentary materials they deemed relevant. Oral presentations and extensive questioning by Samoré served to augment these papers. Throughout this stage of the process, each side met separately with the mediators; there were no joint meetings.[76]

During this period, Samoré took no steps toward finding a solution and did not pressure the parties to make concessions.[77] He did, however, provide them with some general guidelines for structuring the mediation process. First, he informed the delegates that the mediation would address every aspect of the conflict.[78] In actual fact, Cardinal Samoré deviated from this guideline in several important respects. First, he subsequently made it clear that the Straits of Magellan were beyond the scope of the papal mediation, notwithstanding their close historical, political, and geographical ties to the Beagle Channel. Thus, as noted above, the Straits were excluded from the negotiations throughout most of the process. Furthermore, Francisco Orrego reports that Samoré was very willing to declare specific topics off-limits to the parties when he wanted to focus their attention in a particular direction. Specifically, during the early stages of the discussions, he firmly directed Chile not to raise the issue of maritime jurisdiction; Orrego believes that Samoré probably gave parallel instructions to the Argentines regarding their aspirations for islands.[79] This technique may have served to keep the parties focused on those aspects of the dispute where Samoré expected them to make concessions. In any case, Samoré seems to have been entirely comfortable restricting the scope of discussions when it suited his purposes to do so.

The other guidelines that Samoré set out during the initial stage of the mediation were more straightforward. He assured each side that no concessions they made in the course of working toward a solution would be binding until a final treaty was signed. He also informed the delegations that the mediation team would edit their proposals before passing them on to the other party, so as to eliminate any inflammatory language. Finally, he impressed upon them the need for absolute secrecy in conducting the mediation.[80] This he regarded as essential in order to avoid debilitating public debate that might diminish confidence in the proceedings and limit the freedom of action of both governments. Accordingly, it was determined that public communications would be restricted to joint official announcements. For the most part, the two countries followed this guideline throughout the dispute. The most notable exception was the Pope's highly confidential 1980 proposal, parts of which were leaked to the Argentine press within one month.[81]

Several negotiators have observed that Cardinal Samoré's preferred method of mediation was to begin with the easiest matters and then move on to more difficult problems.[82] This technique manifested itself as soon as the initial fact-finding stage came to a close. At Samoré's direction, the delegations began their substantive negotiations by seeking points of convergence on subjects tangential to the key territorial issues, such as navigation and fishing rights.[83] As before, the mediation proceeded through separate meetings with the Vatican team. Each delegation would meet with the mediators to consider possible subjects for joint discussion. Next, the delegation would develop a working paper to be used in preparation for a joint meeting on the topic.[84] Typically, Samoré would conduct follow-up meetings to obtain clarification on specific points. In fact, Francisco Orrego has indicated that the careful and persistent questioning that Samoré employed in seeking clarification of the parties' positions was one of the most consistent characteristics of his mediation technique throughout the dispute, and one that Orrego considered highly effective.[85] The Vatican's expectation was that the preparation of working papers and follow-up meetings would serve to sharpen the issues and pave the way for joint meetings. In actual practice, however, joint meetings were uncommon and resulted only in very limited progress.[86]

In May of 1980, despite the lack of meaningful progress on the ancillary issues covered during the preceding fall and winter, the mediation team shifted the focus of its efforts toward the core problems of the dispute: territorial sovereignty, maritime jurisdiction, and straight baselines.[87] The format of the mediation remained essentially unchanged, but now the cardinal began to relay limited information regarding each side's views along to the other party. As before, the primary method of discussions was separate meetings. The two delegations came together only sporadically, typically when Samoré or the Pope wished to address them generally, or when it was necessary to work out some narrow or technical point.[88] Samoré continued to patiently question each side on the details of its views, the bases for its positions, and its potential for flexibility. The two countries managed some minor concessions, but made no progress on the key issues.

Taking an alternate tack, Samoré asked the two delegations to draft proposals for a comprehensive settlement. The parties' responses, and all subsequent communications relating to their proposals for settlement, were maintained in confidence. Unfortunately, the proposals revealed that the gap between the Chilean and Argentine positions had not meaningfully narrowed. So after issuing a set of questions designed to identify potential points of flexibility, the cardinal drafted his own proposal. This, too, failed to bring the two sides closer. Samoré pressed each side for more open and creative proposals. But a second round of responses from the Argentine and Chilean delegations, in September of 1980, made it clear that there was still no room for agreement. Faced with this apparent stalemate, Samoré met with the Pope to discuss the Vatican's available options. They considered several alternatives, such as suspending the mediation effort—thus leaving the parties to negotiate directly—and making a specific "take-it-or-leave-it" proposal.[89]

On December 12, 1980, the Pope received the two delegations and presented to them his proposal for resolving the conflict, the terms of which had been developed entirely in secret.[90] Under the papal proposal, Chile would retain all of the islands, but Argentina would be entitled to maintain certain limited facilities there and would receive important navigation rights. The key element to this proposal, however, was the creation of a vast ocean area known as the Sea of Peace. In this area, extending to the east and southeast from the disputed chain of islands, Chile would be limited to a narrow territorial sea, in which it would be obliged to afford Argentina equal participation in resource exploitation, scientific investigation, and environmental management. Beyond the Chilean territorial waters would be a much broader band of ocean subject to Argentine jurisdiction, but also subject to the same sharing provisions that applied in Chilean waters.[91]

Despite some reservations regarding the proposal, Chile accepted it very quickly.[92] Argentina, on the other hand, never formally replied to the proposal. However, in March 1981, Argentina delivered a note to the Vatican expressing grave misgivings about the proposal, both because it failed to award any islands to Argentina and because it allowed Chile to maintain a presence so far into the Atlantic.[93] Furthermore, key negotiators from both sides have indicated that the proposal's sharing provisions were highly problematic and probably unworkable.[94] Given that the proposal was totally unacceptable to one party and only marginally acceptable to the other, the question arises whether the Vatican truly expected the parties to accept it, or whether Samoré simply hoped it would advance other purposes, such as constraining hard-line elements in the Argentine military from resuming their menacing posture.

Francisco Orrego is convinced that the Vatican issued its proposal in the genuine belief that it stood a reasonable chance of acceptance. But in so doing, he feels, the mediation team fundamentally misread the Argentines. Orrego attributes this miscalculation to a communication failure on the part of the Argentine delegation; he speculates that one of the Argentine representatives, expressing views not generally shared by the rest of the delegation or the Argentine government, may have given the mediation team reason to believe that its proposal would be acceptable.[95] General Echeverry Boneo, however, has indicated that he gave Samoré unambiguous instructions that all communications from his delegation were to come through him.[96] It is certain, in any event, that the Argentine delegation experienced relatively frequent rotation of its top negotiators, and there appears to have been at least some overlap of leadership roles.[97] Thus, the possibility of miscommunication cannot be ruled out altogether.

Following the papal proposal, negotiations remained stalled for an extended period of time. Chile, having accepted the proposal, was unwilling to dicker with its terms, and so rebuffed Argentina's efforts to renew negotiations.[98] Meanwhile, a series of unfortunate incidents in Chile and Argentina strained relations between the two countries and further hampered the dialogue on the Beagle Channel. These difficulties developed when Argentina closed the border and detained a number of Chilean officials and civilians. Chile responded by arresting Argentine officials in Chile, and the two countries rapidly degenerated into a hostile and unstable posture.[99] The situation in South America, coupled with the stalemate in Rome, placed the entire mediation process in grave danger. Samoré responded to this situation by suspending his work on the core territorial issues and devoting himself completely to resolving these new difficulties, notwithstanding the fact that they were entirely beyond the scope of the original mediation.

This reorientation of the mediation effort resulted in several months of discussions aimed solely at the narrow diplomatic problems that had engulfed the two countries on the home front.[100] For the most part, these discussions proceeded within the existing mediation structure, employing the same procedures that were by now familiar to all participants: separate meetings, probing inquiries by Samoré, and limited exchanges between the parties. For this reason, the process of resolving the diplomatic problems of 1981 has been described as the "mini-mediation" or the "mediation within the mediation."[101] However, in a desperate attempt to keep the Vatican's efforts alive, Samoré also took the unusual step of moving outside the framework of the mediation and directly contacting high-level decision makers in Buenos Aires and Santiago.[102] These efforts eventually paid off. When the Pope, recovering from a nearly successful attempt on his life, issued an entreaty to Chile and Argentina, the two countries quickly acceded to his wishes; shortly thereafter, they released their prisoners and reopened the border.[103]

The year 1981 thus came to an end without any progress on the substantive issues of the mediation, but with the process itself still intact. At the beginning of the following year, however, Argentina again placed the mediation in jeopardy by announcing that it would allow the 1972 General Treaty on the Judicial Settlement of Disputes to lapse at the end of its initial ten-year term.[104] This presented a profound problem to Chile. If the 1972 Treaty were allowed to lapse, Chile would have to decide before the end of the year whether to pursue recourse to the ICJ. Failure to do so might mean that the opportunity would be lost forever. On the other hand, unilaterally appealing to the ICJ would very likely imperil the mediation process and might inspire an extreme response from Argentina. Given that state of affairs, Chile was more reluctant than ever to resume negotiations regarding the underlying substantive issues, as long as the so-called *vacuum juris* continued to exist. Samoré and his team returned to the familiar role of conducting a mediation within the mediation, a process that occupied most of 1982. During this time, however, a fundamental shift in the nature of the process occurred.

By some accounts, it was the arrival of Argentine representative Ambassador Ortiz de Rozas that jump-started the process.[105] De Rozas was a friend of Enrique Bernstein, head of the Chilean delegation, and the two men reportedly began to meet directly on an informal basis. Although some participants in the negotiations have discounted the importance of this relationship in moving the negotiations forward, the direct, informal discussions were a new element in the mediation, and one that assumed increasing importance in the later stages of the process.[106] The Vatican apparently encouraged the direct communications between Bernstein and de Rozas, and even tried to use their discussions to restart negotiations based on the Pope's 1980 proposal. It quickly became apparent, however, that no progress could be made on the substantive issues until the procedural problem presented by the *vacuum juris* was resolved. This objective was finally achieved on September 15, 1982, when the parties accepted a papal proposal to extend the 1972 Treaty solely for purposes of the Beagle Channel dispute.[107]

Yet despite the Vatican's success in moving the parties beyond the diplomatic crisis of 1981 and the *vacuum juris* of the following year, negotiations continued to move very slowly. Chile evinced a greater willingness to negotiate modifications to the papal proposal following the renewal of the 1972 Treaty, but by then it had become clear that the Argentine junta, reeling from its defeat in the Falkland Islands War, was too badly debilitated to consummate an agreement. The death of Cardinal Samoré in February 1983 did nothing to help move things forward, though mediation participants have expressed differing views as to the impact of this development.[108] Further complicating the situation, Argentine delegation head Ortiz de Rozas resigned his position later that month. Under the circumstances, the participants tacitly resigned themselves to waiting out the clock until the new government took over.[109] The Pope attempted to move discussions forward by suggesting that the parties sign a nonaggression agreement in advance of their final settlement. Argentina rejected that proposal.[110]

Nonetheless, this period was not entirely barren. Indeed, the trend toward a broadened, more direct dialogue that had begun with the discussions between Bernstein and de Rozas was reinforced during the summer of 1983. In July of that year, Santiago Benadava, one of the key Chilean representatives, met with Julio Barberi, the Argentine ambassador to Holland, while visiting The Hague on unrelated business. Discussions between the two led to the production of a "nonpaper," setting forth modifications to the papal proposal that they thought might serve as the basis for future negotiations. The basic refinement of this nonpaper was that Argentina would renounce its pretension to the islands and give up the limited facilities on Chilean soil envisioned by the 1980 proposal, while Chile would sacrifice its rights to joint use of the vast Argentine maritime zone and settle for a relatively narrow territorial sea. Benadava and Barberi presented these ideas to their respective governments and received approval to negotiate on that basis. Thereafter, the basic format of The Hague nonpaper served as the foundation for discussions at the Vatican. Using this format, the parties were able to lay much of the groundwork for a final settlement even before such a result was politically feasible.[111]

The final phase of the mediation process began with the return to democratic government in Argentina in December 1983. President Alfonsín's new government was firmly committed to securing an agreement as quickly as possible, and the structure of the mediation changed radically as a result.[112] During this period, direct discussions were far more common than separate meetings. Furthermore, direct channels of communication were opened between career diplomats and politicians in Buenos Aires and Santiago.[113] Indeed, the new delegation heads, Marcelo Delpech of Argentina and Ernesto Videla of Chile, conducted most of their work in South America rather than Rome.[114] By comparison with the preceding five years, negotiations proceeded at a breakneck pace. In his first major foreign policy initiative, President Alfonsín acted to revive the stalled mediation process by sending Deputy Foreign Minister Hugo Gobbi to Rome in December 1983.[115] Based on Gobbi's talks and additional discussions between Delpech and Videla, the two countries agreed to request that the Pope call their foreign ministers together to sign a Declaration of Peace and Friendship. The Vatican agreed, and on January 23, 1984, Argentine Foreign Minister Dante Caputo and Chilean Foreign Minister Jaime del Valle signed the Declaration at a joint meeting in the Holy See.[116]

In April 1984, Vatican Secretary of State Agostino Casaroli met separately with the two delegations and requested their proposals for a final solution.[117] Each side complied with this request. Based on the proposals, Casaroli submitted to the two delegations what he unequivocally described as the Vatican's last proposal on June 11, 1984. Casaroli made it clear that a rejection of this last proposal would end the Vatican mediation.[118] Both sides accepted the proposal.

At this point, the mediation was essentially complete. Teams of experts were called in to work out details regarding dispute resolution mechanisms and the precise contours of the boundary, but progress was swift and the Vatican mediation team played little part in the process. By October, the parties had reached a complete understanding, and the treaty language was finalized on October 18. Following a national referendum in Argentina, the Treaty of Peace and Friendship was signed in Rome on November 29, 1984.[119]

Key Factors in Shaping the Result

Argentine Political Considerations

The domestic political situation in Argentina was clearly one of the most significant factors driving the mediation process, and changes in that situation were quite arguably the primary impetus for the settlement ultimately achieved. The military junta that controlled the Argentine government throughout most of the mediation process was sharply divided between hard-line nationalists and more moderate military leaders. Jorge Videla and Roberto Viola, who held the Argentine presidency back to back from the beginning of the papal intervention until 1981, are generally associated with the latter group. Nevertheless, they were severely constrained in their ability to work toward a peaceful solution by more extreme members of the junta. The military leadership was perpetually concerned that a conciliatory approach toward Chile would be regarded as a face-losing transaction that might destabilize its control and invite challengers from the ranks of the junior officers. It has been reported, for example, that when President

Videla informed the papal nuncio, Pio Laghi, of Argentina's plans to invade the PNL island group in December 1978, he justified the decision by saying that if he did not give the orders for invasion, he would be replaced by extremists within the junta.[120]

The sea change in Argentine politics that ultimately paved the way for the settlement was the Falkland Islands War. Often characterized as a desperate bid to build popular support for the military government in a time of economic crisis, the debacle in the Falklands instead served to fatally weaken the Galtieri government and sour the public on territorially aggressive foreign policy in general. By the time of the presidential election in 1983, public opinion clearly favored a rapid resolution to the problems with Chile. Alfonsín was elected on a platform featuring a pledge to bring the Chilean conflict to an end. As discussed above, the new president moved quickly to make good on that promise. Dante Caputo has indicated that the Alfonsín government regarded a quick settlement as an essential part of its strategy to reduce the influence of the military and implement economically critical military cutbacks.[121] Additionally, the need for regional economic integration had become apparent to everyone, and that process was badly restricted by the conflict in the southern zone. Alfonsín's approach to the Beagle Channel dispute garnered substantial approval among citizens weary of international conflict, and the momentum of that support carried the process to a swift completion.[122]

The Moral Authority of the Pope and Public Opinion

The foregoing discussion might lead to the conclusion that the resolution of the Beagle Channel conflict was entirely the product of historical accident, a lucky break for which the mediator deserves no credit. While it is probably true that the dispute could not have been resolved but for the change in government in Argentina, it does not follow that the Vatican's efforts were without effect. On the contrary, it is almost certain that the papal intervention prevented a war between Chile and Argentina. Every negotiator interviewed for this paper indicated, generally without qualification, that the two countries would have gone to war in the winter of 1978–79 had the Vatican not intervened.[123] Given the evidence suggesting that orders for an invasion had already been given when the Pope announced that he was sending Samoré to Buenos Aires, those assertions appear well grounded.[124] Additionally, the Vatican's efforts served to maintain a dialogue between Chile and Argentina through some very difficult periods, when relations between the two countries might otherwise have declined to a dangerously unstable level. In particular, the Vatican was instrumental in resolving the difficulties that developed following the border closing and detention of prisoners in 1981 and the Argentine repudiation of the General Treaty on the Judicial Settlement of Disputes in 1982.

The Vatican's contribution to the peaceful settlement of this conflict featured two principal elements: the initial crisis intervention, which prevented armed conflict in 1978, and the creation of a forum that kept the situation stable during the potentially volatile period while conditions ripened for the permanent resolution of the dispute. The Vatican was probably better suited to this role than any other mediator. Indeed, the unique nature of the mediator was probably one of the key factors contributing to the peaceful settlement. And what made the Pope the perfect intermediary in this context was that he was uniquely positioned to influence the parties while remaining—and appearing—absolutely neutral. He was, in short, a neutral mediator with leverage.

The Pope's leverage derived from his moral authority in the international community and, perhaps more importantly, within the two countries. Admittedly, the Pope did not have the kind of leverage that could be applied by an interested third-party state with resources to grant or withhold. But he had exactly the kind of power that was so important to Chile when it evaluated possible mediators in 1978: he could not be ignored. If the dispute had been mediated by Henry Kissinger or the king of Spain, Argentina might well have felt at liberty to reject the 1980 proposal and resume a hostile posture. Such a course would certainly have occasioned disapproval in the international community, but nothing approaching the outrage that could be expected with the Pope in the middle. Thus, the Vatican's moral authority afforded leverage, not so much to compel a particular course of action, as to restrict the options of would-be belligerents. Under the circumstances, that is exactly what was needed.

The Pope's moral authority was an even more salient factor within the two countries themselves. Santiago Benadava, a key member of the Chilean delegation throughout the mediation process, has emphasized that even though Chile and Argentina were dictatorships whose relations with the Church were poor during the mediation years, they were not immune to the pressures of public opinion.[125] And public opinion in these two overwhelmingly Catholic countries was profoundly affected by the Pope. The Vatican appears to have been very conscious of this leverage point and exploited it to maximum advantage throughout the dispute. During the initial period of shuttle diplomacy, Samoré made substantial use of the media in publicly exhorting the parties to avoid confrontation. On occasion, he also used the press to chastise the leaders of the two countries for their intransigence.[126] Eventually, the Church began to sponsor peace rallies, pilgrimages, and special masses designed to build public support for the peace effort.[127] This highlights the key point distinguishing the Pope from an ordinary mediator: unlike most neutral intermediaries, the Pope actually had a constituency within the two countries.

Success of the Mediation

Evaluating the impact of particular mediation techniques employed by the Vatican is a more difficult proposition, since it necessarily requires counterfactual speculation as to how effectively the dispute would have been resolved had other techniques been employed. The negotiators interviewed for this chapter generally did not identify specific mediation methods as having greatly impacted the outcome of the dispute. However, a few particularly central aspects of the Vatican's technique deserve comment.

Several mediation participants have expressed a belief that the direct negoti-ations that characterized the last phase of the mediation were significantly more productive than separate meetings.[128] In this view, articulated most vigorously by Marcelo Delpech, chief of the Argentine delegation from late 1983 through the conclusion of the dispute, the format followed during the early stages of the mediation prevented channels of communication from developing between the Argentine and Chilean teams. However, Dante Caputo, Argentine foreign min-ister under President Alfonsín and the official who signed the 1984 Treaty of Peace and Friendship on behalf of Argentina, feels that separate discussions were appropriate during the early stages of the mediation, because of the strained relations and mutual mistrust between the countries at that time.[129]

Clearly, the period characterized by direct talks produced the most substan-tial gains in the shortest period of time. As previously discussed, however, these results are attributable to a variety of factors, the most fundamental of which was simply an increased desire on the part of the Argentine government to reach an accommodation. Even Delpech acknowledges that a settlement was unlikely prior to Alfonsín's election, regardless of the mediation techniques employed.[130] If we assume, with the benefit of hindsight, that the proper objective for the pre-1983 period was simply keeping the parties at the table, then Samoré's system of separate meetings seems highly appropriate. At the same time, the mediation team was flexible enough to permit direct talks where they seemed promising, as it did, for example, when a dialogue developed between Bernstein and de Rozas, and when Benadava and Barberi met in Holland.

Another technique identified as having been particularly effective was the relentless questioning to which Samoré subjected the two delegations. By com-bining this technique with very limited transfers of information between the parties, Samoré was able to act as a kind of informational escrow, immune to the problems of strategic gamesmanship that would certainly characterize any direct interchange of information between the parties at an early stage in the process. This enabled him to identify potential points of convergence and di-rect the discussions accordingly. Francisco Orrego considered this one of the most effective tools employed by Samoré during the mediation. Again, how-ever, it does not appear to have significantly altered or accelerated the course of the mediation.[131]

The most important mediation technique employed by the Pope was clearly the proposal that he developed in December 1980. Although both sides har-bored considerable uneasiness regarding its sharing provisions, most of the ne-gotiators interviewed for this paper feel that it had significant value in clarifying issues and providing a platform for future discussions. The one participant who does not share this view, General Ricardo Echeverry Boneo, thinks that the Vat-ican should have developed a variety of proposals rather than relying on just one.[132] Although it is very difficult to say whether a profusion of proposals would have accelerated the process, one cannot dismiss Echeverry's claim that additional proposals might have sparked creative bargaining and enabled the parties to arrive at an accommodation sooner. On the other hand, if one believes that an agreement was unattainable before 1983, and that the Pope's role prior to that time was largely one of stabilization, then the single proposal begins to look more sensible. By focusing the parties' deliberations within a single, structured context, the 1980 proposal may have served this end more effectively than a multiplicity of overlapping plans. Moreover, it was very likely more difficult to reject the proposal outright, given that the Vatican had put its weight behind this plan as its sole recommendation, than it would have been to dismiss each in a series of mere suggestions. In this regard, it is worth noting that Argentina never explicitly rejected the 1980 proposal, although its negotiators considered it totally unacceptable and never seriously considered accepting it.[133]

Conclusion

Because the outcome of this mediation effort was so significantly shaped by factors such as internal politics and the unique identity of the mediator, specific and generally applicable recommendations are not immediately apparent. However, the Beagle Channel experience does suggest a few general guidelines that may be of value to future intermediaries.

First, the Vatican mediation is a textbook illustration of the value of patience in an unstable, but not yet bellicose, negotiating environment. Stephen Stedman has suggested that when confronted with failure, mediators do best to admit defeat and end the mediation. This position is based on the belief that disputants tend not to appreciate mediation until it is taken away from them. It is also based, at least implicitly, on the assumption that the damage resulting from a suspension of mediation will be more than offset by an increased willingness to work toward a settlement. This may frequently be the case where armed conflict already exists, and there is a premium on getting a settlement as quickly as possible. As the Beagle Channel conflict illustrates, however, this approach is inappropriate when the mediator's goal is to preserve a fragile peace rather than to terminate bloodshed already in progress. Under such circumstances, the mediator plays a dual role, striving both to achieve a workable long-term solution and also to prevent the situation from deteriorating into war. Thus, the mediator of a volatile but noncombative dispute can serve a useful purpose even without obtaining a solution, simply by providing a stable environment within which the situation can be allowed to ripen. And the mediator must be mindful of the fact that efforts to force an early settlement may jeopardize this other important goal.

The Beagle Channel case also illustrates the value of flexibility in a long-term mediation context. Although Samoré worked hard to establish a rigorous structure for the negotiations, he was very willing to work outside that structure when he deemed it necessary or desirable to do so. For example, Samoré moved outside the mediation forum altogether during the diplomatic crisis of 1981, by directly contacting high-level government officials in Buenos Aires and Santiago. He was also willing to relax the highly formal mechanisms for interaction between the parties when opportunities for movement presented themselves;

although the Vatican team took great pains to keep the delegations apart during the tense early stages of the mediation, Samoré permitted and made use of the informal direct meetings between Ortiz de Rozas and Enrique Bernstein and the later meetings between Santiago Benadava and Julio Barberi. The Vatican's success in this regard suggests that mediators must strike a careful balance between the need for a negotiating environment sufficiently structured to maintain stability, and the need to exploit fortuitous developments and alternative problem-solving approaches.

Additionally, Samoré's techniques of information management may well be of value to future mediators. Although these methods probably did nothing to accelerate the resolution of the present dispute, they may well do so in other disputes characterized by informational gamesmanship. Several negotiators were impressed by Samoré's ability to extract candid assessments of the parties' positions through intensive, confidential questioning conducted in separate meetings. It bears noting that this technique requires the mediator to achieve the complete trust of the parties and to convince them of his absolute neutrality. Needless to say, most mediators will have more difficulty than the Vatican in establishing this kind of relationship with the parties.

While the conflict was rooted in a very particular historical and geographical context, the choice of mediator with compelling moral authority, and the techniques used by the mediator to keep war at bay, could be very useful even in post–Cold War cases of secession, internal conflict, or minority rights.

12

The North Korean Nuclear Proliferation Crisis

Rock Tang

Overview

IN 1993, NORTH KOREA refused inspections by the International Atomic Energy Agency (IAEA) and threatened to back out of the nuclear Non-Proliferation Treaty. The prospect of North Korea possibly gaining nuclear weapons threatened regional stability and led the United States to take action in the crisis. The North Korean government, a "rogue state" with fierce philosophical dedication to self-reliance, was able to leverage its power on the nuclear weapons issue into high-level talks with the United States. Some argue that these talks, on issues broader than the nuclear issue, were the primary goal of the North Korean government to begin with. This chapter examines the negotiation process between the United States and North Korea and the implications of these talks for regional and nuclear security. It analyzes the role that second-track diplomacy can play even in a technical crisis, highlighting how the visit of former President Jimmy Carter to North Korea helped set the stage for later official negotiations with the United States. The author compares the strengths and weaknesses of bilateral versus multilateral talks and analyzes the difficulties that the U.S.–North Korean agreement faced in the implementation period.

In an era of nuclear proliferation, with India and Pakistan having tested weapons and the Non-Proliferation Treaty due for review in the year 2000, the negotiation experience between the United States and North Korea could provide important positive and negative lessons for future nuclear crises and the broader political and security contexts in which they operate.

Timeline

1965   North Korea (DPRK) installs a small nuclear reactor obtained from the Soviet Union in Yongbyon.

1974   The DPRK joins the International Atomic Energy Agency.

1985   The DPRK signs the Nuclear Non-Proliferation Treaty (NTP) in Moscow on December 12, in exchange for Soviet promise to transfer advanced nuclear reactors to it.

1992   DPRK signs IAEA Safeguards Accord on January 30, after a delay of more than six years; IAEA Director General Hans Blix visits North Korea in May. The IAEA conducts on-site inspections from June to December 1992.

1993   **January:** IAEA inspection reveals anomalies in North Korea's claims regarding plutonium extraction. **February:** The IAEA requests "special inspections" of two undeclared sites containing nuclear wastes to resolve issue of plutonium extraction. **Mar. 12:** North Korea denies IAEA examination of waste sites and announces it is giving the required ninety-day notice for withdrawal from the NPT. United States and South Korea (ROK) resume Team Spirit annual military exercise. **June:** First high-level U.S.–DPRK meeting. United States prepares to discuss any security issues. The DPRK agrees to "suspend" withdrawal from the NPT. United States sets the following preconditions for continuation of U.S.–DPRK high level talks. The DPRK: (1) does not leave the NPT; (2) does not reprocess spent fuel while the talks continue; (3) does not refuel the 5 MWe (megawatt electric) reactor without IAEA supervision; (4) makes progress in North–South Korean discussions; and (5) makes progress in U.S.–DPRK talks. **July:** Second Round of U.S.–DPRK talks. United States offers to help shift North Korean nuclear power program from graphite-moderated reactors to light-water reactors (LWR). The DPRK agrees to continue "continuity of safeguards" inspections by the IAEA and to discuss with the IAEA the requested "special inspections." North Korea agrees to engage in discussions with the ROK. **August:** The IAEA is able to conduct only partial and unsatisfactory continuity of safeguards inspection. The DPRK refuses to meet with the ROK to discuss promised exchange of envoys. The United States concludes there is no basis on which to proceed with the third round of bilateral talks in September as planned. **December:** In response to perceived North Korean wishes, the United States agrees to enlarge the next high-level bilateral discussion and agrees to a "broad and thorough" discussion of economic and political issues as well as security issues that had been the subject of the discussions thus far.

1994   **January:** Continuing discussion begun in January, the IAEA and DPRK discuss parameters for an effective "continuity of safeguards" inspection (to assure that no further reprocessing had taken place since the original inspection in 1992). **February:** The IAEA agrees on inspection arrangements. The United States and ROK announce that if inspection is satisfactorily completed, and if North–South exchange of envoys proceeds as agreed, then: (1) U.S.–ROK "Team Spirit" exercise would be suspended; and (2) the third round of high-level talks would be held to address political, economic, and security issues in a "broad and thorough" manner. **March:** The IAEA inspection is incomplete. The DPRK refuses to allow critical tests fully agreed to in earlier negotiations. The IAEA declares it cannot declare "continuity of safeguards." North Korea refuses to meet with the ROK to arrange an exchange of envoys. Consequently, third round U.S.–DPRK meeting is not held and suspension of Team Spirit exercises is lifted. **Mar. 31:** The UN Security Council issues a unanimous statement calling on the DPRK to permit full safeguards inspection. China is active in statement negotiation. **April:** The ROK announces that it will no longer hold out for a prior exchange of North–South envoys before third round U.S.–DPRK talks are held. This leaves satisfactory continuity of safeguards inspection by the IAEA as the only remaining condition for third round talks. The DPRK announces that it will refuel the Yongbyon reactor in May. The IAEA and DPRK commence discussions to work out details of IAEA supervision of refueling. U.S. officials confirm that unsupervised refueling would result in breaking off efforts to negotiate with the DPRK. **May:** The DPRK refuses to allow the IAEA to take samples of fuel rods. The IAEA announces it cannot reach agreement on satisfactory arrangements to supervise refueling. IAEA team returns to North Korea to complete inspection procedures begun in March, but North Korea begins refueling the Yongbyon reactor without IAEA supervision. The United States, Japan, and the ROK begin working for UN sanctions against North Korea. North Korea announces that it will withdraw from the IAEA. **June:** Former U.S. President Jimmy Carter visits North Korea and extracts pledge for "good faith" negotiations and summit meeting with South Korean President Kim Young Sam. North Korea freezes its nuclear program in response to Carter's assurance that the United States will not pursue sanctions against North Korea. **July:** U.S.–DPRK high-level negotiations resume in Geneva. **July 8:** North Korean President Kim Il Sung dies of a heart attack. The DPRK calls off summit with the ROK. **August:** U.S.–DPRK negotiators in Geneva outline a potential agreement where North Korea receives light-water reactor technology and more normal relations with the United States, and in return, the DPRK freezes and ultimately dismantles its nuclear program, complies with IAEA requests, and resumes dialogue with South Korea. **Oct. 21:** United States and DPRK negotiators reach agreement for freezing and eventually dismantling the North Korean nuclear program: return of the DPRK to full IAEA safeguards; United States-led consortium provides light-water reactors and interim alternative energy (heavy fuel oil) to North Korea; resumption of the North–South dialogue; and establishment of liaison offices between the United States and DPRK. The implementation is projected to require five or more years. **November:** The IAEA confirms construction is halted on new DPRK 50 MWe and 200 MWe reactors; Five MWe reactor is not being refueled. Fuel rods are under scrutiny.

1995   **January:** The United States delivers first 50,000 tons of oil to North Korea under agreement. North Korea lifts restrictions on imports from the United States. United States eases sanctions against economic activity with North Korea. **March:** Korean Peninsula Development Organization (KEDO) formed in New York by twenty nations with the United States, Japan, and South Korea as key members. **April:** The DPRK refuses to accept South Korean light-water reactors (LWRs). U.S.–DPRK officials' meeting in Berlin ends in stalemate. **May:** U.S.–DPRK meeting convened in Kuala Lumpur in late May to resolve LWR issue. **June 13:** The United States and DPRK conclude an agreement in Kuala Lumpur on provision of light-water reactors through KEDO, with a U.S. firm to serve as program coordinator; arrangements for safe storage of downloaded fuel rods are to begin immediately. **Dec. 15:** KEDO and the DPRK sign the Agreement on Supply of a LWR Project to the DPRK.

Background

North Korea's Suspected Nuclear Weapons Program

The IAEA was created in 1957 to provide nuclear assistance to member states while assuring that its assistance would not be used "in such a way as to further any military purpose."[1] North Korea (also known as the DPRK, the Democratic People's Republic of Korea) joined the IAEA in September 1974, primarily to receive the atomic power-related benefits accompanying membership. The IAEA subsequently provided technical assistance to the DPRK, including assistance to improve the uranium mining and enrichment facilities in Pyongsan and Paekchon.

The IAEA is also charged with safeguarding nuclear materials to verify states' compliance with their obligations under the Nuclear Non-Proliferation Treaty (NPT). To determine a state's compliance, the IAEA guidelines specify three separate steps for investigating the overall safety of member countries' nuclear facilities. Member states must prepare a list of facilities subject to inspection and, within two months, submit a design information report answering fifty-eight questions for each facility included on the list. Second, the IAEA carries out a preliminary inspection to compare information provided by the list against the actual condition of the facilities. Third, the IAEA proceeds with periodic inspections of facilities in accordance with the inspection schedule agreed upon with the respective member state.

Nearly a decade after joining the IAEA, North Korea joined the NPT on December 12, 1985, at the urging of the Soviet Union, from which it was receiving atomic energy-related technology and equipment. The NPT prohibits, among other things, the manufacture of nuclear weapons or explosive devices. Although all members of the NPT are required to sign the IAEA full safeguards accord within eighteen months of admission to the NPT, North Korea delayed signing for six years until January 30, 1992. North Korea's Supreme People's Assembly ratified the accord on April 9, 1992.

INFCIRC 153, known more commonly as the NPT Model Safeguards Agreement, is the template used by states, including North Korea, in their agreement with the IAEA. The Model Safeguards Agreement specifies three types of inspections: ad hoc, routine, and special. "Ad hoc inspections" are used to verify initial inventories of nuclear materials subject to safeguards. "Routine inspections" verify the consistency of reports filed by the state. "Special inspections" are used only when the IAEA considers information given by the state to be inadequate, or when the IAEA seeks greater access than that given by ad hoc or routine inspections.[2]

North Korea prepared responses to IAEA requests for information, but as IAEA on-site inspections progressed, questions and discrepancies emerged. A critical discrepancy concerned North Korea's initial report to the IAEA in 1990 stating that only a tiny amount of plutonium (ninety grams) was extracted from an experimental reactor in Yongbyon. IAEA samples, however, indicated that at least three times the reported amount had been extracted. The IAEA, led by Director General Hans Blix, demanded that North Korea provide a full explanation within a month, despite North Korea's claim that an IAEA technical error in calculation could account for the discrepancy. The IAEA was unpersuaded by Pyongyang's explanation and proceeded on the assumption that North Korea was hiding evidence of having extracted additional plutonium from the experimental reactor.

The anomalies in the North Korean response fueled concern about the possibility of an extensive North Korean nuclear weapons program. North Korea had already delayed signing the IAEA safeguard measures for six years after becoming a member of the NPT and had admitted to extracting a small amount of plutonium from its 5 MWe (megawatt electric) experimental reactor at Yongbyon. The DPRK was also in the process of building additional reactors and reprocessing plants, which could make North Korea a formidable nuclear power. The United States believed that North Korea could have already produced one or two nuclear bombs by 1993. Thus, when North Korea, under considerable international pressure, finally agreed to allow IAEA on-site inspections of its nuclear reactors, anomalies in North Korea's claims regarding plutonium extraction produced anxiety in the international community, in particular, the United States, South Korea, and Japan. Beginning in January 1992, a series of talks between the United States and North Korea attempted to address the differences among the parties.

The First Round of U.S.–DPRK Talks

The first round of U.S.–DPRK talks were held in New York in January 1992 and were attended by U.S. Undersecretary of State Arnold Kantor and North Korean Workers' Party Secretary Kim Yong-sun. This session provided the forum for airing the official position of each side and for discussing a wide range of issues of mutual concern to the two countries. No follow-up meeting was arranged, and the dispute was still far from resolution, but the discussions accomplished both U.S. and North Korean objectives: The DPRK opened high-level talks with the United States, and the United States managed to persuade North Korea to sign the IAEA safeguards agreement.[3]

In February 1993, the IAEA requested "special inspections" of two undeclared sites containing nuclear wastes near the Yongbyon nuclear complex, whose presence was discovered by satellite photos taken by the U.S. military in 1993. The request for special inspections, that is, inspection on demand as opposed to regularly scheduled inspections, was rare and unprecedented in North Korea's case. North Korea immediately condemned the American use of spy satellites as a violation of North Korea's sovereignty and national security and rejected the request.

North Korea denied the IAEA access to the sites for several reasons. First, Pyongyang claimed that the sites in question were purely military facilities unrelated to nuclear weapons development and therefore not subject to inspection under the agreement. In addition, North Korea refused the IAEA's demand on the ground that the IAEA was acting unfairly in its highly unusual request for a special inspection.

On March 12, 1993, North Korea suddenly announced that it was giving the required ninety-day notice for withdrawal from the NPT. This move enhanced suspicions that North Korea might indeed be engaged in a nuclear weapons program and might be hiding evidence from international inspection. North Korea justified its withdrawal by invoking the provision of the NPT recognizing a country's right to withdraw if extraordinary events jeopardized a state's supreme interests. According to the NPT, Article 10, Section 1, "[E]ach Party shall in exercising its national sovereignty have the right to withdraw from the Treaty if it decides that extraordinary events, related to the subject matter of this treaty, have jeopardized the supreme interests of its country."

The Second Round of U.S.–DPRK Talks

North Korea indicated that it would suspend its withdrawal from the NPT if further high-level talks would be scheduled. In response to North Korea's threat to withdraw from the IAEA, the international community, led by the United States in consultation with South Korea and Japan, agreed to further high-level talks under certain conditions. The United States set several conditions to be met prior to continuation of high-level negotiations, including: (1) the DPRK would not withdraw from the NPT, (2) there would be no more reprocessing of spent fuel while the talks proceeded, (3) the DPRK would not refuel the 5 MWe reactor without IAEA supervision, and (4) the U.S.–DPRK talks would make progress.[4] Despite the seemingly firm conditions, increasing tension drove both parties back to the negotiating table before all of the conditions were fulfilled.

The increasing tension created a deepening sense of crisis, culminating in a second round of U.S.–DPRK high-level talks in New York on June 9–11, 1993, and then in Geneva on July 16–19, 1993. First Vice Foreign Minister Kang Sok Ju led the North Korean contingent, while Assistant Secretary of State for Political and Military Affairs Robert Gallucci led the American delegation.

On June 11, exactly one day prior to the announced withdrawal from the IAEA was to take effect, North Korea reversed its stance by announcing that it had now decided to "suspend its withdrawal." In return, the United States gave North Korea assurances against using its armed forces or threatening use of armed force including the use or threat of use of nuclear weapons against North Korea.[5]

In July 1993, at the second high-level U.S.–DPRK meeting, the United States agreed to an earlier proposal from Kim Il Sung to help shift North Korea's nuclear power program from graphite-moderated reactors to light-water reactors.[6] The DPRK, in turn, agreed to allow the "continuity of safeguard" inspections by the IAEA to continue, to discuss with the IAEA the requested "special inspection," and to engage in discussions with the government of the ROK.

At the end of the second round of talks, the parties issued a three-point joint statement: (1) North Korea would begin talks with the IAEA regarding the question of outstanding safeguards, specifically, special inspections; (2) inter-Korean talks would be reopened to discuss matters of mutual concern, including the nuclear issue; and (3) a third round of high-level talks would be held within two months to discuss possible U.S. assistance for North Korea to replace existing graphite-moderated reactors with light-water reactors. The lack of progress on the first two points delayed the third round of talks.[7]

In August 1993, the IAEA was able to conduct only partial and unsatisfactory continuity of safeguard inspections. This fact, in addition to the DPRK's refusal to meet with the South Korean government to discuss a promised exchange of envoys, led the U.S. government to conclude that there existed no basis on which to proceed with the third round of bilateral dialogue with North Korea in September, as originally had been planned.

For the remainder of 1993, IAEA–DPRK negotiations were deadlocked over the issue of access to two nuclear waste sites that North Korea refused to open on the grounds that they were military bases. In late December, however, North Korea made a conciliatory gesture by permitting IAEA inspection activities to resume and changing the film in the cameras installed to monitor reactor activities. This was arranged through the U.S.–DPRK channel in New York, via the DPRK diplomatic mission to the United Nations. The U.S. government now agreed to enlarge the next high-level bilateral talks to include a "broad and thorough" discussion of economic and political issues as well as the security issues that had been the subject of discussion thus far.

The IAEA and the DPRK had been discussing parameters for effective continuity of safeguard inspections since December 1993. The IAEA was concerned that further reprocessing had taken place since the original IAEA inspection in 1992. In February 1994, the IAEA and the DPRK came to agree on inspection arrangements. On March 3, 1994, North Korea allowed the IAEA to resume nuclear inspections for the first time in more than a year, but still refused complete access to all declared and undeclared sites.

During the first half of 1994, North Korea continued to refuse IAEA inspections of fuel rods, essential to determining North Korea's compliance with the NPT. North Korea claimed that it had a unique status with the IAEA in that it was neither a member nor a nonmember, but that it had temporarily suspended its membership. This "unique status," North Korea asserted, allowed it to refuse special inspections.[8] Since inspection of all declared facilities was incomplete, the IAEA announced that it could not assure continuity of safeguards. This led the UN Security Council president to issue a unanimously approved statement on March 31, 1994, calling on the DPRK to permit full safeguards inspections. On the eve of the May 1994 crisis no meaningful progress had been made on the issue of the IAEA continuity of safeguards inspections. The IAEA–DPRK controversy reached an impasse. North Korea continued to refuse IAEA inspections, and the IAEA seemed powerless either to force North Korea to allow inspections or to stop nuclear weapons development.

In May 1994, North Korea accelerated the refueling of the reactor in Yongbyon. International condemnation was quick, but North Korea defended its act by pointing out the necessity of timely replacement of the reactor's fuel rods for safety reasons. North Korea also defended its actions by claiming sovereignty, noting that the NPT and the IAEA safeguard accord could not prevent it from exercising its sovereign power. Furthermore, North Korea charged the IAEA was not impartial by pointing out that other countries such as Japan were already engaged in IAEA-monitored plutonium extraction. If Japan could extract plutonium without IAEA objections, then North Korea reasoned that it, too, should be allowed to do so. North Korea appeared to be proceeding with the separation of plutonium from the spent fuel with or without IAEA inspectors present.

Key Interventions and Major Actors

The United States relied on both official and nonofficial diplomatic channels in its attempt to resolve the conflict. This section focuses on the dynamics of the two key interventions in this dispute, former U.S. President Jimmy Carter's mission to Pyongyang and the third round of high-level U.S.–DPRK talks. Officially, the United States engaged in U.S.–DPRK high-level talks conducted in three rounds between 1993–94. Unofficially, the United States communicated its position through former U.S. President Jimmy Carter's private visit to Pyongyang.

Carter's Mission to Pyongyang

In this critical period of impasse between the second and third rounds of high-level talks, former President Carter visited Pyongyang to mediate between North Korea and the United States. Largely through his efforts, a third round of talks was convened. These talks ultimately resulted in the Geneva Agreed

Framework. Former U.S. President Jimmy Carter's role in his mission to North Korea is controversial. Both Carter and the Clinton administration insist that Carter's trip was purely a private mission and that Carter was given no instructions. Carter, himself, described his trip to Pyongyang as a "private" mission, but his status and prestige as a former president of the United States produced an impact on North Korea as well as the Clinton administration. Whether private or official, Carter's trip to Pyongyang supplemented the official U.S. policy toward North Korea with a second track of diplomacy and was instrumental in avoiding another Korean War.

The mission was a product of Carter's own initiative. As the North Korean crisis mounted in 1994, Carter grew increasingly concerned about the danger of the conflict escalating into a full-scale war over the nuclear issue. He was particularly concerned about "the apparent lack of an avenue of communication with the top leader of North Korea," Kim Il Sung. Carter was convinced that Kim was "the only one who could make the decisions to alleviate the crisis and avoid another Korean War."[9] Under these circumstances, Carter telephoned President Clinton expressing his concern over the developing crisis with North Korea, and Clinton agreed to have his staff give him a background briefing on the issue.[10]

Carter was inclined to accept a long-standing invitation by Kim Il Sung to visit North Korea, but before going, he wanted to hear the official U.S. perspective on his trip. A day after speaking with President Clinton, Carter confirmed the North Korean invitation and verified that the invitation came from President Kim Il Sung himself. Carter then called Vice President Al Gore to inform him that he wanted to accept the North Korean invitation. The next morning, Gore assured Carter that President Clinton and his top advisors approved of his Pyongyang visit.

Carter left Atlanta on June 12, 1994, accompanied by his wife Rosalynn; Marion Creekmore, director of programs of the Carter Center; and Dick Christenson of the U.S. State Department, who would act as interpreter. Carter arrived in Seoul on June 13 and stayed at U.S. Ambassador James Laney's official residence. His first days were spent gathering the opinions of the South Korean government. He held talks with South Korean President Kim Young Sam and discovered that most of Kim's advisors were troubled by Carter's visit to Pyongyang. Many South Koreans expressed concern that Carter might easily fall victim to the North Korean leader's hypnotizing charisma. Carter also talked with U.S. General Gary Luck, commander of the U.S.–ROK Combined Forces, who expressed grave concern over the consequences of another Korean war.

From Seoul, Carter traveled to the truce village of Panmunjom and crossed the demilitarized zone. He arrived in Pyongyang on June 15 and met with North Korean President Kim Il Sung on June 16 to open a round of talks aimed at easing the tension.

Carter's first day in Pyongyang was not auspicious. In his first meeting with Kim Yong-nam, Pyongyang's foreign minister, their discussion did not go far toward resolving the conflict. In response to Carter's proposal on possibilities for ending the impasse, Kim Yong-nam replied that the convening of a third round of U.S.–DPRK talks was a prerequisite to any affirmative move by North Korea. The foreign minister indicated that North Koreans considered sanctions insulting, and Carter left the meeting feeling that sanctions would be unproductive. Carter interpreted the foreign minister's comments as meaning that North Koreans "would go to war rather than yield to economic condemnation and economic pressure."[11] That evening Carter sent Marion Creekmore to Panmunjom to transmit a secure message from South Korea to Washington, explaining the situation and also seeking authorization from President Clinton to propose a third round of talks to defuse the crisis. Carter received the necessary authorization.

Carter's Meeting with Kim Il Sung

On June 16, Carter met North Korean President Kim Il Sung. Carter found Kim Il Sung "to be vigorous, alert, intelligent, and remarkably familiar with the issues."[12] Kim consulted frequently with his advisors, but Carter had the impression that Kim was in command and made the final decisions. Kim thanked Carter for accepting the three-year-old invitation and asked him to speak first. Carter described his "unofficial role," the briefings that he had received, and his visit with South Korean President Kim Young Sam before presenting the position that he had prepared before leaving Atlanta. He outlined the entire situation as he saw it in such a way as to make Kim Il Sung fully aware of "all concerns about North Korean nuclear policies."[13]

Ultimately, Kim Il Sung accepted Carter's proposal for a third round of U.S.–DPRK talks under several conditions. First, the United States needed to support North Korea's acquisition of light-water reactor technology, although North Korea realized that the political realities meant that the funding and equipment would not come directly from the United States. Second, the United States needed to guarantee not to stage a nuclear attack against North Korea, in other words, to give a negative security pledge. Kim insisted that the other outstanding nuclear issues could be resolved at the third round of U.S.–DPRK talks. Kim Il Sung received Carter's assurance that there were no nuclear weapons in South Korea or tactical weapons in the waters surrounding the Korean peninsula, and that the U.S. intention was to see North Korea acquire light-water reactors. In return for U.S. cooperation, Kim Il Sung agreed to freeze North Korea's nuclear program and consider a permanent freeze if its aged reactors were replaced with safer, modern ones. Both men agreed that the Korean Peninsula should be made nuclear-free.

Carter called the White House from Pyongyang on an open line to report on the apparent agreement with the North Korean leader. Carter reported that Pyongyang was now willing not to expel international inspectors as long as "good faith efforts" were made to resolve the dispute. After a discussion with National Security Advisor Anthony Lake, on June 17, Carter announced in Pyongyang that the Clinton administration was now "ready to suspend the UN sanctions effort." Washington also "provisionally agreed" to a third round of high-level talks with Pyongyang to discuss the light-water reactor requested by North Korea. Although the United States and North Korea appeared to have reached an unofficial agreement, President Clinton continued to maintain the official U.S. position by pursuing UN sanctions against North Korea until North Korea's response could be officially verified.[14]

Impact of Carter's Role as Mediator

One of the most significant roles Carter played on his Pyongyang mission was to mediate between South and North Korea. Upon his return to Seoul on June 18, Carter conveyed a message from Kim Il Sung to South Korean President Kim Young Sam. Carter relayed the message that the North Korean leader was willing to meet the South Korean president "anywhere, at any time and without any conditions."[15] The proposal was virtually identical to what Kim Young Sam had already proposed during his presidential campaign in 1992. Consequently, South Korean President Kim accepted the proposal immediately. Preliminary talks were held in Panmunjom regarding the details of the proposed Korean summit. On June 28, the two sides sent delegates of deputy prime minister rank who agreed on the details of the first summit.

Relations between the two Koreas seemed to improve overnight, and the crisis appeared to be close to resolution. On June 21, North Korea extended the visas of two IAEA nuclear inspectors, allowing them to continue monitoring the refueling of its reactor as a gesture of good faith. The following day, the Clinton administration announced that the third U.S.–DPRK high-level talks would be held in Geneva on July 8, 1994.

The Carter mission succeeded in giving North Korea a way to save face. By altering its hard-line position on the nuclear issue, North Korea avoided a UN Security Council resolution imposing economic sanctions. Carter's success stemmed from his ability to maintain his own credibility in both the United States and in North Korea. Kim Il Sung did not perceive that Carter was an emissary of Clinton, especially in light of the divergence in opinion between Carter and Clinton over the efficacy of sanctions. Carter's visit also indicated to the DPRK that Seoul's ties with the United States would play a lesser role in American decisions, thus satisfying a North Korean strategic objective.[16]

The Third Round of U.S.–DPRK Talks

Carter's mission to Pyongyang was a success and opened the way for a third round of official talks. President Clinton praised the private mission: "President Carter was very faithful in articulating the policy of our government ... He provided a forum for Kim Il Sung to respond the way he did."[17] The third round of U.S.–DPRK high-level talks succeeded in producing agreements that served as the benchmark for subsequent U.S.–DPRK negotiations. The third round of talks began on July 8, 1994, were suspended on July 9 due to the death of Kim Il Sung, and resumed on August 5. By August 13, a major agreement was produced on steps to ease nuclear tensions and on establishing liaison offices in each country's capital. A four-point joint statement was also issued reaffirming the principles of the second round talks.

North Korea and the United States agreed that additional discussions were necessary to work out details concerning the replacement of North Korea's graphite-moderated reactor program with LWR technology, safely storing and disposing of the spent fuel, providing alternative energy, and establishing liaison offices. Accordingly, both sides agreed to expert-level talks to be held in Pyongyang and in Berlin.

The third round of talks recessed on August 13 and continued from September 23 through October 17, 1994, in Geneva. These talks continued the process of finalizing and drawing up plans to implement the four-point agreement reached in August. On October 21, 1994, both sides signed the "Agreed Framework between the United States and the Democratic People's Republic of Korea" (Geneva Agreed Framework). The agreement proved that both parties would:

> cooperate to replace the DPRK's graphite-moderated reactors and related facilities with light-water reactor (LWR) power plants ... move toward full normalization of political and economic relations ... work together for peace and security on a nuclear-free Korean Peninsula ... [and] work together to strengthen the international nuclear nonproliferation regime.[18]

For its part, the United States agreed to "make arrangements for the provision to the DPRK of a LWR project with a total generating capacity of approximately 2,000 MWe by a target date of 2003."[19] In addition, the United States agreed to organize under its leadership an international consortium to finance and supply the LWR project to be provided to the DPRK. The United States also agreed to "make arrangements to offset the energy foregone due to the freeze of the DPRK's graphite-moderated reactors and related facilities, pending completion of the first LWR unit," and to provide the DPRK during the interim with an annual supply of 500,000 tons of heavy oil for heating and electricity production purposes.[20]

In return, the DRPK agreed to freeze its graphite-moderated reactors and related facilities within a month of signing the Agreed Framework and to allow the IAEA to monitor the freeze. North Korea also agreed to dismantle its graphite-moderated reactors, but only on the completion of the LWR project. The DPRK agreed to cooperate with the United States to find a safe way to dispose of the spent fuel from the 5 MWe electric experimental reactor.[21]

Form and Specific Mechanisms of Intervention

Choice of Parties

The fact that the two principal states in this negotiating process were North Korea and the United States is somewhat peculiar, given that North Korea's nuclear development threatens South Korea most directly. For the two nations still officially at war, North Korea's development of nuclear weapons legitimately threatens

South Korea with annihilation. Why, then, was the United States negotiating with North Korea? Obviously, the United States had an interest in protecting the roughly 80,000 American troops and civilians in South Korea, but why did South Korea cede leadership in the negotiations to the United States? The answer to this question lies in North Korea's interests in negotiating directly with the United States.

In insisting on direct dialogue with the United States, North Korea was able to achieve two policy objectives at once. By dealing directly only with the United States, the DPRK was able to continue its policy of not recognizing South Korea as a sovereign nation. Furthermore, the DPRK realized that the United States was the only party capable of effectively enlarging the scope of the negotiations from issues about complying with IAEA compliance requests to normalization of U.S. and DPRK relations. Institutionally, the IAEA is incapable of enlarging the scope of discussions to such a broad extent, and in North Korea's view, the IAEA was too biased against the DPRK to act fairly, anyway.[22]

Role of International Organizations

The United States and South Korea originally sought to respond to North Korea through the United Nations and the IAEA, which were the parties legally related to the matter. However, the lack of North Korean response to the IAEA and the United Nations, coupled with hints by the DPRK that a solution could be found through bilateral U.S.–DPRK talks, finally persuaded the United States to consider a direct dialogue with North Korea.

The UN Security Council, in recognition of the delicacy of the situation in May 1993, passed a resolution 13–0 urging North Korea to reconsider its decision to withdraw from the NPT and comply with IAEA requests, instead of urging sanctions as originally planned. The resolution also provided the political justification for the United States to respond to North Korea's request for high-level talks. The resolution specifically stated that all member states were encouraged to urge North Korea to respond positively to the resolution, a suggestion that the United States acted upon in initiating the second round of high-level talks with North Korea.[23]

In addition to providing a diplomatic way for the United States to negotiate with North Korea, the United Nations provided an important multilateral forum throughout the process. North Korea could witness the international condemnation of their actions and felt the threat of UN-sponsored economic sanctions. Discussion in the United Nations defined the severity of the issue and priorities of the major actors and maintained pressure while bilateral talks continued.

The ability of the United Nations to enforce sanctions proved especially important in light of the IAEA's lack of enforcement powers. The IAEA is well suited to monitoring member states' obligations under the Model Safeguards Treaty, but the IAEA's institutional focus and ability to compel adherence is limited. The IAEA has broad investigative powers, but when the DPRK refused to allow IAEA inspectors access to suspected nuclear facilities, the IAEA resorted to requesting the United Nations to threaten sanctions.[24]

Both the IAEA and the United Nations, unlike the United States, simply did not have the authority to enlarge the scope of the negotiations. Without the authority to offer an expanded scope of discussion, both the IAEA and the United Nations were ill suited to act as principal negotiators in this dispute. Both could, however, condemn North Korea for failing to comply with its obligations, and they did just that by threatening sanctions without the rewards North Korea was seeking.

Multilateral versus Bilateral Approaches

The nuclear crisis was ultimately defused through bilateral negotiations. The advantages of a bilateral approach in this context reveal the complexities of regional interests. Most importantly, there may have been no alternative other than to pursue the negotiations through a bilateral framework, because North Korea insisted on dealing primarily with the United States. Asking whether a multilateral or bilateral approach would be more successful in this context implies that the parties have a choice. However, when one party refuses to negotiate in a multilateral setting, the other party will have little choice but to negotiate bilaterally.

Both multilateral and bilateral forums have distinct advantages and disadvantages. Multilateral forums like the Association of Southeast Asian Nations Regional Forum (ARF) or the Council for Security Cooperation in the Asia-Pacific Region (CSCAP) have the potential to promote long-term peace and stability in Northeast Asia. Multilateral forums provide a setting in which parties unwilling to meet in a bilateral context can communicate their views. They are instrumental in confidence-building measures, which help build relationships and lead to transformation in threat perceptions.[25] While multilateral forums are useful for discussing potential problems, the fact that most require agreement by consensus can make them less effective for agreement on a particular plan of action or for carrying out the plan decisively. It should also be noted that multilateral forums always involve bilateral negotiations on the sidelines.

A bilateral framework offers the advantage of pure decisive agreement. Some commentators believe bilateral arrangements are the most effective method to deal with the current conflicts on the Korean peninsula.[26] However, bilateral arrangements must be combined with multilateral diplomacy or meetings to give parties not involved in the bilateral arrangements an opportunity to participate. The continued improvement of bilateral relationships is important to facilitate the development of a cooperative security regime and may be pursued in the context of multilateral forums.

The DPRK talks can be viewed as a necessary component of a larger multilateral negotiation that necessarily includes the ROK and probably Japan and China, as well. For future talks to succeed, a bilateral framework between the United States and DPRK may well be the best approach in light of the parties' objectives; but for long-term stability in the region, these bilateral approaches must expand to include North Korea's neighbors in a multilateral approach.

Key Factors in Shaping the Result

Role of International Law

The Nuclear Non-Proliferation Treaty's imminent revision in 1995 raised additional concerns for the United States. According to Article 10, Section 2 of the NPT, "Twenty-five years after the entry into force of the Treaty, a conference shall be convened to decide whether the Treaty shall continue in force indefinitely, or shall be extended for an additional fixed period or periods. This decision shall be taken by a majority of the Parties of the Treaty."[27] Since the treaty entered into force in 1970, 1995 was the year of this conference. With the NPT's imminent revision, the United States was concerned that North Korea's withdrawal from the NPT might undermine the structure for the entire international nuclear nonproliferation regime.

North Korea judged that the United States had a strong interest in preventing nuclear proliferation and that it would attempt to persuade North Korea to remain a member of the NPT. The primary interest of the United States was to prevent the DPRK from obtaining nuclear weapons, ideally through the extension of the NPT. North Korea had almost no power to prevent the extension of the treaty within its legal framework. As a diplomatic tactic, Pyongyang used its political position on nuclear nonproliferation as a bargaining chip with the United States on a host of security and political issues. The largest bargaining chip was North Korea's capability to destroy Seoul.

Role of Rewards and Sanctions

The international community explored the policy of offering rewards and economic sanctions in its attempt to urge North Korea to submit to IAEA demands. Questions have arisen as to whether economic sanctions were worth pursuing in this situation, given that significant economic sanctions were already in place. To answer this question, we must examine the potential effect of economic sanctions on North Korea.

The North Korean economy is shaped by the concept of self-reliance, or *juche*. Since Albania recently reopened its economy, North Korea has become the most isolated economy in the world.[28] This economic philosophy has resulted in serious food and fuel shortages, to the point that North Korea is unable to meet its basic needs. The North Korean economy has few trading partners, the largest of which is China.

The unique circumstances of the North Korean economy present several dilemmas in the decision to apply sanctions. North Korea imports only what it absolutely needs to keep its economy functioning. This simultaneously limits the scope and volume of potential leverage and means that any sanctions would probably affect key industries. Sanctions could have had a devastating effect, causing the collapse of the economy and, potentially, a military response. The ultimate success of sanctions against North Korea is dependent not only on North Korea's ability to function with sanctions, but on the primary reasons for

North Korea's development of nuclear weapons.[29] Pyongyang's willingness to sign the Geneva Agreement might shed light on the primary reasons for its development of nuclear weapons. If North Korean leaders thought that the development of nuclear weapons was essential to the nation's survival, any sanctions might have triggered a military response. On the other hand, if North Korea was using its nuclear program as a bargaining chip, then the threat of sanctions might have been instrumental in achieving the Geneva Agreement.

Role and Interests of the United States

The United States has a number of strong interests in preventing North Korea from developing nuclear weapons. Not the least of these interests is the fear that any North Korean conflict evolving into a conventional war on the Korean peninsula would force the United States to send troops as part of its treaty obligations to South Korea.

North Korean nuclear weapons development would threaten the entire regional and, to a lesser extent, international nonproliferation regime.[30] The balance of power would be altered in the region, directly threatening Japan and South Korea, America's strongest allies in the region. If North Korea were to withdraw from the NPT, a precedent would be set that might eventually undermine the entire nonproliferation regime. Furthermore, without North Korea's membership in the NPT, efforts to block North Korea's nuclear weapons program would be virtually impossible, opening the way for North Korea to make and sell nuclear technology and weapons to nuclear aspirants like Iran, Iraq, and Libya.[31] The United States faced the daunting prospect of trying to stop a sovereign state already dangerously isolated from most international circles from developing nuclear weapons or assisting other nations in developing them.[32] Realistically, Americans had few alternatives to negotiating with North Korea, because the prospect of a second Korean War was politically impractical: a substantial portion of South Korea's population and approximately 80,000 U.S. citizens live within range of North Korea's rockets and artillery.

The American strategy may be characterized as an example of the carrot and stick approach. As part of its strategy, the United States used the stick of UN sanctions to apply pressure on North Korea to conform to its demands and those of the UN Security Council and the IAEA. The United States also attempted to demonstrate American willingness to use force if necessary, by sending additional reinforcements to South Korea and by commencing joint U.S.–South Korean military exercises. Whether or not the stick approach was effective is debatable. The final Geneva Agreements provisions giving North Korea $4–5 billion worth of economic aid may suggest that, in fact, the carrot approach was more influential in resolving this crisis.

The turning point of the crisis was Carter's mission to Pyongyang. From the Clinton administration's perspective, Carter succeeded in extracting a significant concession from North Korea, thus sowing the seeds of a compromise settlement, when the DPRK hinted that it would trade away its reprocessing plant and put its construction program for 50 and 200 MWe plutonium production reactors on hold if conditions were appropriate. The fact that these two issues were now open for discussion indicated to the U.S. negotiator that the DPRK was putting all its cards on the table. From the American perspective, the main issue then that needed to be settled was the restoration of full-scope safeguards. The Clinton administration sought to move quickly to make the best of this window of opportunity.

After Carter's mediation, North Korean and American interests seemed to converge. U.S. interests lay in stopping North Korea's extraction of plutonium by reprocessing spent fuel. The DPRK had a series of demands on its shopping list, including: a negative security guarantee from the United States, a U.S. guarantee that North Korea could acquire light-water technology, a U.S. guarantee that North Korea's fuel needs would be met in the interim period until the light-water reactors were put into operation, removing existing economic sanctions and preventing new ones, and reestablishing a better long-term relationship with the United States, leading to eventual normalization of U.S.–DPRK diplomatic ties. These were all substantive demands by North Korea that, if fully met, would give the North tangible benefits and rewards for having played the nuclear card with skill and tact.

The U.S. strategy was to pressure and persuade North Korea to abandon its nuclear ambitions by modifying its program away from the development of weaponry and toward the peaceful use of atomic energy. To achieve this objective, the U.S. position all along had been to involve the IAEA in the process of verifying the present and past history of Pyongyang's nuclear program.

Role and Interests of North Korea

North Korea's primary goals were to conduct direct talks with the United States and to strike a package deal on a host of issues as preconditions for resolving the nuclear issue. This strategy also allowed North Korea to temporarily bypass both South Korea and the IAEA on nuclear issues. North Korea demonstrated skilful use of brinkmanship tactics throughout the negotiation process with the United States. DPRK strategy included a variety of techniques such as stalling inspections, neutralizing whatever inspections it agreed to, driving its opponent to the brink of armed conflict, and demanding changes in its prior agreements before backing down.[33]

Role and Interests of South Korea

Despite anger at the United States for being left out of the U.S.–DPRK negotiations, South Korea finally accepted negotiating its position through the United States, since the two allies shared similar views with regard to most issues. Nevertheless, there were a number of instances in which the views of the two allies diverged. Seoul complained that Washington was too conciliatory toward North Korea, having given in to demands in the first and second round of talks without obtaining much in return.[34] This position changed as the threat of war increased in 1994. Seoul encouraged the exploration of all options before requesting UN sanctions. Seoul now felt that a hard-line approach would only exacerbate tensions, realizing that it might be drawn into a war against its will.

Success of the Mediation

The culmination of these three rounds of negotiations is the Agreed Framework between the United States of America and the Democratic People's Republic of Korea. The agreement is, technically, neither a treaty nor an executive agreement. Nevertheless, the agreement serves as the basis for the future of nonproliferation in North Korea. The four elements of the agreement constitute an integral part of the final resolution of the nuclear issue.

First, the DPRK promised "to replace its graphite-moderated reactors and related facilities with light-water reactor (LWR) power plants," and the United States was prepared to make arrangements for the provision of LWRs of approximately 2,000 MWe to North Korea as early as possible and to make arrangements for interim energy alternatives. In return, the DPRK would then "freeze construction of the 50 MWe and 200 MWe reactors, forgo processing, and seal the radiochemical laboratory, to be monitored by the IAEA."

Second, the United States and the DPRK were prepared "to establish diplomatic representation in each other's capital and to reduce barriers to trade and investment, as a move toward full normalization of political and economic relations."

Third, to help achieve peace and security on a nuclear-free Korean Peninsula, the United States was prepared "to provide the DPRK with assurances against the threat or use of nuclear weapons by the United States," and the DPRK remained prepared "to implement the North–South Joint Declaration on the Denuclearization of the Korean Peninsula."

Fourth, the DPRK was prepared "to remain a party to the Treaty on the Non-Proliferation of Nuclear Weapons and to allow implementation of its safeguards agreement under the Treaty." The agreement requires a nongovernmental, independent agency to implement its provisions, the Korean Peninsula Energy Development Organization, or KEDO.

Implementing the Geneva Agreed Framework has been a precarious process since the agreement's first year of existence. Part of the agreement requires the United States to oversee the delivery of two 1000 MWe light-water reactors. The type of reactor to be supplied, however, was left ambiguous. Ambassador Gallucci insisted that the only financially, technically and politically feasible option was for South Korea to provide the reactor, but North Korea refused to accept a reactor from its enemy. After several months of discussion, a compromise was reached by the creation of KEDO, allowing South Korea to provide a light-water reactor based on an original U.S. design.[35]

The most critical challenge facing successful implementation of the agreement lies not with the technical, but with domestic challenges to the agreement in the United States and South Korea. The South Korean government faces popular ambivalence toward the agreement and its implementation. For the agreement to succeed, Seoul needs to maintain popular support. Maintaining popular support will be difficult in light of the recent economic turmoil in South Korea. The unexpected financial crisis raises the critical issue of whether South Korea can keep its part of the bargain in funding 70 percent of the construction costs of the new reactors.[36]

Robert Gallucci, now dean of the Georgetown School of Foreign Service, identifies three major concerns over the successful implementation of the agreement. The most serious concern is the stability of the North Korean government. If the government starts to crumble from economic stress or internal politics or if it feels compelled to commence a military campaign, the Agreed Framework may be ignored. The second major concern is the continued stress between North and South Korea. If an incident causes political controversy, then South Korea may not be able to muster the political support necessary to supply its portion of the $4–5 billion bill for the North Korean light-water reactors. Gallucci identifies the final major vulnerability of the treaty as the ongoing provision of heavy fuel. KEDO has had difficulty in collecting the roughly $50 million it needs to provide heavy fuel to the North Koreans until the light-water reactors are operational. Recent bickering among the funding countries threatens the entire agreement.[37] The United States contributes about $20 million, but collecting from South Korea and Japan has been difficult, since they are already contributing the $4–5 billion for the reactor despite their respective financial worries.[38]

Success is a matter of perspective. In this chapter, the successes of the negotiations are considered from the American perspective, a perspective that includes the larger question of success in nonproliferation. The Americans had four primary interests in the talks with the North Koreans. The first and foremost goal was to stop the DPRK's nuclear program. Second, the United States sought to prevent North Korea from leaving the NPT. Third, the United States wanted to bring North Korea to accept full-scope safeguards including special inspections. The fourth goal was to create an atmosphere that would make North Korea deal directly with South Korea in the future.

According to these standards, the United States was only marginally successful. The DPRK's nuclear program has been suspended, at least for the time being; North Korea remains a member of the NPT; North Korea has allowed some inspections; but North Korea has not dealt on a more open or consistent basis with South Korea. Four years passed before North Korea finally met with South Korea, and little, if any, substantive progress has been made.[39] At most, the two sides have agreed on allowing family reunions.[40] Success is far from complete. North Korea still refuses to allow special inspections, and although it has more dealings with South Korea, it still prefers not to interact. For now, North Korea's nuclear aspirations seem limited to the process of obtaining newer nuclear power plants.

Critics have charged that the United States may have been successful in some regards in slowing down or halting North Korea's nuclear aspirations but that the cost of success has been too high. In addition to the expense, critics maintain that the agreement with North Korea has set a dangerous precedent for nuclear blackmail. Nuclear aspirants can threaten the United States and other nations with continued development of nuclear weapons unless their demands are met. Republicans in Congress have expressed these concerns and have threatened to scuttle the agreement with North Korea and to deny funding for the agreement.[41] So far these efforts have been unsuccessful, but future congressional dissatisfaction may threaten the agreement.

Conclusion

The North Korean experience demonstrates the need for open lines of communication. Carter's unique role as mediator served to bring the parties back to the negotiating table. The importance of his role as a neutral and respected mediator with a genuine interest in seeing a resolution to the crisis gave him legitimacy and offered a way in which both sides could maintain their national pride without stubbornly sticking to their positions. His success lends credence to the belief that informal diplomacy may be instrumental to official diplomacy if the informal diplomat has great prestige and the respect of the parties involved. Carter's position in this crisis is unique, and one certainly cannot expect that an avenue such as that opened by his mediation will exist in every conflict. Nevertheless, his success indicates that an unbiased third party may contribute to dispute resolution and that second-track diplomacy can play a useful role in some conflicts.

The ultimate success of the agreement has yet to be seen. The threat of sanctions and their real effect, in combination with the offer of advanced nuclear technology and a better relationship with the United States, helped to persuade North Korea to compromise. The United States, faced with the real threat of either nuclear proliferation or a regional war, had more than its share of incentives to find a middle ground. The strong incentives of the nations to come to an agreement facilitated the process of conflict resolution. However, coming to an agreement is not the same as implementing one. Whether or not the parties to the agreement will be able to carry through its provisions will depend on whether they will continue to keep open lines of communication and the spirit of resolution.

Part Four

Conclusion

13

Lessons of the Case Studies

John H. Barton and Melanie C. Greenberg

THE CARNEGIE COMMISSION on Preventing Deadly Conflict supported the case studies published in this book on mediation and arbitration in contemporary deadly conflict in order to help define improvements in the world's international mediation and arbitration system. The studies were prepared by political science graduate students and law students from Stanford University's Center for International Security and Cooperation or Stanford Law School and were based in part on interviews with participants in the specific negotiations. This chapter attempts to summarize and integrate the implications of those case studies.

This chapter's judgments are at best statements of tendencies. Stronger statements are almost impossible. The actors in international relations often adjust their strategies in light of their understanding of how other actors are behaving. Moreover, there are always external factors that may control generalizations. Each case took place within the context of an elaborate matrix of negotiations and multiparty relationships; key discussions and breakthroughs in particular mediations frequently result from factors external to the actual mediation forum. But most of all, the case studies show peacemakers working creatively in the face of great odds.

Nevertheless, the examples provide substantial insight into the mediation process; some of these insights were quite surprising to the participants in the project, others matched our expectations. The most important are:

(1) Almost all the recent conflicts involve issues that during the Cold War would have been regarded as purely internal matters in which the participation of the international community would not have been welcome.

(2) A mediator's efforts through the use of positive or negative leverage such as incentives and sanctions, including military force to impose an agreement on the parties, generally work only in the short-term and do not lend themselves well to durable agreements and long-term reconciliation.

(3) The United Nations played an important role in most of the cases studied, by providing the mediator, the forum, or implementing institutions necessary to the mediation effort, and has generally been far more successful than regional organizations in bringing resolution to protracted conflicts.

(4) The value added by the mediator was usually procedural rather than substantive, and the mediator's most important contribution was frequently to provide a procedural or substantive framework within which negotiations could take place. Thus, the impartiality of the mediator was the characteristic most prized by the parties to the conflict.

(5) The international law norms of sovereignty and self-determination can be mutually exclusive and are often bluntly defined; they frequently created a primary barrier to achieving agreement.

(6) Although multiple channels of negotiation and shuttle diplomacy are useful and frequently required, face-to-face discussions between the actual parties—and the accompanying human interplay—almost always proved essential to an ultimately successful negotiation.

(7) In the postconflict phase, institutions that are able to fill in details and assist in the ongoing implementation of agreements are essential. Effective mechanisms and institutions have already been created for arranging and maintaining elections; models are also emerging to handle integration of military forces; institutions that can more effectively deal with amnesty and refugee questions need further development.

(8) The international development banks should explore the development of new international law mechanisms to shape their posture in relation to environmental and natural resource conflicts.

(9) International law institutions should be strengthened and better equipped to deal with minority issues and the building or strengthening of civil society in the postconflict phase.

The Character of the Conflicts Analyzed

The character of the conflicts examined reflects choices made at the beginning of the study and therefore, to some extent, reflects the judgments of the authors as much as the reality of the world. Nevertheless, the cases were chosen to represent the universe of actual conflicts—and there are surprises.

Most tellingly, as indicated in chart 13.1, all but one conflict, the Beagle Channel dispute, and perhaps a second, the Aral Sea Basin crisis, would have been re-

Chart 13.1: The Disputes and Their Subjects

Abkhazia	Independence/autonomy of a portion of a newly independent state
Aral Sea Basin	Avoidance of tensions over environmental and water allocations issues associated with a network of river systems that had become international because of breakup of Soviet Union
Beagle Channel	Border drawing in expanded oceanic exclusive economic zone
Bosnia	Creation of new nation in breakup of Yugoslavia
Cambodia	Constitutional reorganization to accommodate a variety of political movements
Croatia	Creation of new nation with the breakup of Yugoslavia
El Salvador	Termination of guerrilla war
Korea	Compliance with international concerns respecting status of nuclear materials and nuclear nonproliferation treaty
Northern Ireland	Resolution of religious conflict involving desire of one side to transfer sovereignty over region
Rwanda	Intended termination of civil war
South Africa	Constitutional revision to expand political rights to previously disenfranchised majority
West Bank/Occupied Territories	Political autonomy for community in occupied region

garded until recently as a matter of domestic sovereignty—with the frequent overlay of "invited" participation of larger powers—rather than a matter of international politics. (The West Bank is perhaps the "exception that proves the rule" since the dispute predated the establishment of Israeli sovereignty; the declaration of the state of Israel, in a sense ensured that the dispute would remain of interest to the international community.) And only one other, the North Korean nuclear crisis, dealt with weapons of magnitude great enough to affect more than a local balance of power. In short, the agenda has radically changed.

One important group of conflicts found in the new intermedial order arose out of the breakup of multinational states such as the Soviet Union or Yugoslavia. These typically involve questions of legitimacy of the secession of one entity from another and are exemplified by Abkhazia, Bosnia, and Croatia. Similarly (under one legal interpretation), the West Bank dispute derives from the demand for political autonomy in the context of an existing sovereign government with de facto territorial control. A slightly larger number of conflicts involve efforts to integrate conflicting participants into a single community; these conflicts derive from a much wider variety of political, socioeconomic, religious, ethnic, and historical causes and include Cambodia, El Salvador, Northern Ireland, Rwanda, and South Africa. The problems of collapse of empire, and concomitant withdrawal of superpower military, political, and economic support, may be characteristic of the immediate post–Cold War period only. Issues of justice; of oppressed socioeconomic, religious, and ethnic groups; and of the collapse of a developing nation (as in Cambodia and Rwanda) may, however, be paradigms of future deadly conflict. Long-term post–Cold War institutions should be designed to handle the prevention and resolution of these more complex disputes.

Finally, the dispute over Central Asian water exemplifies a different type of conflict that can be expected to proliferate in the future. Although the particular example was a direct result of the breakup of the Soviet Union, the likelihood of conflict over water and other scarce natural resources is on the rise. Future conflict resolution mechanisms should also be designed to handle the unique multiparty nature of resource disputes.

Circumstances Leading to Successful Mediation

These cases offer some basis for evaluating the factors that shape the ripeness or readiness of a conflict for negotiation. Certainly, the most important factor, and one that often underlies other incentives to resolution, is war-weariness—a sense that a conflict has lasted too long and inflicted too much damage, that some form of stalemate is the most likely outcome of even significantly greater efforts to pursue the conflict. When both sides reach the same conclusion, the war enters the stage William Zartman calls a "mutually hurting stalemate."[1] Here, the paradigms are Cambodia and El Salvador. In each, war had been bloody and bitter, and continued conflict appeared unlikely to lead to a better outcome—for any party. In each, the end of the Cold War also brought decisive changes in external factors (in particular, the likelihood of continued military assistance from outside sponsor-states) that intensified the risk of stalemate and the problems of continuing conflict. And, in the case of the Beagle Channel, Argentina's war-weariness from the disastrous Malvinas/Falklands war with the United Kingdom made resolution of conflict with Chile easier.

Specific dramatic events can attract international attention to the conflict and are frequently the catalyst to creating a window for negotiation. The slaying of the Jesuit priests and the mixed success and failure of the FMLN's 1989 offensive created ripeness in El Salvador. By greatly increasing the political and military costs of Israeli occupation of the West Bank, the *Intifada* helped bring both Israel and the PLO back to the bargaining table. The bombing of the market place in Sarajevo and the atrocities at Srebrenica in the summer of 1995 created a sense of moral outrage that added momentum to the mediation efforts.

Changes in government may also signal opportunities in mediation. The new government may be elected on a platform that supports negotiated peace, as in the cases of the Cristiani government in El Salvador or the Rabin government in

Israel. It may also emerge because the previous government was discredited, as in the cases of the military juntas in Argentina following the Malvinas/Falklands war. Further, a new government may have a stronger mandate and firmer control of its own faction, thus lending it greater bargaining flexibility than the prior government, as exemplified by Prime Minister Tony Blair's flexibility to negotiate in Northern Ireland, where John Major had been all but paralyzed by the rifts within his own party, or by the civilian government of Argentina that took power in 1983 following the Malvinas/Falklands war. Conversely, the imminent threat of loss of political power helped bring the PLO to the table, because it offered a legitimating function. Of course, all these factors can affect outside supporting governments as well as internal client groups; the dissolution of the Soviet Union and the emergence of democratic institutions in Russia combined with fatigue with the Cold War made outside forces more willing and able to support or encourage settlements in El Salvador and Cambodia.

As shown in chart 13.2, the evidence is mixed as to the ability of outside entities to achieve a successful resolution through use of positive leverage such as financial assistance, or negative leverage such as direct threats and sanctions, to bring otherwise unwilling parties to the table. Factors to consider include the nature of the leverage (carrots versus sticks), the nature of the mediator or power seeking to use the leverage (the United States, for example, has a larger toolbox of incentives and threats than the Organization of American States, OAS), and the timing of the intervention before, during, or after the "hot" war. A larger question remains as to whether an outside power can ever impose, via mediation, a lasting solution on parties who—absent the intervention—are not yet ready to settle. It is also important to note that in cases in which outside pressure does work, relatively inexorable outside pressures, e.g., that of the IAEA in Korea and of the loss of Soviet assistance in El Salvador, appear more effective than the use of more deliberately orchestrated bargaining chips, e.g., Vance's "take it or leave it" approach to the last UN–EU peace proposal in Bosnia.

Positive leverage seems more helpful than sanctions, but it is difficult to draw a definite conclusion about whether or not financial incentives or other forms of positive leverage constitute the *sine qua non* of a successful negotiated outcome. In North Korea, economic assistance in the form of new nuclear reactors and oil shipments was certainly an incentive to settle the issue of the nuclear weapons threat. In conjunction with negative incentives such as the threat of embargo and sanctions based on the IAEA regime, the positive incentives seemed to play a major role in the final mediated agreement.

In the Aral Sea Basin conflict, the World Bank held great leverage in the form of financial assistance and used it very effectively to encourage the new sovereign powers to reach agreement on regional water use. The example is encouraging, especially because the regional cooperation on water issues could lead to improved cooperation on larger political issues as well. It should be noted that this conflict had not reached the stage of violence, and thus might have been more amenable to outside intervention and leverage. Furthermore, because of the dire financial straits in which the countries found themselves after the

Chart 13.2: Intervention and Success

CASE	FORMS OF PRESSURE	SUCCESS
Abkhazia	Russian embargo	Limited
Aral Sea Basin	Opportunity to obtain funding	Moderate
Beagle Channel	Essentially none	Great (in case of papal mediation, not in case of arbitration)
Bosnia	Substantial—elaborate UN activity	Limited
Cambodia	Plans for UN activity; political leverage in national parties by their sponsors	Limited
Croatia	Elaborate ongoing UN and EU activity	Moderate
El Salvador	Substantial, but primarily as based on the realities of new geopolitical world	Substantial
Korea	Threats of IAEA/UN sanctions; promises of financial/nuclear assistance	Substantial
Northern Ireland	Public relations efforts	Modest
Rwanda	Military assistance, possibility of manipulating foreign assistance	Much initially, but it fell apart
South Africa	Embargo, education, creation of civil society	Great
West Bank	Limited during negotiations, but part of an elaborate process including great outside intervention	Moderate

breakup of the Soviet Union, they were particularly amenable and willing to work for the prospect of economic assistance.

Moral and political encouragement can often play an important, if subtle, role in helping parties agree to mediate and stay at the table. President Clinton's visit to Northern Ireland, his obvious personal interest in the conflict, and his granting of a visa to Gerry Adams at a key moment during the talks played an important role—at very little domestic cost to Clinton—in keeping momentum going. In the Beagle Channel dispute, the Pope's tremendous moral authority kept the parties at the table.

An additional form of effective outside intervention is long-term encouragement and the construction of civilian institutions. As suggested by the South African and Central Asian examples, the international community can help in the long run by strengthening civil society and encouraging the creation of institutions for routine discussion of issues likely to lead to conflict. If human rights institutions and mechanisms to address the allocation and use of natural resources are put in place early enough, conflicts may be averted at an early, nonviolent phase. Since we might expect justice-based disputes (such as minority rights) and natural resource conflicts to increase in the coming years, the establishment of civil institutions to deal with them seems a wise investment of resources.

Negative incentives such as financial sanctions, embargoes, and threats of military force seem less effective to the long-term resolution of a dispute but can help bring about cease-fires between parties unwilling to negotiate with one another. In Bosnia, short-term negative incentives were very important in stopping the fighting and priming the parties to negotiate, even unwillingly. The trade sanctions and embargoes against the rump Yugoslavia weakened the economy sufficiently enough to bring Slobodan Milosevic to the bargaining table. NATO bombing of Bosnian Serb targets helped bring an end to the fighting on the ground. The United States was powerful enough in its own right to negotiate a peace among three unwilling parties, and to back up that peace with military troops. However, the agreement that the United States negotiated only provided a framework for peace; it did not resolve the underlying problem of trying to preserve a multiethnic Bosnia: hard-line nationalist leaders still won in the post-Dayton elections; refugees have not returned to their homes; the institutions designed to promote multicultural civil society have not emerged; and several prominent indicted war criminals remain at large. The combined presence of IFOR troops is still required to ensure that tensions do not erupt into conflict.

In the Israeli–Palestinian conflict, the United States has the leverage and unique ability to bring the two sides together to live up to the obligation and timelines created by the Oslo Accords, as evidenced by the 1998 Wye Plantation talks. It cannot control the internal politics of both parties sufficiently to produce peace. No amount of financial assistance or threat of sanctions is likely to change the level of U.S. influence on these internal dynamics—the parties themselves must turn the corner to embrace a lasting peace. Similarly, outside powers were able to resolve the conflict in the short term in Cambodia, and peacekeeping forces were able to enforce the agreement, but in part because key parties disagreed with the terms of the agreement, the society remains deeply divided and unready to enter the crucial phase of power sharing and democracy building.

But the mere fact that leverage is imperfect or only partly effective does not mean that the international community should avoid intervention. The Arusha Accords in Rwanda provide a good example of the effects of the near-total abdication of international leverage. Although counterfactual analysis is difficult, there is some evidence that had the international community been more willing to police the implementation period, and to exert positive and negative pressure on the Habyarimana government and extremist groups to honor the agreement, genocide might have been averted. This was the essence of President Clinton's "apology" during his visit to Rwanda in 1998—the international community could and should have done more.

Timing is important for the effectiveness of leverage. There may be a period when the situation has deteriorated so much that the international community cannot intervene in a preventive mode, but where the situation is also not yet ready for mediation. Under these circumstances, there may be little the international community can do to mediate the conflict or to hasten its ripeness for mediation. If the international community attempts to intervene too early, its efforts may be unsuccessful. Even if supported by significant leverage, a premature intervention does not succeed in resolving the conflict or shifting its politics, but simply affects the manner in which military conflict continues. The actual outcome of the Arusha negotiations is an example—with devastating results. As noted below, it may sometimes still be better to attempt intervention; moreover, it may be possible and useful to intervene in other than a mediatory mode.

Choice of Mediators

In none of the cases does there appear to have been difficulties in finding a mediator. The UN Security Council and the secretary-general have played major roles. Indeed, as shown in chart 13.3, the United Nations was closely involved as a mediating body in eight out of twelve cases. The exceptions were Northern Ireland, South Africa (in which the mediation was internal), the Beagle Channel (in which it was conducted under the auspices of the Vatican), and the Aral Sea Basin (in which the World Bank took the leading role). Our global procedural mechanisms for encouraging mediation are more effective than we might have expected.

One of the surprises is that regional entities played little or no role in most of the disputes, though in several cases they played a role in earlier, failed negotiations, as in Rwanda and El Salvador. In the El Salvador case, the fact that the OAS excluded Cuba while the United Nations included both the United States and the Soviet Union was important in the parties' choice of the United Nations as a mediating body. Similarly, the regional European organizations were ineffective in bringing about cease-fires in Bosnia and Croatia, largely because of their inability to coordinate action on basic questions such as the recognition of the sovereignty of the seceding states and the lack of a cohesive European military intervention strategy. In all four of those cases, regional political, economic, and military institutions played a role in the late implementation of the mediated settlement.

However, regional organizations played an important role in three of the cases. In Abkhazia, the Commonwealth of Independent States (CIS; with Russia as its most influential actor) applied great leverage to both Georgia and Abkhazia and provided peacekeeping forces to the parties. Not only did the United Nations and the Organization for Security and Cooperation in Europe (OSCE) work closely with the CIS in mediation (a highly unusual but effective arrangement), they also collaborated on so-called "subcontract peacekeeping," through which the United Nations oversaw a peacekeeping operation that was primarily Russian.

Chart 13.3: Negotiating Fora and Role of United Nations and United States

CONFLICT	BASIC FORUM	UN ROLE	U.S. ROLE
Abkhazia	UN and OSCE	Formal source of authority delegated to regional group	Indirect only
Aral Sea Basin	Local groups with World Bank support	None	None
Beagle Channel	Bilateral discussions, organized by Vatican	Essentially none	Essentially none (did urge OAS action at one point)
Bosnia	Dayton talks	Extensive Security Council activity	Central negotiator in Dayton talks; coordinated the pre-Dayton "Contact Group"; exerted occasional pressure pre-Dayton.
Cambodia	P-5 (permanent members of Security Council)	Security Council in background and in implementation	Participant in negotiations
Croatia	Regional and special purpose UN fora	Security Council and Special Representative	Central negotiator
El Salvador	Bilateral discussions	Provided mediator	Background
Korea	Bilateral discussions	Security Council supporting IAEA	Provided key negotiators and helped orchestrate the international activity
Northern Ireland	Commission plus local	None	Strong background encouragement
Rwanda	Regional group	Provided enforcement group	Participant
South Africa	Domestic groups	Background actions only	Background actions only, but Kissinger mission
West Bank	Oslo (plus U.S.)	Little in this phase, enormous in other phases	Avoided in this phase; central role in other phases

In Rwanda, the Organization of African Unity (OAU), under the guidance of Mobutu Sese Seko, failed to broker a pre-Arusha peace. However, under the late guidance of Tanzanian diplomat Ami Mpungwe, the OAU played an important consultative role during Mpungwe's independent mediation of the Arusha Accords, and the OAU oversaw the NMOG (Neutral Military Observer Group) peacekeeping operation. In Northern Ireland, the European Union and Council of Europe have played a critical role in economic and human rights issues, while the United Kingdom's role as a permanent member of the Security Council has kept the United Nations from participating more fully in mediating the conflict.

The United States, other permanent members of the Security Council, and regional powers played significant roles in a number of the mediation cases we studied. Particular countries may be motivated to take a primary role in a mediation because of their strategic interests, as in Russia's role in Abkhazia or the role of the permanent members of the Security Council (with the exception of the United Kingdom) in Cambodia. They may also seek to gain regional and international prestige by helping to solve regional problems, as in the case of Tanzania's role in the Arusha Accords.

Not surprisingly, the United States played an important role in many of the mediations, especially those in which American military force or military alliances had influenced the military and political calculations of the parties (e.g., Bosnia or the second phase of the Oslo process), or where American military interests were at stake (e.g., North Korea). In other cases, the United States provided encouragement from the sidelines, usually focused most often on the achievement of some form of reasonable settlement (e.g., Arusha). And in a few cases, the United States has been essentially absent from the negotiations, either because of minimal strategic interest, or because it believed that the negotiations would go better without it (e.g., the Beagle Channel or the Aral Sea Basin).

In some cases, the United States was effectively disqualified as a mediator because of its perceived lack of neutrality. Thus, the PLO was much more comfortable with Norwegian mediation than with U.S. mediation (notwithstanding the ongoing Madrid talks) to achieve the Oslo breakthrough, and the El Salvador dispute was deliberately brought to a UN official rather than to the United States (which was seen as supporting the Salvadoran government) or to the OAS (in which the United States was perceived as having too much influence). In other cases, it was precisely the perceived *lack* of neutrality that lent the United States force as a mediator (Bosnia, Northern Ireland) able to deploy positive and negative incentives.

In most of the negotiations, a specific channel and specific individual emerged as key. In a few cases, such as the role of Alvaro de Soto in El Salvador and that of Robert Gallucci in North Korea, this centrality reflected their expertise in the specific dispute. Despite their role as mediators, Gallucci and Lord Carrington (in Croatia) represented the interests of their employers. In most cases, however, the choice of mediator appears to be based on a combination of expertise in dispute settlement; possession of a large enough power base to participate; and, most of all, neutrality and impartiality. Thus, in Cambodia, it was the French representative—whose current (if not historical) strategic interests were probably the least affected of all the relevant outside powers by the negotiation—who had the neutrality to be able to present proposals that would help bring the multipower negotiations to a successful result. In Rwanda, the Tanzanian diplomat Ami Mpungwe played a similar role. In the Beagle Channel dispute, the Vatican was chosen because it was expected to be neutral and possessed significant moral authority. Former President Carter acted in North Korea in his role as a well-respected neutral mediator rather than as an expert (with Robert Gallucci able to step in later as an expert).

One of the points made by the participants themselves is that the mediators need a staff. Because a mediator's contribution is frequently more to the process than to the substance of a dispute, they need help and expertise about the substantive issues. If the United States provides the lead mediator, it, of course, has the diplomatic machinery to fulfill this need. But if the United States is not in a central role, there may be a serious lack of experienced staff; in the case of Arusha, for example, the need for gaming to think out the issues and for intelligence information were particularly noted.

Choice of Parties

The choice of which parties will participate in a negotiation gives power and recognition to those parties. This is always a sensitive issue—some parties are almost automatically involved in a specific negotiation; the inclusion of others may involve significant choices with implications for the ultimate success or failure of the agreement.

The choice of including outside national parties in the negotiation has serious implications for regional balance of power and may affect the particular shape of security guarantee arrangements. The clearest example is Abkhazia, where Russia plays an extremely important role, reflecting both its traditional and current power position. In Cambodia, the network of prior support arrangements for specific national entities defined the membership of the negotiating panel, which consisted of these nations plus Indonesia, which played an important role in the form of mediator.

The issue of including subnational representatives is especially sensitive. One problem is that recognition or nonrecognition of the subnational actors by the national actors becomes part of the basic balance of any agreement. In most examples, a nonnational entity demonstrated some form of power before it was recognized in any negotiation. Thus, the PLO was clearly a significant actor in West Bank politics, even though it was not recognized by Israel. The FMLN had made itself central to the future of El Salvador. Bosnia and Croatia had status as entities in the former Yugoslav federation and gained further legitimacy following international recognition of their declarations of independence. Abkhazia was given military support by Russia early on in its conflict with Georgia. In short, it was the operational strength of entities that pushed their inclusion in negotiations. And one of the very difficult issues and arguable misjudgments in the Arusha negotiations was the failure to include the Hutu extremist groups, which shortly precipitated the next round of massacres.

The authority conferred on the parties was frequently masked until the negotiation was concluded. The best example was the "nonofficial" talks at Oslo that led ultimately to a mutual recognition agreement between the PLO and Israel. In Cambodia, the creation of the Supreme National Council made it possible to "invite in" a UN entity that managed "domestic negotiations" among entities that while still somewhat controlled by their patrons, were ultimately recognized as relevant political actors within the nation. In Bosnia, Slobodan Milosevic negotiated on behalf of the Bosnian Serbs, who had not gained recognition for their self-proclaimed republic and whose leaders were indicted war criminals at the time of the Dayton talks.

But there is a greater issue in dealing with subnational representatives. Do the negotiators have power to bind their principals? This was a concern for both Israel and the PLO during the Oslo talks, where each had to be persuaded that the informal talks really did represent substantive negotiations between the principals. Uncertainty was finally resolved by direct higher-level face-to-face negotiations, and by demonstrations by the representatives of ability to affect actions in other fora. It was an even more urgent concern in Arusha, Cambodia, and Northern Ireland, where it was not clear that the subnational leaders had full command of their organizations. Mediators were deeply concerned that any agreement might be undercut by extremist elements within the various communities involved. Thus, for example, Northern Ireland mediation included elaborate games of conditionality and unofficial talks, designed to pressure the Irish Republican Army (IRA) into decommissioning weapons before entering final status talks.

The Role of International Institutions

One of the highlights of the post–Cold War international order is the new prominence of international institutions, often referred to as part of the "international community." International institutions, ranging from the United Nations to local nongovernmental organizations (NGOs), serve a myriad of functions in the premediation phase, the mediation phase, and the implementation phase of post–Cold War conflicts. In the premediation phase, international institutions can help build civil society (a key for conflict prevention), act as fora for discussion of security issues and underlying conflicts, and assist with specific problems such as human and minority rights and refugees. In the mediation phase, these institutions can offer good offices, peacekeeping services, sanctions and rewards, and intellectual input on specific issues. In the implementation period, institutions can aid in truth and reconciliation processes (whether commissions or trials), support security guarantees and provide peacekeeping or economic aid, help in the development of constitutions and legal systems, and assist in the creation or rebuilding of civil society.

In the cases we studied, the United Nations and other international institutions not only provided mediators for disputes, but they also played important background and facilitating roles as well. Through the General Assembly, the Security Council, "Friends" Groups, Observer Missions, peacekeeping forces, and associated agencies, the United Nations was present in every one of the case studies except the Beagle Channel. Regional political and economic organizations such as the OAS, the OAU, the OSCE, and the European Union often served in the background, sometimes as coordinators of military action. (Regional military alliances, such as NATO and ASEAN, Association of Southeast Asian Nations, also provide important support.) NGOs were critical to the success of the Oslo Accords, the Aral Sea projects, the South African peace process, and even the North Korea crisis (representatives of the Carter Center took part in Jimmy Carter's mission). International financial institutions promise a prominent role in the resolution of future resource and environment conflicts, with the Aral Sea process providing a key example.

The United Nations

The United Nations was by far the most important international organization in the case studies we examined. The Security Council played a key role in passing resolutions seeking to shape outcomes (as in the cases of Rwanda, the West Bank, and Abkhazia), in authorizing peacekeeping operations (Bosnia, Rwanda, Cambodia), and in threatening sanctions (North Korea). And members of the permanent five (P-5), acting as sovereign nations (but adopting well-understood P-5 consultative processes), devised the framework for the Cambodian agreements.

Personal envoys of the secretary-general mediated (or "intermediated") in El Salvador and Georgia and went on peace missions to South Africa and the former Yugoslavia. Diplomats from the United Nations played important observer roles in South Africa, where they assisted in the institution building envisioned by the peace negotiations, and in Rwanda, where they acted as proxies or sounding boards for the international community in approving or disapproving provisions of the Arusha Accords.

"Friends" groups, groups of nations either appointed or approved by the secretary-general, played a very interesting role in the Abkhazia and El Salvador conflicts. These groups of diplomats, sometimes acting through their UN missions and sometimes acting in their direct bilateral capacities, emerged as active forces in the mediation efforts. They coordinated policy, briefed the secretary-general on the progress of the talks, helped draft resolutions, and provided resources for the mediation process. In Bosnia, a "contact group" of nations (not officially designated a "friends" group) served a similar purpose.

The United Nations was pivotal in supplying peacekeeping forces to uphold mediated agreements. UN peacekeepers were active in Cambodia, Rwanda, the former Yugoslavia, and (perhaps most effectively) in El Salvador. In addition to carrying out their peacekeeping activities, forces in Croatia set up "safe areas" in which peacekeeping troops sought to protect refugees and to prevent ethnic cleansing.

While these forces were often woefully inadequate to stem the re-eruption of violent conflict, they nonetheless represent a powerful future role for the United Nations in post–Cold War conflict. Bosnia provided the one contrary tale: to be effective, a peacekeeping force must have a peace to keep. The extension of the UNPROFOR (United Nations Protection Force) mandate for Croatia to Bosnia dragged the United Nations into the conflict, making it ineffectual as a mediator.

Finally, the UN agencies played a background role in many of the conflicts we examined. For example, the United Nations Development Program (UNDP) helped establish and bolster NGOs working in the Aral Sea Basin, and the High Commission on Refugees did heroic work in Cambodia, Rwanda, and the former Yugoslavia.

Regional Organizations

As noted above, regional organizations, such as the CIS, the OAU, and the OAS, were not always effective as mediators (with the exception of the CIS) but did play important supporting roles in the mediation process. The strength of regional organizations, namely their strong interest in preventing conflict on their territory, is also their major weakness in that the members may have conflicting interests among themselves or may be less than neutral in their reasons for intervening.

The OAU oversaw the NMOG forces in the Rwanda crisis, and acted as a sounding board for Ami Mpungwe, the mediator. In the Croatian crisis, the European Community presided over the Hague Conference and authorized the use of the monitoring force. In the Aral Sea conflict, the European Union–TACIS (Technical Assistance for the Commonwealth of Independent States) group provided technical assistance and support for water projects and signed a memorandum of understanding with the World Bank and the UNDP to avoid duplication of efforts. In conjunction with the United Nations, the OSCE lent legitimacy and expertise to the Abkhazia negotiations and served as an important monitor group in the Croatia and Bosnia conflicts.

Nongovernmental Organizations

Nongovernmental organizations acted as facilitators and key institution builders in the cases we studied. NGOs play an increasingly important role in countries developing new levels of civil society and in mediation processes in which secrecy and back-channel communication dovetail with higher-profile first-track efforts. In the Oslo negotiations, the think tank FAFO (Institute for Applied Social Science) brought Israelis and Palestinians together under the auspices of an academic conference (a subterfuge that helped bypass an Israeli law forbidding Israeli and PLO representatives from direct contact). As the talks gradually shifted from second-track to first-track status, FAFO was able to maintain secrecy and credibility. When the talks threatened to reach an impasse, FAFO, with backing from the Norwegian foreign ministry, strengthened its role by moving from providing an opportunity to meet to offering more active facilitation.

In the Aral Sea Basin, nongovernmental environmental groups, supported by the West, emerged even before the collapse of the Soviet Union. After the World Bank process began, they acted to help develop popular support for cooperation and to implement programs on the ground. In South Africa, NGOs sponsored numerous nonracial dialogues to build community and political support for the abolition of apartheid and to develop interracial institutions. Similarly, dialogue groups helped forge support for the peace process in Israel and the West Bank and in Northern Ireland. In North Korea, the Carter Center served as part of Jimmy Carter's mission, adding to the impression that Carter's visit was a personal humanitarian one, even though the Center also played a key role in communications with the South Korean government during the visit. When the mediated agreement came before the establishment of effective and useful NGO processes (as in Bosnia and Cambodia), building civil institutions posed a larger challenge in postconflict implementation.

International Financial Institutions

International organizations such as the World Bank and the International Monetary Fund are playing an increasingly important role in international diplomacy. Once dealing only with more purely economic issues, these institutions are now gradually moving to emphasize human rights and civil society building as preconditions for aid. In the Aral Sea Basin, the World Bank went even further by refusing to step into the conflict until the sovereign nations controlling the Aral Sea Basin worked out a water management agreement among themselves. The Bank assisted this process through quiet diplomacy among the leaders of the newly sovereign states. Thus, the Bank filled the vacuum left by Moscow, encouraged civil society building activities by NGOs, used its leverage to influence the scope and form of possible solutions, and encouraged regional institutions and NGOs to cooperate on water issues.

International Law and Institutions Seeking to Resolve Conflicts

Conspicuously lacking in our case studies was an active role for the International Court of Justice, the European Court of Human Rights, or other adjudicative bodies. The processes we studied relied on political and strategic behavior rather than on adjudication of international legal principles. Nevertheless, even in the political and strategic discussions, a number of substantive legal issues recurred and are emerging as items on the new diplomatic agenda, just as issues of borders and expropriation once formed the diplomatic agenda. In the disputes deriving from the breakup of a multiethnic nation, the typical issues are autonomy, definition of borders, and protection or resettlement of the minorities created by the new borders. In the disputes associated with government change and the integration of civil war combatants (e.g., Cambodia and El Salvador), the typical issues include elections, amnesty, integration of the military, and various forms of guarantees ensuring that different groups are successful in their efforts to share power under one functioning government. Technical natural resource and water issues will arise with increasing frequency in the future.

The body of international law dealing with autonomy proved positively harmful. In those cases that confronted the intermixed questions of sovereignty, autonomy, confederation, self-determination, and independence, e.g., Abkhazia, Bosnia, Croatia, Northern Ireland, the legal debate stood in the way of effective dispute resolution. The legal concepts are too blunt to allow for political compromise; there is formally no such thing as partial sovereignty—even though, in practice, sovereignty is always limited by practical and formal international obligations and by responsibilities beyond the management of the nation-state. The absoluteness of the sovereignty concept often becomes an absolute barrier to agreement. Negotiators are forced to try to place the formal sovereignty issues in abeyance for future decision, as might have been a possibility in Abkhazia, or to work carefully with symbols and realities of independence, such as a separate flag or control over separate military forces or educational systems. Sometimes, however, the issue cannot be finessed. Perhaps this explains why the international judicial processes designed to deal with these questions in the Croatian context were not helpful (although they were also used very late in the development of the crisis).

In other areas, international law has provided a framework, and may well have averted many disputes from ever reaching the conflict stage. Nevertheless, the technicalities of international law can create problems, as in the Beagle Channel dispute. Borders and waters have long been a subject of international negotiation, and there is a tradition of diplomats or arbitrators following elaborate principles when drawing land and water borders that take into account historical lines, the borders between differing ethnic communities, the demands of military security, and the need to obtain access to marine resources. Yet, resolution of the Beagle Channel dispute involved separating the treatment of rights over islands from the treatment of rights over associated exclusive economic zones in a way that was legally irrational but politically sensible. And, in the Croatian case, the question of whether to follow the existing constitutional structure or to diverge radically from it in response to the concerns of ethnic communities was central to the context of the negotiations and radically increased the tensions and stakes of the negotiation.

In the area of water resource disputes, international law is extremely abstract and precatory. There are few relevant legal principles that are more precise than a general sense of good faith obligation with respect to upstream/downstream allocations of water. Although the obligation to consult is extremely important, nations find it difficult to reach precise agreements in this context, because they each know the exact implications of any such agreement. It might be very valuable for international donors, in a consultation process, to use their authority to define equitable and more detailed standards for access to natural resources in projects that they finance; the standards would become *de facto* law.

In contrast to the performance of substantive international law, the performance of procedural international law has been excellent in essentially all the examples. Existing processes have successfully led to the availability of international mediators and a reasonable focus of discussion in almost all disputes studied. In spite of the rhetoric of national sovereignty, there has been little serious opposition to the action of the international community in discussing and considering issues that would very recently have been regarded as subject to domestic jurisdiction only.

The panel of legal experts who advised our group also pointed out the success of *emerging* principles of international law, which coincide with political science notions of democratic processes, transparency, and the right of the individual to security. Inherent in the substance of every mediated agreement were adherence to democratic procedures, fair elections, transparent governmental procedures, the primacy of the rule of law, and the promise of human rights to all individuals. Many of the agreements and subsequent implementation agreements incorporated specific international legal norms and covenants (e.g., the annexes of the Dayton Accords, the new South African constitution).

A further surprise arises in connection with the application of international law during the follow-up to an agreement. As indicated above, we are now able (relatively) quickly and easily to incorporate international actions to assist in making an agreement work. This is exemplified by guarantees and UN forces, such as those in Cambodia and Croatia. It is further exemplified more routinely—and therefore more impressively—by institutions for elections, central to the settlements in El Salvador and Cambodia. There was international machinery available for ensuring fair elections, and it made settlement easier. Moreover, as demonstrated by the activity of U.S. Lt. Colonel Marley, advising in the Arusha negotiations, we may be evolving broadly applicable institutions and principles for the integration of military forces.

There are other areas similar to elections and military integration that are routinely subjects of dispute and for which we might well develop or strengthen legal principles or institutions. Are there emerging global norms to distinguish cases in which it is best to give amnesty for past misdeeds to officials of a former government from those in which it is best to impose criminal responsibility? Amnesty, in various forms, was an issue in Cambodia, El Salvador, the former Yugoslavia, Rwanda, and Northern Ireland, for example. Will a future international criminal court embody jurisdiction to resolve questions of amnesty, or is it best left to the political dispute settlement process? Might we do better at applying our body of international law and institutions for refugees (which was created in response to the refugee flows following World War II)? Every one of the "disintegration" settlements considered here has created a flow of refugees, primarily from pockets of one ethnicity in a region allocated in the peace agreement to another ethnic community. These groups are now often no longer welcome in the regions assigned to their community (just as they are unwelcome in the regions assigned to the former community). Can international law be invoked to deal with minority rights in these postconflict situations to make it easier to reach settlements? These are all areas in which traditional international law scholarship based on careful comparisons of standards and experience in different contexts would be highly useful. Some of these issues may be essentially unsolvable, but if they are solvable, there would be great value in developing a body of norms and institutions that could quickly and with relatively little negotiation cost be incorporated into an agreement. They constitute an opportunity.

A key question remains whether future international legal arrangements might serve to help forestall conflict, as by enabling minorities to express grievances legally and politically, rather than militarily, or by encouraging development of a civil society and institutions for dealing with disputes. Although the book did not focus on this issue, the cases give us some insight into what effective international legal intervention might look like.

The rights of minorities or ethnic communities were an issue in over half of the cases studied: Abkhazia, Bosnia, Croatia, Northern Ireland, Rwanda, South Africa, and the West Bank. And the civil rights of communities were also issues in Cambodia and El Salvador. In some of these cases, there has been long-term involvement of international human rights institutions. In Northern Ireland, for example the European Commission of Human Rights has pursued several complaints. The Inter-American Commission on Human Rights has been active in El Salvador. And the ethnic issues of both South Africa and the West Bank have long been a subject of international discussion on the level of academic, judicial, and political exchanges. These outside interventions have clearly contributed to the relative peacefulness of the transition in South Africa and by laying the groundwork for cooperation between racial groups played a role in the negotiated transition. Whether outside interventions by norm-enforcing institutions have been as effective in the other cases is less clear.

It is difficult to define which international law and human rights principles are most likely to be helpful in averting ethnic conflict, let alone envision how such norms would be consistently and effectively applied. Nevertheless, because the application of international legal norms appears promising in helping to prevent future conflict, it deserves future analysis.

More broadly, the use of international human rights law to strengthen civil society appears both useful and desirable. Again, of the cases studied, a strong civil society existed most clearly in Northern Ireland and South Africa—and these are among the most promising situations. In an era of increased travel, direct broadcast satellites, and the Internet, it should be possible to define and enforce international human rights in a way that makes it more difficult for a nation to opt out of participation in a global civil society. Again, analysis is needed as to both mechanisms and effects, but the promise is perhaps the greatest of any available international legal process.

The Negotiation Process Itself

The mechanics of contemporary international diplomacy are significantly different from those of the past, even of the relatively recent past. Consultations with constituencies and leaders back home are much easier than they have ever been because of the spread of (at least reasonably) secure telecommunications systems. At the same time, national governments are almost certainly much more "leaky" than they have ever been—this is another result of the telecommunications and information revolution.

Thus, negotiating representatives generally have significantly less autonomous power than they once did—and mediators have to take the negotiators' relations with their home constituencies into account on a more continual basis. In particular, they have much less ability to work without consultation with home constituencies in developing an "ad referendum" overall balance that must be considered by home constituencies on a package basis. This is exemplified, for example, in the Arusha and the South Africa negotiations; in each, the relations among key negotiators and those competing against them within their own constituency were a central factor in the discussions. As noted above, this also implies that NGOs will play an important role. Not only is this clearly exemplified in the South African and Northern Ireland negotiations, it is also seen in the Croatia and Cambodia negotiations, where the concerns of the international human rights community and of various outside supporters had an impact on the mediations. The increased public participation certainly makes agreement more difficult; it may also make agreement more stable once it is achieved.

It is in this context that one must evaluate the benefits or value added provided by the mediator. Although the framework developed in the methodology chapter is still useful, the actual values appear somewhat different from those believed to be crucial at the time that list was prepared. In almost all cases, the main contributions of the mediator were in maintaining a framework for the negotiations and in facilitating compromise. Persuasion, with certain exceptions, was primarily used to encourage negotiation rather than to shape a bargained result. The effectiveness of leverage depended on a number of factors, including the nature of the leverage, the timing of its use, and the party applying it. A summary of negotiation approaches is presented in chart 13.4.

Persuasion

The role of personal persuasion by the mediator—anticipated as being a critical contribution—was somewhat less than expected. (It is, of course, nearly impossible to evaluate the role of persuasion itself in a context in which that persuasion is almost certainly concentrated in highly confidential discussions.) In some cases, e.g., the actions of the Tanzanian, European, and U.S. officials in Arusha, persuasion seemed central. Norwegian Foreign Minister Johan Holst played a critical persuasive role at one point in the Oslo negotiations. U.S. mediator Richard Holbrooke counted the full economic and military power of the United States among his tools of persuasion. But this pattern was uncommon. What was more common was persuasion to participate in negotiations, as exemplified in most of the Oslo history. Even more frequently, instead of persuasion, the mediator typically questioned the parties to help them develop

Chart 13.4: Negotiating Styles

DISPUTE	PARTICIPANTS	BACK CHANNEL	COMMENTS
Abkhazia	Designated representatives	Several channels	Major protagonists both CIS members
Aral Sea Basin	Relevant bureaucratic officials	Many meetings of many groups	Continuation of working discussions
Beagle Channel	Papal mediator and special representatives	Yes	One phase of shuttle diplomacy later face-to-face
Bosnia	Principals	Several in earlier mediations; closed off in final mediation	Proximity talks
Cambodia	Special ministers of UNSC permanent members	Yes (e.g., China and Vietnam)	Each permanent member represented and helped persuade a local faction
Croatia	Designated representatives	Parallel channels	Dealing with easiest issues first
El Salvador	Designated representatives	Little role	Mediator transmitted proposals; much face-to face
Korea	U.S. and North Korean senior officials	Yes (Carter)	Bilateral discussions in context of UN/IAEA activity
Northern Ireland	Officials from U.K. and representatives from the major Catholic and Protestant political parties	Many channels	Meetings to learn positions of parties
Rwanda	Regional foreign ministry officials and local principals	Side discussions with key third parties	Step-by-step approach
South Africa	Principals		Embedded in elaborate discussions
West Bank	"Unofficial" delegates, later principals	Several channels	Mediator transmitted proposals

proposals, stay focused on the negotiation, and then only rarely proposed compromises to facilitate compromise.

In some of the negotiations, including most phases of the Papal mediation over the Beagle Channel and of the Oslo negotiations, the mediator basically served as a messenger of proposals from one side to the other. But the messenger role was not passive: the mediator actively questioned each side to understand the nuances of the proposal, encourage the party making a proposal to define its goals more precisely, and guide them to consider ways in which their goals could be achieved at less expense to the other side.

In other negotiations, the mediator went further to propose compromises, based on the substantive positions and concerns of the parties. It can be easier for a mediator to propose a compromise position than for either of the parties to take the risk of doing so. This was de Soto's basic approach in the El Salvador negotiations and was attempted in the Papal proposal for resolution of the Beagle Channel—a proposal that was not ultimately accepted but that did include some ideas that were included in the final agreement. Holbrooke adopted this tactic at Dayton, although he frequently concealed who, or what party, had originated the proposal. Moreover, especially if properly staffed, a mediator may be able to analyze the implications and details of a compromise, as Claude Martin may have done in the development of the Cambodian compromise and as representatives of the U.S. Department of Defense were able to do in working at the Bosnian map. The mediator can fit together a number of the uncertainties and provide a basis for each of the parties to evaluate, understand, and perhaps reshape an arrangement that neither one would have been able to articulate or define on their own. For the mediator, this role requires trust and perceived impartiality.

There are also a number of ways to facilitate compromise; it is frequently the mediator who suggests or creates the way. For example, an agreement may be presented as an "interim" arrangement or perhaps a multiphase arrangement—and the underlying reality is that the "interim" or "first phase" arrangement will, in fact, be a long-term resolution of the issue, and the later steps may never be reached until other external factors have changed. The 1994 agreement in Abkhazia, which evaded the thorny issues of sovereignty, might have served this function. Many of the post–world war European arrangements (perhaps unwittingly) served this role. Another method of facilitating compromise is to leave certain aspects for third-party decision—the parties may differ in their expectations as to the outcome of the third-party decision, or the third-party decision maker may provide a convenient scapegoat for the negotiators and their principals. Examples are Bosnia, where the status of Brcko was left for a third-party arbitrator, and Cambodia, where the ultimate composition of the government was to depend upon an election. Clearly, a skilled mediator can be sensitive to such possibilities for facilitating concession and can make suggestions for incorporating such arrangements into an overall agreement. And timing can make compromise possible—the Vatican mediation in the Beagle Channel dispute permitted the parties to keep the dispute on the back burner for a number of years until it became politically resolvable.

Judgment and Knowledge

As noted above, substantive expertise about the conflict on the part of the mediator played relatively little role. The case in which it was most clearly important was Korea, where the technicalities of the nuclear fuel cycle were an important part of the issue. More often, the mediators brought neutrality, process expertise, and, perhaps of course, staff capabilities that provided the necessary reservoir of substantive expertise. The best example was the Beagle Channel case, where the Pope was chosen, on the basis of innate authority and of a presumed ability to manage a fair process, not for his knowledge of oceanic international disputes or the geography of Cape Horn.

Negotiation Dynamics

The dominant contributions of mediation to the dynamics of the negotiation process appear to be (1) creating, shaping, and maintaining a framework and process within which negotiations can proceed and (2) helping to manage publicity and possible statements in such a way as to facilitate agreement.

The clearest example of creating a framework was Oslo. The mediators created a deniable situation in which the parties could meet. As noted above, they also regularly urged the parties back to the table following innumerable breakdowns in negotiation. In the case of El Salvador, part of the role of the UN negotiating structure was to make it harder for either side to leave and thus to increase each side's confidence that the negotiations would proceed to completion. The same was true once the United States succeeded in getting the Bosnia parties to Wright-Patterson Air Force Base. In another way, the World Bank's desire to ensure that those involved in Central Asian water issues do meet—and, if necessary, be funded to meet—plays a central role in facilitating agreement. Financial costs of negotiation were also extremely important in the El Salvador negotiations.

The framework can also involve sequencing the issues. In all the cases for which such information is available, including the Oslo, Arusha, Beagle Channel, Northern Ireland, and Croatia negotiations, discussion began with the easiest issues and moved to the harder ones—some disaggregated difficult issues from the negotiation entirely. In Korea and the Beagle Channel, agreement similarly involved putting off some issues for the future. This is perhaps the area where mediators make the most important judgments, and impartiality—which assists the mediator in hearing the concerns of the parties—may be essential to making these judgments. Obvious examples are the decision whether to concentrate on the existing Yugoslavian constitutional framework in the Croatia negotiations or instead to look at broader ethnic disputes and the decision to include the Croatian blockade of Serbian military facilities as part of the military negotiations in the same dispute.

There is a trade-off in these choices. Resolution of easier issues may build trust, encourage human contacts, and locate common interests to make the harder issues more tractable. Leaving the harder issues for the future or for future negotiations may mean that the difficult issues are never resolved and that the negotiation succeeds but the future of the parties' relationship does not. These cases suggest that the trust-building approach is commonly more effective. By approaching more difficult issues last, the parties and the international community might work in the interim to change the world (or at least the facts on the ground) sufficiently to make later resolution of difficult topics easier. Perhaps most importantly, an iterative process allows the respective constituencies to get accustomed to compromise and to dealing with their opponents. This approach was central in the settlement of such long-term conflicts as Northern Ireland and the Israeli–Palestinian dispute and may, more broadly, be essential in dealing with extremist groups ready to resort to violence.

Defining the framework also involves defining the communication process to be used in the negotiations. At one extreme, there can be "shuttle diplomacy" in which the principals never meet—this was exemplified in the early phases of the Beagle Channel, as well as in the Mideast talks and in the pre-Dayton phase of the U.S. mediation in Bosnia. It permits negotiation in a situation in which the parties do not want to talk directly, or are legally or politically restrained from doing so, or in which they are likely to be vituperative in person. Thus, the diplomacy gives the mediator significant control in managing the flow of information between the parties. Proximity talks, where the parties are brought together in the same location, but are not required to meet face-to-face, take shuttle diplomacy one step further and can considerably shorten the length of negotiations.

Nevertheless, none of the negotiations considered here were ultimately successful until high-level officials from each side met face-to-face. The human chemistry of developing respect and openness to compromise from these contacts was central in a number of the cases, including Oslo, El Salvador, and the Beagle Channel negotiations. This is a central theme of the Norwegian approach—the mediator judges how to bring the principals together and how to shape the circumstances of the negotiations in such a way as to encourage this chemistry. As illustrated at Dayton, however, "chemistry" doesn't always happen; by forcing the parties to eat, drink, and sleep in close proximity to each other, Holbrooke was able to push them to an agreement.

Multiple channels and side negotiations were deployed in all cases: the Oslo Channel and the Washington–Madrid negotiations in parallel; Gallucci and Carter in North Korea supplementing negotiations with the IAEA; China and Vietnam negotiating in Chungdu over Cambodian issues; the United Nations and the regional fora in Croatia. Clearly, the mediator may help to choose the best framework and, in the shuttle context, to provide credibility in the transfer of information from one side to the other and help maintain confidentiality where necessary. But what may be even more important is to suggest or create occasions for (and perhaps even suggest agendas for) back-channel or informal discussions (the "walk in the woods").

As suggested above, information management has now become a critical component of negotiation. Certainly, leaks can torpedo a negotiation, but development of information about a situation can assist in shaping the positions of the various constituencies and thus actually make future agreement more plausible. In the case of the Israeli–Palestinian dispute, the parties ultimately—and self consciously—used the public Madrid–Washington negotiations as a way to prepare their constituencies to accept the results being actually negotiated at Oslo. Consider also the development and release of information about police practices in Northern Ireland, the West Bank, and South Africa. The development and release of the data made possible at least some response to curtail the practices in all cases—and, in turn, helped toward defusing the issue as a source of further tension. The decommissioning study in Northern Ireland must have been designed in part to bring new ideas into the public debate. Similarly, in South Africa, the knowledge and perceived impartiality of the Goldstone Commission provided a basis for bringing into the public domain information that assisted in creating a dynamic that made resolution feasible. In the justice-oriented and natural resource conflicts that are likely to be typical of the future, such careful development and release of information is likely to characterize efforts to persuade constituencies to accept step-by-step compromises.

South Africa also demonstrates a way in which the framework and information factors are combined—the creation of a civil society. Part of the reason that the South African transition is proceeding so effectively is that there have emerged a variety of institutions, at first outside South Africa and later within South Africa, in which the different ethnic and political groups can talk to each other, share a sense of human respect, and begin to consider possible resolutions on a joint basis. The relative absence of such cross-community contacts is one of the problems in Northern Ireland, which has a strong civil society within each community, but few bridges between communities.

Incentives and Leverage

Incentives and leverage, as distinguished from the personal persuasion used by a mediator, played a varying role in the negotiations and were most effective in the short term. As noted above, in the cases where external pressure led to a successful short-term agreement (as in Bosnia), often the implementation of those agreements was problematic and required ongoing external pressure and enforcement. Outside pressures were more effective when they resulted from an unavoidable external or international change, e.g., the impact of the fall of the Soviet Union on El Salvador, and least effective when they appeared arbitrary and orchestrated. Moreover, positive pressures where the parties are offered a promising future seem more likely to be effective than negative pressures. The clear examples are North Korea and the Central Asian water mediation.

Moreover, limited incentives can be useful in the actual process of achieving agreement when the situation is already ripe for agreement. Clear examples are the deadline imposed on the negotiators in the El Salvador dispute by the fact that the UN secretary-general was about to change or George Mitchell's Good Friday deadline in the Northern Ireland talks. But, as suggested by the failures to meet internal deadlines in the Madrid–Washington talks, a self-imposed agreement to negotiate resolutions to specific further issues is unlikely to be successful.

There is certainly also a general linkage associated with resolving issues and regaining the respect and legitimacy associated with membership in the international community, with all the possible benefits (World Bank membership, ultimate eligibility for European Union membership, etc.) that such membership can bring. This desire for international legitimation was key for Bosnia, Croatia, and the Palestinians, and probably North Korea as well.

Effectiveness of Results

This was not, of course, a study of the effectiveness of negotiated results, but a study of negotiation processes. Nevertheless, one is impressed by the number of examples in which an apparently successful negotiation was, in fact, a failure at resolving the underlying dispute and resulted in significant backsliding on the ground: the Oslo Accords and the West Bank, Cambodia, the Arusha Accords and Rwanda, the Dayton Accords and Bosnia.

In making any such evaluation of a negotiation, it is important to consider the differing meanings that can be given to success and failure. Stalling disaster for a period is often valuable. In light of the real uncertainties of the world, few serious politicians will be moved by the argument that the particular peace will lead in a few years to an even worse eruption of violence. (The classic example of a peace with seeds of discord—Versailles—was certainly planned, not a matter of a failure to achieve a more balanced agreement.) Moreover, one never knows how much worse things would have been had there been no agreement.

Although the questions asked of negotiators of course reflect their hindsight, it seems clear that these ineffective results are generally viewed by the insiders as the best that could be achieved in a bad situation. This is not the perspective usually revealed to the media. Misjudgments can and do occur—Hun Sen must have misjudged the likely election outcome in Cambodia. Yet, in the Arbitration Commission of the European Conference for Peace in Yugoslavia, the limitations of the process were clearly recognized. The diplomats knew that it was too little, too late—yet it would have seemed morally wrong and politically unacceptable not to try. And once any form of negotiation process is underway, one must always balance the costs of seeing that process break down without agreement against the costs of a breakdown with an imperfect agreement. Negotiators will seek agreements even when these are imperfect, and these imperfect agreements form part of the fabric of international politics.

Implications

The key conclusions from these case studies can be summarized as follows.

(1) The most typical patterns for future disputes are likely to be conflict over the constitution of a specific national government, cases involving minority rights, and conflict between nations over natural resource issues.

(2) Readiness for agreement is most affected by the war-weariness of the parties. It may be possible to intervene well before armed conflict by

helping, for example, to build a civil society or to design cooperative natural resource projects. But as armed conflict approaches and begins to spread, the international community loses the ability to intervene consensually and may not regain it until a point of war-weariness is reached.

(3) The international community has been very forthcoming in offering mediatory assistance when needed—and the United Nations has played a leading role in this process, almost to the exclusion of regional entities.

(4) The individual mediator is typically a neutral looked to for process expertise rather than substantive expertise in the dispute.

(5) The mediator may have substantial need for staff and intelligence capabilities.

(6) The substantive international law of self-determination is not helpful for resolving disputes and may be harmful.

(7) On the other hand, the evolution of international institutions for negotiation and intervention, and of international law and institutions for facilitating certain aspects of settlement, e.g., elections, has been very positive and helpful. It would be useful to explore the development of similar mechanisms for other recurrent settlement issues, particularly those having to do with amnesty and with minorities.

(8) The mediator provides an important service in encouraging use of the negotiation framework most adapted to the situation.

(9) More frequently than not, the mediator's contribution is less one of persuasion than one of suggesting and staffing compromises and putting forward proposals for resolving specific problems.

(10) Although there are usually multiple channels of negotiation and shuttle diplomacy is sometimes essential, face-to-face discussions—and the accompanying human interplay—are almost always essential to successful negotiation.

(11) Among the most important ways that the international society can encourage peaceful resolution of disputes is through strengthening national capabilities for understanding and resolving disputes, e.g., through strengthening civil society, and developing mechanisms of protection for minorities. This can be done through helping to build institutions and provide education, as well as through developing and using mechanisms for information development and dissemination on issues that require discussion as part of agreement development.

(12) The emerging body of disputes over natural resources and the environment may surface first before the international financial institutions. It is important that they develop fair and credible procedures for dealing with these disputes.

In summary, the role of the mediator is usually more one of facilitation than one of shaping a settlement. (In the case of El Salvador, the name was deliberately weakened to "intermediator.") The key roles are setting frameworks, helping define and communicate positions, encouraging continued negotiation, and only rarely acting to shape the outcome in a particular way. Neutrality is normally an essential requirement. These understandings are reflected in the Norwegian theories that distinguish passive technical hosts, active facilitators, and interested mediators. Although the needs are likely to differ from dispute to dispute (and sometimes within disputes), it is clearly the Norwegian judgment that the first and second of these roles are likely generally to be more effective than the last.

Overall, the study implies that the appropriate international law agenda for improving dispute resolution is not one of studying traditional, difficult topics such as principles of self-determination and sovereignty. Neither is the task one of devising new international dispute intervention mechanisms. Some staffing and intelligence information improvements might be useful, but those institutions are already working quite well.

Rather, the new agenda must recognize that the international and domestic agendas are now completely intermixed. At the prevention level, the international agenda must include ways to help build civil societies and to deal with interethnic and interreligious conflict in nations that may otherwise erupt in violence in the future. And, at the resolution level, it must look at ways to deal with amnesty, refugees, and ethnic tensions as part of dispute settlements, in exactly the same way that it can now routinely offer election services as part of dispute settlement.

Notes

Introduction

1. An article and a book chapter by Stephen Stedman were extremely helpful in developing the framework for the case studies. See Stephen John Stedman, "Negotiated Settlement of Civil War," in *Peacemaking in Civil War: International Mediation in Zimbabwe, 1974–1980* (Boulder, CO: Lynne Rienner, 1989), 1–31. See also Stephen John Stedman, "Negotiation and Mediation in International Conflict," in The International Dimensions of Internal Conflict, ed. Michael E. Brown (Cambridge: MIT Press, 1996), 341–76.

2. Alexander George's classic chapter on the case study method helped us develop a consistent set of questions for this volume. See Alexander L. George, "Case Studies and Theory Development: The Method of Structured, Focused Comparison," in *Diplomacy: New Approaches in History, Theory, and Policy,* ed. Paul Gordon Lauren (New York: Free Press, 1979), 43–63.

3. William Zartman lays out a theory of ripeness in his book *Ripe for Resolution: Conflict and Intervention in Africa* (New York: Oxford University Press, 1989) and in earlier works.

4. See Thomas Princen, *Intermediaries in International Conflict* (Princeton, NJ: Princeton University Press, 1982).

5. Stedman, "Negotiation and Mediation in Internal Conflict," 366–67.

6. Ibid., 343.

7. Ibid., 347.

8. Ibid.

Chapter 1

1. Here and after, *The Blue Helmets: A Review of United Nations Peacekeeping* (New York: United Nations, 1996).

2. Ibid., 572.

3. Ibid., 575.

4. *Federal News Service,* July 27, 1994.

5. Cited in Marieke Kleiboer, "Understanding Success and Failure of International Mediation," *Journal of Conflict Resolution* vol. 40, no. 2 (June 1996): 362.

6. Ibid., 362.

7. Stephen Stedman, "Negotiation and Mediation in Internal Conflict," in *The International Dimensions of Internal Conflict,* ed. Michael Brown (Cambridge, MA: MIT Press, 1996), 351.

8. Thomas Princen, *Intermediaries in International Conflict* (Princeton, NJ: Princeton University Press, 1992), 51.

9. William Zartman, *Ripe for Resolution: Conflict and Intervention in Africa* (New York: Oxford University Press, 1989), 265.

10. Interviews at the Russian Mission to the United Nations, April 1997.

11. Interview with General Hvidegaard, former head of the UN Observer Mission in Abkhazia, in May 1997.

12. Interviews at the Russian Mission to the United Nations, April 1997.

13. Stedman, "Negotiation and Mediation in Internal Conflict," 362.

14. Ibid., 362.

15. Jacob Bercovitch, "The Structure and Diversity of Mediation in International Relations," in *Mediation in International Relations,* ed. Jacob Bercovitch and Jeffrey Z. Rubin (New York: St. Martin's, 1992), 15–16.

16. Princen, *Intermediaries in International Conflict,* 23–24.

17. Cited in Bercovitch, "The Structure and Diversity of Mediation in International Relations," 19.

18. Cited in Stedman, "Negotiation and Mediation in Internal Conflict," 360, 362.

19. Bercovitch, "The Structure and Diversity of Mediation in International Relations," 19.

20. Princen, *Intermediaries in International Conflict.*

21. Kleiboer, "Understanding Success and Failure of International Mediation," 379.

22. Princen, *Intermediaries in International Conflict,* chapter 2.

23. Zartman, *Ripe for Resolution: Conflict and Intervention in Africa,* 277.

24. Cited in Kleiboer, "Understanding Success and Failure of International Mediation," 379.

25. Catherine Dale, "Turmoil in Abkhazia: Russian Responses," *RFE/RL Research Report* vol. 2, no. 34 (August 27, 1993): 49.

26. Lena Jonson and Clive Archer, eds., *Peacekeeping and the Role of Russia in Eurasia* (Boulder, CO: Westview Press, 1996), 10.

27. Ibid., 5.

28. Catherine Dale, "The Case of Abkhazia (Georgia)," in *Peacekeeping and the Role of Russia in Eurasia,* ed. Lena Jonson and Clive Archer (Boulder, CO: Westview Press, 1996), 128.

29. Agence France Presse, August 25, 1997.

30. Zartman, *Ripe for Resolution: Conflict and Intervention in Africa,* 265.

31. Arend Lijphart, "The Power-Sharing Approach," in *Conflict and Peacemaking in Multiethnic Societies,* ed. Joseph Montville (New York: Lexington Books, 1991), 497.

32. Stedman, "Negotiation and Mediation in Internal Conflict," 344.

33. See Kleiboer, "Understanding Success and Failure of International Mediation."

34. See, for example, Stephen Krasner, "Sovereignty and Intervention," in *Beyond Westphalia? State Sovereignty and International Intervention,* ed. Gene Lyons and Michael Mastanduno (Baltimore: Johns Hopkins University Press, 1995), 228–49.

Chapter 2

1. Boutros Boutros-Ghali, as cited in David Rieff, *Slaughterhouse: Bosnia and the Failure of the West* (New York: A Touchstone Book, 1995), 245.

2. Chuck Sudetic, *Blood and Vengeance: One Family's Story of the War in Bosnia* (New York: Norton, 1998), 21.

3. The six republics of Yugoslavia were Serbia, Croatia, Slovenia, Macedonia, Bosnia-Herzegovina, and Montenegro; Vojvodina and Kosovo were autonomous regions.

4. This view, concisely argued in Robert Kaplan's book *Balkan Ghosts,* apparently had a

significant impact on President Bill Clinton and Secretary of State Warren Christopher. David Owen, Balkan Odyssey (San Diego: A Harvest Book, 1995), 171.

5. Richard Holbrooke, *To End a War* (New York: Random House, 1998), 23–24.

6. Warren Zimmermann, *Origins of a Catastrophe: Yugoslavia and Its Destroyers* (New York: Random House, 1996), 210.

7. In her book *Balkan Tragedy: Chaos and Dissolution after the Cold War* (Washington, D.C.: The Brookings Institution, 1995, 47–81), Susan L. Woodward outlines the effects of foreign lending and austerity programs on political stability in Yugoslavia. According to her argument, the republics of Yugoslavia were all affected differently by changes in monetary policy, international lending, and especially by austerity programs put into effect to conform to loan conditions. The resulting imbalances among republics led to a weakening of the federal governing system and to the rise of nationalist leaders able to capitalize on the grievances of their constituents.

8. Milosevic said, "Six centuries [after the Battle of Kosovo Polje], we are again engaged in battles and quarrels. They are not armed battles, but this cannot be excluded." Milosevic, cited in Misha Glenny, *The Fall of Yugoslavia: The Third Balkan War* (New York: Penguin, 1993), 35.

9. Ibid., 35.

10. Laura Silber and Allan Little, *Yugoslavia: Death of a Nation* (New York: Penguin, 1995), 131.

11. For a more detailed discussion of the facts and consequences surrounding Croatia's assertion of independence, see the chapter on Croatia in this volume.

12. Not coincidentally, on March 1, the first shots were fired in Sarajevo, when a gunman fired on a Serb wedding party waving Serbian flags as it marched through a Muslim area.

13. Woodward, *Balkan Tragedy,* 283.

14. "Next in Bosnia," *Economist* (August 10, 1991): 9.

15. Woodward, *Balkan Tragedy,* 281.

16. Ibid.

17. Matthew T. Higham, Michael N. Mercurio, and Steven W. Ghezzi, eds., *The ACCESS Issue Packet on Bosnia-Herzegovina* (Washington, D.C.: ACCESS, 1996), 7.

18. According to accounts:

> Humiliation, terror and mental cruelty were almost universally deployed. Captured men would be told that they were to be executed the following day. . . . They were told that their wives had been raped and then killed, that their children were dead. They were forced, on pain of death, to perform atrocities against each other—mutilation, physical and sexual, and, even mutual killing. They were forced to dig mass graves and collect and bury the bodies of their families and neighbors. Sometimes, those on grave detail would themselves be killed and thrown on top of the bodies they had just delivered. (Silber and Little, *Yugoslavia: Death of a Nation,* 244.)

19. Ibid., 247.

20. "We're becoming collaborators," one worker said. "It's blackmail. The choice we face is either to become agents of ethnic cleansing, or to leave tens of thousands of people to continue living their nightmare." (Silber and Little, *Yugoslavia: Death of a Nation,* 247.)

21. Owen, *Balkan Odyssey,* 49.

22. Ibid., 51.

23. James Baker, cited in Zimmermann, *Origins of a Catastrophe,* 27. These views were supported later by General Colin Powell (chairman of the Joint Chiefs of Staff) in an influential 1992 article in *Foreign Affairs.* In the article, Powell laid out the criteria for U.S. intervention in international crises: "a clearly defined political objective, probability of achieving it by military force, exhaustion of nonviolent approaches, and a knowledge of the consequences of

intervention." (Zimmermann, 214–15.) These criteria were not likely to be met in Bosnia, and the "Powell Principles" strongly influenced both the Bush and the Clinton administrations in the early phases of the war.

24. UNSCR 761 of June 29, 1992, UNSCR 764 of July 13, 1992, and UNSCR 758 of June 18, 1992.

25. Owen, *Balkan Odyssey,* 54.

26. Ibid., 63

27. Silber and Little, *Yugoslavia: Death of a Nation,* 276. In comparing a partition of the country with the Vance-Owen Plan, Owen made an analogy to King Solomon's decision: the unworthy parents, Serbia and Croatia, would have been happy to take a share of a mutilated child, but the plan kept the baby intact, in accordance with the wishes of the good parent, Bosnian President Izetbegovic. (Owen, *Balkan Odyssey,*102.)

28. "A Map for Peace," *Economist* (January 9, 1993): 16.

29. Ibid., and John Mearsheimer and Robert Pape, "The Answer: A Partition Plan for Bosnia," *The New Republic* (June 14, 1993): 24.

30. "Bosnia and Herzegovina: We've Won. Let's Sue for Peace," *Economist* (April 3, 1993): 49.

31. "For Bosnia Muslims, Pact is a Concession and a Gamble," *Boston Globe* (March 27, 1993): 2.

32. Woodward, *Balkan Tragedy,* 306.

33. Ibid., 307.

34. Ibid.

35. First, Milosevic wanted to confirm that the Posavina Corridor, connecting Serbia with Bosnia (and which, according to the plan, would run through Croatian-majority territory) would be strictly policed by UN officials. Owen assured him that it would (and later secured a promise from the Russians that Russian troops would be deployed along the Northern Corridor). Next, he wanted to ascertain that the three-party interim presidency would operate by consensus, rather than by majority vote, so that the Serb nationalists could never be outvoted by a coalition of the Muslim and Croat parties. Finally, he wanted clarification that Serb-held and occupied land turned over to Muslim or Croat sovereignty under the plan would be policed by UN forces rather than by Muslim or Croat police. (Silber and Little, *Yugoslavia: Death of a Nation,* 279.)

36. Ibid.

37. Ibid.

38. Owen, *Balkan Odyssey,* 149.

39. Ibid., 123.

40. Ibid., 129.

41. Ibid., 155.

42. For more on U.S. policy toward the Vance–Owen Plan and the "Lift and Strike" proposal, see "Clinton and Mulroney Fault Balkan Peace Plan," *New York Times* (February 6, 1993): Sec. 1, p. 3; "Ex-Yugoslavia; Peacemongers," *Economist* (February 6, 1993): 52; "A New, Big Ally," *Economist* (February 13, 1992): 49; William Pfaff, "Western Cowardice Allowed the Tragedy in Bosnia to Worsen," *Chicago Tribune* (April 11, 1993): 3; "Clinton, Welcoming Pact, Warns the Serbs," *Boston Globe* (May 3, 1993): 1; "Christopher Sees a Consensus for Firm Action," *Los Angeles Times* (May 4, 1993): Sec. A, p. 1; "United States Plans Fast Thrust of Troops into Bosnia; Move Would Follow Serb Ratification of Pact," *Washington Post* (May 5, 1993): Sect. 1, p. 1.

43. Silber and Little, *Yugoslavia: Death of a Nation,* 288.

44. Ibid.

45. Warren Christopher, quoted in Stephen J. Hedges, Peter Cary, Bruce B. Auster, and Tim Zimmermann, "The Road to Ruin," *U.S. News and World Report* vol. 17, no. 3 (December 12, 1994): 59.

46. Silber and Little, *Yugoslavia: Death of a Nation,* 265.

47. Ibid., 268.

48. Sudetic, *Blood and Vengeance,* 202.

49. Ibid., 203.

50. In fact, a UN official remonstrated a press officer for not using the words "disarmament" and "cease-fire" strongly enough in his report. (Silber and Little, *Yugoslavia: Death of a Nation,* 273.)

51. Sudetic, *Blood and Vengeance,* 129.

52. Ibid., 130.

53. Woodward, *Balkan Tragedy,* 320.

54. Silber and Little, *Yugoslavia: Death of a Nation,* 274.

55. Woodward, *Balkan Tragedy,* 321.

56. Silber and Little, *Yugoslavia: Death of a Nation,* 275.

57. Woodward, *Balkan Tragedy,* 321. The Muslims, who may have inferred from the vague wording of the safe areas resolutions that the United Nations had promised to rush to Srebrenica's aid in the event of a Serb attack, took little comfort from the 150 or so Canadian troops stationed within the enclave. "Oric [the Muslim militia leader in Srebrenica] found himself staring into the barrels of Mladic's tanks and artillery. Behind these weapons was a phalanx of battle-ready troops.... Mladic's men had broken scores of cease-fire agreements, and there was no hint that the Serb general had abandoned his goal to drive the Muslims out of eastern Bosnia forever" (Sudetic, *Blood and Vengeance,* 207.) Even if the Canadian troops kept the Serbs temporarily at bay, they could do little to alleviate the suffering of the refugees and residents in Srebrenica and the other Muslim enclaves. Their fate would not be resolved until the eventual fall and ultimate "cleansing" of Srebrenica in 1995.

58. Silber and Little, *Yugoslavia: Death of a Nation,* 296–97.

59. Ibid., 298.

60. Ibid.

61. Owen, *Balkan Odyssey,* 178.

62. Silber and Little, *Yugoslavia: Death of a Nation,* 288.

63. Owen, *Balkan Odyssey,* 184–85.

64. According to Owen, "the Council embarked on the path of enforcement with no intention of backing it with the necessary resources: the most irresponsible decisions taken during my time as Co-Chairman and taken by four of the permanent members as part of their JAP." (Owen, *Balkan Odyssey,* 190.)

65. Manfred Worner, cited in Roger Cohen, "NATO Talks Fail to Reach Accord on Bosnia Plan," *New York Times* (May 27, 1993): Sect. A, p. 12.

66. Owen, *Balkan Odyssey,* 206.

67. Paul Lewis, "Bosnians Divide Over New Talks to Split Country," *New York Times* (June 23, 1993): Sect. A, p. 1.

68. Owen, *Balkan Odyssey,* 271–72.

69. Ambassador Galbraith received reports that the Croats were holding Muslim prisoners in appalling conditions that might have constituted war crimes. (Silber and Little, *Yugoslavia: Death of a Nation,* 356.)

70. Galbraith even visited those areas, to "[make] the point that we understood the nature of the suffering of the Croatian people." (Silber and Little, *Yugoslavia: Death of a Nation,* 355.)

71. In reality, of course, Tudjman kept a close eye on Bosnian Croat interests throughout the shuttle and subsequent Dayton process. The absurdity of the federation was clear to many observers: "Those very politicians who had advocated carving up Bosnia now spoke out in favor of a common state with the Muslims." (Silber and Little, *Yugoslavia: Death of a Nation,* 358–59.)

72. Silber and Little, *Yugoslavia: Death of a Nation,* 372.

73. David Owen, cited in ibid., 374.

74. There were also complaints, at the time, that the second-tier diplomats who served in the group were ignorant of the Balkans and their history. (Silber and Little, *Yugoslavia: Death of a Nation,* 375.)

75. Ibid.

76. Ibid., 376.

77. Peter W. Galbraith, "Washington, Erdut and Dayton: Negotiating and Implementing Peace in Croatia and Bosnia-Herzegovina," *Cornell International Law Review* vol. 30 (1997): 647.

78. Silber and Little, *Yugoslavia: Death of a Nation,* 382.

79. Susan Rosegrant, "Getting to Dayton: Negotiating an End to the War in Bosnia," A Case Study from the John F. Kennedy School of Government, Harvard University, 1996, 12, quoting Sandy Vershbow, former special assistant to the president for European affairs [stet].

80. Holbrooke, *To End a War,* 65.

81. Warren Bass, "The Triage of Dayton," *Foreign Affairs* 77, no. 5 (Sept. 1998): 95.

82. For a comprehensive account of the events at Srebrenica see Jan Willem Honig and Norbert Both, *Srebrenica: Record of a War Crime* (New York: Penguin, 1997).

83. Warren Zimmermann was the last U.S. ambassador to Belgrade. He was recalled to Washington in 1992. Relations between the rump Yugoslavia and the United States had thus been significantly downgraded for several years.

84. Indeed, Richard Holbrooke devotes the first chapter of his memoir to the incident, and mentions repeatedly throughout the book that the memory of his fallen colleagues inspired him to action at times when the process appeared futile. (Holbrooke, *To End a War,* 3–18.)

85. Ibid., 85.

86. Ibid., 111.

87. Ibid. Holbrooke also noted that the group had worked out its own internal dissent mechanism to handle disagreements within the group before passing them along to higher-ups in Washington.

88. For an excellent summary of the internal dynamics of the Holbrooke team, and the sometimes conflicting views on whether Holbrooke's intuitive manner of approaching the mediation was appropriate, see Rosegrant, "Getting to Dayton," 26.

89. Ibid., 22.

90. Holbrooke, *To End a War,* 192–93.

91. The United States subsequently admitted to having participated in one meeting with Karadzic and Mladic that occurred one evening at Milosevic's hunting lodge. The two hammered out an agreement to withdraw Bosnian Serb forces and heavy artillery form the NATO-enforced "exclusion zone" around Sarajevo. (Rosegrant, "Getting to Dayton," 29.) That Milosevic was able to "produce" Karadzic and Mladic only supported the earlier conclusion that he was able to control them.

92. In fact, the final map agreement fell apart at the last minute because of Mate Granic's objections to conceding to Republika Srpska large chunks of Croat land in eastern Bosnia. (Holbrooke, *To End a War,* 300.)

93. Ibid., 253.

94. Ibid., 200.

95. Ibid., 240, 265.

96. Ibid., 233.

97. Carl Bildt was given a suite in the American building, in recognition of his important role. (Holbrooke, *To End a War,* 233.)

98. Ibid., 204–5. Holbrooke notes that the team studied President Carter's account of Camp David as well as Cyrus Vance's memoirs and William Quandt's case study of the event. The term "proximity talks" dated from UN Middle East negotiations in the 1940s.

99. The team emphasized the multiethnic nature of Ohio to the various Balkan delegations. (Holbrooke, *To End a War,* 234.)

100. Ibid., 232.

101. Ibid., 273.

102. Ibid., 275.

103. Ibid., 281.

104. Ibid., 283. The Defense Mapping Agency used the system PowerScene in Dayton.

105. Holbrooke, *To End a War,* 285.

106. Ibid., 288.

107. Ibid., 240.

108. Michael P. Scharf, *Balkan Justice* (Durham, NC: Carolina Academic Press, 1997), 41–46.

109. Then-Secretary of State Lawrence Eagleburger raised the rhetoric on the war crimes when in December 1992, he named ten names of Serbs who were "suspected" war criminals. The list included Milosevic, Karadzic, and Mladic. (Elaine Sciolino, "United States Names Figures It Wants Charged with War Crimes," *New York Times* [Dec 17, 1992]: Sec. A, p. 1.) But the Clinton administration danced around the term "genocide," preferring to discuss atrocities tantamount to genocide. (Scharf, *Balkan Justice,* 31.)

110. Scharf, *Balkan Justice,* 31.

111. The tribunal at Nuremberg, by contrast, was a multinational court established by the victorious Allied powers. The ICTY in The Hague was given a charter that included jurisdiction over genocide (taken from the 1948 Genocide Convention), crimes against humanity (as understood in customary international law), and war crimes (taken from the 1948 Geneva Convention and its subsequent protocols). For an excellent and comprehensive discussion of the tribunal and the trial of Dusko Tadic, see Scharf, *Balkan Justice.*

112. The tribunal's mandate gave it jurisdiction over all war crimes and crimes against humanity committed in the former Yugoslavia after 1991. (Scharf, *Balkan Justice,* 243.)

113. Interview with Richard Goldstone, Jan. 18, 1998 (McGuinness).

114. Ibid.

115. Ibid. See also, Stephen Engelberg, "Panel Seeks United States Pledge on Bosnia War Criminals," *New York Times* (Nov. 3, 1995): Sec. A, p. 1.

116. Zartman also notes that "[b]ecause the parties may not be of equal strength or position in the conflict, the proper moment for mediation occurs when the upper hand starts slipping and the underdog starts." (I. William Zartman, *Ripe for Revolution: Conflict and Intervention in Africa* [New York: Oxford University Press, 1989], 272.) While this may be an accurate description of the events of the summer of 1995, the Bosnian Muslims and Croatia could not have made the gains they had without the military support of NATO air strikes and the Croatian Army military training made available by the United States.

117. There is also evidence that the United States was aware of arms being provided to the Bosnian Muslims in violation of the international arms embargo, but chose to wink at such shipments. (Holbrooke, *To End a War,* 320.) After Dayton, the presence of armed Mujahiddin from other Islamic countries would cause problems with implementation. Ibid., 321.

118. Zimmermann, *Origins of a Catastrophe,* xi-xii.

119. Holbrooke, *To End a War,* 309.

120. Paul Williams (interview with Frances Cook, Spring 1997).

121. Elizabeth Cousens and Mark Taylor are completing a comprehensive study on the implementation of Dayton. (Forthcoming, 1999.)

Chapter 3

1. It is the view of Lord Carrington that Germany's early recognition of Croatian sovereignty severely hindered the EC Peace Conference on Yugoslavia and shifted the focus of the Yugoslav crisis to the Republic of Bosnia-Herzegovina. Interview with author, May 12, 1997. The secretary-general of the UN, Javier Perez de Cuellar, voiced agreement with Carrington's view in a letter of December 10, 1991, to EC Minister Hans van den Broek (See note 38).

2. Laura Silber and Allan Little, *Yugoslavia: Death of a Nation* (New York: Penguin, 1995), 197. The metaphor was originally Lord Carrington's, who had used it to describe Yugoslavia under the Carrington Plan.

3. Serbs made up 11.6 percent of Croatia in 1981 and 12.2 percent in 1991. (Susan L. Woodward, *Balkan Tragedy* [Washington, D.C.: The Brookings Institution, 1995], 32.)

4. In violation of the 1974 SFRJ Constitution and the Helsinki Final Act of 1975.

5. Quoted by Pia Christina Wood, "European Political Cooperation: Lessons from the Gulf War and Yugoslavia," in *The State of the European Community*, vol. 2, ed. Alan W. Cafruny and Glenda G. Rosenthal (Boulder, CO: Lynne Rienner, 1993), 233.

6. "Joint Declaration of the EC Troika and the Parties Directly Concerned with the Yugoslav Crisis," Europe Documents No. 1725, July 16, 1991, reprinted in *Yugoslavia through Documents: From Its Creation to its Dissolution,* ed. Snezana Trifunovska (Dordrecht: Martinus Nijhoff, 1994), 311.

7. He was authorized pursuant to two declarations on Yugoslavia adopted in the EPC framework at Extraordinary Ministerial Meetings of EC Foreign Ministers on August 27, 1991, and September 3, 1991, respectively. EC Declaration on Yugoslavia, EPC Press Release, P. 82/91 and 84/91, reprinted in Trifunovska, 333–34 and 342–43. During the period of EC intervention, EPC decisions derived from plenary council discussions and EPC opinions were published in press releases on the days following the meetings.

8. "Cease Fire Agreement" and "Memorandum of Understanding on the Extension of Monitoring Activities of the Monitor Mission to Yugoslavia," *Review of International Affairs* vol. xlii (5.X-5.XI 1991): 24, 26.

9. Donald Rothchild, "Successful Mediation: Lord Carrington and the Rhodesian Settlement," in *Managing Global Chaos,* ed. Chester A. Crocker and Fen Olser Hampson (Washington, D.C.: United States Institute of Peace Press, 1996), 476.

10. "Report of the Secretary-General Pursuant to Paragraph 3 of Security Council Resolution 713," UN Doc. S/23169: 8.

11. "Statement by Lord Carrington, the Presidents of the Republics of Croatia and Serbia, and the Minister of National Defence," *Review of International Affairs* vol. xlii (5.X-5.XI 1991): 28.

12. Ibid., 8.

13. On October 3, 1991, a group of four members of the Federal Presidency, consisting of representatives of Serbia, Kosovo, Vojvdodina, and Montenegro, seized control of the presidency's powers to make constitutional decisions, particularly over the actions of the JNA, and declared itself the legitimate Yugoslav head of state. They were supported in this move by senior military officers and the federal secretary for national defense. From this time forward, the JNA followed the directives of this rump presidency, without input by representatives from Slovenia, Croatia, Bosnia-Herzegovina, and Macedonia.

14. UN Doc. S/23169: 5.

15. Ibid., Annex VI.

16. Silber and Little, *Yugoslavia: Death of a Nation,* 193.

17. He was authorized pursuant to two Declarations on Yugoslavia adopted in the EPC framework at Extraordinary Ministerial Meetings of EC Foreign Ministers on August 27,

1991, and September 3, 1991, respectively. (Trifunovska, 363–65.) Milosevic's response to the Carrington Plan.

18. Interpreting norms of international law, the EC Arbitration Commission rendered opinions on several issues submitted by the Republic of Serbia. As to the issue of Yugoslav state succession, submitted on behalf of Serbia by Lord Carrington on November 20, 1991, the Arbitration Commission, in Opinion No. 1, dated November 29, 1991, held that the outcome of succession should be equitable and consensual, settled by terms of agreement between the states concerned, in conformity with the Vienna Conventions of August 23, 1978, and April 8, 1983. As to self-determination of the constituent peoples of Yugoslavia, the Arbitration Commission, in Opinion No. 2, dated January 11, 1992, stated that the Serbian populations of Croatia and Bosnia-Herzegovina were entitled to the minority and ethnic group rights accorded to them by the Carrington Plan. As to the international legal status of internal federative boundaries, the Arbitration Commission, in Opinion No. 3, dated January 11, 1992, upheld the principle of *uti posseditis juris* and the concept of territorial status quo. *Uti posseditis juris,* a generally recognized principle of international law, which derives from a decolonization context, upholds existing administrative frontiers as state frontiers in certain cases of national self-determination. See *Case concerning the Frontier Dispute* (Burk. Faso v. Rep. Mali), 1986 I.C.J. 554, 565 (Dec. 22).

19. UN Doc. S/23169: 5.

20. UN Doc. S/23169: 13.

21. EC Declaration on Yugoslavia, September 19, 1991, EPC Press Release, 90/91.

22. UN Doc. S/23169: 6. After four monitors in a helicopter were shot down by a Yugoslav air force jet, the ECMM discontinued its use of helicopters altogether.

23. According to Ambassador Herbert S. Okun during an interview with the author, June 12, 1997.

24. Christian Democratic Union/Christian Socialist Union Coalition Caucus in the German Parliament, press release, May 7, 1991.

25. UN Doc. S/23169: 5. Ambassador Okun states that EC monitors failed to brief him and Vance fully on the failure to implement deblocking and its significance for cease-fire. Vance and Okun obtained this information from Yugoslav federal officials. (Interview with the author, June 12, 1997.)

26. UN Doc. S/23169: 5.

27. "Report of the Secretary-General Pursuant to Security Council Resolution 721," UN Doc. S/23280: 3.

28. Ibid., Annex III: 15–20.

29. Ibid., Annex II: 13.

30. Ibid., Annex II: 3.

31. Ibid., Annex II: 13.

32. Ibid., Annex III: 15.

33. Ibid., Annex III: 15–20.

34. "Accord Implementing the Cease-fire Agreement of 23 November," UN Doc. S/23363, Annex III.

35. Kohl and Genscher were wrong to invoke the Helsinki Final Act in support of Croatian self-determination. The right to self-determination included in the Helsinki Final Act applies only to consensual changes of borders—thus its relevance to German reunification—but not to unilateral changes. *See* Antonio Cassese, *Self-Determination of Peoples* (Cambridge: Cambridge University Press, 1995), 287.

36. "EC Declaration on the Suspension of the Trade Cooperation Agreement with Yugoslavia," *Review of International Affairs* vol. xlii (5.X–5.XI 1991): 26.

37. "Recognition of the Yugoslav Successor States," *Position Paper of the German Foreign Ministry* vol. xvi, no. 10 (March 10, 1993): 3–4.

38. "Letter dated 10 December 1991 from the Secretary-General of the United Nations addressed to the Minister for Foreign Affairs of the Netherlands," UN Doc. S/23280, Annex IV.

39. "EC Declaration Concerning the Conditions for Recognition of New States," UN Doc. S/23293, Annex I.

40. The Federal Republic of Yugoslavia, founded on April 27, 1992.

41. It also would have been highly unlikely given the international community's great reluctance to intervene in a sovereign state's internal affairs. A joint early recognition/intervention response would have set a too dangerous precedent in support of secessionist movements in the future.

42. Saadia Touval, "Lessons of Preventive Diplomacy in Yugoslavia," in *Managing Global Chaos*, ed. Crocker and Hampson, 411–12.

43. Ibid., 407.

Chapter 4

1. Although much of the following history is noncontroversial, heavy reliance, particularly with respect to controversial components and overall balance, has been placed on Mark Tessler, *A History of the Israeli–Palestinian Conflict* (Bloomington: Indiana University Press, 1994).

2. Bernard Reich, *An Historical Encyclopedia of the Arab–Israeli Conflict* (Westport, CT: Greenwood Press, 1996).

3. Jane Corbin, *The Norway Channel* (New York: Atlantic Monthly Press, 1994), 120.

4. Interview with Jan Egeland.

5. Corbin, *The Norway Channel*, 27.

6. Interview with Jan Egeland.

7. Interview with Geir Pederson.

8. Corbin, *The Norway Channel*, 26.

9. Interview with Jan Egeland.

10. "What's Arafat's Line?—Israel Ends Bar to Role of PLO at Peace Talks," *New York Times* (August 15, 1993): Sec. 4, p. 2.; Interview with Geir O. Pederson; Interview with Jan Egeland.

11. There actually is a long history of unofficial, exploratory talks between Israelis and Palestinians. Madhi Abdul Hadi, "Oslo—The Conflict, the Mediators, and the Breakthrough," *Harvard Newsletter on Negotiation* November 1997.

12. Corbin, *The Norway Channel*, 59–63.

13. Ibid.

14. Ibid., 79–94.

15. Ibid., 110–12.

16. Ibid., 130–34.

17. Ibid., 150.

18. Ibid., 153.

19. Ibid., 177.

20. Ibid., 38.

21. Ibid., 175.

22. Ibid., 186.

23. Interview with Jan Egeland.

24. William Zartman, "Explaining Oslo," 1996 (draft article on file with author).

25. Ibid., 4.

26. Ibid., 2.
27. Interview with Jan Egeland.
28. Corbin, *The Norway Channel,* 18.
29. Interviews with Jan Egeland, Terje Rod Larsen, and Mona Juul.
30. Interview with Mona Juul.
31. Ibid.
32. Interviews with Mona Juul and Terje Rod Larsen.
33. Interview with Mona Juul.
34. Interview with Terje Rod Larsen.
35. Ibid.
36. Ibid.
37. Ibid.
38. Interview with Jan Egeland.
39. Interview with Jan Egeland.
40. Interview with Terje Rod Larsen.
41. Interview with Mona Juul.

Chapter 5

*The author wishes to acknowledge John Bolton, David Gilmore, Steven Ratner, Stephen Solarz, Richard Solomon, and an anonymous French source for their thoughtful input and assistance in this study. Gratitude also goes to Mike Grenier, for his assistance in tracking down secondary sources, and to any reader whose thorough comments on an early draft helped shape the final outcome. Any errors are, of course, my own.

1. Full text in letter dated 30 October 1991 from France and Indonesia transmitting, as representatives of the cochairmen of the Paris Conference on Cambodia, the full texts of agreements signed in Paris, 23 October 1991, by the states participating in the Conference. UN Doc. A/46/608-S/23177 (The United Nations and Cambodia 1995), 132.
2. Ibid.
3. William Shawcross explains the difference in the Cambodian perception of Thai versus Vietnamese occupation, attributing the heightened enmity toward the Vietnamese as stemming from cultural differences:

> The Siamese and the Khmers shared the same religion and similar cultural patterns; this mitigated the effects of occupation by Siam. Relations with Vietnam by contrast involved a sharp cultural clash between Indian-influenced and Chinese-dominated views of society; they were much more brutal and bitter. Unlike the Siamese, the Vietnamese regarded the Cambodians as "barbarians" and attempted to eradicate Cambodian customs in the areas they seized. (William Shawcross, *Sideshow: Kissinger, Nixon, and the Destruction of Cambodia* [New York: Simon & Schuster, 1987], 41.)

4. Jin Song writes: "When the three resistance factions joined together in the CGDK to fight the Vietnamese-imposed Hun Sen regime, a major cohesive factor in their alliance was each member's extreme hatred of Vietnam and nostalgia for power." (Jin Song, "The Political Dynamics of the Peacekeeping Process in Cambodia," in *Keeping the Peace,* ed. Ian Johnstone [Cambridge: University Press, 1997], 55.)
5. The ASEAN states, all signatories to the Paris Agreements, were Brunei Darussalam, Indonesia, Malaysia, the Philippines, Singapore, and Thailand.
6. Telephone conversation with anonymous French diplomat.

7. Song, "The Political Dynamics of the Peacekeeping Process in Cambodia," 61–62. According to Song, Rafeeuddin Ahmed and Heddi Annabi, his senior advisor, "contacted the French in 1988, a month before JIM I, to develop a series of 'non-paper' sketches of many of the elements which later surfaced in the comprehensive settlement presented in Paris." (Ibid.)

8. Michael Haas, *Genocide by Proxy: Cambodian Pawn on a Superpower Chessboard* (New York: Prager, 1991), 131–34.

9. Ibid., 134.

10. Ibid., 136.

11. Telephone conversation with Stephen Solarz, October 15, 1998.

12. Haas, *Genocide by Proxy,* 179. The Vietnamese announcement pressured the French to call the conference quickly, since "after the troop withdrawal, the Vietnamese would be able to declare the Cambodian problem a purely domestic one, with no further need for international action." (Song, "The Political Dynamics of the Peacekeeping Process in Cambodia," 66.)

13. Tommy T.B. Koh, "The Paris Conference on Cambodia: A Multilateral Negotiation that 'Failed,' " *Negotiation Journal* (1990): 86; Haas, *Genocide by Proxy,* 198–200; Steven R. Ratner, "The Cambodian Settlement Agreements," *American Journal of International Law* 87 (1993): 6, fn 24.

14. Telephone conversation with anonymous French diplomat.

15. Haas, *Genocide by Proxy,* 192.

16. Koh, "The Paris Conference on Cambodia: A Multilateral Negotiation that 'Failed,' " 87.

17. According to one French diplomat, the French had to fly to Beijing to convince Sihanouk to come to Paris for the conference, notwithstanding the Tiananmen Square events. Personal telephone communication with anonymous French diplomat, June 10, 1997.

18. Ibid.

19. Ibid.

20. Ibid.

21. Song, "Political Dynamics," 70.

22. Ibid., 69.

23. Article 78, UN Charter.

24. Haas, *Genocide by Proxy,* 273.

25. Susan Blaustein, "Old War, China Card & Sihanouk," *The Nation,* October 30, 1989, 485.

26. Telephone conversation with Richard Solomon, May 15, 1997.

27. According to Gareth Porter:

> A shrewd diplomatic mind is at work behind Sihanouk's seemingly erratic behavior. What casual observers have long described as a "mercurial" personality is in fact a calculated tactic that he has been using for nearly four decades to enhance his diplomatic leverage: by abruptly changing sides, or threatening to do so, he gets concessions from more powerful actors who for one reason or another need his cooperation. (Garth Porter, "Cambodia: Sihanouk's Initiative," *Foreign Affairs* 66 [Spring 1988]: 814.)

28. William Shawcross described Sihanouk between 1941 to 1970 as:

> King, Chief of State, Prince, Prime Minister, head of the main political movement, jazz-band leader, magazine editor, film director and gambling concessionaire.... His exercise of power was so astonishing and so individual that he came to personify his country and its policies abroad as well as at home. He was vain, a petulant showman who enjoyed boasting of his sexual successes.... His speech was high-pitched and idiosyncratic, and his comments were often ambiguous. At the same time he had enormous political skill, charm, tenacity and intelligence. (Shawcross, *Sideshow,* 46.)

29. Claude Martin, the French representative; Robin McLaren, the British representative (who took over from Lord David Gilmore); and Rogachev, the Russian representative, all served immediately subsequent posts as ambassadors in Beijing.

30. Robert S. Ross, "China and the Cambodian Peace Process: The Value of Coercive Diplomacy," *Asian Survey* 31 (December 1991): 1170.

31. Ibid., 1177.

32. Ibid., 1180.

33. "Fortunately, the UN peace process provided both Vietnam and the Soviet Union with a graceful exit from their awkward position *vis-à-vis* Phnom Penh. Not surprisingly, both ultimately gave their full support to UN involvement." (Song, "Political Dynamics," 78.)

34. Telephone interview with Richard Solomon, May 15, 1997.

35. Haas, *Genocide by Proxy,* 250–53.

36. See Blaustein, "Old War."

37. Personal telephone communication with Richard Solomon, May 15, 1997.

38. Personal telephone communication with Stephen Solarz, October 15, 1998.

39. See Janet E. Heininger, *Peacekeeping in Transition: The United Nations in Cambodia* (New York: Twentieth Century Fund, 1994).

40. Personal telephone communication with anonymous French diplomat, June 10, 1997.

41. Haas, *Genocide by Proxy,* 208.

42. Steven R. Ratner, *The New UN Peacekeeping: Building Peace in Lands of Conflict after the Cold War* (New York: St. Martin's, 1995), 144–45.

43. Haas, *Genocide by Proxy,* 222.

44. *The United Nations and Cambodia, 1991–1995:* 7; Australia, Finland and Sweden contributed to the funding of the UNDP fact-finding missions. (Haas, *Genocide by Proxy,* 274, 283–84.)

45. Haas, *Genocide by Proxy,* 281.

46. Ibid., 283–84.

47. Ibid., 273.

48. Song, "Political Dynamics," 72.

49. Ibid., 75; Ratner, "The Cambodia Settlement Agreements," 17.

50. Haas, *Genocide by Proxy,* 287.

51. Telephone Interview with Richard Solomon; Haas, *Genocide by Proxy,* 225.

52. Article 78 of the UN Charter provides, "The trusteeship system shall not apply to territories which have become Members of the United Nations, relationship among which shall be based on respect for the principle of sovereign equality."

53. Ratner, "The Cambodia Settlement Agreements," 9.

54. Letter dated 30 August 1990 from China, France, the Soviet Union, the United Kingdom, and the United States transmitting statement and framework document adopted by their representatives at a meeting in New York, 27–28 August 1990. UN Doc. A/45/472-S/21689. (The United Nations and Cambodia 1995: 88.)

55. Letter dated 11 September 1990 from France and Indonesia, as cochairmen of the Paris Conference on Cambodia, transmitting joint statement on Cambodia issued at the end of talks held in Jakarta, 9–10 September 1990. UN Doc. A/45/490-S/21732. (*The United Nations and Cambodia 1995:* 93.)

56. Letter dated 18 July 1991 from the president of the Supreme National Council transmitting communiqué of the Council's Informal Meeting in Beijing, 16–17 July 1991. UN Doc. A/46/310-S/22808. (The United Nations and Cambodia 1995: 115.)

57. Ross, "Coercive Diplomacy," 1181.

58. Telephone communication with anonymous French diplomat, June 10, 1997.

59. David A. Chandler, *A History of Cambodia,* 2nd ed. (Boulder, CO: Westview Press, 1993), 27.

Chapter 6

1. Gary Bland, "Assessing the Transition to Democracy," in *Is There a Transition to Democracy in El Salvador?* ed. Joseph S. Tulchin, et al. (Boulder, CO: Lynne Rienner, 1992), 170.

2. The FMLN consisted of five Marxist groups: Popular Liberation Forces, People's Revolutionary Army, Central American Workers Party, National Resistance, and Communist Party. James Lemoyne called the Salvadoran guerrillas "the best-trained, best-organized and most committed Marxist–Leninist rebel movement ever seen in Latin America." (James Lemoyne, "El Salvador's Forgotten War," *Foreign Affairs* [Summer 1989]: 105.)

3. Bland, "Assessing the Transition to Democracy," 171.

4. George Vickers, "The Political Reality after Ten Years of War," in *Is There a Transition to Democracy in El Salvador?* ed. Tulchin et al., 34.

5. Roberto D'Aubuisson was the founder of the ARENA party and was heavily involved with death squad activity.

6. Interview with former President Alfredo Cristiani, San Salvador, El Salvador, April 8, 1997.

7. Terry Karl, "El Salvador's Negotiated Revolution," *Foreign Affairs* vol. 71, no. 2 (Spring 1992).

8. Interview with Cristiani, San Salvador, April 8, 1997.

9. Interview with Alvaro de Soto at UN Headquarters in New York, February 18, 1997.

10. Interview with de Soto, February 18, 1997. Interview with Salvador Samayoa in San Salvador, El Salvador, April 10, 1997.

11. Interview with former Costa Rican President Oscar Arias, San Jose, Costa Rica, April 6, 1997.

12. Interview with David Escobar Galindo in San Salvador, El Salvador, April 10, 1997.

13. Father Ellacuria was one of the Jesuit priests murdered in December 1989. According to Cristiani, Ellacuria and he had met three times to discuss the possibility of peace between the government and the FMLN. (Interview with Cristiani, April 8, 1997.)

14. Interview with Samayoa, April 10, 1997.

15. Interview with former Assistant Secretary of State Bernard Aronson, September 17, 1998.

16. Interview with Cristiani, San Salvador, April 8, 1997.

17. Ibid.

18. Ibid.

19. Ibid.

20. Ibid.

21. Interview with former Deputy Defense Minister General Mauricio Vargas, April 9, 1997, in San Salvador, El Salvador. All quotes attributed to Vargas in this article were gathered from this interview.

22. Ibid.

23. Interview with de Soto, February 18, 1997.

24. Karl, "El Salvador's Negotiated Revolution," 153.

25. Ibid.

26. Shirley Christian, "Salvadoran Chief and Rebels Reach Broad Agreement," *New York Times* (Sept. 26, 1991): Sec. A, p. 6.

27. Interview with de Soto, February 18, 1997.

28. Interview with David Escobar Galindo in San Salvador, El Salvador in April 8, 1997.

29. Interview with Aronson, September 17, 1998.

30. Ibid.

31. Interview with Cristiani, San Salvador, April 8, 1997.

32. Interview with de Soto, February 18, 1997.

33. De Soto, "The Negotiations Following the New York Agreement," in *Is There a Transition to Democracy in El Salvador,* ed. Tulchin et al., 140.

34. Ibid.

35. Ibid., 140.

36. ONUCA was meant to be an on-site verification mechanism to monitor compliance by the Central American government with the Esquipulas agreement. The FMLN was opposed to ONUCA, and de Soto met with the FMLN leaders to reduce their hostility toward the organization.

37. Interview with Vargas, April 9, 1997.

38. Interview with de Soto, February 18, 1997.

39. Interview with Arias, April 6, 1997.

40. Ibid.

41. Interview with Cristiani, San Salvador, April 8, 1997.

42. Ibid.

43. Ibid.

44. Ibid.

45. Ibid.

46. Interview with Samayoa, April 10, 1997; Interview with Aronson, September 17, 1998.

47. Interview with Aronson, September 17, 1998.

48. Bland, "Assessing the Transition to Democracy," 176.

49. Interview with Aronson, September 17, 1998.

50. Ibid.

51. Clifford Krauss, "UN Aide Assailed in Salvadoran Talks," *New York Times* (February 1, 1991): A3.

52. Interview with Alvaro de Soto, February 18, 1997.

53. De Soto notes, "This was violated much more than it was respected, but I was able at least to control them to the point that they wouldn't make public proposals that were under discussion or not publicly conducted."

54. Vickers, "The Political Reality after Ten Years of War," 38.

55. Karl, "El Salvador's Negotiated Revolution," 159.

56. Interview with de Soto, February 18, 1997.

57. Interview with Samayoa, April 10, 1997.

58. Interview with Ruben Zamora in San Salvador, El Salvador, April 7, 1997. Ruben Zamora is the moderate leftist founder of the Social Christian Popular Movement, a party of the Democratic Convergence, and served as vice president of the legislature.

59. Interview with Vargas, April 9, 1997.

60. Interview with Cristiani, April 8, 1997.

61. Interview with de Soto, February 18, 1997.

62. Alvaro de Soto and Graciana del Castillo, "Obstacles to Peacebuilding," *Foreign Policy* (Spring 1994): 70.

63. Ibid.

64. Larry Rohter, "Former Rebels Make Impressive Advances in Salvador Elections," *New York Times* (March 26, 1997): Sec.A, p. 5.

65. Interview with Aronson, September 17, 1998.

Chapter 7

1. Republic of Ireland, Department of Foreign Affairs, *Northern Ireland Peace Process: Background Information Note,* December 1996.

2. Landon Hancock, *Northern Ireland: Troubles Brewing* <http://cain.ulst.ac.uk/oth elem/landon.htm> (website visited Oct. 8, 1998).

3. R.F. Foster, *Modern Ireland: 1600–1972* (New York: Penguin, 1988), 154–55.

4. Maire Cruise O'Brien and Conor Cruise O'Brien, *A Concise History of Ireland,* 3rd ed. (New York: Thames & Hudson, 1985).

5. Joseph Ruane and Jennifer Todd, *The Dynamics of Conflict in Northern Ireland: Power, Conflict and Emancipation* (Cambridge: Cambridge University Press, 1996), 224. *See generally,* Bob Purdie, *Politics in the Streets: The Origins of the Civil Rights Movement in Northern Ireland* (Belfast: The Blackstaff Press, 1990).

6. Ruane and Todd, *The Dynamics of Conflict,* 224.

7. Ibid., 150.

8. British mistreatment of detainees, including prolonged and physically demanding interrogation techniques—including hooding; subjection to noise; deprivation of sleep, food, and water; and wall-standing, in which detainees were forced to spend hours standing in a "stress position" against a wall—attracted the attention of Amnesty International, whose report on the subject was a motivating factor for the Irish government to bring a case before the European Commission of Human Rights and the European Court of Human Rights. See *Ireland v. The United Kingdom,* 21 Eur. Ct. H.R. (ser. A) (1978). In that case, the European Commission of Human Rights unanimously determined that the combined use of the techniques constituted inhuman treatment rising to the level of torture. Its decision, however, was modified by the European Court of Human Rights, which determined that although the use of the techniques "undoubtedly amounted to inhuman and degrading treatment," they did not "occasion suffering of the particular intensity and cruelty implied by the word torture." Ibid., paragraphs 167–68.

9. See Kevin Boyle and Tom Hadden, *Northern Ireland: The Choice* (London: Penguin, 1994) 33–48; Martin Melaugh, "Majority–Minority Differentials: Unemployment, Housing and Health in Northern Ireland," in *Facets of the Conflict in Northern Ireland,* ed. Seamus Dunn (New York: St. Martin's, 1995), 131; Alan Smith, "Education and the Conflict in Northern Ireland," in *Facets of the Conflict in Northern Ireland,* 168.

10. Boyle and Hadden, *The Choice,* 35.

11. A.M. Gallagher, *Majority Minority Review 1: Education in a Divided Society* , 2nd ed. (Coleraine, Northern Ireland: University of Ulster, 1995).

12. Boyle and Hadden, *The Choice,* 44.

13. Ibid., 50.

14. Ibid.

15. Ruane and Todd, *The Dynamics of Conflict,* 54.

16. *Police Constable's Annual Report* (1996), 87.

17. Ronald J. Fisher and Loraleigh Keashly, "The Potential Complementarity of Mediation and Consultation within a Contingency Model of Third Party Intervention," *Journal of Peace Research* vol. 28 (1991): 33.

18. David Bloomfield, *Peacemaking Strategies in Northern Ireland: Building Complementarity in Conflict Management Theory* (London: MacMillan Press Ltd., 1997), 123.

19. Joint Declaration of Irish Taoiseach Albert Reynolds and British Prime Minister John Major, Dec. 15, 1993, paragraph 9.

20. Ibid., paragraph 4.

21. Ibid., paragraph 5.

22. Ibid., paragraph 10.

23. I. William Zartman, *Ripe for Resolution: Conflict and Intervention in Africa* (New York: Oxford University Press, 1991), 272.

24. *Frontline: The IRA and Sinn Fein* (PBS television broadcast, Oct. 21, 1997).

25. Ibid.

26. Simultaneously with publication of the Joint Framework Document, the British government published its own, more detailed, plan for new political structures in Northern Ireland. The particulars of the British plan called for the creation of a unicameral assembly of approximately ninety members elected through a form of proportional representation. Under the plan, the assembly would be granted legislative authority.

27. *A New Framework for Agreement,* Feb. 22, 1995, paragraph 7.

28. Ibid.

29. Ibid., paragraph 23.

30. Ibid., paragraph 10.

31. P. Bew and G. Gillespie, *The Northern Ireland Peace Process: 1993–1996* (London: Serif, 1996), 105.

32. Communiqué of the Republic of Ireland and the United Kingdom, Nov. 28, 1995, paragraph 5.

33. Ibid., paragraph 7.

34. Report of the International Body, Jan. 22, 1996, paragraph 8 [hereinafter, Report].

35. In 1995, the United Nations offered to hold an international peace conference in Geneva under UN auspices to break the deadlock in the Northern Ireland peace process over the decommissioning of arms. The offer was rejected by British Prime Minister John Major, who insisted that Northern Ireland was not a matter for the United Nations.

36. Report, paragraph 6.

37. Ibid., paragraphs 25–26.

38. Ibid., paragraph 35.

39. Ibid., paragraph 20.

40. Ibid., paragraph 40.

41. Ibid., paragraphs 38–50.

42. Ibid., paragraph 56.

43. See Nicholas Watt, "Election Plan Cools Early Welcome for Peace Blueprint," *Times of London* (Jan. 25, 1996).

44. Ibid.

45. One of the bombs was located and defused by authorities without injury or loss of life. The other exploded on a double-decker bus in London, killing one person. Police believe that the bomb exploded as it was being transported to its target and that the deceased was an IRA member.

46. *Statement of the Irish Republican Army,* Feb. 9, 1996, paragraph 4.

47. See Section II.B of this chapter.

48. William Graham, "Unionists Bicker as Mitchell Takes Chair," *The Irish Times* (June 13, 1996).

49. Aide-Mémoire sent to Sinn Fein, June 1997, http://www.nio.gov.uk/press/970625hh.htm (visited Oct. 8, 1998).

50. "Adams and Humes 'Optimistic' Over Obstacles," *The Irish Times* (July 19, 1997).

51. Joint Paper from the British and Irish Governments on Decommissioning, June 25, 1997, http://www.nio.gov.uk/press/970625hh.htm (visited Oct. 8, 1998).

52. Gerry Moriarity, "Uncertainty Overshadows SF-UUP Meeting," *The Irish Times* (Sept. 24, 1997).

53. Interview with Senator George Mitchell, independent chairman of the Plenary Session of Multiparty Negotiations (July 17, 1998).

54. See Deaglan de Breadun, "North Parties Gear Up for Bitter Assembly Elections," *The Irish Times* (May 25, 1998); Gerry Moriarty, "DUP Says It Will Not Set Out to 'Wreck' Assembly," *The Irish Times,* May 27, 1998.

55. The Agreement, 10 April 1998, Strand 1, Para. 5, reprinted in 37 I.L.M. 751 (1998).

56. Ibid.

57. The Agreement, Strand 2, Paragraph 1.

58. The Agreement, Strand 3, Paragraph 1.

59. Joint Paper on Decommissioning.

60. See note 34 supra.

61. Telephone Interview with Robert Bradtke, former Deputy Chief Mission, U.S. Embassy in London (June 11, 1997).

62. Ibid.

63. Interview with Senator George Mitchell (July 17, 1998).

64. "British Government Gives Economic 'Peace Aid' to Northern Ireland," *Agence France Presse,* May 11, 1998.

65. Interview with Senator George Mitchell (July 17, 1998).

66. Ibid.

67. Ibid.

68. Ibid.

Chapter 8

1. Tor Sellström and Lennart Wohlgemuth, "Study 1: Historical Perspectives: Some Explanatory Factors," in *The International Response to Conflict and Genocide: Lessons from the Rwanda Experience* (Joint Evaluation of Emergency Assistance to Rwanda, 1996), http://www.reliefweb.int/library/nordic/book1/pb020.

2. Ibid.

3. Ibid., 2–3.

4. Ibid., 4.

5. Ibid., 3.

6. Gérard Prunier, *The Rwanda Crisis: History of a Genocide* (New York: Columbia University Press, 1995), 4.

7. Sellström and Wohlgemuth, "Historical Perspectives," Chap. 2.

8. Ibid.

9. Ibid.

10. Prunier, *The Rwanda Crisis,* 11-12.

11. Sellström and Wohlgemuth, "Historical Perspectives," Chap. 2.

12. Ibid.

13. Prunier, *The Rwanda Crisis,* 13.

14. Ibid., 11–12.

15. John Eriksson, et al., "Synthesis Report," in *The International Response to Conflict and Genocide: Lessons from the Rwanda Experience* (Joint Evaluation of Emergency Assistance to Rwanda, 1996), http://www.reliefweb.int/library/nordic/book5/pb025.html, Chap. 1.

16. Sellström and Wohlgemuth, "Historical Perspectives," Chap. 3.

17. Ibid.

18. Prunier, *The Rwanda Crisis,* 17.

19. Sellström and Wohlgemuth, "Study 1: Historical Perspectives," Chap. 3.

20. Erikkson, "Synthesis Report," Chap. 1.

21. Prunier, *The Rwanda Crisis,* 45.

22. Sellström and Wohlgemuth, "Historical Perspectives," Chap. 3.

23. This number is debated, but Prunier asserts it as the most accurate estimate available. (Prunier, *The Rwanda Crisis,* 63.)

24. Prunier, *The Rwanda Crisis,* 67.

25. Bruce D. Jones, "Roots, Resolution, and Reaction: Civil War, the Peace Process, and Genocide in Rwanda" (paper presented at the University of Toronto conference on Civil Wars in Africa, May 1995), p. 5.

26. Ibid. See also Prunier, *The Rwanda Crisis*, 409.

27. Erikkson, "Synthesis Report," Chap. 1.

28. Sellström and Wohlgemuth, "Historical Perspectives," Chap. 3.

29. Ibid.

30. Prunier, *The Rwanda Crisis*, 101.

31. Ibid. 148–49.

32. Sellström and Wohlgemuth, "Historical Perspectives," Chap. 4.

33. Bruce D. Jones, "The Arusha Peace Process: Report for Study II of the Joint Evaluation of Emergency Assistance to Rwanda" (revised version presented to U.S. Committee for Refugees Conference on 'Early Warning and Conflict Management in Rwanda,' Washington, D.C.; December 18, 1995), p. 2.

34. Ibid.

35. Ibid., 3.

36. Ibid.

37. Théogène Rudasingwa, Rwandan ambassador to the United States, interview by author (taped), Washington, D.C., June 3, 1997.

38. Jones, "The Arusha Peace Process," 3.

39. Jones, "Roots, Resolution and Reaction," 3.

40. Jones, "The Arusha Peace Process," 4.

41. Ibid.

42. Herman Cohen, Rwanda chapter of manuscript in forthcoming book.

43. Ibid.

44. Jones, "The Arusha Peace Process," 4.

45. Cohen, "Chapter 6: Rwanda," 7.

46. Ibid.

47. Alan J. Kuperman, "The Other Lesson of Rwanda: Mediators Sometimes Do More Damage Than Good," *School of Advanced International Studies (SAIS) Review: A Journal of International Affairs* 16 (Winter-Spring 1996): 222.

48. Jones, "Roots, Resolution, and Reaction," 10.

49. Rudasingwa interview.

50. For example, at the opening round the Nigerian ambassador commented on his positive impression of the RPF delegation. This story was related during an interview by the author with Charles Snyder, director of the Office of African Regional Affairs, U.S. State Department, in Washington, D.C., on June 2, 1997.

51. The detailed notes proved decisive as they frequently became the de facto working document at the negotiations. The United States had provided Kagame with some instruction on negotiating tactics. They stressed the importance of prioritizing demands and of having fallback positions spelled out. The United States had provided the training while Kagame was receiving military instruction in the United States as a member of the Ugandan Army.

52. Snyder commented that the RPF upped its demands when its members began to understand their superiority at the negotiating table. A U.S. observer to the talks, Lt. Col. Anthony D. Marley, believed that the RPF would have settled for lower percentages in military. [Lt. Col. Marley, retired, political-military advisor, Africa Bureau, State Department at the time of the Arusha Accords, interview with the author (taped). Las Vegas, Nevada, June 5, 1997.] Also, Snyder interview.

53. The RPF did find allies in the GoR delegation both in Arusha and in Kigali. An ob-

server to the talks indicated seeing confidential GoR position/strategy papers that had been faxed to the RPF.

54. Snyder and Cohen interviews.

55. Howard Adelman and Astri Suhrke, "Study 2: Early Warning and Conflict Management," in *The International Response to Conflict and Genocide: Lessons from the Rwanda Experience* (Joint Evaluation of Emergency Assistance to Rwanda, 1996), http://www.reliefweb.int/library/nordic/book2/pb021.html.

56. Snyder interview.

57. In many ways this contributed to the military success of the RPF. In general, FAR soldiers were primarily concerned with not getting killed. During the February 1993 RPF offensive, many of the FAR soldiers simply fled as soon as the fighting began.

58. Several observers commented on hearing this fear. In one instance, a GoR representative with a scientific Ph.D. from a Western university commented that the Hutu would not be able to compete on a level playing field with the smarter Tutsi. Other stories expressed concerns by the GoR that it would be tricked at the negotiating table by the more intellectually nimble Tutsi.

59. Although Mobutu was never involved, he retained the title of "mediator."

60. During the negotiations, the United States and the Europeans exerted considerable economic leverage on Rwanda. The United States terminated all but U.S. $6 million of its U.S. $20 million in economic aid because of human rights violations. The International Monetary Fund and the World Bank suspended all assistance. In addition, Belgium threatened to withdraw approximately U.S. $30 million if the human rights situation did not improve. (Kuperman, "The Other Lesson of Rwanda: Mediators Sometimes Do More Damage Than Good," 227.) While these efforts did exert pressure on Habyarimana, the unwavering support of France mitigated their full force.

61. Adelman and Suhrke, "Study 2: Early Warning and Conflict Management," Chap. 2.

62. Snyder and Cohen interviews.

63. Adelman and Suhrke, "Study 2: Early Warning and Conflict Management," Chap. 2.

64. Prunier, *The Rwanda Crisis,* 100.

65. Adelman and Suhrke, "Study 2: Early Warning and Conflict Management," Chap. 2.

66. John Byerly, special negotiator, Office of Transportation, U.S. State Department, Interview by author (taped), Washington, D.C., June 2, 1997. Herman Cohen, senior advisor, Global Coalition for Africa, Washington, D.C., June 12, 1997, telephone interview by author. Also, interviews with Snyder and Lt. Col. Marley, retired.

67. After early talks in which the RPF was surprised at its success, Snyder encouraged the RPF not necessarily to take all the concessions it could win. In particular he suggested that they seek a lower percentage in the military. (Snyder interview.)

68. Interview, Lt. Col. Marley, retired.

69. Sellström and Wohlgemuth, "Historical Perspectives," Chap. 4.

70. Ibid., p. 6.

71. Jones, "The Arusha Peace Process," 4 and interview, Lt. Col. Marley, retired.

72. Interview, Rudasingwa.

73. Ami M. Mpungwe, Tanzanian high commissioner to South Africa, Pretoria, June 13, 1997, telephone interview by author.

74. The government was to be extended to include the RPF and to be composed of twenty-one ministers: five MRND (including minister of defense), five RPF (including the vice prime minister and the minister of the interior), four MDR (including prime minister and minister of finance), three PSD, three PL, and one PDC. The transitional parliament was to be composed of eleven members from each of the MRND, MDR, PSD, PL, and RPF, four members

from the PDC, and one member from all other recognized parties. (Sellström and Wohlgemuth, "Historical Perspectives," Chap. 4.)

75. Sellström and Wohlgemuth, "Historical Perspectives," Chap. 4.

76. Jones, "The Arusha Peace Process," 6.

77. Some observers viewed this as bringing into question the RPF's commitment to true
power sharing. (Jones, "The Arusha Peace Process," 4.)

78. Adelman and Suhrke, "Study 2: Early Warning and Conflict Management," Chap. 2.

79. Ibid., 3.

80. Mpungwe considered this arrangement to be the most creative aspect of the Arusha
Accords. (Interview, Mpungwe.)

81. Several members of the observer force felt this was excessive for the RPF and that it
risked repudiation by forces in Kigali. (Jones, "The Arusha Peace Process," 7, and Adelman
and Suhrke, "Study 2: Early Warning and Conflict Management," Chap. 2.)

82. Sellström and Wohlgemuth, "Historical Perspectives," Chap. 4.

83. One militia informer from Kigali indicated that his units could kill 1,000 people in
twenty minutes. (Adelman and Suhrke, "Study 2: Early Warning and Conflict Management,"
Chap. 2.)

84. Prunier, *The Rwanda Crisis,* 199. Members of this refugee population became excellent recruits for the *interahamwe.*

85. Interview, Mpungwe.

86. Sellström and Wohlgemuth, "Historical Perspectives," Chap. 4.

87. Jones, "The Arusha Peace Process," 12.

88. Adelman and Suhrke, "Study 2: Early Warning and Conflict Management," Chap. 2.

89. Ibid.

90. Jones, "The Arusha Peace Process," 11.

91. Hence the media-reported horror stories of Tutsi being massacred while UN troops
were present.

92. Kuperman, "The Other Lessons of Rwanda," 230.

93. Jones, "Roots, Resolution and Reaction," 13.

94. Ibid., 14.

95. Adelman and Suhrke, "Study 2: Early Warning and Conflict Management," Chap. 2;
Kuperman, 221; and Cohen, 14.

96. Jones, "The Arusha Peace Process," 18, and Adelman and Sukhre, Chap. 2.

97. Jones, "The Arusha Peace Process," 9.

98. Ibid.

99. Interview, Lt. Col. Marley, retired.

100. Jones, "Roots, Resolution and Reaction," 16.

101. Kuperman, "The Other Lessons of Rwanda," 237; and Cohen, 14.

102. Shortly after the signing of the Arusha Accords, Habyarimana commented on the proposed UN peacekeeping force, saying, "I think that this force will be there to provide security
to everyone." This sentiment was broadly shared by Rwandans. (Kuperman, 236.)

103. Cohen, 14.

104. Ian Linden, "The Churches and Genocide: Lessons from Rwanda," *Svensk Missionstidskrift* 83 (3/1995): 5–15.

105. Kuperman, "The Other Lessons of Rwanda," 227.

106. Interviews, Cohen and Snyder. Snyder was a U.S. observer at the first Arusha negotiating round in the summer of 1992.

107. Kuperman, "The Other Lesson of Rwanda", 232, and interviews, Cohen and Lt. Col.
Marley, retired.

108. Adelman and Suhrke, "Study 2: Early Warning and Conflict Management," Chap. 2.

109. Ibid., Chap. 4.

110. Prunier, *The Rwanda Crisis,* 227.

Chapter 9

1. Donald R. Morris, *The Washing of the Spears: The Rise and Fall of the Zulu Nation* (New York: Simon & Schuster, 1965).

2. Allister Sparks, *The Mind of South Africa* (New York: Ballantine, 1990), 32.

3. Van Riebeeck himself laid claim to significant lands by right of conquest. He wrote to his superiors at the Dutch East India Company that the Khoikhoi, insisting so strenuously upon the point of restoring to them their own land, that we were at length to say that they had entirely forfeited the right, through the war which they had waged against us, and that we were not now inclined to restore it, as [the land] had now become the property of the Company by the sword and the laws of war. (Sparks, 39)

4. See Leonard Thompson, *A History of South Africa* (New Haven, CT: Yale University Press, 1990), 154–86, for an overview of pre-apartheid segregation in South Africa.

5. Francis Wilson and Mamphela Ramphele, *Uprooting Poverty: The South African Challenge* (Cape Town: David Philip, 1989). The report concluded that policies of separate development, anti-urbanization, forced removals, Bantu education, the crushing of organization, and, in more recent years, destabilization [of the SADC states] have been directly responsible for increasing poverty amongst millions of people. Indeed, it is precisely this dimension of premeditation or deliberate policy in impoverishing people that makes poverty in South Africa different from that in so many other parts of the world. (230)

6. Zola Skweyiya, "Toward a Solution to the Land Question in Post-Apartheid South Africa: Problems and Models," *Columbia Human Rights Law Review* 21 (1989): 213.

7. Andrew Whiteford and Michael McGrath, *Distribution of Income in South Africa* (Pretoria: Human Sciences Research Council, 1994), 62.

8. Lesotho, Botswana, Mozambique, Angola, Swaziland, Zimbabwe, and Zambia. [Joseph Hanlon, *Beggar Your Neighbours: Apartheid Power in Southern Africa* (London: James Currey, 1986).]

9. For the activities of UNITA in Angola and RENAMO in Mozambique, see generally Jeremy Harding, *Small Wars, Small Mercies* (London: Penguin, 1994), 1–79, 237–327.

10. See Hanlon, *Beggar Your Neighbours,* 1.

11. See John Stockwell, *In Search of Enemies* (New York: Norton, 1978) (documenting the extensive involvement of the CIA in the Angolan conflict); Jonathan Kwitny, *Endless Enemies* (New York: Congdon & Weed: Distributed by St. Martin's Press, 1988), 126–52.

12. Angola, Botswana, Lesotho, Malawi, Mozambique, Swaziland, Tanzania, Zambia, and Zimbabwe were the original members of the SADCC in 1980. South Africa joined after the 1994 elections, and the organization renamed itself the Southern African Development Community (SADC).

13. United Nations Children's Fund, *Children on the Front Line* 1989 Update 11 (1989): 38.

14. SADCC, *The Cost of Destabilization: Memorandum presented by SADCC to the 1985 Summit of the Organization of African Unity* (1985), reproduced in Hanlon, *Beggar Your Neighbours,* 265–70.

15. Nelson Mandela, "South Africa's Future Foreign Policy," *Foreign Affairs* 72 (1993): 90.

16. See Ibrahim J. Gassama, "Reaffirming Faith in the Dignity of Each Human Being: The United Nations, NGOs, and Apartheid," *Fordham International Law Journal* 19 (1996): 1464, 1472–76.

17. Ibid., 1472.

18. See General Assembly of the United Nations Resolution 2202 (XXI) of 16 December 1966.

19. On March 21, 1960, the South African police opened fire on a peaceful protest march against pass laws and killed sixty-nine protesters. Soon thereafter, the ANC and PAC, who were responsible for organizing the protest, were banned and forced into exile and underground opposition.

20. UN SCOR, 18th Sess., 1041st mtg. at 6, U.N. Doc. S/5386 (1963).

21. Gassama, "Reaffirming Faith," 1486.

22. Ibid., 1488–91.

23. S.C. Res. 418, U.N. SCOR, 32nd Sess., 2046th mtg. at 1, U.N. Doc. S/RES/418 (1977).

24. This section of the chapter draws from an earlier analysis of mine, see Peter N. Bouckaert, "The Negotiated Revolution: South Africa's Transition to a Multiracial Democracy," *Stanford Journal of International Law* 33.2 (Spring 1997): 375–411. See also Allister Sparks, *Tomorrow is Another Country* (Sandton, South Africa: Struik Publishers 1994); Patti Waldmeir, *Anatomy of a Miracle: The End of Apartheid and the Birth of the New South Africa* (New York: Norton, 1997); Timothy D. Sisk, *Democratization in South Africa* (Princeton: Princeton University Press, 1995); David Ottoway, *Chained Together: Mandela, de Klerk, and the Struggle to Remake South Africa* (New York: Times Books, 1993).

25. See, e.g., Gennady I. Chufrin and Harold Saunders, "A Public Peace Process," *Negotiation Journal* 9 (1993): 155 (discussing the work of the Dartmouth Conference, a regular forum where prominent U.S. and Soviet citizens met from 1960 until the end of the Cold War to discuss the relations between their two nations); Herbert C. Kelman, "Informal Mediation by the Scholar/Practitioner," in *Mediation in International Relations: Multiple Approaches to Conflict Management*, ed. Jacob Bercovitch and Jeffrey Z. Rubin (New York: St. Martin's Press, 1992), 64. The Armenian-Azerbaijan Initiative began in 1993 and is cosponsored by the Foundation for Global Community and the Stanford Center on Conflict and Negotiation. The project is currently facilitated by Dr. Harold Saunders, and a number of meetings between influential citizens have taken place under its auspices.

26. Sisk, *Democratization in South Africa*, 77.

27. Gavin Reilly stated afterwards that the purpose for his meeting with the ANC was "to develop a judgment about the importance of this crummy Marxism which [the ANC purports] to advocate. I'm less concerned about who runs South Africa than I am about the economic system which prevails." Reilly returned reassured that "the leadership of the ANC would be more interested in a viable and vibrant South African economy than they would be in the Marxist form of economy. They were people who can be talked to. . . ." Stefan Kanfer, *The Last Empire: De Beers, Diamonds, and the World* (New York: Farrar, Straus & Giroux, 1990), 354.

28. IDASA is the acronym for the Institute for Democracy in South Africa, an influential nongovernmental organization whose goal was to encourage a democratic settlement in South Africa.

29. For an account of this spirited meeting, see Waldmeir, *Anatomy of a Miracle: The End of Apartheid and the Birth of the New South Africa*, 63–64. According to Waldmeir, the meeting opened with Seterse Choabe, an ANC member, threatening to kill de Lange. At the end of the conference, the two had reconciled, with Choabe embracing de Lange and reminding the latter that "it's our children dying in Soweto."

30. This characterization is Patti Waldmeir's.

31. Sisk, *Democratization in South Africa*, 78. The comments of one participant, Willem de Klerk, echo similar sentiments:

I am convinced that the discussions have greatly improved mutual understanding; created a positive climate of expectations; brought a mutual moderation and realism to our politics; channeled important messages to [the ANC in] Lusaka and [the apartheid government in] Pretoria; and even included the germs of certain transactions. [It] was a bridge-building between NP Afrikaners and the ANC. (Allister Sparks, *Tomorrow Is Another Country,* 84.)

For a more general treatment of the value of pre-negotiation track-two diplomacy, see Janice Gross Stein, *Getting to the Table: The Processes of International Prenegotiation* (Baltimore: Johns Hopkins University Press, 1989).

32. Sparks, *Tomorrow Is Another Country,* 80–81.

33. For a fascinating account of these secret negotiations, see Allister Sparks, "The Secret Revolution," *New Yorker* (April 11, 1994): 56.

34. Sheridan Johns and R. Hunt Davis, eds., *Mandela, Tambo, and the African National Congress: The Struggle against Apartheid 1948–1990* (Oxford: Oxford University Press, 1991), 215.

35. Ibid., 216–25.

36. A 1987 ANC document noted:

There are many indications that the major Western powers are likely to launch an initiative aimed at starting a process of negotiations between the ANC and the Botha regime. . . . It is known that the US, the UK, and the [Federal Republic of Germany] are preparing a document that will, *inter alia,* set out parameters for a negotiated resolution of the South African question. The document includes demands that will be made on the ANC to force it to comply with these parameters. It is said that the Western powers will put maximum pressure on the ANC to achieve these objectives. [Govan Mbeki, *Sunset at Midday* (Braamfontein: Nolwazi Educational Publishers, 1996), 103.]

37. "Charterist" refers to those organizations that align themselves with the goals put forth in the Freedom Charter, adopted at the ANC-sponsored Congress of the People in 1955.

38. Herman Giliomee, "*Broedertwis:* Intra-Afrikaner Conflicts and the Transition from Apartheid," *African Affairs* 91 (1992): 339.

39. The speech is reproduced in part in David Ottoway, *Chained Together: Mandela, de Klerk, and the Struggle to Remake South Africa* (New York: Random House, 1993), 74–76.

40. Sisk, *Democratization in South Africa,* 93–94.

41. In the end, the following twenty parties were represented at CODESA:

the PAC, the [apartheid] government, the NP (as separate delegations, the former as nonvoting), ANC, IFP, Labour Party, Inyandza National Movement (Kangwane), Transvaal and Natal Indian Congresses (joint delegation), Venda government, Boputhatswana government, United People's Front (Lebowa), Solidarity [Democratic Party], Transkei government, National People's Party (opposition party in the Indian House of Delegates), Ciskei government, Kikwankwetla party (Qwaqwa), Itando Yesiswe party (Kwandebele), Ximoko Progressive party (Gazankulu), and the South African Communist Party. (Sisk, *Democratization in South Africa,* 203.)

42. Sparks, *Tomorrow Is Another Country,* 131–32. De Klerk in his opening remarks suggested that the ANC had failed to meet its commitment to disbanding its military wing. Incensed, Mandela rose and told the audience that "[e]ven the head of an illegitimate, discredited, minority regime, as his is, has certain moral standards to uphold," and "[i]f a man can come to a conference of this nature and play the type of politics he has played, very few people would want to deal with such a man."

43. Waldmeir, 200. On the 1992 referendum, see generally Annette Strauss, "The 1992 Referendum in South Africa," *Journal of Modern African Studies* 31 (1993): 339.

44. Rich Mkhondo, *Reporting South Africa* (London: James Currey, 1993), 145.

45. Joe Slovo, "Negotiations: What Room for Compromise?" *African Communist* (3rd Quarter 1992): 36.

46. The entire next issue of the *African Communist* (4th Quarter 1992) was devoted to debating the Slovo proposals and shows the range of ANC opinion.

47. African National Congress, *Negotiations: A Strategic Perspective* (adopted by the ANC National Executive Committee on Nov. 25, 1992).

48. "Report of the Secretary-General to the Security Council in Pursuance of Security Council Resolution 765 (1992)," August 7, 1992, UN Doc. S/24389.

49. "Security Council Resolution: The Question of South Africa," August 17, 1992, UN Doc. S/RES/772 (1992).

50. United Nations Department of Public Information, *The United Nations and Apartheid, 1948–1994* (New York: UN Dept. of Public Information, 1994), 107.

51. See generally, Douglass G. Anglin, "International Monitoring of the Transition to Democracy in South Africa, 1992–1994," *African Affairs* 20 (1995): 519.

52. "Report of the Secretary-General on the Question of South Africa," December 22, 1992, UN Doc. S/25004.

53. Sisk, *Democratization in South Africa,* 112.

54. This important tour of Germany and the United States has unfortunately been ignored by both the academic and the popular press. I owe my information regarding this trip to Stephen Stedman and Justice Richard Goldstone.

55. See, e.g., Neil McMahon, "Kissinger Mission's Failure Bodes Ill for South Africa," *Washington Times* (April 15, 1994): Sec. A, p. 8.

56. Sisk, 296 (quoting a participant in the talks).

57. Ibid.

58. Peter Norbert Bouckaert, "The Negotiated Revolution: South Africa's Transition to a Multiracial Democracy," *Stanford Journal of International Law* 33 (Spring 1997): 375–411.

59. In the complex lexicon of South African racial terminology, the term "black" is used to refer to all non-whites. Thus, the slogan of the Freedom Charter was inclusive of coloureds and Asians, two other significant groups in South Africa. For an inspiring account of the impact of nonracialism on the South African liberation struggle, see Julie Frederickse, *The Unbreakable Thread: Nonracialism in South Africa* (Bloomington: Indiana University Press, 1990). The book spans the entire history of the South African conflict, and uses documentary sources and personal interviews to show the almost hegemonic importance of nonracialism in the South African liberation struggle.

60. "Letter Dated 27 July 1992 from the Secretary-General to Mr. Nelson Mandela, President of the African National Congress," reproduced in United Nations Department of Public Information, *The United Nations and Apartheid,* 445.

61. "Letter dated 23 September 1992 from the Secretary-General to Mr. Frederik Willem de Klerk, President of South Africa," reproduced in United Nations Department of Public Information, *The United Nations and Apartheid,* 452.

62. "Letter dated 29 September 1992 from the Secretary-General to Chief Mangosuthu Buthelezi, President of the Inkatha Freedom Sec.y of South Africa," reproduced in United Nations Department of Public Information, *The United Nations and Apartheid,* 453.

63. "Letter dated 20 November 1992 from the Secretary-General to Mr. Nelson Mandela, President of the African National Congress," reproduced in United Nations Department of Public Information, *The United Nations and Apartheid,* 459; "Letter dated 20 November 1992 from the Secretary-General to Chief Mangosuthu Buthelezi, President of the Inkatha Freedom Party of South Africa," reproduced in United Nations Department of Public Information, *The United Nations and Apartheid,* 459–60.

64. "Statement by the Spokesman for Secretary-General Boutros Boutros-Ghali concerning the loss of life in Ciskei, and details on the United Nations Observer Mission in South Africa (UNOMSA)," September 9, 1992, UN Press Release SG/SM/4807-SAF/141, reproduced in United Nations Department of Public Information, *The United Nations and Apartheid,* 449. The president of the Security Council also condemned this incident, see "Statement by the President of the Security Council, on behalf of the Council, on the shooting of demonstrators in Ciskei," September 10, 1992, UN Doc. S/24541.

65. "Statement by a Spokesman for Secretary-General Boutros Boutros-Ghali expressing 'outrage' at right-wing Afrikaners' 'brazen display' of force and intimidation against multiparty negotiations," June 27, 1993, UN Press Release SG/SM/5028, reproduced in United Nations Department of Public Information, *The United Nations and Apartheid,* 475.

66. See, e.g., "Statement by the Spokesman for Secretary-General Boutros Boutros-Ghali applauding the 'historic agreement' on an Interim Constitution for South Africa," November 18, 1993, UN Press Release SG/SM/5157-SAF/163, reproduced in United Nations Department of Public Information, *The United Nations and Apartheid,* 480; "Statement by the Spokesman for Secretary-General Boutros Boutros-Ghali welcoming the breakthrough agreement in South Africa," April 19, 1994, UN Press Release SG/SM/5268-SAF/172, reproduced in United Nations Department of Public Information, *The United Nations and Apartheid,* 506; "Statement by the Spokesman for Secretary-General Boutros Boutros-Ghali applauding the election process in South Africa," May 6, 1994, UN Press Release SG/SM/5282, reproduced in United Nations Department of Public Information, *The United Nations and Apartheid,* 507.

67. Sparks, *Tomorrow Is Another Country,* 173.

68. Ibid., 173–74.

69. Waldmeir, *Anatomy of a Miracle,* 183.

70. For a discussion of the election, see generally R.W. Johnson and Lawrence Schlemmer, eds., *Launching Democracy in South Africa: The First Open Elections, April 1994* (New Haven, CT: Yale University Press, 1996), especially the essay by R.W. Johnson, "How Free? How Fair?" 323–52.

71. Bouckaert, "The Negotiated Revolution."

Chapter 10

1. Selected sources that focus on the environmental aspects of security include: Jessica Tuchman Mathews, "Redefining Security," *Foreign Affairs* 68 (Spring 1989): 162–77; Richard H. Ullman, "Redefining Security," *International Security* 8 (Summer 1983): 129–53; Norman Myers, *Ultimate Security: The Environmental Basis for Political Stability* (New York: Norton, 1993); Michael Renner, "National Security: The Economic and Environmental Dimensions," Worldwatch Paper No. 89 (Washington, D.C.: Worldwatch Institute, 1989). For a skeptical view, see Daniel Deudney, "The Case against Linking Environmental Degradation and National Security," *Millennium* 19 (Winter 1990): 461–76.

2. For example see Peter Gleick, "Water and Conflict: Fresh Water Resources and International Security," *International Security* 18 (1993): 79–112; and Sandra Postel, "Dividing the Waters: Food Security, Ecosystem Health, and the New Politics of Scarcity," Worldwatch Paper No. 132 (Washington, D.C.: Worldwatch Institute, 1996).

3. Dante A. Caponera, *Principles of Water Law and Administration: National and International* (Rotterdam: A.A. Balkema, 1992),186. This definition covers river and lake navigation as well as issues pertaining to use, development, and conservation in surface, underground, atmospheric, and frozen waters.

4. United Nations, *Register of International Rivers* (Oxford: Pergamon Press, 1978). Updated numbers: Danube (17 following the break-up of Yugoslavia, Czechoslovakia, and the Soviet Union), Niger (10), Nile (10 with the inclusion of Eritrea), Zaire (9), Rhine (8), Zambezi (8), Amazon (7), Mekong (6), Lake Chad (6), Volta (6), Ganges-Brahmaputra (5), Elbe (5), La Plata (5).

5. Kenneth Frederick, "Water as a Source of International Conflict," *Resources for the Future* (Spring 1996): 10.

6. Robin Clarke notes that in Europe there are four river basins shared by four or more countries, yet conflicts are rare due to the approximately 175 treaties regulating these rivers. [Robin Clarke, *Water: The International Crisis* (Cambridge: MIT Press, 1993), 92.]

7. Waterbury, "Transboundary Water and the Challenge of International Cooperation in the Middle East" in *Water in the Arab World: Perspectives and Prognoses,* ed. Peter Rogers and Peter Lydon (Cambridge: Harvard University Press, 1994), 61.

8. For a description of the dispute, see Paul R. Williams, "International Environmental Dispute Resolution: The Dispute between Slovakia and Hungary concerning Construction of the Gabcikovo and Nagymaros Dams," *Columbia Journal of Environmental Law* 19 (1994): 1–53.

9. On the relationship between global ecological interdependence and state sovereignty see Ronnie D. Lipschutz and Ken Conca, eds., *The State and Social Power in Global Environmental Politics* (New York: Columbia University Press, 1993).

10. See Gleick, "Water and Conflict," for the relationship between national security and water scarcity.

11. Miriam Lowi, "Bridging the Divide: Transboundary Resource Disputes and the Case of West Bank Water," *International Security* 18 (1993): 113–38; and Stephan Libiszewski, "Water Disputes in the Jordan Basin Region and Their Role in the Resolution of the Arab-Israeli Conflict," ENCOP Occasional Paper No. 13 (Zurich: Center for Security Policy and Conflict Research, 1995).

12. Thomas Naff and Ruth C. Matson, *Water in the Middle East: Conflict or Cooperation?* (Boulder, CO: Westview Press, 1984).

13. The Rhine River in Europe provides an example of the impact of upstream pollution on a downstream state, the Netherlands. For a description of the negotiation process to reduce chloride pollution in the Rhine, see Thomas Bernauer, "Protecting the Rhine against Chloride Pollution," in *Institutions for Environmental Aid: Pitfalls and Promise,* ed. Robert O. Keohane and Marc A. Levy (Cambridge: MIT Press, 1996), 201–32.

14. For a good overview on attempts to tease out these linkages, see the various working papers that have been generated by the Projects on Environmental Change and Acute Conflict; Environment, Population and Security; and Environmental Scarcities, State Capacity, and Civil Violence based at the University of Toronto. For instance, Thomas Homer-Dixon and Valerie Percival, *Environmental Scarcity and Violent Conflict: Briefing Book* (American Association for the Advancement of Science and the University of Toronto, 1996). Also see the debate on Environmental Scarcity and Violent Conflict in the *Environmental Change and Security Project Report,* Issue 2, The Woodrow Wilson Center, Spring 1996, especially the comments by Jack Goldstone.

15. For an introduction to the topic of environmental refugees, see Myers, *Ultimate Security,* 189–203.

16. Thomas F. Homer-Dixon, Jeffrey H. Boutwell, and George W. Rathjens, "Environmental Change and Violent Conflict," *Scientific American* (February 1993): 38–45.

17. Philip Micklin, "The Water Management Crisis in Soviet Central Asia," The Carl Beck Papers in Russian and East European Studies, No. 905, University of Pittsburgh Center for Russian and East European Studies, 1991: 99.

18. Ibid., 4.

19. Population data from 1995 UN figures. *World Resources 1996–97* (New York: Oxford University Press, 1996).

20. Peter Sinnott, "The Physical Geography of Soviet Central Asia and the Aral Sea Problem," in *Geographic Perspectives on Soviet Central Asia*, ed. Robert A. Lewis (London: Routledge, 1992), 74–97.

21. In 1960 the average area of the sea was 66,900 sq km, but by 1991 it was 33,800. Average volume in 1960 was 1090 cu. km, but by 1991 it was 290 cu. km. During this period salinity rose from 10 grams/liter to 37 grams/liter. [Philip Micklin, "The Aral Crisis: Introduction to the Special Issue," *Post-Soviet Geography* 33 (1992): 269–82.]

22. For example, see Patricia M. Carley, "The Price of the Plan," *Central Asian Survey* 8 (1989): 1–38.

23. Jane Dawson provides a good description of the linkages between environmental activism and nationalism that were prevalent throughout the different regions in the Soviet Union during the 1980s. *Eco-Nationalism* (Durham, NC: Duke University Press, 1996).

24. On the opposition movements to the Siberian River Diversion scheme, see Robert G. Darst, "Environmentalism in the USSR: The Opposition to the River Diversion Projects," *Soviet Economy* 4 (1988): 223–52.

25. For an overview of various opposition and nationalist movements, see James Critchlow, *Nationalism in Uzbekistan* (Boulder, CO: Westview Press, 1991).

26. The plan that received greatest attention was the Sibaral project that Gorbachev abrogated in 1986. This project would have diverted the Siberian rivers to the Aral Sea. See Darst, as well as Philip P. Micklin and Andrew R. Bond, "Reflections on Environmentalism and the River Diversion Projects," *Soviet Economy* 4 (1988): 253–74.

27. Sinnott, "The Physical Geography of Soviet Central Asia and the Aral Sea Problem," 93.

28. Micklin, "The Aral Crisis: Introduction to the Special Issue," 276.

29. Ibid. A report was issued in 1991 outlining the various concepts developed in the contest.

30. Stefan Klötzli, "The Water and Soil Crisis in Central Asia—a Source for Future Conflicts?" ENCOP Occasional Paper No. 11.1994; Sergei A. Panarin, "Political Dynamics of the 'New East' (1985–1993)," in *Central Asia and Transcaucasia: Ethnicity and Conflict*, ed. Vitaly V. Naumkin (Westport, CT: Greenwood Press, 1994); FBIS-Sov-89-115, *FBIS Daily Report: Central Eurasia*, 16 June 1989: 49.

31. The Soviet process of state break-up resembles other cases in which a domestic water system was transformed into an international river basin. On the Indian subcontinent, the partition between India and Pakistan in 1947 left India with control of the waters supplying Pakistan's irrigation canals. On the Indus, see A. Michel, *The Indus River: A Study of the Effects of Partition* (New Haven, CT: Yale University Press, 1967).

32. David R. Smith, "Environmental Security and Shared Water Resources in Post-Soviet Central Asia," *Post-Soviet Geography* 36 (1995): 361.

33. Ibid., 356–57.

34. Ibid.

35. Micklin points out that the BVOs were subordinate to USSR Minvodkhoz and simultaneously lost a good deal of their power when Minvodkhoz was disbanded in 1990. ["The Aral Crisis: Introduction to the Special Issue."]

36. See Klötzli, "The Water and Soil Crisis in Central Asia," and Smith, "Environmental Security and Shared Water Resources in Post-Soviet Central Asia."

37. Smith, "Environmental Security and Shared Water Resources in Post-Soviet Central Asia."

38. Ibid., 351.

39. Micklin, "The Aral Crisis: Introduction to the Special Issue," 278.

40. TACIS—European Commission, "Vol. VI: Legal and Institutional Aspects" (Water Resources Management and Agricultural Production in the Central Asian Republics or known as WARMAP, Tashkent, Uzbekistan, January, 1996), 8. This conforms to the recognized principle of international water law in which you must use your own in such a manner as not to injure others.

41. The functioning of the IWMCC is regulated by the Statute of the Interstate Water Management Coordinating Commission, signed 5 December 1992. For an overview of the legal institutions, see TACIS—WARMAP, "Vol. VI: Legal and Institutional Aspects."

42. This mirrors similar patterns of rapid cooperation among transitional states such as the Visegrad states. See Valerie Bunce, "Regional Cooperation and European Integration in Postcommunist Europe: The Visegrad Group," in *East-Central Europe and the Rise of Germany*, ed. Peter Katzenstein (Ithaca, NY: Cornell University Press, 1998).

43. Interview at the Water Ministry of Uzbekistan (Minvodkhoz), 13 May 1993.

44. Scott Barrett, "Conflict and Cooperation in Managing International Water Resources" (Washington, D.C.: World Bank, Policy Research Working Paper 1303, 1994): 28.

45. In place of the central water authority in Moscow, the IWMCC would approve the limits for water allocation, still using the previous Scheme of Water Resources Use such as the one developed in 1983 for the Syr Darya River Basin (this scheme was updated in 1987). TACIS—WARMAP, "Vol. VI: Legal and Institutional Aspects."

46. The World Bank, "The Aral Sea Crisis: Proposed Framework of Activities," 1993, 19.

47. TACIS–WARMAP, "Vol. VI: Legal and Institutional Aspects," 11.

48. Correspondence with Peter Whitford, The Aral Sea Basin Program.

49. The World Bank, "The Aral Sea Crisis: Proposed Framework of Activities," 1993, vi.

50. Ibid., ii.

51. John Gerard Ruggie, "Multilateralism: The Anatomy of an Institution," *International Organization* 46 (Summer 1992): 561.

52. Thomas Bernauer, "Managing International Rivers," Paper Prepared for the 1995 Annual Meeting of the American Political Science Association, Chicago, Illinois, 16.

53. This is similar to Jackson and Rosberg's argument on quasi-states in Africa. Robert H. Jackson and Carl G. Rosberg, "Why Africa's Weak States Persist: The Empirical and Juridical in Statehood," *World Politics* 35 (October 1982): 1–24.

54. Phone Conversation with Jeremy Berkoff, World Bank Water Economist, November 1993.

55. These agreements provide the basis for ICAS, EC-ICAS, and the ICSDSTEC. The TACIS–WARMAP study finds that "the agreements of 18 February 1992 and 26 March 1993, are framework agreements, i.e., agreements establishing basic principles. Further agreements are required for their implementation." ["Vol. VI: Legal and Institutional Aspects," 9.]

56. The seven main thematic programs broadly are: (1) regional water resources management strategy (including improving the efficiency and operation of the dams and reservoirs); (2) hydrometerological services; (3) water quality management; (4) wetland restoration and environmental studies; (5) clean water, sanitation, and health; (6) integrated land and water management in the upper watersheds; and (7) automatic controls of the BVOs. There is also a supplementary program on capacity building. Progress Report No. 2 from the World Bank Aral Sea Basin Program, September 1995, notes that two of the urgent projects were later merged, leaving eighteen individual projects.

57. "Aral Sea Program—Phase 1, Briefing Paper for the Proposed Donors Meeting," May 1994.

58. Ibid., vi.

59. The World Bank, UNDP, and UNEP signed a Memorandum of Understanding on collaboration between them to define the role of the three organizations in respect to the Aral Sea Program on November 30, 1994.

60. Niyazov of Turkmenistan did not attend the meeting, but he later signed the declaration.

61. Interview, Tashkent, Uzbekistan, 26 February 1997.

62. TACIS–WARMAP, "Executive Summary," Tashkent, Uzbekistan, January 1996.

63. TACIS–WARMAP, "Vol. VI: Legal and Institutional Aspects," 2. TACIS advisors are to assist with the "drafting of international (interstate) agreements on policies and strategies on water and land resources, their use, management, protection and apportionment; the drafting of national and intergovernmental legal and normative acts based on interstate agreements."

64. Environmental Policy and Technology Project Summary: U.S. Aral Sea Program Overview, Prepared for Regional Mission for Central Asia, U.S. Agency for International Development, 2 October 1996. Includes a summary of an unclassified memorandum on the U.S. Aral Sea strategy from Strobe Talbott dated July 22, 1993.

65. In October 1993, Secretary of State Warren Christopher announced a U.S. $15 million program to help alleviate environmental conditions in the Aral Sea region. Then in June 1994, an additional $7 million was pledged.

66. *Ecostan News: Ecological News from Central Asia,* edited by Eric Sievers and Andrei Aranbaev, and ISAR's *Surviving Together* follow the development of such environmental NGOs in Central Asia.

67. There are two aspects to the World Bank's support. First, there is support for the regional programs through the Global Environmental Facility. These programs are smaller in comparison to the Bank's investment lending for projects in water supply, irrigation, and drainage, and other projects at the national level on human needs and poverty alleviation. Correspondence with Peter Whitford, The Aral Sea Basin Program.

68. Abram Chayes and Antonia Handler Chayes, eds., *Preventing Conflict in the Post-Communist World: Mobilizing International and Regional Organizations* (Washington, D.C.: The Brookings Institution, 1996), 15.

69. Ibid., 16. Also see the chapter by Melanie H. Stein, "Conflict Prevention in Transition Economies: A Role for the European Bank for Reconstruction and Development," 339–78.

70. Oran R. Young, *International Governance: Protecting the Environment in a Stateless Society* (Ithaca, NY: Cornell University Press, 1994), 170.

71. Syed Kirmani and Guy Le Moigne, "Fostering Riparian Cooperation in International River Basins: The World Bank at Its Best in Development Diplomacy," World Bank Technical Paper No. 335 (Washington, D.C., 1997).

72. On the role of environmental NGOs see Sheldon Kamieniecki, ed., *Environmental Politics in the International Arena: Movements, Parties, Organizations, and Policy* (Albany: State University of New York Press, 1993); Keohane and Levy, eds., *Institutions for Environmental Aid;* Thomas Princen and Matthias Finger, *Environmental NGOs in World Politics: Linking the Global and the Local* (New York: Routledge, 1994); and Gareth Porter and Janet Welsh Brown, *Global Environmental Politics* (Boulder, CO: Westview Press, 1991).

73. Wolfgang H. Reinicke notes that in fiscal year 1993, 30 percent of all Bank projects included provisions for NGO involvement. "Can International Financial Institutions Prevent Internal Violence? The Sources of Ethno-National Conflict in Transitional Societies," in *Preventing Conflict in the Post-Communist World,* ed. Chayes and Chayes, 294.

74. Cited in *Ecostan,* February 1997 and June 1997. The first meeting took place from No-

vember 22–24, 1996, in Nukus, Karakalpakstan, followed by a second conference between May 16–19, 1997, in Fergana, Uzbekistan.

75. Keohane and Levy, eds., *Institutions for Environmental Aid.*

76. On why countries provide aid, see Bruno Frey, *International Political Economics* (Oxford: Basil Blackwell, 1984), 86–102.

77. These observations come from several on-site visits to state and collective farms in Kazakhstan and Uzbekistan where such projects are underway.

78. Kirmani and Le Moigne, "Fostering Riparian Cooperation in International River Basins," 16.

79. From conversations with Michael Boyd, Harvard Institute for International Development (HIID), Almaty, Kazakhstan, March 11 and 12, 1997.

80. The UN International Law Commission in 1991 issued its draft recommendations or principles, which include four obligations: (1) to inform and consult with water-sharing neighbors before taking actions that may affect them; (2) to regularly exchange hydrological data; (3) to avoid causing substantial harm to other water users; and (4) to allocate water from a shared river basin reasonably and equitably. For a discussion of international water law, see Stephen C. McCaffrey, "Water, Politics, and International Law," in *Water in Crisis,* Peter H. Gleick, ed. In May 1997, the UN General Assembly adopted a Convention on the Law of the Non-Navigational Uses of International Watercourses.

81. I consider water institutions to be the organizational arrangements and practices that constitute the framework for determining the patterns of use and management of a water system. They establish joint decision making over a shared resource and define the environment in which the actors and organizations operate, acting as constraints on behavior. Formal institutional arrangements include water and resource laws, policies, strategies and regulations pertaining to shared river basins.

82. I thank Abram Chayes for making this point.

83. TACIS–WARMAP, "Vol. VI: Legal and Institutional Aspects," 1. One of the TACIS legal advisors found that these institutions "are regulated by separate statutes that are not completely streamlined as to the institutions' respective functions." Hence it was difficult to distinguish between regulatory and development institutions.

84. Postel, "Dividing the Waters: Food Security, Ecosystem Health, and the New Politics of Scarcity."

85. In *Imperium* (New York: Vintage Books, 1995), 254–64, Ryszard Kapuschinki brilliantly captures the Soviet mentality of seeking technical fixes or solutions from the outside rather than ever having to consider hard budget constraints or environmental and social effects of policy choices. Even after the Soviet Union collapsed, research institutes continued to work on the Siberian River Diversion Project. Also see Khasan Iskandarov, "Will Tashkent Become a Port City?—The Idea of Diverting Siberian Rivers Seems to Have Seized the Masses Once Again," *Current Digest of the Soviet Press* vol. XLVI, no 4 (1994): 26.

86. Peter Whitford pointed out that there is a lot of room to improve the efficiency of gravity irrigation through basic infrastructural improvements and the provision of incentives for conservation.

87. Interview with Parliamentarian Kachikayev, Bishkek, Kyrgyzstan, 6 March 1997.

88. Letter sent from A. Matubraimov of the Kyrgyz Parliament to the head of the World Bank in Bishkek, 28 June 1997.

89. The World Bank, "Aral Sea Basin Program, Phase 1," Progress Report No. 3, February 1996.

90. Following the February 28, 1997, meeting, many of these issues appear to be solved. Rim Ghiniatullin has been appointed as chairman of the EC and its status has been clarified.

91. In 1995 the TACIS–WARMAP legal component produced a report by Professor Dante A. Caponera, Senior Legal Advisor, on the "Legal and Institutional Framework for the Management of the Aral Sea Basin Water Resources," Tashkent, April 1995. Many of the local water specialists were angered by this initial report because they perceived it as an attempt to be told how to restructure their water institutions completely from the outside. Yet with time, many of these reactions have been tempered.

92. Interview, Tashkent, 21 March 1997.

93. Each of the five independent Central Asian states produced a report titled "Basic Provisions for the Development of the Nation's Water Management Strategy" that was synthesized with the other four into a report titled "Fundamental Provisions of Water Management Strategy in the Aral Sea Basin," October 1996.

94. Gregory Gleason, "The Struggle for Control over Water in Central Asia: Republican Sovereignty and Collective Action," *Report on the USSR* 3 (June 21, 1991): 11–19.

Chapter 11

1. Michael A. Morris, *The Strait of Magellan* (Dordrecht: Martinus Nijhoff, 1989), 53.

2. Tratado de Límites entre Chile y Argentina, signed in Buenos Aires, July 23, 1881. Published in German Carrasco, *El Laudo Arbitral del Canal Beagle* (Santiago: Editorial Jurídica de Chile: 1978), 19–21. Author's translation.

3. Ibid.

4. Ibid.

5. Ibid.

6. Morris, *The Strait of Magellan*, 77.

7. Ibid.

8. Ibid., 54–55.

9. Ibid.

10. Ibid.

11. Decreto Supremo No. 416 of July 14, 1977; Enrique Gajardo Villarroel, "Las Líneas de Base Rectas," *El Mercurio* (July 17, 1977), reprinted in German Carrasco, *Argentina y el Laudo Arbitral del Canal Beagle,* 17–18; Morris, *The Strait of Magellan,* 80.

12. Gajardo, "Las Líneas de Base Rectas"; Morris, *The Strait of Magellan,* 80.

13. Interview with General Ricardo Echeverry Boneo, Buenos Aires, May 27, 1997 [hereinafter, Echeverry Boneo Interview].

14. Interview with Marcelo Delpech, Buenos Aires, May 27, 1997 [hereinafter, Delpech Interview]; Morris, *The Strait of Magellan,* 83.

15. Morris, *The Strait of Magellan,* 120, 149–55, 184–86.

16. In an interview conducted in Buenos Aires on May 27, 1997, retired Argentine Army General Ricardo Echeverry Boneo, who served as head of the Argentine delegation in Rome for most of the period prior to 1984, showed the author a map that he claimed represented Chilean territorial aspirations, encompassing approximately one-fourth of present-day Argentina. The Chilean military has frequently articulated a similar view of Argentina. Chilean Navy Captain Jorge Roman Farina maintains that "Argentina has always had a hegemonic spirit, has always tried to extend its influence to other sectors." (Cynthia Gorney, "At Tip of South America, Three Tiny Islands Raise Talk of War," *Washington Post* [March 27, 1981]: Sec. A, p. 27.)

17. Morris, *The Strait of Magellan,* 41–45.

18. Ibid., 45–47.

19. Morris, *The Strait of Magellan,* 138–44; Michael A. Morris, "Naval Arms Control in Latin America" in *Controlling Latin American Conflicts: Ten Approaches,* ed. Michael A. Morris and Victor Millán (Boulder, CO: Westview Press, 1983), 156–60.

20. Interview with Francisco Orrego, Santiago, May 29, 1997 [hereinafter, Orrego Interview].

21. On December 14, 1978, Argentine President Videla informed papal nuncio Pio Laghi that Argentina had finalized plans to invade the PNL group the following week. Videla reportedly told Laghi that if he did not give the invasion orders, he would be removed, and those with extreme views would take over. (Thomas Princen, *Intermediaries in International Conflict* [Princeton: Princeton University Press, 1992], 143.) See also, Juan de Onis, "Argentina, Chile Feud Masks Other Troubles," *New York Times* (December 31, 1978): Sec. 4, p. 3. General Ricardo Echeverry Boneo rejects this characterization of Argentine military decision making.

22. Carrasco, *El Laudo Arbitral del Canal Beagle,* 13–14.

23. Ibid., 14–15.

24. Ibid., 15–17.

25. Interview with Julio Philippi, *El Mercurio* (February 26, 1978), reprinted in Carrasco, *Argentina y el Laudo Arbitral del Canal Beagle,* 347. Author's translation.

26. "The Torti Proposal," *El Mercurio* (January 12, 1978), reprinted in Carrasco, *Argentina y el Laudo Arbitral del Canal Beagle,* 51–53.

27. Ernesto Videla, "La Mediación Pontificia en el Diferendo Austral," *Diplomacia* No. 39/1987, reprinted in Carrasco, *Argentina y el Laudo Arbitral del Canal Beagle,* 46.

28. Videla, "La Mediación Pontificia en el Diferendo Austral," 47.

29. Acta de Puerto Montt, published in Carrasco, *Argentina y el Laudo Arbitral del Canal Beagle,* 322–24.

30. Princen, *Intermediaries in International Conflict,* 136.

31. Ibid., 137.

32. Juan de Onis, "Argentina Accepts Mediation for Southern Islands," *New York Times* (November 9, 1978): 3; Barbara Slavin and Rosanne Klass, "Argentina, Chile to Try Mediation," *New York Times* (November 12, 1978): Sec. 4, p. 2.

33. Princen, *Intermediaries in International Conflict,* 140–42.

34. Juan de Onis, "Chile May Take Dispute to OAS," *New York Times* (December 15, 1978): Sec. A, p. 2; World News Briefs, *New York Times* (December 22, 1978): 5.

35. World News Briefs: "U.S. Urges O.A.S. to Act in Chile-Argentina Dispute," *New York Times* (December 13, 1978): Sec. A, p. 6.

36. Tratado General Sobre Solución Judicial de Controversias entre La República de Chile y La República Argentina, signed in Buenos Aires, April 5, 1972. Published in Carrasco, *Argentina y el Laudo Arbitral,* 152–53.

37. Delpech Interview; interview with Santiago Benadava, Santiago, May 30, 1997 [hereinafter, Benadava Interview].

38. Princen, *Intermediaries in International Conflict,* 143.

39. Ibid.

40. Ibid.

41. Echeverry Boneo Interview; Princen, *Intermediaries in International Conflict,* 134.

42. Princen, *Intermediaries in International Conflict,* 139.

43. Echeverry Boneo Interview.

44. Princen, *Intermediaries in International Conflict,* 139–40.

45. Ibid., 139.

46. Orrego Interview.

47. Interview with Dante Caputo, Buenos Aires, May 28, 1997 [hereinafter, Caputo Interview].

48. Echeverry Boneo Interview; Delpech Interview; Orrego Interview; Benadava Interview.

49. Benadava Interview.

50. Delpech Interview; Juan de Onis, "Chile and Argentina Miss an Opportunity," *New York Times* (February 20, 1978): 7.

51. Juan de Onis, "Pope to Take Part in Mexico Meeting," *New York Times* (December 23, 1978): 5.

52. Ibid.

53. Orrego Interview.

54. Princen, *Intermediaries in International Conflict,* 143.

55. Delpech Interview; Caputo Interview.

56. Orrego Interview.

57. The arbitral court accepted Chile's argument that the compromise embedded in the 1881 Treaty had been an exchange of Patagonia for the Straits of Magellan and the islands to the south. Additionally, Argentina's so-called "two ocean principle"—according to which Argentina and Chile would be confined to the Atlantic and Pacific, respectively—was undercut by the arbitral court's conclusions that the entirety of the Straits were Chilean and that the Chilean town of Point Dungeness was on the Atlantic.

58. Echeverry Boneo Interview.

59. Delpech Interview; Morris, *The Strait of Magellan,* 83.

60. Echeverry Boneo Interview; Delpech Interview; Tratado de Paz y Amistad, signed at the Vatican, November 29, 1984 [hereinafter, Treaty of Peace and Friendship].

61. Treaty of Peace and Friendship.

62. Benadava Interview.

63. Ibid.

64. World News Briefs, "US Helping to Resolve Chile–Argentina Dispute," *New York Times* (December 16, 1978): 7; World News Briefs, "US Urges OAS to Act in Chile–Argentina Dispute (December 13, 1978): 6.

65. World News Briefs, "US Helping to Resolve Chile-Argentina Dispute."

66. Caputo Interview; Benadava Interview.

67. Thomas Princen, "Beagle Channel Negotiations," Case 401, Pew Case Studies in International Affairs (Washington, DC: Institute for the Study of Diplomacy, 1988): 14.

68. Ibid.

69. Princen, *Intermediaries in International Conflict,* 143–44.

70. Ibid., 146.

71. Ibid., 147.

72. Ibid.

73. Ibid., 147.

74. Ibid., 148–49.

75. Benadava Interview.

76. Ibid.

77. Ibid.

78. Santiago Benadava, "La Mediación de la Santa Sede en el Diferendo Chileno-Argentino sobre la Zona Austral," in *International Law at a Time of Perplexity,* ed. Y. Dinstein (Dordrecht: Kluwer Academic Publishers, 1989), 39.

79. Orrego Interview.

80. Benadava, "La Mediación de la Santa Sede," 39–40.

81. Princen, *Intermediaries in International Conflict,* 154–55.

82. Echeverry Boneo Interview; Benadava Interview.

83. Benadava Interview.

84. Ibid.

85. Orrego Interview.

86. Princen, *Intermediaries in International Conflict,* 152.

87. Ibid.

88. Echeverry Boneo Interview.

89. Princen, *Intermediaries in International Conflict,* 153–54.

90. Ibid., 154.

91. Papal Proposal in the Beagle Channel Dispute: Proposal of the Mediator.

92. Benadava, "La Mediación de la Santa Sede," 44.

93. Ibid.

94. Echeverry Boneo Interview; Delpech Interview; Orrego Interview; Caputo Interview.

95. Orrego Interview.

96. Echeverry Boneo Interview.

97. At least four individuals—Guillermo Moncayo, Ricardo Echeverry Boneo, Ortiz de Rozas, and Marcelo Delpech—played the role of delegation head during the mediation. Moreover, Moncayo and Echeverry Boneo appear to have shared leadership of the delegation during the early stages of the mediation process; in interviews conducted in 1997, both men claimed to have occupied the central role. Published accounts have likewise attributed the leadership role to both men. See, e.g., Princen, *Intermediaries in International Conflict,* 150, 161.

98. Princen, *Intermediaries in International Conflict,* 155; Benadava Interview.

99. "Argentina Closes Border with Chile after Two Arrests," *New York Times* (April 30, 1981): Sec. A, p. 13; Benadava, "La Mediación de la Santa Sede," 44–45; Princen, *Intermediaries in International Conflict,* 155. [Note dispute among sources.]

100. Orrego Interview; Benadava Interview; Videla, Ernesto, "La Mediación Pontificia en El Diferendo Austral," *Diplomacia* 39 (1987).

101. Benadava Interview.

102. Videla, "La Mediación Pontificia en El Diferendo Austral," 54.

103. Princen, *Intermediaries in International Conflict,* 155.

104. Videla, "La Mediación Pontificia en El Diferendo Austral," 54.

105. Princen, *Intermediaries in International Conflict,* 156.

106. General Ricardo Echeverry Boneo feels that this relationship did not contribute meaningfully to the advancement of the mediation.

107. Benadava, "La Mediación de la Santa Sede," 45–46; Benadava Interview.

108. Ricardo Echeverry Boneo believes that Samoré's death was a turning point in the negotiations, because thereafter Cardinal Casaroli assumed a more direct role in the mediation. In Echeverry Boneo's view, Casaroli's position as the number two man in the Vatican hierarchy enabled him to put more forceful pressure on Argentina. By contrast, Francisco Orrego feels that the transition following Samoré's death was very smooth and did not greatly impact the course of the mediation.

109. Delpech Interview; Caputo Interview.

110. Princen, *Intermediaries in International Conflict,* 158.

111. Benadava, "La Mediación de la Santa Sede," 45–46; Benadava Interview.

112. Interview with Hugo Gobbi, Buenos Aires, May 28, 1997 [hereinafter, Gobbi Interview].

113. Delpech interview; Orrego interview.

114. Orrego Interview; Delpech Interview; Princen, *Intermediaries in International Conflict,* 158.

115. Edward Schumacher, "Three Small Islands Loom Large in Argentina Leader's Plans," *New York Times* (January 5, 1984): Sec. A, p.16.

116. "Argentina Signs Accord with Chile," *New York Times* (January 24, 1984): Sec. A, p. 3.

117. Princen, *Intermediaries in International Conflict,* 160.

118. Ibid.; Echeverry Boneo interview.

119. Princen, *Intermediaries in International Conflict,* 161.

120. Ibid., 143.

121. Caputo Interview.

122. On November 25, 1984, the Alfonsín government held a nonbinding public referendum on the proposed treaty. Seventy-three percent of the Argentine electorate cast ballots, approving the treaty by a four to one margin. Editorial desk, "Victories for Voters in South America; Small Miracle in Argentina," *New York Times* (December 1, 1984): 22.

123. Echeverry Boneo Interview; Delpech Interview; Moncayo Interview; Gobbi Interview; Caputo Interview; Orrego Interview; Benadava Interview.

124. Princen, *Intermediaries in International Conflict,* 143.

125. Benadava Interview.

126. Juan de Onis, "Argentina and Chile Ask Pope to Mediate Border Dispute," *New York Times* (January 10, 1979): 3.

127. Orrego Interview; Benadava Interview.

128. Delpech Interview; Gobbi Interview.

129. Caputo Interview. This view was also expressed by General Ricardo Echeverry Boneo.

130. Delpech Interview.

131. Orrego Interview.

132. Echeverry Boneo Interview.

133. Even Marcelo Delpech and Dante Caputo, who represented the more conciliatory Alfonsín government, considered the 1980 proposal completely unworkable.

Chapter 12

1. IAEA document INFCIRC/153 (Corrected) IAEA, Vienna, 1983.

2. Richard Kokoski, *Technology and the Proliferation of Nuclear Weapons* (New York: Oxford University Press, 1995), 150.

3. Young Whan Kihl, "Confrontation or Compromise? Lessons from the 1994 Crisis," in *Peace and Security in Northeast Asia: The Nuclear Issue and the Korean Peninsula,* ed. Young Whan Kihl and Peter Hayes (New York: M.E. Sharpe, 1997), 197.

4. Ibid., 183.

5. Michael J. Mazaar, *North Korea and the Bomb: A Case Study in Nonproliferation* (New York: St. Martin's, 1994), 121.

6. In a three and a half hour meeting on June 20, 1992, with U.S. negotiator Dr. William J. Taylor, Kim Il Sung asked Dr. Taylor to ask Seoul and Washington whether they would be willing to assist North Korea to shift to light-water reactors. Dr. Taylor relayed the request to National Security Advisor Kim in Seoul and Brent Scowcroft in Washington. (Note: Dr. Taylor is now the senior vice president of the Center for Strategic and International Studies in Washington, D.C., and kindly provided additional insight into the U.S.–DPRK negotiations with his comments on this chapter.)

7. Young, "Confrontation or Compromise?" 197.

8. Kokoski, *Technology and the Proliferation of Nuclear Weapons,* 227.

9. Young, "Confrontation or Compromise?" 190.

10. Robert Gallucci, assistant secretary of state for military and security affairs, briefed

Carter in Atlanta. Gallucci also served as ambassador at large and as chief U.S. negotiator in the second U.S.–DPRK high-level talks.

11. Young, "Confrontation or Compromise?" 191.

12. Ibid., 192.

13. Ibid.

14. Ibid., 193.

15. Ibid.

16. Ibid., 194.

17. "Carter Trip Paves the Way for U.S.-North Korean Pact, *The Carter Center News* (The Carter Center: Atlanta), 11.

18. Agreed Framework between the United States of America and the Democratic People's Republic of Korea, Geneva, October 21, 1994.

19. Young, "Confrontation or Compromise?" 199.

20. Ibid.

21. Ibid.

22. K.D. Kapur, *Nuclear Diplomacy in East Asia: United States and the Korean Nuclear Crisis Management* (New Delhi: Lancers Books, 1995), 168.

23. Hyoung-Chan Choe, "North Korea's Dangerous Nuclear Deal, Process and Prospect," in *Korea: A World in Change,* ed. Kenneth W. Thompson (Lanham, MD: University Press of America, 1996), 173.

24. David Sloss, "It's Not Broken So Don't Fix It: The International Atomic Energy Agency Safeguards System and the Nuclear Nonproliferation Treaty," *Virginia Journal of International Law* 35 (Summer 1995): 873.

25. Janice M. Heppel, "Confidence-Building Measures: Bilateral versus Multilateral Approaches," in *Peace and Security in Northeast Asia: The Nuclear Issue and the Korean Peninsula,* ed. Young Whan Kihl and Peter Hayes, 270.

26. Ralph Cossa, "Multilateralism, Regional Security, and the Prospects for Track II in East Asia," *NBR Analysis* 7 no. 5 (December 1996): 35.

27. *Treaty Series,* Vol. 729 (New York: United Nations).

28. Kimberly Ann Elliott, "Will Economic Sanctions Work against North Korea?" in *Peace and Security in Northeast Asia: The Nuclear Issue and the Korean Peninsula,* ed. Young Whan Kihl and Peter Hayes, 100.

29. Ibid.

30. Tom Plate, "Next on the Diplomatic Agenda: Korea: While the Korean Peninsula Lacks the American Constituency That Ireland Has, Its Future Is Vital for the World," *Los Angeles Times* (April 14, 1998): Sec. B, p. 7.

31. Choe, "North Korea's Dangerous Nuclear Deal," 171.

32. Tim Weiner, "U.S. Says North Korea Helped Develop New Pakistani Missile," *New York Times* (April 11, 1998): Sec. A, p. 1.

33. Ibid., 179.

34. Ibid., 181.

35. Scott Snyder, "Beyond the Geneva Agreed Framework: A Road Map for Normalizing Relations with North Korea," in *Peace and Security in Northeast Asia: The Nuclear Issue and the Korean Peninsula,* ed. Young Whan Kihl and Peter Hayes, 208.

36. Barton Gellman, "U.S., Allies Struggling To Fulfill N. Korea Pact," *Washington Post* (May 2, 1998): Sec. A, p. 15.

37. Jum Mann, "N. Korea Nuclear Deal at Risk, U.S. Fears Financing: Officials Say That Bickering over Funding for $5.1-Billion Reactor Project Threatens 1994 Pact," *Los Angeles Times* (April 10, 1998): Sec. A, p. 12.

38. Robert Gallucci, interview by author, 13 June 1997.

39. "It's Good for the Koreas to Talk: But Don't Expect the Talks, If They Resume, to Get Very Far Very Fast," *Economist,* April 18, 1998.

40. Ibid.

41. Kokoski, *Technology and the Proliferation of Nuclear Weapons,* 231.

Chapter 13

1. I. William Zartman, *Ripe for Resolution: Conflict and Intervention in Africa* (New York: Oxford University Press, 1989), 268.

Bibliography

Chapter 1. Multilateral Mediation in Intrastate Conflicts: Russia, the United Nations, and the War in Abkhazia

Bercovitch, Jacob. "The Structure and Diversity of Mediation in International Relations." In *Mediation in International Relations*, edited by Jacob Bercovitch and Jeffrey Z. Rubin. New York: St. Martin's, 1992.

The Blue Helmets: A Review of United Nations Peacekeeping. New York: United Nations, 1996.

Dale, Catherine. "The Case of Abkhazia (Georgia)." In *Peacekeeping and the Role of Russia in Eurasia,* edited by Lena Jonson and Clive Archer. Boulder, CO: Westview Press, 1996.

———. "Turmoil in Abkhazia: Russian Responses." *RFE/RL Research Report* vol. 2, no. 34, (August 27, 1993): 48–57.

Jonson, Lena, and Clive Archer, eds. *Peacekeeping and the Role of Russia in Eurasia.* Boulder, CO: Westview Press, 1996.

Kleiboer, Marieke. "Understanding Success and Failure of International Mediation." *Journal of Conflict Resolution* vol. 40, no. 2 (June 1996): 360–89.

Krasner, Stephen. "Sovereignty and Intervention." In *Beyond Westphalia? State Sovereignty and International Intervention,* edited by Gene Lyons and Michael Mastanduno. Baltimore: Johns Hopkins University Press, 1995.

Lijphart, Arend. "The Power Sharing Approach." In *Conflict and Peacemaking in Multiethnic Societies,* edited by Joseph Montville. New York: Lexington Books, 1991.

Princen, Thomas. *Intermediaries in International Conflict.* Princeton: Princeton University Press, 1992.

Stedman, Stephen. "Negotiation and Mediation in Internal Conflict." In *The International Dimensions of Internal Conflict,* edited by Michael Brown. Cambridge, MA: MIT Press, 1996.

Zartman, I. William. *Ripe for Resolution: Conflict and Intervention in Africa.* New York: Oxford University Press, 1989.

Chapter 2. From Lisbon to Dayton

Boyle, Francis A. *The Bosnian People Charge Genocide.* Northampton, MA: Aletheia, 1996.

Galbraith, Peter W. Washington. "Erdut and Dayton: Negotiating and Implementing Peace in Croatia and Bosnia–Herzegovina." *Cornell International Law Review* 30 (1997): 647.

Glenny, Misha. *The Fall of Yugoslavia: The Third Balkan War.* New York: Penguin, 1992.

Higham, Matthew T., Michael N. Mercurio, and Steven W. Ghezzi. *The ACCESS Packet on Bosnia-Herzegovina.* Washington, D.C.: ACCESS, 1996.

Holbrooke, Richard. *To End a War.* New York: Random House, 1998.

Lampe, John R. *Yugoslavia as History: Twice There Was a Country.* Cambridge: Cambridge University Press, 1996.

Owen, David. *Balkan Odyssey.* San Diego: Harvest, 1995.

Rieff, David. *Slaughterhouse: Bosnia and the Failure of the West.* New York: Touchstone, 1996.

Rosegrant, Susan. "Getting to Dayton: Negotiating an End to the War in Bosnia." A Case Study from the John F. Kennedy School of Government, Harvard University, 1996.

———. "The Institution That Saw No Evil," *The New Republic,* February 12, 1996.

Scharf, Michael P. *Balkan Justice.* Durham: Carolina Academic Press, 1997.

Silber, Laura, and Allan Little. *Yugoslavia: Death of a Nation.* New York: Penguin, 1995.

Sudetic, Chuck. *Blood and Vengeance: One Family's Story of the War in Bosnia.* New York: Norton, 1998.

UNSCR 761 of June 29, 1992, UNSCR 764 of July 13, 1992, and UNSCR 758 of June 18, 1992.

Woodward, Susan L. *Balkan Tragedy: Chaos and Dissolution after the Cold War.* Washington, D.C.: The Brookings Institution, 1995.

Zartman, I. William. *Ripe for Resolution: Conflict and Intervention in Africa.* New York: Oxford University Press, 1989.

Zimmermann, Warren. *Origins of a Catastrophe: Yugoslavia and Its Destroyers.* New York: Random House, 1996.

Chapter 3. Croatian Independence from Yugoslavia

"Accord Implementing the Cease-fire Agreement of 23 November," UN Doc. S/23363, Annex III.

Case concerning the Frontier Dispute (Burk. Faso v. Rep. Mali), 1986 I.C.J. 554, 565 (Dec. 22).

Cassese, Antonio. *Self-Determination of Peoples.* Cambridge: Cambridge University Press, 1995.

"Cease Fire Agreement" and "Memorandum of Understanding on the Extension of Monitoring Activities of the Monitor Mission to Yugoslavia," *Review of International Affairs* vol. XLII (5.X–5.XI 1991): 24, 26.

Christian Democratic Union/Christian Socialist Union Coalition Caucus in the German Parliament, press release, May 7, 1991.

"EC Declaration Concerning the Conditions for Recognition of New States," UN Doc. S/23293, Annex I.

"EC Declaration on the Suspension of the Trade Cooperation Agreement with Yugoslavia," *Review of International Affairs* vol. XLII (5.X–5.XI 1991): 26.

EC Declaration on Yugoslavia, EPC Press Release, P. 82/91 and 84/91, reprinted in *Yugoslavia Through Documents: From Its Creation to Its Dissolution,* edited by Snezana Trifunovska. Dordrecht: Martinus Nijhoff, 1994, 333–34, 342–43.

"Joint Declaration of the EC Troika and the Parties Directly Concerned with the Yugoslav Crisis," Europe Documents No. 1725, July 16, 1991, reprinted in *Yugoslavia Through Documents: From Its Creation to Its Dissolution,* edited by Snezana Trifunovska. Dordrecht: Martinus Nijhoff, 1994.

"Letter dated 10 December 1991 from the Secretary-General of the United Nations Addressed to the Minister for Foreign Affairs of the Netherlands," UN Doc. S/23280, Annex IV.

"Report of the Secretary-General Pursuant to Paragraph 3 of Security Council Resolution 713," UN Doc. S/23169.

"Report of the Secretary-General Pursuant to Security Council Resolution 721," UN Doc. S/23280, p. 3.

Rothchild, Donald. "Successful Mediation: Lord Carrington and the Rhodesian Settlement." In *Managing Global Chaos,* edited by Chester A. Crocker and Fen Olser Hampson, with Pamela Aall. Washington, D.C.: United States Institute of Peace Press, 1996.

Silber, Laura, and Allan Little. *Yugoslavia: Death of a Nation.* New York: Penguin, 1995.

"Statement by Lord Carrington, the Presidents of the Republics of Croatia and Serbia, and the Minister of National Defence," *Review of International Affairs* vol. XLII (5.X–5.XI 1991): 28.

Touval, Saadia. "Lessons of Preventive Diplomacy in Yugoslavia." In *Managing Global Chaos,* edited by Chester A. Crocker and Fen Olser Hampson. Washington, D.C.: United States Institute of Peace Press, 1996.

Wood, Pia Christina. "European Political Cooperation: Lessons from the Gulf War and Yugoslavia." In *The State of the European Community,* vol. 2, edited by Alan W. Cafruny and Glenda G. Rosenthal. Boulder, CO: Lynne Rienner, 1993.

Chapter 4. The Oslo Channel: Benefits
of a Neutral Facilitator to Secret Negotiations

Corbin, Jane. *The Norway Channel: The Secret Talks That Led to the Middle East Peace.* New York: Atlantic Monthly Press, 1994.

Goldschmidt, Arthur, Jr. *A Concise History of the Middle East.* Boulder, CO: Westview Press, 1996.

Hadi, Madhi Abdul. "Oslo—The Conflict, the Mediators, and the Breakthrough," *Negotiation Newsletter,* Harvard University, November 1997.

Lewis, Bernard. *The Middle East.* New York: Scribners, 1995.

Mansfield, Peter. *A History of the Middle East.* New York: Viking, 1991.

Reich, Bernard, *Arab–Israeli Conflict and Conciliation.* Westport, CT: Greenwood Press, 1995.

———. *An Historical Encyclopedia of the Arab-Israeli Conflict.* Westport, CT: Greenwood Press, 1996.

Savir, Uri. *The Process: 1,100 Days That Changed the Middle East.* New York: Random House, 1998.

Smith, Charles D. *Palestine and the Arab–Israeli Conflict.* New York: St. Martin's, 1995.

"What's Arafat's Line?—Israel Ends Bar to Role of PLO at Peace Talks," *New York Times* (August 15, 1993).

Zartman, I. William. *Explaining Oslo* (draft article on file with the author, 1997).

Chapter 5. The 1991 Cambodia Settlement Agreements

Acharya, Amitav, Pierre Lizé, and Sorpong Peou, eds. *Cambodia—The 1989 Paris Peace Conference: Background Analysis and Documents.* New York: Kraus International, 1991.

Blaustein, Susan. "Old War, China Card & Sihanouk." *The Nation,* October 30, 1989, 485.

Cambodia: Aftermath of the Coup. New York: Human Rights Watch/Asia, 1997.

Chandler, David. "Three Visions of Politics in Cambodia." In *Keeping the Peace: Multidimensional UN Operations in Cambodia and El Salvador,* edited by Ian Johnstone, Michael W. Doyle, and Robert C. Orr. Cambridge: Cambridge University Press, 1997.

Chandler, David P. *A History of Cambodia.* 2nd ed. Boulder, CO: Westview Press, 1993.

Doyle, Michael W. *UN Peacekeeping in Cambodia: UNTAC's Civil Mandate.* New York: International Peace Academy, 1995.

Haas, Michael. *Genocide by Proxy: Cambodian Pawn on a Superpower Chessboard.* New York: Praeger, 1991.

Heininger, Janet E. *Peacekeeping in Transition: The United Nations in Cambodia.* New York: The Twentieth Century Fund, 1994.

Kaufmann, Johan, Dick Leurdijk, and Nico Schrijver. *The World in Turmoil: Testing the UN's Capacity.* Providence, RI: The Academic Council on the United Nations System, 1991.

Koh, Tommy T. B. "The Paris Conference on Cambodia: A Multilateral Negotiation That 'Failed.' " *Negotiation Journal* 6 (1990).

Porter, Gareth. "Cambodia: Sihanouk's Initiative." *Foreign Affairs* vol. 66, no. 4 (1988).

Ratner, Steven R. "The Cambodia Settlement Agreements." *American Journal of International Law* 87 (1993).

———. *The New UN Peacekeeping: Building Peace in Lands of Conflict After the Cold War.* New York: St. Martin's, 1995.

Riding, Alan. "Four Parties in Cambodian War Sign UN–Backed Peace Pact." *New York Times* (October 24, 1991).

Ross, Robert S. "China and the Cambodian Peace Process: The Value of Coercive Diplomacy." *Asian Survey* 31 (December 1991).

Shawcross, William. "Cambodia's New Deal: A Report." *Contemporary Issues Paper 1.* Washington, D.C.: Carnegie Endowment for International Peace, 1994.

Shawcross, William. *Sideshow: Kissinger, Nixon, and the Destruction of Cambodia.* Rev. ed. New York: Simon & Schuster, 1987.

Song, Jin. "The Political Dynamics of the Peacemaking Process in Cambodia." In *Keeping the Peace: Multidimensional UN Operations in Cambodia and El Salvador,* edited by Ian Johnstone, Michael W. Doyle, and Robert C. Orr. Cambridge: Cambridge University Press, 1997.

The United Nations and Cambodia, 1991–1995. The United Nations Blue Book Series, Volume II. New York: United Nations Department of Public Information, 1995.

Chapter 6. El Salvador

Bland, Gary. "Assessing the Transition to Democracy." In *Is There a Transition to Democracy in El Salvador?* Edited by Joseph S. Tulchin, et al. Boulder, CO: Lynne Rienner, 1992.

Christian, Shirley. "Salvadoran Chief and Rebels Reach Broad Agreement." *New York Times* (Sept. 26, 1991).

de Soto, Alvaro. "The Negotiations Following the New York Agreement." In *Is There a Transition to Democracy in El Salvador?* Edited by Joseph S. Tulchin, et al. Boulder, CO: Lynne Rienner 1992.

———, and Graciana del Castillo. "Obstacles to Peacebuilding." *Foreign Policy* Spring 1994.

Karl, Terry. "El Salvador's Negotiated Revolution." *Foreign Affairs* Spring 1992.

Krauss, Clifford. "UN Aide Assailed In Salvadoran Talks." *New York Times* (February 1, 1991).

Lemoyne, James. "El Salvador's Forgotten War." *Foreign Affairs* Summer 1989.

Rohter, Larry. "Former Rebels Make Impressive Advances in Salvador Elections." *New York Times* (March 26, 1997).

The United Nations and El Salvador 1990–1995. New York: United Nations Publications.

Vickers, George. "The Political Reality After Ten Years of War." In *Is There a Transition to Democracy in El Salvador?* Edited by Joseph S. Tulchin, et al. Boulder, CO: Lynne Rienner, 1992.

Chapter 7. The Role of International Mediation
in the Northern Ireland Peace Process

"Adams and Humes 'Optimistic' Over Obstacles" *The Irish Times* (July 19, 1997).

The Agreement, 10 April 1998, Strand One, Para. 5, reprinted in 37 I.L.M. 751 (1998).

Aide-Mémoire Sent to Sinn Fein, June 1997. http://www.nio.gov.uk/press/ 970625hh.htm (visited Oct. 8, 1998).

"Behind the Mask: The IRA & Sinn Fein." PBS television broadcast, Oct. 21, 1997. http://www.pbs.org/wgbh/pages/frontline/shows/ira.

Bew, P., and G. Gillespie. *The Northern Ireland Peace Process: 1993–1996.* London: Serif, 1996.

Bloomfield, David. *Peacemaking Strategies in Northern Ireland: Building Complementarity in Conflict Management Theory.* New York: Macmillan, 1997.

Boyle, Kevin, and Tom Hadden. *Northern Ireland: The Choice.* London: Penguin Books, 1994.

"British Government Gives Economic 'Peace Aid' to Northern Ireland." *Agence France Presse* (May 11, 1998).

de Breadun, Deaglan. "North Parties Gear Up for Bitter Assembly Elections." *The Irish Times* (May 25, 1998).

Fisher, Ronald J., and Loraleigh Keashly. "The Potential Complementarity of Mediation and Consultation within A Contingency Model of Third Party Intervention." *Journal of Peace Research* 28 (1991): 33.

Foster, R.F. *Modern Ireland: 1600–1972.* London: Penguin, 1988.

Gallagher, A.M. *Majority Minority Review 1: Education in a Divided Society.* 2nd ed. Coleraine, Northern Ireland: University of Ulster, 1995.

Hancock, Landon. *Northern Ireland: Troubles Brewing.* http://cain.ulst.ac.uk/ othelem/landon.htm (visited Oct. 8, 1998).

Ireland v. The United Kingdom, 21 Eur. Ct. H.R. (ser. A), 1978.

Joint Declaration of Irish Taoiseach Albert Reynolds and British Prime Minister John Major, Dec. 15, 1993, para. 9.

"Joint Paper from the British and Irish Governments on Decommissioning." June 25, 1997. http://www.nio.gov.uk/press/970625hh.htm (visited Oct. 8, 1998).

Melaugh, Martin. "Majority–Minority Differentials: Unemployment, Housing and Health in Northern Ireland." In *Facets of the Conflict in Northern Ireland,* edited by Seamus Dunn. New York: St. Martin's, 1995.

Moriarity, Gerry. "Uncertainty Overshadows SF–UUP Meeting." *The Irish Times* (Sept. 24, 1997).

———. "DUP Says It Will Not Set Out To 'Wreck' Assembly." *The Irish Times* (May 27, 1998).

O'Brien, Maire, and Conor Cruise O'Brien. *A Concise History of Ireland.* 3rd ed. New York: Thames & Hudson, 1981.

Police Constable's Annual Report (1996): 87.

Purdie, Bob. *Politics in the Streets: The Origins of the Civil Rights Movement in Northern Ireland.* Belfast: The Blackstaff Press, 1990.

Republic of Ireland, Department of Foreign Affairs. *Northern Ireland Peace Process: Background Information Note.* December 1996.

Ruane, Joseph, and Jennifer Todd. *The Dynamics of Conflict in Northern Ireland: Power, Conflict and Emancipation.* Cambridge: Cambridge University Press, 1996.

Smith, Alan. "Education and the Conflict in Northern Ireland." In *Facets of the Conflict in Northern Ireland,* edited by Seamus Dunn. New York: St. Martin's, 1995.

Watt, Nicholas. "Election Plan Cools Early Welcome for Peace Blueprint." *The Times of London* (January 25, 1996).

Zartman, I. William. *Ripe for Resolution: Conflict and Intervention in Africa.* New York: Oxford University Press, 1991.

Chapter 8. The Arusha Accords and the Failure of International Intervention in Rwanda

Adelman, Howard, and Astri Suhrke. "Study 2: Early Warning and Conflict Management." In *The International Response to Conflict and Genocide: Lessons from the Rwanda Experience.* (Joint Evaluation of Emergency Assistance to Rwanda, 1996), http://www.reliefweb.int/library/nordic/book2/pb021.html.

Eriksson, John, et al., "Synthesis Report." In *The International Response to Conflict and Genocide: Lessons from the Rwanda Experience* (Joint Evaluation of Emergency Assistance to Rwanda, 1996), http://www.reliefweb.int/library/nordic/book5/pb025.html.

Jones, Bruce D. "The Arusha Peace Process: Report for Study II of the Joint Evaluation of Emergency Assistance to Rwanda." Revised version presented to U.S. Committee for Refugees Conference on 'Early Warning and Conflict Management in Rwanda,' Washington, D.C., December 18, 1995.

————. "Roots, Resolution, and Reaction: Civil War, the Peace Process, and Genocide in Rwanda." Paper presented at the University of Toronto conference on 'Civil Wars in Africa,' May 1995, p. 5.

Kuperman, Alan J. "The Other Lesson of Rwanda: Mediators Sometimes Do More Damage Than Good." *School of Advanced International Studies (SAIS) Review: A Journal of International Affairs* 16 (Winter–Spring 1996): 222.

Linden, Ian. "The Churches and Genocide: Lessons from Rwanda." *Svensk Missionstidskrift* 83 (3/1995): 5–15.

Prunier, Gérard. *The Rwanda Crisis: History of a Genocide.* New York: Columbia University Press, 1995.

Sellström, Tor, and Lennart Wohlgemuth. "Study 1: Historical Perspectives: Some Explanatory Factors." In *The International Response to Conflict and Genocide: Lessons from the Rwanda Experience* (Joint Evaluation of Emergency Assistance to Rwanda, 1996). http://www.reliefweb.int/library/nordic/book1/pb020.html.

Chapter 9. South Africa: The Negotiated Transition from Apartheid to Nonracial Democracy

African National Congress. *Negotiations: A Strategic Perspective* (adopted by the ANC National Executive Committee on Nov. 25, 1992).

Anglin, Douglass G. "International Monitoring of the Transition to Democracy in South Africa, 1992–94." *African Affairs* 20 (1995): 519.

Bouckaert, Peter. "The Negotiated Revolution: South Africa's Transition to a Multiracial Democracy." *Stanford Journal of International Law* 33 (Spring 1997): 375–411.

Chufrin, Gennady I., and Harold Saunders. "A Public Peace Process." *Negotiation Journal* 9 (1993): 155.

Frederickse, Julie. *The Unbreakable Thread: Non–Racialism in South Africa.* Bloomington: Indiana University Press, 1990.

Gassama, Ibrahim J. "Reaffirming Faith in the Dignity of Each Human Being: The United Nations, NGOs, and Apartheid." *Fordham International Law Journal* 19 (1996): 1464.

General Assembly of the United Nations, Resolution 2202 (XXI) of 16 December 1966.

Giliomee, Herman. "*Broedertwis:* Intra–Afrikaner Conflicts and the Transition from Apartheid." *African Affairs* 91 (1992): 339.

Hanlon, Joseph. *Beggar Your Neighbours: Apartheid Power in Southern Africa.* London: James Currey, 1986.

Harding, Jeremy. *Small Wars, Small Mercies.* London: Penguin, 1994.

Johns, Sheridan, and R. Hunt Davis, eds. *Mandela, Tambo, and the African National Congress: The Struggle Against Apartheid 1948–1990.* Oxford: Oxford University Press, 1991.

Johnson R.W., and Lawrence Schlemmer, eds. *Launching Democracy in South Africa: The First Open Elections, April 1994.* New Haven, CT: Yale University Press, 1996.

Kanfer, Stefan. *The Last Empire: De Beers, Diamonds, and the World.* New York: Farrar, Straus & Giroux, 1990.

Kelman, Herbert C. "Informal Mediation by the Scholar/Practitioner." In *Mediation in International Relations: Multiple Approaches to Conflict Management,* edited by Jacob Bercovitch and Jeffrey Z. Rubin. New York: St. Martin's, 1992.

Kwitny, Jonathan. *Endless Enemies.* New York: Congdon & Weed: Distributed by St. Martin's Press, 1988.

Mbeki, Govan. *Sunset at Midday.* Braamfontein: Nolwazi Educational Publishers, 1996.

McMahon, Neil. "Kissinger Mission's Failure Bodes Ill for South Africa." *Washington Times* (April 15, 1994).

Mkhondo, Rich. *Reporting South Africa.* London: James Currey, 1993.

Morris, Donald R. *The Washing of the Spears: The Rise and Fall of the Zulu Nation.* New York: Simon & Schuster, 1965.

Ottoway, David. *Chained Together: Mandela, De Klerk, and the Struggle to Remake South Africa*. New York: Times Books, 1993.

"Report of the Secretary-General to the Security Council in Pursuance of Security Council Resolution 765 (1992)." August 7, 1992, UN Doc. S/24389.

"Security Council Resolution: The Question of South Africa." August 17, 1992, UN Doc. S/RES/772 (1992).

"Security Council Resolution 418." UN SCOR, 32nd Sess., 2046th mtg. at 1, UN Doc. S/RES/418 (1977).

Sisk, Timothy D. *Democratization in South Africa*. Princeton, NJ: Princeton University Press, 1995.

Skweyiya, Zola. "Towards a Solution to the Land Question in Post–Apartheid South Africa: Problems and Models." Columbia Human Rights Law Review 21 (1989): 213.

Slovo, Joe. "Negotiations: What Room for Compromise?" *African Communist* (3rd Quarter 1992): 36.

Southern African Development Cooperation Conference. *The Cost of Destabilization: Memorandum presented by SADCC to the 1985 Summit of the Organization of African Unity* (1985). Reproduced in *Beggar Your Neighbors: Apartheid Power in Southern Africa,* edited by James Hanlon. London: James Currey, 1986, 265–70.

Sparks, Allister. *The Mind of South Africa*. New York: Ballantine, 1990.

———. "The Secret Revolution." *New Yorker,* April 11, 1994, 56.

———. *Tomorrow Is Another Country.* Sandton, South Africa: Struik Publishers, 1994.

"Statement by the President of the Security Council, on behalf of the Council, on the shooting of demonstrators in Ciskei," September 10, 1992, UN Doc. S/24541.

"Statement by the Spokesman for Secretary-General Boutros Boutros-Ghali concerning the loss of life in Ciskei, and details on the United Nations Observer Mission in South Africa (UNOMSA)," September 9, 1992, U.N. Press Release SG/SM/4807–SAF/141. Reproduced in United Nations Department of Public Information, *The U.N. and Apartheid,* 449.

Stein, Janice Gross. *Getting to the Table: The Processes of International Prenegotiation.* Baltimore: Johns Hopkins University Press, 1989.

Stockwell, John. *In Search of Enemies.* New York: Norton, 1978.

Strauss, Annette. "The 1992 Referendum in South Africa." *Journal of Modern African Studies* 31 (1993): 339.

Thompson, Leonard. *A History of South Africa.* New Haven, CT: Yale University Press, 1990.

U.N. SCOR, 18th Sess., 1041st mtg. at 6, U.N. Doc. S/5386 (1963).

United Nations Children's Fund. *Children on the Front Line.* 1989 Update 11 (1989): 38.

United Nations Department of Public Information. *The United Nations and Apartheid, 1948–1994.* New York: UN Department of Public Information, 1994.

Waldmeir, Patti. *Anatomy of a Miracle: The End of Apartheid and the Birth of the New South Africa.* New York: Norton, 1997.

Wilson, Francis, and Mamphela Ramphele. *Uprooting Poverty: The South African Challenge.* Cape Town: David Philip, 1989.

Whiteford, Andrew, and Michael McGrath. *Distribution of Income in South Africa.* 62 (1994).

Chapter 10. Making Waves: Third Parties and International Mediation in the Aral Sea Basin

Barrett, Scott. "Conflict and Cooperation in Managing International Water Resources." *Policy Research Working Paper 1303.* Washington, D.C.: World Bank, 1994.

Bercovitch, Jacob. "The Structure and Diversity of Mediation in International Relations." In *Mediation in International Relations,* edited by Jacob Bercovitch and Jeffrey Z. Rubin. New York: St. Martin's, 1992.

Bernauer, Thomas. "Managing International Rivers." Paper Prepared for the 1995 Annual Meeting of the American Political Science Association, Chicago, Illinois, 1995.

—————. "Protecting the Rhine against Chloride Pollution." In *Institutions for Environmental Aid: Pitfalls and Promise,* edited by Robert O. Keohane and Marc A. Levy. Cambridge: MIT Press, 1996.

The Blue Helmets: A Review of United Nations Peacekeeping. New York: United Nations, 1996.

Bunce, Valerie. "Regional Cooperation and European Integration in Post-Communist Europe: The Visegrad Group." In *East–Central Europe and the Rise of Germany,* edited by Peter Katzenstein. Ithaca, NY: Cornell University Press, 1998 (forthcoming).

Caponera, Dante A. "Legal and Institutional Framework for the Management of the Aral Sea Basin Water Resources." Tashkent, April 1995.

—————. *Principles of Water Law and Administration: National and International.* Rotterdam: A.A. Balkema, 1992.

Carley, Patricia M. "The Price of the Plan." *Central Asian Survey* 8 (1989): 1–38.

Chayes, Abram, and Antonia Handler Chayes, eds. *Preventing Conflict in the Post–Communist World: Mobilizing International and Regional Organizations.* Washington, D.C.: The Brookings Institution, 1996.

Clarke, Robin. *Water: The International Crisis.* Cambridge: The MIT Press, 1993.

Critchlow, James. *Nationalism in Uzbekistan.* Boulder, CO: Westview Press, 1991.

Dale, Catherine. "The Case of Abkhazia (Georgia)." In *Peacekeeping and the Role of Russia in Eurasia,* edited by Lena Jonson and Clive Archer. Boulder, CO: Westview Press, 1996.

—————. "Turmoil in Abkhazia: Russian Responses." *RFE/RL Research Report* 2, no. 34 (August 27, 1993): 48–57.

Darst, Robert G. "Environmentalism in the USSR: The Opposition to the River Diversion Projects." *Soviet Economy* 4 (1988): 223–52.

Dawson, Jane. *Eco–Nationalism.* Durham, NC: Duke University Press, 1996.

Deudney, Daniel. "The Case Against Linking Environmental Degradation and National Security." *Millennium* 19 (1990): 461–76.

Environmental Policy and Technology Project Summary: U.S. Aral Sea Program Overview, Prepared for Regional Mission for Central Asia, U.S. Agency for International Development. 2 October 1996.

FBIS-Sov-89-115, *FBIS Daily Report: Central Eurasia,* 16 June 1989: 49.

Frederick, Kenneth. "Water as a Source of International Conflict." *Resources for the Future* (1996): 9–12.

Frey, Bruno. *International Political Economics.* Oxford: Basil Blackwell, 1984.

Gleason, Gregory. "The Struggle for Control over Water in Central Asia: Republican Sovereignty and Collective Action." *Report on the USSR* 3 (1991): 11–19.

Gleick, Peter. "Water and Conflict: Fresh Water Resources and International Security." *International Security* 18 (1993): 79–112.

———, ed. *Water in Crisis.* New York: Oxford University Press, 1993.

Homer-Dixon, Thomas F., and V. Percival. *Environmental Scarcity and Violent Conflict: Briefing Book.* American Association for the Advancement of Science and the University of Toronto.

Homer-Dixon, Thomas F., Jeffrey H. Boutwell, and George W. Rathjens. "Environmental Change and Violent Conflict." *Scientific American* (1993): 38–45.

Institute for Soviet-American Relations. *Surviving Together,* 1996.

Interstate Council for Aral Sea Problems (with the assistance of the World Bank). "Fundamental Provisions of Water Management Strategy in the Aral Sea Basin." October 1996.

Iskandarov, Khasan. "Will Tashkent Become a Port City?—The Idea of Diverting Siberian Rivers Seems to Have Seized the Masses Once Again." *Current Digest of the Soviet Press* 46 (1994): 26.

Jackson Robert H., and Carl G. Rosberg. "Why Africa's Weak States Persist: The Empirical and Juridical in Statehood." *World Politics* 35 (1982): 1–24.

Jonson, Lena, and Clive Archer, eds. *Peacekeeping and the Role of Russia in Eurasia.* Boulder, CO: Westview Press, 1996.

Kamieniecki, Sheldon, ed. *Environmental Politics in the International Arena: Movements, Parties, Organizations, and Policy.* Albany: State University of New York Press, 1993.

Kapuscinski, Ryszard. *Imperium.* New York: Vintage, 1995.

Keohane, Robert O., and Marc A. Levy, eds. *Institutions for Environmental Aid: Pitfalls and Promise.* Cambridge: MIT Press 1996.

Kirmani, Syed, and Guy Le Moigne. "Fostering Riparian Cooperation in International River Basins: The World Bank at Its Best in Development Diplomacy." *World Bank Technical Paper No. 335.* Washington D.C.: The World Bank, 1997.

Kleiboer, Marieke. "Understanding Success and Failure of International Mediation." *Journal of Conflict Resolution* 40, no. 2 (1996): 369–89.

Klötzli, Stefan. "The Water and Soil Crisis in Central Asia—A Source for Future Conflicts?" *ENCOP Occasional Paper No. 11.* Zurich: Center for Security Policy and Conflict Research, 1994.

Krasner, Stephen. "Sovereignty and Intervention." In *Beyond Westphalia? State Sovereignty and International Intervention,* edited by Gene Lyons and Michael Mastanduno. Baltimore: Johns Hopkins University Press, 1995.

Libiszewski, Stephan. "Water Disputes in the Jordan Basin Region and Their Role in the Resolution of the Arab–Israeli Conflict." *ENCOP Occasional Paper No. 13.* Zurich: Center for Security Policy and Conflict Research, 1995.

Lijphart, Arend. "The Power–Sharing Approach." In *Conflict and Peacemaking in Multiethnic Societies,* edited by Joseph Montville. New York: Lexington Books, 1991.

Lipschutz, Ronnie D., and Ken Conca, eds. *The State and Social Power in Global Environmental Politics.* New York: Columbia University Press, 1993.

Lowi, Miriam. "Bridging the Divide: Transboundary Resource Disputes and the Case of West Bank Water." *International Security* 18 (1993): 113–38.

Mathews, Jessica Tuchman. "Redefining Security." *Foreign Affairs* 68 (1989): 162–77.

McCaffrey, Stephen C. "Water, Politics, and International Law." In *Water in Crisis,* edited by Peter H. Gleick. New York: Oxford University Press, 1993.

Michel, A. *The Indus River: A Study of the Effects of Partition.* New Haven, CT: Yale University Press, 1967.

Micklin, Philip P. "The Aral Crisis: Introduction to the Special Issue." *Post–Soviet Geography* 33 (1992): 269–82.

———. "The Water Management Crisis in Soviet Central Asia." *The Carl Beck Papers in Russian and East European Studies, No. 905.* Pittsburgh, PA: University of Pittsburgh, Center for Russian and East European Studies, 1991.

———, and Andrew R. Bond. "Reflections on Environmentalism and the River Diversion Projects." *Soviet Economy* 4 (1988): 253–74.

Myers, Norman. *Ultimate Security: The Environmental Basis for Political Stability.* New York: Norton, 1993.

Naff, Thomas, and Ruth C. Matson. *Water in the Middle East: Conflict or Cooperation?* Boulder, CO: Westview Press, 1984.

Panarin, Sergei A. "Political Dynamics of the 'New East' (1985–1993)." In *Central Asia and Transcaucasia: Ethnicity and Conflict,* edited by Vitaly V. Naumkin. Westport, CT: Greenwood Press, 1994.

Porter, Gareth, and Janet Welsh Brown. *Global Environmental Politics.* Boulder, CO: Westview Press, 1991.

Postel, Sandra. "Dividing the Waters: Food Security, Ecosystem Health, and the New Politics of Scarcity." *Worldwatch Paper No. 132.* Washington, D.C.: Worldwatch Institute, 1996.

Princen, Thomas. *Intermediaries in International Conflict.* Princeton, NJ: Princeton University Press, 1992.

———, and Matthias Finger. *Environmental NGOs in World Politics: Linking the Global and the Local.* New York: Routledge, 1994.

Reinicke, Wolfgang H. "Can International Financial Institutions Prevent Internal Violence? The Sources of Ethno–National Conflict in Transitional Societies." In *Preventing Conflict in the Post–Communist World: Mobilizing International and Regional Organizations,* edited by Abram Chayes and Antonia Handler Chayes. Washington, D.C.: The Brookings Institution, 1996.

Renner, Michael. "National Security: The Economic and Environmental Dimensions." *Worldwatch Paper No. 89.* Washington, D.C.: Worldwatch Institute, 1989.

Ruggie, John Gerard. "Multilateralism: The Anatomy of an Institution." *International Organization* 46 (1992): 561–98.

Sievers, Eric, and Andrei Aranbaev, eds. "Ecostan News: Ecological News from Central Asia." *Environmental Change and Security Project Report.* Washington, D.C.: The Woodrow Wilson Center, 2 (1996).

Sinnott, Peter. "The Physical Geography of Soviet Central Asia and the Aral Sea Problem." In *Geographic Perspectives on Soviet Central Asia,* edited by Robert A. Lewis. London: Routledge: 1992.

Smith, David R. "Environmental Security and Shared Water Resources in Post-Soviet Central Asia." *Post–Soviet Geography* 36 (1995): 351–70.

Stedman, Stephen. "Negotiation and Mediation in Internal Conflict." In *The International Dimensions of Internal Conflict,* edited by Michael Brown. Cambridge: MIT Press, 1996.

Stein, Melanie H. "Conflict Prevention in Transition Economies: A Role for the European Bank for Reconstruction and Development." In *Preventing Conflict in the Post–Communist World: Mobilizing International and Regional Organizations,* edited by Abram Chayes and Antonia Handler Chayes. Washington, D.C.: The Brookings Institution, 1996.

TACIS–WARMAP (Water Resources Management and Agricultural Production in the Central Asian Republics). "Vol. VI: Legal and Institutional Aspects." Tashkent, Uzbekistan, January 1996.

TACIS–WARMAP. "Executive Summary." Tashkent, Uzbekistan, January 1996.

Ullman, Richard H. "Redefining Security." *International Security* 8 (1983): 129–53.

United Nations. *Register of International Rivers.* Oxford: Pergamon Press, 1978.

Waterbury, John. "Transboundary Water and the Challenge of International Cooperation in the Middle East." In *Water in the Arab World: Perspectives and Prognoses,* edited by Peter Rogers and Peter Lydon. Cambridge: Harvard University Press, 1994.

Williams, Paul R. "International Environmental Dispute Resolution: The Dispute between Slovakia and Hungary Concerning Construction of the Gabcikovo and Nagymaros Dams." *Columbia Journal of Environmental Law* 19 (1994): 1–53.

The World Bank. Aral Sea Basin Program, Phase 1, Progress Report No. 2, September 1995.

———. Aral Sea Basin Program, Phase 1, Progress Report No. 3, February 1996.

———. "The Aral Sea Crisis: Proposed Framework of Activities." 1993.

World Bank/UNDP/UNEP. "Aral Sea Program—Phase 1, Briefing Paper for the Proposed Donors Meeting to Be Held on June 23–24, 1994, in Paris." Washington, D.C.: Aral Sea Program Unit, World Bank, 1994.

World Resources 1996–97. New York: Oxford University Press.

Young, Oran R. *International Governance: Protecting the Environment in a Stateless Society.* Ithaca, NY: Cornell University Press, 1994.

Zartman, I. William. *Ripe for Resolution: Conflict and Intervention in Africa.* New York: Oxford University Press, 1989.

Chapter 11. The Vatican Mediation of the Beagle Channel Dispute: Crisis Intervention and Forum Building

Acta de Puerto Montt, signed in Puerto Montt, Chile, February 20, 1978 (Act of Puerto Montt).

"Argentina Closes Border with Chile after Two Arrests." *New York Times* (April 30, 1981).

"Argentina Signs Accord with Chile," *New York Times* (January 24, 1984).

Benadava, Santiago. "La Mediación de la Santa Sede en el Diferendo Chileno–Argentino sobre la Zona Austral." In *International Law at a Time of Perplexity,* edited by Y. Dinstein. Dordrecht: Kluwer Academic Publishers, 1989.

Carrasco, German. *Argentina y el Laudo Arbitral del Canal Beagle.* Santiago: Editorial Jurídica de Chile, 1978.

de Onis, Juan. "Argentina Accepts Mediation for Southern Islands." *New York Times* (November 9, 1978).

———. "Argentina and Chile Ask Pope to Mediate Border Dispute." *New York Times* (January 10, 1979).

———. "Argentina, Chile Feud Masks Other Troubles." *New York Times* (December 31, 1978).

———. "Chile and Argentina Miss an Opportunity." *New York Times* (February 20, 1978).

———. "Chile May Take Dispute to OAS." *New York Times* (December 15, 1978).

———. "Pope to Take Part in Mexico Meeting." *New York Times* (December 23, 1978).

Decreto Supremo No. 416, issued by Chile on July 14, 1977 (Chilean Straight Baselines Decree).

Gorney, Cynthia. "At Tip of South America, Three Tiny Islands Raise Talk of War." *Washington Post* (March 27, 1981).

Morris, Michael A. *The Strait of Magellan.* Dordrecht: Martinus Nijhoff, 1989.

———, and Victor Millán, eds. *Controlling Latin American Conflicts: Ten Approaches.* Boulder, CO: Westview Press, 1983.

Papal Proposal in the Beagle Channel Dispute: Proposal of the Mediator.

Thomas Princen, "Beagle Channel Negotiations," Case 401, Pew Case Studies in International Affairs (Washington, DC: Institute for the Study of Diplomacy, 1988): 14.

———. *Intermediaries in International Conflict.* Princeton, NJ: Princeton University Press, 1992.

Schumacher, Edward. "Three Small Islands Loom Large in Argentina Leader's Plans." *New York Times* (January 5, 1984).

Slavin, Barbara, and Rosanne Klass. "Argentina, Chile to Try Mediation." *New York Times* (November 12, 1978).

"The Torti Proposal." *El Mercurio,* January 12, 1978.

Tratado de Límites entre Chile y Argentina, signed in Buenos Aires, July 23, 1881 (Boundary Treaty of 1881).

Tratado de Paz y Amistad, signed at the Vatican, November 29, 1984 (Treaty of Peace and Friendship).

Tratado General Sobre Solución Judicial de Controversias entre La República de Chile y La República Argentina, signed in Buenos Aires, April 5, 1972 (General Treaty on the Judicial Settlement of Disputes).

"Victories for Voters in South America; Small Miracle in Argentina." *New York Times* (December 1, 1984).

Videla, Ernesto. "La Mediación Pontificia en el Diferendo Austral." *Diplomacia* 39: 1987.

Villarroel, Enrique Gajardo. "Las Líneas de Base Rectas." *El Mercurio* (July 17, 1977).

World News Briefs: "U.S. Helping to Resolve Chile–Argentina Dispute." *New York Times* (December 16, 1978).

World News Briefs: "U.S. Urges OAS to Act in Chile–Argentina Dispute." *New York Times* (December 13, 1978).

Chapter 12. The North Korean Nuclear Proliferation Crisis

Agreed Framework between the United States of America and the Democratic People's Republic of Korea, Geneva, October 21, 1994.

"Carter Trip Paves the Way for U.S.–North Korean Pact." *The Carter Center News.* Atlanta: The Carter Center, 11.

Choe, Hyoung-Chan. "North Korea's Dangerous Nuclear Deal, Process and Prospect." In *Korea: A World in Change,* edited by Kenneth W. Thompson. Lanham, MD: University Press of America, 1996.

Cossa, Ralph. "Multilateralism, Regional Security, and the Prospects for Track II in East Asia." *NBR Analysis* vol. 7, no. 5 (1996): 35.

Elliott, Kimberly Ann. "Will Economic Sanctions Work against North Korea?" In *Peace and Security in Northeast Asia: The Nuclear Issue and the Korean Peninsula,* edited by Young Whan Kihl and Peter Hayes. New York: M.E. Sharpe, 1997.

Gellman, Barton. "U.S., Allies Struggling to Fulfill N. Korea Pact." *Washington Post,* May 2, 1998.

Heppel, Janice M. "Confidence-Building Measures Bilateral versus Multilateral Approaches." In *Peace and Security in Northeast Asia: The Nuclear Issue and the Korean Peninsula,* edited by Young Whan Kihl and Peter Hayes. New York: M.E. Sharpe, 1997.

IAEA document INFCIRC/153 (Corrected) IAEA, Vienna, 1983.

"It's Good for the Koreas to Talk: But Don't Expect the Talks, if They Resume, to Get Very Far Very Fast." *Economist,* April 18, 1998.

Kapur, K.D. *Nuclear Diplomacy in East Asia: U.S. and the Korean Nuclear Crisis Management.* New Delhi: Lancers Books, 1995.

Kihl, Young Whan. "Confrontation or Compromise? Lessons from the 1994 Crisis." In *Peace and Security in Northeast Asia: The Nuclear Issue and the Korean Peninsula,* edited by Young Whan Kihl and Peter Hayes. New York: M.E. Sharpe, 1997.

Kokoski, Richard. *Technology and the Proliferation of Nuclear Weapons.* New York: Oxford University Press Inc., 1995.

Mann, Jum. "N. Korea Nuclear Deal at Risk, U.S. Fears Financing: Officials Say That Bickering over Funding for $5.1-Billion Reactor Project Threatens 1994 Pact." *Los Angeles Times* (April 10, 1998).

Mazaar, Michael J. *North Korea and the Bomb: A Case Study in Nonproliferation.* New York: St. Martin's, 1994.

Plate, Tom. "Next on the Diplomatic Agenda: Korea: While the Korean Peninsula Lacks the American Constituency That Ireland Has, Its Future Is Vital for the World." *Los Angeles Times* (April 14, 1998).

Sloss, David. "It's Not Broken So Don't Fix It: The International Atomic Energy Agency Safeguards System and the Nuclear Nonproliferation Treaty." *Virginia Journal of International Law* 35 (1995): 873.

Snyder, Scott. "Beyond the Geneva Agreed Framework: A Road Map for Normalizing Relations with North Korea." In *Peace and Security in Northeast Asia: The Nuclear Issue and the Korean Peninsula,* edited by Young Whan Kihl and Peter Hayes. New York: M.E. Sharpe, 1997.

Treaty Series, Vol. 729, United Nations, New York.

Weiner, Tim. "U.S. Says North Korea Helped Develop New Pakistani Missile." *New York Times* (April 11, 1998).

Appendix: Interviews

Interviews Conducted by the Chapter Authors

Abkhazia

Livu Bota	Special Representative of the UN Secretary-General for Georgia and Head of the UNOMIG
Geuerae Hvidegaard	Former Head of the UN Observer Group in Georgia (UNOMIG)

Interviews with members of the Georgian and Russian Missions to the United Nations

Bosnia

Richard Goldstone	Former Chief Prosecutor, International Criminal Tribunal for the Former Yugoslavia
Richard Holbrooke	Currently U.S. Ambassador to the United Nations. At the time of the Bosnia negotiations, Assistant Secretary of State for European and Canadian Affairs
Charles Redman	Former U.S. Special Envoy to the Former Yugoslavia
Paul Williams	Legal Advisor to the Bosnian delegation to the Dayton Peace Conference

Croatia

Lord Peter Carrington	Former Cochair of the Peace Conference on Yugoslavia
Herbert S. Okun	Former Special Advisor to Cyrus Vance (and former U.S. Ambassador to the German Democratic Republic)
Charles Redman	Former U.S. Special Envoy to the Former Yugoslavia

Oslo Channel

Jan Egeland	Deputy Norwegian Foreign Minister
Mona Juul	Diplomat, Norwegian Foreign Ministry

Geir O. Peterson — Diplomat, Norwegian Foreign Ministry
Terje Rod Larsen — Director, FAFO (Norwegian nongovernmental research organization)

Cambodia

Anonymous French Source
John Bolton — Former U.S. Assistant Secretary of State for International Organizations
Lord David Gilmore — Former British Foreign Secretary
Steven Ratner — Former Legal Advisor, U.S. Department of State
Stephen Solarz — Former Member of U.S. House of Representatives
Richard Solomon — Former Assistant Secretary of State for East Asia and Pacific Affairs

El Salvador

Oscar Arias — Former President of Costa Rica
Bernard Aronson — Former U.S. Assistant Secretary of State
Alfredo Cristiani — Former President of El Salvador
Alvaro de Soto — Executive Assistant to Secretary-General Perez de Cueller and the Personal Representative of the Secretary-General for the Central American Peace Process at the United Nations
David Escobar Galindo — Member of the Government Negotiation Team
Salvador Samayoa — FMLN leader
General Mauricio Vargas — Former Deputy Defense Minister of El Salvador
Ruben Zamora — Moderate leftist founder of the Social Christian Popular Movement, a party of the Democratic Convergence; served as vice president of the Salvadoran legislature

Northern Ireland

Robert Bradtke — Deputy Chief Mission, U.S. Embassy in London
Senator George Mitchell — Independent Chairman of the Plenary Session of Multiparty Negotiations

Rwanda

John Beyerly — Special Negotiator, Office of Transportation, U.S. State Department
Herman Cohen — Former Assistant Secretary of State, Senior Advisor, Global Coalition for Africa
Lt. Col. A.D. Marley, ret. — Political-Military Advisor, Africa Bureau, State Department at the time of the Arusha Accords
Ami M. Mpungwe — Chief negotiator, Arusha Accords; Tanzanian High Commissioner to South Africa

Théogène Rudasingwa	Rwandan Ambassador to the United States
Charles Snyder	Director of the Office of African Regional Affairs, U.S. State Department

South Africa

Justice Richard Goldstone	Former Chair of the Commission on Inquiry; current Justice of the South African Constitutional Court
Stephen Stedman	Senior Research Scholar, Center for International Security and Cooperation, Stanford University

Aral Sea Basin

Yitzhak Alter	WARMAP legal advisor, Tashkent
Jeremy Berkoff	World Bank Water Economist, November 1993
Michael Boyd	HIID, Almaty, Kazakhstan
Barbara Britton	USAID-EPT Project, Almaty, Kazakhstan
Arrigo Di Carlo	WARMAP, Tashkent, Uzbekistan
Rim Abdulovich Ghiniatullin	Water Ministry of Uzbekistan (Minvodkhoz)
Parliamentarian Kachikayev	Bishkek, Kyrgyzstan
David Pearce	Head of World Bank Mission, Almaty, Kazakhstan
Werner Roider	Aral Sea Program, Tashkent, Uzbekistan
Momir Vranes	UNDP, Tashkent, Uzbekistan
Peter Whitford	Manager, Aral Sea Basin Program, Washington, D.C.

Beagle Channel

Santiago Benadava	Legal scholar; Member of Chilean delegation
Dante Caputo	Former Foreign Minister of Argentina
Marcelo Delpech	Head of Argentine delegation from December 1983 through end of dispute
General Ricardo Echeverry Boneo	Chief representative of Argentina to Puerto Montt negotiations; co-head of Argentine delegation to the papal mediation
Hugo Gobbi	Former Deputy Foreign Minister of Argentina
Guillermo Moncayo	Legal scholar; co-head of Argentine delegation during papal mediation
Francisco Orrego	Legal scholar; Chilean representative during direct Puerto Montt negotiations

North Korea

Robert Gallucci	Former U.S. Assistant Secretary of State; Chief U.S. negotiator, second and third round of U.S.–DPRK talks

Index

About the Contributors

John H. Barton is George E. Osborne Professor of Law at Stanford University, where he concentrates on international issues. He regularly teaches an introduction to international law, as well as a variety of specialized international law courses. He was also, for many years, a close collaborator in Stanford's programs on international security and arms control and has authored or coauthored several volumes on arms control issues. He has been a panelist on several international trade disputes between the United States, Canada, and Mexico and is a member of the IUCN's Commission on International Environmental Law. He is a 1958 graduate of Marquette University and a 1968 graduate of Stanford Law School. He was Stanford's principal investigator in the study that led to this volume.

William J. Bien received his J.D. from Stanford Law School in 1997, where he specialized in international commercial law. He completed his baccalaureate degrees in Economics and Chinese from Ohio State University and was awarded Phi Beta Kappa membership. He has studied at the Chinese University of Hong Kong as a Rotary Scholar. Prior to law school Bien worked at the United States International Trade Administration, where he analyzed foreign telecommunications regulations and served on several international negotiating teams. He is currently at the Boston Consulting Group developing telecommunications and financial services strategies.

Peter Bouckaert received a J.D. degree from Stanford Law School in 1997, and has a B.A. from UC Santa Barbara in Law & Society and Black Studies. At Stanford, he was the Senior Articles Editor of the Stanford Journal of International Law, a Fellow in the Stanford Center on Conflict and Negotiation, and the Head Teaching Assistant in the Stanford Program in International Legal Studies. He worked at the Constitutional Litigation Unit of the Legal Resources Centre in South Africa from April 1994 until April 1995 and the South Africa Department of Land Affairs from April 1996 until August 1996. Bouckaert is currently working for Human Rights Watch, where he researches human rights issues in South Africa, Uganda, and Kosovo.

Melanie C. Greenberg is an attorney and conflict resolution specialist focusing on issues of international negotiation and public peace processes. She has served as the Associate Director of the Stanford Center for International Security and Cooperation and the Deputy Director of the Stanford Center on Conflict and Negotiation. She is an Adjunct Professor at Georgetown Law Center and a Lecturer-at-Law at Stanford Law School. Greenberg practiced bankruptcy law at Weil, Gotshal & Manges in Houston and is currently on the executive board of the Lawyers' Alliance for World Security. She holds an A.B. from Harvard University in Comparative Literature and a J.D. from Stanford Law School. She lives with her husband, Lawrence, and children, Anna Rose and Jed, in Washington, D.C.

Alan Hanson completed his law degree at Stanford Law School in 1997. He holds a bachelor's degree from the University of Maryland. Hanson is a practicing attorney in New York City.

Arthur Khachikian was born in Armenia, former USSR, and attended Yerevan State University, Department of Oriental Studies, from 1986 to 1991. He is a doctoral candidate in political science at Stanford University. Since 1991, he has been affiliated with the Stanford Center for International Security and Cooperation (CISAC) as a researcher and a MacArthur Fellow. Mr. Khachikian specializes in international intervention and conflict resolution, intrastate conflicts and international security, ethnicity and ethnic conflict, and regional studies on the former Soviet Union and Caucasus.

Kevin King received his J.D. from Stanford Law School in 1997 and his B.A. degree in 1992 from American University, where he majored in International Studies and Economics. King is currently an attorney with Coudert Brothers, in Washington, D.C., where he specializes in international trade policy and regulation, including U.S. export controls, sanctions regulations, and the Foreign Corrupt Practices Act. Mr. King previously worked for the Securities and Exchange Commission's Office of International Affairs, where he provided assistance to foreign securities regulators and helped coordinate the SEC's interagency law enforcement efforts.

Mark Laudy completed his J.D. at Stanford Law School in 1998. He holds a bachelor's degree from Yale University.

Tali Levy completed a joint degree in law and international relations at Stanford Law School and the Fletcher School of Law and Diplomacy. She holds a bachelor's degree from the University of California, Berkeley. Levy is currently a lawyer at the Alameda County Public Defender's Office.

Margaret E. McGuinness served in the United States Foreign Service from 1988 to 1996. Her overseas postings included Canada, Pakistan, and Germany, where she was Deputy Chief of the Political Section at the U.S. Embassy Office in Berlin. She served as a Special Assistant to Secretary of State Warren Christopher from 1993 to 1994. McGuinness holds a B.A. in International Studies from American University and a J.D. from Stanford Law School. She is currently an attorney in New York.

Barbara Messing completed her J.D. at Stanford Law School in 1997. She holds a bachelor's degree from Northwestern University. Messing is a filmmaker in New York City.

Joel Stettenheim worked as a photojournalist for the SABA news agency and spent over a year in Rwanda, where he reported extensively on the civil war. He holds a B.A. from Haverford College. Stettenheim completed his J.D. at Stanford Law School in 1999.

Rock Tang completed his J.D. at Stanford Law School in 1998. He holds a bachelor's degree from the University of California, Los Angeles. Tang is an attorney in California.

Erika Weinthal is an Assistant Professor of Political Science at Tel Aviv University. She received her Ph.D. in Political Science from Columbia University. Her dissertation, "Making or Breaking the State? Building Institutions for Regional Cooperation in the Aral Sea Basin," focused on the politics of water sharing in Central Asia. She has also received several National Research Council grants for collaborative research in sectoral policy on energy resources in Central Asia. While writing this article, she was a predoctoral fellow at the Center for International Security and Cooperation at Stanford University.